ORGANISATIONAL CULTURE

Concept, Context, and Measurement

Volume II

ORGANISATIONAL CULTURE

CULTURE

Concept, Context, and Measurement

Volume II

Elizabeth Kummerow

The University of Adelaide, Australia

Neil Kirby

The University of Adelaide, Australia

 World Scientific

NEW JERSEY · LONDON · SINGAPORE · BEIJING · SHANGHAI · HONG KONG · TAIPEI · CHENNAI

Published by

World Scientific Publishing Co. Pte. Ltd.

5 Toh Tuck Link, Singapore 596224

USA office: 27 Warren Street, Suite 401-402, Hackensack, NJ 07601

UK office: 57 Shelton Street, Covent Garden, London WC2H 9HE

The image on the cover is taken from WikiPaintings,

http://uploads8.wikipaintings.org/images/giovanni-battista-piranesi/the-lion-bas-reliefs.jpg,

Public Domain, Artwork by Giovanni Battista Piranesi.

Library of Congress Cataloging-in-Publication Data

Kummerow, Elizabeth.

   Organisational culture : concept, context, and measurement / Elizabeth Kummerow, Neil Kirby.

   volumes cm

   Includes bibliographical references and index.

   ISBN 978-9814449519 (hardcover, v. 1 : alk. paper) -- ISBN 978-9814449526 (hardcover,

v. 2 : alk. paper) -- ISBN 978-981-283-782-0 (hardcover : alk. paper)

   1. Corporate culture. 2. Organizational behavior. I. Title.

   HD58.7.K857 2014

   302.3'5--dc23

                          2013027369

British Library Cataloguing-in-Publication Data

A catalogue record for this book is available from the British Library.

In-house Editor: Lee Xin Ying

Typeset by Stallion Press

Email: enquiries@stallionpress.com

Printed in Singapore by World Scientific Printers.

Contents — Volume II

Contents — Volume I

Preface

What is this Book About?

This book is concerned with the concept and measurement of organisational culture. The first volume deals with the historical development of the organisational culture perspective and with existing approaches to the conceptualisation and measurement of organisational culture. It also considers a number of concepts that are closely related to organisational culture, namely, organisational climate, national culture and social representations. The concept of social representations is perhaps a surprising inclusion here, but as we will show, it has striking similarities to the concept of organisational culture, despite developing quite separately from it, within social psychology rather than in organisational psychology and management. The second volume of the book is predominantly methodological. It deals with the empirical investigation of a proposed method for assessing those aspects of an organisation's culture that exist at a deeper level and that have proven to be particularly difficult to reveal. It has been recognised by researchers such as Steven Ott that problems associated with the measurement of organisational culture have prevented the concept from fully realising its useful application in practice, and have made it difficult for the organisational culture perspective more generally to achieve maturity.

An issue that is central to our treatment of organisational culture throughout this book, and that we believe sets the concept apart from other closely related concepts like organisational climate, is the idea that organisational culture exists at different levels. As Edgar Schein has so clearly articulated, an organisation's culture can be thought of as comprising: a surface level associated with artefactual elements (the physical design of the organisation, its dress code, logo, *etc.*) and normative behaviours; a somewhat deeper and less easily discerned level of values that influence the culture's more observable manifestations; and, at its core, an even deeper level of beliefs and assumptions that over time may have become taken-for-granted and unconscious, but that nevertheless profoundly affect how the organisation operates and, in particular, how it responds to challenges and change. While practically useful quantitative measures of normative behaviours and values have been developed to assess the more surface levels of organisational culture, accessing the deeper level of unconscious beliefs and assumptions has proved to be much more difficult. Culture at this deeper level has traditionally been investigated using qualitative methods, akin to those used in anthropology, which require considerable time and lived experience in an organisation, and which are therefore compromised in terms of their practical usefulness, for example, for understanding and facilitating change in organisations. It is the central purpose of this book to propose and investigate a method that, when compared with existing approaches, might provide a more systematic and more economical means whereby to decipher organisational culture at the level of basic beliefs and assumptions. To the extent that such a method could be developed, it would allow this most basic and influential aspect of the concept to achieve a level of theoretical and practical utility that, in our opinion, it has not yet achieved.

To Whom is this Book Addressed?

This book has been written with two audiences in mind. The first volume has been designed primarily for teaching and study purposes, for use in postgraduate level courses in which an understanding of the concept of organisational culture and its measurement is required. We have assumed that such courses will most likely be concerned not only with the theory of organisational culture but also with the practical usefulness of the concept for understanding organisations and how they operate, particularly in response to challenges and change. In the context of addressing these issues, in the first volume we also review the research on the related concepts of organisational climate, national culture, and social representations. A key objective in this regard is to consider how the integration of these concepts with the concept of organisational culture might contribute to a more comprehensive account of the social and cultural aspects of organisations.

The content of this book has been shaped in important ways by the scholarship of others working in the area of organisational culture. A major (and perhaps the foremost) influence has been the work of Edgar Schein. Schein's conceptual treatment of organisational culture — in particular, the distinction that he draws between a culture's surface-level elements and the deeper-level elements that constitute its 'essence' — remains, in our opinion, the most useful and well articulated of its kind. It successfully conveys the complexity of the phenomenon, at the same time as making sense of it in a way that is at once intuitively appealing, theoretically important, and practically useful.

We agree with Schein that one of the key benefits of a cultural analysis of an organisation that is based on a depiction of culture as multi-layered is that it can reveal discrepancies between the elements comprising the different levels of the organisation's culture, and these discrepancies can help to explain complex and sometimes counterproductive aspects of how the organisation operates. The value of an understanding of this kind is perhaps most apparent when seeking to explain why it can be so difficult to achieve change in organisations. The research suggests that the implementation of a proposed change can encounter serious difficulties (and perhaps fail) even when there seems to be broad agreement among the organisation's members about the need for, and usefulness of, the change. What may become apparent from a cultural analysis is that the source of these difficulties lies in collectively- and deeply-held beliefs and assumptions that are not aligned with the proposed change, and that only become apparent as a result of being challenged by the change process. An example of this to which we refer in the book concerns an organisational change designed to promote a more active, informed, and consultative role for workers. Despite their in-principle support for this change, workers are subsequently found to be strongly resistant to it because it challenges their basic belief that it is the role of managers to make decisions and the role of workers to implement these decisions, without being made responsible for them.

Another benefit of Schein's conceptualisation of organisational culture as comprising different levels is that it challenges those interested in methodological issues to discover ways of operationalising those aspects of organisational culture that lie below the surface and that are therefore most difficult to reveal. In the book we acknowledge the 'clinical' method for assessing organisational culture that Schein has developed and that he uses in his work as a consultant to facilitate the change process in organisations. This method involves using group interviews to identify discrepancies between the more surface levels of the organisation's culture — between its artefacts and behavioural norms and its values — that may provide clues as to deeper-level beliefs and assumptions that may act to enable or impede the change process. While economical in terms of the time commitment required for its use, as Schein himself acknowledges, his clinical approach to cultural analysis works best when there is a particular organisational problem or issue to motivate the process. This method does not provide a means whereby to systematically assess an organisation's culture, for the purpose of evaluating changes in that culture over time, or comparing that culture with the culture of other organisations.

In our treatment of the concept of organisational culture, we also draw on the work of Benjamin Schneider. Schneider's explication of the distinction between organisational culture and the related concept of organisational climate, along with his work towards achieving an integration of these two concepts, provided a valuable foundation for our own work and thinking in this area. Importantly also, Schneider's commitment to the integration endeavour — to considering the ways in which related concepts can be used to complement each other — provided the impetus for our further investigation, in the book, of the parallels between organisational culture and national culture, and between organisational culture and social representations.

As indicated, a major focus of the book's content is on methodological issues. In terms of significant influences in this regard, our initial interest in the measurement of organisational culture, and indeed our persistence with this project in the face of the many difficulties posed by the measurement challenge, owe much to a view that was expressed more than two decades ago by Steven Ott. In 1989, Ott drew attention to what he saw as a pressing need to further develop the assessment of organisational culture. In his view, methodological issues constituted the main impediment to the organisational culture perspective achieving maturity and realising its potential as a theoretically and practically useful approach to understanding organisations. We believe that this view is as relevant today as it was then. In grappling with the vexed question of measurement, as it applies to organisational culture, we were greatly assisted by Alan Bryman's comprehensive treatment and critique of research methods in the social sciences. Bryman's explication of the strengths and limitations of quantitative, qualitative and mixed-method approaches, along with his discussion of issues of reliability and validity in relation to each of these approaches, provided invaluable reference material for our exposition of the methodological issues involved in assessing organisational culture.

With respect to our own contribution to work in this area, what we propose in this book, and endeavour to evaluate, is a contextual analysis of organisational culture. In developing this approach, we have drawn on research (our own and that of others) that has highlighted the important role of contextual information — specifically, organisation members' views of the organisation's past, its anticipated future, the ideal for the organisation, and their knowledge of other organisations — in understanding the culture of an organisation. While each of these 'domains' of context has been individually commented on by researchers, and in some cases assessment procedures have been developed to measure them, there has been no previous work towards the kind of integrated contextual analysis that we are proposing. This analysis involves an approach that utilises information from each of these contextual domains, considered separately and in terms of the relationships between domains, in order to provide a more comprehensive account of the different levels of an organisation's culture.

To facilitate the use of this book as a text for teaching and study purposes, we have endeavoured, where possible, to make the chapters relatively self-contained so that their content can easily be understood without reference to other chapters. This has necessitated some level of repetition of material in various chapters. It should also be pointed out that in order to make the content of the first volume of the book as complete as possible, it includes ideas and conclusions that we have drawn from the research that we have undertaken, and that is reported in the second volume of the book. In this sense, there is an unavoidable element of chronological inaccuracy. Notwithstanding these limitations, we hope that our efforts to summarise, expand on, and integrate the various conceptual and measurement issues that we address in the first volume will be of value for teaching and study purposes.

The second volume of the book has been written primarily for those interested in conducting research on organisational culture. To encourage and assist such research, we have provided an account of each of the stages of a research project that we undertook with the aim of developing an approach to deciphering deeper-level organisational culture that would be more comprehensive, systematic and economical than existing approaches. Based on the review material presented in the first volume, and drawing on insights from exploratory research carried out in the first stage of the project, the contextual approach that is proposed and evaluated involves the assessment of organisation members' views about specific aspects of their organisation and its culture — at the present time, in the past, in the anticipated future, in terms of an ideal for their organisation, and if relevant, in terms of how those aspects are manifested in other organisations. Differences between contexts, such as what might be suggested by a respondent's account of the particular aspect of the organisation or issue of interest, as experienced now and in the past, along with respondents' explanations for why these differences might exist, are used to provide clues as to the deeper-level beliefs and assumption that characterise the organisation's culture with respect to that aspect or issue. This information is also used to make predictions about the culture's likely responsiveness to change in relation to that aspect or issue.

In our account of this research project, we have described the research method, the research process, and the results obtained in some detail. We have done this in order to demonstrate how our initial approach was progressively modified, in a 'building-block' fashion, based on the findings of research in each preceding stage. In particular, we demonstrate how aspects of the method — whether the topics that constituted the focus of questioning or the types of questions asked — that initially seemed appropriate, nevertheless failed for various reasons to provide the information about organisational culture that was hoped for. Progressive modifications to these aspects of the method were needed in order to arrive at what we believe can provide the basis for a systematic and economical means whereby to assess the deeper-level beliefs and assumptions that constitute the essence of an organisation's culture.

The research that is reported in the second volume was carried out over a period of three years, during which time the senior author spent between two to three days per week in the research organisation, making general observations and talking to organisation members when there were opportunities to do so, in addition to conducting the more formal interviewing that was used to develop and evaluate the proposed method. In this project, the researcher's lived experience of the research setting, over an extended period of time, helped to ensure a depth of understanding of the organisation's culture of the kind that is advocated by proponents of more qualitative, anthropological, approaches to deciphering organisational culture. This understanding provided a means whereby to validate the information that was obtained using the proposed interview method — a method designed to generate equivalent information about the organisation's culture in a much shorter period of time.

We hope that the research presented in the second volume encourages other researchers with an interest in methodological issues to build on the work that we have begun. While the results that we have obtained appear to us to be promising, they are not used to present an established method for the assessment of organisational culture. Rather, their value lies in the insights they provide about the kind of further research that we believe is needed, to develop a practically useful measure of organisational culture. We will have achieved our aims for this book if it helps to create an impetus for this further research, and if it contributes to the methodological advancement that Ott suggests is needed for the organisational culture perspective to realise its potential contribution to the understanding and improvement of organisations.

How is this Book Organised?

The content of this book is organised into two volumes, each of which comprises three main parts and seven chapters. Volume I reviews the existing literature on organisational culture with reference in particular to the development of the organisational culture perspective and to extant treatments of the concept of organisational culture and its measurement. Consideration is also given to a number of concepts that are closely related to organisational culture. Volume II provides an account of empirical work undertaken by the authors towards the development of a method for assessing organisational culture. A summary description of the content of each volume — in terms of its major parts and associated chapters — is provided below.

Volume I

As indicated, this volume comprises three main parts and seven chapters in all. Part One, comprising Chapters 1 through 3, is focussed entirely on the concept of organisational culture and its development. In Chapter 1, we provide an historical overview of the origins of the contemporary study of organisational culture. Drawing on the work of Ott (1989) and others, consideration is given to the various schools of thought that have been most influential — whether through the articulation of competing or parallel perspectives — in shaping the current view of organisations as cultural entities. Consideration is also given to the popularisation of the organisational culture concept, in particular, with the publication of 'bestseller' management books such as Peters and Waterman's (1982) *In Search of Excellence*. A critique of this, and other popularist approaches to organisational culture is offered particularly with respect to the concept's current status, in the business community, as a catch-all explanation for why firms perform, or fail to perform. Consideration is also given to the difficulties encountered in assessing organisational culture that have restricted the further development of the concept and its application in practice.

In Chapter 2, we address the question of what organisational culture is. Consideration is given to the definitional diversity that characterises treatments of organisational culture and to the lack of agreement that exists about whether culture is something that an organisation *has* — the 'culture-as-variable' perspective — or something that an organisation *is* — the 'culture-as-root-metaphor' perspective. Illustrative examples are provided of research conducted within each of these 'competing' perspectives and the case is made for an approach that exploits their complementarity. In this chapter consideration is also given to Schein's definition and treatment of the concept of organisational culture. Particular attention is drawn to his depiction of culture as a multi-layered phenomenon and to the conceptualisation of what he refers to as the 'essence' of organisational culture. Schein's work in this regard has achieved widespread recognition and acceptance and, as we have indicated previously, has been particularly influential in shaping of our own thinking and research in this area. Chapter 2 concludes with an overview and critique of a conceptual framework that challenges mainstream depictions of organisational cultures as consensual and widely shared. This is the 'three-perspective' framework, derived from the culture-as-root-metaphor perspective, and developed by Meyerson and Martin (1987) and Martin (1992, 2002). The key elements of this framework are described, and this is followed by a critique of its contribution to the debate concerning the nature of organisational culture.

Chapter 3 builds on the conceptual treatment of organisational culture provided in Chapter 2. Consideration is given to the way in which organisational cultures are described, or talked about, in terms of a number of key characteristics. The first part of this chapter focuses on the structural properties, or dimensionality, of organisational culture. Consideration is given to the question as to whether every organisation's culture is unique or whether there are certain universal traits or types that can be used to describe any organisation's culture. It is suggested that this question reflects a parallel concern in the study of personality (not surprising perhaps, given the common representation of organisational culture as being like the 'personality' of an organisation), in which a distinction is drawn between approaches that are *emic* in nature (highlighting the unique aspects of each individual's personality) and approaches that are *etic* in nature (highlighting common types or traits). As in personality research, emic accounts of organisational culture use qualitative means to describe organisational cultures as unique entities, while etic accounts attempt to classify organisational cultures in terms of a finite number of types or traits. In terms of illustrating the latter, an overview and critique is provided of three major typologies of organisational culture, proposed by Schein (1985, 1992, 2004, 2010), Bate (1984), and Harrison (1972), respectively. These typologies are dealt with in some detail because they purportedly focus on the deeper-level elements of organisational culture. Consideration is also given to a number of typologies and trait approaches that are restricted to the more surface-level elements of organisational culture.

In the second part of Chapter 3, the focus is on the strength of organisational culture. We first discuss the commonly used terms 'strong' and 'weak', as descriptors for an organisation's culture, and the associated difficulties that this simple dichotomy poses for conducting the kind of empirical research needed to confirm the theoretical importance of the concept. Payne's (2000) framework for conceptualising the strength of an organisation's culture — one of the few frameworks of its kind — is then considered and critiqued, and a number of suggestions are made regarding additional potential indicators that might be incorporated into measures of cultural strength. In the third and final part of Chapter 3, the focus is on descriptions of organisational culture that emphasise its potential for differentiation, rather than its unitary or integrated character. We consider the possibilities for subcultural differentiation in terms of the emergence of both organisation-specific and occupational subcultures. Consideration is also given to a number of important questions that arise as a result of this differentiation, pertaining for example to: the differential influence of organisational versus occupational subcultures; the possibilities for, and implications of, membership with more than one subculture; the relationship between an organisation's overall culture and its various organisational and occupational subcultures; and the need for leaders and managers to be aware of the extent of subcultural differentiation in their organisation.

In Part Two of this volume, comprising Chapters 4 and 5, consideration is given to a number of concepts that are closely related to the concept of organisational culture. In the case of two of these concepts, namely organisational climate and national culture covered in Chapter 4, the linkages with organisational culture have been explicitly acknowledged in the literature and to some extent also studied. In the case of the third concept, namely social representations covered in Chapter 5, the link with organisational culture, while remarkable, is generally not known and there has to date been no comprehensive analysis of the degree of overlap between these two concepts. With respect to our treatment of organisational climate in Chapter 4, we begin by providing an overview of current thinking about some of the main similarities and differences between the organisational climate and organisational culture perspectives. In particular, we compare these perspectives in terms of: how they have conceptualised the phenomenon of interest; their dominant methodologies; their respective research agendas; and their respective intellectual and theoretical foundations. In the context of this comparison and with particular reference to the issue of measurement, we show that organisational climate measures, which typically focus on norms or values perceived to be characteristic of an organisation, are very similar in their content to those organisational culture measures that focus on these same constructs. Following this comparison, consideration is given to whether or not organisational climate and organisational culture should be regarded as synonymous, or fundamentally different, constructs. We make the case that there is sufficient overlap to justify a more concerted research effort towards establishing a meaningful, and conceptually and theoretically useful, alignment of the two constructs. Finally, in an endeavour to provide a basis for this further work, we examine how organisational climate might be more comprehensively incorporated into Schein's framework for conceptualising organisational culture, and we explore the implications of this for a reconceptualisation of organisational climate and, to some extent also, organisational culture.

In Chapter 4, consideration is also given to the concept of national culture, and in particular, to research on national culture that has been carried out within a work and organisational perspective. It is pointed out that the concept of national culture has had an important influence on the development and application of the concept of organisational culture. However, as with the other related concepts that we consider, research on national culture has tended to proceed separately from research on organisational culture. A brief account is provided of three of the more widely recognised models of national culture that are concerned (either directly or indirectly) with cross-national differences in work-related values. These are the models developed by Hofstede and Peterson (2000), Trompenaars and Hampden-Turner (1997), and Smith, Peterson, and Schwartz (2002). The relationship between the concepts and assessments of national culture and organisational culture are discussed, together with the implications that a consideration of national culture has for the use of the concept and assessment of organisational culture in national and international business contexts.

Chapter 5 considers the overlap between the organisational culture and social representations perspectives, the latter originating in European social psychology and concerned with shared representations (similar to the 'shared beliefs' of organisational culture) at a societal level. As we have indicated, despite the considerable overlap between these two perspectives, they have developed as entirely separate areas of intellectual inquiry. The chapter begins by defining the concept of social representations and commenting on the origins of social representations theory. Consideration is then given to the overlap that is evident in conceptualisations of organisational culture and social representations and to the implications of this overlap for generating new knowledge and understandings in each area. Following this, the two perspectives are compared and contrasted in terms of their dominant research agendas and the research methods that are favoured in each. This comparison is, in part, informed by a review of a sample of organisational culture and social representations articles that we undertook, for the purpose of more systematically comparing the two areas of inquiry. The chapter concludes with some general comments about the value of continued work towards elucidating the synergies between the organisational culture and social representations perspectives, and exploring the ways in which these synergies might be exploited to mutual benefit.

Part Three, comprising Chapters 6 and 7, marks a transition away from the predominantly conceptual focus of Parts One and Two, towards a consideration of methodological issues and an introduction to the contextual analysis of organisational culture that is proposed and evaluated in the research reported in the second volume of the book. Chapter 6 is concerned with extant approaches to the measurement of organisational culture. In this chapter, we describe each of the three main methods that have been used to assess, or decipher, organisational culture, namely: (i) qualitative methods; (ii) quantitative methods; and (iii) an integrated approach that uses some combination of qualitative and quantitative methods. The advantages and disadvantages of each approach are considered, with particular attention given to the capacity of each approach to provide insights into 'deep' as opposed to 'surface' culture, and to provide answers to questions pertaining to a culture's sharedness, differences between the cultures of different organisations and organisational subgroups, and changes in culture over time. Examples are also given of research, including applied research, which has been carried out using each of these approaches. The chapter concludes by making the argument that, despite more than three decades of research into organisational culture, progress towards realising the practical utility of the construct has been disappointing and that this outcome is attributable, in large part, to a lack of methodological advancement in the study of organisational culture.

In Chapter 7, we explore the notion of organisational culture as a context-specific phenomenon and provide an introduction to our proposed framework for conceptualising and analysing organisational culture in terms of five different dimensions, or domains, of context: the *present*, the *past*, the anticipated *future*, *other* organisations, and the *ideal*. Consideration is given to the nature, and extent, of the representation of each of these contextual domains in existing treatments of the concept of organisational culture and in approaches to the measurement of organisational culture. We make the case for a consolidation of these five domains into a single coherent framework that might form the basis of a method for assessing organisational culture that has the capacity to reveal deeper-level cultural beliefs and assumptions. Importantly, the contextual analysis of organisational culture that we propose in this chapter draws on insights from the initial exploratory study conducted as part of the research reported in the second volume of the book.

Volume II

In this volume, which also comprises three main parts and seven chapters, the focus is primarily on empirical work that we ourselves have carried out. The main project in this regard involved a series of three studies undertaken by the first author with the aim of investigating what would be required to develop a measure for organisational culture that would be practically useful, at the same time as capable of providing insights into the deeper-level, and hence more difficult to access, beliefs and assumptions that constitute what Schein refers to as the 'essence' of an organisation's culture. The research site for all three studies was the South Australian operations of a large automotive company, whose local management had given approval for employees (specifically shop floor workers and their supervisors) from two of its divisions to take part in a study of organisational culture. The research was carried out over a period of some three years during which time the researcher (that is, the first author) maintained a level of frequent and regular engagement with the setting and subjects of the research. With respect to the broad structure of our account of this research, Parts Four and Five of this volume provide the details of the three studies that were carried out, along with their main findings. Part Six provides an overall summary and evaluation of this research, and considers the implications for future research that might valuably be undertaken. As an example of the kind of future research that is advocated, Part Six also provides an account of a follow-up study that we conducted subsequent to the main research project. The more specific contents of this volume are summarised below.

In Part Four, comprising Chapters 8 and 9, we provide an account of the initial work that was undertaken towards the development of the proposed method. In Chapter 8, following an introduction to the research organisation and a brief account of the means by which access to this organisation was negotiated, we describe and report the results of the first study in the series. This study was an entirely exploratory study that used the qualitative techniques of observation and in-depth interviewing as a means whereby to gain some initial insights into the organisation's culture, and into the kinds of topics that might usefully be explored and the kinds of questions that might usefully be asked in order to undertake a more structured and systematic investigation of that culture. The findings of this initial study were used to inform the development of a prototype method that was piloted in the second study, an account of which is provided in Chapter 9. The method for this second study took the form of a semi-structured interview designed to investigate respondents' beliefs and assumptions about the 'role of workers' and the 'role of supervisors' in the two divisions studied. Open-ended questions were used to explore respondents' perceptions of, and thinking about, the respective roles of workers and supervisors in relation to different domains of context (the past, the present, the anticipated future, the other, and the ideal). Closed questions took the form of forced-choice rating questions that required respondents to rate the role of workers as more or less 'active' or 'passive', and the role of supervisors as more or less 'directive' or 'consultative'. The design of these rating questions drew on McGregor's (1960) distinction between Theory X and Theory Y beliefs and assumptions, which had emerged in the first study as being particularly relevant to an understanding of culture in the research organisation. The piloting of this method in the second study provided important insights into the strengths and limitations of the prototype method, which was subsequently revised for use in the third and final study in the series.

An account of the third study is provided in Part Five of this volume, comprising Chapters 10 through 12. In Chapter 10, we introduce the third study and describe the main modifications to the method that were made, along with the key design features of the revised interview protocol. As with the original prototype method, the revised method took the form of an issue-focussed semi-structured interview that was designed to provide insights into respondents' deeper-level beliefs and assumptions about the role of workers and the role of supervisors in each of the two divisions. In the revised method, the previous Theory X — Theory Y rating questions were replaced with a series of prompt questions designed to provide a more comprehensive profile of the respective roles of workers and supervisors than had been obtained previously. The revised method also involved a more comprehensive analysis of context with the inclusion, in particular, of questions seeking information about respondents' attributions regarding differences between contexts in their experience of, or thoughts about, the respective roles of workers and supervisors. Chapter 10 also provides procedural information concerning, in particular, the administration of the method in the third study, the approach to data analysis, and the format for reporting the results.

In Chapters 11 and 12, we report and discuss the findings of the third study. In Chapter 11, the focus is on those findings pertaining to the use, in the revised method, of semi-structured interviewing. Consideration is first given to the results pertaining to the use of open-ended questions in combination with closed questions, or prompts. Following this, we examine the way in which qualitative data (generated by allowing respondents to qualify and/or elaborate on their responses) can be used to provide important insights into the meaning of quantitative data (in this case, data that lend themselves to quantification, such as "Yes"/"No" responses). In Chapter 12, the focus is on those findings pertaining to the operationalisation in the revised method of context, in terms of the five dimensions of the present, the past, the future, the other, and the ideal. By way of an introduction to the chapter, the rationale for the treatment of organisational culture as a highly context-specific phenomenon is briefly restated. Consideration is then given to the extent to which references to different contextual domains that are made *spontaneously* might obviate the need for specific questions about context (that is, questions about a given issue in the present, the past, anticipated future, *etc.*). Respondents' causal attributions regarding differences in their experience/thinking between contextual domains (e.g., between the past and the present, or the present and the anticipated future) are also analysed. An important focus of the analysis is on similarities and differences between the two divisions involved in this research. Consideration is also given to the nature of the linkages between the data pertaining to different contextual domains. In the last part of Chapter 12, we consider the methodological implications of the findings reported and provide some preliminary comments about the overall value of the study.

Part Six of this volume, comprising Chapters 13 and 14, has as its main focus, evaluation, future research, and follow up. In Chapter 13, we draw together the main findings of the third study to provide an evaluation of the method developed for use in this study. Consideration is first given to each of the key features of the method and the extent to which it contributes meaningfully to an understanding of organisational culture. A more general evaluation of the method is then offered, with particular attention drawn to the strengths and weaknesses of the method relative to other methods for deciphering and measuring organisational culture. We then draw on insights from this research endeavour as a whole to suggest a number of directions for future research that we believe might valuably be pursued.

In Chapter 14, we provide an account of a follow-up study that we conducted that was suggested by the findings of our earlier work. This study involved the development and testing of a framework for the more systematic analysis of the attributions data that were generated by the previously reported third study. It is presented here as an example of the kind of research that we believe might usefully be undertaken as part of a broad agenda for methodological advancement in the study of organisational culture. The data for analysis in this study took the form of respondents' causal statements about why a reported change, say from the past to the present, or from the present to the anticipated future, had occurred. The analysis that was conducted involved, first of all, coding each attribution (there were some 600 in all) according to a ten-dimension coding framework that we developed for use in this study. Consideration was then given to differences between the two divisions in terms of: (i) simple attribution tendencies in relation to single dimensions of the coding framework; (ii) attribution 'style' as represented by the pattern of relations among dimensions; and (iii) the specific attributions that had most salience for group members. The value of this approach to analysing attributions is discussed, with particular attention given to the implications of the findings for an understanding of the cultures of the two divisions. The important point is made that, despite the relatively elaborate treatment of attributions that was adopted, the size of the data set precluded an examination of 'cross-context' differences in attribution tendencies and 'style' (the idea that attributions about the cause(s) of past-present differences might differ from the corresponding attributions about the cause(s) of present-future differences *etc.*). The possibility that such differences might exist is foreshadowed and highlighted as a further potentially fruitful area for future research.

Acknowledgements

There have been a number of influences that have shaped the development of this book, not the least being the scholarship of others. In the preceding pages we have made reference to a number of writers and scholars in the area whose work has been a valuable source of intellectual enrichment for our own thinking and research, as well as providing the impetus for our continued efforts to find answers to the vexed question of measurement, as it applies to organisational culture. We are particularly indebted in this respect to the work of Edgar Schein, Benjamin Schneider, Steven Ott and Alan Bryman. This book has also been influenced by our experience, over many years, as teachers and supervisors of undergraduate and postgraduate university students enrolled in management and organisational psychology courses, and/or undertaking research in management and organisational psychology, and by our experience in the work cultures of the organisations in which we have been employed or in which we have undertaken research. The impact of this experience has been substantial and we are sincerely grateful to the students and work colleagues who helped to shape it.

There are a number of other important acknowledgements that we wish to make. The chapters in Parts Four and Five of the second volume of this book provide an account of empirical work carried out by the first author. While the data collection for the studies reported in these chapters was completed some years ago, we remain grateful to the research organisation for making this research possible, and we remain indebted to the participants in the research for giving so generously of their time and for so willingly and openly sharing their experiences of their organisational life. We are also grateful to our respective employing organisations — The University of Adelaide Business School and more recently Families SA (the Department for Education and Child Development) in the case of the first author, and The University of Adelaide School of Psychology in the case of the second author — who have supported us in various ways to bring this work to completion, whether by allowing it to be carried out as part of a recognised research role, or by approving much-needed periods of leave to enable the work to continue.

The support of our publisher, World Scientific Publishing, is also gratefully acknowledged. We particularly appreciate WSPC's understanding of the constraints under which this book was written — with both authors juggling the competing demands of work on the project and full time professional jobs — and their generosity in allowing us extra time to complete the book. We would like to especially thank Agnes Ng (Editor, WSPC) for her encouragement and patience during the writing of the book, and Xin Ying Lee (Editor, WSPC) for her very valuable assistance with the arrangement and copy editing of the final manuscript. Special thanks are also due to our good friend Rosie Gronthos for her generous and unwavering support during the final stages of our preparation of the manuscript. Rosie provided us with invaluable pre-submission editorial assistance, in addition to which her constant words of encouragement and optimism about the worth of the project helped to sustain our efforts in the months leading up to submission.

A project of this kind is not without its impact on the home and family front, in particular, in cases like ours where the partners to the project are also life partners. In this sense, our greatest acknowledgement is to our son Eliot, for his patience during the writing of this book, for his understanding of the demands on our time that it created, and for his tolerance of our sometimes overly robust debates about its content. Qualities such as these that have come to mark his character have only strengthened our love and admiration for him. We would also like to thank all the young people in Eliot's friendship group. Their cheerfulness and often-expressed casual interest in our work — "How's the book going?" — were a valuable, and valued, source of encouragement.

And finally, we wish to acknowledge the constant companionship and sometimes overly eager affection of Pablo and Penelope, our two rough-coat Jack Russell dogs. Pablo and Penelope remained at our feet and in our emotional (if not our intellectual) space through the many hours involved in writing this book.

About the Authors

Elizabeth Kummerow

Dr Elizabeth Kummerow's interest in organisational culture has developed over many years in the context of her experience as a higher degree research student, as a university lecturer in management and organisational behaviour, and as a psychologist and manager in various human services organisations in both the public and private sector. Dr Kummerow holds a PhD degree from the University of Adelaide. The various studies that were carried out as part of, and subsequent to, this research — which was concerned with methodological issues in understanding organisational culture — are reported in the second volume of this book. As a university lecturer, Dr Kummerow has more than ten years of teaching experience with the Business School of the University of Adelaide. She has taught at both undergraduate and postgraduate levels, and has been responsible for the development and delivery of courses in general management, human resources management, organisational behaviour, organisational change, leadership, and organisational culture. As a psychologist and manager, Dr Kummerow has worked with human services organisations involved in the provision of supported employment services, and more recently, psychological support services for clients with special and complex needs.

Neil Kirby

Dr Neil Kirby is Senior Lecturer in the School of Psychology at the University of Adelaide in South Australia. He is a member of the Australian Psychological Society and the College of Organisational Psychologists. His teaching and research interests in organisational psychology include organisational culture, the historical development of organisational theories, the role of the organisational psychologist, and the person/organisation fit. Dr Kirby is also Director of the Disabilities Research Unit in the School of Psychology at the University of Adelaide and his interests in disability include the assessment of support needs for achieving independence and quality of life outcomes in community living, and employment for people with disabilities.

PART FOUR
EXPLORING METHOD

Chapter 8

An Exploratory Study of
Organisational Culture (Study 1)

This chapter is the first of five chapters — comprising Parts Four and Five of this volume — that report the results of three empirical studies that were undertaken by the first author towards the development of a measure for the efficient and effective assessment of the deeper-level beliefs and assumptions that constitute Level 3 of Schein's (1985, 1992, 2004, 2010) model of organisational culture. The research site for all three studies was the South Australian operations of a large automotive company, whose local management had given approval for employees from two of its divisions to take part in a study of organisational culture. The research was carried out over a period of some three years during which time the first author maintained a level of frequent and regular engagement with the setting and subjects of the research.

Importantly, the research for these three studies proceeded in a kind of building block fashion, with the development of each subsequent study being informed by insights from the previous study. In this sense, the three studies are best regarded as combining to form a single set, or series. The first study, which is reported in the present chapter, was an entirely qualitative study designed to provide insights into what might constitute a suitable content focus for the proposed method (i.e., in terms of the topic(s) that might be investigated), and how best to elicit the kind of culturally meaningful data being sought (i.e., in terms of the types of questions that might be asked). The second study, which is reported in Chapter 9, involved the trialling of a method that was developed on the basis of insights from the findings of the initial exploratory study, and that represented a first attempt to systematically access deeper-level cultural information about the topic being investigated. Based on insights from the findings of this study, the method was further developed and refined, and the trialling and evaluation of this revised method was undertaken in the third and final study, reported in Chapters 10 through 12.

As indicated, the present chapter provides an account of the initial exploratory study undertaken as part of this research. The chapter begins by presenting the broad rationale for the research — essentially a desire to contribute to the methodological advancement of the study of organisational culture — and then introducing Study 1 as the first in a series of three studies concerned with the development of a practically useful method for the assessment of 'deep' culture. Following this, in the second section of the chapter, the research organisation that was the site for all three studies in this series is described, and a brief account is given of the means by which the researcher gained access to this organisation. In the third section, the research method for Study 1 is described, in terms of: the specific data collection techniques that were used; the number and demographic profile of the participants in the study; and the procedure for data collection. The fourth section introduces the approach to data analysis that was adopted and then reports the results of this analysis in terms of the key content themes that emerged in the data. In the fifth section, the main methodological implications of the findings of Study 1 are discussed, and this is followed in the sixth and final section by some brief concluding comments about the overall value of this study.

8.1 Research Rationale and Introduction to Study 1

In Part One of Volume I, it was argued that Schein's model of organisational culture currently provides the most comprehensive and practically useful approach to the assessment of organisational culture. Schein's model (1985, 1992, 2004, 2010), which is based on the anthropological work of Kluckhohn and Strodtbeck (1961), depicts organisational culture as comprising three levels: the surface and more easily observed level of artefacts and normative behaviours; a second level of less easily discernable values; and a third level of often unconscious or taken-for-granted assumptions and beliefs that have formed as a result of more or less successful attempts, by the organisation, to deal with its problems of internal integration and external adaptation. It was also indicated that the identification of the underlying beliefs and assumptions at Level 3 — which for Schein constitute the 'essence' of an organisation's culture — poses a major problem for the assessment of organisational culture, because organisation members may not be fully aware of them. The importance of assessing this deeper level of organisational culture is underscored by the possibility that there might be discrepancies between a culture's underlying beliefs and assumptions and a description of the culture that is based on a reading of its more surface-level elements. Moreover, such discrepancies, should they emerge, may have important implications for the success or failure of change programs. Thus, a change program that appears to be in the best interests of the organisation, and that organisation members may appear to support, may nonetheless be ultimately resisted because it presents a challenge to the beliefs and assumptions that organisation members hold at a deeper level, and that are not evident in the more surface levels of the organisation's culture.

An example of such a change program (previously mentioned in Chapter 7 of Volume I) might be one that seeks to empower organisation members by providing them with more of a say in decisions about how work is carried out in their particular department. On the face of it, such a change might be seen to offer benefits in terms of accessing workers' knowledge and ideas about how to make work processes more efficient and effective, and workers may even have complained previously about their lack of involvement in decisions that affect them. Nonetheless, it may become evident over the course of endeavouring to implement the proposed change that there is considerable resistance to it, and this resistance may have its roots in members' basic beliefs and assumptions about the respective roles of managers and workers, with the former being expected to make decisions about how work is done, and the latter expected to follow these decisions (and sometimes complain about them).

The traditional means of assessing organisational culture at the deeper level of underlying beliefs and assumptions relies on methods derived from anthropology and sociology that typically involve an investigator spending a considerable amount of time in the organisation in order to gain the depth of understanding that is required. However, as was pointed out in Volume I (see, e.g., Chapter 6), such methods are too time-consuming for practical purposes with respect to understanding and facilitating organisational change. Where such methods have been used, they tend to be applied in a more or less diluted form, in terms of both the time spent in the organisation and the amount of observational and/or interview data that are gathered. This inevitably compromises the validity of the conclusions that are drawn about the nature of the organisational culture being studied. A more efficient method for assessing culture at the deeper level of beliefs and assumptions, which has been developed and used by Schein (2010), involves structured group sessions in which selected members of the organisation, under the guidance of a consultant facilitator, are engaged in a discussion that is designed to elicit information about the organisation's culture in relation to one of more of its basic dimensions (whether beliefs and assumptions about The Nature of Human Nature, The Nature of Human Relationships, *etc.*). However, notwithstanding the fact that seeking information from a group about the organisation's culture is likely to be more efficient than seeking this same information separately from each individual in the group, there are a number of methodological difficulties that can limit the validity of the data that are obtained using a group approach. For example, while it is feasible, in principle, to construct groups whose membership is diverse (e.g., in terms of roles and position in the hierarchy), in reality it is more likely (given the power differentials that are created, both implicitly and explicitly, by the structures of many organisations) that they will comprise a relatively limited range of the organisation's members. Thus, in Schein's case, his groups were comprised predominantly of managers. With the group approach, there is also a risk of dominance of the group by certain individuals whose presence may suppress the offering of contrary viewpoints, and there is a risk of social desirability responding such that group members offer responses that are in line with the company's espoused views, or with the theoretical orientation of the interviewer. The point can also be made that, as yet, there appears to have been no demonstration of the reliability of the group approach to the assessment of the underlying beliefs and assumptions that constitute Level 3 of Schein's model of organisational culture. That is, there has been no demonstration that, in a given context, the repeated use of this method with other similar samples of participants, and with other group facilitators, produces similar findings about the nature of the organisational culture being studied.

As above, in this and the next four chapters of this volume, we provide an account of empirical research that was undertaken by the first author (hereafter referred to as the 'researcher') towards the development of a practically useful method for the assessment of deeper-level culture — essentially, the basic beliefs and assumptions that constitute Level 3 in Schein's model. In the present chapter, we describe Study 1, the first of the three studies that were undertaken as part of this research. This study was a wholly exploratory study that provided important aspects of the conceptual foundation upon which Studies 2 and 3 were built. The study involved the use of qualitative methods including unstructured open-ended interviewing and the gathering of observational data and data from informal conversations with study participants. The main aim of Study 1 was to identify those aspects, or dimensions, of the organisation's culture that seemed to be most relevant to the members of the group being investigated and that might, therefore, constitute an appropriate focus for the measure that the research was seeking to develop. In addition, it was hoped that this study would provide some clues as to the specific kinds of questions that one might ask in order to elicit culturally relevant information pertaining to these dimensions.

The point should be made that the gathering of observational data, pertaining in particular to organisational artefacts and normative behaviours, which commenced in Study 1, continued over the three-year period during which this research was carried out. In other words, it was a common feature of the method employed for all three studies and was used throughout the research as a means whereby to help validate the results obtained from more formal interviewing. Before proceeding to the details of Study 1, the following brief account is given of the research setting and the means by which access to this setting was obtained.

8.2 The Research Setting: Background Information and Access

As indicated above, this research was carried out in two divisions of the South Australian operations of a large automotive company. When the research commenced, the company supported a total workforce of more than 4,000 employees. The two participating divisions were the company's tooling division and one of its production divisions. Study 1 involved employees from the tooling division only, whereas Studies 2 and 3 included employees from both divisions.

The researcher's access to the organisation — in the first instance, to the tooling division — was obtained through a university colleague who was teaching in a management course in which the manager of the tooling division was enrolled. The outcome of an arranged introduction with this manager was that the researcher was able to negotiate access to the organisation (pending approval from senior company management and the unions, which was subsequently granted) for the purpose of conducting a preliminary study of organisational culture in the tooling division. It is perhaps worth noting that the researcher's experience in this regard accords well with Buchanan, Boddy, and McCalman's (1988) depiction of how management researchers often gain access to the organisations in which they carry out their research. According to these authors, gaining access is more often determined by luck (being 'in the right place at the right time') and having contacts in the field, than it is by the superior negotiating skills of the researcher.

By way of some background information on the tooling division, this division was among the oldest in the company, having been in existence since the company's inception in the early 1930s. Its main function was the provision of an in-house tooling service (involving the building and maintenance of press dies, assembly fixtures, and special purpose tools) to the company's fabrication and assembly operations. The division's employees comprised mostly qualified tradesmen, with trade skills in areas such as drafting, pattern-making, fitting, and tool-making. When the research for Study 1 commenced, there were approximately 300 employees in the tooling division. At the time, however, the division was undergoing a major restructure which involved, among other things, the substantial downsizing of the division — some three years later when the research for the third and final study was drawing to an end, there were only 75 employees remaining in this division — as well as the relocation of the division from its original site to the site of the company's main assembly and manufacturing operations, in a different geographical location, some distance away. The point should be made that this restructure was just one of a number of changes which the division had undergone as a result of a decision, taken by the company in the early 1970s, to contract out many of its major tooling projects to Japan.

It was considered (by both the researcher and the manager of the tooling division) that this division would provide a particularly suitable site for a study of organisational culture. Given its long history, and also the tenure of its employees (among the longest serving in the organisation), it was not unreasonable to expect that the division would support a well-established, and hence more readily identifiable, culture that while sharing major aspects of the organisation's overall culture would also have its own unique characteristics, and hence constitute an identifiable subculture. Moreover, it was possible, given the events of recent years, that this was a subculture of the organisation that had experienced, and was continuing to experience, some major challenges to its core beliefs and assumptions.

After some twelve months spent in the tooling division, and with the assistance of tooling division management, the researcher gained access to a second division, in this case one of the company's production divisions (hereafter referred to as the production division). As above, while Study 1 was carried out entirely in the tooling division, Studies 2 and 3 involved the collection of data from both the tooling and production divisions. Importantly, over the life of this project — a period of some three years — the researcher spent between two to three days per week in the research setting, that is, in one or other of the two participating divisions.

In securing access to the production division, the point can again be made that it was not by design, but rather the result of a personal contact — the manager of the tooling division was well-acquainted with the manager of the production division — that this particular division was included in the research. As it turned out, however, a more suitable second site for the research would have been hard to find. The production division was markedly different from the tooling division in a number of respects, suggesting that an examination of subcultural differences between the two divisions would be a worthwhile endeavour. Among the main differences between the divisions, the production division had none of the planning and design responsibilities of the tooling division. It specialised in injection moulding, painting, and the assembly of plastics components, such as bumper bars, consoles, and facia plates for brake lights. Shop floor employees in this division, unlike their counterparts in the tooling division, typically had no formal qualifications. The majority worked as production operators and, as such, possessed general assembly and production skills. The production division was established in the early 1980s — much later than the tooling division — and, as such, its members did not share the very long history of their counterparts in the tooling division. Moreover, in the context of the organisation as a whole, the production division was regarded as being somewhat 'different'. This was because it was the first division in the organisation to make use of semi-autonomous teams — a job design initiative from Japan — to get work done. The organisation used the production division as the site for a trial of this initiative, which was implemented in the early years of the division's operations.

The production division was based at the site of the company's main assembly and manufacturing operations, which as indicated above, was the site to which the tooling division was subsequently relocated. During the three-year period over which this research was carried out, the size of the production division's workforce remained relatively stable at around 300 employees.

8.3 Method

As indicated, Study 1 was conducted entirely in the tooling division. Data collection for this study spanned a period of approximately one year, during which time the researcher spent two to three full days each week as a 'researcher participant' in the division[1]. Divisional members were made aware of the research via a news release that was posted on the divisional bulletin board. This gave a brief introduction to the researcher, provided summary information about the nature of the study (including a brief definition of organisational culture), and invited divisional members to participate in and support the research. A "generalist" rather than a "specialist" approach to data collection was adopted (Siehl & Martin, 1990, p. 243) with information being sought about a range of manifestations (rather than a single manifestation) of the culture of the division. The study was entirely qualitative and drew on three main sources of data: (i) informal conversations with divisional members (at all levels of the hierarchy) during work breaks; (ii) observations of the behaviour of divisional members in work-related and social interactions with one another; and (iii) open-ended in-depth interviews with a sample of divisional members. Notwithstanding the importance of the data from all three sources, the point should be made that the decisions that were subsequently taken regarding the key design features of the measure being developed (e.g., in terms of its key areas of focus, and the questions to be asked) were informed primarily by the data from the in-depth interviews. The techniques of interviewing and the recording (in a diary) of observational data and data from informal conversations with organisation members were a feature of the method for all three studies conducted as part of this research. These methods derive from ethnographic studies and,

---

[1]Thus, the equivalent of six months full-time was spent gathering data for this study.

in this research they were employed in an attempt to access (or promote the emergence of) relevant cultural information pertaining to any, or all, of Schein's three levels of culture, including Level 1 artefacts, rituals, and norms of behaviour, Level 2 values, and Level 3 beliefs and assumptions related to work in the organisation.

As indicated, there were approximately 300 employees in the tooling division when this study commenced. Given the researcher's relatively sustained and prolonged involvement with the division during the study, it was possible for her to become closely acquainted with many of these employees. As such, a relatively large cross-section of the division's membership was represented by the conversational and observational data that were collected. These data and the positions of those providing the data were recorded in a diary on a daily basis for the duration of the study[2]. Individual interviews, of approximately one hour's duration each, were conducted with twenty divisional employees. Table 8.1 provides a description of these employees in terms of their demographic characteristics. As indicated, interviewees were all male and included the general manager of the division, seven supervisory staff (from first-line supervisors to a senior superintendent), two non-supervisory staff, and ten shop floor ('wages') employees (including three with leading hand status). The average age of interviewees was 47 years (and ranged from 33 years to 59 years), their average length of service with the company was 27 years (ranging from 14 years to 35 years), and their average length of service with the division was 23 years (ranging from 3 months to 35 years). Interviewees came from a number of different sections in the division and, in all cases, they worked full-time (i.e., 7.5 hours per day) on the early (i.e., day) shift rather than the late (i.e., afternoon) shift.

Interviews were highly unstructured and took the form of "informal conversations" (Patton, 1990, p. 280) in which interviewees were invited to talk with the researcher about their experience of working in the division. While there were no set interview questions, the researcher had drawn on a number of qualitative accounts of organisational culture (e.g., Barley, 1983; Snyder, 1988) in order to develop a short list of general questions which could be used, if necessary, to get the conversation started or to prompt further discussion. These questions were designed to obtain information about the interviewee's work experience in the organisation and their views about contextual issues such as the relevant history of the organisation, significant events, their ideals and views about the future. These questions included:

- What kind of work do you do here?
- Tell me what it's like around here? What are the good things about working here? What things are not so good?
- What can you tell me about the history of the organisation?

---

[2]As indicated above, the collection and recording of diary data continued through Studies 2 and 3, for both of the participating divisions. These data helped to validate aspects of the measure for organisational culture that was being developed in these later studies.

Table 8.1. Demographic characteristics of Study 1 interviewees.

Interviewee #	Age (yrs)	Years with the Company	Years with the Division	Section	Position
01	40	23	3 months	Total plant	General Manager
02	41	26	24	Die manufacture	Tradeswages
03	49	27	3 months	All manufacturing ops	Manufacturing Manager
04	48	24	17	Die fitting	Foreman
05	48	32	22	Pattern making	General Foreman
06	50	34	34	Pattern making	Tradeswages
07	33	17	17	Jigs	Tradeswages
08	55	28	28	Try-out	Tradeswages
09	49	34	34	Drawing room	Staff, supervisory
10	42	26	26	Drawing room	Staff, non-supervisory
11	54	29	29	Drawing room	Staff, non-supervisory
12	59	14	14	Prototype	Tradeswages (LH)*
13	57	35	35	Machining	Superintendant
14	39	22	22	Prototype	Staff, supervisory
14	40	25	25	Jigs	Tradeswages (LH)*
16	51	26	22	Jigs	Tradeswages
17	50	34	34	Jigs	General Foreman
18	50	27	27	Pattern making	Tradeswages (LH)*
19	50	28	28	Machining	Tradeswages
20	39	23	21	Machining	Tradeswages
	mean = 47.2 yrs	mean = 26.7 yrs	mean = 23.0 yrs		
	sd = 6.9 yrs range 33–59 yrs	sd = 5.5 yrs range 14–35 yrs	sd = 9.8 yrs range 3mths–35 yrs		

* Leading Hand.

- What are some of the most important things that have happened since you came here?
- What sorts of things would you like to see changed here?
- How do you see the future of this organisation?

Only the first two introductory questions were used in all cases. When asked about their current experience of work in the organisation — "Tell me what it's like around here?" *etc.* — many interviewees drew comparisons with working conditions in the past, and/or made comments about what they thought was wrong with the organisation and how it should be different, and/or expressed their concerns about the future of the organisation and their role in it. As such, the contextual questions (pertaining to the past, future, and ideal) were used only in cases where interviewees made no reference to contextual domains other than the present, or where they gave relatively simple answers that they did not elaborate upon.

Interviewees gave their written consent for the interviews to be recorded on audiotape and they were assured, in writing, that their identity would not be revealed in any subsequent reporting of the information that they provided. The transcripts of the interviews ran to some 400 pages.

8.4 Data Analysis and Results

Data analysis involved, first of all, acquiring sufficient familiarity with the data to be able to classify them in some way. To this end, the researcher completed several readings of the interview transcripts and diary data. Following this, the data were grouped according to the main subjects or topics that emerged as being of interest to divisional members. This task was done manually since, at the time, the researcher did not have access to a computer program for analysing qualitative data. It was necessary, therefore, to make multiple copies of the transcripts, so that excerpts of conversations could be cut from the whole conversation and sorted into relevant subject categories. Examples of the kinds of topics that emerged as being salient to participants in the study included: the substantial downsizing of the divisional workforce that took place in the early 1970s and then again in the early 1980s; current promotional practices in the division; the division's operating reward system; the approach to decision-making in the division; the relationship between workers and their supervisors; and changes in the status of tradesmen. In all, 25 such subject categories were identified.

The next step in the analysis was to search for commonalities in what participants said, and how they talked about these various subjects. In this way, it was hoped that a first attempt might be made at describing the culture of the division in terms of a number of underlying "content themes" (Siehl & Martin, 1990, p. 243). Given the treatment, in this research, of organisational culture as a shared phenomenon, it was considered appropriate that the analysis should focus on commonalities, rather than differences, in the data. At the same time, however, this approach required sensitivity to the emergence of differences that might constitute evidence that certain commonalities in the data were limited to specific groups or subcultures. At this stage of the analysis, it became apparent that in order to describe the results in a meaningful way, some kind of general analytical framework was needed that could be used to classify emergent themes according to a small number of broad dimensions or categories[3]. A review of existing frameworks for classifying organisational cultures and cultural themes was conducted and this suggested that the results of the present study could be most usefully described in terms of the framework, or typology, proposed by Schein (1985, 1992, 2004, 2010). This framework — as originally proposed (in the 1985 edition of Schein's book) and in its most recent form (presented in the 2010 edition of Schein's book) — is described in some detail in Chapter 3 of Volume I. As indicated, the original framework comprised five categories of basic (cultural) beliefs and assumptions, which Schein derived largely from the work of Kluckhohn and Strodtbeck (1961). Over the years, Schein has adapted the framework somewhat, with the revisions undertaken in this regard including some minor rewording and reorganisation of the original five categories.

Drawing on Schein's original framework, there were two categories of basic beliefs and assumptions that seemed to be particularly relevant for the classification of emergent themes in this study. The first of these was the nature of human nature, comprising beliefs and assumptions that, at an organisational level, are concerned with the way in which workers and managers are viewed. The second was the nature of human relationships, comprising beliefs and assumptions about how group members should relate to one another to ensure the optimal functioning of the group. As indicated in Chapter 3, in the most recent version of the framework (Schein, 2010), these two categories, along with the category The Nature of Human Activity, have been combined into a single category. Of some relevance also, but less strongly supported by the data, was the category Humanity's Relationship to Nature, comprising beliefs and assumptions about how organisation members view the relationship of the organisation to its external environment (whether in control of, coexisting in, or controlled by). This category was subsequently reclassified within the Nature of Reality and Truth category (Schein, 2010).

It was also the case that emergent themes from the present study — specifically those pertaining to the nature of human nature — could be further classified according to McGregor's (1960) distinction between Theory X and Theory Y managerial assumptions about the nature of workers. With respect to this analysis, there was good evidence to suggest that divisional practices and procedures, as well as the "managerial climate" of the division — defined by McGregor (p. 134) as "the psychological climate of the relationship" between superiors and subordinates — reflected predominantly Theory X assumptions (though interviewees did not speak about their experiences in this regard in terms of any such theory).

---

[3]The subject categories that had been identified were never intended to serve this purpose — they simply offered a preliminary means of sorting the data. Moreover, as was to be expected, it sometimes happened that the same theme emerged in interviewees' comments about more than one subject.

We turn now to a discussion of the results of the thematic analysis of data from Study 1. The main focus of this discussion is on the thematic content of data pertaining to the best represented of Schein's categories — as above, the nature of human nature and the nature of human relationships — since it was these findings that were of particular relevance to the development and testing of the proposed method for assessing deeper-level culture. Themes pertaining to the nature of human nature are described first with reference, as appropriate, to McGregor's distinction between Theory X and Theory Y assumptions. Following this, themes pertaining to the nature of human relationships are described. The discussion of results concludes with a brief account of emergent themes pertaining to humanity's relationship to nature — that category of beliefs and assumptions in Schein's model that, while relevant, was less well-represented in the Study 1 data set than either of the two previous categories. Within each broad category, themes are further grouped according to the particular domain (i.e., subject area) of their experience (i.e., whether experience of the division's reward system, its approach to decision-making, *etc.*) to which interviewees referred. While excerpts from the data are used to illustrate each of the themes discussed, it was not deemed necessary, given the exploratory nature of the study, to provide more than a few illustrative examples in each case.

8.4.1 *Themes pertaining to the nature of human nature*

The results of the thematic analysis of data pertaining to four subject areas — promotional practices, reward and recognition, performance appraisal, and superior/subordinate perceptions — provided the basis for making inferences about assumptions in this category. These results are as follows:

8.4.1.1 *Promotional practices*

Theme 1: 'Required personnel' are not promoted
One of the key themes to emerge from the data in this domain is related to the notion of required personnel. The term was used to describe divisional members who, because of their competence in their current position, were required in that position, and were there-fore unlikely to be considered for a promotion to a more senior position, or even for a transfer to another position at the same level. The following excerpts serve to illustrate:

> There are some that have tried [for promotion] and have banged their heads against the walls for years, waiting to get out and go somewhere else, into another department and improve themselves. They just weren't allowed to go... They were too clever in their present job. (staff, non-supervisory)
>
> When a job becomes available, there's always a notice on the board: 'There is a vacancy coming up. People who want to apply, have to apply on a form. And let your supervisor know that you're going to apply for this different job'. But if you're a very clever chap in the position you're in, you always get a knock back. (staff, non-supervisory)

He's a great organiser, and work, he knows what he's doing. Now there's a bloke who will never get on. He will never get on with this company…because they don't want him to. Number 1, he's too good at his job where he is, so to take him out of that job, and have it filled by someone who's not as good… (wages employee)

Interestingly, the label 'required personnel' was also seen to work against employees who were seeking early retirement:

Now someone will put in an A.V.O. [Avoid Verbal Orders][4], but he'll be knocked back [from early retirement] because he's considered required personnel. (wages employee)

As suggested by these data, competence or being good at one's job was not perceived as a guarantee of reward. On the contrary, it could lead to the employee becoming locked into his current position, with little hope of advancement. Moreover, this was a practice in which the needs of the division (at least, its immediate, short-term needs) clearly had priority over the needs of individual employees. In this sense, the practice can be seen to be more consistent with a Theory X orientation, than a Theory Y orientation.

Theme 2: Non-performance factors influence promotion

The data in this domain contained frequent references to how to get ahead in the organisation. There was a perception that certain personal factors, not related to performance, significantly influenced one's chances of promotion within the company. Reference was made, for example, to the importance of membership with the Freemasons, knowing the "right" people, owning a four-wheel drive, being apprenticed in the same year as the boss, being a "yes" person, having an "ability to talk" (a reference to self-promotion), and engaging in social and sporting activities (e.g., fishing, lawn bowls, golf) with the right people. The following excerpt provides a revealing illustration of the perception among divisional members that conformity with the group (and its underlying rules for membership) was an important criterion for promotion:

You promote a 'yes' person, not a 'no' person. Individuality is definitely out, not acceptable, and if you had someone like that, well you would not promote him… or you could see that you have a chance to bring him along your lines and therefore he becomes one of the big group and sings the same songs, and forgets actually what he really is about, puts that in the background. (wages employee)

As above for the data pertaining to Theme 1, these data can be seen to be more consistent with a Theory X orientation than a Theory Y orientation. They provide further evidence of

---

[4]The Avoid Verbal Orders form was a standard form that had been designed to encourage divisional members to communicate important matters in writing, rather than verbally.

a perception among divisional members that the needs and requirements of the group (organisation) take precedence over the needs and requirements of individual members of the group.

Theme 3: Promotion from within no longer the norm

A common concern which was expressed by divisional members was that the past practice of promotion from within the division no longer applied. There was an increasing trend toward the recruitment of divisional managers from other divisions of the company and this seriously undermined members' expectations that, so long as they met certain requirements (e.g., being "next in line" for a promotion and satisfactory performance), they could reasonably expect to advance their position and status within the division. This change in promotional practices in the division was seen by some divisional members as a consequence of the company's attempt to reduce the overall number of management personnel, while at the same time avoiding lay-offs:

> Instead of making them up off the shop floor, they started to bring them in, because they wanted to use the staff they already had [in other divisions] ...if they really desperately needed a staff person out there, they wouldn't make one up because they're trying to lower the amount of staff people now. They would look for some area where they're already paying someone a staff wage, and they'd bring them into the shop. (wages employee)

Others were more negative in their interpretation of the change. As they saw it, the division was being used, by the company, as a convenient "dumping ground" for poor performing managers from other divisions:

> I suppose the 'higher ups' thought they had to do something with [X]. He might have been on a limb in the job he was in before. (wages employee)
>
> We feel that we've only been getting what other departments don't want, and that's the general consensus on it. (staff, supervisory)

This latter view is nicely illustrated in Figure 8.1, which shows a cartoon, drawn by a wages employee from the tooling division, and depicting the artist's interpretation of what a 'promotion' to this division really meant[5].

Again, a Theory X orientation, with its emphasis on the organisation's needs taking precedence over the individual's needs, is suggested by these data.

---

[5]This was one of a number of cartoons drawn by the same artist, which were circulating among shop floor employees in the division during this period. Cultural artefacts such as these provided another window into divisional members' perceptions of life in the division at the time.

Figure 8.1. Insider's impression of winning a 'promotion' to the Tooling Division

8.4.1.2 *Reward and recognition*

While the above data are concerned specifically with members' perceptions of promotional practices in the division, numerous other references were made by divisional members to more general aspects of the division's operating reward system. The analysis of these data suggested the following seven general themes.

Theme 1: Money a major motivator of work performance

A commonly held view among divisional personnel was that money constituted the primary, and in some cases, the only benefit of working. Numerous references were made to the higher than average wages which employees in the division received (compared with similarly qualified tradesmen working in other industries) and to the fact that there was usually plenty of overtime available which offered a healthy supplement to employees' regular pay. With respect to this latter point, one interviewee (a wages employee) held the view that overtime was "the only thing that makes it worthwhile still working here."

It is interesting in the present context to consider also the views of those divisional members who had left the company at some stage (either voluntarily or because they had been retrenched), taken up work elsewhere, and then subsequently returned because of the better pay and conditions offered by the company. In the case of employees who had been made redundant, their return was in spite of the considerable resentment and antagonism that they reportedly felt toward the company at the time. The following excerpt, in which the comments of both the interviewer (I) and the respondent (R) (a supervisor) have been retained, serves to illustrate:

> I: What was your feeling about the company [after being sacked]?
> R: If I could've got a bomb I would've blown this place up. It hurt to be put off because since I left school I've never been fired from a job yet, so it hurt.
> I: What was your initial reaction to the telegram asking you to return to work?
> R: It [the telegram] got screwed up and thrown in the corner. It took me a month from the time I got the telegram to reapply for the job.
> I: Why did you come back?
> R: Money, money. I was working at [X] and when I went, when I was due to go on annual leave, I'd seen what some of the boys from [X] were getting paid. You'd lost all your demerit money and all the bonuses they paid, and they just paid you out for annual leave on the flat rate and it was awful.

One final point that can be made in relation to this theme is that, consistent with Theory X assumptions, there was a perception among supervisory staff that money and other tangible rewards and benefits (such as good leave conditions and access to overtime) *should* be sufficient to motivate employee performance. There was little apparent appreciation of the potential motivational value of more intrinsic, less tangible rewards, such as those identified as motivational factors in Herzberg's Two-Factory Theory of motivation (Herzberg, Mausner, & Snyderman, 1959). The following excerpt serves to illustrate:

> I've always found this company good to work for, never knocked the company, but it annoys me to hear other people knock the company when they don't really give their lot. They get good conditions, good pay, four weeks leave, plus all the PDO's [Programmed Days Off], plus public holidays. They can take their pick if they want to work overtime and earn extra money. The working conditions are good. (staff, supervisory)

Theme 2: Use of overtime as a control mechanism

As suggested above, a commonly held view among divisional members (at least at the shop floor level) was that one of the major benefits of coming to work was the opportunity to supplement one's basic income with overtime pay. There was also a perception that this reliance on overtime served to weaken employee resolve in relation to industrial action in the division (one condition of which was the imposition of overtime bans). As one interviewee observed, overtime pay (or the threat of losing it) was, for many, a more powerful motivator than the possible violation of the principles to which one claimed adherence in supporting strike action:

> You know if there's any union trouble here, and it's a matter of banning overtime, you'll find that while the heat of the moment is on, yes, ban overtime, because no-one wants to stand out in a group and say: 'No, I don't believe that.' Afterwards, they'll go around trying to undermine that: 'The overtime's been banned, we've got to stop that, we're losing money.' It doesn't matter what the principle is, or what's happened. (wages employee)

Similarly, another interviewee observed:

> Actually, as a body, they're [the union] pretty weak. They always have been — they're governed by overtime. If the boss says there's plenty of overtime, you'll never get anybody wanting to do anything. (wages employee)

This interviewee went on to suggest that the company (management) used overtime as a mechanism to control the level of industrial action in the division:

> As soon as you've got no overtime, [the workers say]: 'Well, do you want to do it [take strike action] now? Yeah, why not?' And as soon as the company gets wind of that, there's a day's overtime comes out.

Theme 3: Intrinsic value of the work to the individual and pride in skill

While it was clear that monetary incentives had always been a key element in the division's reward system, there was evidence to suggest that, for some employees at least, their motivation derived from the work itself. References were made, for example, to the satisfaction derived from "a job well done" and "when something works out" (wages employee); the enjoyment and challenge associated with "experimental work" (leading hand); and the satisfaction derived from being given "a fair amount of freedom to do and achieve an ultimate result in a job" (leading hand). A closely related theme, and one which no doubt underpinned such views about the intrinsic worth of the work, concerned the tradesman's pride in his skill. It was apparent that, in the past, there was considerable status associated with being a tradesman. Tradesmen were among the most technically proficient people in the industry and, as one interviewee (a leading hand) noted, a trade in the past was regarded as "an honourable profession" and "an admirable ambition". While trade qualifications reportedly no longer carried such status, it was evident from comments such as "there's nothing much that we couldn't do" (leading hand), "we've got a lot of very technically competent people here" (staff, supervisory), and "the expertise on the floor is still there" (wages employee) that, within the division, the skill and expertise of tradesmen continued to be held in high regard.

It is interesting to note that, despite views such as the above (which were expressed by supervisory staff as well as shop floor employees), there was little evidence to suggest that the efforts of individual tradesmen were positively acknowledged by their supervisors. As one employee pointed out:

> You never get told that you're doing a good job, you only get told when you're doing a bad job. (staff, non-supervisory)

Moreover, to the extent that one derived satisfaction from the work itself, this was regarded as one's own "personal thing", regardless of "whether somebody else cares or not" (wages employee).

Theme 4: Use of non-tangible rewards surreptitiously

The data in this domain also provided evidence that praise and other non-monetary rewards, to the extent that they were used at all, were used surreptitiously. One interviewee (a supervisor) indicated that, because he was constrained in the use of financial incentives (tradesmen's wages were fixed by an award), he tried to reward above average performers by making them "feel important" or by giving them "a better or more interesting job". He indicated, however, that he was careful not to administer such rewards "openly". This was because, on the one hand:

> Management doesn't like it that you get too sort of pally with them [the workers] because it makes it rather difficult when you have to discipline people.

On the other hand, it was likely that subordinates rewarded in this way would earn a reputation as the "teacher's pet" and consequently be ostracised by their peers.

Theme 5: Hard work rewarded with more hard work

Another theme to emerge from the data in this domain concerned a perception among shop floor employees that, not only was there no longer any incentive for them to work hard — opportunities for promotion were now practically non-existent, the past system of awarding bonuses for good work had been abandoned, and employee wages were now fixed by an award — but there was a positive disincentive for them to do so. As illustrated by the following excerpts, the experience of some employees was that the reward for hard work was simply that one was given more work:

> Well, I show a lot of interest here, but ten guys won't, but I do, and that's why I get all the bloody work. (wages employee)
> But here actually, the only thing you get out of the firm for doing more is that you will also get the next job quicker. While the one that's not doing anything, he will not even be given a job. (wages employee)

In a similar vein, there was a perception that skills and experience were no longer necessarily an asset to the individual. For example, one employee complained that, because of the skills and experience which he had acquired as a result of his past efforts to get ahead in the organisation (efforts which were not subsequently rewarded with promotion), he was now relied upon to take on work which he did not necessarily want to accept, but which his less conscientious and less ambitious peers were incapable of performing. In his own words:

> I'm still one of those that move around [to different sections] whether I like it or not. And often now the moves aren't very good... But you can't go and get the bloke that's been sitting on his tail in a certain section. You'll never get him to move, because he just says he doesn't know how to do it. (wages employee)

Theme 6: Service incentives no longer valued

Even though employee service with the organisation was no longer valued in the same way that it had been in the past — prior to the major retrenchments which took place in the division in the early 1970s and then again in the early 1980s, longer-serving employees could reasonably feel assured of a 'job for life' (see Theme 7 below) — the company continued the practice of granting service awards to longer-serving employees. Current attitudes towards these incentives, however, appeared to be quite negative, with divisional members criticising them on the grounds that they were no longer of much value financially. Consider, for example, the following excerpt in which the interviewee (a wages employee) describes the circumstances surrounding, and his response to, his receipt of the 'gold watch' service award, for 25 years' service with the company:

> ...it was one of those appreciation things, you know, they give you after 25 years. You get a watch and you get a handshake from the manager... They sort of take you into the office and give you a cup of coffee and sort of 'We appreciate your work', and you get a watch and one and a half Scotch Finger biscuits. They put them on your saucer so you can't take two from the middle. You see that's why I'm wearing my Hungry Jack's watch.

When asked where his gold watch was, the interviewee replied:

> In the cupboard. Who needs it? What is a watch today, after 25 years' service? What's this? What appreciation is this? This one [he points to his Hungry Jack's watch], I bought a whopper [a hamburger made by the Hungry Jack's fast food chain] and I got the watch for nothing. That's what you get after 25 years' service. Terrific isn't it?

In a similar vein, but in relation to the award granted for 50 years' service:

> There has been one [employee] who spent 50 years here, and they gave him a fridge. What would a car cost them? $5,000? 'Look, here's a nice new car.' What a great incentive that

would be for people to stay on. Like we get a clock or a watch for 25 years. I worked it out. It was 20 cents per year that we got out of them. A great incentive! (staff, non-supervisory)

Theme 7: Changes in the 'reward contract' over time

There was good evidence from the data in this domain to suggest that, over the years, the division's reward system had undergone considerable change. This was a change, not in the types of rewards that were offered, but rather in the availability of those rewards which had traditionally been in use. For example, as indicated above, divisional members no longer had the opportunities for promotion from within the division that they had in the past; similarly, the past system of pay increments for high performers was no longer in use (this system had reportedly been abandoned due to a lack of funds, in addition to which wages were now fixed by an award). Perhaps the most significant change to the division's reward system, however, was the change that was effected by the major downsizing of the division that was undertaken in the early 1970s. Specifically, the division's workforce was reduced to approximately half its original size (of approximately 1000 members), with the sacking of all those shop floor employees with less than ten years' service with the company. The retrenchments were apparently carried out within a very short period of time (less than one week) and with no advance warning given to employees. Moreover, at this time, there was no obligation on the part of the company to pay retrenchment money; those made redundant were compensated for one week's notice only. That this was a critical event in the history of the division was abundantly clear from members' accounts of the period. For example, some divisional members talked about the atmosphere of fear and uncertainty that prevailed in the division just prior to the retrenchment notices being handed out. In the words of one such employee:

> There was a horrible air of scariness about the place. Everybody knew something was happening, but they didn't know what. (staff, supervisory)

Other divisional members described the shocked reactions of those who were dismissed:

> ...they just walked off the plant in stunned amazement. (staff, supervisory)
> ...there was just blokes standing around with their mouths gaping wide open. (staff, supervisory)

And still others (notably those who had been dismissed and subsequently returned to the division) commented on their own personal reaction to the experience:

> If I could have got a bomb, I would've blown this place up... (staff, supervisory)
> ...it is terribly disappointing, you feel betrayed. It's like somebody stealing your car, breaking in your house, and... well, I will not go as far as rape, but it's almost like that. (wages employee, leading hand)

One important consequence of this event was that it undermined what appeared to be a tacit agreement between employees and the company — referred to in the literature as the 'psychological contract' (Rousseau, 1989) — that if employees did the 'right thing' and were loyal to the company, then they would be rewarded with long-term job security. The following excerpts serve to illustrate:

> ...prior to '71 it was unknown that anyone would be sacked because of lack of work; if you were a tradesman you were secure. (wages employee)
>
> ...this couldn't happen, you know, this couldn't happen, we had a job for life, we did the right thing, you know, why would they want to do it to us. (wages employee, leading hand)
>
> You had given, or thought that you'd given your best, and your loyalty and all of a sudden, without any explanation you were redundant, you were out... that was a great shock. (wages employee, leading hand)
>
> ...everybody just thought 'Well, 'til the age of 65, or retirement age, I'm safe and secure', which then '71 or '70 already, changed abruptly and became very confusing and very demoralising, absolutely demoralising. (wages employee)
>
> ...the years when I sort of started, once you got in the company and once you got on staff, that was it, you've got a job for life, you've got a good job, they'll look after you... (staff, supervisory)

This expectation of a job for life was clearly a very important, though implicit, aspect of the division's reward system and it can reasonably be argued that its disconfirmation by the events of the early 1970s had contributed, in part, to the negativity which character- ised the current attitudes of divisional members. Some of this negativity is evident in the data presented above. In addition, numerous comments were made by divisional members to the effect that the morale of the workforce had declined, that employees no longer felt any loyalty toward the organisation, and that productivity had dropped significantly such that many employees now did no more than was required.

An important conclusion suggested by the above analysis was that an understanding of the historical context of organisation members' experience can help one to better under- stand members' perceptions of, and responses to, their current experience. This analysis also provided some confirmation of the view, expressed by a number of organisational culture scholars (Pettigrew, 1979; Sathe, 1985; Schein, 1985), that critical events in the history of an organisation can bring to the surface beliefs and assumptions which have previously been taken-for-granted and unconsciously held.

Considered as a whole, the various themes described above can be seen to be more consistent with Theory X, rather than Theory Y, assumptions about the nature of workers. In particular, there was an emphasis on the role of economic self-interest in motivating employee performance and there was evidence of the use of money (in this case, overtime pay) as a mechanism by which to control employee behaviour. Moreover, while there was a sense in which tradesmen in the division experienced their work as inherently satisfying, there was little evidence to suggest that intrinsic rewards (such as the sense of achievement provided by the work itself) were explicitly recognised by divisional management and exploited for their motivational potential. Finally, in terms of its basic orientation (whether Theory X or Theory Y), the organisation's reward system appeared to have changed very little from the past to the present. There had, however, been considerable erosion of this system over time (rewards traditionally in use were no longer available and employee assumptions about a job for life had been undermined by the events of the early 1970s) and this, it was argued, helped to explain the negativity which was evident in divisional members' accounts of their current experience.

8.4.1.3 *Performance appraisal*

While references to the appraisal of employee performance tended to be made in the context of more general discussions about the organisation's reward system, there were sufficient data on this topic to warrant their treatment as a separate domain. The analysis of these data suggested the following four common themes:

Theme 1: Appraisal as a basis for remuneration and promotion decisions

The data in this domain provided evidence to suggest that divisional members who were involved in formal performance appraisal — this system applied to staff only and not to wages employees — tended to regard appraisal primarily as a vehicle for the administration of pay rises and promotions. This view emerged in the context of complaints about the fact that, in the current climate of financial restraint and staff rationalisation, the system no longer worked as people believed it should. In the words of one employee:

> A lot of people don't think it's worthwhile. I mean there's no value in it. The only value is like I said, if there is any merit money around. Another time it's supposed to be used is for human resources management, I think. All this information on who you are and what you are, and what you're doing and what you'd like to do, is supposed to be recorded by Personnel, who then when there is a position vacant, they're supposed to go through all the records and press a button, and out pops somebody's name, but that doesn't happen. (staff, non-supervisory)

In a similar vein, another employee indicated that, as he saw it, the organisation's appraisal system was no longer being used:

> The system is there to be used, but as far as I know I don't think it is being used…because there's about 15 staff people out there that have been out there since J.C. was a boy. (staff, supervisory)

Theme 2: Appraisal decisions based on the organisation's needs

Consistent with a Theory X perspective, there was evidence to suggest that decisions made on the basis of appraisal information (such as, promotion and work allocation decisions) were designed principally to satisfy the organisation's needs. To the extent that these decisions also satisfied the individual needs of the employees concerned, this appeared to be more by coincidence than by design. Consider, for example, the following excerpt:

> I fill them [appraisal worksheets] out for the people who've worked for me, and somebody fills one out for me, and it goes right through the system there, recorded by Personnel... So when the company needs somebody in a particular position, they have a look through the records of what people have done, and what their ability is, and where their strengths are, and that's how a selection is done. So I suppose in my case, they must've looked at everybody that was here... I must have some strengths that are good for what we're trying to do here, at this particular time. (staff, supervisory)

The notion of required personnel, referred to previously in relation to promotional practices, was also mentioned in the context of comments about performance appraisal. For example, one employee (a non-supervisory member of staff) described how, in his very first performance appraisal, he had specified a further development goal which involved a request for a transfer to another section of the division. He indicated that his manager at the time made no effort to accommodate this request, but refused it outright — "You can't do that, you can't do that" — on the grounds that the employee was "required in his current section".

Theme 3: Principles of performance appraisal not enacted in practice

In the stated objectives of performance appraisal — outlined in the company's formal guidelines pertaining to the practice — considerable emphasis was given to the importance of active employee involvement in the appraisal process. Such involvement, it was argued, would facilitate the employee's development "in line with [her/his] abilities and interests", it would promote "better communication" (presumably between the employee and her/his supervisor), and it would help to ensure the achievement of appraisal objectives (presumably by engendering the employee's greater commitment to these objectives). This emphasis on the value of a client-centred focus was also evident in the design of the system which allowed for: (i) the appraisal of the employee by her/his supervisor; (ii) employee self-appraisal; and (iii) the appraisal of the supervisor by the employee.

While the formal documentation on performance appraisal was available to all those involved in the process (including the appraisers and those being appraised), there was good evidence from the present study to suggest that the system was not operating in accordance with the values espoused in this documentation. In particular, there appeared to be little support, in practice, for employee self-appraisal. On the one hand, it was suggested that supervisors failed to take the self-appraisal comments of their subordinates seriously and that this had resulted in reluctance, on the part of subordinates, to provide this information:

> Initially you spill all your beans — 'I've done this, I've done that.' You go into the office where your supervisor sits, and the management, the head of that particular department.

'Right, [subordinates name], we'll read out your ... [laughs here] ... look at that. Did you, did you do that? Well, you're a good boy.' And the supervisor and that, they have a good laugh at your expense. You know, you feel that degraded... Now, well I can't think of anybody here that fills out an appraisal. You say to the supervisor 'You go ahead and say what you think', and it's brought back to you, you read that, you approve it, or say that is correct, incorrect, sign it. I think that some don't even sign it. (staff, non-supervisory)

On the other hand, there were those who were opposed to employee self-appraisal, in principle, and who argued that the responsibility for appraisal should rest exclusively with one's supervisor. In the words of one divisional member:

I totally disagree with the system and won't fill it [the self-appraisal form] in. As far as I'm concerned, it's my boss's job to tell me what to do and my job to tell those below me what to do. (staff, supervisory)

It is interesting to note that this latter view was consistent with evidence suggesting that divisional members had traditionally had little experience of the kind of active role for employees implied in self-appraisal approaches. For example, while wages employees in the division were not involved in the formal appraisal system, there had reportedly been some past initiative by the company to develop a dossier of general information on employees at this level. As indicated in the following excerpt, however, wages employees were somewhat reluctant to provide the information requested and viewed the exercise with some suspicion:

They [wages personnel] were asked to fill in a form with what their qualifications were, what their interests were, and what they would like to achieve, and a lot of them just put in their name, address, trade, and their age. The rest of it, which was the information people wanted, just wasn't put in... There wasn't the interest out there, and people [wages] thought that they [the supervision] were prying, looking... trying to get underneath them and find out what was going on. It wasn't. I took it as an exercise to try and find out what skills people had and what they wanted to achieve, but these people just didn't want to do it. (staff, supervisory)

Finally, while the appraisal system had been designed to allow for appraisal of supervisors by their subordinates, in practice, there appeared to be no support for this option and no evidence of it ever having been implemented. In the words of one divisional member:

Well, if you like to go back to sweeping the floor... I mean people aren't stupid. The company might think they are but they are not totally stupid... I mean, would you write down... you've got a wife, kids, trying to run a car, and every other thing... and sit down and tell your boss he is a complete dickhead and then walk out. I mean, what's he going to think? (staff, non-supervisory)

Theme 4: Performance appraisal seen as an administrative formality

The fourth theme to emerge from the data in this domain concerned a perception, by some divisional members, that performance appraisal was little more than an administrative formality. Consider, for example, the following account by one divisional member of his experience of being an evaluator:

> It's a bit daunting for a start… When you are new or when you come into that position and have to do it, to be able to write up about somebody I suppose, it's a bit of a task. But after a while it becomes fairly repetitious — just drag out the previous year's and almost rewrite what you saw before. (staff, supervisory)

In a similar vein, one divisional member indicated that he was aware of an appraisal having been conducted retrospectively, that is, after the decision had been taken to grant the employee being appraised a promotion. There was also evidence that apprentices in the division, though they were appraised using a different system from that described above for staff, shared similar views about the appraisal process. For example, two apprentices indicated that their most recent progress reports had been completed by a supervisor whom they had never met, and who had never observed them at work. Finally, as suggested by the following excerpt, the timing of appraisals — in the case of staff, annually on the individual's birthday — seemed to further confirm the perception of appraisal as an administrative formality, rather than as a tool by which the individual's development and motivation could be enhanced:

> They come around once a year on your birthday, not in a particular period that you've put in a good effort, come up with a good answer and saved the company some money. It's not pulled up then or done then. It [the good effort, good idea] might be a month after your birthday, so 11 months later you do this appraisal. That's forgotten — that pat on the back — because it happened 11 months ago. (staff, non-supervisory)

In conclusion, the data in this domain, along with the emergent themes that they suggested, provided further evidence that the culture of the division supported predominantly Theory X, rather than Theory Y, assumptions. Despite the participative values that were espoused in the formal documentation associated with the company's performance appraisal system, the evidence suggested that, in practice, those being appraised had a relatively passive role in the process. Moreover, there appeared to be a general acceptance of this role and a belief in the inherent 'correctness' of one's superiors taking primary responsibility for the process and for the decisions that followed from it. There was also little evidence of appraisal being used as a vehicle by which the individual's and the organisation's needs and goals might be mutually satisfied (a Theory Y perspective). On the contrary, the organisation's needs appeared to be the dominant consideration in appraisal decisions and there appeared to be little awareness of the potential of appraisal to motivate employee performance and facilitate employee growth.

8.4.1.4 *Superior/Subordinate perceptions*

While the data in this domain provided insights into how superiors and subordinates were viewed, the perspectives offered were principally those of subordinates. That is, subordinates talked about how they thought their superiors saw them; they talked about how they saw their superiors; and they talked about how they saw themselves, in the context of their relationship with superiors. The analysis of these data suggested the following four common themes.

Theme 1: Workers seen as 'numbers'

A common perception among wages employees was that their superiors regarded them, and treated them, not as valuable human resources, but as production resources or numbers whose worth lay solely in their ability to do the work to which they had been assigned. In the excerpts that follow, one interviewee (a wages employee) contrasts his current work experience with his experience in a previous job, in terms of how he thinks he is seen by his supervision:

> There [past job] I was fully appreciated. Here I am appreciated in my trade; they have recognised me in that direction, yes, but only as doing the job, not as a person.

The interviewee went on to talk about how his past supervisor attempted to accommodate the individual needs of subordinates (e.g., the interviewee had a preference for working independently rather than in a team), the result of which was that there was "less friction" in the work unit and an ability to "achieve more". As he saw it, his present supervision lacked this kind of interest in the individual and in "the broad prospect of the whole relationship". Rather, the attitude toward subordinates was that:

> [You are] here to work, to do a job that I give you.

In a similar vein, another wages employee expressed the view that:

> Really they [supervision] don't treat us as people. We're not people to them, we're a particular number, and what they can get out of us, and that's it.

This same employee likened the relationship between superiors and subordinates to that between a "master and slave", where the attitude of the former toward the latter was: "We know what's good for you, and you'll accept it". Evidence for this theme was also indicated in references by divisional members to workers being regarded, and treated, as "second class citizens", "peasants", "pawns", and even "cattle".

Theme 2: Workers seen as expendable

Closely associated with the above view was a perception among subordinates that their superiors regarded them as expendable. Consider, for example, the following reference to the major downsizing of the division which was undertaken in the early 1970s and which, according to some divisional members, resulted in the loss of some of the company's best employees:

> They [the company] thought it would make no difference, [to] let these people go, and if the work picks up again, there will be enough unemployed on the street which can be employed and taken into a job. (wages employee)

In a similar vein, but at a more individual level:

> If they don't need me, they'll just put me out in the street, no 'ifs', no 'buts'. It's business and that's how they work it. (staff, supervisory)

Interestingly, there was some evidence from the present study to suggest that the attitudes and behaviours of subordinates in the division corresponded to their perceptions of how their superiors regarded them — that is, as easy to replace and of value only in terms of their ability to get the job done. There was evidence, for example, that workers were motivated primarily by self-interest. Apart from economic self-interest (to which reference has already been made), there were indications that, in a more general sense, workers were inclined to put their own needs and interests before the needs and interests of the organisation. Employee commitment to the organisation, at least at the present time, was reportedly very low, with one divisional member (a wages employee) estimating that only 1% of shop floor employees had any sense of loyalty toward the company. This theme is further illustrated in the following two excerpts, the first in which reference is again made to the events of the early 1970s, and the second in which the interviewee draws attention to the tendency for organisational outcomes (in this case, the efficient operation of equipment) to be compromised in the name of protecting one's own interests:

> Well, it was [a difficult time for the company], yes, but it wasn't for me. How can I put it? It wasn't for me. I just went with it at that stage. There was nothing that I had to worry about, because I'd nearly paid my house off, because I'd worked a lot of overtime, and I wasn't really concerned at what happened to this company. I knew that I had the potential and skill to go anywhere and get a job. I just used to come in here…do the job that I was required to do, and that was it. (wages employee)

They [superiors] say: 'Oh well, patch it up, patch it up, patch it up.' They try to save their dollars — their expense account — so they look good and, of course... well, anybody... I do the same thing myself, to make your side of the thing look rosy and as a result the whole demise... it [the tooling division] runs itself down very markedly. I think that's fairly simple, that people try to look after their own jobs and make themselves look good, and the rest of the situation gets a little bit hopeless. (wages employee)

The dominance of self-interest as a motivator of employee behaviour was also indicated in the admission by one divisional member (also a wages employee) that his attendance at company training courses "is selfish — it's for me and not for the company".

Finally, there were a number of references to the less than optimal productivity of workers in the division. One divisional member (a supervisor) noted the tendency of workers to perform only at the minimum required level, unless "pushed to work harder". Similarly, in the words of another divisional member (also a supervisor):

I don't think they're [shop floor employees] purposely trying to sort of make the company go down; they just haven't got that interest any more to do more than sort of required. They'll just do what's their minimum requirement.

It is worth noting the implication in the above excerpt that workers' past attitudes and behaviours were different from their attitudes and behaviours at the present time. Indeed, these comments were made in the context of a discussion by the interviewee about changes in the division from the past to the present — in particular, a change whereby the division was no longer valued by the company as a whole, and a change whereby the traditional promote-from-within practice had given way to external promotions (i.e., the promotion of personnel from other divisions of the company to senior positions within the division). The point can again be made that information about the historical context would appear to be essential for an understanding of information pertaining to the present context.

Finally, the above suggestion of a link between subordinates' perceptions of how their superiors regarded them and the subsequent attitudes and behaviours of subordinates, can be seen to have some support in the literature. For example, as Schein (1985, 1992, 2004, 2010) has suggested, subordinates (at least those who remain with the organisation) tend to adapt to the underlying assumptions of their superiors — that is, they come to behave, and think, in the way in which their superiors expect them to behave and think. And it is in this way, according to Schein, that the initial assumptions that superiors hold about their subordinates come to be confirmed and reinforced.

Theme 3: Superiors seen as the ultimate and legitimate authority

A third theme to emerge from the data in this domain concerned a perception among subordinates that their superiors (i.e., their supervisors and managers) were the ultimate and legitimate authority. Thus, while subordinates might not agree with some of the decisions made by their superiors, they believed in the inherent right of their superiors to make such decisions and see that they were implemented. Consider, for example, the following excerpt in which one employee describes his response to a company decision — namely, the appointment of someone from outside of the division to a senior position within the division — with which he and his work colleagues disagreed:

> I thought to myself at the time: How can we do anything to stop it [the appointment]? I mean why do we want to stop it? The guy's [new appointment] been given to us; he's obviously a management-type person, or else he wouldn't have got the job. It's the company's management decision to make. I mean, who are we to say: 'This is the way I feel personally'? (staff, supervisor)

In a similar vein and in the context of his complaints about a recent directive from divisional management (regarding the need for employees to be more punctual with respect to their start time and break times), another employee (an apprentice) expressed the view that: "They [management] are just enforcing laws that they have a right to enforce". Interestingly, the directive referred to here took the form of a written bulletin enunciating a list of rules, one example of which is the following rule pertaining to the lunch break:

> Lunch break is 12.30 pm to 1.00 pm total. This is 12.30 pm from your work place to start lunch and 1.00 pm at your work place to commence work again. The traditional five (5) minutes prior to 12.30 pm for hand washing is ok, but five (5) minutes only.[6]

This bulletin is another example of the artefactual data that were gathered over the course of conducting this research; it can be regarded as a tangible manifestation of what is essentially a Theory X control mechanism. Like the interviewee above, a third interviewee (a supervisor) indicated that, while he thought that workers should have more say about matters such as where they worked, ultimately "it is the management's right to put people where they think fit".

Associated with the above, there were some divisional members who saw it as inappropriate for subordinates to question, or openly disagree, with their superiors. One employee (a wages employee), who was a particularly strong proponent of this view, commented that "Your supervisor is in that position because he is superior". Interestingly, the researcher was confronted with this view when a question that she put to a senior member of staff (concerning the implications for the division of the forthcoming merger of the company with another major automotive company) was met with the response: "You shouldn't ask about things that don't concern you or for that matter us".

Finally, the importance placed on deference to authority appeared to influence role relationships at all levels of the divisional hierarchy. One employee (a wages employee

---

[6]Emphasis in original.

with leading hand status) made the following comments about how he thought apprentices should behave in the context of their relationship with their superiors (i.e., tradesmen):

> Your job is to pick up the hand towels for the tradesman, have them washed. Your job is not to question the tradesman all the time, but look at what he's doing, but don't say: 'Don't do it like that.' You're there to be guided.

There was, however, little evidence to indicate that these expectations were currently being met and, ironically, tradesmen appeared to regard their subordinates (i.e., apprentices) in much the same way as they believed their superiors regarded them. The following excerpts serve to illustrate:

> They're [apprentices] shocking, they're disrespectful, they don't want to learn. They're only doing this for a job; they're not doing it because they want to do it. It's something they'll pass the time with, get good money. They've no ambition. (wages employee, leading hand)
>
> A lot of young people are not interested in the job anyhow; they just have something to fill in. I mean there are a few good ones in there, but the majority… (wages employee)

Theme 4: Subordinates see themselves as powerless and of limited worth

The data in this domain provided insights, not only into subordinates' perceptions of their superiors, but also into subordinates' corresponding perceptions of themselves. Specifically, there was evidence that, within the context of their relationship with their superiors, subordinates defined themselves as largely powerless and of limited relative worth. As they saw it, their role was a predominantly passive one that required them simply to comply with the instructions and directives of their superiors. In the words of one employee (a wages employee): "Because he carries the stripes, I've got to do it his way". Moreover, there were some subordinates who, whilst they grumbled and complained about their situation, nevertheless conceded that: "It's not for me to judge higher ones" (wages employee) and "It's only what I sort of gather myself, not that I know anything" (staff, supervisory).

The above observations regarding how superiors and subordinates were defined, within the superior-subordinate relationship, can be seen to correspond closely with Bate's (1984) notion of subordination. Of relevance also is Bate's argument that, to the extent that subordinates define themselves as powerless, and behave accordingly, the managerial view of authority as the central and indispensable means of managerial control is reinforced.

Overall, and as for the subject categories previously discussed, the thematic content of data pertaining to how superiors and subordinates were regarded was suggestive of a Theory X, rather than a Theory Y, orientation. The data in this domain also provided some support for arguments in the literature about the cyclical (or mutually-reinforcing) nature of the processes whereby such an orientation might evolve and be maintained. The essence of these arguments, as applied to the present data, is that Theory X assumptions breed Theory X behaviours, and that these behaviours in turn confirm and reinforce the Theory X assumptions on which they are based.

8.4.2 *Themes pertaining to the nature of human relationships*

As Schein has suggested, assumptions about the nature of human nature can be expected to give rise to, or be reflected in, assumptions about the nature of human relationships. Thus, in the present study, one would expect that the above findings regarding how superiors and subordinates were viewed would have implications for how relationships between these two groups were conducted. That this was indeed the case is illustrated in the following discussion of the thematic content of data pertaining to communication and decision-making in the division (this domain of data being the primary domain from which inferences about beliefs and assumptions in this category could be made). The analysis of these data suggested four common themes of relevance to beliefs and assumptions about the nature of human relationships.

Theme 1: Decision-making is top down and autocratic

A common theme to emerge from the data in this domain was that the division's, and the company's, approach to decision-making, whether at a strategic or operational level, tended to be autocratic. There was no indication of active participation in the process, either by those responsible for implementing the decisions that were made, or by those likely to be most affected by these decisions. With respect, first of all, to strategic decision-making, this appeared to be the exclusive domain of the company's executive group, based interstate and overseas. Consider, for example, the following excerpts:

> I still say this company's a puppet for [its parent company]. [The parent company] makes the major decisions. I think very little of management in South Australia get to make any decisions other than 'Oh, I might go to the canteen now' or 'I might not'. They can't make any decisions really on whether they're going to introduce bonus schemes, or 'Should we let the fellows go five minutes early?' or anything like that. It's basically all got to come from [the company's head office in Australia]. (wages employee)
>
> As far as we know, [the parent company] makes the rules for this place… They wouldn't know us from a bar of soap. So you can say we're just a number, and when that number's time is up, rub it out. (staff, supervisory)
>
> We're not even brought in on the finance side of things, only the, you know 'You're spending too much, cut it out'. The financial decision as to whether to make something in-house or overseas is made by the finance experts interstate, main office, head office, that do their sums over there. (wages employee)

> They're [divisional management] only the puppets, because they get told what to say and they say it because that's their job. (staff, supervisory)

Similarly, when asked about whether or not staff in the division had any involvement in the recruitment of divisional management, one employee replied:

> There's just no communication in that direction. It's all decided by people higher up, the directors — in [the company's head office in Australia], and in [the parent company] I suppose. (staff, non-supervisory)

In the same way that senior members of the division were not consulted about decisions which affected them, or which they might be required to implement, so too were shop floor employees excluded from decisions of a more operational nature. In the following excerpt, a wages employee expresses his dissatisfaction with the fact that engineering personnel in the division did not consult directly with tradesmen about the problems that they (the engineers) experienced:

> They [the engineers] talk to the foreman and the foreman's got to come back to me. I said to [name of foreman] one day, I said 'Look, you've got all these guys here. Why don't they come and converse with us. Like, I built the bloody thing. I'd like to know where their problems are, or what's going on'. (wages employee)

Another wages employee commented on the tendency for divisional management to work in almost complete isolation from the shop floor, such that when problems arose, no thought was given to the possibility of seeking input from the shop floor as to how these problems might be resolved:

> They [internal management] are a group that is not to be touched... They are sufficient that they can handle it, and if they have problems, then they should go higher up, to [the company's head office in Australia] or so on, but not with the workforce itself, trying to iron these things out.

And a third wages employee pointed out that, while there had been talk of introducing a problem-solving committee which would include representatives from the shop floor, this had not eventuated and the dominant approach, as he saw it, continued to be one in which:

> All you get is [management saying] 'That's what we're going to do'. [Workers say] 'Oh, hang on, how about we go and discuss it?' [Managers say] 'Well, we've kicked it around and we can't see anything better than that, so that's it!' (wages employee)

Interestingly, the above perceptions of decision-making practices in the division (and the organisation generally) were not consistent with statements about the company's new "people focus", which were made by the company's manager, and which appeared in the local press at the time:

> 'We used to be a bureaucratic, unresponsive operation' Mr [X] said. 'Now we are giving people the accountability and the responsibility to run their own business.'
>
> People were another essential part of the winning formula. 'We're putting the focus on people' Mr [X] said. 'It's people who are going to run the business, make it survive and make it grow.' He said decision-making, authority, and responsibility were now shared, right down to the shop floor.

Theme 2: Communication via indirect rather than direct means

There was evidence from the data in this domain to suggest that the division's grapevine, and even the local media (i.e., newspapers, motor magazines), were often the means by which divisional members first learned about important decisions that had been made. Examples of such decisions — about which the researcher was told in an informal conversation with a small group of divisional members — included the decision of the company to merge with another company and the decision to rationalise various aspects of the company's operations. Interestingly, even the decision of their own manager to resign was a decision that was not communicated directly to divisional members. Rather, they learned about this decision, initially through rumours, and subsequently via a written bulletin posted on the division's public bulletin board. Interestingly, this bulletin had been written and signed, not by the general manager who was resigning, but by his immediate superior. This style of communication seemed, to the researcher at least, to be unusually impersonal. Surely it would have been more appropriate for the general manager to communicate this information directly to his subordinates? When the researcher put this view to the personnel with whom she was talking, however, their surprise at the question indicated that they regarded the practice as in no way unusual. On the contrary, this form of communication was one with which they were entirely familiar and which they regarded as entirely appropriate. Of relevance here is the argument in the organisational culture literature (Louis, 1980; Schein, 1985, 1992, 2004, 2010) that when one encounters a discrepancy between one's own perceptions and the perceptions of the group (i.e., 'insiders'), one may in fact be passively experiencing some aspect of the group's culture.

Theme 3: Communication via the chain of command

Another feature of communication practices in the division, as indicated by the data in this domain, was that communication, whether upwards or downwards, was directed through the chain of command. One consequence of this was that shop floor workers reportedly never received direct feedback from senior company personnel (whether local management or management from interstate) about the quality of the tooling projects that they completed. Rather, as suggested by one employee (a wages employee):

> They told that to [my boss's] boss, and it gets passed down the line.

There was also evidence that violations of the chain of command were met with considerable disapproval. In the following excerpt, one employee (a wages employee) describes the reaction of his superiors to his transfer to a new position — a change which was not negotiated through the usual channels, but which was the result of a decision taken by his immediate superior (i.e., his foreman) and a senior superintendent in the division:

> And my superintendent and my general foreman at the time were rotten because firstly they really knew nothing about it. It was talk between a foreman and a senior superintendent, and it didn't go through the chain of command, you know, down through the ladder. And they tried to stop it and all that, but fortunately, management saw reason and said 'He's the one for the job and that's it'. (wages employee)

Theme 4: Recent changes in communication and decision-making practices

Finally, the data in this domain provided evidence to suggest that, in recent times, communication and decision-making practices in the division may have changed somewhat. Specifically, there was a perception among some divisional members that information was exchanged more freely now than it had been in the past, and that rules of hierarchy and authority were no longer observed, or enforced, with quite the same degree of strictness. Consider, for example, the following excerpt in which reference is made to a change in the division towards greater information dissemination to employees at the shop floor level:

> Well, they're being told more than what they have been told. They're being told more, not everything, but they're being told something, which is good, and this is what they've been after for a long time, to get told some of the decisions that are going to be made in this place... This has only happened in what, the last six months. Up till then, they [the workers] really had to drag everything out of them [management]. (staff, supervisory)

A change in the relationship between shop floor employees and their immediate supervision had also been observed, such that:

> The big barrier's not there, like the iron walls and everything have been pulled down in general, like, you know, the staff don't go 'round with their nose up in the air and that sort of thing. (staff, non-supervisory)

And finally, there was a suggestion that some decision-making was being pushed down the divisional hierarchy (at least, to the level of supervisory staff). For example, in a reference to retrenchment decisions, in which people at his level had typically had no say, one divisional member (a section supervisor) indicated that: "Nowadays, I believe that we would have more of a say…".

While the above changes might be interpreted as tangible evidence of the company's espoused commitment to a stronger people focus (see above), the attributions of divisional members regarding why these changes had occurred suggested an alternative explanation, namely, that the changes were the result of circumstances over which divisional management had little control. For example, there was a perception among some divisional members that the devolution of responsibility downwards was simply a consequence of the significant downsizing of the division — a reduced workforce meant that those who remained had to take on more responsibility and had to work together more closely simply to get the job done. As one divisional member put it:

> You go to [divisional management] with a problem and these guys are that busy because there's been so many people taken away from them, that you go with a problem and say 'Look, so and so and so and so,' and [management] says 'Yeah, okay. Well look, first of all get your facts and figures, build up a case…', and then it's back to you again, so then you find you've got another job to do which, going back to the good old days, there used to be somebody to do that. (staff, supervisory)

In a similar vein:

> …everybody's sort of had to get in and do it, because there's just not the number of people to rely on, that you had… and people have just sort of bonded together for that reason, because if they want to get the job done, they have to do that. (staff, non-supervisory)

A second factor that was seen as influential in the above changes was that management personnel and supervisory staff no longer enjoyed the same job security as they had in the past. Whereas these positions had previously carried a kind of informal guarantee of life-long employment, in recent years, the threat of redundancy had become something with which personnel in these positions, like their counterparts on the shop floor, increasingly had to contend. As one employee (a wages employee) noted:

> They're not the bosses any more so much, because they know they can go tomorrow just the same as we can, so you know, it's a little bit more liberal.

Finally, there was the argument that past events in the history of the division (which had eroded the division's reward system, substantially reduced opportunities for promotion from within, and undermined employees' trust in management) had left the workforce feeling so demoralised and demotivated that they no longer accorded their superiors the same authority that they had in the past. In other words, supervisory and management personnel no longer enjoyed the solid power base that they had once enjoyed. As one employee (a wages employee) put it:

> After all, they're only human beings, and they're only people, and you're not to be scared of them. I mean, what can they actually do to you that they haven't already done? ...They can't do any more, and I'm not scared of them and they can do what they like.

On the basis of the above themes, it could reasonably be inferred that the culture of the division was one that supported strong hierarchical assumptions. The relationships between divisional members appeared to be determined very much by the relative positions that they occupied in the chain of command and there was evidence that the 'power distance' (Hofstede, 1980) between superiors and subordinates was relatively high. While there were claims about the company having become more people-focussed in recent years, there was little to suggest that practices in the tooling division had changed significantly to reflect this new focus. Moreover, to the extent that changes had occurred, divisional members attributed these to circumstances outside of the control of divisional management, rather than to an explicit attempt on the part of divisional management to change the power structure in the division. Indeed, from the available evidence, the latter appeared to be predominantly paternalistic, that is, "based on [the] assumption of autocracy and on [the] assumption that those in power are obligated to take care of those not in power" (Schein, 1985, p. 134).

8.4.3 *Themes pertaining to humanity's relationship to nature*

As indicated above, assumptions in this category are concerned primarily with the issue of control and its articulation in the organisation's (group's) definition of its relationship with its external environment. Schein (1985) draws attention to the link between assumptions in this category and Rotter's (1966) notion of 'locus of control', the argument being that organisations, like individuals, can develop beliefs about the extent to which they are able to control what happens to them. Data from the present study which had a bearing on assumptions in this category came from divisional member accounts of the decline of the division and, in particular, their attributions about the reasons for the decline. A recurrent theme in these data concerned the tendency for divisional members to externalise the source of their problems, that is, to attribute problems to factors outside of their control. In the following discussion, an account is given of the major factors that divisional members saw as contributing to the decline of the division.

A common perception among divisional members was that the decline of the division had been brought about by increased competition in the local market. In the period from the early 1960s through to the mid-1970s, the number of car manufacturers in Australia increased from two to five. As suggested in the following excerpts, one important consequence of this change for the company was that it could no longer support the number of new model releases that it had in the past:

> It was probably about, I guess, 10 to 15 years ago when there were actually five manufacturers in Australia and decisions were taken not to have a new model every year that business started to wind down. (staff, supervisory)
>
> In years gone by we used to put out a complete new model, which took 18 months to two years to tool up for... they cut down the number of models coming out... the cost I suppose, the increase, the Japanese coming into the market. (wages employee)

In a particularly insightful analysis of the problem, one interviewee argued that it was not competition *per se* which had caused the decline of the division, but rather the company's failure to redefine itself, and its position in the marketplace, in such a way as to be able to deal more effectively with this competition. In the employee's own words:

> I would say that the competition increased here. Japanese cars were coming in, and well, before the company was supreme in Australia, and there was nothing else. They never in my opinion found a way of adjusting to be part of a big group of manufacturers. They were still clinging, still in my opinion are clinging mentally, to the supreme role they once had. And that I think is the biggest problem here with management. (wages employee)

The above observation is noteworthy because it captures a phenomenon which has been well-documented in the organisational culture literature (e.g., Kantrow, 1984; Kilmann, 1984; Schein, 1985, 1992, 2004, 2010), namely, the tendency for organisations to maintain behaviours and mindsets which, in the past, were associated with success, but which are no longer appropriate for the organisation in its current environment.

A second major factor seen as contributing to the decline of the tooling division was government intervention in the automotive industry. In the following excerpts, reference is made to the impact of the Button Plan — a government initiative to modernise the Australian automotive industry, which was introduced by Senator John Button in the mid-1980s and which involved, among other things, the substantial reduction, over time, of tariffs on imported motor vehicles:

> Well, I suppose they were starting to scream about tariffs on imported vehicles, and I believe they were starting to relax tariffs around that time, or were talking about it. Imported vehicles were becoming more and more prevalent... And that [the Button Plan] sort of spelt the death knell, I suppose, for toolrooms in Australia, because the imported vehicle was becoming easier and easier to get. (staff, supervisory)
>
> The government is at fault too because old Senator Button has just brought in laws that the motor vehicle industry must apply to and must agree to. (wages employee)

Third, the decline of the tooling division was attributed to one or more "wrong" decisions made by "the company" (a general term used by divisional members to refer to company executives, whether based interstate or overseas). Examples of these wrong decisions, as perceived by interviewees, included: the decision to manufacture a 'world' car — a standardised product whose component parts were manufactured in different parts of the world — and the associated introduction of a smaller model vehicle; the decision to subcontract tooling projects to outside vendors (within Australia and off-shore); and the decision to sell the facility to another company. With respect to the latter, the following except illustrates one interviewee's perception of the adverse, and irrevocable, impact of this decision:

> Now it's [the tooling division] a pile of rubbish, purely because it's just gone down, down, down, for one reason or another. It was let go down because [Company X] was going to buy it and it got worse. Once we sold this site, once [the company] decided to sell this site, it went down you know. That's a decision made for some reason or other. (staff, supervisory)

Finally, there were some interviewees who attributed the decline of the division to problems within the division itself. As with the above attributions, however, there was no suggestion that the group, as a whole, should share responsibility for these problems. Again, it was a case of: "It is they who are at fault, not us". Consider, for example, the following excerpts in which attention is drawn to the role of divisional management and senior divisional personnel in the decline of the division:

> You see management lost track, through dealing with the trade unions and again, I think, lack of enthusiasm, to the fact that they lost control of the workforce... There's no control of the workforce at present... They lost control of the workforce, as if anyone did anything wrong, or didn't perform or what have you, they lost the ability to sack someone. (staff, supervisory)
>
> Let's be honest, I think that if I want to go down to the real nuts and bolts of the whole tooling division situation at the moment, it's a matter that you've had superintendents that have had a budget to work to, and they've tried to do everything on a shoe string... And they've tried to save their dollars or their expense account so they look good... People try to look after their own jobs and make themselves look good, and the rest of the situation gets a little bit hopeless. (wages employee)

In contrast, some divisional members saw the fault as lying with workers rather than with those in authority. As indicated in the following excerpt, there was a perception that the attitudes of workers had changed such that workers today lacked the commitment, and pride in the product, of workers in the past:

> That's why half this place is going downhill, because their product isn't really up to standard... because of the attitude of everyone around the place. A lot of people, their

attitudes change, they're not as dedicated. You know, a lot of the cars before here, because that's what it's all about — building cars — they put a lot of pride in their cars. But now, oh well, they just get guys off the street. (wages employee)

In a similar vein, another divisional member expressed the view that the retrenchments of the early 1970s (in which the 'last on, first off' rule was applied) had resulted in the loss of some of the best workers in the division:

We had lost actually the cream and [the company] has never recuperated that. They have admitted themselves that was the biggest mistake ever. (wages employee)

In summary, and drawing again on Rotter's (1966) notion of locus of control, the findings reported above suggested that the tooling division supported a predominantly external, rather than internal, orientation. As indicated, divisional members attributed the problems confronting the division to factors that they perceived to be beyond their control and there was little indication that they felt any sense of shared responsibility for these problems. As they saw it, they did not cause the problems, and neither were they responsible for fixing them. There was also a tendency for divisional members to engage in what Bate (1984) has called depersonalisation (see Volume I, Chapter 3, Section 3.1.3). That is, where the problems of the division were attributed to human factors (and this was predominantly the case), specific individuals who might have been seen as being responsible were rarely named; rather the human element was depersonalised and referred to using vague terms such as "they", "the company", "management", and "the workers". According to Bate, this kind of attributional style, to the extent that it is embedded in the organisation's culture, will act to impede effective problem-solving and decision-making in the organisation.

Finally, the point should be made that, while the data presented above provided some basis for making inferences about beliefs and assumptions pertaining to the organisation's view of its relationship vis-à-vis its external environment, there was a limit to what they could reveal in this regard. As Schein suggests, assumptions in this category lie at the heart of an organisation's strategic orientation and are concerned with the way in which the organisation thinks about, and defines, its overall mission or primary purpose. In the present study, the level of organisational membership to which the researcher had access (primarily, shop floor workers and their immediate supervision) necessarily limited the extent to which data relevant to assumptions in this category could be obtained. A more thorough exploration of assumptions in this category could only have been achieved if the researcher had had more access to senior management within the division than was granted (e.g., the researcher was not permitted to attend meetings of divisional management), and if access to company management (both in South Australia and interstate) had also been negotiated.

8.5 Methodological Implications of the Findings of Study 1

As indicated in the introduction to this chapter, the aim of Study 1 was to provide some initial insights into the culture of the organisation being studied, and how the data gathered might be used to inform the development of a measure for organisational culture — in terms of the specific topics that might be explored and the specific questions that might be asked. On the basis of the findings reported above, there are a number of suggestions that can be made, including:

(1) **Level of access as a determinant of the issue to investigate.** Given the level of access that the researcher had been able to negotiate in the research organisation, an appropriate focus for a subsequent and more systematic investigation of the culture of the organisation would seem to be topics related to Schein's categories concerned with the nature of human nature and the nature of human relationships respectively. The results of Study 1 provided evidence to suggest that organisation members at the level being investigated (for the most part, shop floor workers and their supervisors) would be able to provide more useful, and more detailed, information about topics related to these categories than about topics related to the other categories in Schein's typology.

(2) **Theory X — Theory Y as a useful interpretive framework.** In Study 1, McGregor's (1960) distinction between Theory X and Theory Y assumptions provided a very useful framework for the interpretation of emergent themes from which beliefs and assumptions about the nature of human nature could be inferred. Consideration might therefore be given to how this distinction could be incorporated into the design of a method for the more systematic assessment of organisational culture.

(3) **The value of an explicit focus on context.** Based on the results of Study 1, such a method might also include specific questions about the context of organisation members' experience. In particular, information about the historical context of organisation members' experience would seem to be crucial for understanding members' accounts of their present experience. For example, in the tooling division, information about changes over time in the division's operating reward system (including the undermining of the tacit agreement that employee loyalty would be rewarded with long-term job security) proved essential for understanding the current climate of negativity in the division (at least, as reflected in organisation members' feelings about those aspects of their organisational experience about which they spoke). As indicated, this climate was characterised by low employee morale and commitment to the organisation, and a tendency for employees to work to minimum requirements only. The finding that the data considered contained a number of spontaneous references to the past suggests that organisation members' experience in relation to other contexts (such as the anticipated future), if asked about explicitly, might also provide useful information for understanding the aspect(s) of culture being investigated.

(4) **Causal attributions as a possible 'window' into organisational culture.** Study 1 also provided some evidence that attributions data might be of value for understanding organisational culture. For example, the finding that divisional members tended to attribute cause externally provided important insights into the meaning, to members, of changes that had occurred in the division (such as the change towards more open and participative styles of communication and decision-making that was reported). In view of this, the development of a method for the more systematic assessment of organisational culture might benefit from the inclusion of some specific questions about members' causal attributions.

(5) **The value of a semi-structured interview approach.** Finally, on the basis of the insights provided by Study 1, the specific method developed might most usefully take the form of some kind of semi-structured interview. Compared with questionnaire measures of organisational culture, in which both questionnaire items and response categories are typically formulated in advance, such an approach would provide respondents with the opportunity to elaborate on, and qualify, their responses. In this way, it would be possible to obtain relatively detailed and context-specific information about the particular topic(s) being investigated.

8.6 Conclusions

Study 1, as the first in a series of three studies, was designed to provide some initial insights into what might be required — in terms of the possible topics or issues to investigate, and the kinds of questions to ask — to develop a measure for the more systematic assessment of an organisation's deeper-level culture. Drawing on Schein's conceptualisation of organisational culture, the aim was to develop a means whereby to more efficiently and effectively assess the Level 3 beliefs and assumptions that, for Schein, constitute the essence of organisational culture.

The study was carried out in a large automotive company using participant observation and largely unstructured interviews with workers and supervisors from one division of the company. The data were analysed in terms of the main categories of Level 3 beliefs and assumptions to which Schein draws attention in his model of organisational culture. It was found that the content themes that emerged in these data could, for the most part, be classified within two of these categories, the first pertaining to beliefs and assumptions about the nature of human nature, and the second pertaining to beliefs and assumptions about the nature of human relationships. This helped to bring into sharper focus the issue (or issues) that might most usefully be investigated in the method under development.

The results of Study 1 also suggested that there were two types of questions that might usefully be incorporated into a measure of organisational culture, such as that being proposed. The first of these was contextual questions, that is, questions that ask about respondents' experience of an issue, not just at the present time, but as it was in the past, as envisaged in the future, and perhaps also as it ideally should be. The second type entailed questions that sought information about respondents' attributions regarding the causes of various organisational outcomes or events (whether experienced or anticipated). Of particular interest in this regard were questions that asked about the reasons for any perceived differences between the different contexts of respondents' experience — regarding, for example, any changes from the past to the present, or any changes in the anticipated future.

In the following chapters, we investigate the extent to which the above methodological lessons from Study 1 might usefully be applied to the development, and ongoing testing — in the same research setting — of a measure for the more effective and efficient assessment of the deeper-level beliefs and assumptions that, for Schein, constitute the essence of organisational culture.

Chapter 9

Piloting a Prototype Method (Study 2)

In this chapter, we provide an account of the second study conducted as part of our three-study investigation into the development of a method for the systematic assessment of an organisation's deeper-level culture. The chapter begins with an introduction to Study 2 in terms its central aim of piloting a prototype method for assessing 'deep' culture that was developed on the basis of insights from Study 1. The key design features of this prototype method are also briefly outlined in this introduction. The second section of the chapter describes the research method that was used for Study 2. Specifically, a more detailed description of the prototype method (which took the form of a semi-structured interview) is provided; the Study 2 sample is described in terms of its size and the relevant demographic characteristics of study participants; and the procedure for data collection is outlined. In the third section, the approach to data analysis is described and in the fourth section, the results of Study 2 are reported and discussed. The chapter concludes with some summary comments about the main implications of the findings of Study 2 for the refinement of the prototype method, with particular attention given to what emerged as the main strengths, and limitations, of this method.

9.1 Introduction to Study 2

On the basis of insights provided by the findings of Study 1, reported in Chapter 8, some first steps were taken toward designing a method for the systematic assessment of certain aspects of organisational culture. The aim of Study 2 was to pilot this method with a small sample of participants from the research organisation in order that some evaluation of the method, in terms of its ability to tap cultural phenomena, could be obtained. It was thought that a useful test of the method would be its potential to detect differences in the subcultures of different divisions within the organisation in which these studies were carried out and, to this end, the subjects for Study 2 were drawn from both the tooling division and the production division. As indicated in Chapter 8, given the markedly different histories and demographics of these two divisions, it was quite conceivable that they would support separate and distinctive subcultures.

The method developed for use in Study 2 can be described in terms of the following three general design features:

(1) The method took the form of a semi-structured interview in which open-ended and closed questions were combined. This particular format was chosen for its potential to exploit the strengths of both qualitative and quantitative approaches. On the one hand, it allowed participants some scope to provide the kind of 'rich' data which the results of this, and previous, research had shown to be so essential for cultural understandings. On the other hand, it provided a means whereby these data might be collected in a more systematic and more efficient manner than would be the case if an entirely unstructured qualitative approach were used.

(2) The interview was designed to provide information from which beliefs and assumptions pertaining to The Nature of Human Nature — one of the categories in Schein's (1985, 1992, 2004, 2010) typology — could be inferred. It was considered that this category of beliefs and assumptions constituted an appropriate area of focus for the second study. As indicated, not only had it been well represented by the data from Study 1, but it had also emerged as a particularly relevant category for describing beliefs at the level of organisation membership to which the researcher[1] had been granted access. In order to infer beliefs in this category, questioning in Study 2 focussed specifically on how members viewed the role of workers and the role of supervisors in their organisation. Moreover, consistent with the findings of Study 1, and also with Schein's suggestion about the relevance of McGregor's (1960) Theory X — Theory Y typology for classifying assumptions concerning the nature of human nature (or at least that subset of assumptions concerned with roles and role relationships), interviewing in Study 2 sought specific information about members' perceptions of the extent to which the respective roles of workers and supervisors reflected a more or less Theory X or Theory Y orientation.

(3) Based on the results of Study 1, which highlighted the importance of understanding organisation members' experience in its historical context, the method developed for use in Study 2 sought to systematically examine the way in which contextual data can inform an understanding of organisational culture. To this end, the interview included a number of specific questions designed to provide information about various aspects of the context of organisation members' experience.

9.2 Research Method

As indicated above, in this section, we provide a more detailed description of the interview protocol that was developed for use in Study 2. We also comment on the rationale for the

---

[1]As indicated in Chapter 8, this is a reference to the first author who undertook the empirical work for the three studies that are reported in Parts Four and Five of this volume.

inclusion of specific questions in this protocol. Following this, the participants in Study 2 are described, and the procedure for administering the interviews is outlined. The reader is reminded that, while the interviews constituted the central focus of data collection in Study 2, the 'diary' data referred to in Study 1 continued to be collected during Study 2, in this case from both of the participating divisions. As indicated previously, these data (essentially, records of the researcher's conversations with, and observations of, divisional members) served the important purpose of helping to validate aspects of the method being developed.

9.2.1 *The interview protocol*

In the interview protocol (see Appendix A) the same general format of questioning was followed in both sections of the interview (the first concerned with the participant's experience of the role of workers in her/his division and the second concerned with the participant's experience of the role of supervisors). This format is described in some detail below:

Initial open-ended question. This question provided an initial opportunity for the respondent to describe, in her/his own words and without any prompting from the interviewer, how she/he saw the role of workers (or, alternatively, the role of supervisors) in her/his division at the present time. It was intended as a kind of quick "What's it like around here?" question which would serve to capture the respondent's immediate impression of the issue about which she/he was being asked. In addition, it was anticipated that the response to this question would provide some indication of the extent to which the respondent could clearly articulate a role for workers and a role for supervisors respectively.

Theory X — Theory Y rating. This question was designed to provide a one-off measure (in terms of a single descriptor) of the respondent's perception of the role of workers (supervisors) in her/his division at the present time. The question involved, first of all, presenting the respondent with two contrasting descriptions of a role for workers (and subsequently, a role for supervisors), each of which was read out to the respondent by the interviewer. The first of these descriptions was designed to reflect a predominantly Theory X orientation to the role of workers (supervisors) and the second, a predominantly Theory Y orientation (see Appendix A). In formulating these descriptions, the researcher drew on some of the most salient aspects of McGregor's (1960) conceptualisation of the distinction between Theory X and Theory Y assumptions. Rather than use McGregor's labels, however, an attempt was made to identify alternative labels that could be understood more easily by respondents. Accordingly, the role of workers was described as being either 'passive' (corresponding to a Theory X orientation) or 'active' (corresponding to a Theory Y orientation); the role of supervisors was described as being either 'directive' (corresponding to a Theory X orientation) or 'consultative' (corresponding to a Theory Y orientation).

Once the descriptions of these contrasting orientations had been read out to the respondent, she/he was asked to think about the role of workers (supervisors) in her/his division at the present time and to indicate, on a six point scale, from *very passive* to *very active* (and, for the role of supervisors, from *very directive* to *very consultative*) the extent to which this role reflected a more or less Theory X or Theory Y orientation.

It was anticipated that, taken together, the initial open-ended question and the Theory X — Theory Y rating question would provide some insight into the more surface normative elements of the organisational culture with respect to the particular issues being investigated. The second question is also not unlike the kinds of questions that one finds in measures of organisational climate (see, e.g., Litwin & Stringer, 1968; Stern, 1970). The similarities include: (i) it is a closed question; (ii) it focuses on the respondent's perception of a *current* characteristic of the organisation; (iii) the respondent is not asked to evaluate the characteristic (i.e., say how she/he feels about it); and (iv) the respondent is not asked to explain what the characteristic means to her/him (and hence, in the absence of further information, there is no way of knowing whether there are qualitative differences in the meaning which individual respondents attribute to the characteristic). It will be noted here that, in Chapter 4 of Volume I, we have argued for a reconceptualisation of organisational climate to include an explicit affective dimension that is incorporated into the measurement of the construct (such that respondents are asked how they feel about the issue being assessed). Accordingly, we would not consider our Theory X — Theory Y rating question to, by itself, be tapping an aspect of the climate of the two divisions.

The aim of the remaining questions in the interview protocol was to push beyond the surface-level insights provided by the two initial questions to reveal aspects of the organisation's deeper-level culture with respect to the issues being explored. More specifically, these questions sought information about the meaning of respondents' perceptions of the respective roles of workers and supervisors (as indicated in their responses to the first two questions), as well as information about the cultural beliefs and assumptions underlying these perceptions. In order to elicit this information, three broad categories of questions were developed, each of which is described below.

Evaluation questions. The aim of the questions in this category was to provide some initial insights into the respondent's personal position with respect to the issues under investigation. Two questions were asked, both of which it was thought could provide information about the respondent's personal evaluation of the role of workers (supervisors), as she/he perceived it, and as indicated in her/his response to the previous Theory X — Theory Y rating question. The first of these questions asked about the respondent's level of satisfaction/dissatisfaction with the role of workers (supervisors) in her/his division; the second sought information about the respondent's perception of the effectiveness/ineffectiveness of divisional workers (supervisors). These questions were an attempt to investigate the extent to which an affective component of organisational climate — in this case, pertaining to respondents' feelings about the roles of workers and supervisors respectively — might be able to be assessed. Moreover, it was considered that such a measure might provide insights into aspects of organisational culture at Level 3 (i.e., comprising basic beliefs and assumptions). In particular, a negative organisational climate, here measured by questions concerning satisfaction and effectiveness, might indicate a discrepancy between organisational norms at Level 1 and underlying beliefs and assumptions at Level 3, in this case pertaining to the roles of workers and supervisors respectively.

For both of the above questions, the respondent was required to indicate her/his response on a seven-point rating scale (from *extremely satisfied* to *extremely dissatisfied* in the case of the first question and from *extremely effective* to *extremely ineffective* in the case of the second). It should be noted that, in the case of the effectiveness question, some additional information was also sought. Specifically, the respondent was asked to explain her/his response to this question and, if possible, to do so by making reference to an illustrative example drawn from her/his own experience. The aim of this subsequent probing was to gain some insight into the criteria that the respondent used in making her/his assessment of the effectiveness of workers (supervisors). It was anticipated that this information would, in turn, provide clues about the respondent's beliefs regarding what constituted an appropriate role for workers (supervisors).

Personal experience questions. Whereas all of the questions in the interview protocol up to this point had asked about the role of workers (supervisors) directly, the questions included in this category attempted to elicit this information using a more indirect approach. It was considered that one such approach would be to focus on an aspect of the respondent's personal experience in relation to the role of workers (supervisors). Accordingly, for the role of workers, the respondent was asked to describe the 'best' and 'worst' worker with whom she/he had ever worked in the division, or whom she/he had ever supervised. Similarly, for the role of supervisors, the respondent was asked to describe the 'best' and 'worst' supervisor she/he had ever had in the organisation. In attempting to establish a profile of the respondent's best/worst worker (best/worst supervisor), specific information was sought about: (i) the particular characteristics and qualities which the respondent most admired/most disliked about this individual; (ii) the individual's view of the organisation; and (iii) the nature of the individual's relationships with other members of the organisation (i.e., with supervisors and co-workers in the case of workers, and with subordinates in the case of supervisors). In the same way that Fiedler used his concept of the 'least preferred co-worker' to investigate an individual's leadership style (Fiedler, 1967), it was hoped that these questions would provide insights into the respondent's beliefs about the respective roles of workers and supervisors. Thus, it was anticipated that the qualities that the respondent attributed to her/his best worker, for example, would reveal something about the respondent's personal beliefs regarding what constituted an appropriate role for workers.

A further rationale for focusing on the respondent's actual experience (in this case, of a best/worst worker and a best/worst supervisor) was that it was thought that the respondent would probably be more articulate about this experience (than about experience acquired indirectly) and also more at ease in talking about it. The information provided might, therefore, be expected to be more valid in the sense of revealing more about what the respondent *actually* thought. It is also worth noting that the emphasis on personal experience, while most explicit in this category of questions, was an important general feature of the interview protocol. A not uncommon strategy in this regard was to ask the respondent to clarify her/his responses to particular questions — the effectiveness questions above and the context questions below — by, if possible, illustrating with an example drawn from her/his own experience.

Context questions. Building on the insights provided by Study 1, the questions in this category were designed to provide a context, or framework, within which the respondent's account of her/his current experience (concerning, in this case, the respective roles of workers and supervisors) could be understood and interpreted. As shown in the interview protocol, three separate aspects, or domains, of context were investigated, namely: (i) the historical context; (ii) the anticipated future context; and (iii) the 'other' context (referring, in this case, to the respondent's experience of other organisations). Although the 'ideal' has been proposed in Chapter 7 of Volume I as being another important dimension of context, respondents in the present study were not asked directly about what they considered to be the ideal role for workers and supervisors respectively. It was considered that this line of questioning, being very direct, might create some uncertainty among respondents about what specifically they were being asked about. Instead, and as indicated above, an attempt was made to approximate this question by asking respondents about the best and worst workers and supervisors that they had ever worked with and/or supervised. The specific questions that were asked in relation to each of the contextual domains listed above are now discussed, along with the rationale for their inclusion in the protocol.

With respect, first of all, to the historical context, the respondent was asked to comment on the role of workers (supervisors) in their division in the past and, in particular, to indicate how this role had changed (if at all) from the role of workers (supervisors) at the present time. Based on the results of Study 1, it was anticipated that historical data of this kind might assist in the more accurate interpretation of data pertaining to the present context. Historical data might, for example, provide important insights (not provided by present-time data) into the meaning of the respondent's level of satisfaction or dissatisfaction with the current role of workers (supervisors), as she/he perceived it. From Study 1, it will be recalled that information about members' past experience of life in the tooling division helped to explain the climate of negativity which prevailed in the division at the time that this study was conducted. As indicated, there was good evidence to suggest that this negativity was, at least in part, due to the gradual undermining, over time, of the psychological contract which had traditionally defined employer–employee expectations in this division. The negativity was not, as might have been assumed in the absence of historical data, a result of members' dissatisfaction with the division's predominantly Theory X orientation toward the role of workers and supervisors. On the contrary, this orientation appeared to be a relatively widely shared and deeply embedded part of the division's culture. An important implication of this finding is that any attempt to improve the climate of the tooling division by introducing changes (e.g., in the division's work practices and in its reward and control systems) designed to promote the development of a more Theory Y orientation, might be expected to be met with some cultural resistance.

An additional argument in favour of the inclusion of specific questions about the historical context is that most conceptual treatments of organisational culture are quite explicit about the role of an organisation's history in shaping its culture. For example, in discussing Schein's (1985, 1992, 2004, 2010) treatment of the 'essence' of organisational culture attention was drawn to the historical character of cultural beliefs and assumptions and to Schein's view that, in order for a group (or organisation) to develop a culture, it must have some history in time. An important methodological implication of this view would seem to be that, in order to confirm that a cultural phenomenon is genuine (and not just a manifestation of some aspect of the organisation's more temporary state, or climate), one would need to demonstrate some connection between this phenomenon and the organisation's past. In the method developed for use in this study, it was therefore hoped that the inclusion of specific questions about the past would provide the historical data necessary to validate inferences about cultural beliefs regarding the respective roles of workers and supervisors.

Finally, an attempt was made to anchor the respondent's notion of the past in real time. To this end, the respondent was asked to specify how far back (i.e., "How long ago…?") the past experiences to which she/he referred extended. The rationale for including this question was simply that individual respondents, when talking about the past, might be referring to different periods in time.

Having asked about the respondent's experience in relation to the historical context, the focus of questioning in this category then turned to a consideration of the respondent's anticipated future experience. Specifically, the respondent was asked to comment on her/his expectations regarding how the current role of workers (supervisors) in the division might change (if at all) in the future. Again, it was the early work carried out in the tooling division that provided the rationale for the inclusion, in the method developed for use in this study, of questions about the anticipated future context. As indicated in Chapter 8, at the time that Study 1 was carried out, the tooling division was undergoing a major transition and, not surprisingly, this had given rise to considerable anxiety among divisional members, many of whom were now faced with an uncertain future. An interesting question suggested by contextual information of this kind concerned the extent to which information about the future expectations of organisation members might provide additional insights (over and above those provided by historical data) into the culture of the organisation. Accordingly, some attempt was made to investigate the particular contribution that information about the future context might make to the interpretation of data pertaining to the present context.

As shown in the interview protocol, questioning in relation to this contextual domain also sought information about the respondent's beliefs regarding why future change may, or may not, occur. Drawing again on the results of Study 1, there was a possibility, worth investigating, that attributions data of this kind might provide additional clues about the culture of the organisation with respect to the particular issues being investigated.

Finally, the questions in this category sought information about organisation members' experience in relation to other contexts. As indicated, the respondent was asked about her/his awareness of the role of workers (supervisors) in other organisations. The decision to include a focus on this contextual domain was based on the fact that participants in Study 2 included employees from both the production division and the tooling division. As indicated in Study 1, the production division was a relatively newly established division, whose workforce comprised mostly production operators with no formal qualifications. It was reasonable to expect, therefore, that many of the employees in this division might have had some experience of working elsewhere and that this experience, in turn, might have influenced their perceptions of, and attitudes toward, their current experience. Of course, one also needed to acknowledge the possible influence of indirect, as opposed to direct, experience of other organisations — that is, experience acquired through, say, reading about other organisations or through contact with people who worked elsewhere — and, to this end, where knowledge of other organisations was indicated, the respondent was asked to indicate the source of this knowledge.

9.2.2 *Participants in Study 2*

In contrast to Study 1, which was conducted entirely in the tooling division, Study 2 was conducted both in the tooling division and in the production division. In selecting participants for this study, an attempt was made to get some broad representation of each division's membership[2], in terms of demographic characteristics such as gender, seniority, work area, and work shift. The rationale for this more inclusive approach to sampling was that it would provide some insight into the extent to which each division supported an overall divisional culture (as opposed to a number of separate divisional subcultures). In selecting participants for this study, it was also considered desirable that, as far as was possible, each participant should be representative of the average divisional member working at the same level as the participant, in the same section, and on the same shift. To this end, the researcher consulted with both supervisory staff and union representatives from each division as to who might qualify as 'typical' within a given category of interest. On the basis of this information, a number of potential candidates for participation in Study 2 were identified. Of those who were subsequently approached, there was only one who declined to participate in the study, this being on the grounds of anxiety about the use of an audiotape to record the interview (see details on procedure below). The final sample for Study 2 comprised twelve participants, six from the tooling division and six from the production division. The size of the sample, while small, was not considered to be unreasonably so, given that the aim of the study was simply to pilot the method which had been developed.

Table 9.1 provides a summary of the main demographic characteristics of the Study 2 sample, considered separately for participants from each division. It can be seen that all of

---

[2]The sample size for Study 2 was, however, too small to warrant any attempt to achieve statistical representativeness.

Table 9.1. Demographic characteristics of Study 2 respondents, shown for both the Tooling Division (TD) and the Production Division (PD).

| | | | | | Years in | Years with the | Years with the | | | |
Resp #	Gender	Age (years)	Marital Status	Country of Birth	Australia	Company	Division	Section	Position	Shift
						Tooling Division (TD)				
TD1	Male	46	Married	UK	16	16	16	Machining	Tradeswages	Day
TD2	Male	52	Married	UK	37	29	29	Pattern making	Tradeswages (LH)*	Day
TD3	Male	54	Married	Australia	—	39	35	General	General Foreman	Afternoon
TD4	Male	41	Married	Australia	—	23	23	Fitting	Tradeswages (LH)	Afternoon
TD5	Male	43	Married	Australia	—	27	25	Die manufacture	Tradeswages	Day
TD6	Male	53	Married	Australia	—	36	36	Try-out	Superintendant	Day
		Mean = 48.2				Mean = 28.3	Mean = 27.3			
		Sd = 5.6				Sd = 8.4	Sd = 7.6			
		Range 41–54				Range 16–39	Range 16–36			
						Production Division (PD)				
PD1	Male	36	Married	UK	25	16	8	Production control	Supervisor	Day
PD2	Male	36	Married	UK	12	12	3	Materials	Materials Handler	Day
PD3	Female	48	Married	UK	23	10	8	Assembly	Operator	Day
PD4	Male	49	Married	UK	29	20	6	Materials	Materials Handler	Night
PD5	Female	23	Married	Australia	—	3.5	3.5	New model	Operator	Afternoon
PD6	Male	38	Married	India	26	11 months	11 months	General	Acting Supervisor	Afternoon
		Mean = 38.3				Mean = 10.4	Mean = 4.9			
		Sd = 9.5 Yrs				Sd = 7.3	Sd = 2.9			
		Range 23–49				Range 1–20	Range 1–8			

* Leading Hand.

the participants from the tooling division were male[3], whereas participants from the production division included four males and two females. Participants from the tooling division were, on average, older than their counterparts from production, with the average age of the former being 48 years, compared with 38 years for the latter. It was also the case that tooling division participants had considerably longer tenure (both with the company and with their division) than did their counterparts from production. As indicated, the average length of service of tooling division participants was 28 years with the company, and 27 years with the division. In contrast, production division participants had an average length of service with the company of only 10 years, and with the division, of only five years. It is perhaps worth noting that the differences between tooling division and production division participants in terms of the above demographics were consistent with differences in these demographics at a divisional level.

It can also be seen from Table 9.1 that, consistent with the aforementioned aim of sampling widely from each division's membership, the sample for each division included both 'wages' employees (four from each division) and supervisory staff (two from each division); it included participants from a range of different work areas (or sections); and it included participants from each of the different shifts operating within the division (day shift and afternoon shift in the case of the tooling division, and day, afternoon, and night shifts in the case of the production division).

Finally, attention might be drawn to both the marital status and country of birth of participants in Study 2. With respect to the former, it can be seen from Table 9.1 that all participants from both divisions were married. With respect to the latter, it can be seen that, whereas the majority of tooling division participants were Australian-born, all but one of the participants from the production division were born outside of Australia. In all cases, however, participants born outside of Australia had been residents in Australia for a considerable period of time (with the range for the entire sample being from 12 years to 37 years).

9.2.3 *Procedure*

Each of the twelve participants in Study 2 was interviewed individually using the interview protocol described above. While some consideration was given to the use of group, as opposed to individual, interviews — indeed, Schein (1992) argues that, since culture is a shared (i.e., group) phenomenon, it should be studied as such — the adoption of this strategy was rejected on a number of grounds. First, as Schein himself has observed, the use of group interviewing in cultural analysis works best when there is a particular organisational problem or issue (related, e.g., to the implementation of some change in the organisation) to motivate the process. Schein indicates that, in his experience, where this has been lacking, the analysis has failed due to a lack of interest on the part of the group. This would seem to mitigate

---

[3]With the exception of the manager's administrative assistant, the entire membership of this division was male.

strongly against the use of group interviewing in the present research or organisational culture research of this kind, since this research was in no way driven by the kind of problem-solving agenda which Schein regards as so essential to the success of cultural analysis at the group level. The point might also be made that Schein's group work has typically involved groups of managers, rather than organisation members at lower levels of the hierarchy, as in the present study. It is not unreasonable to expect that the challenges of group work for this latter cohort — in particular in the absence of an explicit problem-solving agenda — will be even greater than Schein has found them to be for the former cohort.

A second reason for rejecting the use of group interviews in the present research was that group interviews, generally, have been found to suffer from a number of important limitations. Some of the most commonly cited of these (see, e.g., Easterby-Smith, Thorpe, & Lowe, 1991, and Patton, 1990) include: (i) problems associated with the management of dominant group members and, conversely, the management of members who lack the confidence and/or verbal skills to share their views; (ii) the existence of social pressures within the group which press group members toward conformity with particular views; and (iii) problems associated with confidentiality such that, in groups where the members know each other, it is not possible to guarantee the confidentiality of the information provided. Group interviews also pose the problem of deciding what constitutes the optimal composition of the group. For example, should the group include more senior members of the organisation, or will this have the effect of inhibiting communication? While Schein (1992, p. 149) provides some guidelines for how to go about making this decision in the case of problem-solving groups — he argues that consideration should be given to the nature of the problem, organisation members' perceptions of who the "culture carriers" are, and organisation members' perceptions of the degree of openness and trust which characterises the climate of the organisation — these guidelines were clearly of limited usefulness in the case of the present research.

A third and final argument against the use of group interviewing in the present research was that, given the nature of the research (i.e., it was not part of an organisational development consultancy), the researcher had no authority as a change agent to try to negotiate permission to work with groups, as opposed to individuals. Indeed, it was the researcher's impression that it would have been extremely difficult to secure management's approval for the release, from their work, of more than a few divisional members at any given time.

In terms of further information regarding the procedure for administering the Study 2 interviews, the following points can be made. Each of the participants in Study 2 was consulted as to a time for the interview that would be mutually convenient to the participant and to her/his immediate superior. In all cases, the interviews were conducted within the participant's working hours, with the duration of each interview being approximately one and a half hours. Participants gave their written consent for the interview to be recorded on audiotape and subsequently transcribed — it was explained that this would help to ensure the accuracy of data collection — and each participant was assured in writing that all of the information which she/he provided would be treated with the strictest confidentiality.

9.3 Approach to Data Analysis

As for Study 1, the task of analysing Study 2 data was conducted manually. In order to get some indication of the value of the method for detecting differences between the two divisions, and also in the interest of maintaining a good research relationship (divisional personnel had expressed an interest in the findings that were specific to their own division), the data for each division were analysed separately. This analysis produced an account of each division in terms of how participants responded to each of the questions they were asked. Consistent with the approach adopted in Study 1, within each division, the focus was on identifying any commonalities that emerged in the data for that division. In this way, it was possible to compare, and contrast, the divisions in terms of participants' views about the respective roles of workers and supervisors. While it was considered that the results of such an analysis would be of interest in their own right, it must be remembered that the primary objective of the analysis of Study 2 data was evaluative. That is, the aim was to determine the extent to which each of the questions included in the interview protocol might contribute something to an understanding of cultural phenomena in the two divisions being studied. In this sense, in the results reported below, it is the methodological findings, rather than the more descriptive findings, which are given precedence.

9.4 Results and Discussion

We turn now to a consideration of the results of the analysis of the Study 2 data. The particular format that we have adopted for reporting these results is as follows. First, for each of the questions asked, the responses of tooling division participants are summarised, followed by a summary of the responses of production division participants. Attention is then drawn to any similarities or differences between the divisions that are suggested by these data. Following this, and where relevant, consideration is given to the methodological implications of the findings. In particular, consideration is given to the extent to which the question asked 'worked', or 'didn't work', in the sense of providing culturally relevant insights of the kind that were anticipated.

It should be noted that, in this section, it is only the results of the analysis of data pertaining to the role of workers that are presented in their entirety. This is because many of the same methodological points were suggested by these results as by the results of the analysis of data pertaining to the role of supervisors. For the purpose of economy, we draw on the latter only as appropriate, to provide additional support for critical points which are made concerning the method[4]. Finally, it should be noted that, due to time constraints, it was not possible to ask all questions (pertaining to both the role of workers and the role of supervisors) of all participants.

---

[4]The results of the analysis of data pertaining to the role of supervisors are reported in Kummerow (2000).

9.4.1 *Open-ended question*

Q1: What do workers do in this division?

For both divisions, the responses to this initial open-ended question tended to be brief, ranging from one word answers to single short sentences. The content of these responses is described below, first for the tooling division and then for the production division.

Tooling division: This question was asked of four of the six tooling division partici-pants. Of these, three made reference to the work role of workers, one (a supervisor) indi-cating that workers "build tools", another (a wages employee) that they "build dies", and a third (a supervisor) that they "work". A fourth participant (a wages employee) indicated that workers "do as they are told".

Production division: All six of the production division participants responded to this question. In two cases, the reference was to the work role of workers, with one participant (a supervisor) indicating that workers "produce a motor car" and another (a wages employee) that workers "work". Two participants (both wages employees) made refer-ence to the subordinate role of workers, one indicating that workers "do the job they've been given to do" and the other that they "do as they are told". And two participants made reference to the general level of activity of workers, one (a wages employee) indicating that workers did "not much", and the other (a supervisor) that they did "as little as possible".

Taken as a whole, the above findings suggest that the initial open-ended question may not have been particularly meaningful to respondents. As indicated, they seemed unable to provide very articulate, or very detailed, responses to this question. At the same time, however, the responses given do serve to provide a very general indication of how the role of workers, in both divisions, was viewed. Moreover, to the extent that this role might be classified as more or less Theory X, or Theory Y, the data would appear to be suggestive of the former rather than the latter. Finally, the point can be made that, while some of the responses to the initial open-ended question — for example, responses indicating that workers do "as little as possible" and that workers "do as they are told" — might seem to have been said in jest, it was not the researcher's impression that this was the case. On the contrary, respondents appeared to be quite sincere in formulating their answers to this question.

With respect to the associated findings for the role of supervisors, the summary com-ments above apply equally to these findings. That is, in response to the question "What do supervisors in this division do?", participants gave similar types of responses, indicating for example that supervisors "control the organisation", do "nothing", do "more than what they used to", "sit back and take the money" and do "as little as possible".

Table 9.2. Role of workers: Theory X — Theory Y rating and satisfaction rating for Tooling Division and Production Division respondents.

		Tooling Division	
Respondent # and Position		**Theory X–Theory Y Rating**	**Satisfaction Rating**
1	Wages	Moderately Active	Moderately Satisfied
2	Wages Leading Hand	Moderately Passive	Extremely Satisfied
3	Supervisor	Slightly Active	Moderately Satisfied
4	Wages Leading Hand	Slightly Passive	Moderately Satisfied
5	Wages	Very Passive	Extremely Dissatisfied
6	Supervisor	Workers In All Categories	
		Production Division	
Respondent # and Position		**Theory X–Theory Y Rating**	**Satisfaction Rating**
1	Supervisor	Slightly Passive	Moderately Satisfied
2	Wages	Moderately Active	Moderately Satisfied
3	Wages	Moderately Passive	Extremely Dissatisfied
4	Wages	Moderately Passive	Moderately Dissatisfied
5	Wages	Moderately Passive	Moderately Dissatisfied
6	Supervisor	Slightly Passive	Moderately Satisfied

9.4.2 *Theory X — Theory Y rating*

Q2: What is your perception of the current role of workers in this division? (Rated on a six-point scale from *very passive* to *very active.*)

Respondents' ratings for this question, which were analysed separately for each division, are summarised in Table 9.2[5] and discussed in some detail below.

Tooling division: All participants from the tooling division responded to this question. As indicated in Table 9.2, responses varied considerably, and were represented by five of the six response categories listed (namely, *very passive* through to *moderately active*). This finding was somewhat surprising and not consistent with what was expected, given the predominantly Theory X orientation to the role of workers in this division, suggested by the results of Study 1. In other words, based on Study 1, it was expected that tooling division respondents in Study 2 would more consistently rate the role of workers in their division as passive, rather than active. It is interesting in this regard to consider respondents' elaborations on their ratings, since qualitative data of this kind (to the extent that they were available) helped to clarify the meanings that respondents attributed to their ratings.

---

[5]Table 9.2 also provides a summary of the associated ratings for Question 3, which asks about respondents' satisfaction with the current role of workers in their organisation.

As indicated in Table 9.2, there were two respondents from the tooling division who rated the current role of workers in their division as active — moderately active in the case of one participant (a wages employee) and slightly active in the case of the other (a supervisor). As suggested by the qualitative data associated with these ratings, however, these respondents appeared to differ in their interpretation of the term active. In the case of the former, the respondent appeared to be using the term to imply a strongly assertive, almost reactionary, role for workers. This respondent rated the current role of workers as moderately active on the grounds that, as he saw it, workers today were much more inclined than they had been in the past to challenge managerial decisions likely to affect them. By way of illustration, the respondent described a recent situation in which workers had successfully argued against the imposition of a decision, by divisional management, to introduce a roster system that would require day shift workers to periodically work on the afternoon shift. It was suggested by the respondent that a key factor influencing management's decision not to proceed with this change was the threat (if not explicit, then implied) of industrial action. In the respondent's own words:

> ...our manager here... he didn't want to rock the boat, he didn't want any industrial upheaval or anything like that, and [so] we got that stopped, and the guys were quite happy. (wages employee)

The point should be made that the interpretation of active by this respondent was different from that which was intended by the researcher, and which she had attempted to convey in the definition of active provided in the interview protocol. In particular, in emphasising a more enriched role for workers, the definition implied (though did not make explicit reference to) the existence of collaborative, rather than adversarial, relationships between workers and their supervisors.

In contrast to the above, the qualitative data associated with the slightly active rating of the second respondent suggested that, in this case, the term active was being used to mean initiative. According to this respondent, the role of workers in the division could be described as slightly active because, rather than "do things blindly", workers would alert their supervisors to problems (whether anticipated or actual) on the job and seek additional job-related information if this was required. The respondent's verbatim comments, in full, were as follows:

> I say slightly active...because people will come up with some suggestion that they can see something that you're telling them that's wrong — they will certainly talk about it, and bring it to your attention. They're not passive [in] that they'll just do things blindly. And in a lot of cases, you'll sort of give a person a job, but not give him one hundred percent instructions on how to do it, and so he'll be active enough to seek out this information, and either come back to you or ask someone else. (staff, supervisory)

As shown in Table 9.2, there were three respondents from the tooling division who rated the current role of workers in their division as more or less passive. The specific ratings given, along with respondents' elaborations on their ratings, are discussed below.

A slightly passive role was reported by one respondent (a wages employee with leading hand status) who argued that, while workers did not "blindly follow" instructions and were generally "alert as to what could be done", they were reluctant to make suggestions regarding how the job might be done better, since they had learned though experience that their efforts in this regard were typically not recognised or rewarded by their supervisors. Interestingly, while this respondent acknowledged the benefits of a more active role for workers, he pointed out that the ideal role comprised both active and passive elements. It was good for workers to have some input into the job but, because they didn't have "all the information", they sometimes needed to be able to accept decisions and instructions from their supervisors without question. A second respondent (also a wages employee with leading hand status) rated workers as playing a moderately passive role because, as he saw it, "most people do as they're told". At the same time, however, it was suggested that there were some sections of the division that supported a more active role for workers. The respondent (a wages employee with leading hand status) cited his own section as one such example, indicating that: "Supervision in our area are [*sic*] open to suggestions". In the case of the third respondent (a wages employee), the role of workers was rated as very passive on the grounds that workers were very reluctant to question the instructions of their supervisors in the event that they disagreed with these instructions. According to this respondent, this was the case particularly for migrant workers who had been brought up to respect the supervisor as the ultimate and legitimate authority. In the respondent's own words:

> I'm talking here of guys who are say from a European background, immigrants and that who have probably come up under that — that you don't question your supervisor sort of thing. (wages employee)

Finally, as shown in Table 9.2, there was one respondent from the tooling division (a supervisor) who indicated that he was unable to provide an overall rating of the current role of workers in the division because, as he saw it, there were some workers who played a more or less active role, and others who played a more or less passive role. The respondent was subsequently asked to describe what, for him, constituted the defining characteristics of active and passive workers respectively. With respect to the former, it was suggested that:

> The one that's very active is still the one that's willing to go on and do his job, and use his own initiative, and question whatever you're going to do. And the active ones, the real active ones are not the ones that come up and ask you how to fix something. They come up and tell you there's a problem, and that 'Maybe, we can fix it this way'. Whether that be a problem with... like a supervisor with a problem in the shop, whether it's an industrial

problem, or whether it's a physical problem on the job, it's all the same sort of thing. (staff, supervisory)

Interestingly, this respondent's notion of an active role for workers appears to be somewhat broader than conceptualisations of active which are suggested in the comments of other respondents from this division. As indicated above, the latter (whether made in the context of evaluating the role of workers as active or passive) contain references to behaviours, such as: bringing work-related problems to the attention of supervisors; asking supervisors for more information about the job if this is required; providing input into how to go about doing the job; and making suggestions for how the job might be improved. While these references convey the idea of at least some degree of job enrichment for workers, contrary to what was intended, active workers in this case appear to have little additional involvement and input beyond the domain of their immediate task or job. In the case of the present respondent, however, active workers are seen to have a role, not only in solving "physical" problems on the job, but also in solving industrial relations problems and in helping supervisors to solve more general problems "in the shop". Finally, with respect to the characteristics of passive workers, this respondent indicated that:

As you say, his output could be quite reasonable, but he's the type of person that you'd have to still go along and say 'Well, this is the next stage to do, and this is how you should do it', and that's what you do, and he does that.

Production division: All participants from the production division responded to this question. As can be seen from Table 9.2, there was somewhat less variability among the participants from this division, compared with their counterparts from the tooling division, in their ratings of the current role of workers in their division. Five respondents rated the role of workers as passive, while one rated it as active. With respect, first of all, to the former, there were three respondents (all wages employees) who indicated a moderately passive role for workers, and two (both supervisory staff) who indicated a slightly passive role. The qualitative data associated with these ratings — each of these respondents elaborated, to a greater or lesser extent, on her/his rating — suggested that the interpretation of passive by these respondents was generally consistent with that intended by the researcher. For example, reference was variously made to the role of workers in the division as "followers of instructions", to workers' lack of input in decision-making, to a lack of information dissemination to workers (at least, those below the level of leading hand), to the tendency of workers to unquestioningly accept the decisions of those above them, and to workers' lack of ambition beyond simply coming to work, working eight hours, and getting paid for it. Some illustrative examples of the verbatim comments of these respondents are provided below, the first two being associated with a moderately passive rating and the second two, a slightly passive rating:

> I'd say they're more on the passive side, at present... We have no say in what goes on, so they [the workers] just go along with management's decision. (wages employee)

> ...there's not enough information that goes down. It goes from supervisor to leading hand and it mainly stops there. It doesn't get shared amongst everybody. There's a few people that — they'll say what they think outright, but most of them will just be given an order and they take it. (wages employee)

> ...but the average worker's not having any input, it's only the leading hands that are having the input. (staff, supervisory)

> All they [the workers] really want to do is they want to go to work for eight hours, do the eight hours, give X amount of parts and go home and feel very happy about it, and they get paid for it. (staff, supervisor)

Interestingly, the last respondent above expressed the view that, in a company as large as the present company, it was appropriate that workers should play a predominantly passive role, since the resources that would be required "to get involved with the people who have ideas" were simply not available. In this sense, the respondent regarded it as important to have "set methods and ways of doing things".

With respect to the single respondent from this division who indicated an active role for workers, the specific rating given was moderately active. While the criteria upon which this assessment was based were not specified, it could be inferred from comments made by the respondent in response to subsequent questions that his interpretation of an active role for workers was reasonably consistent with that intended by the researcher. For example, in response to the question about whether or not the role of workers in the division would change in the future, the respondent (a wages employee) pointed to evidence, at the present time, that divisional management were becoming more supportive of an active role for workers. As he saw it:

> Now management is beginning to recognise in little ways that...you can have one supervisor standing over one operator and that still won't make them produce any more parts. But you can get the worker to enjoy what he does and all of a sudden, 50% goes up in the work [output], because it's no longer a bind, it's no longer a job, it's something he enjoys doing. By that I mean, they're getting us involved in everybody else's areas, and they're beginning to show an active concern. (staff, supervisory)

The above findings, along with those for the role of supervisors, provide a number of insights that have implications for an evaluation of the present method. These are summarised in point form below:

(1) Although the interview protocol did not include a question asking respondents to explain their X/Y rating, this information, when it was provided (either spontaneously or in

response to prompting by the interviewer), gave valuable insights into the extent to which respondents' interpretations of the key concepts of active and passive (and, in the case of the role of supervisors, consultative and directive) were consistent with the interpretations intended by the researcher. It would, therefore, seem desirable that rating questions of the kind asked in the present interview, should always be followed by a question that seeks clarification of the response given. In an interview, this might involve a specific question asking the person to explain their response or to give an example. This might also be included in a questionnaire where the respondent could be asked to provide an example or be given an opportunity to write a comment on their rating.

(2) Following on from the point above, qualitative data associated with the ratings of tooling division respondents, provided some evidence that, in this division, an active role for workers had been interpreted somewhat more narrowly than intended. Specifically, there appeared to be little awareness among the respondents from this division of an enriched role for workers beyond that which entailed giving workers more involvement in, and responsibility for, their immediate job. An important methodological implication of this finding is that, even though a researcher may attempt to impose her/his own definition of particular concepts (in this case, active and passive to describe the role of workers, and consultative and directive to describe the role of supervisors), these concepts will still be subject to interpretation by respondents and, as such, will be attributed meanings which are context-specific (in the sense of reflecting respondents' experience) and which may, or may not, be consistent with the meanings intended by the researcher.

Further support for the argument above can be found in the interpretation of a consultative role for supervisors, suggested by the comments of one participant from the tooling division. As indicated, this participant (himself a supervisor) argued that, because first-line supervisors typically had more subordinates than senior supervisors, and because they had to "come up with an answer for all of [their workers'] problems", it was necessary for them to be more consultative in their style of supervision than senior supervisors. This participant appeared to be using the term consultative simply to imply an increased level of interaction with workers on the part of first-line supervisors. No doubt this interpretation, which was quite inconsistent with that intended by the researcher was, at least in part, grounded in the participant's personal experience of the role of supervisors.

(3) The finding, for the tooling division, that one respondent misinterpreted active to mean reactionary highlights a possible limitation of the method. As indicated in the interview protocol, in attempting to describe two contrasting roles for workers (supervisors), examples were given of the specific kinds of behaviours in which workers (supervisors) who played that role might engage. It is possible that, to the extent that any one of these behaviours had particular salience for a respondent, the respondent might focus on this behaviour as the sole criterion upon which to base her/his evaluation of the role of workers (supervisors). Thus, in the case of the respondent referred to above, undue

emphasis may have been given to that aspect of the definition of an active role for workers which alluded to workers being prepared to question and/or challenge decisions (work practices *etc.*) that they did not understand or that they disagreed with.

(4) Finally, as indicated in the findings reported above, and also in the findings reported for the role of supervisors, there were some respondents from the tooling division (specifically, two in the case of the role of workers and three in the case of the role of supervisors) who indicated that it was either impossible, or difficult, for them to give a rating of the role of workers, or the role of supervisors, in their division *as a whole*. These respondents suggested that there was some variability in the roles played by workers and supervisors respectively and they attributed this variability to individual differences, sectional differences, and in the case of supervisors, seniority differences. This finding highlights a potential problem with the unit of analysis specified in the interview questions (i.e., the division) and raises questions about the possible existence of divisional subcultures (within different sections and/or at different levels of the hierarchy). In a more general sense, this finding also draws attention to a limitation of methods which use forced choice questions and which provide no opportunity for respondents to indicate that they *cannot respond*.

9.4.3 *Evaluation questions*

Q3: How satisfied are you with the role that workers play in this division at the present time? (Rated on a seven-point scale from *extremely satisfied* to *extremely dissatisfied.*)

Tooling division: As shown in Table 9.2, five participants responded to this question. Of these, four (including one supervisor and three wages employees) indicated that they were either moderately or extremely satisfied with the role played by workers in their division, and one (a wages employee) indicated extreme dissatisfaction with the role of workers. While the interview protocol did not include a question asking for clarification of respondents' satisfaction ratings, two of the above respondents nevertheless offered this information, one spontaneously and the other in response to prompting by the interviewer. For the first of these respondents (a wages employee with leading hand status), his satisfaction rating was extremely satisfied and his rating of the role of workers was moderately passive. While it was intended that these two ratings should be linked (i.e., the former should indicate the degree of satisfaction/dissatisfaction with the latter), in the case of this respondent, his clarification of his satisfaction rating suggested that this might not be the case. From the following comments by the respondent, it appears that instead of rating his satisfaction/dissatisfaction with the role of workers in the division, the respondent was rating his satisfaction/dissatisfaction with the quality of the workers for whom he was directly responsible:

> My lot seem to work pretty good together — we all work together. So I'd say I'm satisfied working with the ones I work with. (wages employee, leading hand)

In the case of the second respondent (also a wages employee with leading hand status), his qualifying comments suggested that he had interpreted the satisfaction question as intended. This respondent's satisfaction rating was moderately satisfied and his rating of the role of workers was slightly passive. In qualifying the former, the respondent commented that:

> I'd say that I was quite happy about [workers] being slightly passive, but there is room for improvement, and being a little bit more active in it could improve things…It would add more to the job — make the job easier actually for all around I think, if you've got more people putting their ideas into how it should be done and that sort of thing. (wages employee, leading hand)

Production division: All participants from the production division responded to this question. As indicated in Table 9.2, compared with their counterparts from the tooling division, the majority of whom reported some degree of satisfaction in response to this question, production division respondents were evenly divided in their satisfaction ratings. Three respondents (all wages employees) reported dissatisfaction with the role of workers in their division, and three respondents (including two supervisors and one wages employee) reported satisfaction. With respect to the former, the specific ratings given were moderately dissatisfied (two respondents) and extremely dissatisfied (one respondent). While each of these ratings was associated with a moderately passive rating for the role of workers, whether or not these two ratings were actually linked remains unclear since these respondents were not asked for (and neither did they offer) any clarification of their satisfaction ratings.

With respect to the latter, a rating of moderately satisfied was given by all three respondents. In two cases (the respondents were both supervisors), this rating was associated with a rating of slightly passive for the role of workers. One of these respondents elaborated spontaneously on his response, indicating that he would "like to see [the role of workers] even more passive". When asked to explain why, the respondent said:

> Because I'm a firm believer in you set up systems, and when systems are set up and they're foolproof, then you can go ahead and do your job. That's the way I sort of feel. When I come to work, I like to know what I'm going to be doing and that's what I get done — in a company this size. (staff, supervisory)

These data would appear to indicate that, for this respondent, his satisfaction rating was directly linked to his previous rating of the role of workers. In the case of the third respondent (a wages employee), his satisfaction rating was associated with a rating of moderately active for the role of workers. No elaborative data were available on this respondent's satisfaction rating.

In conclusion, the following points can be made:

(1) Compared with their counterparts from production, tooling division respondents appeared to be somewhat more satisfied with the role of workers in their division (ratings

of which were highly variable). As indicated, production division respondents were evenly divided in their satisfaction ratings and there was some evidence, in this division, of seniority differences in these ratings. Specifically, wages employees indicated that they were dissatisfied with the predominantly passive role that they perceived workers to play, whereas supervisors indicated that they were satisfied with this role.

(2) The findings for the role of supervisors indicated a similar pattern of responding to that reported above for the role of workers. That is, as a group, tooling division respondents were more inclined than their counterparts from production to indicate satisfaction with the role of supervisors in their division (ratings of which were again variable). In fact, all but one of the production division respondents indicated that they were dissatisfied with the role of supervisors in their division and, in this case, participants' ratings tended to be associated with perceptions of a directive role for supervisors.

(3) Finally, while the findings for both the role of workers and the role of supervisors indicated that there were some differences between the two divisions in respondents' satisfaction ratings, it is difficult to draw any conclusions about what these differences might mean. This is because respondents typically were not asked for (and neither did they offer) any qualification of their satisfaction ratings. Indeed, where qualitative data of this kind were available, they provided evidence of the potential for misinterpretation of the satisfaction question. As indicated, there was one respondent above whose clarification of his satisfaction rating suggested that, instead of rating his satisfaction with the role of workers, he was rating his satisfaction with workers more generally.

With respect to point 3 above, the findings for the role of supervisors contained evidence of the satisfaction question having been similarly misinterpreted. For example, one respondent (a supervisor from the tooling division) offered the following explanation for why he was only moderately satisfied (and not extremely satisfied) with the role of supervisors in his division (which, as he saw it, combined both directive and consultative elements):

> Well, over the last few years, I think some of our foremen have lost a bit of interest in the place, and this is not necessarily their fault. You've got to have 100% interest to get the extremely satisfied position, and I don't think we'll get that here under the situation that we're in. (staff, supervisory)

Similarly, a second respondent (a supervisor from the production division), when asked about why he was extremely dissatisfied with the role of supervisors in his division (which he had judged to be very directive), indicated that:

> ...because I don't believe that we've really got very many good supervisors. We've possibly got one good supervisor in the whole area. (staff, supervisor)

As above, the satisfaction ratings for these respondents appeared to be more a reflection of respondents' satisfaction with supervisors generally, than a reflection of their satisfaction with the role of supervisors specifically.

Misinterpretations such as these raise some doubt about the value of the satisfaction question. While this question was designed to provide some insight into respondents' personal views about the respective roles of workers and supervisors — such information being seen to have potential cultural significance — the question may be criticised on the grounds of being overly academic. In other words, while it is likely that most organisation members will be able to comment with ease on their satisfaction with concrete aspects of their experience (such as, workers and supervisors), it may be unrealistic to expect them to be able to comment, in an informed manner, on abstractions (such as, in this case, the role of workers and the role of supervisors).

Q4: How would you rate the effectiveness of the workers in this division at the present time? Give reasons for your rating. (Rated on a seven-point scale from *extremely effective* to *extremely ineffective*.)

Tooling division: This question was asked of five participants from the tooling division. Of these, one (a supervisor) indicated that he was unable to provide an overall rating of worker effectiveness in the division because, as he saw it, some workers were more effective than others. This respondent suggested that approximately 50% of tooling division workers were slightly to moderately effective, 25% were extremely effective, and 25% slightly ineffective. The ratings of the other four respondents were as follows: moderately effective (two respondents, including one wages employee and one supervisor), slightly effective (one respondent, a wages employee), and neither effective nor ineffective (one respondent, a wages employee).

The four respondents above who gave an overall rating of worker effectiveness were subsequently asked to explain their ratings. As indicated, it was anticipated that the explanations offered would provide information about the criteria used by respondents to rate worker effectiveness and that these criteria would, in turn, reveal something about respondents' personal beliefs regarding what constituted an appropriate role for workers. Table 9.3 provides a summary of the main criteria that respondents from both divisions appeared to use in evaluating the effectiveness of the workers in their division.

As indicated, respondents from the tooling division variously made reference to the importance of work skills, such as, efficiency and producing a quality product, and to the importance of work behaviours and attitudes, such as, being prepared to think about, and take responsibility for the job, and caring about and showing pride in the job. A somewhat different perspective was provided by one respondent who judged worker effectiveness according to the extent to which workers were prepared to speak out about their ideas, and be assertive in relation to getting these ideas acted upon by supervision. By way of illustration, a sample of the verbatim comments from which these effectiveness criteria were

Table 9.3. Criteria used to judge worker effectiveness, shown separately for respondents from the Tooling Division and the Production Division.

Effectiveness Criteria	Tooling Division Respondent (R) #	Production Division Respondent (R) #
Work Skills		
Ability to do job quickly (efficiency)	R4, R5	R4
Ability to do job well (quality of work)	R4, R5	R1, R4
Work attitudes and behaviours		
Thinks about the job	R3	
Takes responsibility for the job	R3	
Shows imagination in relation to the job	R4	
Has input into how to do the job		R4, R5
Comes up with ideas for improving the job		R4, R5
Cares about the job	R5	
Feels pride in the job	R5	
Willing to speak out, assertive	R1	
Shows a desire to learn new skills		R2
Willing to take on more work		R2
Reliable		
Trustworthy		R2
Tries hard		R2
Conscientious		R3
Wants to make good quality parts		R3
Has a good attitude toward work		R3
"Gives 100%"		R6

inferred is provided below. The first excerpt is associated with an effectiveness rating of moderately effective, and the second with an effectiveness rating of slightly effective.

...there's a tendency to have people do exactly as you'd want them to do. You're not using their brain power. I always say that half a dozen brains are better than one, and a lot of cases we're not utilising that brain power, because of the way we get things done, and the way we're sort of set up. We haven't got time to go round asking everyone's opinion, and when we continually give a man a job, and let him go away and do it to our instructions, therefore he stops thinking about it...If they were given a little bit more responsibility we'll say, it might make them think about the job in depth a little bit more, and therefore we'll get better value out of them. (staff, supervisory)

Well, I suppose because of the condition — not knowing the future here — the future workloads, and what have you, and not being able to find out the information. More or less no one gives a damn now really. But I suppose when it gets down to it, they've still got a bit of pride in the job they're going to do. It may not be as fast as they could possibly do it, but I mean they don't want to bugger the job up or something. They might overrun the hours because the drive is no longer there. (wages employee)

The first excerpt above is interesting in the sense that, while a Theory Y orientation might initially be inferred from this respondent's comments, a more careful reading of the excerpt suggests an alternative interpretation. It is true that, when considered out of context, the change which the respondent is advocating, namely, to give workers more responsibility, can reasonably been seen as implying a Theory Y orientation. Importantly, however, this change is considered only in terms of how it might benefit the organisation, specifically, by enabling the organisation to get "better value out of [workers]". There is no corresponding consideration of the potential benefits of the change to workers themselves (i.e., in terms of increased worker motivation and satisfaction). This subordination of the individual's needs and interests to the needs and interests of the organisation is, of course, one of the distinguishing features of a Theory X orientation. Considered in its entirety, then, the excerpt above serves to illustrate that it may not always be possible to categorically group data according to whether they are more consistent with a Theory X or a Theory Y orientation. Attempts to formulate questions according to this framework are also likely to encounter difficulties. This is because, as illustrated by this excerpt, the finding that a respondent agrees with a statement, such as, "Workers should have more responsibility" cannot necessarily be interpreted to mean that the respondent holds strongly Theory Y assumptions.

A second point that can be made in relation to the above data is that, contrary to expectations, it was not always easy to infer effectiveness criteria from respondents' explanations of their effectiveness ratings. There was sometimes a degree of uncertainty surrounding the inference process, which made it necessary for the researcher to take some interpretive licence when analysing these data. The second excerpt above provides a good illustration of the difficulties encountered in this regard. For example, it is not clear from a negative comment such as "no one gives a damn now" whether, for this respondent, 'giving a damn' constituted an important effectiveness criterion. While this was the interpretation adopted in the present analysis, such an interpretation is clearly open to question. The same kind of uncertainty surrounds the respondent's comments about time overruns and a concern, on the part of workers, not to "bugger the job up". Whether it can be inferred from these comments (as was done in the present analysis) that, for this respondent, efficiency and work quality constituted important effectiveness criteria, is an interpretation which is, again, open to question.

Production division: This question was asked of all participants from the production division. Four respondents (including one supervisor and three wages employees) judged the workers in their division to be moderately effective, one respondent (a supervisor) considered them to be neither effective nor ineffective, and one respondent (a wages employee) considered them to be moderately ineffective. It can be seen from Table 9.3 that, as a group, respondents from the production division, like their counterparts from the tooling division, varied in terms of the criteria they used to judge worker effectiveness. As for the tooling division, reference was made to the importance of skills associated with the quality and quantity of the work produced, and to the importance of behaviours and attitudes suggestive of a more enriched role for workers (such as, having input into the job and coming up with ideas for how the job might be improved). In addition, in the production division, there was an emphasis on the importance of behaviours and attitudes such as conscientiousness, being a "trier", reliability, and trustworthiness. That there was no evidence for these latter criteria in the tooling division data possibly highlights a cultural difference between the two divisions.

Some examples of the verbatim comments from which the above effectiveness criteria were inferred are provided below. For all three excerpts, the associated effectiveness rating was moderately effective.

> Well, out of the 100% of workers here, maybe 25% you'd get more than your money's worth out of their work…You would have 25% that would be moderately effective and you could rely on, and the other 50% I believe you wouldn't really trust them because, if you give them a free rein, then they would go back[wards]. (staff, supervisory)
>
> They all seem very conscientious. They all strike me as if they do want to make good quality parts in here. We've got very few with a poor attitude to work. We've got a few, but on the whole most of them have got a good attitude to their work. (wages employee)
>
> I suppose they've got to be effective…Well, they're getting production out…And I suppose they're getting a certain quality out — what is required. (wages employee)

As above for the tooling division, there was some uncertainty surrounding the process of inferring effectiveness criteria from the explanations that production division respondents offered for their effectiveness ratings. For example, in the first excerpt above, it is not entirely clear whether, for this respondent, the qualities of reliability and trustworthiness constituted important criteria for judging worker effectiveness. While, for the purpose of the present analysis, it was assumed that they were, such an assumption is clearly open to question. The findings for the production division suggested the further difficulty that, contrary to expectations, the criteria used by respondents to evaluate worker effectiveness might not always be their own. For example, in the third excerpt above, there is a sense in which the criteria implied in this respondent's comments may be those of the company (at least, as perceived by the respondent), rather than those of the respondent himself.

Finally, the data on worker effectiveness (both for the production division and the tooling division) provided some interesting insights into respondents' perceptions regarding why workers were not as effective as they might be, and how worker effectiveness might be enhanced. For example, in response to prompting, one respondent from the production division (a supervisor who had judged the workers in the division to be neither effective nor ineffective) suggested that, in order to improve worker effectiveness, one of two possible approaches could be adopted. On the one hand, stricter controls and more rigid management systems could be introduced, such that the organisation would operate "virtually like an army". On the other, the organisation could be divided into "a lot of little cells", each of which would be managed as an independent unit, very much according to "private enterprise" principles. The participant indicated that he favoured the former "military" approach on the grounds that the company was too big, and that it lacked the kind of leadership talent that would be required (at all levels) to support the latter approach. Given the potential of data such as these to reveal respondents' assumptions about how workers should be managed, consideration might be given to the inclusion, in the revised interview protocol, of a formal prompt asking participants to indicate how they think worker effectiveness might be enhanced.

The above findings, along with those for the role of supervisors, suggest the following conclusions and methodological points:

(1) The prompt question asking participants to explain their effectiveness rating was useful insofar as it provided some insight into the criteria used by participants to evaluate the effectiveness of the workers in their division. However, there was some evidence, albeit slight, of a difference between the divisions in this regard. As indicated above, whereas qualities such as conscientiousness, reliability, and trustworthiness appeared to be of some significance in the production division (i.e., as criteria for evaluating worker effectiveness), there was no reference to these qualities in the corresponding data for the tooling division. In the case of the role of supervisors, the findings were somewhat more conclusive. In the tooling division, the criteria used to evaluate supervisor effectiveness typically emphasised the control aspect of supervision. One participant (a supervisor) went so far as to suggest that the supervisors in his division could become "a lot more effective" if they were given "100% control over their people". In contrast, in the production division, the criteria for evaluating supervisor effectiveness tended to emphasise human relations qualities, such as, being approachable, encouraging worker involvement in the job, and asking workers for their ideas.

(2) While the questions about worker effectiveness (including the closed rating question and the associated clarification prompt) went some way toward achieving what they were intended to achieve, these questions were not without their limitations. As indicated above, there were difficulties associated with the process of inferring effectiveness criteria from participants' explanations of their effectiveness ratings. These same difficulties were encountered in the subsequent analysis of data pertaining to the role of supervisors. Moreover, there was some evidence to suggest that, contrary to what was intended, participants might not use their own criteria in evaluating worker (supervisor) effectiveness. These limitations possibly suggest the need for some revision of the effectiveness questions.

(3) Finally, while it was anticipated that participants' responses to the effectiveness questions would, to some extent at least, be linked with their responses to the previous X/Y rating and satisfaction questions, this was not always the case. On the one hand, some of the criteria used by participants to evaluate the effectiveness of workers and supervisors (e.g., conscientiousness and reliability in the case of workers, and ambition and level of education in the case of supervisors) were unable to be classified within a Theory X — Theory Y framework. On the other hand, there was some evidence to suggest that individuals may not always be consistent in their responses to the questions they are asked. A nice example of this was provided by one participant from the tooling division (a wages employee) who judged the role of supervisors in his division to be very directive, indicated that he was extremely dissatisfied with this role, and then went on to evaluate the effectiveness of supervisors in terms of the extent to which they met the control requirements of the job.

9.4.4 *Personal experience questions*

As indicated in the interview protocol, there were two main personal experience questions — the first (Question 5) comprising five parts, and the second (Question 6) comprising four parts. The format for the presentation of results in this section is as follows. For each question, the findings for each part of the question are presented first, along with some brief summary comments, where these are deemed necessary. Following this, there is a discussion of the main methodological implications of the findings for that question, considered as a whole.

Q5: Think about the best worker that you have ever had (worked with, known) in this division.

(a) What was it that you admired or liked about this worker?

   Tooling division: All participants answered this question. Of these, there were five for whom the worker identified as their best worker was someone who the respondent had known, or worked with in the tooling division, in the past. Only one respondent described a worker with whom he was familiar, and whom he admired, at the present time. Respondents attributed a range of different qualities to their best workers, a summary of which is provided in Table 9.4. As indicated, four broad categories of best worker qualities were suggested, namely: (i) work knowledge, skills, and abilities; (ii) work behaviours and attitudes; (iii) interpersonal skills and behaviours; and (iv) personal qualities and characteristics. For tooling division respondents, the first of these categories was the best represented. Four of the six respondents from this division (including three wages employees and one supervisor) made reference to their best worker's competence in terms of his job knowledge, skills, and/or abilities. More specifically, the best worker was variously described as an individual who "understood the job thoroughly", who was able to "plan the job very well mentally", who was highly efficient in the sense of being able to "finish his job very, very quickly" and who was "brilliant at the job".

Qualities associated with the second category — work behaviours and attitudes — were mentioned by two respondents only. One of these respondents (a supervisor) described the considerable initiative of his best worker (in this case, a leading hand):

> I liked this particular person because he didn't wait to be told to do things. He did things on his own initiative... He went around — he was a leading hand this chap — and he looked after the equipment. He had the equipment up to scratch. He had it where it was needed, and he thought about the job one jump ahead of the person that was

Table 9.4. Tooling Division (TD): Characteristics of workers judged to be 'best' workers as described by individual respondents.

Respondent # and Position	Work Knowledge, Skills, & Abilities	Work Behaviours & Attitudes	Interpersonal Skills & Behaviours	Personal Qualities & Characteristics
TD1 wages	• Skill and ability to do the job		• "Personality" in the sense of being able to communicate with, and form social relationships with co-workers	
TD2 wages			• Ability and willingness to teach others	
TD3 supervisor	• Good job knowledge • Thorough understanding of the job and the function of the tools	• Shows initiative • Always "one jump ahead"		
TD4 wages	• Good job knowledge • Fast worker • Conceptual and planning skills • Imagination in relation to the job			
TD5 wages	• Ability to do the job well, "brilliant at the job"		• Good understanding of the strengths and weaknesses of other workers	• Ability to stay calm when disagreements arise
TD6 supervisor		• Competitive approach to the job, always trying to do the job better than co-worker		

doing it and, therefore, had everything ready for the person that was doing it. (staff, supervisory)

It is noteworthy that, implicit in this respondent's comments, is the idea that a 'good' leading hand is someone who organises the work for his subordinates. The other respondent (also a supervisor) indicated that his best worker's competitive approach to work — "he always wanted to compete with me all the time, to be better than me" — was a quality which he admired since it provided him (the respondent) with a strong incentive to do better himself.

In terms of interpersonal skills and behaviours, it can be seen from Table 9.4 that there were three respondents (all wages employees) who made reference to qualities in this category. Specifically, one respondent indicated that what he admired most about his best worker was the worker's ability and willingness to teach others. The respondent described how this was a quality which he himself had benefited from since, when he first started with the company, this worker had been a kind of mentor to him:

...he taught me a lot of things. ...Virtually, about the job. ...When I first started with the company, I didn't know the business at all, and he took me under his wing and showed me different things. (wages employee)

A second respondent described his best worker's sensitivity to individual differences, in particular, his capacity for understanding workers who "may not be so fast or so good". A third respondent commented on the positive social relationship that his best worker had been able to establish with co-workers. According to this respondent, the existence of such a relationship (which had its roots in common outside interests, whether "football, or fishing, soccer, or whatever") could facilitate communication between workers and help workers to get on better with one another. From a cultural perspective, it is worth noting that this reference to the importance of qualities associated with the purely social dimension of work (and work relationships) was the only one of its kind in the tooling division data. It is also worth noting the suggestion, by this respondent, that an important precedent to the formation of social relationships between workers in the tooling division was that workers should respect one another for their job skills and abilities. In the respondent's own words:

...I do believe that people respect one another for their skill and their ability to do the job...And then, from then, you form a relationship in as much as what your common interests are outside. (wages employee, leading hand)

Finally, in terms of the personal qualities and characteristics of best workers, it can be seen from Table 9.4 that there was a single reference only to a quality in this category. In this case, the respondent (a wages employee) indicated, that because the tooling division supported a culturally diverse workforce, exchanges between workers could, at times, "get a bit heated". In this sense, the respondent admired his best worker's ability to "control [his] temper".

Apart from the above findings, there was one other point of interest that emerged from the analysis of tooling division data pertaining to best worker characteristics. Three respondents from this division (including one wages employee and two supervisors) suggested, without any prompting from the interviewer, that the qualities which they had attributed to their best worker were qualities which were part of the worker's innate personality make-up and which, as such, could not be developed in workers through training. The verbatim comments of one of these respondents speak for themselves:

> The best tradesmen are [the] ones that have an imagination, and can see what a job's got to look like when it's finished. There's not too many that have got this imagination... I don't think you can cultivate it. (wages, leading hand)

A second respondent, in reflecting on the considerable initiative displayed by his best worker, made the comment that:

> ...it's a matter of personality. Not everyone is that way inclined [*sic*]. I mean if we had a factory full of those workers, we wouldn't have a problem in the world, and we wouldn't need a lot of the supervision that we've got...Not everybody has the natural ability to be able to do those things. (staff, supervisory)

And a third respondent (a supervisor) indicated that, for many workers, it was simply not "naturewise", meaning that it was not in their nature, for them to be competitive or to strive to do better. As he saw it, such workers:

> ...only want to plod along and do what they always do. They are not interested in change, and not interested in doing something quicker. (staff, supervisory)

The important point can be made that this view of best workers as 'born and not made', to the extent that it is shared widely among the division's membership, has potentially serious implications for the effective implementation of training programs designed to develop the competencies (whether technical, interpersonal, or other) of the workers in this division. Prior to implementing such training, some assessment of the sharedness of this view might, therefore, be recommended.

Production division: All participants responded to this question, three describing a current best worker and three, a past best worker. Like their counterparts from tooling, respondents from the production division attributed a range of different qualities to their best workers. These qualities are summarised in Table 9.5, in terms of the same four categories used to classify the corresponding tooling division data, and discussed in more detail below.

Table 9.5. Production Division (PD): Characteristics of workers judged to be 'best' workers as described by individual respondents.

Respondent # and Position	Work knowledge, Skills, & Abilities	Work Behaviours & Attitudes	Interpersonal Skills & Behaviours	Personal Qualities & Characteristics
PD1 supervisor	▪ Logical and methodical thinking ▪ Ability to work independently i.e., "without detailed instructions"	▪ Shows initiative ▪ Strives to achieve		
PD2 wages		▪ Effort and perseverance, gives "100% all the time" ▪ Willing to learn, develop new skills	▪ Willing to share knowledge ▪ Easy to get on with	▪ Even tempered
PD3 wages	▪ Does a "good job"		▪ Helps co-workers with work-related problems	▪ A nice temperament
PD4 wages		▪ Effort and perseverance, "gives 100%"		▪ "Practices what he preaches" i.e., actions consistent with words
PD5 wages	▪ Well-organised ▪ Knows the job		▪ Friendly nature ▪ Easy to work with ▪ Willing to help others	▪ "All round nice person"
PD6 supervisor		▪ Effort on the job, giving "total eight hours work a day"		

In terms of work knowledge, skills, and abilities, it can be seen from Table 9.5 that there were three respondents from the production division (including one supervisor and two wages employees) who, in describing their best worker, made reference to one or more qualities in this category. Compared with the corresponding tooling division data, there were fewer references in these data to the importance of job specific knowledge, skills, and abilities. Rather, the emphasis appeared to be more on general competencies, such as, logical thinking, the ability to work independently, and organisational skills. This difference between the divisions, while it lacks the support of an extensive data set, is nevertheless consistent with what one would expect given differences in the nature of the work performed in each division — that is, general production and assembly work in the production division, and more specialised engineering and tooling work in the tooling division.

Compared with their counterparts from the tooling division, production division respondents placed somewhat more emphasis on the work behaviours and attitudes of their best workers. It can be seen from Table 9.5 that there were four respondents from this division (compared with two from the tooling division) who described their best worker in terms of qualities in this category. Three of these respondents (including two wages employees and one supervisor) drew attention to their best worker's effort on the job and to the fact that she/he consistently "gave 100%". It is worth noting the link between these data and the previous emphasis on conscientiousness as an important criterion by which production division respondents judged the effectiveness of the workers in their division. The point can also be made, as previously, that the lack of evidence (in this case, from the best worker data) suggesting the importance of qualities such as effort, perseverance, and conscientiousness in the tooling division, possibly highlights a cultural difference between the divisions.

In terms of interpersonal skills and behaviours, it can be seen from Table 9.5 that there were three respondents from the production division (all wages employees) who attributed qualities associated with this category to their best worker. The emphasis in these data was on the best worker's willingness to help, and ability to get on with, co-workers. In addition, there were four respondents (the three above and a fourth wages employee) who mentioned a personal quality that they admired in their best worker, in particular, their best worker's positive disposition and even temper. By way of illustration, a sample of the verbatim comments of these respondents is provided below:

> He was a very easy chap to get on with — very easy and even-tempered. I mean, we had our disagreements but there was no long animosity after…He was also willing to share his knowledge. (wages employee)
>
> They[6] are very helpful. If they think that you have got a problem, they'll help you out with it…Always, always in the same mood. Never…you know, like some people will help you and then another day, they'll shrug you off…no, always the same, a nice temperament, you know, [a nice] type to work with. (wages employee)

---

[6]This participant used the plural 'they' to refer to her best worker.

[She was] extremely friendly towards me when I first started. She's still very friendly with me now. She was very good at showing me what I had to do. She was just an all-round nice person — easy to work with and she knew what she was doing. (wages employee)

Considered as a whole, these data provide some evidence to suggest that, in the production division, the social and personal qualities of workers may be more highly valued (by workers, if not also by supervisors) than they are in the tooling division. Again, this finding can probably be explained in terms of differences between the divisions in the nature of the work performed in each (or, perhaps more accurately, in how the work in each is organised). In the production division, work is typically performed by groups or teams, with each member of the team performing one part only of the total task (or assembly) which the team has been assigned. In contrast, in the tooling division, work is more often performed by individuals who work independently on an entire job, from start to finish. Skills associated with effective teamwork are, therefore, likely to be attributed more importance in the production division than in the tooling division.

Q5 (b) How important is it to you that workers have these particular characteristics (attitudes, behaviours)? Why?

Tooling division: All participants responded to this question and, in all cases, the qualities attributed to best workers were regarded as being either important, or very important. The reasons given for why these qualities were important varied. Three respondents (including two supervisors and one wages employee) made reference to the benefits, to the individual, of their best worker's qualities. In one case, it was argued that a good knowledge of the job was important because it enabled the individual to make decisions about the job more easily; a second respondent drew attention to the pride and self-esteem associated with being "brilliant at the job"; and a third respondent argued that the desire to compete with, and do better than, one's co-workers gave the individual more incentive and more interest in the job.

In contrast to the above, there were two respondents (both wages employees) for whom the emphasis was more on the social implications of their best worker's qualities. In one case, it was suggested that being good at one's job was important because it contributed to a positive relationship with one's superiors and it also enhanced one's own satisfaction with the job. In this respondent's own words:

Well, you've got to be successful in your job, because if you can do your job well, and successfully, and quickly, then your supervision are happy with you, and you're happy in your job. (wages employee)

In the other case, it was suggested that the ability to form social relationships with co-workers was important because "[in order] to work with somebody, you've got to get on with them". As indicated previously, however, it was this respondent's view that the formation of relationships of this kind was contingent on the individual first of all having respect for the skills and abilities of co-workers.

Finally, there was one respondent (a wages employee) who suggested that it was important for newcomers — for "anyone learning the trade" — to have access to someone who was willing and able to teach others. The respondent did not comment on his reasons for this view.

Production division: As above, all participants from the production division responded to this question, and all participants regarded the qualities they attributed to their best worker as being either important or very important. It was also the case that the reasons given for why these qualities were considered to be important were similarly varied.

Two respondents (both wages employees) suggested that, given the nature of the work in the production division (very routine, and typically performed by groups), and given the amount of time that one spent at work, it was essential for workers to have a pleasant disposition and be able to get on with one other. One of these respondents also suggested that, because workers depended upon one another to get the job done, it was important that they had a good knowledge of, and were well-organised in relation to, their individual tasks. The verbatim responses of these respondents were as follows:

> There's nothing worse than coming into work and, like, just bitching all day. You know, some people just bitch all day, and you think 'Oh, God, I can do without this'. Because the work's boring, so you do need...you know, you spend the biggest part of your life in here, and you just don't want to listen to people bitch all the time. (wages employee)
>
> Because you're working with those people for eight hours, five days a week, and if they're not organised and they don't know their job, it makes your job twice as hard. And if they're not friendly, it just puts you in an awkward position for eight hours, because it's a long time in there. (wages employee)

A further two respondents stressed the importance of their best worker's effort on the job. One of these respondents (a wages employee) argued that "giving 100%" was an important quality because it led to more efficient operations and this, in turn, provided the individual with a sense of satisfaction in a job well done. The respondent went on to suggest that, once the individual's satisfaction was aroused in this way, there was a kind of "flow-on" effect, such that the motivation of other members of the group tended to increase and the performance of the group, as a whole, tended to improve. In contrast with this view, the other respondent (a supervisor) argued that, in an organisation as large as theirs, where close supervision of individual workers was not possible, it was very important to have workers who made considerable effort on the job — who were "willing to give you eight hours". In such an organisation, it was considered too easy for workers who didn't really want to work to "hide" and "bludge around"[7].

---

[7] 'Bludge' is Australian vernacular meaning to avoid work or responsibility.

A different perspective again was provided by a fifth respondent. In this case, the respondent (a supervisor) argued that being a good operator (in the sense of showing initiative and being able to think logically and methodically) was an important quality because, in recent years, there had been a trend in the division toward the allocation of more responsibility to the shop floor. This meant that some of the functions previously performed by supervisory staff were now being performed by leading hands, and some of the functions previously performed by leading hands were now the responsibility of production operators.

Finally, a sixth respondent argued that the consistency of his best worker — "he practises what he preaches" — was an important quality because it gave those around him reason to "believe in" him and "respect everything" he did.

Q5 (c) What was this worker's view of the organisation?

Tooling division: All participants responded to this question. Best workers were perceived to hold a range of different views of the organisation, a summary of which is provided below.

Two respondents (both wages employees, one with leading hand status) reported that their best worker had a negative view of the organisation. In one case, it was suggested that the best worker considered the organisation (specifically, the tooling division) to be poorly managed. The point was made that this was a view that was shared widely among divisional members and which had developed over the years as the division had been allowed to decline. In the other case, the best worker's negative view was attributed to a perception, by the worker, that he had been poorly treated by the company.

A third respondent (a wages employee with leading hand status) implied that his best worker was indifferent to the organisation. In this case, the worker reportedly viewed the organisation simply as "a place to come and earn money". The fact that the worker performed his job as competently as he did was, according to this respondent, the worker's way of meeting his "obligation to the company". A fourth respondent (a supervisor) indicated that, while his best worker was "pretty positive" in his view of the organisation, like many others he had a tendency toward cynicism because despite the need for change in the division "it goes on and on and on, and nothing ever happens".

The remaining two respondents (a wages employee and a supervisor) ascribed a highly positive view of the organisation to their best worker. Interestingly, in each case, the best worker was an individual with whom the respondent had worked in the past (15 years ago in one case and 30 years ago in the other). One respondent pointed out that, although workers in the division in the past typically did not express their views about the company explicitly, there was nevertheless a feeling of pride in the company, which was evident in the defensive attitudes that workers adopted toward outsiders who said "anything against the product or the company". The other respondent indicated that, while he could not remember exactly what his best worker's view of the organisation was, he supposed that it would have been very positive. In the respondent's own words, this was because:

> It was an excellent company to work for at that time. ...[it] was a company which you felt was progressing, it had something to offer you, it had a future to offer you, it had stability to offer you. (staff, supervisory)

The reader will recall that the Study 1 data contained many such references to a more positive past in the tooling division — a past in which members felt more or less assured of a job for life, in which those who wanted to get ahead could get ahead, and in there was a strong sense of member loyalty to the organisation and pride in the product it produced.

On the basis of the results reported above, it appears that in the tooling division at the present time, a worker's classification as a best worker is not contingent on the worker having a positive view of the organisation. As indicated, there were two respondents who ascribed a distinctly negative view of the organisation to their best worker. The finding that the most positive views were reported for past best workers raises the possibility that, in this division, a best worker's view of the organisation may be linked in some way with the organisation's life stage, with negative views being associated with a period of relative decline for the division, and positive views being associated with a period of relative prosperity. To the extent that this is the case, it highlights the need, not only to establish a best worker's status as a present or past best worker, but if the latter, to also determine the approximate time (year) to which the respondent is referring when she/he describes this worker (in other words, to establish how far back the past actually extends).

Production division: All participants responded to this question. Four respondents (including one supervisor and three wages employees) reported that their best worker had a negative view of the organisation. In all cases, this view was attributed to some aspect of how the company, or the division, was managed. Specifically, the reasons given included: the perception that more senior divisional members were, in some cases, not doing their jobs (one respondent); the perception that credit was often not given where it was due, with more senior divisional members claiming credit (which was undeserved) for the achievements of those below them (one respondent); dissatisfaction with traditional (bureaucratic) management methods perceived to be still in practice in the division (two respondents); inadequate recognition by more senior personnel of the abilities and worth of shop floor employees (one respondent); a lack of organisational skill at more senior levels (one respondent); and the failure of those responsible for implementing various change programs (e.g., information sharing programs) to follow through on those programs (one respondent)[8].

---

[8] Some respondents gave more than one reason for their best worker's negative view of the organisation.

Of the remaining two respondents, one (a wages employee) indicated that, while her best worker had never commented on his view of the organisation, she supposed that it would be "pretty good" because of the marked contrast between this worker's previous work experience in a communist country and his current work experience in an environment where conditions of work generally were regarded as more favourable. The other respondent (a supervisor) suggested that his best worker's view of the organisation was neutral, that is, neither positive nor negative. This respondent's best worker was similar to the tooling division best worker described previously, in that his involvement with the organisation reportedly did not extend beyond doing his job and getting paid for it. The respondent went on to suggest that, in his opinion, all good workers in the production division were similarly inclined in this regard, suggesting that, at least at this level, deeper involvement with the organisation may not be regarded as a particularly important factor in the assessment of an employee's worth. In the respondent's own words:

> I think most of the good workers, they're quite happy to get paid once a week for doing their job. I don't believe the involvement goes much deeper with the company. I think they'd be good workers no matter who they worked for; they're just that type of people. (staff, supervisory)

The main conclusion that can be drawn from these data is that, as for the tooling division, a worker's classification as a best worker in the production division was not contingent upon the worker having a positive view of the organisation. In fact, as indicated, the views of production division best workers were perceived to be predominantly negative. Unlike the tooling division, there was no evidence in these data to suggest that past best workers might differ from present best workers in their view of the organisation. A likely explanation for this finding lies in the age of the production division. At the time of this study, the division had been in operation for less than ten years and, as such, its members were unlikely to have developed the kind of historical perspective (at least, with respect to the division) that was so evident in the experience of members of the tooling division. It was also the case that each of the three past best workers described by production division respondents was a worker with whom the respondent had been associated in this division (rather than elsewhere in the company)[9]. In this sense, then, the past as referred to by these respondents was a more recent past than that referred to by the two tooling division respondents above.

Q5 (d) How did this worker relate to supervision?

Tooling division: All participants responded to this question. Best workers were reported to have generally positive relationships with supervision, with ratings ranging

---

[9]Respondents from the production division, like their counterparts from tooling, were not specifically asked to indicate the time (year) of their association with their best worker. However, from a close reading of the production division transcripts and, in two cases, knowledge of the identity of the best worker being referred to, this information could easily be deduced.

from "reasonable" through to "very good". No negative relationships were reported, although one respondent (a wages employee with leading hand status) indicated that workers no longer respected supervision as they had done in the past. Two reasons were given for this. First, supervisors were reported to have become increasingly negative in their attitudes — this was attributed to their perception that the organisation didn't care about them — and this had led to correspondingly negative attitudes among workers. Second, it was argued that supervisors in the tooling division had failed to adapt their style of supervision to suit the more "modern" approaches that were evident elsewhere in the company. The old style of supervision, whereby workers were expected, simply, to "accept orders", while it was still practised in the tooling division, was no longer entirely acceptable to workers who had acquired some degree of familiarity (albeit indirectly through hearing about changes elsewhere in the company) with alternative, less directive approaches.

Respondents used very similar criteria by which to judge the relationship between their best worker and his supervisor(s). A common theme in these data was that a positive relationship between a worker and his supervisor was one that was devoid of conflict. It was a relationship in which the worker showed respect for his supervisor and complied with his wishes. This theme emerged in the responses of five respondents (including one supervisor and three wages employees). A related theme, which emerged in the responses of three respondents (one supervisor and two wages employees), was that a positive worker-supervisor relationship was one in which the competence of the worker was such that only minimal contact with the supervisor was required. By way of illustration of these themes, a sample of respondents' verbatim responses is provided below:

> I think [he] relates reasonable... I think he's only too pleased to try and help and assist wherever he can. But I do believe now, at this particular time, there's quite a lot of people that have lost a lot of respect...You should always have respect for your supervisor and know he's the boss. (wages employee, leading hand)
>
> Fairly good, I'd say [referring to the worker's relationship with his supervisor]. He wasn't a rebel, or he didn't stir people up, or anything like that...He did his job, he didn't argue, he did what he was told. (wages employee)
>
> He was very good with supervision. He was easy to deal with and cooperative. (staff, supervisory)
>
> Very well, I think [referring to how the worker related to his supervision], because he always kept [them] happy and they didn't pester him or anything like that. They stayed off his back, so he was happy, because he was producing the results. (wages employee, leading hand)

Production division: The pattern of responding for production division respondents was less clear than that described above for respondents from the tooling division. Two respondents reported a generally positive relationship between their best worker and her/his supervisor(s); in two cases the relationship appeared to be more or less neutral; one respondent suggested that the nature of the relationship depended on the supervisor; and one respondent described a somewhat negative relationship. The criteria upon which these relationships were judged also varied more than they did for the tooling division. These criteria are outlined briefly below.

Of the two respondents who reported a positive relationship between their best worker and her/his supervisor(s), one made reference to the relative absence of problems, in this case, between himself (the respondent was a supervisor) and the worker. The respondent indicated that, apart from times when he had to "pacify" this worker (the worker reportedly had a somewhat difficult personality), he "related quite well" to the worker and "didn't have a problem" with him. The second respondent (a wages employee) attributed the positive relationship between her best worker and supervision to the friendliness of the worker and to the worker's knowledge of the job which, it was suggested, had earned her the respect of supervisors who would "go to her and ask her what was going on, more so than the leading hand".

In the case of a third respondent (a wages employee), a neutral relationship was implied in the respondent's comment that "I think he [the worker] just gets along with supervision, type of thing". This respondent pointed out that, because his best worker was an ex-leading hand, he had had more experience with supervision than ordinary shop floor workers and, as such, he "knew what it was like to talk to supervision". A neutral relationship was also implied in a fourth respondent's comment that her best worker "just relates to [supervision] when he's got to". This respondent indicated that, unlike many other workers in the division who often sought the attention of their supervisor(s) in order to avoid work, her best worker preferred to work independently and actively sought supervision only if he had "a problem that he needs their help with".

A fifth respondent (a supervisor) indicated that his best worker — who was very similar to the best worker described above — related differently to different types of supervisors. He enjoyed a positive relationship with supervisors who allowed workers to work independently, but related poorly to supervisors who desired more control over their workers. In the respondent's own words:

> Depending on the supervision, the worker, because of the nature of the beast...they tend to like to be left alone to do their job. So they get on with their job and they like very minimal supervision, and they like to go to supervision when they have a problem. They don't like the type of supervision that stands behind them all the time. (staff, supervisory)

Finally, a sixth respondent (a wages employee) indicated that, while the relationship between his best worker and supervision was somewhat volatile and argumentative, the worker's grievances were never without foundation and supervision always conceded that the worker had a point. In the respondent's own words:

> Well, he seemed pretty volatile at times and [supervision] had many confrontations with him. But there was never an argument without any backing. He always had some fact or a

valid reason for the argument and [supervision] would always say 'We understand what you're talking about, but there's nothing we can do'. (wages employee)

The respondent went on to suggest that, as he saw it, the main reason for the conflict that sometimes arose between his best worker and supervision was that the worker believed that supervision (as well as more senior management) should be more prepared than they were to make difficult decisions that took them outside of the "safe parameters" within which they usually operated.

Two concluding points are suggested by the above findings. First, it would appear that, in the production division, a worker's classification as a best worker is not contingent on that worker having a positive relationship with supervision. Second, and in contrast with the associated findings for the tooling division, respondents from production varied considerably in the criteria they used to judge the quality of the relationship between their best worker and supervision.

Q5 (e)   *How did this worker relate to her/his co-workers?*

Tooling division: All participants responded to this question. Four respondents (including one supervisor and two wages employees) indicated that the relationship between their best worker and his co-workers was generally positive; one respondent (a wages employee) described a somewhat "reserved" relationship; and one respondent (a supervisor) implied that the relationship was variable (in this case, the best worker was reportedly disliked by some of his co-workers, and more or less tolerated by others).

There was considerable variability among respondents in the criteria they used to judge these relationships. For the four respondents who indicated a positive relationship, these criteria were as follows. In one case, the basis of the relationship appeared to be common outside interests. This respondent suggested that workers in the tooling division generally got on "very well" with one another because, apart from the "odd one or two that are slightly different", they were similar in terms of "their interests and general sort of day-to-day running of their lives". A second respondent indicated that, while his best worker had considerable personal and family problems, he did not allow these problems to "affect his working life". The worker reportedly "got on well with everyone" despite these problems. A third respondent indicated that his best worker "got on well with" co-workers because "they respected him for his ability [and] for the help that he gave them on the job". Finally, the fourth respondent ascribed his best worker's positive relationship with co-workers to the fact that the worker did not interfere in the work activities of his co-workers. In the respondent's own words:

Basically I'd say he stayed out of their hair. He didn't go around trying to tell them how to do the job or anything like that...He didn't isolate himself from others; he got along with them very well. But he also didn't impose his will or anything onto them — try to tell them that they're doing it wrong or anything else like that. (wages employee, leading hand)

The assessment, by one respondent, of a somewhat "reserved" relationship between his best worker and co-workers was based on the respondent's perception that there were cultural differences between his best worker and co-workers (his best worker was an Italian immigrant) which somehow inhibited the development of a more intimate relationship and which explained why his best worker was "a bit of a loner". Finally, with respect to the one variable relationship that was reported, the respondent in this case indicated that his best worker was disliked by about one third of his co-workers because "his work output was higher [and] it made them look worse than they would [otherwise]". Of the other co-workers with whom this best worker was associated, there were some who reportedly "didn't mind" the worker, and others who "just tolerated" him.

There are two concluding points suggested by the above findings. First, it would appear that, in the tooling division at the present time, it is not essential for a worker to have a positive relationship with co-workers in order to be classified as a best worker. Second, respondents' judgements about what constituted a positive relationship between their best worker and his co-workers did not seem to be informed by any common criteria. On the contrary, the data provided evidence of considerable variability in this regard.

Production division: All participants responded to this question and, in all cases, the nominated best worker was reported to have a generally positive relationship with her/his co-workers. In terms of the criteria used to judge this relationship, there were five respondents (including two supervisors and three wages employees) who made reference to some aspect of their best worker's attitudes and behaviour toward other workers. Specifically, one respondent reported a "very good" relationship between his best worker and co-workers, indicating that his best worker was a "very helpful, very cooperative sort of guy to his fellow workmates". A second respondent emphasised his best worker's treatment of co-workers as equals: "He never put you down, he never made you feel small". A third respondent, in describing her best worker's relationship with co-workers, made the point that "Everybody likes him". A fourth respondent described her best worker as "friendly" toward others, easy to approach, and straightforward in the sense of giving co-workers a "straight" answer to their questions, rather than giving a "roundabout answer like of lot of [supervisors] do". Finally, the response of a fifth respondent suggested that the "generally good" relationship that was reported in this case was due to the best worker making a habit of greeting co-workers at the beginning of his work shift. Beyond this act of courtesy, however, the worker reportedly avoided getting too involved with co-workers, either on the job or socially, outside of work. The criterion used by a sixth respondent (a wages employee) to judge his best worker's relationship with co-workers — which, in this case, was described as "pretty fair" — was not clear.

Apart from the above findings, there were three respondents from this division (all wages employees) who implied, or stated explicitly, that their best worker might not enjoy an equally positive relationship with all of her/his co-workers. One respondent indicated that his best worker could not abide co-workers who were "lazy" and who had the attitude that "That's not my job". A second respondent implied that his best worker, who believed that everyone should be prepared to work as hard as he did, might not be liked so well by co-workers who were inclined to "have a bit of a bludge or take it easy". And a third respondent indicated that, while her best worker was liked by his immediate co-workers, he was disliked by workers on different shifts who appeared to be jealous of his ability and the recognition (presumably from his supervision) that this had earned him.

It can be seen from the above that there was considerably more consistency in the production division data pertaining to the relationship between a best worker and her/his co-workers than there was in the associated tooling division data. As indicated, a common theme to emerge in these data concerned the perception that positive relationships among co-workers were founded on qualities such as friendliness, cooperation, equality of treatment, being approachable, and helpfulness. Interestingly, a quality such as being good at one's job, while it might contribute positively to relationships with some co-workers, could contribute negatively to relationships with others.

We turn now to a consideration of the above findings in terms of what they reveal about the usefulness of Question 5 for generating cultural information of the kind that was being sought. A number of insights were provided in this regard and these are discussed below.

(1) On the basis of the above findings, it can be concluded that Question 5 was valuable insofar as it served to differentiate the two divisions, at least to a point. For example, differences were indicated in the qualities that respondents attributed to their best worker. In the tooling division, there was an emphasis on the technical competencies of best workers, whereas in the production division, the emphasis was more on qualities such as conscientiousness and the ability to get on with others. Differences were also indicated in the criteria that respondents used to judge their best worker's relationship with her/his supervisor(s) and with co-workers. With respect to the former, there was an emphasis in the tooling division on the importance of cooperation and a lack of conflict as defining characteristics of a positive relationship between a best worker and his supervisors. In the production division, these criteria did not emerge as being particularly important. With respect to the latter, there was evidence that, in the production division, qualities such as friendliness, cooperation, and helpfulness provided the foundation for a positive relationship between a best worker and her/his co-workers. In the tooling division, these particular qualities were accorded markedly less importance. As indicated, the differences between the divisions that were suggested by the above findings were consistent with what one would expect given differences in the nature of the work performed in each division. The point might also be made that these differences were consistent with the researcher's impression of differences in the culture of each division, based on the years spent in each division.

(2) While a number of patterns, or commonalities, emerged in the data for each division (these patterns constituting a source of differentiation between the divisions), it was also the case that, within each division, there was often considerable variability between respondents in their responses to the questions they were asked. For example,

in both divisions, there was considerable variability in the responses to Question 5(a), asking about best worker characteristics. This variability is illustrated in Tables 9.4 and 9.5, which show that for each division respondents' answers could be represented by all four categories of best worker characteristics that had been identified. Respondents within a division were also shown to vary in the criteria they used to evaluate their best worker's relationship with her/his supervisor(s) and co-workers respectively. As indicated, evaluations of the best worker-supervisor relationship in the production division appeared to be based on a variety of different criteria, as were evaluations of the best worker-co-worker relationship in the tooling division.

   An important methodological implication of the kind of variability observed in the above findings is that it is impossible to know whether the responses of all, or only some, of the respondents within a division are important from a cultural perspective. Consider, for example, the reference by two respondents from the tooling division to the work behaviours and attitudes of their best worker (see Table 9.4). The question arises as to whether the qualities referred to (e.g., initiative and a competitive approach to work) are qualities which are regarded as important by these two respondents only, or whether there are other respondents from this division who also regard these qualities as important but who, for whatever reason, did not think to mention them when describing their best worker. Of course, the obvious way to answer this question would be to ask other respondents from the division specifically about their perception of the importance of these qualities. In this sense, while an open question, such as Question 5(a), would appear to be limited with respect to its capacity to reveal what is cultural and what is not, the advantage of such a question is that it can highlight issues of potential cultural significance (in this case, these may be characteristics of best workers, or criteria for judging a best worker's relationships with her/his peers and/or superiors) that might subsequently be asked about more directly through the use of some form of closed question or prompt. The approach being alluded to here — namely, the use of qualitative methods (e.g., open-ended questions) to inform the development of indices for quantitative research — is one which has been advocated, and used, by a number of organisational culture researchers (see, e.g., Hofstede, Neuijen, Ohayv, & Sanders, 1990; Rentsch, 1990; Siehl & Martin, 1988).

(3) A third methodological issue raised by the above findings relates specifically to Question 5(b), which asked respondents to indicate how important their best worker's qualities were (in the sense of constituting desirable qualities for workers more generally) and why. The finding that all respondents from both divisions considered their best worker's qualities to be important is, on reflection, perhaps not surprising. In other words, while it is possible, it is very unlikely that a respondent would argue that a quality attributed to her/his best worker would not be an important quality for workers, in general, to possess. The further point can be made that, while it was antici- pated that some common themes might emerge in the reasons given by respondents for why their best worker's qualities were important, this was not the case. As indicated,

there was considerable variability in these data, which perhaps might also have been expected, given the range of different best worker qualities to which they referred. Thus, it would seem that Question 5(b) is somewhat redundant. It appears to add little of value to the information already generated by Question 5(a) and, in this sense, can probably be omitted from any subsequent revision of the interview protocol.

(4) A fourth methodological issue concerns the question of whether or not parts (c), (d), and (e) of Question 5, which asked about the best worker's view of the organisation, relationship with supervision, and relationship with co-workers, respectively, were redundant questions in the sense that information of relevance to the issues they address had already been provided in respondents' responses to part (a) of Question 5. From Tables 9.4 and 9.5, which provide a summary of respondents' responses to Question 5(a), it can be seen that, in neither division were there any spontaneous references to the best worker's view of the organisation, or to her/his relationship with supervision. In both divisions, there were, however, several spontaneous references to some aspect of the best worker's relationship with co-workers. The overall conclusion suggested by these findings is that questions of the kind asked in parts (c), (d), and (e), which seek information, in this case, about specific characteristics that best workers might possess, do have the potential to generate additional information, over and above that which respondents provide spontaneously. Whether or not this additional information is also useful, is a question which points 5 and 6 below attempt to address.

(5) The above findings suggest that, in terms of their potential to provide culturally relevant information, parts (c), (d), and (e) of Question 5 may be useful only insofar as respondents responded negatively to them. Thus, for example, if best workers were perceived to have negative views of the organisation (this was the case for a majority of best workers in the production division), then it could reasonably be concluded that it was not necessary for a worker to have a positive view of the organisation in order to be classified as a best worker. The corollary of this argument in the case of positive responses to these questions is, however, much more difficult to sustain. Thus, the finding that all best workers in the tooling division were perceived to have a positive relationship with their supervisor(s) does not justify the conclusion that such a relationship was essential to one's classification as a best worker in this division. These two factors — that is, a worker's relationship with her/his supervisor(s) and her/his status as a best worker — may, indeed, be quite unrelated. Of course, where positive responses to these questions confirm what has already been said, one might more confidently argue that the attribute in question may be one that is highly valued. A case in point is the finding that respondents from the production division, both spontaneously and in response to part (e) of Question 5, reported positive relationships between their best worker and co-workers.

The fact remains, however, that what is of most interest from a cultural perspective is how organisation members define a best worker. In other words, what are the particular worker qualities (attitudes, behaviours, *etc.*) that are most highly valued in the organisation? Is it necessary, for example, for a worker to think highly of the organisation in order to be regarded as a best worker? Does a worker have to relate positively with her/his supervisor(s) and/or co-workers in order to be thought of as a best worker? The above findings suggest that parts (c), (d), and (e) of Question 5 were limited with respect to their capacity to provide information of this kind which, it would seem, might have to be sought through a much more direct form of questioning.

(6) The argument above about the importance of understanding organisation-specific meanings highlights a further limitation of parts (c), (d), and (e) of Question 5. Again, from a cultural perspective, it would seem to be less important to know that a best worker has a positive view of the organisation, or that she/he has a positive relationship with supervisors and/or co-workers, than it would be to know what organisation members actually mean by the term 'positive' when they apply it to these concepts. For example, is a positive relationship between a best worker and her/his supervisor(s) one which emphasises deference to authority (as indicated, there was some evidence that this was the case in the tooling division), or is it one which is characterised more by participation and power sharing? While an attempt was made, in the present analysis, to infer these meanings from the responses given, it was sometimes difficult to make confident judgements in this regard because of ambiguous, or inadequate, information. For example, if a best worker is described as relating to supervision only as required, in order to solve a problem (this was the case for one respondent from the production division), it is not clear from this description whether the ability to work independently is, or is not, an important criterion for judging a worker's relationship with supervision. Again, information of this kind may be best sought through a more direct question, such as, in this case: "How should a worker behave in order to get on well with her/his supervisor(s)?". Of course, questions of this kind, which seek to establish the basis for relationships among organisation members are, in terms of Schein's typology, more concerned with beliefs and assumptions pertaining to The Nature of Human Relationships than they are with beliefs and assumptions pertaining to the nature of human nature (this latter category being the one of interest in the present study).

(7) One final methodological issue raised by the above findings is that the term 'best worker' may need to be more clearly specified by the researcher than it was. This is because there were some respondents who, when asked about their best worker, described a worker with leading hand status. Given the extra responsibility of workers at this level — leading hands have a semi-supervisory role — they can be regarded as a somewhat different group from ordinary shop floor workers. In one case, the best worker described was actually a supervisor. In this case, it appeared that the respondent (himself a supervisor) had interpreted the term even more broadly, to mean 'best employee'. Since this was not the interpretation that was intended, this respondent was subsequently asked to describe the best shop floor operator that he had ever known. These findings serve to illustrate that even concepts which appear to the researcher to

be quite unambiguous in their meaning, can be interpreted differently by different research respondents.

The above arguments regarding the strengths and weaknesses of Question 5 are supported equally well by the findings for the role of supervisors as they are by the findings for the role of workers. As above, these findings drew attention to some divisional differences in respondents' descriptions of their best supervisor. For example, in the tooling division, there was an emphasis on the job knowledge, skills, and abilities of best supervisors (these were qualities that earned supervisors the respect of others), whereas in the production division, best supervisors appeared to be admired more for their people skills. At the same time, and as above for the role of workers, the responses of participants within a division often varied considerably and, again, this raised the question as to whether or not the various qualities attributed to that division's best supervisors were qualities which were regarded as important by all participants from the division, or as important only by those participants who made specific reference to them. As above, Question 5 was also found to be limited with respect to its capacity to provide culturally relevant information such as, in this case, whether or not it was necessary for a supervisor to have a positive view of the organisation, or a positive relationship with other employees (whether subordinates, peers, or superiors), in order to be classified as a best supervisor. It was also the case, as above, that the criteria upon which these evaluations were made were sometimes difficult to ascertain.

Finally, the findings for the role of supervisors drew attention to one additional methodological issue that, while it was not identified in the review of findings for the role of workers, is nevertheless equally relevant in the context of those findings. This issue relates specifically to respondents at a supervisory level who, when asked to talk about their best supervisor (or best worker), made reference to an individual they had known, or worked with, in the past. The point is that, in these cases, information should be sought about the respondent's position (whether subordinate, peer, or superior) in relation to her/his best supervisor (or best worker) at the particular time to which reference was being made. This is because a respondent's perspective in this regard may influence the criteria upon which she/he judges a supervisor (or worker) to be a best supervisor (or best worker).

We turn now to a consideration of the findings for Question 6, which asked about participants' worst worker (and worst supervisor).

Q6: *Think about the <u>worst</u> worker that you have ever had (worked with, known) in this division.*

(a) What was it that you disliked, or regarded as problematic, about this worker?

Tooling division: All participants answered this question. Five participants described a worst worker whom they had known, or worked with, in the organisation in the past (of these, four mentioned a worker from the tooling division and one mentioned a worker from elsewhere in the organisation). One participant only described a worker who was currently employed in the division.

A summary of the qualities that respondents attributed to their worst worker, in terms of the same four categories used to classify the qualities of best workers, is provided in Table 9.6. It can be seen that the second category was the best represented, with five of the six participants from this division (including two supervisors and three wages employees) making reference to one or more problems associated with the work behaviours and attitudes of their worst worker. For example, worst workers were variously criticised for the following: laziness, a lack of interest in the job, low work motivation, negative attitudes towards all aspects of work (including the decisions taken by managerial and other personnel), and a lack of interest in learning. As indicated in the following excerpts, there were two participants who regarded their worst worker's poor attitude to work as an extension, or manifestation, of what was seen as the worker's problematic attitude to life in general:

> I suppose they were apathetic to anything, you know, they've got a negative outlook on life and this passes over into the job, in which case they're not interested. They don't want to do anything. Anything that they're really doing is wrong, and all decisions made by other people, or [by] the management structure, are wrong, and totally negative. (staff, supervisory)
>
> He has a totally different outlook on life. He virtually doesn't have any goals in life or any ambitions and, therefore, doesn't get enthused about anything. It's very, very difficult to teach him anything because basically he's not interested on a lot of occasions. (wages employee, leading hand)

Apart from the above, there were two respondents (both wages employees) who made reference to problems associated with their worst worker's work knowledge, skills, and abilities. One of these respondents suggested that, in terms of these qualities, his worst worker was "not as good as 90% of the tradesmen here". The respondent went on to express his dissatisfaction with the division's current reward system which was such that less competent workers (such as his worst worker) not only received the same remuneration as more highly skilled workers, but they also ended up with less to do, since the bulk of the work was allocated to the workers judged to be most competent to complete it. In the respondent's own words:

> ...they're getting [the reference is to incompetent workers], well, exactly the same amount of money as you, [and] they're no worse thought of, and you're not better thought of... what tends to happen is that particular person, if he's not as good in his job as you, he will be left alone, and the people that are quite good will be manipulated to do more, and more, and more. (wages employee, leading hand)

The reader may recall that this perception of there being a positive disincentive for workers to be good at what they do, was a common theme to emerge in the Study 1 data

Table 9.6. Tooling Division (TD): Characteristics of workers judged to be 'worst' workers as described by individual respondents.

Respondent # and Position	Work knowledge, Skills, & Abilities	Work Behaviours & Attitudes	Interpersonal Skills & Behaviours	Personal Qualities & Characteristics
TD1 wages	▪ Limited skill and ability — "not as good as 90% of the tradesmen here"			
TD2 wages		▪ Lazy		
TD3 supervisor		▪ Entirely negative attitude towards work: lack of motivation to work; lack of interest in the job; views all decisions made by management as wrong		▪ Entirely negative outlook on life
TD4 wages		▪ Lack of interest in the job ▪ Unwilling to learn new skills		▪ Different outlook on life from others: a total lack of ambition and no enthusiasm about anything
TD5 wages	▪ Limited skill in terms of working "with his hands"	▪ Lack of interest in being on shop floor (aspired to a higher level position) ▪ Lack of interest in learning		
TD6 supervisor		▪ Lack of motivation to perform and lack of interest in the work (despite ability and good job knowledge)		

for this division. The second participant to make reference to a quality in this category indicated that his worst worker was not particularly skilled in working "with his hands".

The final point can be made that the relatively poor representation, in the above findings, of the first category of worker characteristics (i.e., work knowledge, skills, and abilities) — it will be remembered that, in the tooling division data for best workers, this was the best represented category — was perhaps not surprising given that most workers in the tooling division were qualified tradesmen who would have been required to demonstrate a certain level of competence in order to gain their qualifications. In this sense, skills deficits are unlikely to constitute a major, or commonly perceived problem, for the workers in this division.

Production division: All participants responded to this question. In two cases, the time of the respondent's association with the worker described was not established. A third respondent indicated that he was unable to think of one worker, in particular, whom he would classify as a worst worker, and so he subsequently described the qualities of worst workers in general. Of the remaining three respondents, there were two who described a past worst worker, and one who described a present worst worker.

The qualities attributed by production division respondents to their worst worker are summarised in Table 9.7, using the same four categories as previously. As indicated, category 3 — interpersonal skills and behaviours — was the best represented category, with all six respondents from this division making reference to some aspect of their worst worker's interaction with others. Specifically, worst workers were criticised for being disruptive of others (two participants), for "riding" on the efforts of co-workers (three participants), for "dobbing"[10] co-workers in, in order to gain favour with supervision (one participant), for treating others poorly (one participant), and for being disrespectful of supervision (one participant). As shown in Table 9.7, there was also a strong emphasis in these data on problems associated with the worst worker's work behaviours and attitudes. With respect to qualities in this category, worst workers were criticised for not working to their full potential (one respondent), for being lazy (two respondents), for an inability to concentrate on the job (one respondent) — in this case, the worst worker was considered to be, by nature, unsuited to the work — and for generally poor attitudes to work, reflected in low productivity, and a lack of respect for, and poor treatment of, equipment and people alike (one respondent). The following excerpts provide a sample of the verbatim responses that informed the above analysis:

> …he's very capable…he could do the job quite easily and make time for himself, but once he did make time for himself, you'd get nothing else. He just stopped and disrupted everyone else. He'd do anything and everything [rather] than what he's supposed to do, and of course, as a supervisor, when he's disrupting other areas, and not doing his function, even though his work's right up to date, that's what I classified as a worst worker. (staff, supervisory)

---

[10] 'Dob' (somebody in) is Australian vernacular meaning to inform on somebody.

Table 9.7. Production Division (PD): Characteristics of workers judged to be 'worst' workers as described by individual respondents.

Respondent # and Position	Work Knowledge, Skills, & Abilities	Work Behaviours & Attitudes	Interpersonal Skills & Behaviours	Personal Qualities & Characteristics
PD1 supervisor			▪ Capable worker who could do the job but with very disruptive behaviour (particularly when time on his hands)	
PD2 wages		▪ Did not work to full potential	▪ Lets friends down, would "bludge" on friends	
PD3 wages		▪ Unable to concentrate on the job	▪ Disruptive of others (wanted them to "play his game")	▪ By nature, not suited to the work (unable to "be confined to do something for eight hours a day")
PD4 wages		▪ Lazy ("bludge" whenever the opportunity arose)	▪ "Dob in" workmates in order to gain favour with supervisor ▪ Rides on the efforts of workmates (i.e., "bludge" on workmates)	
PD5 wages		▪ Lazy	▪ Rides on the efforts of workmates ("…she made everyone else try to cover for her")	
PD6 supervisor		▪ Poor attitude to work: wouldn't work; didn't care about the job; didn't look after equipment	▪ Poor treatment of other people ▪ Disrespectful of supervision	

> When you think about the worst worker type of thing, you know, I think it was people who you didn't respect, that go running to the foremen all the time, type of thing, bludge every opportunity they get…Some people, you know, would dob their mates in at the least drop of the hat, type of thing. They think it might get them somewhere…That person would bludge on his fellow workmates type of thing. (wages employee)
>
> …I knew he could do a lot better. He was one that would be 25% rather than 50% and you knew he had the potential to get the 100% and he [did] it several times. He let his friends down, he would bludge on his friends. (wages employee)

Q6 (b) *What was this worker's view of the organisation?*

Tooling division: All participants responded to this question. In four cases, worst workers were reported to hold negative views of the organisation. Specifically, there was one respondent (a wages employee with leading hand status) who indicated that, as he saw it, his worst worker held the same view as the majority of his co-workers, namely, that the organisation was not run very well. Two respondents (a supervisor and a wages employee with leading hand status) described a worst worker who was openly critical of the organisation. In one case, the worker reportedly had "nothing much good to say about the [organisation]" and, in the other, the worker reportedly told people how much "he hates the place". A fourth respondent (a supervisor) indicated that his worst worker "didn't like [the organisation] at all". In this case, the worker reportedly had little interest in the organisation and viewed it simply as a means to an end:

> …he was ambitious to set up his own business outside, which he did do. He actually [did] that while he was here…He didn't have any interest in the company at all. It was just a means of doing his apprenticeship and getting a trade behind him, and that was all he was interested in. (staff, supervisory)

A similar view to the above was expressed by a fifth respondent (a wages employee), who reported that his worst worker's view of the organisation was such that "[it] owed him a living and he was here to collect his money and that was it". In this case, however, there was no reference to the worker holding distinctly negative views of the organisation. Finally, a sixth respondent indicated that he could not say how his worst worker viewed the organisation, since this was not a subject that they had discussed. At the same time, however, there was a suggestion that the worker, who was reportedly "biding his time" in his current position (he was a shop floor employee) until a preferred position (in administration) became available, might view the organisation as providing the means by which he could satisfy his personal goals and objectives.

Production division: All participants responded to this question. Of these, five were able to comment on their worst worker's view of the organisation — perceptions of these views ranged from distinctly negative to more or less indifferent — and one was not able to comment. These responses are elaborated upon briefly below.

One respondent (a supervisor) described a worst worker whose view of the organisation — and indeed every aspect of his experience of the organisation — was distinctly negative. In the respondent's own words:

> They[11] wouldn't be very happy with the organisation. As far as they were concerned the organisation sort of stunk, you know. The union stunk, management stunk, everybody stunk. [They thought] that they should be running show. (staff, supervisory)

A second respondent (also a supervisor) was very critical of his worst worker's view of the organisation that, as he saw it, was such that "he's only here to get as much as he possibly can out of it". It was suggested that this worker was guilty of serious exploitation of the organisation, to the point where he had engaged in illegal acts, such as, stealing company property and selling drugs on site.

Three respondents (all wages employees) described a worst worker who appeared to be more or less indifferent in her/his view of the organisation (i.e., neither hating the organisation, nor being strongly committed to it). Specifically, in all three cases, the worst worker was an individual who reportedly saw the organisation simply as a place to come and earn money. For two of these worst workers, it was also implied that, if they were able to earn more money elsewhere, then they would readily leave the organisation. Finally, there was one respondent (a wages employee) who indicated that, since she never talked to her worst worker — this was because "I didn't like her" — she was unable to comment on the worker's view of the organisation.

It can be seen from the above findings that, while there were no worst workers in either division who were reported to have a positive view of the organisation, it was also not the case that *all* worst workers from both divisions had distinctly negative views. As indicated, there was evidence from both divisions to suggest that a worst worker could be more or less indifferent in her/his attitude toward the organisation. These findings, along with the fact that there were two respondents (one from each division) who were unable to comment on their worst worker's view of the organisation suggest that, in neither division, was a worker's classification as a worst worker contingent upon that worker having a negative view of the organisation. Indeed, if these findings are considered together with the previous findings for best workers (as indicated, there were best workers in both divisions with positive, negative, and neutral views), the more general conclusion might be reached that, in neither division, did the view that workers held of the organisation appear to have much bearing on the way in which workers were evaluated.

Q6 (c) How did this worker relate to supervision?

Tooling division: All participants responded to this question. Four (including two supervisors and two wages employees) judged the relationship between their worst worker

---

[11]The respondent was using the plural 'they' to refer to his worst worker.

and his supervisor(s) to be negative. Of these, three made reference to their worst worker's non-compliance with supervision. In these cases, the worst worker was variously described as refusing to do as he was told, responding reluctantly, or not at all, to supervision, and being difficult to supervise in the sense of not wanting to do the work. Reference was also made by these respondents to the supervision needs of their worst worker. One respondent was particularly critical of what he saw as the overly lenient treatment of workers such as his worst worker:

> In here I find that most supervision...if you're a rebel and you stir things up, they'll put you to one side, not stir you up, and let you go your own way and do what you want. (wages employee)

In this respondent's view, the proper management of such workers would be to "get rid of them". A second respondent (a supervisor) indicated that, in his opinion, "strong [supervisory] measures" were needed to "get on top of" workers such as his worst worker. This respondent also pointed out that he was unsure of the reasons for his worker's non-compliance, whether lack of intelligence, lack of interest, or "playing dumb". A third respondent (also a supervisor) indicated that the style of supervision that he used with his worst worker, namely "speaking to him, and trying to encourage him to do his work" had no effect whatsoever, in terms of changing this worker's behaviour.

The above findings are consistent with the associated findings for best workers, in the sense that, in both cases, a worker's compliance with supervision appeared to constitute an important criterion upon which that worker's relationship with supervision (whether positive or negative) was judged. Not surprisingly, whereas a positive relationship was one that was characterised by a lack of supervision (the idea that best workers could work independently), a negative relationship was one in which strict supervisory control was seen as being necessary, if not practised.

In the case of the fourth respondent above, the basis for his assessment of a negative relationship between his worst worker and supervision was unclear. This respondent (a wages employee with leading hand status) suggested that his worst worker's poor relationship with supervision — the worker was described as relating "not very well" to supervisors — was underpinned by personal insecurity and a basic fear of supervisors, which the worker disguised with shows of bravado and efforts to gain popularity.

The response of a fifth respondent from this division implied a more or less neutral relationship between the respondent's worst worker and supervision. In this case, the worker was reportedly ignored by his supervisor because the latter was aware that the worker, who was "only a cadet" (similar to an apprentice) had no intention of remaining in his current section on completion of his training. Finally, a sixth respondent (a wages employee with leading hand status) indicated that his worst worker had much the same relationship with supervision as did the majority of workers in the division. This relationship was "reasonable", but with some loss of respect on the part of workers for supervisors, over the years.

Production division: All participants responded to this question. It could reasonably be inferred from the responses of four of these participants that the relationship between the participant's worst worker and her/his supervisor(s) was negative. For example, there were two respondents (a wages employee and a supervisor) who drew attention to their worst worker's negative attitudes towards, and lack of respect for, their supervisors. In one case, the worst worker reportedly regarded his supervisors as "a bunch of wankers" and, in the other, supervisors were seen as "a mob of dickheads". According to one of these respondents, the most appropriate way to deal with workers of this kind was not to transfer them to another department or shift, as was typically done, but rather to confront the problem directly by dismissing them. In the respondent's own words:

> The best way is to face it in confrontation. Get it out of the way and get rid of him. ...get the union involved and everything, and if they didn't want to work, you're far better off getting rid of him. (staff, supervisory)

A third respondent (a wages employee) judged the relationship between her worst worker and supervision from the perspective, not of the worker (as above), but of the worker's supervisor. In this case, it was suggested that the worker was disliked by her supervisor — "he wasn't real keen on that particular person...he used to watch her all the time" — because she was the kind of individual who was "just outright lazy". The fourth respondent (a wages employee), in commenting on his worst worker's relationship with supervision, merely indicated that "management were after sacking [the worker] for a long, long time". While the exact nature of this worker's relationship with supervision was not made clear, the respondent's response strongly implied that it was a negative relationship.

Finally, there were two respondents from this division (a supervisor and a wages employee) who described a relationship between their worst worker and supervision that was difficult to classify (in terms of whether it was negative, neutral, or positive). In one case, the respondent (in this case the worker's supervisor) indicated that, while his worst worker often required strict supervisory discipline in order to get the job done — "once I started getting right onto the level of having to threaten to sack him, or get close to giving [a] disciplinary procedure...he'd do it" — there were nevertheless times when he and this worker related "quite well" and would be "quite friendly" towards one another. In the other case, the respondent indicated that it was typical of worst workers generally to "toe the line" in the presence of supervisors but, in their absence, to "try to get away with whatever they can".

In summary, in neither division, was it the case that *all* of the worst workers described were reported to have a distinctly negative relationship with their supervisor(s). This finding suggests the tentative conclusion that, in neither division, was a worker's classification as a worst worker contingent on that worker having a negative relationship with her/his supervisor(s). The corresponding finding for the production division, namely, that not *all* best workers had a positive relationship with their supervisor(s), suggests the further conclusion that, at least in this division, evaluations of workers more generally may be influenced very little by perceptions of how workers get on with their supervisors.

A second point that can be made with respect to the above findings is that, while there were four respondents from each division who reported (or at least implied) a negative relationship between their worst worker and her/his supervisor(s), there was markedly more inconsistency in the production division data that were generated by this question than there was in the corresponding tooling division data. For example, there was no evidence of any common thematic content in these data (such as the emphasis, in the corresponding tooling division data, on the importance of compliance with authority). Participants evaluated the relationship between their worst worker and her/his supervisor(s) from different perspectives (in two cases, from the perspective of the worker and, in one case, from the perspective of the supervisor), and some relationships were described which were difficult to classify in terms of whether they were negative, neutral, or positive. While the difference between the divisions in this regard may be nothing more than an anomaly of the small sample size, it is perhaps worth noting that a similar pattern of responding emerged in the corresponding findings for best workers.

Q6 (d) How did this worker relate to her/his co-workers?

Tooling division: All participants responded to this question. While each of the worst worker-co-worker relationships that was described contained some negative element, only two of these relationships could be classified as being distinctly negative. In both cases, this assessment appeared to be based on a perception by the respondent that the worker somehow didn't fit into the group, as a whole. Specifically, one respondent (a wages employee with leading hand status) indicated that his worst worker was unpopular with his peers because of his self-interested attitude — "he's for himself and that's it" — which was manifested in a refusal to participate in activities (such as, contributing to the purchase of gifts for co-workers who were retiring or getting married, and giving assistance to workers who were "in strife", whether at work or outside of work) that helped to build a more cohesive work unit. Another respondent (a wages employee) indicated that his worst worker, who was anticipating a transfer from his current position on the shop floor to an administrative position, was unpopular with his co-workers because of his superior attitude toward them. In the respondent's own words:

> ...no one had any time for him because he sort of looked down upon us, sort of thing. He thought he was going to be more or less God Almighty and we were just the trash. (wages employee)

A further two respondents described worst worker-co-worker relationships that appeared to be neither particularly negative, nor particularly positive. In one case, the respondent (a supervisor), who had chosen to talk about worst workers generally, indicated that, while such workers typically had a reputation with co-workers for being "bludgers or spongers", and while co-workers might complain amongst themselves about such workers and "have a bit of a dig at them", it was not the case that these workers were, in any way, ostracised by the group. Rather, it was suggested that, in general, "they get on alright with other workers". In the other case, the respondent (a wages employee) indicated that his worst worker was tolerated by his co-workers. This worker reportedly had a problem with alcoholism and, according to the respondent, his work colleagues correctly understood his behaviour (including shows of bravado, attempts to gain popularity, and public criticism of the division) to be a front for his underlying insecurity. In the participant's own words:

> People can see that it's a front...probably they feel sorry for him. They sort of tolerate him and ignore [him] in that respect. But he's not shunned or outcast. People talk to him and everything. (wages employee)

Finally, there were two respondents from this division who indicated that their worst worker's relationship with co-workers was such that the worker got on well with some co-workers, but was unpopular with others. One of these respondents (a wages employee) indicated that, while his worst worker had a reputation for being "very, very lazy", and while his co-workers were inclined to "treat him as a joke", he nevertheless had some friends and some enemies. The other respondent (a supervisor) indicated that, while his worst worker probably got on "okay" with his age peers, older co-workers were very disapproving of this worker's poor attitudes to work.

On the basis of these findings, it would seem reasonable to conclude that, in the tooling division, it is not necessary for a worker to have a negative relationship with his co-workers in order to be thought of as a worst worker.

Production division: All participants responded to this question. Given the previous emphasis that respondents had spontaneously given to problems associated with their worst worker's interpersonal skills and behaviours (see the findings for Question 6(a), reported above), it was anticipated that the relationships between worst workers and co-workers described in response to this question, would be predominantly negative. However, this was not the case. In fact, there were two respondents from this division who reported a distinctly positive relationship between their worst worker and his co-workers. One of these respondents (a supervisor) indicated that, while most people knew his worst worker to be a "rogue" — the worker reportedly used the organisation to generate his own personal income (e.g., from drug sales and from doing "foreigners"[12] at work) — he was

---

[12]Local organisational jargon used to refer to private jobs completed in company time, and using company equipment and materials.

nevertheless considered to be a "loveable rogue". It was suggested further that, for a small fee, the worker would "do anything and everything" for his co-workers[13]. The other respondent (a wages employee) indicated that, while her worst worker was disruptive of others, and while there were days when he performed very poorly, he was nevertheless liked by all of his co-workers. The respondent attributed the worker's popularity to his cheerful disposition and to his desire to see those around him equally happy. In the respondent's own words:

> They liked [the fact that] he was always happy. If somebody was down in the dumps, he'd really want to cheer them up, you know. He didn't like to see anybody unhappy. He was a happy soul. (wages employee)

In a similar vein to the above, though depicting a reasonable, rather than distinctly positive, relationship, there was one respondent (a wages employee) who indicated that, while the "worker side" of his worst worker "left a lot to be desired", the worker "wasn't bad" as far as his "personal relationship" with others was concerned.

One possible explanation for the apparent contradiction between the above findings and the free responses of these participants to part (a) of Question 6 — being disruptive of others and allowing co-workers to do the work were the qualities which these participants spontaneously ascribed to their worst worker — is that it may be picking up on a kind of organisational equivalent of what Fiedler (1967) meant by a relationship-oriented, as opposed to task-oriented, personality. According to Fiedler's theory (and with reference specifically to the personality measure derived from it), a relationship-oriented individual is an individual who describes her/his least preferred co-worker (i.e., the worker with whom she/he can work least well) in very favourable terms (such as, pleasant, friendly, cheerful, and agreeable). The idea here is that the relationship-oriented individual places so much value on personal relations that she/he is able to think positively even about the worker with whom she/he least prefers to work. In the case of the present findings then, it is conceivable that while a worst worker might be criticised for, say, disrupting the work of co-workers, she/he may still be liked by these co-workers.

With respect to the remaining three respondents from this division, there was one (a supervisor) who expressed the view that worst workers typically had quite strong personalities and that, as such, they would always attract a small core of followers (i.e., other workers) who would see them as "heroes" and seek to emulate their behaviour. This respondent did not comment on his perception of the relationship between worst workers and co-workers more generally. A second respondent (a wages employee) described a relationship that might be classified as indifferent. This respondent argued that, since most workers were inclined to loaf if the opportunity arose, his worst worker's poor

---

[13]Presumably, the reference here is to assistance given in relation to the extramural interests and activities of co-workers.

performance (the worker had a reputation for being lazy and allowing his workmates to do the work), "probably didn't matter" to them too much. Finally, a third respondent (also a wages employee) indicated that the relationship between her worst worker and co-workers was negative. This was the only relationship of its kind reported by production division participants, the assessment in this case being based on the participant's experience that her and her colleagues continually had to make up for the below average effort and output of this worst worker. In the respondent's own words:

> Not very well [referring to how the worst worker related to co-workers], because everyone had to cover for her...it's a big area...everyone has to do their own job. Otherwise everyone else is behind and [then] you have to do twice as much to cover one person at the beginning, especially if it's the first operation...Everyone does that sometimes, but we don't mind it. If someone is having an off day, you cover for them because normally you know that they're up with their job. But when it's all the time, you get sick of it. (wages employee)

In conclusion, and as for the tooling division, a worker's classification as a worst worker in the production division does not appear to be contingent on that worker having a negative relationship with co-workers. As indicated, some of the worst workers from this division reportedly enjoyed a very positive relationship with their co-workers. Importantly, however, it would seem that a distinction needs to be drawn between relations among workers that revolve around getting the job done, and those which operate at a more personal level. As indicated, there was some evidence (from the above findings and those pertaining to part (a) of Question 6) to suggest that, in this division, a worker could get on well with her/his co-workers in a personal sense, while at the same time having poor working relations with them. A possible limitation of part (d) of Question 6 in this regard, is that it does not specify whether the respondent should comment on the working relationship, or on the personal relationship, between her/his worst (or best) worker and co-workers.

On the basis of the above findings, there are several points that can be made regarding the value of Question 6 for eliciting information of the kind that was sought. These are as follows:

(1) In its current form, Question 6 does not appear to provide significant additional insights about what worker qualities are valued/not valued by the organisation, over and above those which were provided by Question 5. In other words, within each division, the qualities that respondents attributed to their worst worker were, to a large extent, the opposite of those that they had attributed to their best worker. A comparison of the findings reported in Table 9.5 with those reported in Table 9.7 provides a clear illustration of this. As indicated, whereas the best workers in the production division were admired for the effort that they put into the job, as well as for their

ability to work well with others, the worst workers in this division were criticised for being lazy and for having poor working relations with co-workers. Although the corresponding findings for the tooling division were somewhat less illustrative in this regard, it was nevertheless still the case that the qualities attributed to the worst workers in this division were consistent with what one might have expected, given the qualities that had been attributed to the best workers in the division. Whereas the latter were admired for their technical competence (i.e., job-specific knowledge, skills, and abilities), the former were criticised, not so much for their lack of technical competence — as indicated, this would have been unlikely since most of the workers in this division were trade qualified — but rather for their poor attitudes toward the job (e.g., lack of interest in the job and lack of interest in learning new skills) and for their poor work motivation. The further point can be made that, in the same way that the interpersonal skills and personal qualities of the best workers in this division were accorded relatively little significance, so too was there a lack of emphasis on these qualities (or, at least, deficits in relation to these qualities) for the worst workers in this division.

(2) While Question 6 can be regarded as being somewhat redundant (for the reasons outlined in point 1 above), it was valuable insofar as it generated information that, when combined with the findings for Question 5, enabled a number of more general conclusions to be drawn about the value of particular worker qualities. For example, the finding that, in neither division, were worst workers consistently negative with respect to their view of the organisation, when combined with the finding that, in neither division, were best workers consistently positive with respect to their view of the organisation, suggested the more general conclusion that a worker's view of the organisation (similar perhaps to the notion of organisational commitment) was a quality which had little bearing on how the workers, in either division, were judged. In a similar vein, the emergence of a deference to authority theme in both the best worker and the worst worker data for the tooling division — for best workers, a positive worker-supervisor relationship was one in which the worker complied with supervision and, for worst workers, a negative worker-supervisor relationship was one in which the worker did not comply with supervision — suggested the more general conclusion that, in the tooling division, deference to authority was a quality which was relatively highly valued.

(3) Given that Question 5 and Question 6 were essentially the same question, but with a different focus (best workers in the case of Question 5, and worst workers in the case of Question 6), the same criticisms that were made previously of Question 5 can also be made of Question 6. For example, the same difficulty arises with respect to the interpretation of variability in respondents' responses. That is, it is difficult to know, without asking, whether the different qualities which respondents within a division variously attributed to their worst worker were important to all respondents within that

division (suggesting that they might be part of the division's culture), or important only to those respondents who made specific reference to them. Although the researcher used her knowledge of the research setting to make some assumptions in this regard — for example, it was argued that skill deficits were unlikely to be a major concern in the tooling division — the previous argument still applies, namely, that information of this kind is probably best acquired directly through the use of some form of closed question or prompt.

The criticisms made previously of parts (c), (d), and (e) of Question 5 — which asked about the best worker's view of the organisation, her/his relationship with supervision, and her/his relationship with co-workers — can also be made of these questions asked about worst workers (i.e., parts (b), (c), and (d) of Question 6). The problem remains that, in the final analysis, these questions (whether asked about best workers or worst workers) do not contribute much to an understanding of the group's interpretation of what it means to be a best worker, or a worst worker. In particular, they provide inadequate and inconclusive information about the value of the qualities they ask about — a worker's view of the organisation and the nature of her/his relationship with supervision and with co-workers — to the group as a whole. It remains unclear, for example, as to whether or not a worker's relationship with her/ his supervisor(s) is so important in the group that, if negative, the worker is likely to be classified as a worst worker and, if positive, the worker is likely to be classified as a best worker. As suggested previously, a more direct form of questioning may be needed to elicit information of this kind.

(4) One final methodological point is that, in this broad category of questions, it might have been more informative to have asked about 'good' workers and 'bad' workers, rather than about best workers and worst workers. The latter may be individuals who have been classified as such because of particular idiosyncratic characteristics that they possess which make them stand out from others (the worst worker from the tooling division who reportedly suffered from alcoholism being a possible case in point). As such, the qualities attributed to these individuals may reveal more about the individuals themselves (and what they value) than they do about the organisation in which they work (and what it values). Questions about good workers and bad workers, on the other hand, might be more likely to elicit descriptions in terms of more general characteristics which would be shared by a number of individuals and which, as such, may provide more of a window into values which are supported by the organisation (division) as a whole.

Another possibility would be to ask about the 'ideal' worker. Although there is no negative equivalent for the ideal, the above results suggested that responses concerning the worst worker provided little additional cultural information over and above that provided by responses concerning the best worker. Of course, responses concerning the ideal worker might tend to be more unrealistic than responses concerning a good worker, and the concept itself may have less salience for respondents (in particular, wages employees) than the concept of a good worker.

Finally, on the basis of a review of the corresponding findings for the role of supervisors, it can be concluded that these findings give rise to the same methodological arguments as those made above, on the basis of the findings for the role of workers. Of particular interest, perhaps, is the finding that, of the worst supervisors identified, there were two (both from the production division) who reportedly possessed personal characteristics which one might reasonably assume would place them outside of the norm for their group. In one case, the evaluation was based on the supervisor's interpersonal relationships with a number of subordinates (which were seen as exploitative and inappropriate); in the other case, the evaluation pertained to the supervisor's reported problem with alcohol. This finding provides further support for the argument made in point 4 above, namely, that questions about best workers/worst workers (and, in this case, best supervisors/worst supervisors) may be limited in the sense that they may elicit information about worker (supervisor) characteristics that are idiosyncratic, rather than necessarily culturally relevant.

Apart from the confirmatory value of the findings for the role of supervisors, these findings drew attention to one additional methodological issue of relevance to an evaluation of Question 6. Specifically, there was some evidence in these findings to suggest that a distinction might need to be drawn between what the individual values and what the individual thinks the organisation values. In describing their worst supervisor, there were three respondents, all of whom were wages employees (two from the tooling division and one from the production division), who suggested that their worst supervisor was probably not regarded as such by the organisation. In one case, the respondent suggested that her worst supervisor was simply complying with the expectations of those above him; a second respondent indicated that his worst supervisor was "a real company man", meaning that he followed the directives of his superiors "without question" and did not "rock the boat"; and a third respondent suggested that, from the company's perspective, his worst supervisor was "probably a very good person" since he was "always thinking about the job". While it is impossible to know, without more information, what the cultural significance, if any, of these responses might be, there are two possible cultural interpretations which come to mind. On the one hand, it may be that the organisation supports separate worker, and management (company) subcultures. On the other hand, the organisation's culture may be one that supports strong us/them assumptions, such that workers and management are, by definition, viewed as opposing entities. These speculations aside, the argument remains that the questions in this category (whether they ask about best/worst workers and supervisors, or good/bad workers and supervisors) might usefully seek information, not only about what the individual values in this regard, but also about what the individual thinks the organisation values in this regard.

9.4.5 *Context questions*

As indicated in the description of the interview protocol in the method section, the questions in this category were designed to provide contextual information that would assist in the more accurate interpretation of respondents' accounts of their present experience (regarding, in this case, the respective roles of workers and supervisors). To this end, respondents were asked to comment on: (i) their experience of the role of workers (supervisors) in their organisation in the past; (ii) their expectations regarding the future role of workers (supervisors) in the organisation; and (iii) their experience of the role of workers (supervisor) in any other organisation(s) that they had worked in, or that they knew about. To ensure some comparability of the data across the various contextual domains of interest (including the present context), it was considered desirable that respondents base their responses to these questions on the same Theory X — Theory Y framework that they had used, in Question 2, to evaluate the current role of workers (supervisors). Prior to the administration of the questions in this category, each respondent was therefore reminded briefly of the X/Y rating which she/he had given in response to Question 2.

The findings for each of the context questions are reported below, along with a more general discussion, at the end, of the methodological implications of these findings.

Q7: What was the role played by workers in this division in the past? Did it differ from the role of workers at the present time? How? Give examples. How long ago was this?

Tooling division: All participants responded to this question. Four participants (all wages employees) reported some change, from the past to the present, in the role of the workers in their division and two (both supervisors) reported no change. With respect to the former, the perception of three of these respondents was that divisional workers had played a more passive role in the past than they did at the present time. In one case, it was argued that, whereas workers today were prepared to challenge managerial decisions likely to affect them (using the threat of industrial action, if necessary), workers in the past had been more inclined to simply accept such decisions. A second respondent argued that, given the high degree of job specialisation in the past, there was not the same requirement then, as there was now, for workers to possess a range of skills and to be versatile with respect to the use of those skills. In the respondent's own words:

> In the old days, you used to do a little bit of a job, you didn't finish the whole job. Now, we do the whole thing virtually from start to finish. People are more versatile than they used to be and more active in what they do...they're prepared to do things that years ago they wouldn't [do]. They'd only do a certain job and that was it, you know. (wages employee)

A third respondent attributed a more passive role to workers in the past on the grounds that supervisors, at the time, were more dictatorial and, as such, there was little inducement for workers to "speak out with any ideas" or to "add something to the job". Interestingly, a kind of win-lose perspective was indicated in this respondent's attempt to explain the role changes that he perceived to have taken place (reportedly, over the preceding ten years or so). He said:

> At one time, the supervisor was almost sort of God. But now, I don't know whether the workers have come up, or whether the supervisor has been dragged down, but they've got a lot closer together. (wages employee)

It is worth noting that the responses of the first two respondents above imply an interpretation of the active/passive (Theory Y — Theory X) dichotomy — respondents had been introduced to this in Question 2 — which was not entirely consistent with that which was intended. In the first case, the respondent appeared to be contrasting a reactionary with a compliant role for workers; in the second, the distinction seemed to be between a role for workers which emphasised skill versatility and one which emphasised skill specialisation. The point can be made here, as previously, that interpretive inconsistencies such as these raise questions about the imposition, in the present method, of *a priori* dimensions (in this case, contrasting a Theory X with a Theory Y orientation) by which to try to represent organisation members' experience. The results suggest that the use of questions of this kind in organisational culture research requires pilot studies to check that their interpretation by respondents is consistent with that intended by the researcher.

Of the four respondents who reported a change, from the past to the present, in the role of divisional workers, there was one who, at least initially, attributed a more active role to workers in the past. This participant used the term active in the same way as the participant above, namely, to imply a reactionary or oppositional role for workers. As an example of divisional workers playing a more active role in the past, the participant described a strike by workers in 1985 in which workers maintained a 24-hour campsite vigil outside of the division, as a protest against the threatened closure of the division. Given that this respondent had been with the division for many years (his length of service with the division at the time of this study was 25 years), he was subsequently asked if he could comment on the role of divisional workers in the more distant past. The information provided in response to this question, and in response to an associated prompt, was of particular interest and, as such, it is considered in some detail below.

When asked about the role of divisional workers in the more distant past, the participant indicated that:

> Well, [workers] didn't really have a role. Everyone was so happy, there was plenty of work. You could work here six or seven days a week if you sort of chose [to]. That was it — everyone knew more or less what was going on. There was a lot of people here. It was a more friendly atmosphere. (wages employee)

On further consideration, however, and having been reminded of the active/passive orientations described in Question 2, the participant acknowledged that, in terms of these orientations, there was no difference between the role of workers at this time, and the role of workers at present which the participant had judged to be very passive. In other words, workers then, as now, did pretty much as they were told, and they were not involved in, and neither did they question, the decisions made by those in authority. These data are interesting because they suggest that, while the role of the workers in this division appears to have changed very little over time, at least in an objective sense, the context in which that role is played out may have changed considerably — from one of certainty and security in the past, to one of uncertainty and insecurity at present. If this was the case — certainly, the results of Study 1 would appear to support such a conclusion (see, e.g., the discussion in Chapter 8, Section 8.3.1.2, Theme 7) — then one might question the *actual* source of the dissatisfaction which this respondent expressed in response to Question 3 (in response to this question, the respondent indicated that he was extremely dissatisfied with the current role of the workers in his division). It is possible, for example, that the emphasis on the role of workers in the present study may simply have provided a focus for the respondent's dissatisfaction, the real cause of which may have been changes in the experience of work associated with the declining fortunes of the division (e.g., increased job insecurity, fewer opportunities for promotion, and reduced access to overtime).

An important implication of the above argument is that training designed to alleviate worker dissatisfaction through a redefinition of the role of workers may, in this situation, be misdirected. Indeed, the finding reported here might usefully be interpreted in terms of Alderfer's concept of frustration-regression, as articulated in his theory of motivation (Alderfer, 1972). According to Alderfer, the frustration of higher-order needs can lead to a regression to lower-order needs, and where this occurs, the *ostensible* cause of workers' lack of motivation (e.g., complaints about the quality of safety equipment) may mask the *real* cause of their lack of motivation (e.g., not being consulted about the choice of their safety equipment). Interviewers therefore need to be cautious about accepting responses to questions at face value, without checking (e.g., by asking for an example) on the meaning attributed to the response by the respondent. This caveat would seem to be particularly applicable to organisational culture research.

Finally, with respect to the two respondents who reported no change in response to this question, there was one who argued that, in his experience (the respondent had been with the division for some 35 years), the workers in this division had always played a slightly active role. The basis for this assessment was that, according to the respondent, workers had always been prepared to question the instructions of their supervisors if they anticipated problems with these instructions — they did not just "do things blindly". Workers had also always had the initiative to seek out the additional information that might be required to complete a job for which they had been given partial instructions only. The second respondent indicated that, as far as he could tell, the role played by divisional workers — in response to Question 2, this respondent had attributed a predominantly active role to some workers and a predominantly passive role to others — had not changed from the past to the present. In his own words:

> I don't think there's any difference. I don't think they've changed. If they have, it's been a very gradual change and I've never noticed it. (staff, supervisory)

Production division: All participants responded to this question. Four respondents (including two supervisors and two wages employees) attributed a more active role to divisional workers in the past; one respondent (a wages employee) suggested that workers in the division in the past played a more passive role; and one respondent (a wages employee) reported no change. A more detailed account of these findings is provided below.

All four respondents who attributed a more active role to divisional workers in the past had rated the current role of divisional workers as passive, with the specific ratings given ranging from slightly passive (two participants) to moderately passive (two participants). In describing the past role of divisional workers, three of these respondents (including one supervisor and two wages employees) made reference to the Team Concept, a Japanese model of work organisation on which operations in the production division were originally based. During this period in the division's history, it was reported that: (i) workers were more interested in, and committed to, the success of the division (one respondent); (ii) workers were involved in group meetings for the purpose of solving problems on the shop floor (two respondents); and (iii) workers and management interacted more as equals in the sense that workers had the opportunity to respond to the proposals put forward by management, even to the extent that they could openly disagree with these proposals "without being reprimanded" (one respondent).

A number of reasons were offered for why the team concept — which had been abandoned some four years after its introduction — had failed. According to one respondent (a wages employee), the team meetings that were an integral part of this initiative, and which should have been "worthwhile to the company", frequently suffered from a lack of focus, with team members losing sight of the true purpose of the meetings. In the respondent's own words:

> ...[the meetings] didn't always work very well, because they very often went off line. [They] got to be bitch sessions, so they stopped them, and I can see why they stopped them, because they were becoming just a bitch session and, for some people, it was just [time] off the shop floor for half an hour or an hour. (wages employee)

A second respondent (also a wages employee) argued that the problem with the team meetings was that there were some team members who simply did not contribute. It was suggested that, in a team of say ten members, there would be three or four who would be actively involved, while the rest would be more "passive" and happy to "go along with whatever decisions [were] made".

Both of the above respondents also made reference to what they saw as management's role in the failure of the team concept. In one case, it was argued that, while the workforce as a whole was initially very enthusiastic about the innovation, management did not provide the kind of ongoing support and feedback that was needed in order to ensure its success. As illustrated in the following excerpt, this lack of support for an innovation by the very people seen to be responsible for its introduction, was regarded by this respondent as a key factor influencing the current attitudes of divisional workers towards renewed efforts, by divisional management, to increase the involvement of workers in divisional activities:

> Look, we made charts...and I don't think anybody ever looked at them, and so now when [management] come along and they ask you to chart something, the attitude is 'Oh, stuff that, I've done that before and nobody even bothered to look at them'. And it's true [that] once they've done something to people on the shop floor...[they've] got a long memory, and they resent [management] trying to get them to do it again, even though this time they might be genuine. (wages employee)

In a similar vein, the second respondent reported that the team concept "wasn't really pushed by upper management" who had the final say in whether or not suggestions for change made by shop floor workers were approved for implementation. The fact that upper management frequently did not support workers' ideas was attributed, by this respondent, to a general resistance to change at this level — a reluctance to do something "different from what they'd known" — as well as a concern that the team concept provided workers with "too much freedom and latitude", thereby undermining their own positions of power in the organisation.

Without making reference specifically to the failure of the team concept, the third respondent above (a supervisor) did offer some comments on his perception of why the role of divisional workers had changed. In this case, it was suggested that the commitment and enthusiasm displayed by divisional workers in the early set-up phase of the division, had been "gradually browbeaten out of [workers]". While there was no indication of how this was done, its impact, according to the respondent, was that many of the division's original employees had left the company, whilst those who remained developed the attitude that: "I'm here for eight hours, and I don't give a shit what they do any more, because I've been there, done that, so what the hell for?". This respondent also expressed the view that current efforts on the part of divisional management to encourage a more active role for workers were being met with limited success only. He attributed this to differences between managers and workers in how these efforts were perceived. Managers, on the one hand, were convinced of the "morale-boosting" value of what they were doing, believing that "commitment [was] going back on the shop floor". Workers, on the other hand, perceived that their representation was inadequate and that, in reality, input from the shop floor was rarely sought below the level of leading hand.

As indicated, there were four respondents who attributed a more active role to divisional workers in the past. The last of these respondents argued his case somewhat differently from the three respondents whose responses have been described above. This respondent (a supervisor) spoke about the company more generally and argued that, because of the downsizing which had taken place over the years, a climate of uncertainty had developed which had induced many of the company's more active personnel (both staff and wages employees) to voluntarily leave the organisation. The personnel who remained were, according to this respondent, the kind of individuals who lacked the confidence and self-direction to take control of their lives in this way. In the respondent's own words:

> ...I think it was a little bit more active prior...because I think *the organisation* diminished in size...we got rid of shall we say our more active people...they would have seen the writing on the wall, and in any situation where there was a possibility of you losing your job, people who know they have the ability and people who don't mind taking the risk...[they are] the good people who opt out and jump off the ship before it sinks, to get on to something else. And you [are] left with the people who are unsure and are scared, and they will hang on to the last minute and possibly go down with the ship...So I suppose we've got slightly more passive as time has gone on. (staff, supervisory)

It is worth noting the assumption in this respondent's use of the terms active and passive that individuals are, by nature, either active or passive. Contrary to what was intended, these were not seen as qualities, or orientations, which were under the control of, and therefore able to be shaped by, the organisation and the particular style of leadership and management which it supported. The point should also be made that this respondent, unlike the three participants above, was a relative newcomer to the company and the division. At the time of this study, he had been with the division and the company for eleven months only; in contrast, the tenure of his colleagues at the time of the study was between six and eight years with the division, and between 10 and 20 years with the company. Unlike his colleagues, then, this respondent did not have a firsthand knowledge of the early set-up of the division and was, therefore, not able to bring the same personal history to bear on his discussion of the role played by divisional workers in the past.

Of the remaining two respondents from this division, there was, as indicated, one who reported no change, from the past to the present, in the role of division workers, and one who attributed a more passive role to divisional workers in the past. With respect to the former, this respondent (a wages employee) simply indicated that, as she saw it, the role of divisional workers in the past was "basically the same" as it was at the present time (the participant had previously rated the current role of divisional workers as moderately passive). With respect to the latter, this respondent's attribution of a more passive role to divisional workers in the past — the respondent had previously rated the current role of divisional workers as moderately active — appeared to have been influenced, at least in part, by his experience elsewhere in the company. The respondent (a wages employee) indicated that, prior to commencing work in the production division (some three years ago), he had worked for nine years in another division where the managers, relative to his current managers, had been "quite strict on the workers". The respondent subsequently provided an example, in this instance from his more recent past, of the more passive role which he believed was played by divisional workers in the past. He recounted how, in the early months of his employment with the production division, he had come up with an idea for the treatment of a particular waste product that, if implemented, could save the company a considerable amount of money. Despite having confirmation of the worth of his idea from one of the company's technical experts, the respondent's supervisor at the time did not support the idea and instructed the respondent to dispose of the product in question. The respondent described his compliance with this instruction as follows:

> He said: 'Scrap it.' I said: 'Whatever you say.' So I scrapped it. That was his job — his job as foreman was to say 'Scrap it'. So you scrap it. To me, that was very passive. (wages employee)

Apart from the above findings, one other finding of interest that emerged from the analysis of the present data set was that there were two respondents (both wages employees) who, despite being reminded of their previous X/Y rating of the current role of divisional workers, initially responded to Question 7 by talking about some seemingly unrelated aspect of their past experience in the division. One of these respondents made the comment that she was "a lot more fussy" (presumably, with respect to the quality of her work) now than she had been in the past; the other respondent made reference to the fact that, in the past, "you didn't have so many women in the workforce". A possible interpretation of these responses is that they provide further evidence of the difficulty experienced by respondents in conceptualising a role for workers in terms of the kinds of abstract, or theoretical, dimensions with which they had been presented.

There are a number of methodological issues that are raised by the above findings. These are discussed in point form below:

(1) The findings for Question 7, like those for Question 2, provided evidence of problems associated with the conceptualisation of a role for workers (in this case, a past role) in terms of the active/passive dichotomy described. In particular, respondents from the tooling division seemed to have difficulty with the concept of an active role for workers, which was variously interpreted to mean a role in which workers actively opposed those in authority and engaged in win-lose negotiations with them (two respondents), and a role in which workers practised multi-skilling as opposed to task specialisation (one respondent). There was also the comment by one respondent from this division that, in the more distant past, divisional workers "didn't really have a role", implying perhaps some further difficulty with the framing of one's experience in terms of this dichotomy. While the problems in this regard were by no means exclusive to the tooling division, they were more evident in the data for this division than in the corresponding data for the production division. It is possible, therefore, that the active/passive dichotomy had less relevance for the members of this division,

than for the members of the production division. Indeed, as indicated in Study 1, it was the researcher's impression, based on an association of several years with this division, that divisional members had had little exposure, over time, to a more enriched role for workers of the kind that the definition of an active orientation was intended to imply.

(2) With respect to the usefulness, in the present method, of seeking information about the historical context of respondents' experience, the findings for the production division were more informative in this regard than were the findings for the tooling division. One explanation for this may be that, because there was less interpretive inconsistency indicated in the findings for the production division (see point 1 above), these findings provided a more coherent picture of the value of historical data. In particular, they provided some support for the idea that past experience helps to shape current perceptions and that knowledge of past experience can, therefore, provide important insights into the meaning of current perceptions. For example, the finding that the workers in the production division were perceived to play a predominantly passive role at the present time — interestingly, the researcher's own impression of this role was that it was relatively active, at least when compared with the corresponding role of workers in the tooling division — is perhaps better understood when it is viewed in the context of the more active role which the workers in this division reportedly played in the past (as manifested in their involvement in activities associated with the team concept). In a similar vein, the finding that there was one respondent from this division who, in contrast to his colleagues, rated the current role of divisional workers as active, makes more sense when it is viewed in the context of this respondent's past experience in another division of the company, in which workers reportedly played a very passive role. The preceding arguments, while they are based on the responses of a small number of respondents only, nevertheless draw attention to the potential value of historical data of the kind generated by Question 7 and, as such, provide at least tentative justification for the retention of this question in any subsequent revision of the present method.

(3) The findings for Question 7 confirmed the importance of establishing a time frame for respondents' experience. While the researcher was not as diligent as she might have been in seeking information of relevance in this regard (this was partly due to time constraints), when this information was obtained it served to amply illustrate that organisation members can differ considerably in terms of what, for them, constitutes the past. For example, as indicated in point 2 above, there were some respondents from the production division for whom the past constituted the early years of the division's set-up; for another, shorter-serving, respondent from this division, his past was defined by his experience in the division in which he had first commenced work with the company. Similar differences were found among the respondents from the tooling division. Interestingly, while all of the respondents from this division had a considerable divisional history upon which to draw (the shortest-serving respondent from this

division had been with the division for sixteen years), there were some respondents who, when asked about their past experience, made reference to the recent past (less than five years ago), and others who talked about the more distant past (at least ten years ago). This latter finding suggests that a distinction might need to be drawn between an individual's chronological past and her/his psychologically salient past.

(4) The fourth and final point is that the above findings draw attention to the need to consider, not only the content of organisation members' past experience (in this case, whether workers in the past played a more active, or a more passive role than workers at the present time), but also the affective response of organisation members to that experience. As indicated, the findings for the production division provided evidence that the members of this division had had some past exposure, via practices associated with the team concept, to a more active role for divisional workers. Importantly, however, members' experience of this role did not appear to have been particularly positive. Given our proposition that organisational climate should be defined in terms of the feelings associated with the surface elements of organisational culture (i.e., at Levels 1 and 2), this finding might be indicative of a past climate that was somewhat negative with respect to the more active role for workers entailed in the team concept. Among the perceived drawbacks of the team concept, it was suggested that workers' efforts in relation to their more enriched role — including making suggestions for change and recording work-related information — were not actively encouraged by divisional management. The legacy of this experience was that recent efforts, by the division's current management, to resurrect certain aspects of the team concept had reportedly been met with some resistance from workers. An important implication of this latter finding is that, without a knowledge of the historical context of organisation members' experience — in terms of both its content and affective dimensions — management's understanding of, and ability to deal effectively with, such resistance is likely to be curtailed.

A review of the corresponding findings for the role of supervisors provides additional support for the points above regarding the methodological implications of the findings for the role of workers. For example, the findings for the role of supervisors served to further illustrate the value of historical data. In the case of the tooling division, these data depicted a relatively long history of no change in the more or less directive role which divisional supervisors were perceived to play. In the case of the production division, perceptions of the past role of divisional supervisors differed, depending on the particular time frame within which the respondent was operating. Moreover, these differences helped to explain differences among the respondents from this division in their perception of the current role of divisional supervisors. Interestingly, there was one respondent from the production division who based his evaluation of the past role of divisional supervisors, not on personal experience (this respondent had been with the company for a very short time only), but rather on what he had heard from fellow employees. These data drew attention to the possibility that knowledge acquired through socialisation may be just as important in influencing the way in which organisation members interpret their experience as knowledge acquired through direct experience.

The final point can be made that, while the concepts of directive and consultative seemed to present fewer difficulties than the corresponding concepts of active and passive (in terms of the meanings which respondents attributed to them), it was still the case that there were some respondents who, despite being prompted to do so, did not evaluate the past role of supervisors in terms of these concepts. This again brings into question the use, in the present method, of the Theory X — Theory Y framework.

Q8: Do you think that the role played by workers in this division at the present time is likely to change/stay the same? If you think that it will change, how will it change? Why will it change in this way? If you think that it will stay the same, why?

Tooling division: Five participants responded to this question. Of these, three (including one supervisor and two wages employees) responded in a way that suggested that they did not anticipate any change in the role of divisional workers in the future, and two (a supervisor and a wages employee) suggested that the role of divisional workers might become more active. These findings are discussed in more detail below.

With respect to the respondents whose responses implied no change, there was one (a supervisor) who predicted that, in the future, there would be fewer workers in the division with characteristics similar to those of his best worker (an individual whom the respondent had described as having an ability to think ahead, showing an interest in the job, and being self-motivated, in the sense of being able to "do things without being goaded and driven into it"). The reason for this, it was argued, was that there had been a change in the broader social context such that people today were more self-interested, and more expecting of immediate gratification for their efforts, than they had been in the past. The implication was that workers today constituted a different 'breed' from workers in the past. A second problem, as this respondent saw it, was that the industrial relations environment had changed such that much of the power and authority that was once invested in the supervisory role was now held by the unions. These views are expressed verbatim in the following excerpt:

...the tendency nowadays is for people on the job, and this is part of our social thing I think, that people want to do less for more rewards, that's the basis of it. In fact, some of the young people that we get in now think that the world owes them a living; they want the best conditions and everything right from the word go, before they've actually learnt anything...I mean it was a bit the same when I was young, but we were under far stricter discipline than what you can apply now. You can't apply the discipline now like you could because of the social system, not only in here but outside. I mean in our day you could get a cuff under the ear [whereas] you certainly can't do that now...The power of the unions now too [has] got that way where a person has got to do something really wrong for you to be on safe ground to take some action against him...It's all wrapped up in legality now. (staff, supervisory)

Interestingly, there is an implicit assumption in the above excerpt that strict supervisory control and discipline are the appropriate means by which to improve worker performance. Such an assumption is, of course, consistent with a Theory X, rather than a Theory Y, view of workers.

The response of a second 'no change' respondent conveyed this respondent's considerable pessimism about the future of the division more generally. It was suggested that, because the company no longer regarded the division as integral to its operations, it had allowed the division to decline to the point where divisional members no longer had any opportunity for promotion and where the only remaining inducement to work was the challenge of the work itself. The implication was that, given this state of affairs, it was unlikely that anything whatsoever would change in the division in the future. In the respondent's own words:

> Well, we seem to have stagnated these last few years. The way I see it, this company really doesn't want us. That's the feeling I get. We're put to one side virtually and we've stagnated. There's been no one promoted, they've just been tied up. So we're in a situation...we'll get jobs in that no one else wants to do and we'll do them...Or no one else can do them and we've done them. That's the challenge — in the work, not in you're looking forward to being promoted or whatever, that doesn't come into it. (wages employee)

Finally, a third 'no change' respondent indicated that, as he saw it, change was unlikely because the age and length of service of the majority of the division's members was such that they were all "sort of in a groove" and they were "very hard to shake up".

Both of the respondents who anticipated a more active future role for divisional workers conceptualised this role in terms of a closer relationship between supervisors (or management) and workers. In one case, the respondent's response recalled the above theme of the diminishing power of supervisors. This respondent (a wages employee with leading hand status) indicated that, as he saw it, workers and supervisors were beginning to interact much more closely with one another. The reason for this was that supervisors had reportedly lost some of the control that they had once enjoyed and, as a result, were less dictatorial now than they had been in the past. In commenting on the diminished control of supervisors, the respondent made the following observation:

> I don't think the supervisor can really fire somebody now — definitely not straight out. He's got to put him on report so many times, almost sort of put it before a board before [he] can get rid of anybody. He can't just say 'You're out'. (wages employee, leading hand)

The second respondent (a supervisor) argued that advances in technology would necessitate a closer working relationship between workers and management in the future. Essentially, this respondent's argument was that, as the skill requirements of jobs increased (a consequence of advances in technology), so too would it be necessary for the level of education and training of workers to increase. This, in turn, would lead to some equalising of the status of workers and management and would make it possible for these two groups to communicate more directly with one another. Apart from advances in technology, the diminishing size of the tooling division was also considered, by this respondent, to be a factor that would bring about a closer working relationship between workers and management. These views were expressed verbatim, as follows:

> Yes, [the role of workers] will change. Well, technology itself is going to change, so [the worker's] got to change with it. We will need, in this organisation, higher educated people in the trades groups, to be able to keep up with the technology we've got...you're getting onto a level where you're going to have very similar two people, the management and the tradesman...you're going to be still very highly educated people to be able to converse with each other a lot more. And because also the tooling division is getting smaller in numbers, and will get smaller in numbers, and you'll have a much closer relationship between man-agement and [workers]. (staff, supervisory)

There are two general points that can be made in relation to the above findings for the tooling division. First, these findings provided further evidence to suggest that the active/passive dichotomy may lack relevance for the respondents from this division. Not only were direct references to this dichotomy lacking in respondents' responses to Question 8, but there was also a sense in which the responses given by some respondents failed to properly address the question (a case in point being the first respondent above who antici-pated that workers in the future would be more self-interested than their counterparts in the past had been). Moreover, the problem of interpretive inconsistency was once again encountered. For example, in one case, a more active future role for divisional workers was conceptualised as involving, simply, "a bit more interaction between the supervisors and the men", brought about by the fact that supervisors could no longer be as dictatorial as they had once been.

The second point concerns respondents' explanations for why the role of the workers in the division would or would not change in the future. The general impression conveyed by these data was that there was a lack of perceived control over outcomes in this regard, with respondents variously making reference to the influence of factors such as changes in the society at large, changes in the industrial relations context, advances in technology, and the downsizing of the division. The reader may recall that this tendency for respondents from the tooling division to attribute cause externally was noted previously in the findings for Study 1. In view of this, and also given the argument by Bate (1984) that some organisa-tions (groups) are culturally predisposed to think in this way — Bate classified this as depersonalisation, a cultural orientation whereby organisation members commonly attribute their problems to non-human factors, or to factors outside of their control — the argument might again be made that questions which seek information about respondents' causal attributions (whether in relation to experienced, or anticipated, changes) may be particularly useful for eliciting information about the organisation's (group's) culture.

Production division: All participants responded to this question. Four participants (including two supervisors and two wages employees) anticipated no change in the role of divisional workers in the future; one participant (a wages employee) anticipated a change towards a more active role; and one participant (a wages employee) anticipated a change towards a more passive role. These findings are elaborated upon below.

With respect, first of all, to the 'no change' respondents, all of these respondents had previously judged the current role of divisional workers to be more or less passive. In arguing that this role was unlikely to change in the future, one of these respondents (a supervisor) drew attention to the very traditional style of management that he believed prevailed in the division. According to this respondent, the majority of the division's managers had been with the company for a very long time, they had all been indoctrinated in the same way — in the respondent's own words, "very similar to an army situation" — and, as a result, it was likely that they would "continue to run the place [in] exactly the same way" as it had always been run. A second respondent (a wages employee) argued that a change in the role of divisional workers was unlikely because, while divisional management might espouse a commitment to a changed role for workers — management might, for example, espouse the importance of sharing information with workers — it was the respondent's experience that this commitment was never borne out in practice.

The other two 'no change' respondents (a supervisor and a wages employee) shared the view that, while there was the potential for divisional workers to play a more active role in the future — made possible by the restructuring of the award being undertaken at that time[14] — it was unlikely that this potential would be realised. The reason, according to one respondent, was that there were not enough workers with the motivation and interest to benefit from opportunities for greater involvement. In the respondent's own words:

> ...it's my belief that you'll get a few, a minority, that'll try their best, but you'll have the majority that'll just sit here and let the rest of the ship cruise, sail into the sunset, you know. They'll just sort of lay back passively [with the attitude] 'What do you want me to do?' (staff, supervisor)

---

[14]Towards the end of the 1980s, a major restructure of the vehicle industry award was undertaken in Australia. This was a tripartite initiative involving the government, the unions, and local automotive manufacturers. Among its main objectives were the simplification of existing award classifications and the introduction of industry-wide procedures for increasing employees' skills and knowledge. Award restructuring can be seen as the precursor to enterprise bargaining, the mechanism for negotiating wages and conditions of work (in this case at an organisational rather than industry level) that is in use today.

This respondent argued further that, unless the "good people" were encouraged and given "some sort of incentive" to continue to perform, the role of divisional workers in the future might become even more passive than it was at the present time. The other respondent argued that efforts to encourage a more active role for divisional workers were unlikely to come to much because of the cynicism with which workers viewed such efforts. As indicated in the following excerpt, this respondent clearly saw some parallels between the practices associated with the team concept of the past, and those associated with the more recent award restructuring:

> Well, when I saw this restructuring, what they're going to do type of thing, and read some of that, I think 'Heck, we had that years ago' and they're talking about reintroducing it...I mean, [the production division], I always thought was way ahead of all that years ago, and they chucked it out. Management got rid of it, you know. (wages employee)

This respondent also expressed some concern about the ability of the division's current management to bring about a change towards a more active role for divisional workers. According to the respondent, the main problem in this regard was that ineffective managers were never removed, but simply transferred to other managerial roles of equally high status. In this way, the poor performance of the ineffective manager continued to have an impact.

Of the remaining two respondents from this division there was, as indicated, one who anticipated a change towards a more active role for divisional workers and one who anticipated a change towards a more passive role for divisional workers. The first of these respondents argued that, because of improved managerial attitudes toward workers, the role of divisional workers in the future was likely to be even more active than it was at the present time (this respondent had previously rated the current role of divisional workers as moderately active). According to this respondent, there was a growing recognition among divisional managers that shop floor workers constituted a valuable resource and that the way to increased productivity lay not in more, and stricter, supervision but rather in efforts to increase the job satisfaction of workers. In the respondent's own words:

> It will change, it's going to get better. ...management is beginning to recognise in little ways that people who run the shop floor, the people on the shop floor...you can have all the supervision in the world, you can have one supervisor standing over one operator and that still won't make them produce any more parts. But [if] you can get the worker to enjoy what he does...all of a sudden 50% goes up in the work [output] because it's no longer a bind, it's no longer a job, it's something he enjoys doing. By that I mean they're getting us involved in everybody else's areas and they're beginning to show an active concern. (wages employee)

In the case of the second respondent, it was initially argued that, whether or not there would be a change towards a more active, or a more passive role, for divisional workers in the future would depend entirely upon management:

> It's up to management...[workers] are passive basically. If management want them to be passive, they will be. If they want them to be actively involved, they've got to give them the first nudge. (wages employee)

After reflecting on how her own attitudes towards work had changed — nowadays, she felt that she should "just come in, ask what they've got to do, and do it...like the little robot" — the respondent reached the conclusion that, in the future, divisional workers would probably play an even more passive role than they played at the present time (the latter having previously been rated as moderately passive).

One general point that can be made in relation to the above findings is that the respondents from the production division seemed to experience less difficulty than their counterparts from the tooling division, in framing their anticipated future experience in terms of the active/passive dichotomy. Not only were there more direct references to this dichotomy in respondents' responses to this question — that is, the terms active and passive were used more frequently — but there was also more evidence of respondents having interpreted these terms as intended. This finding is not inconsistent with evidence suggesting that the members of the production division, compared with their counterparts from tooling, had had some exposure, over time, to work practices that, on the one hand, implied a passive role for workers and, on the other, implied a more active role for workers.

The point can also be made that the attributions data for the production division provided an interesting comparison with the corresponding data for the tooling division. Whereas tooling division respondents seemed to attribute outcomes (in this case, related to the future role of divisional workers) to the influence of factors external to the division, production division respondents seemed to place more emphasis on the influence of factors internal to the division. As indicated above, there were references by the latter to the role of divisional management (their style, attitudes, competence, *etc.*) in influencing future outcomes; the attitudes of divisional workers were also seen as important in this regard; and there was a reference, by one respondent, to problems associated with the division's operating reward system (which reportedly provided workers with little incentive to become more actively involved). Given the previous argument about the possible cultural significance of attributions data, it would seem appropriate that, in revising the present method, allowance should be made for the further investigation of organisation members' attributions.

In terms of a more general assessment of the value of Question 8, a review of the above findings, for both divisions, suggests a number of reasons for why this question might usefully be retained. These are as follows:

(1) While there was some variability, within each division, in the content of respondents' comments about the anticipated future context, the general impression conveyed by

these data was one of considerable pessimism about the future. In fact, there was only one respondent from the total sample who expressed any optimism about the future. This was a respondent from the production division who believed that things would "get better" because divisional managers were gradually coming to regard shop floor workers as a valuable resource. There was also evidence of a perception in both divisions that, if there was to be some future change — importantly, a majority of respondents from each division anticipated no change, or very little change, in the future — then this change was unlikely to be taken up very easily, or incorporated very rapidly. There were references, for example, to the likelihood of change being a "slow process"; to the likelihood that the workforce would be "very hard to shake up"; to the indoctrination of management personnel in traditional ways of thinking and behaving; and to the cynical attitudes of workers toward change.

The above observations suggest that information about the future context of organisation members' experience might be valuable insofar as it may provide insights into the likely responsiveness of the organisation (group) to change, and it may also serve as a kind of gauge for the affective or organisational climate dimension of the organisation's (group's) culture. With respect to this latter point, the idea here is that organisation members' views about the future (whether positive or negative) may reveal more about how members feel about their current situation (organisational climate) than information pertaining to the present time only.

(2) Apart from the general mood of negativity that they conveyed, the future context data — particularly those for the tooling division — were noteworthy because of the number of references to the past that they contained. As indicated, respondents from the tooling division variously made reference to the better prospects for promotion which existed in this division in the past (one respondent), to the greater control and authority invested in the supervisory role at the time (two respondents), and, by association, to the relative lack of power, in the past, of employee unions (one respondent). While respondents from the production division were somewhat less inclined to talk about the past, reference was nevertheless made to the division's past experience of the team concept (one respondent) and also to the veteran status of the division's management, many of whom had been with the company as apprentice tradesmen (one respondent). These observations draw attention to the possibility that information generated in response to questions about the future context may provide clues as to which aspect of organisation (group) members' experience (e.g., whether members' experience of the past, or whether their anticipated future experience) may have been most influential in shaping the organisation's (group's) culture. Drawing on the above findings, the tendency for respondents from the tooling division to talk about the past, when asked about the future, suggests that this division may be more strongly rooted in the past than in the anticipated future.

(3) A third and final argument in favour of seeking information about the future context is that such information may reveal the extent to which organisation members share a

clearly articulated, and coherent, view of the future. Despite the emergence in the above findings of a sense of shared negative affect about the future, there was, as indicated, considerable variability in the content of respondents' comments about the future (and what it might hold with respect to the role of divisional workers). This kind of variability, it might be argued, might have implications for the ability and willingness of the members of the group (organisation) to accommodate changes in relation to the issue in question. In particular, change may be more difficult in groups whose members lack a clear direction for the future, than in groups whose members are able to clearly articulate such a direction.

Finally, a review of the corresponding findings for the role of supervisors draws attention to a number of parallels between these findings and the above findings for the role of workers. Once again, the attributions data provided evidence to suggest that the divisions might differ in terms of members' causal attributions (in this case, concerning whether or not there would be a change in the role of divisional supervisors in the future). As above, respondents from the tooling division were more inclined to attribute outcomes in this regard to the influence of factors outside of, rather than within, their control (including, e.g., changes in company policy, an increase in the power of unions, improved educational standards in the population as a whole and, hence, a better educated workforce, and advances in technology). In contrast, while the corresponding data for the production division contained some external attributions (e.g., one respondent commented on how global competition would force a redefinition of the supervisory role), there were also references in these data to the influence of factors internal to the division (e.g., one respondent made reference to the influence of a new manager who had "brought a breath of fresh air into the place", while another respondent argued that, in his opinion, it would be the resourcefulness of the workforce which would ultimately convince supervisors of the value of a more consultative approach). These findings provide further support for the case made above in favour of an extension of the current investigation of organisation members' attributions.

The findings for the role of supervisors also served to further support the above argument that information generated in response to questions about the future context may be of value insofar as it may provide clues as to the dominant orientation of the organisation's (group's) culture. Once again, there was evidence of a relatively strong past-orientation in the tooling division, with the respondents from this division being much more likely than their counterparts from the production division, to make reference to their past experience when asked about their anticipated future experience. Reference was made, for example, to the higher status enjoyed by supervisors in the past ("...a supervisor was held on a higher pedestal years ago"), to the style of supervision which was regarded as acceptable in the past (which was such that workers had little autonomy and were "treated like slaves"), and to the way in which supervisors were traditionally inducted into the role (with "no training at all virtually").

One last point that can be made in relation to the findings for the role of supervisors is that these findings, in contrast to the findings for the role of workers, provided some evidence of a difference between the divisions in respondents' perceptions of the likelihood of future change (concerning, in this case, the role of divisional supervisors). Specifically, a majority of respondents from the production division (four out of the five who responded to this question) regarded a change in the role of divisional supervisors as inevitable or, at the very least, quite possible. Moreover, there was good agreement among these respondents about the nature of the anticipated change which, in general terms, was seen as involving the devolution of some of the supervisor's current responsibilities to leading hands, and a redefinition of the supervisory role to incorporate activities such as planning, giving technical advice, coaching and consulting. In contrast, in the tooling division, a change in the role of divisional supervisors was not only seen as less likely, but of the two respondents who seemed confident that change would occur, one was very negative about what he saw as the undermining of the power and authority which was rightfully invested in the supervisory role. Finally, the data for the tooling division also contained elements of the kind of negative affect to which reference was made above.

Q9: Are you aware of the role played by workers in other organisations? Give examples. What was the nature of the other organisation(s) and how did you come to know about it?

Tooling division: This question was asked of four participants only (due to time constraints). Of these, there were two (a supervisor and a wages employee) who indicated that they were unaware of the role played by workers in other organisations. In one case, the respondent explained that this was because he had "only ever worked here". A third respondent (a wages employee) indicated that he had some knowledge, acquired through friends who worked there, of the role of workers in the local branch of a chemicals company. In this firm, workers reportedly had "far greater input" as indicated, for example, in their representation in meetings of the company board, in which decisions were made about personnel recruitment and promotion. The respondent indicated that he was very much in favour of this particular practice because, in his opinion, it would help to ensure that people would be hired, or promoted, on the basis of merit, rather than on the basis of family connections — "your father may be on staff" — or the ability to win favour with those in authority — "the blue-eyed boy syndrome".

Finally, in response to this question, the fourth respondent (a supervisor) indicated that he could comment only on the role played by workers in other tooling facilities that he had visited in Australia. It was noted that, while these facilities were very similar to the tooling division (the participant had been with this division for 36 years) in terms of how they were structured, they were generally much smaller and, as a result, "management have been much closer to the people". The respondent also made reference to the poorer physical conditions (e.g., facilities such as rest-rooms) and lack of security, leading to high employee turnover, which he had observed in tooling facilities that were non-unionised.

While no firm conclusions can be drawn on the basis of the above findings, an emerging pattern was that, among the members of this division, direct knowledge of the role of workers in other organisations (i.e., knowledge based on personal experience of having worked elsewhere) might be limited.

Production division: All participants from the production division were asked about their knowledge of the role of workers in other organisations. Three respondents (including two wages employees and one supervisor) were able to respond to the question on the basis of their personal experience of having worked elsewhere. Of these, one recalled his years as an apprentice in an organisation in the United Kingdom. In describing what the workers in this organisation did, the respondent made no reference to the active/passive dichotomy, but rather drew attention to the culture of low productivity which this organisation supported:

> There I [saw] a different culture...I have never seen so many people do so little, honestly. I mean, I think back now...I can understand why the government wanted to privatise [the organisation]...They were some of the best dart players and card players in England, I can tell you that. (wages employee)

The second respondent commented on her experience, some twenty three years previously, in a job in which employees were paid according to a piece-rate system. Such a system, it was argued, fostered very passive attitudes in employees, such that:

> They didn't want to question things. The only time they got upset was when the machines didn't work, and they weren't earning money. (wages employee)

The third respondent responded to the question on the basis of his experience in a number of other organisations. The respondent indicated that, compared with his current organisation, these other organisations supported a climate of much greater trust between workers and management. The size of the organisation was regarded as an important factor here, with reference being made to the experience of working in smaller companies that were set up in such a way as to enable managers to interact "on a one-to-one basis with the people". According to the respondent, a further problem for his current organisation in this regard was that the rationalisation of the workforce, over the years, had led to considerable job insecurity:

> ...the place has been going for so long, as I've said, it's just sort of lumbered on and lumbered on. And the people who are left have the distrust in them, they foster that, you know. If you're scared, everyone around you is going to be scared... (staff, supervisory)

In addition to the three respondents above, there was one other respondent from the production division (a supervisor) who reported having some knowledge of the role of workers in other organisations. In this case, however, the respondent's knowledge in this regard had been acquired only indirectly — that is, through contact with a relative who worked elsewhere. The respondent suggested that, while the role of workers in his relative's organisation was very passive (compared with the role of workers in his own organisation), far from creating dissatisfaction, this role was one which workers enjoyed because it provided them with a clear and unambiguous understanding of what they were expected to do. In the respondent's own words:

> ...it's a completely different sort of lifestyle up there. The role there is virtually...you've got an area, you're told what to do, and you work that way, and they seem to be a lot happier in what they're doing. It seems to be an 'us-and-them' sort of situation, but at least they get some sort of...you know where you stand. You know what the rules are...and everybody understands it. (staff, supervisory)

The respondent went on to point out that a recent attempt, on the part of this organisation's management, to develop a more participative work culture, had encountered some difficulties. The problem, as he saw it, was that practices associated with "worker participation" and "worker democracy" had the disadvantage of creating considerable role ambiguity for superiors and subordinates alike:

> ...it's leaving grey areas. ...who's the boss, and who's not? What areas are you going to put the controls on? Where does it stop? If you leave that open, you create grey areas of demarcation.

Finally, there were two respondents from this division (both wages employees) who indicated that they were unable to comment on the role of workers in other organisations. In one case, the respondent was an older employee with some twenty years' service with the current organisation and, in the other the participant was a young employee in her first job.

In conclusion, the above findings for the production division confirmed the expectation that, given their demographic characteristics, the members of this division would be more likely than their counterparts from the tooling division to have had direct experience of working in other organisations. Given the small sample size, and also given problems associated with depicting this experience in terms of a common framework (in this case, the active/passive dichotomy), it is not possible to comment with any confidence on how this experience might have influenced respondents' experience of their current organisation. At the same time, however, one might reasonably expect there to be some kind of association in this regard and, in this sense, the further investigation of organisation members' other experience would seem to be warranted.

Finally, with respect to the corresponding findings for the role of supervisors, it was not surprising, given the nature of the question being asked — Question 9 was, in a general sense, concerned simply with the extent of the respondent's knowledge of other organisations — that the same pattern of responding emerged in these findings as in the above findings for the role of workers. That is, respondents from the production division were more likely than their counterparts from the tooling division to report some direct knowledge of the role of supervisors in other organisations. The same conclusion is, therefore, suggested by these findings as by the findings for the role of workers.

9.5 Overall Evaluation of the Study 2 Method

As indicated in the introduction to this study, the aim of the study was to pilot a first attempt at the more systematic assessment of certain aspects of an organisation's (group's) culture, specifically, beliefs and assumptions pertaining to the nature of human nature (Schein, 1985, 1992, 2004, 2010). Based on the results of the study, a number of conclusions were able to be drawn regarding which features of the method seemed to work well — insofar as eliciting information of the kind that was being sought — and which did not. A summary of some of the main insights that were obtained in this regard is provided below and, where appropriate, reference is again made to how these insights might inform the subsequent refinement of the method. The strengths of the method are discussed first, followed by a discussion of the method's limitations. It should be noted that, while references to the parallel inquiry into the role of supervisors have not been included below (in order to avoid unnecessary 'clutter' in the text), the conclusions drawn apply equally to this data set as to the data set for the role of workers.

The results of Study 2 suggested the following five main strengths of the method:

1. Capacity to differentiate groups. The results of the study provided reasonable evidence of the method's capacity to detect differences between the divisions, in this case, in members' experience of the role of divisional workers (supervisors). There was evidence, for example, that respondents from the two divisions differed in the criteria which they used to judge the effectiveness of the workers (supervisors) in their division, as well as in the criteria used to classify a worker (supervisor) as a best worker (best supervisor). Differences were also indicated in respondents' past experience of the role of workers (supervisors) in their division and in the extent of their experience of the role played by workers (supervisors) in other organisations. The point can be made that the differences identified in this regard were, on the whole, consistent with the researcher's impression of cultural differences between the divisions.

2. Explanations and elaborations as a key to understanding. The results of the study confirmed the importance of asking respondents to explain, or elaborate on, their responses to the questions they were asked. While this information might have been sought more consistently than it was — this point has implications for the subsequent revision of the method — when it was provided (whether in response to prompting, or spontaneously), it proved valuable for a number of reasons. For example, it served to clarify the meanings of respondents' ratings of the respective roles of workers and supervisors — whether more or less passive or active in the case of workers, or more or less directive or consultative in the case of supervisors — and, in so doing, revealed the extent to which these meanings were consistent with one another and also consistent with the meanings intended by the researcher. Similarly, in the case of respondents' satisfaction ratings, qualifying and elaborative data proved valuable insofar as they provided a check on whether or not a respondent's expressed satisfaction, or dissatisfaction, was actually related to the topic under investigation. For example, there was one instance in which these data revealed that, instead of rating his satisfaction/dissatisfaction with the role played by the workers in his division (as he had been asked to do), the respondent had rated his satisfaction/dissatisfaction with the quality, or calibre, of the particular workers for whom he was directly responsible.

In the present study, the opportunity to explain, or elaborate on, their responses also allowed those respondents who felt unable to express an opinion about some aspect of their division *as a whole*, to indicate that this was so. While it might be argued that the obvious way to deal with such contingencies, at least in the case of forced-choice questions, would be to include a "cannot respond" or "don't know" response category, there is a danger that, if given the opportunity *not* to express an opinion about a particular issue, respondents may be less likely to think seriously about the issue than they would be if no such opportunity existed. In this sense, an advantage of the present method, which includes no formal response categories of this kind, is that respondents are unlikely to admit that they are unable to answer a question, without first having given the question (along with its various response options, where these were specified) some, hopefully careful, thought.

3. Vindication of a semi-structured interview format. The above arguments regarding the value of qualifying and elaborative data are not intended as a case against the degree of structure which was adopted in the present method. Given the more systematic approach to the assessment of organisational (group) culture that was sought, it would have been inappropriate for the method to have taken the form of a completely unstructured interview. In seeking information about a particular aspect of organisational (group) culture — in this case, beliefs and assumptions about the respective roles of workers and supervisors — it was important to obtain a body of coherent information of relevance to the topic at hand. Clearly, this would not have been possible without the use of some fairly highly focussed questions, the responses to which could be shown to be linked in meaningful ways. As indicated, the results of the study provided evidence of a number of such linkages — for example, the link between respondents' past experience of the role of workers (supervisors) and their current perceptions of this role — and, in this sense, the adoption of a more structured format for the present method can be seen to have been vindicated.

4. Potential cultural significance of contextual data. Another feature of the method that seemed to work well was the inclusion of specific questions about the context of respondents' experience. As indicated above, there was some evidence to suggest that knowledge of respondents' past experience could valuably inform an understanding of respondents' perceptions of their current experience. For example, the knowledge that respondents from the production division had had some past experience of a more active role for divisional workers (through their involvement in the team concept) helped to explain the perception, among these respondents, that the workers in their division at the present time played a predominantly passive role. Another important insight provided by the data pertaining to the past context was that, within a given group, individuals could differ in terms of what, for them, constituted the meaningful past. The finding that respondents referred to different periods of time when they talked about the past and that, for a given respondent, her/his chronological past could differ from her/his subjectively important past, highlighted the need to seek more specific information about the time frame of respondents' past experience in the subsequent revision of the method.

Questions about the future and other contexts, while they were of less obvious value than questions about the past context, were nevertheless also shown to generate information of potential cultural significance. With respect to the former, there was evidence to suggest that information about the future context might provide some insight into the affective dimension of an organisation's (group's) culture and that this, in turn, along with members' ability, or lack thereof, to clearly articulate a future, might provide clues as to the organisation's (group's) likely responsiveness to change. With respect to the latter context, the finding that respondents from the tooling division had had less experience of other organisations than their counterparts from the production division suggested the possibility that experience of other organisations might help to explain the degree of embeddedness of an organisation's (group's) culture.

There was also evidence to suggest that contextual information may be of value in that it may highlight differences between organisations (or subcultures) in the particular aspect, or domain, of context (whether the present, the past, the anticipated future, or the other) which is most dominant in members' thinking (and which may, therefore, have been most influential in shaping the culture of the organisation (or subculture). As indicated, the finding in the present study that respondents from the tooling division, when talking about their anticipated future experience, frequently made reference to their past experience, confirmed the researcher's impression that this division (more so than the production division) supported a culture which was very strongly rooted in the past.

Overall, the above arguments would seem to provide fairly strong grounds for the further investigation of the way in which organisation (group) members' experience in relation to different domains of context might inform an understanding of the organisation's (group's) culture.

5. **Potential cultural significance of attributions data.** Finally, the results of the study provided further support for the argument (suggested by the results of Study 1) that attributions data may be of value for understanding organisational culture. As indicated, there was evidence to suggest that the two divisions might differ in terms of members' attributions concerning why things may, or may not, change in the future. It would be interesting in the forthcoming study to look more carefully at members' causal attributions and, in particular, to try to establish the extent to which these reflect a consistent, or common, style. A useful modification to the present method in this regard would be to seek information, not only about members' perceptions of the cause of anticipated changes, but also about their perceptions of the cause of changes already experienced.

The results of Study 2 suggested the following four shortcomings of the method:

1. **Theory X — Theory Y dimensions difficult to operationalise.** One feature of the method which was found to work less well than expected was the attempt to arrive at some classification of the respective roles of workers in the two divisions, in terms of McGregor's (1960) Theory X and Theory Y dimensions. As indicated, a number of problems were encountered in this regard. For example, with respect to the Theory X — Theory Y rating question, it was found that respondents' interpretations of the key terms used to describe these dimensions — passive and active in the case of the role of workers, and directive and consultative in the case of the role of supervisors — were not always consistent with the interpretations intended. It was also the case that the description of each of these dimensions in terms of a number of characteristic behaviours (attitudes) — this was necessitated by the complexity of the dimensions — gave rise to the problem of some respondents basing their rating, not on a consideration of the full range of characteristic behaviours (attitudes) specified, but rather on the basis of a consideration of a single behaviour (attitude) which may have had particular salience for the respondent.

Another limitation of this feature of the method to which attention was drawn was that, contrary to what was intended, it was not always possible to classify respondents' responses to the subsequent context questions in terms of the Theory X — Theory Y dimensions. In other words, despite being prompted to do so, there were some respondents who failed to draw on these dimensions when describing the role of divisional workers (supervisors) in the past, the anticipated future, and in relation to the other context. This finding, along with the interpretive inconsistencies referred to above, raised questions about the extent to which these dimensions were relevant or salient to respondents themselves, insofar as offering them a framework within which they could meaningfully classify their experience. Even though there was evidence to suggest that respondents from the production division may have been somewhat more at ease than their counterparts from the tooling division, in the application of these dimensions — this was attributed to the members of this division having had some actual experience of the contrasting roles of workers and supervisors which these dimensions attempted to represent — the problem remains that one cannot assume, *a priori*, that these dimensions will necessarily be relevant to organisation members.

In view of the above arguments, there would seem to be little value in attempting to directly measure a collective phenomenon, such as organisational culture, using hypothetical dimensions such as those identified by McGregor.

2. Evaluation of the role of workers (supervisors) posed difficulties. The evaluation questions constituted a second feature of the method that proved to be less useful than anticipated. As indicated, in the case of the satisfaction question, there was evidence to suggest that respondents' satisfaction ratings may not always have been related to the topic under investigation (the example was given above of the respondent who rated his satisfaction/dissatisfaction with the quality of the workers for whom he was directly responsible). This finding suggested the conclusion that, while respondents might easily be able to rate their satisfaction/dissatisfaction with those aspects of their experience that are tangible and concrete (their subordinates, supervisors, conditions of work, *etc.*), it might be unrealistic to expect them to rate their satisfaction/dissatisfaction with more abstract notions, such as in this case, the role of workers (supervisors). In this sense, it was argued that the satisfaction question possibly suffered from being overly academic.

In the case of the effectiveness question, respondents' explanations of their effectiveness ratings proved to be less revealing than it was hoped they would be, insofar as providing insights into their beliefs about what constituted an appropriate role for workers (supervisors). As indicated, it was sometimes difficult to infer effectiveness criteria — that is, the criteria used, by participants, to evaluate the effectiveness of the workers (supervisors) in their division — from respondents' explanations of their effectiveness ratings. There was also evidence that, in some cases, respondents based their evaluations of the effectiveness of workers (supervisors) not, as intended, on criteria which they themselves considered to be important but rather on criteria which they believed the organisation (presumably management) regarded as important. The failure of the method to adequately distinguish between respondents' personal values and the values which respondents believed were supported by the organisation, is a subject to which attention is again drawn in point 3 below.

3. Best/worst worker (best/worst supervisor) data provided limited cultural insights. Finally, the results of the study highlighted a number of flaws in the design of the personal experience questions (that asked about respondents' best/worst worker and best/worst supervisor). As indicated, one of the main problems in this regard was that these questions provided, at best, equivocal information only about the particular worker (supervisor) qualities and characteristics that were/were not valued in each division. For example, the variability indicated in the responses to part (a) of these questions (that sought information about the qualities of respondents' best/worst worker) left some doubt as to the importance, to the *group*, of those qualities that were not mentioned by a majority of respondents. One possibility that was suggested in this regard was that the qualities identified by some respondents as being important may have been equally important to other respondents who, for whatever reason, had simply forgotten to mention them. In a similar vein, there was a degree of uncertainty about the cultural significance of the qualities that respondents ascribed to their best/worst worker (supervisor) in response to the latter parts of these questions (which asked about the worker's (supervisor's) view of the organisation and the nature of her/his relationship with supervision and with co-workers). For example, as indicated, the finding that all respondents from the tooling division attributed a positive worker-supervisor relationship to their best worker could not necessarily be interpreted to mean that, in this division, a worker's classification as a best worker was *dependent upon* her/him having this quality.

There were a number of additional shortcomings of the personal experience questions to which the results of the study drew attention. For example, there was some evidence that the focus on extremes — in this case, best and worst workers (supervisors) — may have resulted in the identification of worker (supervisor) characteristics that were idiosyncratic rather than, as intended, more generally approved of, or more generally disapproved of. It was also the case that, while the questions pertaining to worst workers (supervisors) were valuable insofar as they elicited information which, to a large extent, confirmed the findings of questions pertaining to best workers, they were redundant in the sense that they provided few additional insights of relevance to an understanding of the cultures of the two divisions being investigated.

On the basis of the above limitations, a number of suggestions were made (more or less explicitly) regarding how the personal experience questions might usefully be modified. Briefly summarised, these suggestions included: (i) the removal of Question 6, pertaining to worst workers (worst supervisors); (ii) a shift in the focus of the inquiry to seek information about good workers (good supervisors) as opposed to best workers (best supervisors); (iii) the use of a more direct form of questioning along the lines of "What does a worker (supervisor) have to do to be thought of as a good worker (good supervisor)?"; (iv) the possible inclusion of specific prompts about behaviours in which a worker (supervisor) might engage in order to be thought of as a good worker (good supervisor); and (v) the drawing of a distinction between the respondent's personal values regarding what makes a good worker (good supervisor) and the respondent's beliefs about what the organisation values in this regard.

4. Restricted sample. A final limitation that needs to be acknowledged with respect to the above comments is that participants in the study were restricted to workers and their immediate supervisors. It is possible that managers, and particularly managers who have received formal training, might be more likely to interpret the questions (e.g., those relating to the Theory X — Theory Y framework) as intended by the researcher. They might also be more likely to answer questions about best and worst workers (supervisors) in line with the values of the organisation, rather than in terms of their own personal values. If such differences between different levels or job roles within an organisation were to be found, it would have important implications for studies seeking to investigate possible subcultures. Apparent differences suggesting different subcultures might be partly due to the respondents in those apparent subcultures providing different answers to questions because they have interpreted the questions in different ways.

9.6 Conclusions

Overall, Study 2 can be judged to have been a useful study with respect to its main aim of piloting the prototype method that we had developed, based on insights from Study 1. The study enabled us to evaluate the design features of the method, and in particular, to ascertain the efficacy of the questions in the interview protocol for generating meaningful information about the issue being investigated — in this case, the category of cultural beliefs and assumptions in Schein's typology concerned with the nature of human nature. The results of the study provided a clear demonstration that the untested use of the questions proposed — that is, their use without a careful evaluation of the kind undertaken in this study — may have led to conclusions being drawn, and inferences being made, that were at best uncertain, and at worst inaccurate, in terms of capturing an aspect of the culture of the group(s) studied.

We turn now to Part Five of this volume in which we report on the third and final study in our research towards the development of an effective and efficient method for the assessment of deeper-level culture. In Study 3, our exploration of method continues, but with modifications to the interview design and protocol, based on the lessons learned from Study 2.

Appendix A

STUDY 2 INTERVIEW PROTOCOL

Part A: The Role of Workers

Open-ended question

Q1: What do the workers in this division do?

Theory X, Theory Y rating

Q2: In some organisations (or work groups) the role of workers is primarily a *passive* one. Workers are seen by their supervisors, and see themselves, primarily as people who follow instructions and carry out orders. This does not mean that workers are lazy, or that they don't get things done, but rather that what they do, and how they do it, is usually decided upon by someone else. Workers who play a passive role tend to do pretty much as they are told to do, and accept things mostly without question.

In other organisations (or work groups) workers play a more *active* role. This means that they have more input into, and take more responsibility for, decisions that affect them. They are more inclined to take the initiative for solving their own problems and, if they have an idea about how to improve things, they will say so. Workers who play an active role are also more likely to challenge, rather than simply accept, things that they don't understand, or that they disagree with.

Now, think about the role of workers in this division at the present time. Tick the description that corresponds most closely to your perception of the role of workers in this division.

very passive	----
moderately passive	----
slightly passive	----
slightly active	----
moderately active	----
very active	----

Evaluation questions

Q3: How satisfied are you with the role that workers play in this division at the present time? Please tick one.

extremely satisfied	----
moderately satisfied	----
slightly satisfied	----

neither satisfied nor dissatisfied   ----
slightly dissatisfied   ----
moderately dissatisfied   ----
extremely dissatisfied   ----

Q4: How would you rate the effectiveness of the workers in this division at the present time? Please tick one.

extremely effective   ----
moderately effective   ----
slightly effective   ----
neither effective
nor ineffective   ----
slightly ineffective   ----
moderately ineffective   ----
very ineffective   ----
Give reasons for your rating.

Personal experience questions

Q5: Think about the *best* worker you have ever had (worked with, known) in this division.

a) What was it that you admired or liked about this worker?
b) How important is it to you that workers have these particular characteristics (attitudes, behaviours)? Why?
c) What was this worker's view of the organisation?
d) How did this worker relate to supervision?
e) How did this worker relate to his/her co-workers?

Q6: Think about the *worst* worker you have ever had (worked with, known) in this division.

a) What was it that you disliked, or regarded as problematic, about this worker?
b) What was this worker's view of the organisation?
c) How did this worker relate to supervision?
d) How did this worker relate to his/her co-workers?

Context questions

Q7: What was the role played by workers in this division in the past? Did it differ? How? Give examples. How long ago was this?

Q8: Do you think that the role played by workers in this division at the present time is likely to change/stay the same? If you think that it will change, how will it change? Why will it change in this way? If you think that it will stay the same, why?

Q9: Are you aware of the role played by workers in other organisations? Give examples. What was the nature of the other organisation(s) and how did you come to know about it?

Part B: The Role of Supervisors

Open-ended question

Q1: What do the supervisors in this division do?

Theory X, Theory Y rating

Q2: In some organisations (work groups) the role of supervisors is primarily a *directive* one. That is, the supervisor's job is limited to giving workers instructions about what to do, and then making sure that these instructions are carried out.

In other organisations (work groups) supervisors plays more of a *consultative* role. That is, in addition to providing direction, the supervisor also encourages workers to come up with their own ideas which she/he then discusses with them. The supervisor tries to provide workers with the guidance and support that they need to perform their work effectively and to gain satisfaction from it.

Now, think about the role of supervisors in this division at the present time. Tick the description that corresponds most closely to your perception of the role of supervisors in this division.

very directive	----
moderately directive	----
slightly directive	----
slightly consultative	----
moderately consultative	----
very consultative	----

Evaluation questions

Q3: How satisfied are you with the role that supervisors play in this division at the present time? Please tick one.

extremely satisfied	----
moderately satisfied	----
slightly satisfied	----
neither satisfied	
nor dissatisfied	----
slightly dissatisfied	----

moderately dissatisfied ----

extremely dissatisfied ----

Q4: How would you rate the effectiveness of the supervisors in this division at the present time? Please tick one.

extremely effective ----

moderately effective ----

slightly effective ----

neither effective

nor ineffective ----

slightly ineffective ----

moderately ineffective ----

extremely ineffective ----

Give reasons for your rating.

Personal experience questions

Q5: Think about the *best* supervisor you have ever had in this division.

a) What was it that you valued most about this supervisor?

b) How important do you think it is for supervisors to have these particular characteristics (attitudes, behaviours)? Why?

c) What was this supervisor's view of the organisation?

d) How did this supervisor relate to employees in general?

e) How did this supervisor relate to you in particular?

Q6: Think about the *worst* supervisor you have ever had in this division.

a) What was it that you disliked, or regarded as problematic, about this supervisor?

b) What was this supervisor's view of the organisation?

c) How did this supervisor relate to employees in general?

d) How did this supervisor relate to you in particular?

Context questions

Q7: What was the role played by supervisors in this division in the past? Did it differ? How? Give examples. How long ago was this?

Q8: Do you think that the role played by supervisors in this division at the present time is likely to change/stay the same? If you think it will change, how and why? If you think it will stay the same, why?

Q9: Are you aware of the role played by supervisors in other organisations? Give examples. What was nature of the other organisation(s) and how did you come to know about it?

PART FIVE
ANALYSING CONTEXT

Chapter 10

Towards a Refinement of the Method
(Study 3, Part 1)

Insights from the findings of Study 2 were used as the basis for a number of modifications to our proposed method. In this and the next two chapters (i.e., Chapters 10 through 12), we provide an account of the third and final study in this series, the main aim of which was to comprehensively evaluate the key features of the revised method, again through trialling it in the two participating divisions of the research organisation. Given the magnitude of Study 3, the substantive contents of this study are presented in the three chapters that comprise Part Five of this volume. The present chapter introduces Study 3 and describes the main modifications to the method that were made, along with the key design features of the revised method. This chapter also provides procedural information concerning the method and its administration, the approach to data analysis, and the format for the reporting of results. In the next two chapters, we report and discuss the main findings of Study 3. Chapter 11 is concerned with the findings pertaining to the use of semi-structured interviewing in the revised method, and Chapter 12 is concerned with the findings pertaining to the operationalisation of various domains, or dimensions, of context.

In terms of the broader evaluation of the method used in Study 3, the point should be made that this is presented in Part Six of this volume, rather than in the chapters comprising Part Five. Specifically, in Chapter 13, we provide an evaluation of the revised method (in terms of each of its key features and also more generally in terms of how it compares to other methods for assessing organisational culture), and we also consider the possibilities for future research that are suggested by the combined results of the three studies that make up the present research.

10.1 Introduction to Study 3

The results of Studies 1 and 2, which were reported in Chapters 8 and 9 respectively, constituted the building blocks for a third and final study designed to evaluate the key elements of our proposed (and revised) method for assessing the deeper-level beliefs and assumptions that comprise what Schein (1985, 1992, 2004, 2010) refers to as the 'essence' of an organisation's culture. As indicated in Volume I (see, in particular, Chapters 2 and 6), organisational culture at this level — Level 3 in Schein's framework — has proven to be more difficult to assess effectively and efficiently than organisational culture at the more surface levels of artefacts and normative behaviours (at Level 1), and values (at Level 2).

The main reason for this difficulty is that Level 3 beliefs and assumptions tend to be mostly taken-for-granted and unconsciously held by members of the organisation. This is assumed to occur as a result of repeated adaptations that the organisation and its members make over an extended period of time, to the external and internal challenges that they face. This process eventually gives rise to normative behaviours and associated beliefs and assumptions about what constitutes the right way to deal with such challenges. Over time, organisation members become progressively less aware of these beliefs and assumptions, and it becomes more difficult for them to answer direct questions (e.g., such as those in a questionnaire) about them. This means that a more indirect approach to the assessment of culture at this level is required.

As has already been pointed out in Chapter 6 of Volume I, Schein (1985) began his attempts to measure deeper-level culture by having individuals (or alternatively groups) discuss questions related to the categories of basic beliefs and assumptions outlined in the work of Kluckhohn and Strodtbeck (1961). As indicated in later editions of his book, Schein (1992, 2004, 2010) has since moved away from this kind of direct approach to assessing an organisation's overall culture, and has adopted a more issue-focussed approach (often concerning change) in which group discussions are used to surface the more deeply held cultural beliefs and assumptions that are related to that issue.

In terms of our own research in this area, our aim, as indicated, was to develop a method for the assessment of deeper-level cultural beliefs and assumptions that is more systematic and more efficient than traditional anthropological, or ethnographic, approaches (that involve the investigator spending a considerable amount of time in an organisation, observing and recording behaviour and activities from which deeper-level culture might be inferred). The first study in our research (reported in Chapter 8) was an entirely exploratory study. It was valuable insofar as the findings enabled us to identify a topic (or issue) that would be suitable as a focus for the method being developed. This study also provided insights into the types of questions that might usefully be included in the method. In particular, the findings drew attention to the possible value of questions about contextual aspects of respondents' experience of the issue (e.g., the issue as experienced in the past and as envisaged in the future), and questions about respondents' attributions concerning, in particular, the causes of changes in the issue as experienced from one contextual domain to another (e.g., from the past to the present). Subsequently, the insights from Study 1 were used to inform the development of a prototype measure. This measure was essentially our first attempt to systematically investigate an aspect of organisational culture (in this case, the role of workers and supervisors) by asking the kinds of questions that the findings of Study 1 suggested might usefully be asked in this regard. This measure was trialled, and its key features evaluated, in the second study in this research.

As above, drawing on insights from the findings of Study 2 (reported in Chapter 9), we subsequently revised the method being developed and this revised method was trialled and evaluated in our third and final study (reported in this and the following two chapters). Broadly speaking (and as will be seen below), the revision of the method that was undertaken involved retaining, and as deemed necessary, making modifications to, those aspects of the method that showed promise with respect to the assessment of organisational culture, and removing those aspects of the method that seemed to be ineffective, or redundant, in this regard. As with Study 2, the main aim of Study 3 was evaluative. This study, like the one before it, sought information about the extent to which the method (in its revised form) offered a useful means by which to investigate aspects of an organisation's deeper-level culture.

10.2 Key Design Features of the Revised Method

In this section, we describe the key design features of the method for assessing organisational culture that was used in Study 3. Where relevant, reference is made to how the method differs — in its design — from the method used in Study 2. Four key design features are described, each constituting a separate sub-section of the discussion below.

10.2.1 *Issue-focussed interview*

The method took the form of what Sackmann (1991) has called an 'issue-focussed' interview. In Study 3, however, the focus of interviewing was somewhat narrower than it was in Study 2. Whereas the method, in its original form, had been designed to tap prevailing views about both workers and supervisors[1] — through questioning about the respective roles of workers and supervisors — the revised method was concerned only with how workers were viewed. The decision to narrow the focus of interviewing in Study 3 in this way was based on the finding, from Study 2, that information pertaining to the role of supervisors was largely redundant in the sense that it provided few additional *methodological* insights over and above those which had been provided by information pertaining to the role of workers. In attempting to infer organisation (group) members' beliefs about the essential nature of workers, the specific focus was, once again, on the role of workers. However, in the revised method, interviewing was structured around two separate subtopics (each of which had been addressed, but not clearly differentiated, in Study 2). The first of these was concerned with what workers do (i.e., their duties and activities), and the second was concerned with the defining characteristics of 'good' workers (previously, 'best' workers).

At this point, it is perhaps worth drawing the reader's attention again to the exploratory nature of the present research. The aim of this research was not to describe divisional culture in a car company per se but rather, as indicated, to test out a new method for investigating workplace culture. In view of this, it was important, indeed necessary, that the

---

[1] Such views can be regarded as constituting an organisational subset of beliefs and assumptions about The Nature of Human Nature — one of the categories of beliefs and assumptions in Schein's typology (1985, 1992, 2004, 2010).

method took the form of an issue-focussed interview. Had the interview lacked a specific focus (e.g., if respondents had been allowed to talk very generally about their experience of organisational life), it would have been very difficult to evaluate the extent to which particular features of the method had, or had not, 'worked'. This issue-focussed approach is similar to that used by Schein (2010) in his attempts to uncover deeper levels of organisational culture by focusing on a particular issue (often concerning change) that organisation members are facing. However, unlike Schein, who uses a group approach, the current method used individual interviews. This was because, in our view, individual interviews would provide a means of assessing the extent to which responses were similar, or different, without the possibility of group dynamics leading to a consensus (or lack of it) that did not properly represent the independent views of those participating.

10.2.2 *Semi-structured interview*

In the revised method, the semi-structured interview format, whereby open-ended and closed questions were combined, was also retained. This feature of the method differed, however, insofar as modifications had been made to the specific questions that were asked, in addition to which there was a more direct link between the open-ended and closed questions than there had been previously. For each sub-topic being addressed, respondents were first of all presented with an open-ended question about that topic. Thus, in Part A of the interview, respondents were asked, first of all, to comment on their perception of what it was that the workers in their division did at the present time (in terms of their main duties, as well as any other activities in which they were engaged); in Part B of the interview, respondents were asked about the characteristics of those workers in their division who were generally regarded as being good workers. The decision to ask about good workers rather than best workers was based on evidence from Study 2 that the latter question elicited answers that tended to be more personal and idiosyncratic, and therefore potentially less informative about the organisation's (group's) culture. The inclusion in the revised protocol of these initial open-ended questions (similar to that asked in the original protocol) was supported by evidence from Study 2 suggesting that, while such questions may not elicit very detailed, or very articulate responses, they nevertheless give a sense of respondents' spontaneous thinking about the issue under investigation. It can also be argued that such questions serve the additional purpose of providing a platform from which to begin to explore the issue in more depth.

In the revised protocol, for each sub-topic being investigated, the initial open-ended question was followed by a series of closed questions, or prompts. These prompts were linked directly to the subject of the open-ended question and were designed to elicit additional information of relevance to this question. Thus, in Part A of the interview, respondents were prompted as to the involvement of the workers in their division in a number of specific activities in which workers might reasonably be expected to engage (including, e.g., attendance at meetings of various kinds, record-keeping activities, participation in training and development programs, and participation in social activities). In Part B of the interview, respondents were prompted as to the importance, in their division, of a number of specific worker characteristics (including, e.g., initiative, compliance, efficiency, and team skills), each of which could potentially influence judgements about whether or not a worker was a good worker. In both Part A and Part B of the interview, a given prompt was presented *only* if the information sought by that prompt had not already been provided spontaneously, that is, in response to the open-ended question.

There were two main reasons for the inclusion, in the revised protocol, of this form of prompting. First, there was evidence from Study 2 to suggest that the open-ended questions alone might be limited with respect to their capacity to reveal what is cultural and what is not. As indicated, the responses to such questions can be quite variable and this creates the problem of not knowing whether aspects of their experience to which some respondents refer in answering these questions might not be equally relevant to other respondents who, for whatever reason, simply failed to mention them. A hoped-for outcome of the revised method was that the particular combination of open-ended and closed questions (or prompts) adopted would go some way toward resolving this problem. In particular it was hoped that, for each sub-topic addressed, the information generated by the prompts, when combined with that elicited spontaneously (i.e., in response to the open-ended question) would provide a more accurate, and more complete, picture of those aspects of respondents' experience that had relevance for the group, as a whole. The second reason for the inclusion of specific prompts of the kind described above was that it provided a means whereby relatively detailed information about the topic in question might be elicited relatively quickly. It was hoped that this, in turn, might increase the likelihood of drawing the respondent's attention to aspects of her/his experience that, because of their taken-for-granted nature, might not normally be mentioned and might require considerable time to bring them to the surface if qualitative methods alone were being used.

It is important to point out that the choice of an appropriate set of prompts for each of the sub-topics addressed in the revised protocol was not made arbitrarily. Rather, it was guided by insights from Study 2 (in particular, concerning the kinds of worker activities and worker qualities that participants in this study seemed to value), as well as the researcher's[2] more general knowledge of the two research divisions and their respective orientations to the role of workers. In addition, and as for the development of the Theory X — Theory Y rating questions in Study 2, the development of these prompt sets was guided, in part, by McGregor's (1960) distinction between Theory X and Theory Y assumptions about the essential nature of workers. Drawing on the most salient aspects of McGregor's conceptualisation of these contrasting views, an attempt was made to include, in each prompt set, some prompts that could be classified as indicative of a Theory X

---

[2]As indicated in Chapter 8, this is a reference to the first author who undertook the empirical work for the three studies that are reported in Parts Four and Five of this volume.

orientation to the role of workers and some prompts that could be classified as indicative of a Theory Y orientation. For example, in Part A of the interview, the involvement of workers in meetings which require their active participation (e.g., planning and work group meetings), would imply more of a Theory Y orientation to the role of workers, whereas the involvement of workers *only* in those meetings in which they play a passive role (e.g., information meetings), would suggest more of a Theory X orientation. In Part B of the interview, a quality such as being prepared to question, and suggest alternatives to, current approaches — to the extent that it is valued — would be suggestive of a Theory Y orientation; a quality such as compliance — to the extent that it is valued — would be suggestive of a Theory X orientation.

The attempt, in the revised protocol, to incorporate the Theory X — Theory Y distinction into the design of each of the prompt sets can be seen, at least partially, as a response to the problems that were encountered with the Theory X — Theory Y rating question that was included in the original protocol. As suggested by the results of Study 2, attempts to access theoretical dimensions such as those identified by McGregor, through the use of direct questioning about these dimensions, are unlikely to be successful. A more effective alternative may be to use a less direct method, such as that being proposed, whereby information is sought from which one can infer the relevance, or otherwise, of these dimensions. An implication of this approach is that just as personality researchers experimented with different questions that were designed to indirectly reveal dimensions of an individual's personality, rather than trying to assess these dimensions directly, so too in seeking to assess dimensions of organisational culture, considerable experimentation with questions may need to occur before arriving at those questions most likely to access the particular aspect(s) of deeper-level culture of interest.

In addition to the particular combination of open-ended and closed questions (prompts) described above, an important feature of the semi-structured interview format that was adopted was that it assumed a degree of in-built flexibility. That is, although the revised protocol had a relatively high degree of structure, in its actual administration, the interviewer provided respondents with considerable latitude to elaborate on, or qualify, their responses. The reason for this was that, as suggested by the results of Study 2, qualitative data of this kind can provide important insights into the meanings which respondents themselves attach to the answers that they give, and these meanings, in turn, can have important implications for understanding the culture of the organisation (group) being studied. Interviewing in Study 3 also allowed a certain amount of what Measor (1985, cited in Bryman, 1988, p. 46) has called "rambling", whereby respondents spontaneously move away from formally designated topics to explore issues which are of more immediate interest to them. Where this occurred, the additional data generated were not discarded but, rather, were used to build upon insights gained from data generated by questions included in the formal schedule. Finally, allowance was made for the tendency of some respondents to pre-empt standardised questions. For example, it was not uncommon for respondents from the older tooling division to pre-empt standardised questions about the past[3], by referring spontaneously to their past when responding to questions about the present. Where this occurred, the respondent was allowed to continue uninterrupted for the time taken to give her/his particular train of thought closure, after which the interviewer would redirect the focus of interviewing.

The above feature of the method has important implications for the skills of the interviewer. It requires the interviewer to maintain an effective balance between, on the one hand, accommodating a level of 'rambling' that is useful (insofar as maintaining rapport and generating data that may be culturally significant) and, on the other hand, ensuring a sufficiently tight focus on the interview to ensure that time is not wasted obtaining information that is irrelevant to cultural considerations. It has already been pointed out in Chapter 6 of Volume I that little information tends to be provided on the formal interviewing skills required of researchers involved in qualitative studies of organisational culture, in spite of the considerable evidence that exists regarding common interviewer biases, including the inadvertent use of leading questions. The work of Margaret Mead and the critique of her work by Freeman (1983) were mentioned as an example of how a well-intentioned attempt at a scientific approach to this kind of assessment in anthropology can produce inaccurate results.

10.2.3 *The operationalisation of context*

As indicated, the results of Study 2 provided evidence to suggest that the more systematic examination of the context of organisation members' experience might contribute valuably to the assessment of organisational culture. In particular, the treatment of context as a multi-dimensional phenomenon — comprising a number of different dimensions, or domains — emerged as a promising avenue of inquiry in this regard. In this section, we first describe the treatment of context in the revised method and how this differs from the treatment of context in Study 2. Then, by way of a more general rationale for this particular design feature, we consider some of the evidence in the organisational culture literature — pertaining to both conceptualisations of organisational culture and its operationalisation — that would seem to support the conclusion based on our own research that a method for the assessment of deeper-level culture might valuably include an explicit focus on different dimensions of context. Importantly, this discussion draws on material already presented in Chapter 7 of Volume I. The decision to summarise aspects of this previous discussion in the present chapter was made, in part, for the benefit of the reader, and also because this discussion draws attention to the fact that there does exist at least some theoretical grounding for this feature of the method.

---

[3] See Section 10.3.1 for a description of questions about context.

10.2.3.1 *Context in the revised method*

Given evidence from Study 2 attesting to the value of an explicit focus on context, this feature of the design of the original method was retained. As previously, information was sought about the respondent's past experience with respect to the issue under investigation, her/his anticipated future experience, and her/his experience in relation to other organisations. However, an important modification that was made to this aspect of the method was the inclusion of a focus on what was called the 'ideal' context. Questioning in relation to this contextual domain sought information about the respondent's views regarding how things *ought to be* — in this case, what workers *should* do (in terms of their duties/activities) and what the defining characteristics of good workers ideally *should* be. To clarify further, and with reference to the particular treatment of context adopted in the present research, the ideal context might reasonably be seen as constituting the evaluative dimension of context.

In terms of the rationale for this change, questions about the ideal context were, broadly speaking, intended to take the place of, or offer a (hopefully) better alternative to, questions in the original protocol which sought information about what the respondent her/himself valued, or considered to be important. Examples of such questions from the original protocol include the effectiveness question, in which the respondent was asked to explain her/his rating of worker effectiveness, and the personal experience questions which asked about the characteristics of the respondent's best worker and worst worker respectively. As indicated, these questions were designed to provide information about the particular worker behaviours (attitudes *etc.*) which the respondent her/himself regarded as being important, and which she/he would take into account in evaluating a worker's worth. In the final analysis, however, these questions were shown to suffer from a number of methodological shortcomings and it seemed that a more direct form of questioning might be needed in order to more readily access the kind of information being sought. Thus, in the revised protocol, the respondent was asked explicitly about her/his own values regarding the role of workers. The point can also be made that the addition of these questions to the revised protocol provided a means by which to more easily detect differences between what the respondent valued and what the respondent perceived the organisation to value (the former being the subject of questioning in relation to the ideal context and the latter, the subject of questioning in relation to the present context). While the original protocol did not explicitly seek information about this distinction, it nevertheless emerged as being a relevant distinction for some of the participants in Study 2.

It is worth noting that the treatment of context adopted in the present research has, as far as we are aware, no precedent in the literature. However, as indicated in Chapter 7 of Volume I, existing conceptualisations of organisational culture do provide some support for the notion that context might usefully be thought of as a multi-dimensional phenomenon. In the following section, we provide a brief overview of some of the extant evidence in this regard.

10.2.3.2 *Context in existing conceptualisations of organisational culture*

As indicated above, the discussion in this section draws on material already presented in Chapter 7 of Volume I (though in its present form, constituting a much abridged version of the latter). For each contextual dimension considered, we first comment on existing conceptualisations of organisational culture in which reference is made (more or less explicitly) to the relevance, or importance, of that dimension. Following this, we offer some brief speculative comments about how changes in the operating environment of contemporary organisations might impact upon the relative importance, or salience, of that dimension for understanding organisational culture.

The historical context. As we have suggested in Chapter 7, the historical context is acknowledged more or less explicitly in most scholarly treatments of the concept of organisational culture. The view of culture as comprising shared ways of interpreting and dealing with problems — that ultimately become part of an organisation's assumed or taken-for-granted knowledge — clearly necessitates the passage of a certain period of time. The emphasis on the historical context in this respect draws attention to a potential source of differentiation between 'strong' and 'weak' organisational cultures. Thus, for example, Wilkins and Ouchi (1983) argue that an important condition for the development of 'clan' cultures — cultures characterised by a high level of consensus among members — is a long history, combined with a relatively stable group membership. More 'practitioner-oriented' treatments of the concept of organisational culture also emphasise the importance of the passage of time. A case in point is Kantrow's (1984) depiction of the development of an organisation's culture as being analogous to the build-up of a coral reef. An important practical implication of this view is that culture change is likely to be much more difficult to achieve than many management training programs would suggest.

While treatments of the past — as an important contextual dimension for understanding organisational culture — have generally emphasised the passage of time and an implied slow passive accumulation of significant events, as we suggested in our discussion of this issue in Chapter 7, it may be that what is important for culture formation in organisations is the *number* of significant events over a given time span in the past, and not just the passage of time. We also argued in Chapter 7 that, given the increased pace of change in modern organisations, and the increased prevalence of professional subcultures, the formation of culture in some organisations may have been more rapid and more active than one might have predicted, given the common representation of this process as slow and passive, and analogous to the development of a coral reef.

The future context. While conceptual treatments of organisational culture have given more emphasis to the historical context than to any other contextual domain, there are some treatments in which the emphasis is on an implied future context. Thus, for example, it has been argued that an organisation's culture can influence the strategic choices that are made by an organisation (e.g., Donaldson & Lorsch, 1983; Schein, 1985, 1992, 2004, 2010). Conversely, it has been suggested that cultural meanings might themselves be influenced by the expectations that organisation members have about the future (e.g., Pettigrew, 1979). It would seem reasonable, therefore, that any attempt to understand an organisation's culture should take account of the expectations that organisation members have about the future, and how these might shape, and be shaped by, the organisation's culture.

As above for the past as context, one might expect that changes in the operating environment of contemporary organisations will also impact on the future as context. In Chapter 7, we suggested that the pace of change in modern organisations, along with the variety of challenges that modern organisations face — related, for example, to increased competition (local, national, and international), government legislation, changes in the workforce and in the role and influence of unions — might contribute to an increased concern with how the organisation is likely to perform in the future.

The other context. As indicated in Chapter 7, the relevance of the 'other' context for understanding organisational culture is implied in conceptualisations that draw attention to a group's social isolation from other groups, as a factor influencing the strength or embeddedness of the group's culture. Thus, for example, Wilkins and Ouchi (1983) have argued that lack of exposure to "institutional alternatives" (p. 473) is more likely to produce clan cultures, and Louis (1983) has suggested that a group's social isolation from other groups — the "impermeability of [its] organisational boundaries" (p. 47) — will contribute to the development of localised cultures. In discussing the other, as context, consideration was also given in Chapter 7 to the types of changes in modern organisations that might impact on the relevance of this contextual dimension for understanding organisational culture. Specifically, it was argued that changes such as fewer 'jobs for life', higher turnover, an increased prevalence of professional subcultures, immigration leading to increased workforce diversity, the changing influence of unions, and more access to media information about other organisations, might all act to reduce the relative isolation of organisation members from other organisations (and organisational realities), and the consequent 'impermeability of organisational boundaries' to which Louis refers.

The ideal context. The importance of an ideal context for understanding organisational culture can be inferred from conceptualisations that draw attention to the prescriptive nature of cultural beliefs and assumptions, and that depict culture as a knowledge system, or system of shared cognitions, about the rules that define acceptable and unacceptable behaviour. Cultural knowledge of the kind being referred to here is the equivalent of Sackmann's (1991) 'recipe knowledge' — knowledge that provides organisation members with 'theories of action' to guide their behaviour and decision-making when faced with situations affecting the organisation. The view that culture influences organisation members' thinking about how they should behave — their intended, if not their actual, behaviour — suggests that responses to questions of the kind asked in the present research, regarding for example what workers *should* do, or how they *should* behave, are likely to be subject to some degree of cultural constraint. This effect is likely to be more pronounced in cultures with a long and stable history in which organisation members have had little exposure to alternative perspectives than in cultures with a shorter history, higher member mobility, and/or more exposure to other organisations. In the former more 'culture bound' organisation, the ideal is more likely to be considered by the organisation's members to be similar to how things have always been in the organisation. In the latter less culture bound organisation, a less constrained notion of the ideal is likely to emerge.

As with the other contextual dimensions, the relative importance and salience of the ideal for understanding organisational culture may have changed over time. As we argued in Chapter 7, in modern organisations the available sources of information for shaping one's notion of the ideal may have increased. For example, factors such as the experience of workers in other similar organisations (resulting from the increased mobility of the workforce), along with greater access to information (e.g., from the media and from unions) about current and anticipated developments in similar organisations, or in organisations more generally, might be expected to have increased the knowledge/experience base upon which notions of the ideal are formed.

An important methodological issue with respect to the ideal context concerns the kind of ideal that is asked about, or that is understood by those answering questions about the ideal. Three different kinds of ideal seem possible. First, questions about the ideal could be asked in terms of what could be done, and should be done, that is consistent with the organisation's stated mission and current resources. This question is essentially about the extent to which the organisation lives up to its rhetoric. In this case, the ideal could be readily and immediately achieved if management was, for example, to insist on existing procedures being carried out as intended. A second option would be to ask questions about an ideal that might involve significant changes to the aims and structure of the organisation, and that might be beyond the organisation's present resources to achieve. In this case, while the ideal might be realistic, it might take some time to achieve, perhaps a number of years. It is also possible that the change required to achieve this more ambitious ideal may involve a transformation of the organisation's culture. Such a change may be difficult to understand, and even if understood, it may be difficult to achieve. A third option would be to ask about an ideal in the context of a brain-storming exercise, in which participants are asked to think freely about how the organisation should be, without reference to the organisation's present situation, its environmental context, or its current resourcing. The second and third options might be used most effectively with managers, to promote the generation of ideas for strategic planning; these options might be more difficult to use effectively with workers (since the kind of ideal being asked about may be one that is difficult for workers to envisage). Of course, there is a fourth unrealistic ideal in which participants might whimsically describe their ideal organisation, manager, supervisor, fellow workers, or working conditions in such a way as to make this ideal virtually impossible for any existing organisation to achieve.

A final qualification to questions about the ideal involves the extent to which they refer to the whole organisation, the participant's own department, or to some specific function of the organisation, such as the service it provides to its clients. The fact that there are these different kinds of ideals and that the ideal may refer to the whole organisation or to one aspect of it only, means that careful questioning and clarification of answers may be needed to ensure that all participants interpret questions about the ideal as it is intended they should.

We turn now to a consideration of the treatment of context in existing approaches to the measurement of organisational culture. As indicated above, the content of the following section draws on material already presented in Chapter 7.

10.2.3.3 *Context in existing approaches to the measurement of organisational culture*

As indicated in Chapter 7 of Volume I, while conceptualisations of organisational culture (considered as a whole, rather than singly) draw attention to what might be regarded as different dimensions (or domains) of context, this same emphasis is not reflected in actual operationalisations of organisational culture. This is the case for both quantitative and qualitative measures, though the former can most readily be criticised in this regard. In the discussion below, consideration is given first to the treatment of context in quantitative measures of organisational culture, and second to the treatment of context in qualitative measures.

Quantitative measures. Questionnaire measure of organisational culture can be seen to be particularly limited with respect to their treatment of context. Indeed, researchers using such measures — particularly where these take the form of off-the-shelf questionnaires — cannot really claim any commitment to context, since the relevance of the categories, or dimensions, with which the questionnaire is concerned, in the context being studied, can only be speculated upon. Even where an attempt is made to develop questionnaire items which have some contextual grounding (e.g., by using the results of preliminary qualitative work conducted in the field to inform the subsequent development of the questionnaire[4]), the problem remains that most questionnaire measures of organisational culture are concerned only with organisation members' perceptions of, and beliefs about, the organisation *at the present time*. These measures provide no information about how these perceptions and beliefs might have been shaped by members' experience in relation to other contextual domains.

Notwithstanding the prevalence of questionnaire measures of organisational culture that focus exclusively on the present context, there are some questionnaire measures that also seek information about the ideal context. Two notable examples are the Kilmann-Saxton Culture-Gap Survey (Kilmann & Saxton, 1983) and Harrison's (1975) questionnaire for diagnosing organisation ideology (and its revised edition, Diagnosing Organizational

---

[4]Examples of studies that use this approach are reported in Chapter 6 of Volume I (see Sections 6.3.1 and 6.3.2).

Culture, by Harrison & Stokes, 1992). Apart from dealing with different manifestations of organisational culture — in the former, the focus is on behavioural norms and, in the latter, it is on values and overt beliefs — these measures differ from one another in that they define the ideal differently. The Kilmann and Saxton measure asks about the ideal as it relates to the respondent's *current work group*. Specifically, respondents are asked to choose, from a series of norm pairs, those norms that they believe should be operating in their work group in order to improve performance, job satisfaction, and morale. In the Harrison measure, respondents are asked to think about the kind of organisation that they would ideally like to belong to, and the associated ideologies of that organisation. The point can be made that, in terms of its conceptualisation of the ideal, the method that we are proposing has more in common with the Kilmann and Saxton measure than it does with the Harrison measure. In our revised interview protocol, respondents are asked to imagine that they are in charge of their current division and then, from this perspective, to talk about the kinds of duties and activities in which they believe workers should be engaged, and the kinds of behaviours (attitudes *etc.*) which they believe workers should display.

While our proposed method is similar to the Kilmann and Saxton measure in terms of its conceptualisation of the ideal, it differs from this measure and from the Harrison measure in terms of its use of information about the ideal. As indicated, a potential advantage of asking about the ideal in the present method is that information about this contextual domain, when considered *in combination with* information about other contextual domains — namely, the present, the past, the anticipated future, and the other — may provide insights into the strength, or boundedness, of the organisation's (group's) culture. Evidence of a strongly bounded culture would be suggested by the finding that respondents' thinking about the ideal was constrained by other contextual domains. This would be the case if their ideal was found to be similar to other contexts such as the present, the past, the anticipated future, and/ or other organisations. Evidence of a weaker, or less bounded, culture might be indicated either by the relative absence of demonstrable links between respondents' experience in relation to the ideal and other contexts, or by the influence of particular contexts such as the other or the future, that are different from the present and past contexts.

In questionnaire measures, such as the two above, information about the ideal is *contrasted with* information about the present in order to determine the extent of the gap, or discrepancy, between the actual culture, as perceived by organisation members, and members' ideal culture. Moreover, in the case of the Kilmann and Saxton measure, members' ideal culture, to the extent that it is different from their actual culture, is viewed as the preferred culture and, hence, the one towards which the organisation should endeavour to move. Of course, this approach might be seen to imply that culture change towards some projected ideal can be achieved relatively easily, and that it will not be undermined by elements of the organisation's deeper-level culture that may be incompatible with this ideal. In reality, however, this is unlikely to be the case. For example, if an organisation's underlying culture is one that supports strong Theory X assumptions about the nature of workers, then an attempted change in that organisation towards increasing the decision-making responsibilities of workers (the desirability of which may be espoused by organisation members) is likely to be strongly resisted. Kilmann and Saxton's approach also ignores the possibility that a marked discrepancy between members' actual and ideal may constitute evidence of a culture that is high in what Bate (1984) has called 'antipathy'. The members of such a culture, in responding to a questionnaire such as that developed by Kilmann and Saxton, might be expected to consistently position themselves in opposition to the organisation, with respect to the issues about which they are asked.

Qualitative measures. As indicated in Chapter 7 of Volume I, whereas quantitative (questionnaire) measures of organisational culture are generally regarded as being ill-equipped to generate context-specific understandings, approaches which use qualitative methods such as in-depth interviewing and observation enable the collection of data that are relevant to the specific organisational context being studied (see Chapter 6 of Volume I, Section 6.1.3). Many qualitative studies of organisational culture acknowledge the influence of the historical context by seeking information about critical incidents in the organisation's history, although they do not always convincingly show how these incidents have shaped the organisation's culture. In Chapter 7, Pettigrew's (1979) study of organisational culture in a private British boarding school and Sathe's (1985) study of culture change in an engine company were given as examples of qualitative research of this kind — where claims are made about past events having influenced the organisation's culture, but without a clear demonstration of how this occurred. Unlike studies of this kind which seek information about the historical context in terms of the past generally, or in terms of critical events in the organisation's history, in the present method, questioning about each of the different contextual domains of interest is concerned with the *same* basic issue (the duties and activities of workers in Part A of the interview, and the defining characteristics of good workers in Part B). In this sense, the present method may be better equipped to identify linkages, where these exist, between organisation members' experience in relation to these different domains (whether between the past and the present, the present and the anticipated future, *etc.*).

While many qualitative studies entail at least a general recognition of the importance of an historical perspective, it is probably true to say that the primary focus of qualitative approaches, like that of quantitative approaches, is on the present context. Moreover, as far as we are aware, there are no qualitative studies of organisational culture that explicitly seek to understand culture as being shaped by, or serving to shape, organisation members' future expectations, their interpretations of their experience of other organisations, or their notions of the ideal. Where qualitative approaches do seek information about these other contexts — and this is more the exception than the norm — this tends to be for purposes other than a comparison with associated information about the present or past contexts. For example, in Dick and Dalmau's (1988) study, questioning about the future simply invites respondents to envision an ideal state for the organisation, and in Sackmann's (1991) study, information sought about employees' previous work in other organisations is used only to establish a demographic profile for participants in the study. Similarly, while Sackmann's study does include questions concerning 'recipe' or prescriptive knowledge, the focus seems to be mainly on existing normative behaviours — the dos and the don'ts of the organisation's current culture. There is no attempt to ascertain whether respondents share a deeper-level belief about the inherent 'rightness' of these norms or recipes, for example, by asking them about how organisation members ideally should behave.

10.2.3.4 *A concluding comment on context*

It can be seen from the above discussion that the kind of contextualist approach being proposed in the present research is very different from anything that has been attempted previously. As indicated, while conceptualisations of organisational culture variously draw attention to the importance of a number of different dimensions of context, there is no *single* treatment of culture that incorporates a focus on all of these dimensions. There are also no studies of organisational culture (whether using qualitative or quantitative methods) that attempt, systematically, to operationalise different dimensions of context and examine the way in which they might be interrelated.

10.2.4 *The use of causal attributions*

In addition to the key design features described above — specifically, the use of issue-focussed interviewing, the adoption of a semi-structured interview format, and the opera-tionalisation of context — the revised method, compared with the method in its original form, sought to more systematically examine the value of attributions data as a source of information about the organisation's (group's) culture. To this end, the revised interview protocol sought information about respondents' perceptions of the cause of both experi-enced changes (i.e., changes from the past to the present) and anticipated changes. Building on insights from Study 1 and Study 2, it was thought that the analysis of this information could provide insights into the extent to which the two research divisions might be able to be differentiated on the basis of cultural differences in attribution style.

10.3 Research Method

In this section, each of the key elements of the research method is described. We begin with a description of the interview protocol, in terms of its structure and the format for questioning that was adopted, and with reference also to the guides that we developed to support the administration of the interview and the recording of interview responses. This is followed by a description of the Study 3 sample, in terms of its size and the relevant demographic characteristics of study participants. The section concludes with an overview of procedural considerations concerning the administration of the interview, and the recording and transcribing of interview data.

10.3.1 *The interview protocol*

A copy of the interview protocol that was developed for use in Study 3 can be found in Appendix B. It can be seen that, along with the actual interview questions, the protocol includes guidelines for administration[5]. These guidelines were developed in an attempt to provide what might be required to make the protocol suitable for use by a person (or persons) other than the present researcher. It would be recommended, however, that prior to conducting the interview, the interviewer should familiarise her/himself with both the interview questions and the administration guidelines. As indicated, an important aim of interviewing in the present method was to generate 'rich' information and, to this end, it was necessary for the interviewer to administer the interview in such a way as to create something of the atmosphere of a conversation.

Accompanying the interview protocol was a Response Summary Sheet — a form on which to record the interviewee's responses. A copy of this Response Summary Sheet can be found in Kummerow (2000). Given that all of the interviews for Study 3 were recorded on audiotape, this form was used in this study *only* for the purpose of noting down respondents' answers to questions about the present context. It was important to have a written record of this information because the researcher needed to remind respondents of what they had said about the present before asking them to comment on their experience of the issue (whether the duties and activities of workers, or the characteristics of good workers) in relation to other contextual domains. Of course, in circumstances where permission to tape-record interviews was not granted, a form such as the Response Summary Sheet could arguably be put to very good use. In such circumstances, it would probably be preferable for one person to conduct the interview and another to act as a scribe and record interviewees' responses.

In terms of the design and structure of the Study 3 interview — and by way of further clarifying some of the points made in the introduction to this chapter — it can be seen from the interview protocol that the same general format of questioning was followed for each of the two sub-topics being investigated. Specifically, respondents were asked about each sub-topic in the context of: (i) their present experience (What is x like at the present time?); (ii) their past experience (What was x like in the past? Was it different from the way it is at present?); (iii) their anticipated future experience (What do you think x will be like in the future? Will it be different from the way it is at present?); (iv) their experience of other organisations (What is/was x like in other organisations?); and (v) their ideal experience (What would x be like if you were running this organisation? Would you want it to be different from the way it is at present?). Within each of these contextual domains (with the exception of the other context), the same pattern of open-ended question(s) plus prompts was followed. While a different prompt set was developed for each sub-topic (Part A prompts differed from Part B prompts), within each sub-topic, the same prompt set was

---

[5]These are italicised and appear in square brackets.

presented across contextual domains. No specific prompts were presented when asking respondents about their experience of other organisations since questioning in relation to this contextual domain was intended simply to provide a rough indication of the extent of respondents' experience and/or knowledge of organisational life beyond the boundaries of their current organisation.

It can also be seen from the interview protocol that, in Part A of the interview, an attempt was made to obtain objective information about the extent of workers' involvement in the activities in which they were, reportedly, currently engaged. Specifically, respondents were asked to estimate the percentage of workers engaged in each activity and, where appropriate, the frequency of occurrence of each activity. These estimates subsequently provided the standards against which respondents were asked to compare their experience of these activities in relation to other contextual domains. Thus, questioning about the past context, for example, sought to establish whether or not, in the respondent's experience, the involvement of workers in these activities in the past was the same as, or different from (in the sense of being greater than, or less than), the involvement of workers in these activities at the present time. While an alternative to the present approach would have been, simply, to ask respondents to rate the extent of workers' involvement in the activities in which they were engaged, there was evidence from Study 2 to suggest that the meanings attributed to ratings of this kind may differ from one group (culture) to another, reflecting, at least in part, differences between groups in the nature of their past experience. Thus, in Part A of the interview, where the behaviours of interest were behaviours about which respondents should be able to provide more or less objective information, the use of rating scales was rejected in favour of the more factually-oriented line of questioning that was adopted.

Of course, in Part B of the interview, where the information sought took the form of value judgements by respondents — in this sense, there were no objective measures for this information — there was no option but to use rating scales. Thus, in this part of the interview, respondents were asked to rate, on a five-point scale (from *very important* to *disapproved of*), the importance of the particular worker qualities that they mentioned, or about which they were asked. Ratings of this kind were obtained for four of the five contextual domains of interest, namely, the present, the past, the anticipated future, and the ideal. In the case of the first three of these domains, the focus was on the respondent's perception of what the organisation (division) valued, or regarded as important; in the case of the ideal context, the focus was on what the respondent, her/himself, valued or regarded as important.

The Study 3 interview protocol, like the protocol in its original form, also included questions designed to generate 'time-line' information. In the revised protocol, however, these questions were asked, not only in relation to experienced changes (as was the case in the original protocol), but also in relation to anticipated future changes. With respect to the former, it can be seen that, for each change from the past to the present which a respondent mentioned (whether spontaneously, or in response to prompting), she/he was asked to indicate approximately when the change had occurred (i.e., in what year) and for how long before the change (i.e., for how many years) things had been the same. With respect to the latter, it can be seen that, for each anticipated future change that a respondent mentioned (whether spontaneously, or in response to prompting), she/he was asked to estimate when (i.e., in how many years' time), in her/his opinion, the change was likely to occur. As previously, these questions sought to anchor the respondent's past and, in this case also her/his future, in *real time*. The value of such questions, as suggested by the results of Study 2, was that they could potentially provide insights into the extent to which individuals, or groups, differed in terms of what, for them, constituted the psychologically meaningful past (as distinct from the chronological past), and the psychologically meaningful future.

Finally, and as indicated in the introduction to this study, information was sought about respondents' causal attributions. Thus, for each change from the past to the present which a respondent mentioned (whether spontaneously, or in response to prompting), she/he was asked to comment on her/his perception of why the change had occurred; similarly, for each anticipated future change that the respondent mentioned (whether spontaneously, or in response to prompting), she/he was asked to indicate why, in her/his opinion, the change would occur.

10.3.2 *Participants in the study*

As was the case for Study 2, Study 3 was carried out in both the tooling division and the production division. Given the events occurring in the tooling division at the time — the final stage of the division's major restructure was underway and this involved a further reduction in the size of the workforce, as well as the physical relocation of the division from its original site to a new plant within the company's main assembly and manufacturing complex — decisions regarding the selection of participants from this division were necessarily constrained. One problem in this regard was that it was difficult to select participants who would be broadly representative of the division's membership (in terms of demographics such as age, tenure, seniority, *etc.*). This was because, during the period over which this study was conducted, the demographics of the division were changing constantly, with divisional members variously, and at different times, accepting retrenchment packages or transferring to the new site. In terms, simply, of the numbers, the workforce comprised approximately 190 members at the time when participants were being selected for this study; by the time that data collection was complete, this had declined to approximately 75 members. The point should also be made that this was a period of considerable stress for many divisional members and, as such, the researcher had to exercise greater than usual sensitivity when soliciting members' involvement in the study. The researcher therefore decided that, rather than risk creating further anxiety for these individuals, she would not proceed with those negotiations in which individuals agreed to participate, but with obvious reservations. As it turned out, it was necessary to exercise this option on one occasion only.

In view of the above constraints, the tooling division sample was necessarily made up of individuals selected principally on the basis of their availability at the time, as well as their willingness to participate in the study. The point should be made that the kind of opportunistic approach adopted here draws attention to a well-documented characteristic of fieldwork in general, namely, that the researcher must work within the constraints imposed by the research context and that, very often, this necessitates a trade-off between what is theoretically desirable, on the one hand, and what is practically possible, on the other (see, e.g., Buchanan, Boddy, & McCalman, 1988, and Easterby-Smith, Thorpe, & Lowe, 1991).

Table 10.1 provides a description of the tooling division sample in terms of its main demographic characteristics. It can be seen that the sample comprised twelve divisional members, all of whom were male. Of these, six were 'wages', or hourly paid, employees and six were salaried staff. Four of the salaried staff were foremen, responsible for the direct supervision of wages employees, and two held more senior positions as general foremen. Using the figures available at the time of sample selection, the sample represented approximately 6% of the division's total workforce at that time. Approximately 4% of the division's wages employees, and approximately 25% of the division's salaried staff, were represented. It was also the case that seven of the division's ten major sub-sections were represented. In terms of summary statistics, it can be seen from Table 10.1 that participants in the sample had a mean age of 48.8 years (sd = 7.6 years); a mean length of service with the company of 25.7 years (sd = 10.8); and a mean length of service with the division of 23.2 years (sd = 10.7). From Table 10.1, it can also be seen that all but one of the participants from the tooling division worked on day shift.

With respect to the selection of participants from the production division, this was not subject to the kinds of constraints that influenced selection from the tooling division. As such, in sampling from this division, an attempt was made to achieve some broad representation of the demographic characteristics of the wider membership of the division. Having identified a list of potential participants, the researcher sought the advice of a number of supervisory staff regarding which of these individuals were likely to be most suitable for inclusion in the study. Individuals whose English proficiency was reportedly limited were excluded, as were individuals who were employed on permanent night shift. With respect to the latter, the work schedule of these individuals presented problems insofar as their availability for interviewing was concerned. Once identified, individuals deemed suitable for participation in the study were individually approached by the researcher (with their supervisor's permission) and invited to take part.

A description of the demographic characteristics of the final sample for the production division can be found in Table 10.2. The point should be made that, while this sample originally comprised twenty divisional members — and not nineteen as indicated in the table — there was one participant (a wages employee) whose data, unfortunately, could not be included in the analysis. This was because the recording of this participant's interview was of such poor quality — the cause of this was not known to the researcher — as

Table 10.1.　Demographic characteristics of Study 3 respondents from the Tooling Division.

						Tooling Division (TD)				
Resp #	Gender	Age (years)	Marital Status	Country of Birth	Years in Australia	Years with the Company	Years with the Division	Section	Position	Shift
TD1	Male	53	Married	md*	md*	30	30	Die manufacture	Tradeswages (LH)**	Day
TD2	Male	47	Married	UK	17	17	9	Machining	Tradeswages	Day
TD3	Male	55	Married	Germany	md*	33	33	Jigs	Foreman	Day
TD4	Male	49	Married	Australia	—	33	33	Try-out	Foreman	Day
TD5	Male	51	Married	Australia	—	28	20	Die fitting	Foreman	Day
TD6	Male	52	Married	Australia	—	35	25	Pattern making	General foreman	Day
TD7	Male	53	Married	Australia	—	30	30	Pattern making	Tradeswages (LH)**	Day
TD8	Male	52	Married	Australia	—	6	6	Jigs	Tradeswages (LH)**	Day
TD9	Male	28	Single	Australia	—	6	6	Jigs	Tradeswages	Day
TD10	Male	56	Married	Australia	—	40	36	General	General foreman	Afternoon
TD11	Male	42	Married	md	md*	25	25	Quality Control	Foreman	Day
TD12	Male	48	Defacto	UK	25	25	25	Pattern making	Tradeswages (LH)**	Day
		mean = 48.8				mean = 25.7	mean = 23.2			
		sd = 7.6				sd = 10.8	sd = 10.7			
		range 28–56				range 6–40	range 6–36			

*Missing data.
**Leading Hand.

Table 10.2. Demographic characteristics of Study 3 respondents from the Production Division.

						Production Division (PD)				
Resp #	Gender	Age (years)	Marital Status	Country of Birth	Years in Australia	Years with the Company	Years with the Division	Section	Position	Shift
PD1	Male	30	Single	md*	md*	8	8	Testing	Operator	Day
PD2	Male	41	Married	UK	30	19	9	Materials	Clerical (LH)**	Day
PD3	Female	44	Widowed	Australia	-	5	5	Moulding	LH**	Afternoon
PD4	Female	57	Married	UK	23	17	10	Quality control	Inspector	Alternate
PD5	Male	28	Separated	Australia	—	9	9	Testing	Operator	Day
PD6	Male	49	Married	UK	md*	9	8	Materials	Forklift driver	Day
PD7	Male	32	Separated	UK	14	9	8	Testing	Operator	Day
PD8	Female	43	Married	Australia	—	4	4	Assembly	Operator	Day
PD9	Male	40	Married	Australia	—	20	7	Testing	Operator	Day
PD10	Female	56	Married	UK	30	15	9	Moulding	Inspector	Day
PD11	Male	30	Married	UK	27	5	5	Moulding	Die Setter	Afternoon
PD12	Male	53	Married	UK	30	30	9	Quality control	Inspector	Alternate
PD13	Female	30	Separated	Australia	—	5	5	Moulding	Operator	Day
PD14	Male	39	Married	Australia	—	18	8	Paint & assembly	Senior supervisor	Day
PD15	Male	36	Married	Australia	—	20	10	Paint & assembly	Senior supervisor	Afternoon
PD16	Male	37	Married	UK	24	17	9	Materials	Supervisor	Day
PD17	Male	37	Married	UK	33	15	8	Moulding	Supervisor	Day
PD18	Male	38	Married	UK	14	14	6	Testing, P&A	Supervisor	Day
PD19	Male	35	Married	Australia	-	3	3	Paint & Assembly	Operator	Day
		mean = 39.7				mean = 12.7	mean = 7.4			
		sd = 8.8				sd = 7.2	sd = 2.1			
		range 28–57				range 3–30	range 3–10			

*Missing data.
**Leading Hand.

to make the interview very difficult to transcribe. In terms of its size, the sample for the production division represented approximately 6% of this division's total workforce of 320 members at the time that the study was carried out. As indicated in Table 10.2, fourteen of the nineteen participants from this division were male and five were female. This gave a male:female ratio of 3:1, compared with the male:female ratio of 6:1 for the division as a whole. Fourteen participants were wages, or hourly paid, employees and five were salaried staff, representing 5.5% and 15% of the total membership of each of these categories, respectively. All of the staff in the sample had supervisory responsibilities, with two being senior supervisors and three, first-line supervisors.

It can also be seen from Table 10.2 that there were seven divisional sub-sections represented in the sample. The two sub-sections not represented were intentionally overlooked because the wages employees in both of these sections, unlike their counterparts elsewhere in the division, were in all cases trade qualified. Finally, in terms of summary statistics, it can be seen that participants in the sample had a mean age of 39.7 years (sd = 8.8 years); a mean length of service with the company of 12.7 years (sd = 7.2 years); and a mean length of service with the division of 7.4 years (sd = 2.1 years). It should be noted that the variability indicated in participants' length of service (with both the company and the division) was quite consistent with the variability that characterised the division's entire membership in this regard. In other words, whereas the tooling division comprised mostly longer-serving employees (typically with more than twenty years' service with the company and the division), the production division comprised employees whose length of service varied considerably. Given the widely accepted view of culture as being historically-based, one might reasonably expect that organisation members' interpretations of events will differ depending on the length of members' association with the organisation. In sampling from the production division, an attempt was therefore made to identify participants who had been with the company, and the division, for varying periods of time. Specifically, the sample included: (i) participants who had been with the company for fifteen years or more, and who had also spent a considerable amount of time in the division (five years or more); (ii) participants who had been with the division since its inception (some eight years ago) and who had not worked for any significant length of time elsewhere in the company; and (iii) participants who were relatively new to the division (with four years of service or less) and who had no significant experience elsewhere in the company.

One final point that should be made regarding the selection of participants for this study is that an attempt was made to obtain sufficient numbers of participants from each division to allow individual differences, between and within divisions, to emerge. At the same time, however, the sample size for each division was relatively small and this, combined with the large numbers of variables to be considered (prompt questions, e.g., were asked in relation to each of four different contextual domains), made the widespread use of statistical tests of such differences inappropriate. Moreover, given the nature of this research, the conclusions drawn were based not just on insights obtained from the analysis of quantitative data, but rather on insights obtained from the analysis of quantitative data in combination with qualitative data. An important focus of the analysis in this sense was that it sought information about the degree to which respondents' interpretations across a range of variables (e.g., their perceptions of a given issue in relation to different domains of context) were consistent. In view of these considerations, the results of statistical tests, where these were carried out, are simply noted, rather than reported in detail.

10.3.3 *Procedure*

Participants in Study 3 were interviewed individually by the researcher for approximately two hours each, on two separate occasions. All of the interviews were conducted outside of working hours. Participants were asked to indicate their preferred location for the interview, whether: (i) a private office at their place of work; (ii) their own home; (iii) the researcher's work office; or (iv) the researcher's home. Eight of the nineteen participants from the production division were interviewed in their own homes, with the remaining eleven being interviewed in a private office made available in the division for this purpose. Of the twelve participants from the tooling division, eleven were interviewed in their own homes and one was interviewed in the researcher's home.

All participants gave their written consent to participate in the study and to have their interviews recorded on audiotape. Participants were assured that the information that they provided would be entirely confidential and that their identity would not be revealed in any account, either written or verbal, of the results of the study. On completion of the interviews, each participant received a copy of her/his recorded interview and subsequently also, when it had been prepared, a copy of the interview transcript. The purpose of making this material available to participants was twofold. On the one hand, it was simply an act of courtesy; on the other, it provided participants with the means whereby they could review what they had said and make any corrections they deemed necessary. With respect to this latter point, it is worth noting that no such corrections were made.

10.4 Approach to Data Analysis

Interview data (in the form of complete transcripts of each participant's interview) were analysed using both quantitative and qualitative methods. With respect to the former, data generated by both open-ended and closed questions were quantified. The quantification of responses to closed questions was very straightforward since these questions typically required the respondent to give simple "Yes/No" answers or, alternatively, to select the 'best' answer from a number of *a priori* response categories. The quantification of responses to open-ended questions was more difficult. Responses were content analysed to identify a finite number of categories into which common or similar responses could be grouped. For example, an analysis of responses to the question "What do workers in this organisation at the present time have to do to be thought of as good workers?" suggested three broad categories of responses, concerned with: (i) work skills (e.g., job knowledge and quality of work); (ii) work behaviours (e.g., attendance and showing initiative); and (iii) interpersonal skills and behaviours (e.g., politeness and getting on well with others). The responses in category (ii) were further divided into: (a) work behaviours that one might expect to be valued in an organisation which promoted a predominantly passive role for workers (Theory X orientation); (b) work behaviours that suggested a more active role for workers (Theory Y orientation); and (c) work behaviours that were neutral in the sense of reflecting neither a predominantly passive nor a predominantly active role for workers.

It was also the case that, where responses to the open-ended questions described worker activities, or alternatively, good worker characteristics that were the same as, or similar to, those which were the subject of the prompt questions, they would be classified with the same label as the associated prompt. Thus, for example, the prompt labelled 'work group meetings' (see Part A of the interview) was used to classify all references, by participants from the production division, to the past involvement of the workers in this division in team meetings (held as part of the team concept). This facilitated the comparison of prompt data with open question data and enabled an assessment to be made of the extent to which the worker activities and characteristics that were the subject of the prompt questions were mentioned spontaneously, in response to the open-ended questions.

Interview data were also analysed qualitatively using a text analysis computer program known as 'Ethnograph' (Seidel, Kjolseth, & Seymour, 1988). In the present study, ethnographic analysis was undertaken primarily to clarify the meaning of results obtained from the quantitative analysis. The aim was *not* complex theory building and, hence, for any given interview, selected segments of text only were extracted for analysis. Specifically, a given segment was extracted if it either: (i) clarified or provided new insights into the meaning of quantitative data; or (ii) introduced a topic or theme which was different from, or tangential to, the topic of the formal interview question.

Finally, the point should be made that, consistent with the approach taken in the previous two studies, the main focus of the analysis of Study 3 data was on methodological issues. Once again, and in contrast with the approach taken in most qualitative studies of organisational culture, the aim was *not* to provide a summary description of each division's culture based on the data collected. Rather, it was to evaluate the method being developed in terms of its capacity to elicit culturally meaningful data (i.e., data from which aspects of the culture of each division might be inferred).

10.5 Format for Reporting Results

As indicated in the introduction to this chapter, the results of Study 3 are reported in the next two chapters — Chapters 11 and 12. These results are primarily concerned with the analysis of data from Part A of the Study 3 interview (concerned with the duties and activities of workers). These data were found to provide a sufficiently comprehensive and detailed assessment of the method and its capacity to reveal deeper-level beliefs and assumptions concerning the topic.

Broadly speaking, there were two main methodological issues that the analysis of the Study 3 data sought to address. The first of these — which is the subject of the results reported in Chapter 11 — was concerned with the use, in the present method, of a semi-structured interview format. The second — which is the subject of the results reported in Chapter 12 — was concerned with the treatment, in the method, of context as a multi-dimensional phenomenon. More specifically, Chapter 11 presents the results of two separate analyses, the first of which examines the value of combining open-ended questions with closed questions, or prompts, and the second of which examines how qualitative data (in the form of respondents' elaborations on, and qualifications of, their responses) can inform our understanding of the meaning of quantitative data. In Chapter 12, the results of the analysis of data pertaining to each of the contextual domains of interest — namely, the present, the past, the future, the other, and the ideal — are presented. In this chapter, the nature of the linkages between the findings for these different contextual domains is also investigated, and attention is drawn to the possible cultural implications of these linkages. In particular, an examination is provided of attributions made in response to questions about the relationships between different contexts, and why there are differences between those contexts.

Finally, as for the reporting of results in the two previous studies, the results of Study 3 (in any given section) are reported separately for the tooling division and the production division. Also as previously, attention is drawn to both similarities and differences between the divisions, and these are discussed in terms of their possible significance for understanding the culture of each division.

10.6 Conclusions

In this chapter we have provided a background and introduction to Study 3. The method developed for use in this study was described, in terms of its general design features and the rationale for their incorporation into the revised method (with reference to both insights from the findings of Study 2 and supporting evidence from the literature). In this chapter, detailed information was also provided about the interview protocol (its structure, the specific questions asked, the procedure for administration, *etc.*), and the approach to data analysis and the reporting of the results for Study 3. In the following two chapters — Chapter 11 and 12 — the findings of Study 3 are reported and discussed. Chapter 11 is concerned with the findings pertaining to the use of semi-structured interviewing as a key feature of the design of the Study 3 method, and Chapter 12 is concerned with the findings pertaining to the operationalisation of various dimensions, or domains, of context and the use of attributions data.

Appendix B

STUDY 3 INTERVIEW PROTOCOL
The Role of Workers

Part A: Duties/Activities

THE PRESENT CONTEXT

Open-ended questions (OQ)

OQ1. Organisations (divisions) generally have a list of duties for workers to carry out. In this division at the present time, what are the main duties that workers *actually* carry out?

OQ2. Apart from doing their immediate job, is there anything else that workers in this division do at the present time?

Prompts (P)

[In this section, the respondent is presented with a number of activities in which workers in the division might get involved. The purpose of these 'prompts' is to jog the respondent's memory so that aspects of the role of the worker not referred to in response to the open-ended questions above (either because the respondent has simply forgotten to mention them or because they are taken for granted and therefore not usually spoken about) can be elicited. As indicated, for each activity the interviewer must establish whether or not workers in the division are involved in the activity at the present time, and if so, to what extent. If the activity has been mentioned previously (i.e., in response to either of the open-ended questions), there is clearly no need to ask about it again. However, for each activity mentioned spontaneously, the interviewer should subsequently obtain an estimate of the extent of worker involvement in the activity.

In this section, as elsewhere, respondents should not be restricted to one-word responses. To the extent that longer responses are needed to clarify the meaning of what is being said, these should be encouraged. At the same time, a Response Summary Sheet is provided on which to record a brief summary of the respondent's answers. Summary data on the present will provide a useful aid to questioning in subsequent stages (e.g., when trying to establish whether or not the past role of workers in the division differed from their present role). The Response Summary Sheet should be completed for each successive stage of questioning. In introducing the prompts, the format outlined below is suggested.]

Workers in different organisations (divisions) may do different things in addition to their immediate jobs. You have said that in this division at the present time, in addition to their immediate jobs, workers..... *[Paraphrase response to OQ2 above]*. Here are some other things that workers may do in addition to their immediate jobs. Indicate which, if any of these, workers in this division do at the present time. For each of the activities you have mentioned, answer each of the questions concerning the extent of worker involvement in the activity.

P1.   Do workers attend meetings?

        Yes/No

        If "Yes":

                What meetings?

                [Ask the respondent to briefly describe each kind of meeting.]

                What percentage of workers attend at the present time?

                [Ask for each type of meeting.]

                How often are the meetings held?

                [Ask for each type of meeting.]

[Go on now to ask the respondent about worker involvement in meetings which she/he has not mentioned above. A list of different types of meetings is presented below. Ask only about those meetings to which the respondent has not already referred. Establish whether or not workers attend these meetings and, if so, ask what percentage of workers attend and how often the meetings are held. Respondents who indicate from the outset that workers are not involved in any meetings (namely, a "No" response above) may also be presented with these prompts.]

(a)   *Planning meetings* in which decisions are made about such things as the future directions of the division, forthcoming work schedules, forthcoming equipment needs, and training needs.

(b)   *Information meetings* (such as 'State of the Nation' meetings) in which workers are given information by those above them about such things as the current performance of the division, future directions of the division and anything else considered to be of relevance to the shop floor.

(c)   *Work Group meetings* in which workers collaborate with other divisional personnel (e.g., technical people, union officials, or supervisors) to discuss ways in which the effectiveness of the division (or a particular section) might be enhanced (in terms of quality of work produced, output, worker satisfaction, *etc.*).

(d)   *Safety meetings*

(e)   *Union meetings*

P2.   Do workers help other workers in their work if and when they need help?
          Yes/No
          If "Yes":
              What percentage of workers engage in this activity at the present time?

P3.   Do workers record information about what they do which is given to those above them?
      [For example, workers might record quality and productivity data.]
          Yes/No
          If "Yes":
              What percentage of workers engage in this activity at the present time?
              How often is this information recorded?

P4.   Do workers attend training or professional development programs?
      [Need to specify that this does not include apprenticeship training; also need to specify that this does not include training that the worker does in her/his own time and that is not sponsored by the company.]
          Yes/No
          If "Yes":
              What % of workers are involved in training at the present time?
              How much time is spent in training?
              [This could be evaluated in terms of hours per week/month; alternatively, the respondent might be able to specify the length of time that particular training courses run for.]

P5.   Do workers participate in social activities?
      [A distinction is made here between formal and informal social activities. Formal social activities are those that are organised by the company (i.e., by an established committee or by some other elected body or individual). Some examples are: Christmas functions, sporting events, family days, and film evenings. Informal social activities are more impromptu. There is no committee or individual formally responsible for their organisation. Some examples of informal social activities are: drinks after work, card games or other leisure activities in work breaks, and celebrations of employee birthdays, engagements, etc.

      If the respondent mentions more than one activity in either category, it is not necessary for her/him to comment on the frequency of worker involvement in each activity separately. Rather, the respondent should provide an overall estimate of how often (weekly, monthly, annually) workers are involved in activities in that category.]

              Formal
              Yes/No
              If "Yes":
                  What % of workers participate in these activities at the present time?

How often are they held?

Do staff also attend?

Yes/No

Informal

Yes/No

If "Yes":

What % of workers participate in these activities at the present time?

How often are they held?

Do staff also attend?

Yes/No

P6. When they are at work, do workers talk to their supervisors either about work, or about social things?

[It should be specified here that this does not include worker-supervisor interactions that are part of formally organised meetings.]

Yes/No

If "Yes":

What % of workers do this?

How often do workers do this?

What % of these interactions are supervisor-initiated compared to worker-initiated?

What % of these interactions are negative and concerned with problems?

What % of these interactions are neutral and concerned with problems?

What % of these interactions are concerned with information giving?

What % of these interactions are positive and concerned with praise for achievements?

What % of these interactions are concerned with personal/social issues?

THE PAST CONTEXT

Open-ended questions

OQ1. Main duties

(a) What were the *main* duties of workers in this division in the past? Were they the same as, or different from, the main duties of workers in this division at the present time? *[If the respondent asks what is meant by the 'past', point out that it can either be during the time that she/he has been with the division, or before that. For some respondents, it may be the case that the past extends further back than their year of commencement with the division, or even the company.]*

    Same/Different/Don't know

    If "Different":

        In what way were the main duties of workers different in the past?

    If "Same":

        How long have the main duties of workers remained the same?

            For as long as I have been here/Like this before I started

            If "Like this before I started":

                For how long?

                How do you know about this?

(b) How did workers carry out their main duties in this division in the past? Were the methods used the same as, or different from, current methods?

    Same/Different/Don't know

    If "Different":

        In what way were past methods of doing the job different from current methods?

    If "Same":

        How long have the methods of doing the job been the same?

            For as long as I have been here/Like this before I started

            If "Like this before I started":

                For how long?

                How do you know about this?

[Ask the remaining questions for each change that the respondent mentions in response to OQ1(a) and OQ1(b) above.]

        When did the change first become apparent?

            More then 20 years ago

            Between 10 and 20 years ago

            Between 5 and 10 years ago

            Less than five years ago

        Were you there?

            Yes/No

            If "No":

                How do you know about the change?

        To what do you attribute the change?

OQ2.   Other activities

Apart from their immediate job was there anything else that workers did in this division in the past, that was different from what workers do at the present time?

Same/Different/Don't know
If "Different":

In what way were the other activities of workers different in the past?

Prompts

[Use the Response Summary Sheet as an aid to questioning here. Refer first to the respondent's unprompted response to OQ2 in the Present Context (if the response to this question is "no other activities" proceed straight to the prompts section.) Establish whether or not things were different in the past with respect to these activities (this activity). Then ask about each of the activities in the prompts section that have not yet been discussed in relation to the past context. The suggested format for questioning is outlined below.]

You have said that, at the present time, in addition to doing their immediate job workers in this division .... *[Paraphrase response to OQ2. in the Present Context, and then go on to do the same for each of the prompts.]* Do you think that this was any different in the past?

Same/Different/Don't know
If "Different":

In what way was it different?

[Ask the following questions for each of the changes (whether unprompted or prompted) that the respondent mentions in this section.]

When did the change first become apparent?
More then 20 years ago
Between 10 and 20 years ago
Between 5 and 10 years ago
Less than five years ago

Were you there?
Yes/No
If "No":

How do you know about the change?
To what do you attribute the change?

[If, in the Present Context, the respondent has described one or more 'other' activities which workers do at the present time, but goes on in this section to indicate that worker involvement in these activities (this activity) was the same in the past as it is at present,

then go on to ask the following questions. As above, these questions are designed to find out whether the respondent has a sense of the past which extends back further than the year in which she/he commenced work with the division, or the company.]

> If "Same":
>> How long has the involvement of workers in these activities (this activity) been the same?
>>> For as long as I have been here/Like this before I started
>>> If "Like this before I started":
>>>> For how long?
>>>> How do you know about this?

THE FUTURE CONTEXT

Open-ended questions

OQ1.   Main duties

(a)   In the future do you think that the *main* duties (i.e., the duties comprising the actual job) of workers in this division will be the same as, or different from, the main duties of workers in this division at the present time?
> Same/Different/Don't know
> If "Different":
>> In what way will the *main* duties of workers be different in the future?
> If "Same":
>> For how long do you think that the *main* duties of workers in this division will continue to be the same as they are at present?

(b)   In the future, do you think that the methods used by workers to do the job will be the same as, or different from, current methods?
> Different/Same/Don't know
> If "Different":
>> In what way will the methods used by workers to do the job be different in the future?
> If "Same":
>> For how long do you think that the methods used by workers to do the job will continue to be the same?

[Ask the remaining questions for each change that the respondent mentions in response to OQ1(a) and OQ1(b) above.]

When do you think the change will occur?
>   Within the next six months
>   Within the next year
>   Within the next 2 years
>   Within the next 5 years
>   More than 5 years away

Why do you think the change will occur?
Do you think that the change you anticipate is a good thing? Is it desirable?
Please explain.

OQ2.   Other activities

>   In this division in the future, do you think that the things that workers do in
>   addition to their immediate jobs, will be different from the things that they do
>   at the present time?
>>   Same/Different/Don't know
>>   If "Different":
>>>   In what way will the *other* activities of workers be different in the
>>>   future?

Prompts

[Use the Response Summary Sheet as an aid to questioning here. Refer first to the respondent's unprompted response to OQ2 in the Present Context (if the response to this question is "no other activities" proceed straight to the prompts section). Establish whether or not the respondent thinks that things will be different in the future with respect to these activities (this activity). Then ask about each of the remaining activities in the prompts section that have not yet been discussed in relation to the future context. The suggested format for questioning is outlined below.]

You have said that, at the present time, in addition to doing their immediate job workers in this division..... *[Paraphrase response to OQ2 in the Present Context, and then go on to do the same for each of the prompts.]* Do you think that this will be different in the future?
>   Same/Different/Don't know
>   If "Different":
>>   In what way will it be different in the future?

[Ask the following questions for each of the changes (whether unprompted or prompted) that the respondent mentions in this section.]

>   When do you think the change will occur?
>>   Within the next six months
>>   Within the next year

> Within the next 2 years
> Within the next 5 years
> More than 5 years away

Why do you think the change will occur?

Do you think that the change you anticipate is a good thing? Is it desirable?

[If, in the Present Context, the respondent has described one or more 'other' activities which workers do at the present time, but goes on in this section to indicate that worker involvement in these activities (this activity) will be the same in the future as it is at present, then go on to ask the following question. As above, this question is designed to find out what the respondent's notion of the future is, and how far beyond the present it extends.]

> If "Same":
>
> > For how long do you think that the involvement of workers in these *other* activities (this other activity) will continue to be the same as it is at present?

THE OTHER CONTEXT

Open-ended questions

[The aim of the first question in this section (OQ1) is to establish the familiarity of the respondent with the role of workers in other organisations.]

OQ1.   Are you aware of what workers in other organisations do?

> Yes/No
>
> If "Yes":
>
> > For each organisation with which you are familiar, indicate the source of your knowledge about the organisation. Indicate 'self' if you have personal experience of the organisation, 'other' if you have heard about it from friends or acquaintances who have worked there, and 'media' if you have read about it in newspapers or heard about it on radio or TV.

[The second and third questions in this section (OQ2 and OQ3) are asked in relation to the organisation about which the respondent has the most experience. OQ2 is asked <u>only</u> if the organisation is similar to the one in which she/he currently works. Note that the respondent is not presented with any of the prompts in this section.]

OQ2.   Main duties

How do workers in..... *[name of other organisation, or alternative identifier]* carry out their main duties? Are the methods that they use the same as, or different from, the methods used by workers in this organisation?

Same/Different/Don't know

If "Different":

In what way are they different?

OQ3.   Other activities

Are the things that workers in..... *[name of other organisation or alternative identifier]* do in addition to their immediate job different from the things that workers in this organisation do in addition to their immediate job?

Same/Different/Don't know

If "Different":

In what way are they different?

THE IDEAL CONTEXT

Open-ended questions

OQ1.   Main duties

If you were running a division like this one, would you make any changes to the *main* duties of workers (i.e., the duties which comprise the actual job), in terms of what these duties are and/or how they are carried out? Please explain your response.

OQ2.   Other activities

If you were running an organisation like this one, what sorts of things do you think workers *should* do in addition to their immediate jobs? Please explain your response.

Prompts

[Use the Response Summary Sheet as an aid to questioning here. Refer first to the respondent's <u>unprompted</u> *response to OQ2 in the Present Context (if the response to this question is "no other activities" proceed straight to the prompts section). Establish whether or not the respondent thinks that worker involvement in these activities (this activity)* <u>should</u> *change or remain the same. Then ask about each of the remaining activities in the prompts section that have not yet been discussed in relation to the ideal context. The suggested format for questioning is outlined below.]*

You have said that, at the present time, in addition to doing their immediate job, workers in this division..... *[Paraphrase response to OQ2 in the Present Context, and then go on to do the same for each of the prompts.]* If you were running a division like this one, would you make any changes to the involvement of workers in this activity? Please explain your response.

Part B: Characteristics of Good Workers

THE PRESENT CONTEXT

Open-ended question (OQ)

[The following OQ asks about the characteristics of a 'good' worker from the <u>organisation's</u> perspective, that is, from the perspective of power-holders in the organisation. The question is not concerned with the respondent's personal views about what the characteristics of good workers <u>should be</u>, this information being sought in the final section on the Ideal Context. While it is acknowledged that personal and organisational ideologies with respect to what makes a good worker might be the same, it is important that the respondent understands that, in this question, she/he is being asked to comment on the latter. It may be necessary to include a 'don't know' response option, for respondents who seem unsure of what a good worker is from the organisation's perspective.]

Different organisations (divisions) can have different ideas about what makes a 'good' worker. Think about the workers in your division at the present time who are generally regarded by those above them (i.e., by their managers and supervisors) as being good workers. Why are these workers thought of by those above them as good workers?

Prompts (P)

[The purpose of the prompts is the same here as it is in Part A, namely, to jog the respondent's memory so that the characteristics of good workers not referred to spontaneously in response to the initial open question (perhaps because they are taken-for-granted), can be brought into consciousness and articulated by the respondent. In this way, a more complete picture of the characteristics of good workers (as defined by the division at the present time) is obtained. In introducing the prompts, the format outlined below is suggested. Do not present those prompts that the respondent has made reference to previously in response to the open-ended question.]

Different organisations (divisions) can have different ideas about what makes a good worker. You have said that in your division at the present time, workers who are thought of as good workers by those above them (i.e., by their managers and supervisors) are workers who..... *[Paraphrase response to OQ]*. Here are some other characteristics of workers that may or may not be important in determining whether a worker in your division at the present time is thought of as a good worker by those above her/him. Think about each characteristic. Is it 'very important', 'moderately important', 'slightly important', or 'not important' in determining whether a worker is thought of as a good worker? Perhaps the characteristic is 'disapproved of' so that, if a worker shows this characteristic, she/he might even be thought of as a 'bad' worker? Let's start with 'initiative'. In order to be thought of as a good worker by those above her/him, how important is it for a worker in this division at the present time to 'show initiative on the job'?

[Present each of the prompts in turn, prefacing each with the words: 'In order to be thought of as a good worker by those above her/him, how important is it for a worker in this division at the present time to....?'. This will help to keep the exercise focussed by reminding respondents that they are required to evaluate the characteristic in terms of its importance to the division, and <u>not</u> in terms of its importance with respect to their own personal values and beliefs. Most characteristics are rated on a five-point scale: 'very important', 'moderately important', 'slightly important', 'not important', 'disapproved of'. However, in two cases, an additional response category, 'no opportunity', is included to accommodate the possibility that, due to structural properties of the division, workers may have no opportunity to exhibit a particular characteristic (behaviour, attitude, etc.). As indicated in Part A, respondents should not be discouraged from qualifying the ratings that they provide since it is often a qualifying comment that casts new light onto what a rating actually means. At the same time, however, the interviewer should be skilled in helping the respondent to 'get to the point' relatively quickly so that the next prompt can be presented.]

P1. Show initiative on the job.
      Very important
      Moderately important
      Slightly important
      Not important
      Disapproved of

P2. Do as she/he is told and follow instructions exactly.
      Very important
      Moderately important
      Slightly important
      Not important
      Disapproved of

P3. Come up with ideas for how to improve things that are discussed with her/his supervisor.
      Very important
      Moderately important
      Slightly important
      Not important
      Disapproved of

P4. Plan out her/his own work and set her/his own goals.
        Very important
        Moderately important
        Slightly important
        Not important
        Disapproved of
        No opportunity

P5. Consistently produce high quality work.
        Very important
        Moderately important
        Slightly important
        Not important
        Disapproved of

P6. Maintain a high output of work.
        Very important
        Moderately important
        Slightly important
        Not important
        Disapproved of

P7. Be prepared to question existing ways of doing things and suggest alternatives.
        Very important
        Moderately important
        Slightly important
        Not important
        Disapproved of

P8. Spend time helping other workers in their work.
        Very important
        Moderately important
        Slightly important
        Not important
        Disapproved of

P9. Actively seek to learn new skills (either in own time or company time).
        Very important
        Moderately important
        Slightly important
        Not important
        Disapproved of

P10. Show that she/he is committed to the organisation and its welfare.
>   Very important
>   Moderately important
>   Slightly important
>   Not important
>   Disapproved of

P11. Be able to work well in a team.
>   Very important
>   Moderately important
>   Slightly important
>   Not important
>   Disapproved of
>   No opportunity

THE PAST CONTEXT

Open-ended question

In this division in the past, were the characteristics of hourly paid workers who were thought of by their supervisors and managers as good workers different from the characteristics of good workers at the present time?

[If the respondent asks what is meant by the 'past', point out that it can either be during the time that she/he has been with the division, or before that. For some respondents, it may be the case that the 'past' extends further back than their year of commencement with the division or the company.]
>   Same/Different/Don't know
>   If "Different":
>>   In what way were the characteristics of good workers different in the past?

Prompts

[Use the Response Summary Sheet as an aid to questioning in this section. Refer first to the respondent's <u>unprompted</u> response to the OQ in the Present Context. Establish whether the characteristics of good workers referred to spontaneously in response to this question (i.e., referred to before any of the prompts were introduced) were different in the past. The suggested format for questioning is outlined below.]

You have said that in this division at the present time, in order to be thought of by her/his supervisors and managers as a good worker, it is important for a worker to..... *[Present each of the characteristics mentioned in response to the OQ in the Present Context, in turn]*. Do you think that this was any different in the past?

>Same/Different/Don't know
>
>If "Different":
>
>>In what way was it different? In other words, was this characteristic more or less important in the past than it is at the present time?

[Go on now to ask the respondent about each of the characteristics listed in the prompts section which have not yet been discussed in relation to the past context. Obtain a rating of the importance of each of these characteristics in the past, using the same rating scales as previously. The suggested format for questioning is outlined below.]

You have said that in this division at the present time, it is..... *[Remind the respondent of her/his 'importance' rating]* for a worker to..... *[Present each of the prompts in turn]* in order to be thought of by those above her/him as a good worker. Do you think that this was any different in the past? That is, was this particular quality more or less important in the past?

[The following questions ask about the timing, and perceived cause, of changes from the past to the present in the worker qualities that are valued in the division. In asking these questions, the changes that are mentioned by the respondent (whether spontaneously or in response to prompting) should be considered as a whole, rather than separately. It is possible (though unlikely) that the respondent will mention only one such change, in which case this instruction does not apply.]

>When did the change(s) first become apparent?
>>More then 20 years ago
>>Between 10 and 20 years ago
>>Between 5 and 10 years ago
>>Less than five years ago
>
>Were you there?
>>Yes/No
>>If "No":
>>>How do you know about the change(s)?
>>To what do you attribute the change(s)?

[If the respondent says "Same" in response to both the OQ and the P above, ask the following questions which are designed to find out whether the respondent has a sense of the past which extends back further than the year in which she/he commenced work with the division or the company.]

>If "Same":
>>You have indicated that, in this division in the past, in order to be thought of as a good worker by those above her/him, a worker had to do much the

same as she/he has to do at present. How long have the characteristics of good workers been the same?

> For as long as I have been here/Like this before I started
> If "Like this before I started":
>> For how long?
>> How do you know about this?

THE FUTURE CONTEXT

Open-ended question

In this division in the future, do you think that the characteristics of daily paid workers who are thought of as good workers by those above them, will be different from the characteristics of good workers at the present time?

> Same/Different/Don't know
> If "Different":
>> In what way will the characteristics of good workers be different in the future?

Prompts

[Use the Response Summary Sheet as an aid to questioning in this section. Refer first to the respondent's <u>unprompted</u> response to the OQ in the Present Context. Establish whether or not the respondent thinks that the characteristics of good workers referred to spontaneously in response to this question (i.e., referred to before any of the prompts were introduced) will be different in the future. The suggested format for questioning is outlined below.]

You have said that in this division at the present time, in order to be thought of by her/his supervisors and managers as a good worker, it is important for a worker to..... *[Present each of the characteristics mentioned in response to the OQ in the Present Context, in turn]*. Do you think that this will be different in the future?

> Same/Different/Don't know
> If "Different":
>> In what way do you think it will be different? In other words, in this division in the future, will this characteristic be more or less important than it is at the present time?

[Go on now to ask the respondent about each of the characteristics listed in the prompts section which have not yet been asked in relation to the future context. Obtain a rating of the predicted importance of each of these characteristics in the future, using the same rating scales as previously. The suggested format for questioning is outlined below.]

You have said that in this division at the present time, it is..... *[Remind the respondent of her/his 'importance' rating]* for a worker to..... *[Present each of the prompts in turn]* in order to be thought of by those above her/him as a good worker. Do you think that this will be any different in the future? That is, will this particular quality be more or less important in the future?

[The following questions ask about the timing, and perceived cause, of anticipated changes in the worker qualities that are valued in the division. In asking these questions, the changes that are mentioned by the respondent (whether spontaneously or in response to prompting) should be considered as a whole, rather than separately. It is possible (though unlikely) that the respondent will mention only one such change, in which case this instruction does not apply.]

> When do you think the change(s) will occur?
>> Within the next six months
>> Within the next year
>> Within the next 2 years
>> Within the next 5 years
>> More than 5 years away
>
> Why do you think the change(s) will occur?
> Do you think that the change(s) you anticipate is a good thing, is it desirable? Please explain.

[If the respondent says "Same" in response to both the OQ and the P above, ask the following question that is designed to find out what the respondent's notion of the future is. In other words, for how many years does the respondent think that things will continue as they are at present?]

> If "Same":
>> You have indicated that, in this division in the future, in order to be thought of by those above her/him as a good worker, a worker will have to do pretty much the same as what she/he does at the present time. For how long do you think that the characteristics of good workers in this organisation will continue to be the same as they are at present?

THE OTHER CONTEXT

Open-ended questions

[The aim of the first question in this section (OQ1) is to establish the familiarity of the respondent with the role of workers in other organisations.]

OQ1. Are you aware of the worker characteristics that are considered to be important in other organisations?

  Yes/No

  If "Yes":

  For each organisation with which you are familiar, indicate the source of your knowledge about the organisation. Indicate 'self' if you have personal experience of the organisation, 'other' if you have heard about it from friends or acquaintances who have worked there, and 'media' if you have read about it in newspapers or heard about it on radio or TV.

[The second question in this section (OQ2) is asked in relation to the organisation about which the respondent has the most experience. Note that the respondent is not presented with any of the prompts in this section.]

OQ2. Are the characteristics of good workers in..... *[name of other organisation, or alternative identifier]* different from the characteristics of good workers in this organisation at the present time?

  Same/Different/Don't know

  If "Different":

  In what way are they different?

THE IDEAL CONTEXT

Open-ended question

If you were running a division like this one, what sorts of characteristics (attitudes, behaviours, *etc.*) would you consider it important for daily paid workers to have? In other words, what sorts of things would a daily paid worker have to do for you to think that she/he was a good worker? Please explain your response.

Prompts

[Use the Response Summary Sheet as an aid to questioning here. Refer first to the respondent's <u>unprompted</u> response to the OQ in the Present Context. Using the same rating scales as previously, ask the respondent to rate the importance, to her/him personally, of each of the characteristics of good workers referred to spontaneously in response to this question (i.e., referred to before any of the prompts were introduced). The suggested format for questioning is outlined below.]

You have said that in this division at the present time, in order to be thought of by her/his supervisors and managers as a good worker, it is important for a worker to..... *[Paraphrase response to the OQ in the Present Context].* If you were running a division like this one, how important would it be to you that daily paid workers..... *[Present each of the characteristics mentioned in response to the OQ in the Present Context, in turn.]*

[Go on now to ask the respondent about each of the characteristics listed in the prompts section which have not yet been asked in relation to the ideal context. Using the same rating scales as previously, ask the respondent to rate the importance, to her/him personally, of each of these characteristics. The suggested format for questioning is outlined below.]

You have said that in this division at the present time, it is..... *[Remind the respondent of her/his 'importance' rating]* for a worker to..... *[Present each of the prompts in turn]* in order to be thought of by those above her/him as a good worker. If you were running a division like this one, how important would it be to you that daily paid workers..... *[Present each of the prompts in turn].*

Additional Questions for Part B

1.   What percentage of daily paid workers in this division at the present time do *you* consider to be good workers?
2.   What would need to be done to make the remaining workers good workers?
3.   Was the percentage of good workers in this division in the past different from the percentage of good workers in this division at the present time?

         Same/Different/Don't know

         If "Different":

             What was the percentage of good workers in this organisation in the past?

             When did this change first become apparent?

                More than 20 years ago

                Between 10 and 20 years ago

                Between 5 and 10 years ago

                Less than 5 years ago

             Were you there?

                Yes/No

                If "No":

                     How do you know about this change?

             To what do you attribute this change?

Chapter 11

The Use of Semi-Structured Interviewing (Study 3, Part 2)

As indicated in Chapter 10, in which we introduced Study 3, our proposed method for investigating organisational culture in this third and final study incorporated the following key elements: a semi-structured interview format involving the use of open-ended and closed (i.e., prompt) questions, as well as questions inviting respondents to qualify and/or elaborate on their responses; a consideration of different dimensions, or domains, of context, including the present, the past, the future, the other, and the ideal; and an analysis of respondents' attributions regarding perceived differences between these different contextual domains (e.g., between the past and the present, or between the present and the anticipated future). In the present chapter, we summarise those results pertaining to the use of semi-structured interviewing in the Study 3 method. Consideration is first given to the results pertaining to the use of open-ended questions in combination with closed questions, or prompts. Following this, we examine the way in which qualitative data (generated by allowing respondents to qualify and/or elaborate on their responses) can be used to provide important insights into the meaning of quantitative data (in this case, data that lend themselves to quantification, such as yes/no responses). In Chapter 12, we summarise the results pertaining to the operationalisation of context and the analysis of attributions.

11.1 Combining Open-Ended Questions with Closed Questions or Prompts

The critical question for the evaluation of this feature of the design of our proposed method is whether or not the use of prompt questions, following on from the open-ended questions, provides additional information of value, over and above that provided by the open-ended questions alone. In an attempt to answer this question, the results of an analysis of the difference between the open question data and the prompt data for the *present* context — these data pertain to respondents' perceptions of what it is that the workers in their division do at the present time — are presented and discussed. A number of possible reasons for the discrepancy between respondents' free and prompted responses are suggested and these are evaluated through a more detailed examination of the data pertaining to two worker activities, labelled 'information meetings' and 'attend training'. This latter analysis draws on respondents' accounts of both their present and past experience of the involvement of divisional workers in these activities.

11.1.1 *Findings for the present context*

The analysis of the open question data is reported first, followed by the analysis of the prompt data.

11.1.1.1 *Open question data*

Respondents were first of all given the opportunity to comment freely, that is, without any prompting from the interviewer, on their perceptions of what constituted the main job of workers in their division at the present time. For both divisions, responses to this initial open-ended question typically took one of two forms. Many respondents gave a brief description of the broad function of either their division as a whole (e.g., for the tooling division, "building dies", and for the production division, "making parts") or the particular section in which they worked, or for which they were responsible (e.g., for the tooling division, "prototype work"). Other respondents provided a list, which was more or less inclusive, of the key operations of their division (e.g., for the production division, "materials handling, moulding parts, inspection, assembly of parts, painting of parts") or section (e.g., for the production division, "writing job schedules, keeping track of stock, issuing job cards"). A minority of responses (only three in the total sample) could not be classified in this way. One respondent from the production division made reference to the expectation that workers should "do as they are told" and two respondents from the tooling division made reference to the expectation that workers should "do a fair day's work for a fair day's pay".

It is worth making the point that the responses to this initial open-ended question (particularly those given by respondents who were themselves workers) were probably not the considered responses that one might expect if the question had been of a more probing nature. On the contrary, they were probably very similar to the kinds of well-rehearsed and economical responses that one would expect to get to the commonly encountered question "What do you do for a living?".

Following the presentation of this very general open-ended question, respondents were asked whether or not there were any other activities, in addition to those which they had already mentioned constituted the main job of workers, in which workers in their division engaged at the present time. Again, this was an open-ended question and respondents were given no prompting by the interviewer that might suggest possible answers to the question. The responses to this question, along with the responses to the subsequent prompts, are summarised in Table 11.1. It should be noted that, in terms of its construction, Table 11.1 lists all of the 'other' activities, or activity categories, to which respondents made reference (whether in response to the open-ended question or in response to subsequent prompting). In order to facilitate the comparison of open question data with prompt data, those activities that were the subject of specific prompts are grouped separately and appear, in the table, in italics. In the event that a respondent mentioned a prompted activity spontaneously — it was anticipated that this would occur since the prompts asked about other

Table 11.1. Workers' 'other' activities: A comparison of the open question and prompt data for the Tooling Division and the Production Division for the present context.

Activity Category	Tooling Division (n = 12)		Production Division (n = 19)	
	Open Q		Open Q	
Primary task	2			
Work maintenance			7	
Quality activities			4	
Efficiency activities			1	
Job rotation			1	
Communicate with workers	1		1	
Safety awareness	2			
		Prompt		*Prompt*
Planning meetings		*1*		*4*
Information meetings		*8*	*1*	*18*
Group problem-solving		*2*		*5*
Safety meetings	*3*	*8*	*1*	*13*
Union meetings	*2*	*9*		*15*
Help other workers		*11*		*16*
Record work-related information		*3*		*15*
Attend training		*12*		*12*
Formal social	*2*	*10*	*2*	*17*
Informal social	*2*	*10*	*3*	*16*
Communicate with supervisors	*1*	*9*		*19*
	no other activities		no other activities	
	n = 3		*n* = 7	

Notes:
1. Activities, or activity categories, which constituted the subject of specific prompt questions are shown in italics.
2. Multiple references by a single respondent to any given activity, or activity category, are not reported.
3. Respondents were not prompted about activities that they had already mentioned spontaneously, that is, in response to the open-ended question. Thus, the numbers of respondents represented in the 'Open' and 'Prompt' cells of the table are independent of one another.

activities in which workers could potentially engage — the respondent was not subsequently prompted about that same activity. Thus, the numbers of respondents which are represented in the 'Open' and 'Prompt' cells of the table are independent of one another.

The point should be made here that, while the aim of the present research is to develop a method for assessing Schein's (1985, 1992, 2004, 2010) Level 3 beliefs and assumptions, the concern is with defining the broad parameters of such a method and identifying the *general* types of questions that might most usefully be asked. As such, further research would be needed to determine which specific open-ended and closed questions would be most suitable for tapping beliefs and assumptions in each of the categories that make up Schein's (2010) typology (notwithstanding the fact that the focus in Study 3 is on beliefs and assumptions about The Nature of Human Nature). The search for such questions might also reveal the extent to which Schein's major categories, which were based on anthropological research, are sufficient to describe the cultures of organisations.

It can be seen from Table 11.1 that, in response to the second open-ended question, one quarter (3/12) of the respondents from the tooling division and just over one-third (7/19) of the respondents from the production division indicated that the workers in their division at the present time were engaged in no other activities. It can also be seen that the remaining respondents from each division made reference to a range of other activities. With respect, first of all, to the results for the tooling division, reference was made to worker involvement in safety activities (whether formal, in the sense of attendance at safety meetings or informal, in the sense of maintaining a general awareness of safety requirements) and industrial relations activities (i.e., attending union meetings). Reference was also made to worker participation in formal and informal social activities (the former being initiated by the organisation, usually with the involvement of a formally constituted social committee and the latter being more impromptu and initiated by individual workers). Finally, two respondents from this division made reference to worker involvement in 'primary task' activities, that is, activities that would appear to constitute an integral part of the main job of workers in the division.

The picture for the production division open responses was somewhat different. As can be seen from Table 11.1, there was a strong emphasis in this division on worker involvement in 'work maintenance' activities, that is, activities designed to maintain the flow of work and support production operations (e.g., housekeeping, fork truck driving, and relieving other workers). Approximately one-third of the respondents from this division (7/19) made one or more references to worker involvement in activities of this kind. The next best represented activity category for the production division was 'quality activities', with two respondents making reference to the rework responsibilities of workers in the division, and two referring to a more general quality function for workers. As for the tooling division, reference was also made to worker participation in formal and informal social activities.

11.1.1.2 *Prompt data*

Following the presentation of the two open-ended questions described above, respondents were presented with a series of closed questions or prompts. As indicated, the prompts for this part of the interview took the form of specific questions about worker involvement in a range of potentially relevant other activities. Some of the prompts described very general activities (e.g., work-related social activities and communication with one's supervisor), while others described activities that more obviously implied a more active and self-directing role for workers (such as, involvement in planning and group problem-solving activities).

The reader is reminded that it was the initial qualitative work, undertaken in Study 1 and described in Chapter 8, that provided the basis for the subsequent design of the prompts developed for use in Study 3. This earlier work suggested that McGregor's (1960) distinction between Theory X and Theory Y beliefs was a useful framework for understanding the culture of the tooling division, and that it might subsequently also be of value for comparing this culture with the culture of the production division. Of course, similar research would be needed to determine suitable prompts for accessing information about other topics — whether related to the nature of human nature category or to other categories in Schein's typology. Once identified, these prompts might prove to be useful for understanding differences between organisations, in particular, differences that are grounded in organisational culture.

It can be seen from Table 11.1 that, for both divisions, there was a large discrepancy between spontaneous and prompted responses in terms of both the range of activities in which workers reportedly engaged, and the numbers of respondents who indicated worker involvement in these activities. Thus, the activity profile suggested by an aggregation of spontaneous with prompted responses is significantly broader than that suggested by the spontaneous responses alone. Also, there was generally more agreement among respondents about worker involvement in prompted activities than in activities referred to in response to the open-ended question. For example, Table 11.1 shows that, for the tooling division, five of the prompted activity categories were represented in responses to the open question, whereas in response to prompting all 11 of these categories were represented. The pattern of responding was similar for the production division. As indicated, whereas only four of the prompted activity categories were represented by the spontaneous responses, all 11 of these categories were represented by prompted responses.

With respect to the numbers of respondents indicating worker involvement in particular activities, Table 11.1 shows that, in the tooling division for example, there were no respondents who made spontaneous reference to the involvement of workers in this division in either information meetings or training programs. However, in response to prompting, a majority of respondents from this division reported worker involvement in both of these activities (eight indicated worker involvement in information meetings and 12 indicated worker involvement in training). Again, the pattern of responding was similar for the production division. One respondent only made spontaneous reference to worker involvement in information meetings but, in response to prompting, 18 respondents reported worker involvement in this activity. Similarly, no respondents made spontaneous reference to the involvement of workers in this division in training compared with 12 who indicated worker involvement in this activity in response to prompting.

11.1.2 *Interpreting the discrepancy between open question and prompt data*

It is clear from the above results that, if the interview had included open-ended questions only, this additional information about the activities of workers in each division would not have been obtained. The question arises as to why respondents from both divisions failed to mention worker involvement in particular activities in response to the open-ended question, but subsequently, in response to prompting, indicated that workers were involved in these activities. One possible explanation for this discrepancy, which receives some support in the literature, is that more structured approaches to data collection (such as the present use of specific prompts) can have the effect of 'putting words into people's mouths'. A good illustration of this is provided by Lewis and Furnham (cited in Lewis, 1990) in their study of opinions about how unemployment in Britain could be reduced. In this study, open-ended questions — respondents were simply asked, without prompting, for their views on how unemployment could be reduced — were combined with a forced choice procedure whereby respondents were required to indicate the extent of their agreement or disagreement with a number of 'solutions' that had been identified *a priori* by the researchers. The result was that some solutions (e.g., reducing immigration) received strong support in the forced choice procedure but were mentioned considerably less often in response to the open-ended questions. Thus, according to Lewis (1990), a problem with the forced choice procedure is that it can inflate the popularity of certain proposed solutions and inhibit respondents who genuinely have nothing to say from indicating that this is the case. In this sense, the forced choice procedure can have the effect of putting words into people's mouths.

While this explanation for a discrepancy between 'free' responses and forced choice responses seems reasonable in the context of Lewis and Furnham's study, it is less plausible in the context of the present results which reflect respondents' perceptions of what *actually* happens (i.e., what workers in their division actually do), rather than their opinions about what *ought* to happen. There seems little reason to doubt the validity of the present results, particularly given the significant numbers of respondents (in some cases, the entire sample) who, in response to prompting, reported that workers in their division engaged in particular activities. It might be anticipated, however, that the effect of putting words into peoples' mouths would be more likely to influence results for that part of the interview concerned with respondents' opinions about the activities that workers *ideally* should be involved in. If this were the case, one might expect that, for questions in this later part of the interview, the discrepancy between spontaneous and prompted responses would be even more pronounced than that observed for the present set of questions. However, as will be seen when the results for the ideal context are reported, this was not the case.

There are three other possible explanations for the present discrepancy between spontaneous and prompted responses. First, it may be that respondents were simply unclear as to the meaning of the initial open-ended question concerned, in this case, with other worker activities (that is, activities in which workers engaged in addition to those which reportedly constituted their main job). However, with the subsequent presentation of the prompts, any ambiguity about the meaning of this question would be resolved since, as it will be recalled, the activities which were the subject of the prompts were intended as possible answers to the question. While this explanation is plausible, it is not consistent with the researcher's[1] experience of administering the interviews. Respondents showed little hesitation in framing their responses to either of the initial open-ended questions suggesting that, for the most part, they had a good understanding of what they were being asked to comment upon.

These impressions aside, however, evidence for the plausibility of this explanation should be contained within the actual interview data. It can be argued that, if initial confusion about the meaning of the open-ended question was the problem, then the pattern of responding reported above, which pertains to perceptions of the present role of workers, should not emerge in subsequent questions about the role of workers in the past and anticipated future. This is because, as indicated, the earlier presentation of the prompts in the context of respondents' present experience would have removed any ambiguity about the meaning of the open-ended question. Hence, when asked what is effectively this same open-ended question on a second and third occasion, in the context of their past and anticipated future experience respectively, respondents should be quite clear as to what was required. In fact, one might expect that their responses to the open-ended question, when asked on these subsequent occasions, would be primed by the earlier prompting about their present experience of the other activities of workers. (In other words, one would expect that significantly more prompted activities would be mentioned in spontaneous references to the other activities of workers in the past and anticipated future than in spontaneous references to other activities of workers at the present time.) Although respondents were not actually asked the same question again — rather, they were asked whether or not the role of workers was different in the past, or likely to differ in the anticipated future — it would still seem reasonable to argue that the questions asked concerning the respondent's present experience should make it clear what respondents were being asked to comment upon, so that this should not be a problem subsequently when asked about the other contextual domains.

A second explanation for the present discrepancy between spontaneous and prompted responses is that some activities may be more central and more salient than others to members' definitions of the role of workers in their division. One might expect that these activities would be more likely to be mentioned in responses to open-ended questions about what workers do than activities that are more peripheral to prevailing definitions of the role of workers (even though these latter activities may occupy a reasonable amount of workers' time). As such, specific prompting may be required in order to make apparent the involvement of workers in these latter activities. Alternatively, a third explanation is that, given the view of organisational culture as comprising unconscious beliefs and assumptions, it may be that certain activities have come to be so much a part of organisation members' thinking about 'what workers do' as to have acquired the status of assumed knowledge. An important implication of this third explanation is that such activities would

---

[1] As indicated in Chapter 8, this is a reference to the first author who undertook the empirical work for the three studies that are reported in Parts Four and Five of the present volume.

be unlikely to be mentioned spontaneously (in response to the open-ended question) but, rather, would require prompting to bring them to the surface of respondents' awareness.

To determine which of the above explanations (if any) is most plausible in the context of the present results, it is necessary to explore more fully the nature of respondents' experience of the activities of workers in their division. Some valuable insights in this regard were provided by the analysis of data generated by other questions in the protocol, in particular: (i) questions from the present context about the extent of workers' current involvement in various activities; and (ii) questions from the past context concerning whether or not workers' involvement in these activities had changed over time and, if so, why. Since similar observations were made for most of the activities mentioned in response to both the open-ended and prompt questions, only the data for two of these activities, labelled 'information meetings' and 'attend training', are reported here. These two activities were chosen because, as indicated in Table 11.1, for both activities there was a marked discrepancy in the data for both divisions between respondents' spontaneous and prompted responses.

11.1.2.1 *Findings for 'information meetings'*

It can be seen from Table 11.1 that, for both divisions, there was a marked discrepancy between the number of spontaneous and prompted references to workers' current involvement in information meetings. It should be noted that, in the prompt procedure (see Appendix B), information meetings were defined as meetings in which workers were given information by those above them about such things as the current performance and future directions of either their division or the organisation as a whole. This prompt was included to cue respondents to the involvement of workers in both divisions in what were commonly referred to as *state of the nation* meetings (held for the purpose of disseminating information of this kind). As indicated, for the tooling division, no respondents indicated worker involvement in information meetings in response to the open-ended question, compared with eight respondents (two-thirds of the sample) who reported worker involvement in this activity when prompted. The picture was similar for the production division. One respondent only made spontaneous reference to the involvement of workers in this division in state of the nation meetings while, in response to prompting, a further 18 respondents (95% of the sample) reported that workers attended these meetings.

What then might these discrepancies mean? When asked about the extent of workers' current involvement in information meetings, respondents from the tooling division reported that, although the meetings were typically attended by all workers, they were held infrequently (only once or twice annually). It also became apparent from questions about respondents' past experience of worker involvement in this activity that the meetings had been introduced relatively recently (on average, five years ago). Given that tooling division respondents had an average length of service with the division of approximately 23 years, it can be argued that, as a group, they shared quite a long history of no worker involvement in this activity. Also, when asked about why the meetings were introduced, a common response was that it was an attempt by management to quash increasing rumours about the possible closure of the division. These findings suggest that, from a cultural perspective, the experience of worker involvement in this activity may not yet have been sufficiently extensive (in terms of how long workers had been involved in the activity, how frequently they were involved in it, and perceptions about why the activity was introduced) to have effected a change in traditional ways of thinking about what workers do.

The explanation for the production division findings is essentially the same as that for the tooling division findings. There were, however, some differences between the two divisions with respect to the specific nature of respondents' experiences of the involvement of workers in information meetings. While respondents from the production division also indicated that information meetings had been introduced relatively recently (on average, three years ago), and that they were typically attended by all workers, the meetings were reportedly held much more frequently than those in the tooling division (every one to three months). Hence, workers in the production division appear to have had much greater exposure to this activity in recent years than their counterparts in the tooling division. While this might suggest that the activity had come to be taken-for-granted with respect to divisional member thinking about what workers in the division do, this is unlikely given the relatively short history of the activity and given what we know about the length of time required for culture evolution and change (see, e.g., Schein, 1985, 1992, 2004, 2010).

A consideration of respondents' attributions about why the meetings were introduced provides some additional insights here. Most respondents associated the introduction of information meetings with the arrival, in the late 1980s, of a new divisional manager who was perceived by divisional members to be more committed to the involvement of shop floor workers in divisional activities than most previous managers reportedly had been. In fact, it was the researcher's understanding from a number of conversations with this manager, that this was an integral part of his overall strategy for improving the efficiency of the division. It was also the case that, during the period of the researcher's association with the division, a number of other initiatives designed to increase worker involvement in divisional activities were beginning to be introduced.

The above findings, together with the researcher's more general observations, suggest the interesting possibility that the introduction of any new worker activity which assumes values that somehow challenge more traditional thinking about the role of workers is unlikely to lead to a redefinition of that role unless all of the following conditions are met:

(1) The activity has occurred for a relatively long period of time;
(2) Workers have had significant exposure to the activity;
(3) Positive attributions (as above) are made about the reasons for worker involvement in the activity; and
(4) The activity constitutes one of a range of management initiatives that have been fully implemented to increase worker involvement, rather than simply a 'token' effort by management to bring about change.

11.1.2.2 *Findings for 'attend training'*

With respect to the activity labelled 'attend training', Table 11.1 shows that prompting was again required to highlight the involvement of workers in this activity. In fact, as indicated, no respondents from either division spontaneously mentioned worker involvement in training. However, in response to subsequent prompting, all of the respondents from the tooling division and almost two-thirds of the respondents from the production division reported that the workers in their respective divisions attended training. Interestingly, all seven of the production division respondents who reported that workers were not involved in training were wages employees (i.e., they themselves were workers). These results (as with the above results for information meetings) suggest the interesting possibility that discrepancies between free and prompted responses could provide important information about the extent to which the representations that organisation members have of certain issues — that is, their way of thinking about, or framing, these issues — are consciously or unconsciously held. Such discrepancies might differ from one issue to another and they might also differ between subcultures (e.g., between a management and a worker subculture). Furthermore, such discrepancies might be of interest with respect to issues that are the subject of organisational change programs. Assessments before and after change programs might be expected to show that such issues are commented on more freely (i.e., with less need for prompting) after the change program than before it. Paradoxically, a sign that certain changes have become part of the organisation's culture might be that after a time they are no longer commented on spontaneously because they have come to be taken-for-granted, such that, in order to elicit information about them, organisation members will require prompting. As above for information meetings, in attempting to explain the discrepancy between free and prompted responses for 'attend training', it is useful to consider some of the additional data pertaining to respondents' experience of the involvement of workers in this activity.

In contrast to the findings for information meetings, there was considerable variability, among respondents from both divisions, in their estimates of the extent of workers' involvement in training programs. For the tooling division, estimates of how many workers attended training ranged from 5% to 50%. Estimates of the amount of training received ranged from 20 hours per worker per year to 50 hours per worker per year. The picture was similar for the production division, with estimates of the numbers of workers involved in training ranging from 5% to 100%, and estimates of the amount of training received ranging from two hours per worker per year to 50 hours per worker per year. This lack of agreement among respondents from both divisions about the extent of workers' involvement in training may reflect on the status of the activity in each division. In other words, to the extent that training was regarded as a somewhat peripheral activity, one might expect members' knowledge of the activity to be limited. This explanation is not inconsistent with the author's impression of the status of training in each division.

Another explanation, which is also supported by the researcher's experience, is that training in both divisions was a less uniform activity than the so-called state of the nation meetings. In other words, where all workers were required to attend state of the nation meetings which were held on a more or less regular basis, the involvement of workers in training seemed, more often than not, to reflect individual initiatives whereby individual workers would express an interest in, and seek approval for, participation in particular training courses that were being offered. To the extent that this was the case, estimates of the extent of worker involvement in training could be expected to vary considerably.

At this point, it is useful to turn to a consideration of the data pertaining to the history of worker involvement in training. Data from the tooling division are considered first, followed by a consideration of data from the production division.

Tooling division: Past experience of training. In answering questions about the past, all of the tooling division respondents reported that, in the past, there was less training (5/12 or 42% of the sample) or no training at all (7/12 or 58%) for workers in this division. Estimates for the whole sample of when the change towards increased training had occurred ranged from between two years ago to eight years ago. However, 80% of these estimates were between two and four years ago, suggesting a fair degree of agreement among respondents from this division about when this change had occurred. There was also good agreement among respondents about why the change towards increased involvement in training had occurred. Of the 11 respondents for whom attributions data were available, eight made reference to the requirement, associated with the recent restructuring of the award,[2] for workers to become multi-skilled. Other attributions included: the impact of technological change requiring workers to become better trained (one respondent); a recognition on the part of management of the need to increase the knowledge, efficiency, and flexibility of workers (two respondents); an attempt to replace skills lost through the downsizing of the division over recent years (one respondent); and an increasing emphasis on quality in line with international developments (one respondent). All respondents also agreed that, prior to the change reported, the status of this activity in the division had remained the same (i.e., less training than that received currently or no training at all) for a period which extended back to at least the respondent's start date with the company. In two cases reference was made to a past that extended back beyond the respondent's date of commencement to the early years of the start-up of the division (some fifty years previously). These results suggest that it may be important to question the times at which certain events or changes occurred.

The above historical data are interesting for a number of reasons. First, there was more consensus among respondents about the history of worker involvement in training in the tooling division than about the extent of workers' current involvement in training. Second,

---

[2] As indicated in Chapter 9, towards the end of the 1980s, a major restructure of the vehicle industry award was undertaken in Australia. This was a tripartite initiative involving the government, the unions, and local automotive manufacturers. Among its main objectives were the simplification of existing award classifications and the introduction of industry-wide procedures for increasing employees' skills and knowledge. Award restructuring can be seen as the precursor to enterprise bargaining, the mechanism for negotiating wages and conditions of work (in this case at an organisational rather than industry level) that is in use today.

the data suggest that, when viewed in its historical context, the involvement of workers in this division in training has been relatively brief. This would tend to support the argument that training may not constitute a centrally important activity with respect to divisional members' thinking about what it is that workers in the division do. One might therefore expect that respondents would be unlikely to mention worker involvement in this activity without prompting. As indicated above, this was indeed the case. The point should also be made that the majority of workers (wages employees) in the tooling division were qualified tradesmen who had gained their trade qualifications after successfully completing their training as apprentices when they first commenced work with the company. In this sense the training of these workers was probably regarded, by divisional members in general, as being complete. The notion that training should continue to constitute a centrally important activity for workers in this division might, therefore, be seen as an admission of inadequate apprenticeship training.

Finally, the data are interesting because they provide some insight into the context that may have shaped respondents' perceptions of the nature of workers' involvement in training at the present time. As indicated, respondents in this division had experienced a relatively long history of little or no worker involvement in training. The question arises as to whether or not this may have led to a tendency to overstate the case with respect to the current involvement of workers in this activity. In other words, would the same objective amount of training be perceived differently by respondents from a division in which workers had participated in training on a regular basis over a much longer period of time? If this were the case, it would be consistent with the view — shared widely among organisational culture scholars and supported by the results of Studies 1 and 2 of the present research — that the historical context can significantly influence the meaning that respondents attach to particular events. The further point can be made that one of the problems with questionnaire measures in this regard — whether measures of organisational culture or some other organisational phenomenon — is that they assume that questionnaire items and the various Likert-type response categories associated with these items (e.g., *very likely, very unlikely, strongly agree, strongly disagree*) will mean the same thing to all respondents.

Production division: Past experience of training. The experience of production division respondents regarding the history of worker involvement in training was much less uniform than that reported above for tooling division respondents. As a group, production division respondents appeared to have less shared history of worker involvement in this activity than their counterparts from the tooling division. Just over half of the respondents from the production division reported that there was no change in worker involvement in training from the past to the present (with half of these having previously reported that workers attended training at the present time and half having reported that they did not). The remaining respondents indicated that there was a change from the past to the present, with the majority of these reporting that, in the past, there was either less training than at the present time or no training at all. Estimates of when the change towards more training had occurred were similar to those reported for the tooling division and ranged from between one to four years ago.

Attributions about why the change had occurred included: pressure from the government and unions associated with the introduction of award restructuring (three respondents); the more positive attitudes of the recently appointed manager to training (one respondent); part of a more general effort to make better use of the division's human resources (one respondent); and an initiative by the respondent himself to increase the amount of training provided to the workers in his section (one respondent). All respondents agreed that, prior to the change reported, the status of this activity in the division had remained the same (i.e., less training than that received currently or no training at all) for a period which extended back to the respondent's start date with the company (which for longer-serving production employees can be distinguished from their start date with the division).

Interestingly, the majority of respondents who reported a change from the past to the present (with less or no training in the past) were longer-serving employees with 15 or more years' service with the company. In contrast, of those reporting no change from the past to the present, the majority were shorter-serving employees who had spent most of their time with the production division and whose length of service with the company ranged from between four and nine years. These findings are consistent with the argument that the historical context of an individual's experience of any given change may influence the salience of that change to the individual. In the present example, longer-serving employees with a relatively long history of little or no worker involvement in training were more likely to report a change in this activity than shorter serving employees who were nevertheless present when the change occurred. The argument is that these latter employees are likely to be more accustomed to change (from the outset, the production division has been a site for management innovations) since they do not have a significant history of 'no change' against which to evaluate their current experiences.

These results suggest that demographic information — related, for example, to a respondent's age, gender, length of tenure with the organisation, ethnicity, *etc.* — may be important for an understanding of individual differences in responses to questions about topics such as the role of workers. For example, gender might be an important demographic in understanding perceptions of the role of workers, as impacted by a work-family policy. In particular, females might be found to have a better knowledge of the policy, in terms of when it was introduced, its contents and any changes that have occurred, because of the greater relevance of the policy to their working lives.

The question remains, however, as to the implications of the above findings for an understanding of why, to the extent that workers in the production division were currently involved in training, this only became apparent when respondents were prompted about it and did not emerge in their responses to the open-ended question. In attempting to answer this question, it is interesting to consider the data for shorter-serving and longer-serving respondents separately. If 10 or more years of service is used as the 'cut off' to differentiate longer-serving from shorter-serving respondents, the sample for the production division can be seen to comprise 10 longer-serving respondents and nine shorter-serving respondents. Of the longer-serving respondents, there were eight (including all five supervisors in the sample) who, in response to prompting, indicated that the workers in their division were currently involved in training. Given the length of service of these respondents, as well as the timing of the introduction of the change (relatively recently), the same explanation as that offered above for the tooling division may apply here. In other words, for these respondents, training may constitute a peripheral rather than a central activity in terms of their definitions of the role of workers. It is possible also that the pattern of responding for this group contains some social desirability bias. As indicated, the group included all five of the supervisory staff in the sample and, it may be that these individuals, in responding positively to the prompt, were expressing their overt support for company policy regarding the importance of training. Further research would be needed to confirm the relative influence of social desirability effects. However, the results suggest that researchers should be alert to the likely greater influence of these effects on some members of the organisation than others (e.g., managers who may have a stronger vested interest than workers in promoting certain organisational practices, such as training).

Of the nine shorter-serving respondents (all of whom were wages employees), there were four who, in response to prompting, indicated that the workers in their division were currently involved in training, and five who indicated that the workers in their division were currently not involved in training. Shorter-serving respondents were, therefore, less inclined than their longer-serving counterparts to agree about worker involvement in this activity.

This lack of agreement alone would suggest that, for these respondents, this activity is not centrally important in their definitions of what workers do. Further support for this conclusion can be found in findings reported in the next section — pertaining to respondents' qualifications of, and elaborations on, their responses — that provide evidence of a degree of cynicism among employees in this division, associated with their perception that training was provided only when production demands allowed it.

11.2 The Use of Qualitative Data to Give Meaning to Quantitative Data

The critical question for the evaluation of this feature of the design of our proposed method is whether or not the additional time required to allow respondents to elaborate on, and/or qualify, their responses is justified in terms of the insights that the data generated can provide. In attempting to answer this question, the results of an analysis of the qualitative data associated with the same two worker activities as above — 'information meetings' and 'attend training' — are presented and discussed. Particular attention is drawn to the emergent themes in these data and the similarities and differences between the divisions that they serve to highlight. While the analysis in this section, as in Section 11.1 above, is concerned primarily with respondents' *present* experience, it also draws on aspects of respondents' past experience. Specifically, attributions data (generated by questions about the past context) are analysed in order to gain insights into respondents' personal explanations for the current status of the two worker activities examined.

In terms of the structure for this section, the findings for 'information meetings' are reported first, followed by the findings for 'attend training'. For each of these worker activities, particular attention is given to the following:

(1) Similarities and differences, within and between divisions, in the way in which respondents defined the issue in question (i.e., "What are information meetings?" and "What is training?");
(2) Similarities and differences, within and between divisions, in the thematic content of respondents' elaborations on the issue in question; and
(3) Attributions data reflecting respondents' views about the events (actions *etc.*) that had shaped the present situation, with respect to each of the issues in question (essentially, attempts to explain the current involvement of workers in information meetings and in training).

Before reporting the results of this analysis, there are a number of points of clarification (concerning, e.g., certain specific features of the data set and the style of presentation of the data) that need to be made, as follows:

(1) With the exception of the attributions data, all of the data included in the present analysis pertain to respondents' accounts of their *present* experience. At the same time, however, these data were often embedded in responses pertaining to some other contextual domain. For example, in the course of talking about her/his experience of training in the past or anticipated future, a respondent might, by way of drawing a comparison, comment on training in the division at the present time. These comments, along with all other data pertaining to the respondent's experience of training at the present time were extracted for inclusion in the present analysis.

   The fact that respondents could, and did, refer to other contexts (e.g., the past and anticipated future) when responding to questions about a given context (e.g., the present), suggests that this information could be important in determining contextual influences on aspects of an organisation's culture. For example, if respondents' answers to questions about the present or anticipated future were found to contain multiple references to the past (with few or no references to the other or ideal contexts), then this might be indicative of a strongly embedded culture. It should also be noted that, if the present study had included *only* questions about the present context, then the additional data about the present context that were generated in response to questions about other contexts would not have been obtained.
(2) It will become apparent from the data reported in this section that the perspective from which different respondents provided information sometimes differed. For example, it

was not uncommon for supervisory staff to talk about a particular issue (e.g., training) from the perspective of what they as individuals did in the organisation. Shop floor (i.e., wages) employees, on the other hand, were more likely to talk about the issue from the perspective of their perception of how things were done in the organisation.

(3) All of the data presented in this section take the form of respondents' comments, quoted verbatim. In reporting these data, the same style protocol has been adopted as previously for Studies 1 and 2. Specifically, no attempt has been made to correct grammatical errors in any of the quoted material. However, where clarification of a respondent's meaning is required, or where it is necessary to substitute a name with a more neutral title, such changes have been inserted into the quoted material and enclosed in square brackets.

Points (4), (5), and (6) below pertain specifically to the results of the thematic content analysis.

(4) In reporting the results of the thematic content analysis, emergent themes that were common to both divisions are described first, followed by a description of emergent themes that were unique to each division. Within each of these two categories ('common' and 'unique' themes), themes are described in order of how strongly they were supported by the data (in terms of the number of respondents' comments reflecting each theme), from those with the most support to those with the least support.

(5) For each theme described, all of the data (i.e., all respondents' comments) reflecting that theme are presented. Also, contradictions to any given theme in the form of minority views are also highlighted. This approach was adopted in order to provide a clear indication of the extent to which given themes were supported by the data. It can be contrasted with the more common practice in qualitative studies of reporting data selectively, typically with no indication given of the criteria used in selecting the data that are reported. Accordingly, if only confirmatory data are reported, the reader does not know if there were any divergent views that were expressed.

(6) Finally, the reader may note that, in some cases, the same data are presented in support of more than one theme. This occurs when a respondent has made a comment (concerning some aspect of her/his present experience of information meetings or training) containing more than one central idea or theme. Since the comment could not be fragmented further without risking a change in meaning, it was left intact and simply reproduced where appropriate. Since this occurred very infrequently, it was felt that there was little reason for concern about redundancy in the data presented.

11.2.1 *Findings for 'information meetings'*

As indicated above, in reporting these findings, consideration is given first to similarities and differences between the divisions in how respondents defined information meetings.

Following this, consideration is given to similarities and differences between the divisions in the thematic content of the qualitative data pertaining to information meetings. And finally, consideration is given to the nature of respondents' attributions regarding the current involvement of workers in information meetings (i.e., why it is as it is, and how it may have come to be this way).

11.2.1.1 *What are information meetings?*

As indicated in Table 11.1, in response to prompting, eight of the 12 respondents from the tooling division and 18 of the 19 respondents from the production division reported some involvement of the workers in their division in information meetings[3]. It is interesting to note that, of the eight respondents from the tooling division, there were only two who offered this information in response to an initial *general* prompt: "Do workers in your division at the present time attend meetings of any kind?" The remaining six had to be asked *specifically* about the involvement of workers in their division in information meetings. In contrast, in the production division, 15 respondents provided this information in response to the initial general prompt, whereas only three had to be presented with the subsequent more specific prompt[4]. This finding is consistent with the frequency data reported above, suggesting that workers in the production division had had markedly more exposure to this activity than their counterparts in the tooling division.

Tooling division. Of the eight tooling division respondents who reported some worker involvement in information meetings, five gave some indication of their perception of what these meetings involved. The remaining three simply indicated that workers were involved in such meetings, without elaborating on the nature of these meetings. The most common perception of the purpose of information meetings was that they provided a venue for the dissemination of information about the performance of the company as a whole. This view was indicated, more or less explicitly, in the comments of four respondents, as follows:

> ...[talking about] tooling projects, the way the car was selling and all that sort of general company situations... (wages employee, leading hand)

> Well the only thing that I've been to a meeting of is when the future of the company, when they've been going bad and they'll have a meeting right, of telling you what's going on. (wages employee, leading hand)

> Occasionally we were involved, like they used to, [the divisional manager] used to call a mass meeting sometimes. ...for a specific reason, if there was a special occasion like the launch of the new model, they'd say how it was going, how we did. (wages employee)

---

[3] It can also be seen in Table 11.1, that there was one respondent from the production division who provided this information spontaneously, that is, in response to the initial open-ended question.
[4] This difference between the divisions was statistically significant (Chi square $= 7.53$, $p < .01$).

> The state of the nation meetings, or state of the company or whatever, is given to provide the workers with information, not really to take from them any information. (wages employee, leading hand)

Also contained in two of the excerpts above is the idea that information meetings were held, not on a regular basis, but only when some specific event or set of circumstances seemed to warrant this form of communication to workers (e.g., a downturn or, alternatively, the launch of a new model).

In contrast to the above, one respondent from this division was emphatic that the sole purpose of the information meetings was to inform workers about how the current relocation effort was proceeding and to notify them of the likely implications of this change for the division as a whole and for them as individual employees. According to this respondent, performance information (related, e.g., to product quality) was not disseminated in these meetings:

> Hang on a minute. The information update was only on the future of the tooling division and what will happen with the people. It has never involved quality or whatever. (first-line supervisor)

Production division. Compared with the tooling division, there seemed to be more variability among respondents from the production division in their perceptions of what constituted the main focus of information meetings. In all, there were 15 respondents from this division whose elaborations on the subject included some reference to the specific content of information meetings. While these respondents all agreed that the meetings were for the dissemination of performance information, respondents differed in their accounts of how local the information was. For example, the following comments by eight respondents suggest that an important focus of information meetings was the dissemination of highly localised information pertaining to the performance of the respondent's particular section or work group:

> Well, you just go through how your area is going — its reject rates, its absenteeism, safety, you just go through your performance. It entails how to improve it, where we're going wrong, things like that. With management [you] sit down and go through these things. (wages employee)
>
> State of the nation talks... they're mainly about how your area runs. (wages employee)
>
> ...they go in and they just talk about [the section]... how good that's going, how many rejects. (wages employee)
>
> ...we had monthly feedback sessions to the groups where we monitored key performance indicators and then once a month, we would, when we collated the end of month figures, we would sit them down and we would talk about those, that is, their key performance

indicators, so they really knew where they were, what it meant, what went into them. ...we would present them with anything that we thought was relevant, coming forward, like we did a lot of, we kept right up to date with the latest developments in [the new model]... it was just monthly feedback meetings, it was done by operating group, by the supervisor, by shift. (senior supervisor)

We do that on about a monthly basis because we do the charts and all that, the performance charts. ...Yes, [you get] performance indicators for the areas that they're working in. Absenteeism and stuff like that, car sets, injury visits to the medical centre and all that stuff. (senior production control supervisor)

...each respective supervisor of their own particular section takes the troops in and lets them know about the absentee rates, their scrap rate, the productivity per car sets, mostly just to keep them informed of what is going on. And like if the company made a profit — like the last one was that the company announced a [substantial] profit — and what happened was that before it was announced on the press, they had all the groups in and told them that this is what is going on. (first-line supervisor)

...we try on a monthly basis to give a state of the nation type talk and we schedule every-body right across the floor in all areas and departments. ...[the plant manager] comes along, [the technical manager] comes along, our superintendent may give a talk, I always give a talk on how the group performs, give them that feedback and normally just general company type issues. (first-line supervisor)

...we have a monthly meeting where we discuss with the group... we discuss safety, pro-duction, scrap, absenteeism, quality, our customer's perception of quality, and we added one in, I believe a new one, with suggestions — we try to encourage people on the floor to put in suggestions. (first-line supervisor)

In contrast to the above, the following comments by six respondents contain no refer-ence to the dissemination of local work group information in information meetings. Rather, the focus appears to be broader and concerned primarily with the dissemination of divisional or company-wide performance information:

They hear about how the plant's been running for the last month or six weeks or whatever. They get told something about the future sometimes. (wages employee)

Well, we have a state of the nation (meeting) but that's just like our every three months' meeting where we sit and watch a video of the state of the whole of the company, not just production. Really we're not involved in any meetings as just for [our division]. (wages employee)

State of the nation meetings — how the company is going virtually. ...it's all about the company and their operations here. (wages employee)

...they're only telling you what's happening in the industry, that's all... (wages employee)

> About the only meetings we attend, as like state of the nation or actually how production is going. ...That's mainly just getting all the people together and just saying how the cars are selling, and what the industry is going like. (wages employee)

In the case of the following two respondents, it was unclear from their description of information meetings, whether or not the information disseminated in these meetings included any local content:

> Just to tell us... if we're up or if our parts are down... Just, you know, [to tell us] how the cars are selling. (wages employee)

> Well, we have the state of the nation. That involves... they tell you the quality, how the quality record's going, how many rejects we've had for so many months, how the sales, how the market is... If they've got any grievances, the bosses that is, management. If they've got any grievances they'll bring them up at this meeting and see if people have got ideas as to how to overcome them... (wages employee)

One possible explanation for the apparent inconsistency in respondents' perceptions of the nature of information meetings is that respondents were referring to different meetings. In fact, after responding to the initial prompt, two of the above respondents went on to distinguish between local production meetings, in which workers from individual sections (work areas) were given feedback about the performance of their section, and state of the nation meetings in which workers received divisional and company-wide performance information:

> Well one [meeting], like the first one, is how your section's going... like whether you're getting many rejects on the table... and the bigger, the state of the nation, is how the company's going. (wages employee)

> State of the nation was different... that was one that [the plant manager] put on purely to sort of give them the big burst; that was the plant-wide stuff... It's usually like major things, like financial reports, you know, this is where we are, this is where we were, this is where we're going, you know, everything's rosy, everyone's happy, we've really got to stay on top of the overtime, and blah, blah and all that... (senior supervisor)

The point should be made, however, that the term 'state of the nation' appears to have been used generically by some respondents to refer to any meeting in which performance feedback was provided to employees. As such, in the absence of more specific information, there remains some uncertainty about whether the meetings to which some of the respondents above were referring were local production meetings or more widely-focussed state of the nation meetings. The important lesson provided by these data, however, is that they challenge our tendency, as researchers, to assume that respondents' interpretations of our questions are consistent with our own, and that the responses they provide to any given question can be taken to mean the same thing. On the basis of such assumptions, we proceed to aggregate data and report trends in these data that may, in fact, be entirely spurious. This, of course, is a particular problem where quantitative methods constitute the sole approach to data collection, since such methods, unlike qualitative methods, typically do not allow respondents to elaborate on the responses they provide. This problem can be partly overcome by making questions more specific (perhaps based on pilot study information), by providing an 'other' response option, and/or by including a request to provide an example or to comment on the other response option.

11.2.1.2 *Thematic content analysis: Themes common to both divisions*

The analysis of the thematic content of the qualitative data pertaining to information meetings suggested the following three themes that were common to both divisions.

Theme 1: Attendance at meetings not self-motivated

Respondents from both divisions made comments that indicated that the involvement of workers in information meetings was not self-motivated. On the contrary, it seems that it was mandatory for workers to attend such meetings, the implication being that, if this were not the case, the meetings would be considerably less well attended than they were at the present time. In the production division, there were five respondents who expressed this view:

> But [100% of workers attend] because it's compulsory, it's done in company time and the line goes off. (wages employee)
>
> Well, I would say ninety five percent of the people go because they're virtually told that they've got to go. (wages employee)
>
> ...but [there has] always been maybe one state of the nation, once or twice a year, where the workers would have to go. (wages employee)
>
> [They don't go] unless they are instructed to. ...Now when I say instructed, they get told that we're going to have a state of the nation meeting as we call it, and we all go into the canteen, and one of the bosses usually gives a run down on how things are going. (wages employee)
>
> They're supposed to [attend] but they don't. (wages employee)

Similar views were expressed by two respondents from the tooling division. Note that, in the first excerpt below, the respondent (a first-line supervisor) presents an image of workers as being motivated entirely by economic self-interest. As he saw it, workers were disinclined to participate in any work activities for which they were not compensated financially. This view of workers is, of course, entirely consistent with Theory X assumptions about the nature of workers (McGregor, 1960).

> [Workers attend meetings] only if they have to. ...If the company is paying you for it, if it is in company time, they go there. If it is not in company time, even if it is in their own interest, if they don't get paid they don't go. ...They used to keep those meetings for about once a month and everybody went until... because you had to clock off at 4 o'clock. ...And they clocked off at 4 o'clock and that was it. They only went to the meeting because it was better than working. (first-line supervisor)

> The state of the nation meetings have always been on a two times a year, three times a year basis and workers are expected to attend. (wages employee, leading hand)

The above data raise some concerns about the extent to which any intention, on the part of management, to make workers feel more valued as a result of their involvement in meetings such as information meetings, is being realised. The overall impression created by these data is one of obligatory, rather than self-motivated, involvement.

Theme 2: Role of workers essentially passive

A small number of respondents from both divisions commented on the role of workers in information meetings. It was clear from these data that, despite the numbers of workers attending these meetings, and the fact that they were invited to contribute with questions, the role of workers in information meetings remained essentially passive. As indicated in the following comments by two respondents from the production division, few workers responded to the invitation to ask questions and those who did tended always to be the same workers:

> Like some people do, like, the whole lot do get involved, but it's only like three main people who've got questions and questions firing. (wages employee)

> ...afterwards when they ask for comments or ask for questions, you get very few people stand up... like at most meetings, they won't. (wages employee)

A third respondent from the production division made the point that workers were not asked for their views at all, but were simply told about decisions that management had taken:

> The only time you really get any information is if something has happened or, you know, something's wrong, then they'll come and say 'Well we're changing this'. ...they don't come out and ever say 'Well we're looking at changing this. What do you think?' You know, they come out and say 'We're changing this'. (wages employee)

In a similar vein, two respondents from the tooling division alluded to the relatively passive role of workers in information meetings. In the first excerpt below, the point is again made that it is always the same workers who contribute in question time. Moreover, the reluctance of many workers to contribute is attributed to their perception that they have little power to influence key organisational outcomes. In the second excerpt, the respondent makes the point that state of the nation meetings are intended primarily for the dissemination of information downwards. Their main purpose is not to facilitate two-way communication between workers and management.

> Well there's always a question time, and it is always the same people that ask questions... Teamwork's teamwork, but what happens is at these information type meetings... you get the same people, you don't actually get a team response. You know what I mean? You will get people that will come up... they'll be the same people all the time, and others just sit back. And I mean we're all guilty of it. I mean, I go to some meetings and I think to myself 'Well they haven't brought up any relevant points that [are] going to stir me up', so I don't normally get involved in things that I find irrelevant. If something I think is really gonna bug me, okay, but I think a lot of the people are prepared to go along with... because maybe in some ways they're a bit like me, you can say a lot but you're not gonnna have a big influence on any change in a big organisation like this one. It's very regimented and you've got your chain of command and a bloke on a shop floor is going to have... alright he might change a couple of things in his area, he might get a light put in the corner so he can read a drawing better, which is all a help, don't get me wrong, but he's not gonna have a big influence on the running of the place. And I think that tends to quieten people down. They realise that fact. People aren't completely stupid. (first-line supervisor)

> [Workers] get involved in as much as after a state of the nation meeting it's open for questions. So if they've got any problems then is the time to state the problem. Beyond that, they don't really have any involvement whatsoever. The state of the nation meetings, or state of the company, or whatever, is given to provide the workers with information, not really to take from them any information. (wages employee, leading hand)

In the tooling division there were also a number of respondents who, in the context of their comments about information meetings, made more general references to the nature of the communication between shop floor workers and their supervision. In the first excerpt below, it is suggested that supervisors feel threatened by, and hence discourage, a more active and involved role for workers. In the second excerpt, the respondent makes the point that workers often have difficulty gaining access to information that has direct relevance for them.

> But down there, they don't like it, they don't like you being involved... To me, I got the feeling that supervisors feel as if you're trying to give too much and you might be sort of be after their job or something like that. (wages employee, leading hand)

Like we're having at the moment, our program's starting up, and its not until you sort of ask questions... You've got to sort of like dig deep... Yeah, [I would want] the information given freely instead of workers [having] to work it out for themselves, or having to really dig deep. (wages employee)

The point should be made here that it is perhaps an over-simplification to equate the degree of support for any given theme (in terms of the number of respondents' comments which reflect that theme) with the theme's centrality to respondents' thinking about the particular issue under investigation. For example, while the present theme does not appear to be strongly supported by the data, the absence of any views to contradict those reported above suggests that the theme may, in fact, be of some significance in informing our understanding of the nature of workers' current involvement in information meetings.

Theme 3: Meetings held as the need arises

A small number of respondents from both divisions suggested that information meetings were held only as the need arose, that is, when there was specific information, whether negative (e.g., relating to declining productivity) or positive (e.g., relating to the launch of a new model) which management wished to communicate to workers. This theme emerged in the comments of three respondents from the production division and two respondents from the tooling division. Specifically, respondents from the production division commented that:

[Meetings are held] only when they've got information to tell the people... Or when the situation arises, such as a shortage of work or a drop in sales. Then, you know, we get 'told' [to improve performance]. (wages employee)

The only time you really get any information is if something has happened or, you know, something's wrong... (wages employee)

...there's not really much to report at the moment 'cos nothing's happening, there's not a heap of cars being sold and it's probably bad news anyway... (wages employee)

The two respondents from the tooling division commented that:

Well, the only thing that I've been to a meeting [for] is when the future of the company, when they've been going bad and they'll have a meeting, right, [for] telling you what's going on. (wages employee, leading hand)

Occasionally we were involved, like they used to, [the divisional manager] used to call a mass meeting sometimes... For a specific reason, if there was a special occasion like the launch of the new model, they'd say how it was going, how we did. (wages employee)

While it is not entirely clear, it appears that this contingency applied only to information meetings in which company-wide information was disseminated; it did not apply to the sectional or work group meetings, mentioned previously, and referred to in the elaborations of some of the respondents from the production division.

11.2.1.3 *Thematic content analysis: Themes unique to each division*

The analysis of the thematic content of the qualitative data pertaining to information meetings revealed two themes that were unique to the production division. Each of these themes is described below. For the tooling division, no unique themes were identified by this analysis.

Theme 1: Information meetings contingent on production demands

Four respondents from the production division made explicit reference to their perception that either the attendance at information meetings, or the frequency with which these meetings were held, was contingent on the level of production in the division. When production demands were high, meetings were either not held or not attended by certain key workers or groups of workers:

> Well, yes, [all workers] are supposed to [go], but we don't always do it if we're busy or something. I quite often cop out if I'm busy... I think, I haven't got time to go to that. (wages employee)

> No, they haven't been [held on a regular basis]. Since the introduction of the new model, it has been whenever there has been time. And that is the whole philosophy regarding all meetings, right. It has sort of died a death and [been] put to the back burner until we get some sort of stability, because of the model introduction... (first-line supervisor)

> ...unfortunately, the last couple of months we've missed out, with the [new model]. ...unfortunately, our first function is that we have to provide parts to build a car, and when the heat's on, certain things get dropped off. It's unfortunate, but this only happens once every two years anyway with a new model. And the last couple of months we've missed out on our monthly talk to the groups. (first-line supervisor)

> [All workers] are supposed to [attend] but they don't. ...it depends on the section. If the section is busy, they just ignore them... they miss out. (wages employee)

The notion that information meetings were of secondary importance, relative to other activities in the division (associated, e.g., with the production demands referred to above), was implied in the comments of a further 10 respondents from this division. Of these, four reported that information meetings had been held more regularly in the past than they were at the present time. Given the data above, it would seem reasonable to assume some association between this observation and the introduction, in recent times, of a new model vehicle:

> It used to be once a month. I reckon [it is now] about three or four times a year. (wages employee)
>
> Occasionally, not as often as we used to... Well, I don't think I've been to one now since January. So it's not as often as it should be. We used to have them regular. We used to have them at least every two months and now I would say it's about four months since I've been to one. (wages employee)
>
> *Interviewer:* Do workers in the production division attend meetings? *Respondent:* Not as much these days as we used to. (wages employee)
>
> ...from the shop floor initially they were pretty sceptical because, you know, these sorts of programs start and stop, start and stop, and then in fact that's what happened. (first-line supervisor)

The remaining six respondents simply pointed to the irregularity with which information meetings were currently held. Again, while these respondents offered no explanations as to why this was the case, their comments below nevertheless give some indication of perceptions about the relative importance of information meetings:

> I'd say they've always been there, but on and off. Sometimes you'd have them and then you might go for a few months and you wouldn't have them. Then they might develop again. (wages employee)
>
> I'd say [meetings are held] maybe every couple of months, maybe more. It just depends. (wages employee)
>
> ...I think it's supposed to be once a month, but I reckon it averages out once every three months. (wages employee)
>
> It depends, they vary. Sometimes you get them every six months or you have them every couple of months. It just depends. (wages employee)
>
> ...sometimes you can get a couple [of meetings] in, you know, one each month, and then don't have it for two months, so it's not as regular [as it should be]. (senior supervisor)
>
> ...occasionally a month will slip by where we don't give a meeting, but we try on a monthly basis to give a state of the nation type talk... (first-line supervisor)

Theme 2: Divergent views about information meetings

Respondents from the production division had varying perceptions of the value of information meetings. For example, there were four respondents who expressed positive views about information meetings. Of these, three elaborated further on their perception of the implications of such meetings for employee relations within the division:

> ...on the average [the meetings] are pretty good. (wages employee)

> ...I think when you give the people the information back, I mean they don't all appreciate it, but I think say ninety percent of them do... And, you know, to me it instils a little bit more pride in what you're doing. (wages employee)

> ...it generated interest, it got them together. It did at least force the supervisor, even if he didn't want to, to communicate with his people in a structured way... and it was a pretty good get together... (senior supervisor)

> ...if we don't give one they say, 'How come we haven't had a monthly feedback?'. And that's good, because they want to know their position and they want to know their future, and I want to know mine as well, so we're all in the same boat. (first-line supervisor)

In contrast to the above, there were four respondents from this division who, for varying reasons, were critical of information meetings. For example, one respondent made the point that, even though there was an opportunity in these meetings for workers to ask questions, the concerns which they raised were often not attended to seriously or acted upon:

> ...even at the state of the nation meetings they'll say 'Well, we need your input for this... If you don't like the way this is done...', but then you can turn around and say 'Well, I don't like the way that's being done', and they say 'Well, bad luck'.

> ...and like I said, they say the same things, the workers say the same things. I mean we get bad parts from [the moulding section] so 'Why don't you do something about moulding?' and the bosses give us the same answer. And every meeting is exactly the same... it doesn't matter how much you complain about what's wrong up your end, they've got just as many problems down their end. But then a lot of our guys don't see it like that. All they can think of is 'We're getting all these shit parts and we don't want them anymore, do something about it'. Whereas moulding have got the same problem, even I can see that. (wages employee)

Two other respondents were critical of the content of information meetings, arguing that the information presented lacked relevance for workers on the shop floor and that it was communicated in a way which made it difficult for workers to understand:

> ...we really felt like early on, I mean, it just went way over their heads. It was too far up the management scale to be meaningful to them. [It was] sort of pie-in-the sky stuff that a lot of them really weren't interested in anyway. ...if you're going to communicate to them,

> it's got to be something that is directly relevant to their working day. They're not really interested in company profit and loss really. (senior supervisor)

> ...quite often they throw a lot of figures around, which most people don't understand. Figures don't mean a lot to a lot of people... quite often people come up [and say] 'What was he talking about?' And you have got to try and explain what he was saying. And that happens so many times. In fact, every meeting I've ever been to, I've had people come up to me and say, 'Oh I didn't really understand anything'. (wages employee)

A fourth respondent pointed out that the communication in information meetings was very much one-way — from management down to the workers. This respondent argued for a more active role for workers, in particular, with respect to the collection of the performance data presented in these meetings:

> It's all management [communicating to the workers]... They come up with these graphs and say, 'We've done this — rejects, medical visits... This is not good enough, that's not good enough. [You] have to improve this, improve that. You people out on the shop floor, you should know all the safety hazards...'. What you [should] do is get the figures for the month, you get one person, like let's say you've got yourself this month, I give it to you. The figures for the month could be accident reports and the costing, and rejects, right? So you've got one day, a whole day to do all that. Next time it's somebody else's turn. (wages employee)

In contrast with the production division, there was only one respondent from the tooling division (out of eight who reported some worker involvement in information meetings) who provided any insight into his evaluation of these meetings. As indicated in the excerpt below, this respondent was critical of what he perceived to be a failure on the part of management to keep promises that were made in information meetings:

> After that, for many occasions, the company has shown that what they were saying proved to be untrue. I kept a lot of records which I threw away where our leaders told us 'We will look after you. We [will] do this and we [will] do that' and it was completely untrue. (first-line supervisor)

The finding that tooling division respondents were less inclined than their counterparts from production to comment on their perception of the value of information meetings is not inconsistent with the previous observation that this activity appeared to be somewhat peripheral to definitions of the role of workers in this division.

The above interpretation of the results depends on the evaluation of all the data taken together. While interpretations of this kind are open to bias on the part of the researcher, perhaps in favour of a particular theory, the presentation of all the data at least provides the reader with the opportunity to judge the extent to which the interpretation offered is consistent with the data. In many studies of organisational culture, however, only excerpts of the data that support the researcher's interpretation are presented, so that the reader has no means by which to judge the validity of the interpretation.

11.2.1.4 *Attributions data*

Respondents from each division were asked *specifically* about changes in their experience of worker involvement in information meetings from the past to the present. Where changes were reported they were then asked to comment on their perceptions of the reasons for these changes. The point should be made that these attributions data, while they could be generated only by asking respondents to focus on differences between the past and the present, nevertheless represented explanations for why the present was the way it was. As such, it seemed appropriate to report on the findings of the analysis of these data in the present section (which, as indicated previously, is concerned primarily with qualitative data reflecting the *current* context of respondents' experience), rather than in some other section of the results. Findings for the tooling division are reported first, followed by findings for the production division. Within each division, the main focus of the analysis was on attributions that respondents had in common.

Tooling division. As indicated below, the attributions data for this division could be summarised in terms of one major theme.

Major Attribution: Information meetings introduced to quell employee anxiety

Six respondents from the tooling division reported a change in their experience of information meetings from the past to the present. In all cases, it was indicated that, in the past, there were no information meetings for workers in this division. All six respondents pointed to a link between the introduction of information meetings and the decline of the division (which culminated in its substantial downsizing and eventual relocation). This was reportedly a period of high anxiety for divisional employees, marked by the proliferation of rumours and the growing unrest of a workforce that felt increasingly uncertain about its future. The excerpts below suggest that management's primary aim in introducing information meetings at this time was to try to deal with the negative employee relations' consequences of the decline of the division. The reader's attention is drawn to the last two excerpts which contain evidence of the growing distrust that workers in the division felt towards management:

> The information update was only on the future of the [tooling division] and what will happen with the people. (first-line supervisor)

> [Management were] probably I guess trying to gradually indoctrinate people into the move and the way things were slowing down. (wages employee, leading hand)

> [It was a] management decision. They probably woke up that they should be telling everyone, passing on more information, probably to make a happier work force or to stop rumours. [I would] say [that] the rumours became a lot more prevalent over the last four or five years, the rumours of the tooling division closing down. A lot of the meetings were

held to pass on information about that, [to] stop false rumours, [to] sort or give us facts and information. (first-line supervisor)

[The meetings were introduced] probably when work started to become irregular. ... previously we had continual work from our own models... you might have a bit of a period of three or six months when there was a bit of a lull, but there was always something coming, there was something in the pipeline. But when things started to become, you know like there's nothing coming, it was like 'We won't have anything to do for two years' and that's when rumours started amongst people out on the shop floor and so management obviously tried to put people in the picture that, you know, 'No need to worry, we've got this job and we're looking at this, and we are trying to do this, trying to keep the workforce happy'. (first-line supervisor)

...some of the things that had to be told to the people when [the divisional manager] took over couldn't be told and then retold. It had to come from [the divisional manager's] mouth, otherwise they used to say 'That's bullshit, you know, we don't believe you'. And the only way that they would think that what they were being told was honest was for him to stand up in front of everybody and tell them. And half the time they didn't believe him anyhow. (first-line supervisor)

[The meetings were introduced] because I think, or what I heard was, in the past... see they had that big sacking a few years, I don't know what year it was, but a few years ago they put off a lot of people... [It was in the] early 70s and the people don't trust them. The workers didn't trust the management of the company. And they were kicking up because they heard a lot of whispers, and I think the workers wanted to know what was going on. And they kept going to the union all the time and asking the union to find out what's going on. (wages employee, leading hand)

Production division. In the production division, there were 13 respondents who reported a change in their experience of information meetings from the past to the present. Of these, 12 indicated that, in the past, there was either no formal performance feedback to workers at all, or less than that which was currently made available. Respondents' explanations for the increase in performance feedback in recent years varied and suggested the following three themes or attributions.

Attribution 1: Information meetings seen as a new management initiative

Seven respondents attributed the change to a change in management, with particular reference to the appointment in the late 1980s of a new divisional manager. As indicated in the excerpts below, five of these seven respondents made explicit reference to some aspect of the new manager's style reflected in:

(1) A recognition on the part of management of the value of increased worker involvement in divisional operations;

(2) A recognition on the part of management of the need for workers to receive feedback on their performance;

(3) The new manager's commitment to communication;

(4) The new manager's preference for the visual (i.e., graphic) presentation of performance information; and

(5) The new manager's commitment to formalising the process of providing workers with feedback on their performance.

It is worth noting that four of the respondents whose comments are quoted below were supervisory staff.

> Well, it was an idea, same thing as the team concept, to try and get people involved, you know. If you are involved in a thing, you can... you have more input to the thing, you know, more idea of what's going on. Like years ago, you were sort of always in the dark, you didn't know what was going on, you know. But at least now if you're interested, you can find out, or you can know what's going on. (wages employee)

> [The meetings were introduced because] I think that the management that we've got now realised the people's needs, that they do need feedback on how the company is performing, and [that they need] some sort of outlook on what sort of future they're going to have with the company. (first-line supervisor)

> It's only in recent times [that information meetings have been introduced]... after [the divisional manager] came... I think he probably spent about 12 to 18 months just sniffing around the place and making small subtle changes, and then he got really heavily into this communications... [He] wanted to communicate with people and really let them know. (senior supervisor)

> No, it's only when [the divisional manager] came along. [He's] a stickler for graphs and stuff... (senior supervisor)

> They had [state of the nation meetings] there before, but not on a regular formalised basis. [Then] it was only when there was a requirement to have it, if that makes sense... once [the divisional manager] came in, he wanted a formalised state of the nation. (first-line supervisor)

While somewhat less specific in their attributions, the remaining two of these seven respondents also expressed the view that management was responsible, at least in part, for the increased emphasis, in recent times, on performance feedback to workers:

> We didn't used to get any at all to begin with, so it's since [the divisional manager] has taken over, he has sort of brought this in. (wages employee)

> [The meetings were introduced] because the people wanted to know more information... I don't know if it's the workers, or the union, or management [that] have decided to give us more information. Like [the Managing Director] had us over in the canteen to tell us how

bad the cars was going, see, that would never have happened years ago, never... I think [the Director of Manufacturing] is the one that's bought a bit more [feedback] to the workers. (wages employee)

Attribution 2: Information meetings seen as a vehicle for providing positive feedback

While a change in management constituted the most commonly cited reason for the increase, in recent years, in information meetings for workers, a number of other explanations for this change were also offered. Two respondents pointed to the role of information meetings in the communication of good news to workers. As they saw it, information meetings in their current form had been introduced at a time when the company was experiencing a significant upturn in its performance associated with the market success of the most recently released model. In the first excerpt below, the respondent (a wages employee) is distinctly cynical about what he sees as a form of management propaganda designed to secure the commitment of workers to company objectives. In the second excerpt, the respondent (a supervisor) portrays the initiative in a much more positive light, suggesting that the workers were both surprised and encouraged by the experience of receiving positive feedback about their performance.

It really, it's all been connected with the [new model], because [it] was so successful. They could actually show people on charts that we were coming up to [the level of] our main competitor. And, you know, they could show people nice propaganda instead of doom and gloom as before, because the plant, the production plant was never making any sort of money for years up there [or] so they tell us, you know. But I can't see a big business pumping money into a plant unless, in the long term, they think they're going to make money out of it. But they always said that production was down, it was all doom and gloom. But the last couple of years it has picked up, it has been better you know......they could say, they could show you positive charts 'cos the [new model] went Number 1 seller, so you could see our red line up there and [our competitor's] blue line down there, sort of thing. So whether they were trying to psych the people up saying, 'Yes, you're number one', all that crap. And the people up there... they're not Japanese-type people, they're not American-type people, they're just Australian workers in the factory, sort of thing, you know. (wages employee)

But they actually brought out state of the nation to say how well we were doing, and that was totally... people thought 'Blimey, that's the first time we've ever been sat down and [told] you're doing a good job, and look how well we're doing here, and we're going in the right direction...'. And they came out of those meetings thinking 'Oh yeah'. So the state of the nation for the first time ever was used in a positive manner. (first-line supervisor)

Attribution 3: Information meetings introduced to quash rumours

Another reason for the change, cited by two respondents, was that information meetings had been introduced to curb the spread of rumours within the organisation. In the second excerpt below, the respondent makes the point that, in his opinion, information meetings were introduced primarily to provide workers with more reliable and consistent information than that which was available to them through the company grapevine.

> [Information to workers] stops rumours, and things like that, 'cos rumours are deadly, you know... (wages employee)

> ...up until state of the nation was introduced in a global [i.e. company-wide sense], there was always... one plant would have a bit of information, you'd go to the canteen, people would say 'What's going off here?'. 'Oh, I didn't hear that...'. Come back here and you could even hear something about [what] was going to affect your plant that another plant was talking about. And when they had state of the nations, they were planned so that they were all done within a certain time frame, people felt a little bit more informed. And I believe that was the first idea of state of the nation... to let everyone know at the same time. That was its first purpose... that's what I believe anyway. (first-line supervisor)

In addition to the above, there were two respondents from the production division who made attributions that were not shared by any other respondent. One argued that information meetings provided management with the means by which they could familiarise workers with management problems. This respondent was critical of the behaviour of management in this regard, arguing that management failed to reciprocate by seeking a better understanding of the problems of workers:

> I think they were introduced mainly to make workers, people producing things, aware of the problems that management have... to show they're [the workers] not the only people with problems and that we should all work together... But it's never worked the other way. We've started to go to meetings now with management and get told about production. But management have never gone onto the shop floor to do manual work to find out [about] the problems that we have. (wages employee)

The other respondent indicated that his first experience of information meetings coincided with his transfer from afternoon shift to day shift. The perception of this respondent was, therefore, that the change in his experience of information meetings (from no involvement in this activity in the past to his current level of involvement) could be attributed to the change in his work shift. However, subsequent questioning revealed that the respondent was uncertain about the actual history of information meetings within the division. He indicated that he did not know whether, in the past, there were no information meetings for workers at all or, alternatively, whether information meetings were provided for workers on day shift only.

> When I was on afternoon shift, there was none... Afternoon shift people just didn't get to go to them. They might have had one a year or something, but that's it... I don't know if they had them at all [in the past]. I'm not too sure if they did before. (wages employee)

The reader may note that the number of respondents represented by the above data is 13 and not 12, as might have been expected. The reason for this apparent inconsistency is that two of the respondents represented above are each quoted on two separate occasions (i.e., in attempting to explain the change in their experience of worker involvement in information meetings, they each made two attributions); further, attributions data were not available for one of the 12 respondents who reported a change towards increased worker involvement in this activity in recent years.

Finally, one respondent from the production division reported that, in the past, there had actually been more performance feedback to workers than that which was currently made available. This respondent attributed the current status of this activity to the phasing out of various initiatives (e.g., weekly team meetings) introduced as part of the team concept.

11.2.1.5 *Concluding comments about the analysis of qualitative data on information meetings*

The above analysis of qualitative data on information meetings provided a number of valuable insights into the meaning that this particular worker activity had for respondents from both divisions. These are discussed in point form below.

(1) With respect first of all to the analysis of the definitional data, there was some evidence to suggest differences (both between and within divisions) in the way in which respondents defined information meetings. While there was general consensus among tooling division respondents that information meetings involved the dissemination of company-wide performance information, respondents from the production division variously referred to information meetings as meetings in which local (sectional) performance information was disseminated or, alternatively, as meetings in which company-wide performance information was disseminated. This lack of agreement among production division respondents about what constituted the main focus of information meetings suggested the possibility that, in this division, there existed more than one type of meeting that could be classified as an information meeting. As indicated, the findings of this analysis of definitional data have important implications for careful consideration and checking of the understanding of questions by respondents and also for the extent to which quantitative data from one division can be aggregated reliably and compared with quantitative data from another division.

(2) A second, deeper level of insight into the meaning of the quantitative data on information meetings was provided by the analysis of the thematic content of respondents' elaborations on this subject. As indicated, there were a number of emergent themes in these elaborations that were common to both divisions. For example, respondents from both divisions made the point that attendance at these meetings was obligatory rather than self-motivated, and that it was primarily because of this that the meetings were currently so well-attended. It was also suggested that, despite the opportunity for

workers to ask questions in these meetings, their role in the meetings remained an essentially passive one. Finally, it was noted that some information meetings (namely, those in which divisional or company-wide, rather than sectional or work group, information was disseminated) appeared to be held, not on a regular basis, but rather in response to certain specific events (either positive or negative) about which management thought workers should be informed.

It should be noted that the above representations of information meetings were not consistent with a developing rhetoric in the organisation that espoused values of worker involvement and empowerment, more consistent with a Theory Y approach. In this sense, these representations might be regarded as being more closely aligned with Schein's (1985, 1992, 2004, 2010) Level 3 cultural elements, when compared with the aforementioned organisational rhetoric that can be seen as more aligned with the surface-level elements at Levels 1 and 2.

(3) The thematic content analysis also revealed that, with respect to some aspects of their experience of information meetings, the two divisions were qualitatively different. For example, a number of respondents from the production division shared the view that the level of production in the division significantly influenced both the attendance at information meetings and the frequency with which they were held. High levels of production inevitably led to compromises in the involvement of workers in this activity. This was not a theme that emerged in the tooling division data. Respondents from the production division were also more inclined than their counterparts from the tooling division to make evaluative comments regarding their experience of information meetings. While their evaluations of these meetings tended to be mixed (i.e., some positive and some negative), the important point can be made that, at least in the production division, respondents appeared to have had sufficient exposure to this activity to have formed an opinion about its value.

(4) It was argued that the results of the thematic content analysis could have important implications for the achievement of managerial objectives associated with the introduction of information meetings. If, as suggested by the organisational rhetoric that espoused a more Theory Y approach to the management of workers, a hoped-for outcome of providing workers with more performance feedback was that workers would feel more valued by the organisation, and hence more committed to its goals, then the results of this analysis would suggest that only partial progress toward the achievement of this objective had been made.

(5) Finally, the analysis of attributions data provided evidence of divisional differences in respondents' attributions about why information meetings, in their current form, had been introduced. There was also evidence of differences in the degree of sharedness of attributions. In the tooling division, there was general consensus among respondents that information meetings had been introduced to deal with the uncertainty and rumours associated with the decline of the division. In contrast, respondents from the production division were more variable with respect to their perceptions of why the

meetings had been introduced. The most common attribution pointed to a link between the current emphasis on performance feedback to workers and the arrival of a new divisional manager whose managerial style was characterised, in part, by a commitment to more open communications with workers. It can be argued that this attribution is potentially more optimistic than that made by tooling division respondents. The latter suggests a view of management as reactive and inclined to adopt initiatives such as information meetings only when problems arise, whereas the former suggests a view of management as being more aware of the human relations value of more open communications with workers. A number of other attributions were also made by respondents from the production division, including the introduction of information meetings for the purpose of communicating good news to workers (whether as a form of management propaganda or as genuinely positive feedback) and also to curb the spread of rumours within the organisation. These attributions were, however, shared by a minority of respondents only.

(6) An important methodological implication of the above findings, when considered as a whole, is that it is hard to imagine how the insights they provide could have been obtained using a more structured quantitative approach to data collection. The qualitative data are typically highly context-specific, meaning that it would be very difficult, if not impossible, to identify *a priori* the range of possible questions that one would need to ask in order to generate the responses obtained. The only way in which this might be approximated with more quantitative approaches would be to provide respondents with the opportunity to comment on and/or give examples to illustrate their responses. However, the success of such a strategy is highly dependent upon respondents being willing, and able, to provide such additional information.

11.2.2 Findings for 'attend training'

The format for reporting the results in this section is essentially the same as that adopted above for information meetings. That is, consideration is given to similarities and differences between the divisions in: how respondents defined training; the thematic content of the qualitative data pertaining to training; and respondents' attributions regarding the current involvement of workers in training. As will be seen, however, this section presents the results of an additional analysis, namely, the analysis of the very first comments that respondents made in response to prompting about worker involvement in training.

11.2.2.1 What is training?

As shown in Table 11.1, in response to prompting, all of the tooling division respondents and 12 of the production division respondents reported some involvement of the workers in their division in training. No respondent mentioned this worker activity spontaneously. Specifically, respondents were asked: "Do workers in your division at the present time attend training or professional development programs?" It was perhaps not surprising, given the wording of this prompt, that the training activity typically reported by respondents from both divisions took the form of formal training courses that were provided in-house or externally through one of the local colleges of further education. For the tooling division, all references were to worker involvement in formal training. For the production division, nine of the 12 respondents (75%) reporting some worker involvement in training and all of the seven respondents reporting no worker involvement in training were referring to formal training. However, for the remaining three respondents who reported some worker involvement in training (25% of this group), it was clear that the reference in each case was to training that was provided on-the-job. There was, therefore, some inconsistency (albeit marginal) among production division respondents in their interpretations of what constituted 'training'.

This finding draws attention to the point made previously in relation to information meetings, namely, that had the present method relied solely on the use of the particular closed questions that were asked, interpretive inconsistencies of this kind would not have been revealed. Of course, with the benefit of hindsight, one might argue that more specific closed questions might have been asked in order to tap this difference between formal and on-the-job training. However, the problem remains that, without some knowledge of the organisation and its culture (e.g., through the use of a pilot study), the researcher cannot know what questions are the 'right' questions to ask. In this sense, all closed questions that are designed *a priori* must be seen to be susceptible to the kind of interpretive inconsistency reported here. As indicated above, the only way in which this problem might be partly solved is to ask respondents to comment on, or provide examples to illustrate their responses. These additional data may serve to reveal discrepancies between respondents in their interpretations of the questions.

11.2.2.2 *Initial comments about worker involvement in training*

It became apparent in the early stages of analysing the qualitative data on training that there were some interesting insights to be gained from a review of the very first comments that respondents made in response to the prompt question. Unlike the corresponding data on information meetings, these initial comments actually gave some indication of how respondents from each division perceived and thought about training in their respective divisions. For example, the following initial comments by three respondents from the tooling division suggested some uncertainty about the nature and amount of training provided in that division:

> Well, they were bringing those courses in, yes. That would probably be in the last two years. All this new — what do they call it — to make you more skilled. (wages employee, leading hand)

> I think they would attend training [if they had the opportunity]... Yes, some are. (wages employee, shop steward)

> We set up a training room. I don't really think we used it very much. They did have some welding classes and some hydraulic classes and some pneumatic classes and stuff like that

which was all training... And so I would have to answer yes [to the question]. (senior supervisor)

A further three respondents from the tooling division made initial comments which, more or less explicitly, pointed to a relatively low level of training activity in the division:

[In the] latter years, there have been a few courses on. (wages employee, leading hand)

They had a training program... about 12 months before they sort of closed down. (wages employee, leading hand)

I reckon not enough [time is spent in training]. (wages employee)

This same impression was conveyed by the initial comments of eight production division respondents. These respondents suggested that not only were training opportunities for workers in the division limited, but they were also restricted to particular individuals or groups within the division:

No. Oh, that's not quite right. In the moulding area sometimes die setters do get to do some training. (wages employee)

[Laughs] Some do, some don't. ...It depends on how much money they got and how much time they got. (wages employee)

Interviewer: Are there any other meetings that workers attend? *Respondent:* Maybe a training course which they send some of the workers to. (wages employee)

There is, spasmodically there's these die setting courses that they send people on. (wages employee)

Yes, some do. I couldn't put a figure on how many but, yes, some have gone down to Regency Park, places like that to [do training]. (wages employee)

We have had, yes a bit of training, actually yes, we do attend training. (wages employee)

There is I would say the opportunity, what is the word, yes there is training there, they have had training for painters, they have had training for injection moulding... (first-line supervisor)

Not a great deal, no. I mean the sort of training that we do, we try and do in-house. (first-line supervisor)

The initial comments from the production division also contained one reference to the company's legal obligation to provide training and one reference to a temporary interruption in training activity that the respondent attributed to current production demands:

By law I think we're obliged to spend 1% of our salary on training anyway and in this plant it's more than that, and I can't tell you exactly what it is but I think it's somewhere around about 5% at any one time. (senior supervisor)

We've got a paint course going at the moment and then along came [the new model] — it's been held off for the last three weeks. (first-line supervisor)

For the production division, some of the "no" responses to the prompt were also of interest. The first two responses below are notable for the certainty which they project, while the third response expresses a view similar to that above, namely, that there was a tendency in the division for production demands to take precedence over training needs.

[There is] no such thing [as training]. (wages employee)

No-one's been to training for yonks. No. (wages employee, acting leading hand)

No. We only do that when we've got spare time. (wages employee)

11.2.2.3 *Thematic content analysis: Themes common to both divisions*

The analysis of the thematic content of the qualitative data pertaining to 'attend training' suggested the following three themes that were common to both divisions.

Theme 1: Organisation's needs take precedence over individual's needs

A key theme which emerged in the tooling division data and which was also present, although to a lesser extent, in the production division data was that training was primarily a response to the organisation's needs. The potential for training to satisfy higher-order individual needs, such as the need for self-esteem and the need for self-fulfilment (Maslow, 1954), was not evident in respondents' thinking about the provision of training in their respective divisions. This separation of the organisation's and the individual's needs is consistent with Theory X assumptions about the nature of workers (McGregor, 1960), whereby workers are perceived to be motivated primarily by lower-order needs, such as the need for job security and a basic wage. As indicated in the following comments by five respondents from the tooling division, the perception of training in this division was that it was primarily about replacing lost skills, learning what the organisation wanted you to know, and developing competence in the use of new technology. None of the excerpts contains any reference to the notion that training might potentially increase the motivation and self-esteem of individual workers. The last excerpt, in particular, suggests an approach to training and selection that is reminiscent of Taylor's (1911) recommendations for the 'scientific' management of workers. This excerpt also contains the idea that training was reactive, that is, provided in response to a problem that had arisen.

...obviously [the company] introduced [multi-skilling] to benefit themselves of course, there is no doubt about that. But it possibly is [part of a wider industrial] reform, and that is the way of thinking, [whereby] you can have a more versatile workforce. (wages employee, shop steward)

When you start to lose skills, you've got to replace them somehow or other and the only way you're going to do it is to get a person willing to start to better himself. (first-line supervisor)

[The approach to training] is a bit like the army, it's sort of what [the company] wants you to know is what they'll let you know... I mean you have to have a work relation to the schooling you allocate for the people from a company's point of view, you must have that sort of thing, but I don't think a company should be narrow minded in the way they present it. (wages employee)

Give me the authority from the bosses up top that I can educate them [the workers] and if they are unwilling that I can put it to them that 'Either you do it this way, how it should be done. I don't want any shonky work. You do it that way, how it should be done, that we create a product, or you are fired'. (first-line supervisor)

...I think the training is pretty adequate. I think the main training areas are apprentices. Beyond the apprentices, the training involvement then is technological change involvement. That is, we are now introducing NC [Numerical Control] machining and such like, so everybody should be put on those machines even if only for a very short time, so they're aware of exactly what that thing is doing and what they need to do to achieve what that machine requires. (wages employee, leading hand)

Well training... once I found out from the leading hand that a person is not capable in doing the job, I encouraged the leading hand to look after him, and help him out so that he knows what he is supposed to do. I also encouraged the people in [the spray gun shop]... that every one knew how to make [a spray gun], and once that was done, then I selected the people for a job that they could do best. Now we had Bill on the drill. He was magic. Putting Fred on the drill, who couldn't do it, didn't want to do it, or whatever, it just didn't work out. But also Bill on the drill knew exactly how to make a gun, not as good as Fred who was bending tubes or doing something else. They all knew how to make guns but after I found out who can do things better and faster, not necessarily faster, but better because our aim was quality... (first-line supervisor)

A similar view of training emerged in the production division data. The following comments by two respondents from this division highlight the role of training in satisfying production needs in the division. In the first excerpt, the suggestion is that training is provided only when the need arises (in this case, the need for a new fork lift driver to cope with the division's materials handling requirements). In the second excerpt, the implication is that training is of value only to the extent that it will subsequently be applied on-the-job.

Well, drivers get training but that's if they need a new driver they train someone up. (wages employee)

[There's] no point in sending an operator to a trouble shooting course because unless they are going to be a die setter, they're not going to get any benefit out of it, and I think the courses are about $400 each, which I'm sure the company can claim on its tax purpose or whatever, but they haven't got a heap of money to throw around up there, and what's the point of sending a 45 year old lady to a die setting course and she's Polish and she's not going to understand it? (wages employee)

While the above data provide evidence that a predominantly Theory X view of workers may underlie the approach to training in each division, there was one respondent from the tooling division whose perception of worker involvement in training implied a more Theory Y view of workers. As this respondent saw it, the company's aim in providing workers with training was to help workers develop an increased sense of responsibility for the job and enhance their interest and involvement in their work. Whether or not this aim had been achieved, however, was not commented upon.

The company is trying to get the worker to feel as though he is responsible for what he's doing. Like at one stage when you go into work the expected thing is you are there for eight hours because of the fact that you've got a clock there. You clock on, you clock off. So the attitude of the worker is that well, I'm here for eight hours, I'll do the work and that's it. But what the company's trying to get into people is that not only are they doing eight hours work, but they're doing eight hours of interesting work, and they're trying to get them more involved in that work. (wages employee, leading hand)

It is perhaps worth pointing out that the respondent who expressed this minority view worked in a section of the tooling division which was separate from the main area that housed the division's machining, manufacturing, and try-out operations (and from which the majority of respondents in the present study were drawn).

Theme 2: Negative attitudes toward the current emphasis on training

In both divisions, there existed negative attitudes towards the formal training that was currently made available to workers. However, as above for Theme 1, this result was more pronounced for the tooling division than for the production division. In all, there were five respondents from the tooling division whose elaborations on the subject of training contained some form of criticism. For example, two respondents were critical of the current emphasis on multi-skilling, suggesting that it resulted in workers acquiring skills which were unlikely to be maintained because of their questionable relevance to the actual work in which workers were engaged:

I mean since I started a couple of years ago, as I was saying, you could take any course, and it didn't matter... it had nothing to do with die making for instance. What is the sense in that? (wages employee, leading hand)

Well you can retrain yourself to do lots of things, but these things are useless to you unless you carry on working in that capacity. I mean I could go to a course and be retrained as a computer operator. After a couple of months, that would be totally useless to me because I would have forgotten everything I had learned, and unless you're working with it, things are so complicated nowadays you can't retain them in your memory. (senior supervisor)

Another respondent warned against the financial implications of having too many trained workers:

I think that [training] will reach a level and then they have got to be careful because if you have got too many [trained workers], you can't use them because everybody will be demanding extra money. (wages employee, shop steward)

There was also a perception that older employees, who had acquired valuable experience over the long-term, were being discriminated against unfairly by the current reward system which was designed to link remuneration and opportunities for promotion to the number of skills acquired through training:

How can he ever move up the ladder? He's too old. He's got all the brains and the skills that's necessary to put him there, and it's too late. Now, with this thing that's come in [the reference is to award restructuring], if he can't pass courses and sit for exams and do well, which are supervisory type stuff, you just don't make it. (first-line supervisor)

Finally, one respondent expressed the view that the most valuable training available to workers was still that provided on the job:

I mean to me, to me personally, I don't think schooling is the big advantage to a tradesman. I went to trade school. I learnt nothing there. I learnt all my skills from work. (wages employee, leading hand)

Two of the nine respondents from the production division who reported some worker involvement in formal training expressed negative attitudes towards this training. Specifically, these respondents were critical of the quality of the training provided, with the second respondent quoted below pointing to the questionable practice of classifying, as training, any worker activity which did not involve direct production (including basic housekeeping activities, such as, "painting" and "cleaning up"). As suggested subsequently by this respondent, the aim of this practice was to ensure compliance with recent government legislation that required companies to spend a certain percentage of their payroll on training.

And what happened was when we went down, downturn in our schedule this year, all of a sudden everyone was getting this training everywhere, and I still believe a lot of it was just a total waste of time. And we could have trained in better ways. (senior supervisor)

...I think that it was last August. They stopped the plant two and a half hours early every day to get people training. Now you have seen what happened around here with the training didn't you? *Interviewer:* People were cleaning up and painting and... *Respondent:* But they recorded that as training. Now, pushing a broom is not training, sitting in an office upstairs and showing them how to do problem-solving techniques... Well that was training, but people have seen that all over before, and yet nothing after that training has been of any value to the company, so I again question 'What is training?'. (first-line supervisor)

It is perhaps worth noting that, while the above data are similar in that they all reflect negative attitudes towards training, one can nevertheless detect a difference between the divisions with respect to the specific grounds upon which respondents are critical of training. A key issue for tooling division respondents was the questionable relevance of the training provided (given both the ageing population of the division and also the nature of the work traditionally performed in the division); for production division respondents the issue was whether or not the training provided constituted 'real' training. From a cultural perspective, this difference may not be insignificant and may reflect the different cultural contexts into which training for workers has been introduced.

An important caution in interpreting data of this kind is that positive or negative comments should not be accepted at face value without checking their source, since such comments may be the result of 'spill over' from some other issue. For example, in the above context, negative attitudes to training or to information meetings may be due to frustration with a lack of consultation of workers by managers.

Theme 3: Workers motivated by economic self-interest

A third theme that emerged in the accounts of training provided by respondents from both divisions concerned the motivation of workers to participate in training courses. In the following comments by two respondents from the production division (both of whom had previously reported some worker involvement in training), the suggestion is that workers are reluctant to attend training if this requires an investment of their own time, for which the company does not compensate them financially. The implication here is that workers are primarily motivated by economic self-interest which is, again, a view of workers that is typically associated with Theory X assumptions:

Well, they used to pay them overtime if it was in their own time, but they don't pay that any more, and some workers are telling management to stick it. (wages employee)

...if people don't get paid to go on extra training, quite often they won't go. ...Well, knowing the people, I know a few of them won't do anything unless they get paid by the company and unless they are going to gain something out of it, and a lot of them don't consider gaining knowledge as a gain. (wages employee)

A similar view was expressed by one respondent from the tooling division:

> That is why the attendance was that low because a lot of people said that I am not spending my time... the training time was two hours, the company paid you one, and you paid one out of your own time. (first-line supervisor)

While the number of respondents represented by the above data is small, the reader will recall a related theme that emerged in the context of respondents' elaborations on information meetings. As indicated previously, a perception in both divisions was that workers attended information meetings primarily because it was compulsory that they do so, and not because they were necessarily motivated by a desire to be better informed about, and hence more involved in, company and divisional operations. In the same way, the present theme raises questions about the genuine commitment of workers to enhancing their skills and knowledge through formal training. These data have important implications for what management might be trying to achieve through the increased involvement of workers in activities such as information meetings and training. If the aim is to effect a more positive human relations environment, then the perception that workers engage in these activities because they have to, or because their participation offers a means of avoiding work, must be seen as a potentially serious impediment to the achievement of this aim.

In the context of the present discussion on worker motivation, the following comments by two respondents from the production division are also of interest. The implication in the first is that, given the low levels of motivation of workers compared to staff, it is questionable what training, if any, can usefully be provided to workers. In the second, the implication is that company sponsorship of worker participation in more general training courses (in which they could acquire skills that were potentially marketable outside of the organisation) is undesirable on the grounds that workers are not sufficiently committed to the company to stay there in the event that other options were to become available. Both of the respondents quoted had previously reported some worker involvement in training.

> ...what training courses do you give wages people? ...like staff are more motivated to do things on their own. (first-line supervisor)

> There are courses available from the company to anyone who wishes to benefit themselves and benefit the company. I mean they won't pay for you to go and do a car re-spraying course or anything like that because what the company finds is that they pay for the training and then the person shoots through and gets a better job. (first-line supervisor)

11.2.2.4 *Thematic content analysis: Themes unique to each division*

The analysis of the thematic content of the qualitative data pertaining to 'attend training' revealed two themes that were unique to the tooling division and four themes that were unique to the production division. The results for the tooling division are discussed first, followed by the results for the production division.

Tooling division. The following two themes were unique to the tooling division:

Theme 1: Involvement in training an individual initiative

In the tooling division, there was some evidence to suggest that, although training was offered according to divisional (organisational) needs (as above), the actual involvement of workers in this training was largely an individual initiative. In other words, it was up to the individual worker to express an interest in, and seek approval for, attendance at particular training courses that were being offered. In this sense, the division's role with respect to training would appear to be essentially passive. There was no indication that workers in the division were actively encouraged by their supervisors and managers to attend training. This theme is reflected in the following comments of four respondents from this division:

> Well, they were bringing those courses in... to make you more skilled. Everybody had the opportunity. It was open to everybody. (wages employee, leading hand)

> No-one is forced to go. They are made aware that these courses are on and they let me, or a supervisor, know they want to attend, and those arrangements are made. (first-line supervisor)

> There are courses that they can attend, like a welding course, electrical courses, that they can do part in company time, part in their own time... they would see the notice come out saying that they wanted welding courses, electrical courses and you could put your name down for whatever you wanted to do. (first-line supervisor)

> Yeah, well I was in charge of the training side of things. ...Not in charge of training the people themselves, but just organising those people to be trained in certain, how would you say, post-trade little courses and what have you. They were available and it was up to the individual to become involved. (first-line supervisor)

Theme 2: Training more appropriate for younger workers

In the tooling division, the training implications of the introduction of award restructuring were perceived to have more relevance for younger employees than for longer-serving employees. This theme emerged in the comments of four respondents, as follows:

> A lot more people will be involved in training with award restructuring, particularly the younger people. It's not going to have a great effect on a person like me. I'm sort of getting a bit too old to learn new tricks and all that sort of thing now. Award restructuring is for the younger people and the next generation coming up, more so than the older people. (first-line supervisor)

Well, I believe that any knowledge is good knowledge as long as you're a young kid... When you get over fifty years of age and they turn around and say the only way you can get to become Grade 7 [a more advanced supervisory grade] is to go back to school and get your intermediate and then go and get this certificate, who is going to remember how to two times two? (first-line supervisor)

I think restructuring is going to make people go and do [training]. If they're prepared to go on... particularly the boys [i.e., younger workers] are going to have to do a lot more. They tell me that there's supposed to be a grandfather clause in it for us older guys. (wages employee, leading hand)

I think the young ones will [be involved in more training]. (wages employee, leading hand)

Production division. As indicated, there were four themes pertaining to 'attend training' that were unique to the production division. These are as follows:

Theme 1: Divided views on the effectiveness of on-the-job training

As indicated above, in response to prompting about worker involvement in training, respondents from both divisions typically made reference to the involvement of workers in formal, rather than on-the-job, training. At the same time, however, the subject of on-the-job training appeared to be of some significance to respondents from the production division. Twelve respondents from this division made reference to the fact that on-the-job training continued to constitute a common approach to the training of workers in the division. In contrast, none of the tooling division respondents made reference to this form of training when talking about their present experience of training in the division. This finding was perhaps not surprising given that almost all of the wages employees in the tooling division were qualified tradesmen who, in most cases, had negligible responsibility for providing on-the-job supervision and training to the division's few remaining apprentices. It could also be argued that respondents from this division might be less likely to be explicit about any on-the-job training that was provided, since this might be seen by them as an admission that the existing trade skills of workers in the division were somehow inadequate.

In the production division, attitudes towards on-the-job training appeared to be some-what divided. For example, the implication in the following comments by four respondents (two of whom had previously reported some worker involvement in formal training and two of whom had reported some worker involvement in on-the-job in training) is that on-the-job training constituted an effective means of teaching job skills to new or existing workers:

...if a person came from [the car trim fabrication section], and you wanted to show them [how to do the job] ...you put an experienced operator and you stay with them, until they feel they're capable of being left ...and then they go back later, and see that they're going all right. And they are implementing ...it is being implemented that. (wages employee)

...what I normally do is get my key people to train any new people, and I believe in job rotation and that means that when you do job rotation everyone gets trained to do the job properly. (senior supervisor)

I mean the sort of training that we do, we try and do in-house... Well, as a new worker you would be shown the basics right throughout and if you came to my area for example, you would be [shown] right through moulding... We have people trained up in a way that we would feel confident, that we train them up ourselves; they've got the capability to actually run through like a system, if you like. (first-line supervisor)

That works with the obvious thing where you bring in either a new employee, or you're training up because of award restructuring, the employee can do a certain function within the group, so then he is trained up so that he can do every single function within that group, and he is trained either by the leading hand or another experienced operator. (first-line supervisor)

In contrast, the four respondents quoted below (two of whom had previously reported no worker involvement in training and two who had reported some worker involvement in formal training) were all critical of the quality of the on-the-job training that was provided. In addition, it was either implied or argued explicitly that such training did not constitute 'real' training:

I mean our spray painters get put in the booth and get stuck with someone who has sprayed before. I mean is that training? ...As far as I'm concerned training is learning to do a job the right way, by the right people, by professionals. ...There's [on the job training] for everything. You get put on a job by whoever is doing it and get shown how to do it, but the only thing that you are doing then is getting taught the bad habits of the person who was there before. There's no official training, there is no people with authority that have done the training themselves, that have got some sort of recognition that they can do the job right. (wages employee)

...the spray painting we got here is if your overalls fit, you are sort of a spray painter. They don't have any formal training or anything like that. ...there's a few of us that got trained properly and the rest of them nowadays just get thrown in the booth and they say 'This is the gun, this is the part, paint it'. (wages employee)

I think [management] have got the feeling that everybody should know their job, without being trained. ...Well, that's like as I said to you before. When I started learning spray painting, the foreman came in, no [it] was the leading hand actually, he was in there for about an hour, two hours showing me how to do it and that was it, he just walked out. (wages employee)

It depends [on] what the definition of training is. If it is you telling me as the leading hand of the area, sitting me down and saying 'This is what you have to do, that is what you do' and that is recorded as training, then I do not consider that as training... When you come into [the production division] you are taken around, shown where the toilets are, shown where the canteen is, told the fundamentals and all this sort of thing. Then you are taken to the [work] area and then you are [told] that is what is going to be your job, and then you stand there, and then you are given to a leading hand and you are shown, if you are mould-ing, this is what you do in this particular job. Then you are taken on this [job] and that is what you do there and this is it. There is no formalised follow up. There are no written job procedures. Unless you have something to measure a person's performance by, in a formalised sort of a fashion, you are only relying on what the person. [says]: 'Yes, they are okay, they seem to be going alright, no particular problems there, they do everything I ask them'... Now is that training? (first-line supervisor)

It is worth mentioning that, although the small numbers of respondents represented by the above excerpts preclude statistical significance testing, seniority does appear to be a factor influencing respondents' perceptions of the effectiveness of on-the-job training. Supervisory staff tended to be positive in their attitudes towards this form of training (three out of the four respondents expressing positive attitudes were supervisory staff), whereas wages employees tended to be negative (three out of the four respondents expressing nega-tive attitudes were wages employees).

Theme 2: Amount of training contingent on production demands

It will be recalled that, in response to prompting about the involvement of workers in train-ing, two respondents from the production division made initial comments that contained the idea that training needs were secondary to production demands. When production demands were high, the involvement of workers in the division in training diminished significantly (or sometimes even completely) while, when production demands were low, training activity in the division was increased. In the subsequent more detailed analysis of the qualitative data on training, it was found that this was a view shared by a number of other respondents from the production division. In all, six of the 19 respondents (32%) from the production division (including the two mentioned above) made comments that reflected this view. These six respondents included three who, in response to prompting, had reported some worker involvement in training (25% of this group), and three who, in response to prompting, had reported no worker involvement in training (43% of this group). The comments of the former were as follows:

Some do, some don't. ...It depends on how much money they got and how much time they got. ...if they've got time to train people, they'll train them, but if all of a sudden they get busy, they won't train anyone else. ...A good case was just before Easter. They were doing a big training thing and all the people they could cover away from their jobs, which were most of them except for the duco mixers and spray painters, got to go and we didn't, 'cos they can't afford to lose us from our jobs in here. (wages employee)

We brought [the local college of Technical and Further Education] in here to do a spray painting course and we got half way through and had to stop it because of [a new model] introduction...

They had this downturn and we didn't really look at what we were training them [in]. We just gave them training for the sake of training...

And what happened was when we went down, downturn in our schedule this year, all of a sudden everyone was getting this training everywhere, and I still believe a lot of it was just a total waste of time. And we could have trained in better ways. (senior supervisor)

We've got a paint course going at the moment and then along came [the new model] — it's been held off for the last three weeks...

Most of the training they do is when we're going bad — when we've got excess labour around the plant, they send them on all the training courses they can get their hands on. ...and there's an avalanche of courses like within three months — people get sick to death [of training]. (first-line supervisor)

The comments of the latter three respondents were as follows:

...at the moment the opportunity is there for the company to train people because the industry is depressed and there is not enough work for the workers that they have got. As the industry goes up again they will have even less time, so if they're not training people now when they've got the time and the labour, they're certainly not going to do it when everybody's working solid. (wages employee)

No. We only do that when we've got spare time. Like when there was a down turn two months ago... they decided that they would use that time to take one of those [relief groups] and relieve on the lines so that that person on the lines, say in moulding or assembly or whatever, could go into a training... It did stop because we started to get busy for [the new model]...

If we're very slow, then they'll say 'We'll use this time for training.' (wages employee)

...at the moment if you want to learn something, they can say 'We haven't got time to show you that'. (wages employee)

That the above theme did not emerge in the tooling division data was perhaps not surprising given the distinctly different systems of production which operated in the two divisions. Using Woodward's (1965) typology for classifying production systems (i.e., technology), the production division could be described as supporting 'mass production' technology (with work organised around a number of different production lines, each mass producing various component parts), whereas, in the tooling division, work was organised around a 'unit or small batch' production system (for the design and manufacture of press dies, assembly fixtures, and special purpose tooling and equipment). Production demands in the tooling division were, therefore, unlikely to be as urgent on a day-to-day basis as they were in the production division.

It will be recalled that the present theme also emerged in respondents' elaborations on information meetings. There is evidence, then, that the demands of production in this division may take precedence over, not just one, but a range of activities not directly related to production. To the extent that this is the case, it sends a clear signal to workers about what it is that management *actually* values and this, in turn, is likely to undermine those values which management may be hoping to communicate through the increased involvement of workers in the division in activities such as training and information meetings.

Theme 3: Bias in the selection of employees for training

Two of the production division respondents who reported some worker involvement in training suggested that selection decisions for participation in training courses were often biased in favour of the foreman's (first-line supervisor's) preferred candidate, rather than necessarily the most deserving candidate.

> Well, normally it's the foremen that pick who goes, or it's the leading hands. And so it's either the leading hands or the leading hands' mates that go all the time. (wages employee)

> I know people in this plant that have been here nearly as long as me, and [have] never, ever been asked to go on a course. Yet, there are new people that have come in — they've got die setting, they've got all sorts of things — and people resent this. ...I've never been on a course. I've been asked [by the foreman] three times and three times I've been knocked back [by management]. The only courses I've been on is for health and safety, and I've worked here all these years...

> ...foremen have favourites and you'll get this all the time; that some people will get nothing and another person would [get everything]. (wages employee)

This same view was expressed by a third respondent who, in response to prompting, had reported no worker involvement in training:

> See you get different... they've just done different things for different people. (wages employee)

Theme 4: Training as a cost

A key idea in each of the following excerpts by three respondents from the production division is that training is essentially a one-off cost, rather than a potentially valuable investment in the human resource capabilities of the organisation. The first two respondents quoted had initially reported some worker involvement in training, while the third respondent had reported no worker involvement in training. The third respondent also implied that this particular attitude to training, which was not one to which he subscribed personally, was somewhat short sighted.

> Well, I'd like to see more training but training can be so expensive you know. The employer doesn't like to have training. (wages employee)

> Now, we've had a lot of people that have come in who have had no intention of working in [the production division], you spend six months training them up and they leave, and even that basic training, there's a lot of money. (first-line supervisor)

> ...they will not have [a training person] here because it's a surplus head. ...But look at what they'd gain by having all the people training properly. You know, it's so sad really. (wages employee)

11.2.2.5 *Attributions data*

As above for information meetings, respondents from each division were asked *specifically* about changes in their experience of worker involvement in training from the past to the present. Where changes were reported they were then asked to comment on their perceptions of the reasons for these changes. Findings for the tooling division are reported first, followed by findings for the production division. Within each division, the main focus of the analysis was on attributions that respondents had in common.

Tooling division. All respondents from the tooling division reported a change from the past to the present in their experience of training for workers in the division. In all cases, it was reported that there was either no training in the past or less than that which was currently made available. Two common attributions — the first more widely shared than the second — emerged in respondents' explanations for the current status of this activity. These were as follows:

Attribution 1: Increased training seen as a response to external pressures

The majority of respondents (nine out of 12, or 75% of this group) indicated that they saw the change towards increased training at the present time as having been externally rather than internally driven. It can be seen from their comments below that a range of external forces for change were identified including: pressure from the government; nation-wide reforms in the industry; pressure from the union; changes in government legislation; and the introduction of award restructuring. The reader's attention is drawn to the distinctly cynical tone of the first two excerpts below.

> If it was left to [the company] it wouldn't happen. But that is the new plan right around the country isn't it, that they want people to be more skilled, so they have got to sort of give people courses that they can do... That will get to the stage where they [management] will

say... as it diminishes... they will say that we don't need that anymore anyway. (wages employee, leading hand)

The company's been forced to do this [become more quality conscious, increase training, *etc.*]. They never do anything until they're forced to. (first-line supervisor)

Yes, quite recently [workers] have been asked to participate in quite a few educational trainings, like pneumatics, PLC [programmable logic control]... It is now the tendency... I think that it started about two years ago... it is now the tendency of a company to train their people to acquire a better quality job... It is a government push... It is a government-sponsored thing that people should do more and know more... (first-line supervisor)

...obviously [the company] introduced [multi-skilling] to benefit themselves of course, there is no doubt about that. But it possibly is [part of a wider industrial] reform and that is the way of thinking where you can have a more versatile workforce. (wages employee, shop steward)

Interviewer: Why do you think training was brought it? *Respondent:* I think it was the law. I think [it was] the legislation. (senior supervisor)

...since they brought that, what do you call it, where they had to supply worker training... It was a union sort of work thing. (wages employee)

Well, I think it was involved with the restructuring, you know, the government's restructuring program, retraining and so forth. (senior supervisor)

Interviewer: Why do you think that they introduced [training]? *Respondent:* Well, I think it was more about this restructuring situation, I think that's really where it's all starting to stem from. (wages employee, leading hand)

...there was very little training being offered until the introduction of restructuring. (wages employee, leading hand)

Attribution 2: Training increased to further develop existing skills or replace lost skills

The remaining three respondents simply referred to the implications of increased training for enhancing the skills, knowledge, and flexibility of workers. While the first respondent quoted below implied that the change had been driven primarily by internal circumstances (namely, the loss of skills through the retrenchment of divisional employees over past years), the last two respondents offered no insights into their perception of why management might want to increase the efficiency and flexibility of workers. In fact, the clear impression conveyed by the comments of the third respondent below is that his uncertainty about the issue prompted a response designed primarily to 'fit' with what he thought the interviewer wanted to hear.

It was just trying to build up some of the skills of the workers... When you start to lose skills, you've gotta replace them somehow or other, and the only way you're going to do it is to get a person willing to start to better himself. (first-line supervisor)

I think they're trying to develop the tradesman into learning a bit more scope, like, that he can sort of do a bit more here and a bit more there. (wages employee, leading hand)

I don't know [why training was introduced]. Probably to make a more efficient organisation, give more knowledge to the people that's working on the tooling. *Interviewer:* So it's a management attempt to improve efficiency? *Respondent* [laughing]: Yeah, that sounds all right! (first-line supervisor)

It is interesting to note that, in none of the attributions above, is there any clear reference to a more Theory Y orientation to training, whereby the value of training for satisfying the needs of individual workers, as well as the organisation's needs, is recognised.

Production division. In contrast to the tooling division, only eight out of 19 respondents from the production division reported a change from the past to the present in their experience of training for workers in the division. Of these, six indicated that, in the past, divisional workers had either less training than at the present time, or no training at all, and two respondents indicated that there was more training for divisional workers in the past. With respect to the former, various attributions were made regarding the change towards more training at the present time. These are summarised below.

Attribution 1: Increased training seen as a response to external pressures

Like their counterparts from the tooling division, three respondents pointed to the impact of various external pressures. Specifically, the first two respondents quoted below attributed the change to a change in government legislation requiring organisations to spend a certain percentage of their total payroll on the training of employees. The third respondent attributed the change to the introduction of award restructuring.

I think a lot of the times they look at the training account and they say 'We better train some people'...We've put more hours into it, but it is not quality hours. And when I say that, what I am saying is, because the companies now have to spend a percentage of their salaries on training, we tend to train for the sake of training. But I don't believe we've really looked at it diligently enough to come up with the needs of the people on the shop floor. (senior supervisor)

I think that legislation now says they have to record on what the training is because the award restructuring has put the emphasis in it, because the companies now get fined if they don't have at least 1% whatever... It is legislation that has forced it onto the company. (first-line supervisor)

Since this job restructuring really — they're doing more training now than they've done before... it's part of the restructuring. (wages employee)

Attribution 2: Training increased in order to further develop skills

In contrast to the above, two respondents implied that training initiatives in the division had, at least in part, been motivated by a concern to develop the potential of the division's human resources (particularly with regard to skill development). However, it remains unclear as to whether the concern for people alluded to is intended to serve the interests of the organisation only, or the interests of both the organisation and its workers.

> The idea is to try and, you know, improve people or improve the work potential. (wages employee)
>
> I guess because we finally got a couple of managers that realised that... you got more out of training than it actually cost you. You know, people can't do a job unless they know how to do it. I mean you can't ask a person to spray paint if he doesn't know how to operate a spray gun, for example... (senior supervisor)

The remaining respondent in this group (a supervisor) indicated that he himself had initiated on-the-job training for the workers in his section. In the excerpt below, the respondent points out that his decision to introduce training had been motivated by a concern to help new workers deal with the frustrations associated with working on new and unfamiliar tasks. He also points to the positive implications of training both for his own, and his workers', sense of achievement. While the comments below imply a very Theory Y orientation to training, the respondent himself makes it clear that the approach he describes is very much an expression of his own personal philosophy, rather than an indication of company-wide values regarding the training of workers:

> *Interviewer:* Tell me, though, this increased emphasis on training, is this just something that you've done... or is there a divisional drive towards [increased training]? *Respondent:* I've got a personal thing myself for that type of [training], that's my personal sort of input. I had frustrations when I came up through the company and I know that a lot of people have got those frustrations, so I do my darnedest to relieve it, in a lot of cases. And it's a twofold type situation. I mean you get a sense of achievement when you can see an operator come into a plant and he's growing in knowledge, and you can see him develop, and that gives me a sense of achievement. And it also gives the employee a sense of achievement because he can see how he's come up and had a chance to improve himself... [But] I wouldn't say there's a real drive [by the division], no. (first-line supervisor)

With respect to the two respondents who reported more training for divisional workers in the past, there was one who argued that there had been a shift in focus, away from the use of external training courses in the past, towards more in-house training at the present time. The implication was that the current approach represented an attempt to make training more relevant to workers' specific training needs:

> Actually they used to send people out to TAFE [Technical and Further Education] colleges; they used to send them out to TAFE in the old days to do die setting courses and things like that. They used to actually send them to TAFE but then they started bringing TAFE

in... They have to package the course up. They have to make a bit of this, a bit of this, and a bit of this. So you haven't got a full variation of... you've got a variation of all different courses but not any specific things. (wages employee)

In the case of the second respondent, his experience of training was reportedly limited to a single training course, offered to spray painters in the division, and conducted in-house over a five-month period during the mid-1980s. The respondent indicated that he did not know why this training was no longer provided.

11.2.2.6 *Concluding comments about the analysis of qualitative data on 'attend training'*

As was the case for information meetings, the results of the above analysis of the qualitative data on training provide some valuable insights into the meaning of this particular worker activity for respondents from both divisions. Importantly, these insights provided a context (or meaning framework) within which to better understand and interpret the quantitative data on training. With respect to the latter, it will be recalled from Table 11.1 that all of the tooling division respondents and almost two-thirds of the production division respondents reported that the workers in their respective divisions attended training. In all cases, this information was provided in response to specific prompting, rather than spontaneously in response to the open-ended question. Additional quantitative data revealed marked discrepancies, among respondents from both divisions, in their estimates of the numbers of workers involved in training and the amount of training received (per worker per year). The researcher's general contextual knowledge suggested that these discrepancies might be due to the non-uniform nature of training activities in each division (reflected, e.g., in sectional differences in worker access to training, and the expectation, in the tooling division at least, that workers should initiate their own involvement in training). What, then, are the specific insights provided by the results of the above more detailed analysis of the qualitative data on training? There are four main points that can be made in this regard, as follows:

(1) With respect first of all to the analysis of the definitional data, it was found that there was some variability among production division respondents in how they defined training. While the majority of respondents from this division thought of training as formal training, it was clear from the responses of a minority that their references were to training provided on-the-job. No such discrepancy existed for tooling division respondents, all of whom defined training as formal training. As with information meetings, the point can be made here that this interpretive inconsistency, while reflected in the comments of a minority of respondents only, was not evident in the quantitative data on training. The argument that data pertaining to a particular issue cannot be reliably aggregated where there are differences in respondents' definitions of the issue also applies here.

(2) Second, the above results highlighted the potential value of conducting a separate analysis of the initial comments that respondents make in response to open questioning about a given issue. These data can reveal elements of respondents' spontaneous thinking about the issue which are perhaps less likely to emerge in more considered responses. As indicated above, the initial comments of respondents from both divisions, when asked about the current involvement of workers in their respective divisions in training, conveyed the clear impression that training constituted a peripheral, rather than a central, activity with respect to respondents' thinking about the role of workers in their division. Specifically, the initial comments of some tooling division respondents suggested that there existed in the division a degree of uncertainty about the availability of training for workers; the comments of others implied that the level of training activity in the division was relatively low. This latter impression was also conveyed by the initial comments of some production division respondents. In addition, initial comments from respondents in this division contained references to the differential access of different groups within the division to training, the company's legal obligation to provide training, and the subordination of training needs to production demands. The point was also made that initial comments associated with "no" responses can be as 'telling' as those associated with "yes" responses in terms of their capacity to reveal respondents' spontaneous thinking about an issue.

(3) The results of the thematic content analysis indicated that, as was the case for information meetings, there existed both similarities and differences between the divisions in the thematic content of respondents' elaborations on training. For example, respondents from both divisions talked about training in a way which suggested a predominantly Theory X orientation to the provision of training for workers. In other words, the emphasis was on the role of training in serving the organisation's needs, with no indication of a significant role for training in the satisfaction of individual worker needs. In both divisions, there was also some evidence of negative attitudes towards the formal training that was made available to workers. A third theme common to both divisions concerned the motivation of workers to attend training. It was suggested that workers were reluctant to attend training in their own time unless they were paid by the company to do so. Reference was made to the similarity between this theme, which suggested a view of workers as motivated primarily by economic self-interest, and a previous theme which emerged in the data on information meetings suggesting a view of workers as externally motivated (in the sense of participating in various activities because they have to, and not because they want to).

In addition to the above common themes, the thematic content analysis also revealed a number of themes that were unique to each division. For example, the elaborations of some tooling division respondents on training contained the idea that it was largely up to the workers themselves to initiate their own involvement in training. There was no sense in which the organisation was seen to be actively encouraging workers to pursue development of this kind. That this theme did not emerge in the production division data may reflect changes in this division, over recent years, whereby management had introduced a number of initiatives (e.g., problem-solving groups, performance feedback sessions for individual sections, and the graphic display of outcome data in work areas) which were designed specifically to increase the involvement of workers in the daily operations of the division. As such, management in this division could be seen to be more actively encouraging and supporting the involvement of workers in a number of non-production activities. A second theme that was unique to the tooling division concerned the perception that recent training initiatives in the division were of relevance only to the division's younger employees. The emergence of this theme in the tooling division data, and not in the production division data, probably reflects differences in the demographics of the two divisions, with employees in the tooling division being, on average, older and longer serving than their counterparts in the production division.

The elaborations of production division respondents also contained a number of themes that were unique to that division. As indicated, the subject of on-the-job training was clearly of some significance to respondents from this division, with some offering positive evaluations of this form of training and others suggesting that it did not constitute 'real' training (which, in their view, was training provided by qualified professionals). The point was made that the absence of any references to on-the-job training by tooling division respondents probably reflected the status of employees from this division as qualified tradesmen, whose on-the-job skills and competencies were already well-established. Another theme that was unique to the production division concerned the view that the amount of training available to divisional workers was contingent on production demands. When production demands were high, the level of training activity in the division was low; when production demands were low, there was spare time available for the provision of training. It was noted that this same theme emerged in the production division data on information meetings, suggesting that the particular contingency described may apply to a range of worker activities in this division. Finally, there were two additional, though less well-represented, themes that emerged in the production division data on training. The first pointed to a degree of bias in the selection of workers for participation in training courses and the second highlighted the perception of training as a cost.

(4) The fourth and final point concerns the insights offered by an analysis of the data pertaining to respondents' past experience of training. As was the case for information meetings, there was evidence to suggest that tooling division employees may be a more homogeneous group in this regard than their counterparts in production. As indicated, all respondents from the tooling division reported that, in the past, there was either less training in the division than that which was currently available or no training at all. In contrast, less than half the respondents from the production division reported a change in their experience of training from the past to the present. Moreover, while most of these respondents indicated an increase in training activity over recent

years, there was a minority who reported a decrease. With respect to their attributions regarding these changes, there was again less variability among tooling division respondents than among production division respondents. For the former, the impact of external pressures was the most commonly cited explanation for the increase in training over recent years. For the latter, the increase in training was variously attributed to external pressures, a recognition by management of the need to develop workers' skills, and in one case, the commitment of the respondent himself to developing the potential of his workers. The point was made that the less consensual views of production division respondents (regarding their experience of training) could not be accounted for simply by differences in the demographics of this group, and that an alternative explanation in terms of contextual factors might need to be considered.

Overall, then, it can be seen that the above findings for the activity labelled 'attend training' highlight the value of qualitative data for understanding the meaning of quantitative data. This same general conclusion applied with respect to the findings for information meetings. Again, the point can be made that, if the present method had relied solely on quantitative techniques of data collection, it is unlikely that the above insights into the nature of respondents' experience of, and thinking about, training could have been obtained. It is difficult to imagine how one could design, *a priori*, a set of specific questions capable of generating the range of highly context-specific information reported above. As we have argued on several previous occasions, the only way in which some checks on differences in interpretation could be obtained is to ask respondents to comment on, and/or provide examples of, what they are referring to in their responses. As suggested, however, this technique relies on respondents being willing and able to provide such additional information. While qualitative questioning (e.g., asking for examples) can help to ensure that respondents' understanding of questions is at least similar, the success of this approach relies to some extent on the skill of the interviewer to detect what might be misunderstandings in the responses given, and then to probe those responses to ascertain their meaning for the respondent.

11.2.3 *Methodological issues arising from the analysis of qualitative data*

There are a number of important methodological issues arising from the findings reported above, all of which have implications for an evaluation of the particular approach to combining qualitative and quantitative methods adopted in the present study.

1. Issue specific analyses. The first issue concerns the present approach to analysing qualitative data. Rather than conduct a single analysis of the entire qualitative data set for a given interview, the approach adopted above was to dissect this data set and conduct separate analyses of the qualitative data pertaining to specific issues addressed by the interview (in this case, concerning respondents' experience of worker involvement in information meetings and in training). One of the problems with this approach is that, if viewed separately from each other, the findings of these separate issue-specific analyses can under-represent the prevalence of emergent themes or attributions that are identified. This is because the same theme or attribution may emerge in the context of respondents' comments about, not one, but a range of different issues. In fact, it will be recalled from the results of the thematic content analyses reported above, that two such themes were identified, each of which emerged in respondents' elaborations on information meetings and training. The first theme, which was a theme common to both divisions, concerned the lack of motivation workers to participate in non-production activities; the second concerned a perception among production division respondents that, at any given time, the involvement of workers in non-production activities was largely dependent on the demands of production at that time. An important implication of this particular feature of the present method is that, in order to provide accurate information about the prevalence of any given theme or attribution, the researcher must, at some point, draw together the findings of each of the separate issue specific analyses that she/he has conducted with the aim of identifying what they have in common.

The above comments are not to deny the value of the present approach to interviewing, whereby respondents are presented with a series of prompts (closed questions) designed to provide information about a range of specific issues. In fact, it might be argued that, compared with completely unstructured approaches to interviewing, the present approach may be more effective in bringing to the surface those themes and attributions that may be of particular significance in a given context. This is because, in focussing respondents' attention on a number of specific issues there are, in a sense, more opportunities for particular themes and particular attribution styles to find expression. A related advantage of this approach is that there may also be more opportunities for both the emergence and subsequent evaluation of possible explanations for the presence (or absence) of these themes and attributional styles. In fact, the findings associated with the above theme, concerning the perception that production demands determined the level of worker involvement in non-production activities, provided some evidence to support this view. It will be recalled that this was a theme that was unique to the production division. There was no indication of this particular contingency also applying in the tooling division. In attempting to explain this difference between the two divisions, reference was made to the different production systems operating in these divisions. Interestingly, however, this explanation did not become apparent initially, in the context of respondents' elaborations on information meetings (which contained the first references to this theme), but was only suggested subsequently by the findings of the analysis of the associated data on training.

2. Significance of repeated themes. The second methodological issue raised by the above findings is not unrelated to the first in the sense that it too is concerned with the question of how prevalent, or how significant, a given theme is in the context being studied. As suggested above, one indicator of the significance of a given theme is the extent to which the theme emerges in respondents' comments about, not one, but a range of issues of potential relevance to their experience of organisational life. Another indicator is simply the sharedness of the theme, reflected in the numbers of respondents whose comments contain some expression of the theme. However, these two criteria are not the sole criteria by which a theme's significance can be evaluated. A third, somewhat less obvious criterion, is the extent to which disconfirming evidence and/or contradictory themes are absent. Where this is the case, one might be justified in arguing that a given theme, which is not strongly supported by the data (in the sense that it emerges in the comments of a minority of respondents only) may be of more significance than would initially appear to be the case, given the relatively low level of available confirming evidence. Of course, such an argument is convincing only if one reports data comprehensively (as in this study), rather than selectively as is often the case where qualitative methods alone are used. An important practical implication of such an approach, however, is that it imposes definite limits on the amount of data that one can reasonably be expected to collect (since the comprehensive reporting of all relevant data is possible only if a thorough analysis of the entire data set has been carried out). It is also the case that researchers who adopt this approach would need to make use of one of the available computer programs for text analysis, rather than attempt to analyse their data manually. In the present study, the use of one such program, namely, Ethnograph (Seidel, Kjolseth, & Seymour, 1988) made it possible to systematically analyse a relatively large data set.

3. Use of data from other contextual domains. The third issue is related to a point made previously, namely, that many of the data reported above, while they pertained to the *present* context of respondents' experience were embedded in, and hence were drawn from, responses pertaining to some other contextual domain. In fact, this was the case for almost half of the excerpts quoted in the two sub-sections above in which the results of the thematic content analyses are reported. Specifically, of a total of 95 excerpts quoted (all pertaining to the present context), 46 were drawn from responses to questions about the respondent's past, anticipated future, or ideal experience (regarding the involvement of workers in information meetings and in training)[5]. An obvious implication of this finding

---

[5] An examination of this entire data set indicated that there were no significant differences between the two divisions with respect to the contextual domain from which the quoted excerpts (pertaining to information meetings on the one hand, and training on the other) were drawn. However, there was some evidence to suggest that, within each division, there were differences between each of the issues investigated. For example, for the production division, most of the comments about information meetings that were quoted were embedded in responses pertaining to the present context. A minority of these comments only were drawn from responses pertaining to the past, anticipated future, and the ideal. With respect to the comments about training, however, these were drawn from responses pertaining to three contextual domains, namely, the present, the past, and the anticipated future, with each of these domains being equally well-represented. For the tooling division, one half of the comments about information meetings that were quoted were embedded within responses pertaining to the present context, while the other half were drawn from responses pertaining to the ideal. In contrast, comments about training from this division were almost all drawn from responses pertaining to either the present context or the anticipated future. It is difficult to know what the significance of these findings might be. Of particular interest is the finding that, for each division, the anticipated future context was well

is that, if respondents had only been asked about their experience with respect to the present context (and not with respect to these other contextual domains), these data, and the valuable insights they provide about the present, would not have been obtained.

The same argument applies with respect to the attributions data. These data inform us of respondents' perceptions about why the present is as it is. However, as indicated, they could only be generated by asking respondents about the past. The point should be made here that attributions are, by their very nature, contextual in that they presuppose the existence of a past, anticipated future, and/or ideal for the organisation's culture that may help people to explain some aspect of their present. While not as *obviously* related to the organisation's culture, outside influences that contribute to the proposed other, as a context, might also assist in explaining the present. For example, with respect to training, one attribution in the data presented was that the involvement of workers in training was due to management responding to external government requirements, rather than this being an internal management initiative.

The above observations might usefully be considered in the context of conceptual treatments of organisational culture that emphasise its dynamic, rather than static, nature. This notion that an organisation's culture has a past, a present, and a future is one that is examined in more detail in the next chapter. In the next chapter, data are presented which provide support for an approach to understanding culture that seeks specific information about respondents' experiences with respect to a number of different contextual domains. In a sense, the above observations can be seen to foreshadow the major claim of the next section, namely, that an understanding of these various aspects of context is crucial for an understanding of culture.

4. Importance of elaborative data on both "yes" and "no" responses. The fourth and final issue relates to the present approach of analysing the qualitative data associated with both yes and no responses to the closed questions (or prompts). This approach can be contrasted with that adopted in many questionnaire designs that include a qualitative component. Questionnaire respondents are typically asked to comment only on their yes responses, with no opportunity provided whereby they can elaborate on their no responses. An important insight provided by the findings reported above is that elaborations on both yes and no responses to any given question can contain the same thematic content. This was found to be the case for several of the themes that emerged in the elaborations of

---

represented with respect to comments about training, but not with respect to comments about information meetings. This finding may reflect the current emphasis in the industry on multi-skilling and the implications of this reform for the retraining of employees, if not now, then in the near future. In this sense, training can be seen to be very much on the agenda for the future, making it perhaps more likely that respondents will refer to their current experiences and perceptions of training, not just in the context of their comments about the present time, but also in the context of their comments about the anticipated future. The observation, made previously, that tooling division respondents in particular, felt some anxiety and uncertainty in relation to the introduction of multi-skilling, may also be of significance here.

production division respondents on training. One such theme concerned the perception of some production division respondents that worker involvement in activities not directly related to production (e.g., training) was contingent on production demands. This theme emerged in the elaborations of respondents who had previously reported some worker involvement in training as well as in the elaborations of respondents who had previously reported no worker involvement in training.

It is interesting to consider this finding in the context of Australian research conducted by Clarke, Ruffin, Hill, and Beaman (1992). These researchers found evidence to support their argument that the practice, common in quantitative research in the social sciences, of converting verbal probability terms (such as those used to represent response categories for Likert-type items) to numerical scales, for the purpose of carrying out statistical analyses, rests upon a number of questionable assumptions. In particular, their findings questioned the assumption that all respondents assign comparable meanings to these probability terms. Their findings also questioned the assumption that these terms, once converted to numerical scales, represent mathematically equidistant and symmetrical points on these scales (so that the difference between, say, *very likely* and *likely* can be assumed to be equal to the difference between *unlikely* and *very unlikely* and, furthermore, that responses such as *very likely* and *very unlikely* can be taken to represent probabilities that are equal in magnitude, but opposite in direction). The point can be made that, although the yes/no response categories referred to above are crude in comparison with those investigated by Clarke *et al.*, the same general conclusion applies, namely, that one cannot assume that those respondents who give a yes response necessarily constitute a qualitatively different group from those respondents who give a no response. An implication of this finding for the design of questionnaires that incorporate a qualitative component is that respondents should be given the opportunity to comment both on their yes responses and on their no responses. Of course, even with such a modification, the fact remains that most questionnaires are designed to generate written information only. A clear advantage of face-to-face interviews in this respect is that the data they generate have both a verbal and a non-verbal dimension. Thus, the meaning of a given response can be inferred, not just from the verbal response (i.e., the words, as written down) but also from the way in which the response is communicated. It has been the researcher's experience, for example, that yes and no responses can be communicated with greater or lesser conviction, with the degree of conviction being reflected, at least in part, in the tone of the respondent's voice. This, of course, places responsibility on the skills of the interviewer who, without appropriate training, might miss such cues or be more likely to interpret them (e.g., a no response taken to be yes because of the nonverbal cues) in terms of a preconceived explanation for the data.

The suggestion above that differences between respondents who give a yes response and those who give a no response may be more apparent than real is further supported by the finding that respondents can differ with respect to their interpretations, or definitions, of the particular issues about which they are asked. As indicated above, an analysis of the qualitative data on training revealed some inconsistencies, among respondents from the production division, in their definitions of training. While the majority of respondents defined training as formal training, there were some who defined it as training received on-the-job. Specifically, this latter group comprised three respondents who had previously indicated that, yes, workers in their division did attend training. The question arises as to whether these three respondents may, in fact, have more in common with respondents who had previously answered no to the question about worker involvement in training (all of whom were referring to 'formal' training) than they do with other yes respondents (who, unlike themselves, were referring to 'formal' training and not to on-the-job training). To the extent that this is the case, it provides support for the view that differences between yes and no responses should not be taken at face value, but rather, they should be interpreted in the light of insights provided by an analysis of the qualitative data associated with these responses.

One final illustration of the value of analysing the qualitative data associated with both yes and no responses is provided by the above analysis of the very first comments made by respondents in response to the training prompt. As indicated, these comments provided some useful initial insights into the way in which training was perceived by some of the production division respondents. In particular, they conveyed the impression that training was accorded relatively low status as an activity for the workers in this division.

11.3 Conclusions

In this chapter, we have reported the results of Study 3 concerned with the use in the proposed method of semi-structured interviewing. Consideration was given first to the results pertaining to use of open-ended questions in combination with closed questions, or prompts. One outcome of this feature of the method was that it resulted in more information being generated about the issue being investigated than would have been the case had the interview protocol included open-ended questions only, or alternatively, closed questions only. The marked discrepancy between respondents' spontaneous and prompted responses raised questions about the cultural significance of this discrepancy. In particular, the finding that there were some worker activities that, while not mentioned in response to the open-ended question, were subsequently mentioned by a majority of respondents (from both divisions) in response to prompting, led to a consideration of the evidence regarding, on the one hand, the likely salience of these activities for respondents and, on the other, the possibility of information about these activities being a part of respondents' assumed (or taken-for-granted) knowledge. These ideas were explored in some depth with reference to the data on worker involvement in two activities, namely, information meetings and training.

In this chapter, we also considered the results pertaining to that feature of the method that allowed respondents to elaborate on and/or qualify their responses. The analysis of the thematic content of the qualitative data that were generated in this way (including definitional data, general explanations or elaborations, and attributions) provided valuable insights into the highly context-specific meanings that the issues being investigated had for respondents. These data revealed important interpretive differences between the two divisions, and indeed also between the researcher and the participants in the research. The point was made that insights of the kind provided by this analysis would be unlikely to have been obtained had the method involved a more highly structured interview format (or the use of a more traditional quantitative method, such as a questionnaire).

In the next chapter, we report the results of Study 3 concerned with the operationalisation, in the proposed method, of various dimensions of context, including the present, the past, the future, the other, and the ideal. As in the present chapter, consideration is also given to respondents' attributions regarding the reasons for experienced and/or anticipated differences between contexts (i.e., differences in respondents' experience with respect to a given issue between the past and the present, or between the present and the anticipated future).

It is perhaps apposite at this point to remind the reader that Chapters 11 and 12 (i.e., this chapter and the next) are primarily concerned with the reporting of the Study 3 results. For a comprehensive evaluation of all of the key features of the method used in Study 3, the reader is referred to Chapter 13 (in particular, Sections 13.1 and 13.2).

Chapter 12

The Operationalisation of Context
(Study 3, Part 3)

In the present chapter, we report the results of Study 3 concerned with the operationalisation, in the proposed method, of various dimensions of context, including the present, the past, the future, the other, and the ideal. The chapter begins with a brief restatement of the rationale for the treatment of organisational culture as a highly context-specific phenomenon. This is followed, in the second section, by a discussion of the extent to which, in the Study 3 data set, there were spontaneous references to different contextual domains. This was an important consideration in view of the subsequent assessment of the benefits of an explicit focus on different dimensions of context (i.e., by way of specific questions about respondents' experience of a given issue in the present, the past, anticipated future, *etc.*). In the third and major section of this chapter, we report the results of the analysis of contextual data elicited through specific questioning. In particular, consideration is given to respondents' accounts of their experience (perceptions) of the role of workers (specifically, what workers do) in relation to each of the contextual domains of interest[1]. Consideration is also given, where relevant, to respondents' causal attributions regarding differences in this experience between contexts (e.g., between the past and the present, or the present and the anticipated future). An important focus of the analysis reported here (as for the data considered in the previous chapter) is on similarities and differences between the two organisational units that participated in this research. In this third section, attention is also drawn to the nature of the links between contextual data from different domains and to the methodological implications of the findings reported. The chapter concludes with some brief summary comments about the overall value of Study 3 and an introduction to the content of Part Six, the final part of Volume II and of this book.

Before proceeding to the substantive content of this chapter, the reader is advised that, given the amount of data generated by questions about context, it was not possible to report the results of the analysis of these data in their entirety. It was decided, therefore, that only the results of the analysis of open question data would be reported in full, and that the results

---

[1] It should be noted that the results for the present context are not presented in a separate section; rather, they are integrated, as appropriate, into the discussion of results for each of the other contextual domains of interest, namely, the past, the anticipated future, the other, and the ideal. This is because respondents' experience of the role of workers *at the present time* constituted the base from which they considered the role of workers with respect to these other contextual domains.

of the analysis of prompt question data would be referred to selectively, in order to illustrate particular methodological points. These latter results are reported and discussed in full in Kummerow (2000). We would again reiterate that the central concern of the three studies undertaken as part of the present research was with methodological issues in understanding organisational culture; the aim was not to produce a definitive account of the cultures of the two participating organisational units. In view of this, and as suggested above, the reporting of results serves the primary purpose of illustrating particular methodological points.

12.1 Organisational Culture as Context-Specific

As we have indicated previously, a common conceptualisation of organisational culture is that it is highly context-specific and that, in order to really understand the culture of any given organisation (i.e., the pattern of shared meanings that help organisation members to 'make sense of' their experience of organisational life), one must seek an understanding of the context within which that culture has evolved and possibly also been transformed. The results of Study 2, considered together with the various conceptual treatments of culture that one finds in the literature (as reported in some detail in Chapter 7 of Volume I), suggested the possibility that an organisation's culture might usefully be thought of as comprising a number of specific dimensions, or domains, of context including: a past, a present, a future, an 'other' (reflecting organisation members' experiences in, or of, other organisations), and an ideal (reflecting organisation members' views about how things ideally should be). Accordingly, a key feature of the present method was that it attempted to operationalise each of these different domains of context by asking specific questions about them, with the aim being to generate information that could assist in the drawing of inferences about underlying assumptions concerning, in this case, the role of workers.

It is worth noting that, while the present chapter focuses exclusively on the contextualist approach adopted in this research, a partial illustration of this approach has already been provided by findings reported in the previous chapter. As indicated, information about the *present* context of respondents' experience (in relation to the involvement of divisional workers in information meetings and in training) was often embedded in respondents' answers to questions, not about this contextual domain, but rather about one, or other, of the other contextual domains about which they were asked. As was suggested, if the present method had focussed on the current context of respondents' experience only, the valuable insights that these additional data provided about the present would not have been obtained.

12.2 Spontaneous References to Contextual Domains in Responses to Questions About the Present

Before proceeding to the above-mentioned analysis of contextual data obtained through specific questioning, it is important to consider the extent to which, when asked about the present, respondents spontaneously make reference to aspects of their experience which pertain to some other contextual domain (e.g., the past, anticipated future, the other, or the ideal). If this can be shown to occur to a significant degree, then it might be argued that specific questions about respondents' experiences with respect to these other contextual domains may be redundant. It may be, for example, that one does not need to ask specific questions about the past since, if given time, respondents may refer spontaneously to aspects of their past experience in the course of responding to questions about the present. In order to explore this question more fully, data from the present interviews were analysed further to determine the number and nature of spontaneous references to contextual domains other than the present, which emerged in responses to questions about the present. The point can again be made, as above, that in the previous chapter in which data on the present context are reported, it was found that some of these data came from responses to questions about other contexts (i.e., the past and anticipated future). These data would not have been available had the interview included only questions about the present.

12.2.1 *References to the past in responses to questions about the present*

The results of this analysis are shown in Tables 12.1 and 12.2. It can be seen from Table 12.1 that, in the context of their responses to questions about the present, a majority of respondents from each division (9/12 or 75% of tooling division respondents, and 17/19 or 89% of production division respondents) made one or more spontaneous references to the past. For the production division, the maximum number of references to the past by a single respondent was five, with most respondents making three references or less. For the tooling division, the maximum number of references to the past by a single respondent was four, with the majority of respondents making only one or two references to the past. While these findings might initially suggest a relatively strong tendency among respondents from both divisions to refer to the past when asked about the present, it must be remembered that, in this part of the interview, each respondent was asked a total of 13 questions about the present (two open-ended questions concerning, respectively, the main duties and other activities of workers in the division, followed by six prompt questions (the first of which comprised six parts) asking about specific activities in which workers in the division might engage). If it is the case that prompting respondents about specific aspects of their organisational experience at the present time leads them to reflect on the nature of this experience in the past, then one might have expected the number of spontaneous references to the past, made by individual respondents from either division, to have been, on average, greater than that reported.

Table 12.2 shows that, for each division, the spontaneous references to the past that were made covered a fairly broad range of topics (or activity categories). At the same time, however, there were certain specific topics that were better represented than most (in terms of the percentage of the total number of references which they accounted for, and also in terms of the number of respondents who referred to these topics). For the tooling division, the best-represented topic was Sports and Social Activities. Seven respondents from this division (58% of the sample) spontaneously commented on the involvement of the workers in this division in the past in sports and social activities that no longer occurred or that now

Table 12.1. Spontaneous references to contexts other than the present context, contained within responses to questions about the present context, shown for the Tooling Division (TD) and the Production Division (PD).

Respondent #	PAST TD	PAST PD	FUTURE TD	FUTURE PD	OTHER TD	OTHER PD	IDEAL TD	IDEAL PD
R1	3		1		1			
R2	3	1	1					1
R3	2	2	1				1	
R4		3					1	3
R5	2	2						
R6	1	3						
R7	2	1						1
R8		1						
R9		2					1	
R10	4	3		1				1
R11	1	5		2				2
R12	2	1						
R13		1						
R14		5		1				1
R15		2						2
R16		3						1
R17		2		2				1
R18		2		2		1		1
R19								
Number of respondents	9	17	1	7	1	1	3	10
Total references	21	39	1	10	1	1	3	14

Note: Multiple references by a single respondent to any given activity, or activity category, are not reported.

occurred less often, with these references accounting for 35% of the total number of spontaneous references to the past that were made by respondents from this division. The point can be made that this finding was consistent with the more general observation that employees from the tooling division, in their day-to-day conversations with the researcher[2], were frequently reminiscent of the very positive social climate that had prevailed in the division in its early years. Information Meetings was also a reasonably well-represented topic in this division. References to this topic were made by five respondents (42% of the

---

[2]As indicated in previous chapters, this is a reference to the first author who undertook the empirical work for the three studies that are reported in Parts Four and Five of this volume.

Table 12.2. Activities, or activity categories, that were the subject of the spontaneous references reported in Table 12.1, shown for both the Tooling Division (TD) and the Production Division (PD).

	PAST		FUTURE		OTHER		IDEAL	
	TD	PD	TD	PD	TD	PD	TD	PD
Involvement of workers (general)		1						
Housekeeping		1						1
Specialisation versus multi-skilling		1		1				
Job rotation								1
Reward		1						
Meetings (general)		4						
Demographics		1						
Planning activities	1	2		1				1
Information meetings	5	4	1					1
Group meetings		7		1	1	1		2
Safety meetings	2			2				2
Union meetings	1	2						
Help other workers	2	1					2	
Record work-related information		1		4				1
Training activities	2	3		1			1	2
Sports/Social activities	7	7						
Worker-supervisor communication	1	3						3
Total references	21	39	1	10	1	1	3	14

Notes:

1. Multiple references by a single respondent to any given activity, or activity category, are not reported.

2. Activities, or activity categories, that constituted the subject of specific prompt questions are listed in italics (bottom half of table) and can therefore be distinguished from other activities.

sample) and accounted for 25% of all spontaneous references to the past made by respondents from this division. For the production division, the best-represented topics were Sports and Social Activities and Group Meetings. Each of these topics accounted for 18% of the total number of spontaneous references to the past made by respondents from this division and each was referred to by seven respondents (representing 37% of the sample from this division).

12.2.2 *References to the future, other, and ideal in responses to questions about the present*

The findings for the other contextual domains of interest (namely, the anticipated future, the other, and the ideal) contrasted markedly with those reported above for the past. As indicated in Table 12.1, there were far fewer respondents from each division who, in the course of responding to questions about the present, made spontaneous references to these other contextual domains. Nevertheless, the findings associated with these other contextual domains provided evidence to suggest some differences, albeit marginal ones, between the two divisions. It therefore seems reasonable to comment briefly on these findings.

With respect to the future, it can be seen that there was only one respondent from the tooling division who made spontaneous reference to the future in the context of answering questions about the present. This compared with seven respondents from the production division (37% of this group). While this difference between the divisions was not statistically significant, it was nevertheless consistent with the common perception among tooling division employees (to which reference has been made previously) that the division was in a state of decline and that, as such, its future was at best highly uncertain and at worst non-existent (in the sense of critical aspects of the division's current or past identity being be preserved in the future). With respect to the number of references to the future made by a single respondent, in no case (for either division) did this exceed two. From Table 12.2, it can be seen that, for the production division, no topic was mentioned significantly more than any other topic. The best represented topic (which was a reference to a change, in the future, in the involvement of the workers in this division in the recording of work-related information) was mentioned by four respondents (21% of the sample) and accounted for 40% of all the spontaneous references to the future that were made by the respondents from this division.

The findings for the ideal context were similar to those reported above for the future in that, compared with their counterparts from the tooling division, there were more respondents from the production division who, in the course of commenting on their present experience, made spontaneous reference to some aspect of their ideal experience (their views about how things ideally should be). Specifically, there were 10 respondents from the production division (53%), compared with three respondents from the tooling division (25%), for whom this was the case. As above, while this difference between the two divisions was not statistically significant, it was nevertheless consistent with some of the more general differences that were observed to exist between the two divisions. Again, this difference might be explained in terms of the perception among tooling division employees that the future of their division was highly uncertain. It may be that, in the absence of some sense of continuity between their present state and an anticipated future state, organisation members are less inclined to think about, or be able to articulate, a preferred or ideal state. An alternative explanation is suggested by the general impression of the tooling division as supporting a stronger, and more easily identifiable culture than the production division (consistent with the relatively long and stable past experience of employees in this division). If, as a group, respondents from the tooling division were more 'culture bound' in their thinking than their counterparts from the production division, then one would expect that they would be less likely to perceive a need for change and, hence, less likely to speculate on a preferred state which differed significantly from their existing state

As reported for the past and future contexts, the number of spontaneous references to the ideal by a single respondent was in all cases relatively small. In neither division did the maximum number of references per respondent exceed three and, in most cases, respondents made only one or two references each. It was also the case that, for neither division, was there any one topic that was referred to significantly more frequently than any other topic.

Finally, with respect to the other context, Table 12.1 shows that there was only one respondent from each division who, in the context of commenting on her/his present experience, spontaneously referred to some aspect of her/his experience of other organisations. It was also the case that each of these respondents made one reference only to her/his experience with respect to the other context.

12.2.3 *Methodological implications*

Overall, the above results suggest that respondents — at least at this level of a manufacturing organisation — are unlikely to provide much information about their experiences with respect to contextual domains other than the present unless they are specifically asked to do so. In other words, questions about the present (whether they are open-ended and relatively general, or closed and more specific) are unlikely to elicit a lot of information of this kind. It was clear from these results, however, that when respondents did provide additional contextual information, they tended to refer more to their past experience (in their current organisation), than to their anticipated future experience, their experience of other organisations, or their ideal experience. This is perhaps not surprising given that one's past constitutes an already experienced phenomenon (compared with, say, one's anticipated future or one's ideal). In this sense, people are probably able to articulate their past experience more readily, and with more confidence, than they are able to articulate their thoughts with respect to these other contextual domains.

The finding that there were so few spontaneous references to other organisations probably reflects the fact that even the shortest serving participants in the study had been with their current organisation (and division) for at least several years. The longest serving participants in the study (who were from the tooling division) had in excess of 20 years service with their current organisation (and division). In this sense, it is perhaps not surprising that almost all of the spontaneous references to the past that were made were concerned with past experiences that respondents had in their current organisation, rather than past experiences that they had in other organisations. It might also be that respondents would be more likely to refer spontaneously to their experiences in other organisations if these experiences differed markedly from experiences they had in their current organisation. As will be seen later in this chapter, the results of an analysis of data pertaining to the other context provided evidence to suggest that this was not the case.

The point should be made, however, that even given the focus on the past reported here, there were still relatively few spontaneous references to past experiences that might have shaped the way in which respondents thought about, and talked about, their present experiences. This suggests that a lot of potentially relevant contextual information may be implicit and, therefore, require some form of prompting to bring it to the surface.

The above conclusions might need to be qualified when dealing with organisations undergoing a major change of some kind. For example, in an organisation which is about to be taken over by another organisation, it would not be surprising if there were more spontaneous references to concerns about the organisation's future. Similarly, in a government organisation that has recently been privatised, one might expect more spontaneous references to what work was like in the past. In an organisation with a high turnover of professional staff, there might be relatively more spontaneous references to what work is like in other organisations and perhaps also to the ideal for such organisations.

12.3 An Introduction to Contextual Data Elicited Through Specific Questioning

The results of the analysis of the contextual data that were elicited through specific questioning are summarised in Tables 12.3 and 12.4. As indicated, Table 12.3 summarises the findings for the tooling division and Table 12.4 summarises the findings for the production division. By way of an introduction to the discussion of these results (in Sections 12.4 through 12.7), and to assist the reader in interpreting the data in these tables, an explanation is first given of how these tables were constructed. In this introductory section, we also make some general observations about the nature of the responses to questions about context.

12.3.1 *Guide to reading Tables 12.3 and 12.4*

With respect first of all to the format of questioning that was followed in this part of the interview, it will be recalled that the initial focus was on the *current* context of respondents' experience. Specifically, respondents were presented with two open-ended questions — the first asked about the main duties of workers in their division at the present time, and the second asked about other activities in which workers in their division were currently engaged. These open-ended questions were followed by a series of closed questions or prompts concerning possible other activities in which workers in any organisation might engage. It was anticipated that respondents might mention some of these prompted activities spontaneously, that is, in response to the second open-ended question about other activities. This same format of questioning was then duplicated across each of the four other contextual domains concerning, respectively, respondents' experience of what workers did in the past, their anticipated experience of what workers would do in the future, their experience of what workers in other organisations did, and their ideal experience (reflected in their beliefs about what workers ideally should do). Unlike the present, however, the focus with respect to these other domains was on perceived (or desired)

Table 12.3. Summary of responses to open-ended and prompt questions for five contextual domains for the Tooling Division.

DUTY/ACTIVITY	PAST		PRESENT		FUTURE		OTHER	IDEAL	
	Open	Prompt	Open	Prompt	Open	Prompt	Open	Open	Prompt
(No knowledge)							(6)		
(No change)	(4)				(2)		(1)	(4)	
(Don't know)					(1)				
(Change, unspecified)					(1)				
Primary task	3		11		2		1		
Technology	2				4		1		
Work maintenance			2						
Quality	1								
Efficiency			1		1		1	1	
WA-Production layout									
WA-Job rotation									
WA-Workload									
WA-Specialisation vs MS	3				5		1	2	
WA-Responsibility/Acct	2				3		1	3	
WA-Teamwork									
WA-Work schedules							1		
Communication general			1					1	
Health & safety general	1		2		1			1	
HRM-Reward							1	1	
HRM-Selection									
Individual Skills/Atts/Behs							1	2	
Industrial relations									
Compliance with superiors			4						
Planning meetings		2		1		4	1		5
Information meetings		6		8		4	1		7
Group problem-solving				2	1	4	1		4
Safety meetings	7	3		8		7	1		2
Union meetings	4	2		9		2			2
Help other workers		2		11		3			2
Record work-related info		2		3		2	1		4
Attend training	1	11		12	1	8			4

(Continued)

Table 12.3. (*Continued*)

DUTY/ACTIVITY	PAST Open		PRESENT Open		FUTURE Open	OTHER Open	IDEAL Open	
Formal social [Social]	3	6	2	10	5	2	3	4
Informal social			2	10				
Wkr-sup communication		4		10	3	2		5

Notes:
1. Activities, or activity categories, which constituted the subject of specific prompt questions, are listed in italics.
2. WA: A broad 'Work Arrangements' category to capture activities related to how work is organised or arranged.
3. MS: Multi-skilling.
4. HRM: A broad category to capture specific Human Resources Management practices.

Table 12.4. Summary of responses to open-ended and prompt questions for five contextual domains for the Production Division.

DUTY/ACTIVITY	PAST Open	PRESENT Open	FUTURE Open	OTHER Open	IDEAL Open
(No knowledge)				(3)	
(No change)	(2)		(2)	(4)	(3)
(Don't know)			(1)		
Primary task	1	18	3		
Technology	6		10		
Work maintenance	1	10			
Quality	3	5			1
Efficiency	2	1	1		2
WA-Production layout	1				3
WA-Job rotation		1			5
WA-Workload	3		1	1	
WA-Specialisation vs MS	2		1		
WA-Responsibility/Acct	2		1	2	4
WA-Teamwork				1	
WA-Work schedules					
Communication general	1	1			
Health & safety general	3	2		2	1
HRM-Reward	2		1	3	2
HRM-Selection				1	
Individual Skills/Atts/Behs	4		1	5	

(*Continued*)

Table 12.4. (*Continued*)

DUTY/ACTIVITY	PAST		PRESENT		FUTURE		OTHER	IDEAL
	Open		Open		Open		Open	Open
Industrial relations							2	1
Compliance with superiors			1					
		Prompt		Prompt		Prompt		Prompt
Planning meetings		6		4		3	9	7
Information meetings	1	12	1	18		4	1	5	8
Group problem-solving	6	10		5	2	4		2	6
Safety meetings		6	1	13		6			13
Union meetings		6		15		3	1		5
Help other workers		8		16		3			5
Record work-related info		9		15		10			8
Attend training		8		12	1	11	3	5	11
Formal social [Social]	2	10	2	17	1	8	6	2	7
Informal social			3	16					
Wkr-sup communication	3	10		19		5	3	4	8

Notes:
1. Activities, or activity categories, which constituted the subject of specific prompt questions, are listed in italics.
2. WA: A broad 'Work Arrangements' category to capture activities related to how work is organised or arranged.
3. MS: Multi-skilling.
4. HRM: A broad category to capture specific Human Resources Management practices.

changes in the main duties and other activities of workers, rather than on the actual duties and activities that defined the role of workers with respect to any given domain. It was also the case that, for the other context, respondents were presented with the initial open-ended questions only and were not asked the subsequent prompts. As indicated previously, this was because the first two studies had indicated the limited knowledge that these workers had of other organisations, and thus the aim of questioning with respect to this contextual domain was simply to obtain a rough indication of the extent of respondents' experience and/or knowledge of organisational life beyond the boundaries of their current organisation. With the above information in mind, the following details are now offered regarding the actual construction of Tables 12.3 and 12.4.

(1) With the exception of data pertaining to the present context, all of the data presented in Tables 12.3 and 12.4 are 'change' or 'difference' data. That is, the numbers shown indicate the number of respondents who reported some difference between their perceptions of what workers in their division did at the present time (as indicated by the profile of worker activities shown under Present) and their experience of what workers (whether in their own or other organisations) had done in the past, their beliefs about what

workers would do in the future, and their beliefs about what workers ideally should do. All of these difference data are absolute in the sense that no information is given in the tables about their specific nature, whether quantitative (and, if so, what the reported direction of the difference was) or qualitative. To have incorporated this additional information would have made the tables unnecessarily complex and difficult to read.

(2) For each division, the number of respondents reporting no difference between their experience with respect to the present context and their experience with respect to the four other contextual domains about which they were asked are indicated (shown in parentheses). In addition, for the contextual domain, other, the number of respondents in each division who reported having no knowledge of what workers in other organisations did are indicated (again, shown in parentheses).

(3) In line with McGregor's (1960) distinction between Theory X and Theory Y assumptions about the nature of workers, it was originally hoped that all of the data from this part of the interview could be classified according to whether they reflected a more or less active or passive role for workers. It soon became clear, however, that many of the data could not easily or meaningfully be described in this way. This was the case even for data generated by those prompts that were included specifically because they asked about activities that could potentially signal a more active role for workers. As the reader will recall from the results presented in the previous chapter, there was some evidence in the thematic content of respondents' comments about the involvement of workers both in information meetings and in training to suggest that the potential for these activities to provide workers with a more active role was not being realised to the extent that it might have been. In view of these difficulties it was, therefore, necessary to consider alternative approaches to classifying the data.

One such approach involved the application of some of the broad groupings that have been used to order the content of student texts on organisational behaviour (e.g., Gibson, Ivancevich, & Donnelly, 2000). Potentially relevant groupings included Organisational Processes (incorporating topics such as organisational communications, the reward system, and decision making), Organisational Structure (with micro issues, such as job design, being of particular relevance in the present context), and Organisational Development (incorporating topics such as job training and career development). Like the previous approach, this approach also proved to be inadequate, largely because the groupings described were too broad and hence not sufficiently informative, to capture the context-specific nature of the particular data set to which they were being applied.

The system for classifying the data that was eventually adopted was developed in collaboration with a work colleague. Rather than apply an existing classification scheme (such as that described above), an attempt was made to identify the key groupings suggested by the data themselves. This exercise was undertaken only in relation to those data generated by the open questions that could not be classified according to any of the prompted activity categories. With respect to the latter, it can be seen from Tables 12.3 and 12.4 that the activities about which respondents were prompted are listed as activity categories in their own right (highlighted in italics). This separation of prompted from non-prompted activity categories serves to highlight differences between prompted and spontaneous responses, the analysis of which will be reported subsequently. It can also be seen that the emergent or non-prompted activity categories that were identified included some which were stand alone categories (e.g., Primary Task and Work Maintenance) and others which were subsumed under the two broader groupings of Work Arrangements (WA) activities[3] and Human Resources Management (HRM) activities.

(4) The reader may have noted that some of the so-called activity categories that are listed (e.g., Technology and Reward) seem to be less appropriate given that the questions were about worker activities. These categories emerged in the difference data only, suggesting that some respondents may have had difficulty in answering the open questions that required them to comment on changes in what workers do (whether with respect to their past experience, their anticipated future experience, or their ideal experience). As a result, in responding to these questions, these respondents may simply have resorted to commenting on more general changes in the work environment or changes that indirectly affected work activities (e.g., technological changes), rather than attempt to identify specific changes in the duties and activities of workers. Alternatively, however, it might be argued that the responses included in these activity categories may be culturally significant in that they may highlight issues of central concern to respondents at the time of interviewing (a case in point is the emphasis on technological change that is particularly evident in data from the production division). While not intended, it may be that the open questions about changes in what workers do are, in this instance, functioning as projective questions.

(5) As indicated, the initial open-ended questions (asked with respect to each of the five contextual domains) sought information about, first of all, the main duties of workers and, secondly, other activities in which workers were engaged. It was originally anticipated that the responses to these questions might be treated separately, with the latter providing insights into the extent to which the role of workers extended beyond task execution activities to include conceptual activities, such as, planning, decision making and problem-solving. However, it became increasingly clear as interviewing proceeded, that respondents were not distinguishing consistently between main duties and other activities. In other words, the main duties that were mentioned by some respondents were cited by other respondents as other activities, and vice versa. For this reason it was decided that, within each of the contextual domains, the responses to the open-ended questions should be aggregated. As such, no distinction is made in Tables 12.3 and 12.4 between main duties and other activities[4].

---

[3] Activities in this category were concerned with the way in which the work was organised or arranged.

[4] This highlights a difference between the present time data reported in these tables and the present time data reported in Table 11.1 (see Section 11.1.1.1). With respect to the latter, only responses to the second open-ended question, concerning worker involvement in 'other activities', were reported.

(6) The numbers shown in Tables 12.3 and 12.4 represent numbers of respondents, rather than numbers of references to activities (or changes in activities) within a given activity category. In other words, even though a respondent might have mentioned more than one activity which could be classified in a given activity category, that respondent would be represented only once in any given cell. While this approach to presenting the data results in some loss of the emphasis that multiple references give to particular activity categories, it has the advantage of allowing a direct comparison of the divisions in terms of each of the listed activity categories.

(7) As mentioned previously, there is a distinction in the tables between prompted and non-prompted activity categories, the main aim of which was to facilitate a comparison of spontaneous and prompted responses (within each division across the five contextual domains, as well as between divisions for a given contextual domain). As can be seen, however, some respondents mentioned prompted activity categories spontaneously, that is, in response to the initial open-ended questions. It will be recalled that this result was as expected, since the activities about which respondents were prompted were selected specifically because of their potential relevance to the role of workers.

12.3.2 *General observations about the nature of the responses to questions about context*

In reporting the results summarised in Table 12.3 and Table 12.4, it is useful first of all to draw the reader's attention to the following general observations regarding what these two sets of results have in common. First, it can be seen that, for each division, there was a marked difference between responses to the open-ended questions and responses to the prompts. Specifically, prompted activity categories were generally poorly represented in responses to the open-ended questions. These activity categories were typically much better represented when respondents were asked about them specifically. The reader will recall that this effect has been noted previously in relation to the data pertaining to the present context, reported in Chapter 11. As shown in Tables 12.3 and 12.4, however, this difference between spontaneous and prompted responses can be observed in the pattern of responding for each of the contextual domains about which respondents were asked.

Of particular interest is the finding that this difference emerged even in responses to questions about the ideal context. This is contrary to what one would expect to find if responding had been influenced significantly by social desirability biases. In this event, it might be predicted that the number of respondents making spontaneous references to prompted activity categories (particularly to those categories which could be seen to be characteristic of a more active, and arguably a more desirable, role for workers), would be likely to exceed the numbers reported in Tables 12.3 and 12.4. The reason for this lies in the considerable exposure of respondents, up to this point in the interview, to the prompted activity categories. It will be recalled that the format of questioning was such that, by the time respondents were asked for their views about what workers ideally should do, they had already been presented with the prompted activity categories on three separate occasions (in relation to their present experience, their past experience, and their anticipated future experience).

From a cultural perspective, this finding may be of some significance. It was suggested in the introduction to Study 3 that a possible indicator of the strength of an organisation's culture may be the degree to which 'free' or unprompted responses to questions about the ideal can be shown to be culture bound (in the sense that they suggest a view of organisational life which does not deviate significantly from what organisation members have already experienced). With respect to the above finding it might be argued further that, where there are possibilities for social desirability responding to occur (such as in the present interview in which respondents are presented with a range of possible other activities in which workers might engage), stronger cultures might be more resistant to these effects than weaker cultures. This finding and its implications will be examined in more detail subsequently.

In the present study, respondents were workers and their immediate supervisors. The point can again be made that social desirability effects might be more likely to occur with more senior levels of management, since at these levels there is likely to be a greater awareness of what it would be socially desirable to say in response to such questions. In such cases, it might be necessary to check for social desirability by asking for clarification and, in particular, for examples that illustrate what is said about the particular aspect of the organisation being investigated.

A second general observation that can be made regarding the findings summarised in Tables 12.3 and 12.4 is that the majority of respondents from both divisions reported some changes in their experience of organisational life (in their respective divisions) over time. That is, most respondents pointed to some differences between the past and the present in what workers in their respective divisions did. Most respondents also indicated that what workers would do in the anticipated future, and what they ideally should do, would somehow differ from what they did at the present time. These findings are consistent with the view that organisational culture is a dynamic, rather than a static, phenomenon (Trice & Beyer, 1993). An important implication of this view is that, in order to achieve more than a superficial understanding of the culture of any given organisation, one should seek information that reflects this basic characteristic of culture. Clearly, any method for investigating organisational culture which focuses only on the present context of organisation members' experiences (this is the case for the majority of existing questionnaire measures of organisational culture) will be seriously limited in this regard. At the very least, one's approach should seek to locate organisation members' experiences within some kind of time perspective rather than give the impression of a static culture. In this sense, it might be argued that questions about the past and anticipated future, such as those asked in the present interview, should constitute standard questions for inclusion in any measure of organisational culture.

We turn now to a more detailed examination of the results summarised in Tables 12.3 and 12.4. As will be seen, the main focus of the forthcoming discussion is on reported changes in the profile of worker activities for each division — from the past to the present, in the anticipated future, in relation to other organisations in which respondents have worked (or of which they have some knowledge), and with respect to respondents' beliefs about the activities in which workers ideally should engage. Particular attention is drawn to similarities and differences between the two divisions, in terms of the changes reported, and consideration is given to the possible cultural significance of these similarities and differences. It will also be noted that the findings associated with each of the four contextual domains of interest — the past, the anticipated future, the other, and the ideal — are discussed separately and in this order.

12.4 The Past Context

The discussion in this section is presented in four main parts. First, we report the results of the analysis of the open question data. Second, we provide an overview of the main similarities and differences between the divisions that are represented by the prompt data shown in Tables 12.3 and 12.4. Third, drawing on both the open question and prompt data (including the detailed analysis of the latter reported in Kummerow, 2000), we provide a summary of the key findings of the analysis of past context data, in particular, in terms of the additional insights of value that these data provide. Fourth, and finally, we provide an historical overview of the role of workers in each division.

12.4.1 *Findings for the open questions*

It can be seen from Tables 12.3 and 12.4 that, in response to the initial open questions, four respondents from the tooling division (33% of this group) and two respondents from the production division (11% of this group) reported that there was no difference between the past and the present in what the workers in their respective divisions did. In other words, a majority of respondents from each division (67% from the tooling division and 89% from the production division) reported some changes from the past to the present in either the main duties or other activities of workers in their division. It can be seen that, for the tooling division, these changes are described by eight activity categories, with the best represented of these (in terms of the number of respondents who made reference to one or more activities associated with each category) being:

(1) Primary Task (with two respondents indicating that, in the past, the division undertook less experimental prototype work than it did at the present time, and one respondent indicating that, in the past, more work of this kind was performed in the division);

(2) Specialisation (with all three respondents pointing to more task specialisation in the past); and

(3) Formal Social (with all three respondents pointing to the greater involvement of workers in the past in social activities organised by the company).

For the production division, the changes reported are described by 17 activity categories. As a group, then, production division respondents were not only more likely than their counterparts in the tooling division to refer spontaneously to some change, from the past to the present, in what workers in their division did (89% compared with 67%), but their experience of change (as reflected in their unprompted responses) also appears to have been broader, in the sense of encompassing more different types of change (17 activity categories represented compared with eight for the tooling division). The best-represented unprompted activity categories for the production division were:

(1) Technology (with six respondents indicating that, in the past, the division was technologically less sophisticated than it was at the present time);
(2) Group Problem-Solving (with six respondents reporting more worker involvement in problem solving groups in the past, associated with the implementation of the Team Concept); and
(3) Individual Skills/Attitudes/Behaviours (with four respondents pointing to differences between the past and the present in how conscientious workers were, how secure they felt in their jobs, and their level of job satisfaction).

The point should be made that, for neither division, were any of the unprompted activity categories particularly well represented. As indicated, for the tooling division, the best-represented activity categories were mentioned by only three respondents each (i.e., by only 25% of the respondents from this group) and, for the production division, the best represented categories were mentioned by only six respondents each (i.e., by 33% of the respondents from this group). It is perhaps surprising that there was not more agreement, particularly among respondents from the tooling division (who, as noted previously, constituted a more homogenous group than the production division, in terms of respondents' age and length of service), about changes over time in what workers did. Interestingly, when respondents were asked specifically about whether or not the involvement of workers in particular activities had changed over time (the prompt questions), there was a marked increase in the level of agreement among respondents about changes in certain of these activities. For example, Table 12.3 shows that, for the tooling division, prompting resulted in an additional 11 respondents making reference to changes over time in the involvement of workers in this division in training. Similarly Table 12.4 shows that, when both unprompted and prompted responses are taken into account, a large majority of respondents from the production division can be seen to have reported a change over time in the involvement of workers in this division in group problem-solving activities. Again, the question arises as to what these discrepancies between prompted and unprompted responses might mean.

With respect to the spontaneous (unprompted) responses reported in Tables 12.3 and 12.4, it might be argued that when respondents are asked open questions about changes over time in the activities of workers in their division, their responses are likely to be based, not on some detailed schema of all of the various activities which might make up the role of workers, but rather on what they perceive to be the general and most salient aspects of the role of the workers in their division. In this sense, the open question data can probably be taken at their face value, that is, they can be interpreted to mean that the role of workers, as it is broadly defined by respondents from both divisions, has changed little over time. While the prompt data suggest that worker involvement in certain specific activities may have changed over time, it may be that these changes have been insufficient to redefine, in the minds of respondents, what workers do in their respective divisions. A closer examination of the data on training for the tooling division (including both the quantitative and qualitative data) can help to illustrate this point.

As indicated, all respondents from the tooling division reported a change, from the past to the present, in the involvement of the workers in this division in training, with the majority providing this information in response to prompting. In terms of the direction of the change, all respondents also indicated that there was either no training for workers in the division in the past, or that the level of training available was less than it was at the present time. However, as reported in Chapter 11, the findings regarding the *current* involvement of workers in this division in training were highly inconsistent, with estimates of the percentage of workers currently attending training ranging from 5% to 50%, and estimates of the amount of training received by each worker annually ranging from 20 to 50 hours. The point can also be made that all of the references to the type of training received were to training in specific skills (such as welding, pneumatics, *etc.*). There were no references to worker involvement in training of the kind that might indicate that the role of workers in the division was undergoing a change of any significance (e.g., training of the kind that might be associated with initiatives such as total quality management programs). Finally, the reader will recall that the majority of respondents from this division attributed the change towards increased training at the present time to a recent initiative, by the government and unions, to multi-skill workers through award restructuring. In other words, there was a perception that the company's current commitment to training was, at least to some extent, the result of external pressures. Clearly, the change in training described by these data is unlikely to have the same impact on the way in which these organisation members think about the role of workers in their division as would the introduction of training which was provided on a more regular basis, and which was designed by management to facilitate the development of skills, attitudes and behaviours which differed from those associated with the traditional role of workers in the division.

The above conclusion is not intended to understate the possible significance of those changes in specific worker activities about which there was considerable agreement among respondents (whether from the tooling division or from the production division), and which were revealed largely through prompting. It may be that these changes are indicative of culture change in progress (in this case, concerning organisation members' beliefs and assumptions about the role of workers).

The discussion thus far has been concerned mainly with changes, over time, in the profile of worker activities, as represented by the open question data for each division. Attention was drawn to the number of activity categories that were represented by these data and the point was made that, even for the best represented of these activity categories (in terms of the number of respondents reporting a change, from the past to the present, in one or more activities associated with each category), there was a relatively low level of agreement among respondents about the changes that had occurred. This finding was interpreted to mean that the role of workers in both divisions, as broadly defined by respondents, had remained relatively stable over time. It was also noted, however, that in terms of specific activities in which workers were engaged, the prompt data provided good evidence that there had been some changes, over time, in the involvement of workers in these activities.

12.4.2 *Prompt questions: Some initial findings*

Before proceeding to a discussion of some of the initial findings for the prompt questions, it is useful to inform the reader of the general approach to the analysis of prompt data that was adopted. For each of the contextual domains of interest — the past, the future, and the ideal[5] — prompted activities were first of all grouped into those for which similarities between the divisions (in terms of the number of respondents indicating change, whether from the past to the present, the present to the anticipated future, and in the ideal) were indicated, and those for which differences were indicated[6]. The activities within each of these two groups were then analysed further, with particular consideration given to the nature (direction) of the changes reported, the timing of these changes (for the past and future contexts), and respondents' attributions regarding the causes of these changes (again, for the past and future contexts).

With respect to the first part of this analysis, it can be seen from Tables 12.3. and 12.4 that, for the past context, there are four activity categories for which *similarities* between the two divisions can be identified. These are:

(1) Planning Meetings (defined for respondents as meetings in which decisions are made about such things as the future directions of the division, as well as forthcoming work schedules, equipment needs, and training needs);

---

[5]The reader will recall that the prompt questions were not asked in relation to the other context.
[6]The nominated criterion for the classification of a 'similarity' was that the difference between the number of respondents from each division indicating a change with respect to the activity should be less than 20%; the criterion for the classification of a 'difference' was that this difference should be 20% or more.

(2) Information Meetings (defined for respondents as meetings in which workers are given information, by those above them, about such things as the current performance and future directions of the division);

(3) Union Meetings; and

(4) Social Activities[7].

With respect to planning meetings and union meetings, the similarity between the divisions lies in the finding that there was a minority of respondents only from each division who reported a change, from the past to the present, in the involvement of workers in each of these activities. For planning meetings, there were two respondents from the tooling division who reported a change (17% of this group) and six respondents from the production division who reported a change (32% of this group). For union meetings, there were four respondents from the tooling division who reported a change (33% of this group) and six respondents from the production division who reported a change (32% of this group).

In the case of information meetings and social activities, the similarity lies in the finding that at least half of the respondents from each division reported that the involvement of workers in these activities had changed from the past to the present. For information meetings, there were six respondents from the tooling division who reported a change (50% of this group) and 13 respondents from the production division who reported a change (68% of this group). For social activities, there were nine respondents from the tooling division who reported a change (75% of this group) and 12 respondents from the production division who reported a change (63% of this group).

In can also be seen from Tables 12.3 and 12.4 that there are two prompted activity categories, namely Group Problem-Solving and Attend Training, for which *major differences* between the divisions (in terms of the number of respondents reporting a change from the past to the present) are suggested. For group problem-solving, no respondents from the tooling division, compared with 16 respondents (84%) from the production division, reported a change. For attend training, all of the respondents from the tooling division, compared with eight respondents (42%) from the production division, reported a change.

---

[7]In the interview, an initial distinction was drawn between formal (i.e., organised by the company) social activities and informal (i.e., impromptu) social activities. Specifically, respondents were asked to comment on the involvement of divisional workers in each type of social activity at the present time. However, in subsequent questioning (about the past, future, and ideal contexts), there was no similar emphasis on this distinction (partly because of time constraints and also because respondents seemed to find it increasingly difficult to draw the distinction, in particular, in relation to their anticipated future and ideal experience). Hence, with respect to questions about these latter contextual domains, no distinction between formal and informal social activities was made and respondents were asked simply to comment on changes in the involvement of workers in social activities generally. In Tables 12.3 and 12.4, this change is signified by the inclusion of the activity [Social] in the same cell in which Formal Social is listed.

As will be seen, the results of these various analyses are referred to selectively in the following summary of the main findings of the analysis of data pertaining to the past context.

12.4.3 *The past context: Summary of key findings*

This section offers a summary of the main findings of the analysis of data (both open question and prompt data) pertaining to the past context. The key question to be considered in this section is whether or not the additional insights provided by an historical perspective, over and above those obtained through questioning about the present context only, justify the additional time and effort required to obtain these insights. The findings suggest that an approach that seeks specific information about the historical context can provide the following specific benefits.

1. An understanding of the historical context of organisation members' experiences can highlight important differences between work groups (in this case, between two divisions of a single company) that may not be revealed using research methods that focus only on the present context of organisation members' experiences. In the present study, the findings pertaining to the activity categories Group Problem-Solving and Social Activities[8] provided good examples of support for the above conclusion. With respect to the former, the two divisions were perceived to support similarly low levels of worker involvement in group problem-solving activities *at the present time*. As indicated in Tables 12.3 and 12.4, respectively, there were only two respondents from the tooling division, and only five respondents from the production division, who reported any current involvement of the workers in their division in problem-solving activities. While there was some variability in respondents' estimates of how often such activities were held, estimates of the number of workers involved at any given time were similarly low (5% or less) for both divisions.

The point should also be made that there was no evidence in respondents' qualifications of their current experience with respect to this activity category to suggest any marked qualitative differences between the two divisions. Neither of the two respondents from the tooling division who reported some current involvement of the workers in their division in problem-solving activities made any comments to indicate their personal evaluation (whether positive or negative) of this aspect of their experience. The picture was similar for the production division. Of the five respondents from this division who reported some current involvement of divisional workers in group problem-solving activities, three were neutral in their comments about the experience (i.e., they expressed neither positive nor negative attitudes); one respondent evaluated the experience positively, suggesting that

---

[8]The detailed analysis of the data for Group Problem-Solving and Social Activities are reported in Kummerow (2000).

group problem-solving meetings should be held more often; and one respondent evaluated the experience negatively, suggesting that such meetings served a "finger pointing" purpose, whereby workers were blamed for problems that management were unable to solve. In summary, then, an analysis of the present time data (including both the quantitative and the qualitative data) provided no substantial evidence to suggest that the divisions differed with respect to respondents' current experience of worker involvement in group problem-solving activities.

In contrast, the analysis of data pertaining to the past context suggested that the two divisions differed markedly in terms of their respective histories of worker involvement in group problem-solving activities. While the tooling division had a relatively long and stable history of little or no worker involvement in such activities, there were, in effect, two periods in the history of the production division during which workers had considerable involvement in group problem-solving (the first, and perhaps most significant, during the years of the team concept when production operators worked in semi-autonomous teams and the second, associated with a more recent quality assurance (QA) initiative which involved a team approach to solving work-related problems). Furthermore, there was good evidence to suggest that, for members at all levels of the production division hierarchy, the experience of group problem-solving in relation to both of these initiatives (i.e., the team concept and QA initiative) had been a predominantly negative one. In fact, the point was made that the reported failure of the more recent QA initiative may have been due, at least in part, to the residual effects of divisional members' negative experiences in relation to the earlier team concept initiative. It was also suggested that the QA initiative might have been more successful had it been implemented with a more obvious commitment, on the part of those implementing the program, to learning from the lessons of the past. Given that some of the same problems were reportedly encountered in relation to both of these initiatives (in particular, problems associated with a lack of team leadership, a lack of interest and commitment on the part of team members, and a failure on the part of management to follow-up on the ideas generated by the teams), there is a sense in which the experience of the QA initiative might be seen as an instance of divisional history repeating itself.

To the extent that past experience influences organisation members' attitudes towards future change, one might anticipate that the members of the production division may respond with some cynicism and resistance to any future attempt, on the part of divisional management, to introduce group problem-solving initiatives similar to those already experienced. If such a change was indeed anticipated, management would be well advised, not only to acknowledge and seek to understand this cynicism and resistance, but also to develop strategies for its effective management.

As above for group problem-solving, an analysis of the historical context of respondents' experience with respect to worker involvement in social activities, revealed differences in divisional histories that would have remained largely obscured had the focus been solely on the present context of respondents' experience. While the two divisions appeared to be roughly equivalent in terms of the current involvement of divisional workers in social activities[9], the history of the tooling division was distinguished by a long period during which a very active and very positive social climate had prevailed. Furthermore, respondents were typically nostalgic in their recollections of this period. In contrast, the production division had a much less well-defined history with respect to this activity category. Where changes were reported (in the involvement of divisional workers in social activities over time), there was far less consensus among respondents about either the direction or the cause of these changes. The finding that the tooling division supported a very positive social climate in the past provides one important clue as to the foundation upon which this group's past identity may have been formed. Moreover, while it would be unrealistic (given changes in the demographics of this group) to suggest that any attempt should be made to resurrect this aspect of the division's past, a knowledge of it (and what it meant for divisional members) could make management more sensitive to the range of factors that may have contributed to the current low levels of member satisfaction and morale in this division. In other words, the current 'depressed' climate in the division may reflect more than just member anxiety about job security. We would draw attention here to our use of the term climate, as we have suggested it should be used, to represent the affect dimension of an organisation's culture (or particular aspect of it).

2. An understanding of the historical context of organisation members' experiences can facilitate the more accurate interpretation of data pertaining to members' perceptions of their current experience. This conclusion was most strongly supported by the findings reported for the activity category Attend Training. As indicated (see also Chapter 11), with respect to their present experience, all of the respondents from the tooling division, compared with two-thirds of the respondents from the production division, reported some current involvement of the workers in their respective divisions in training. The point was made that, while this difference was only marginal in terms of its magnitude, its direction was nevertheless the reverse of what had been expected. Qualitative data (from observations and informal conversations with divisional members), which the first author continued to gather over the course of all three studies comprising this research, provided evidence to suggest that the production division was more committed than the tooling division to the development of its human resources. Compared with the tooling division, in which human resources development initiatives seemed to be distinctly lacking, the production division supported a range of such initiatives, including training initiatives. Hence, the finding that there was more agreement among tooling division

---

[9]As discussed in Kummerow (2000), the divisions could be differentiated only on the basis of the type of social activity (with retirement functions constituting a common social activity in the tooling division but not in the production division) and not on the basis of either the number of social activities identified or the estimated extent of worker involvement in these activities.

respondents than among production division respondents about the current involvement of divisional workers in training was somewhat surprising.

An understanding of the historical context of respondents' experience with respect to this activity category provided a possible explanation for this inconsistency between the findings suggested by the interview data and those suggested by what were essentially informally gathered qualitative data. As indicated (see also Chapter 11), the two divisions were found to differ markedly with respect to their training histories. Specifically, it was found that the tooling division had a very long history during which there had been little or no involvement of divisional workers in ongoing training and development (i.e., training and development beyond that provided to trade apprentices). Furthermore, there was good agreement among respondents from this division that the recent increased emphasis on training in the division had been a response to recent moves, by the unions and the government, to multi-skill workers through award restructuring. In contrast, the history of training in the production division was far less well defined. Less than half of the respondents from this division perceived any change, from the past to the present, in the involvement of divisional workers in training. Furthermore, compared with their counterparts from the tooling division, there was less consensus among these respondents about both the direction (whether more or less training in the past than at the present time) and the cause of the perceived change.

On the basis of these findings, it was suggested that the yardstick against which respondents from each division had evaluated their present experience of worker involvement in training was different. For tooling division respondents, the yardstick was a very long past during which the level of worker involvement in training had remained low. For respondents from the production division, the yardstick was more ambiguous — in general, a shorter past with differing member perceptions about the nature of changes that had occurred. It could be argued, therefore, that as a group, respondents from the tooling division were probably more sensitive than production division respondents to shifts in the emphasis placed on worker involvement in training, and accordingly more likely to interpret such shifts as instances of specific change.

An important methodological implication of the argument presented above is that researchers cannot assume that they are comparing 'like with like' when they compare the responses of two groups of subjects to a particular set of questions (even if both groups are located within the same organisational context). As the present example illustrates, subjects' interpretations of, and subsequent responses to, the questions that they are asked are likely to be influenced by their own context-specific experience. Given that this is likely to be different (to a greater or lesser extent) for different groups, one must question the extent to which, in the absence of information about the historical context of their experience, groups can be meaningfully compared with one another.

3. For any given work group, an understanding of the chronology of individual members' histories can help to explain variability among members in the way in

which they perceive and evaluate their current experience of group life. This conclusion was most strongly supported by findings reported for the production division in relation to changes, from the past to the present, in the communication relationship between workers and their immediate supervisors. As reported in Kummerow (2000), among those respondents who reported a change, some (the majority) pointed to a trend towards more open worker-supervisor communication at the present time, whilst others indicated that worker-supervisor communication had become increasingly strained in recent years. While there was some evidence of sectional differences between these two groups of respondents (with a range of different sections being represented by the former, and all but one respondent from the latter being from the same work section), their contrasting perceptions of change could not be explained in terms of differences with respect to any other demographic variables (including, age, seniority, length of service, *etc.*).

There was, however, some evidence that the two groups differed in terms of the yardstick against which they were evaluating change. Specifically, respondents who reported a trend towards more open worker-supervisor communication at the present time tended to use the distant past as their yardstick, whereas respondents who reported a change towards a growing tension in worker-supervisor communication used the more recent past as their yardstick. In other words, for respondents in the former group, the historical experience that informed their evaluations of change spanned a relatively long period of time, while for respondents in the latter group, it spanned a relatively short period of time. Moreover, as indicated, this difference between the groups was not reflected in a parallel difference in respondents' length of service (in particular, the latter group comprised employees with relatively long service with the organisation as well as employees with relatively short service with the organisation).

These findings suggest that organisational culture researchers, in seeking to explain variability in organisation members' perceptions, should give consideration to the historical context of organisation members' experience. In particular, attention should be focussed on the chronology of individual member histories — how far back the individual's history extends. Furthermore, it should not be assumed that this information will always be reflected in the individual's age or length of service (even though, intuitively, this might appear to be the case). As the findings reported above suggest, an individual's chronological past (spanning the period of her/his tenure with the organisation) may not necessarily be the same as her/his psychologically salient past. This, of course, has broader implications for efforts to identify subcultural groupings on the basis of the demographic characteristics of the group being studied.

4. For any given work group, an understanding of the group's history, in terms of its content (i.e., the events which make it up) and chronology, can provide important insights into the nature and extent of the group's exposure to change. These insights may, in turn, facilitate the more accurate prediction of the group's likely responsiveness to future change, in addition to providing clues about how to manage such

change. Considered as a whole, the findings for the past context provided good evidence to suggest that the two divisions differed in terms of both the nature and the extent of their exposure to changes, over time, in the role of divisional workers. Specifically, the history of the tooling division with respect to the role of workers appeared to be long and relatively stable, whereas that of the production division was shorter and marked by more change. By way of illustration, attention is drawn to some of the findings pertaining to changes, over time, in the involvement of divisional workers in activities about which respondents were specifically prompted. As indicated previously, these findings are reported in detail in Kummerow (2000).

With respect first of all to the findings for the tooling division, a majority of respondents from this division reported that the workers in their division at the present time were not involved in planning, group problem-solving, or record-keeping activities. These activities were reportedly the domain of leading hands and/or supervisory staff. Furthermore, according to these respondents, the role of divisional workers with respect to these activities had remained the same for a period which extended back at least as far as the respondent's start date with the division (which, on average, was some 23 years ago) and, in some cases, beyond this to the year in which the division first commenced operations (some 50 years ago). The findings for the tooling division also showed that, in recent years, there had been a number of changes in the division — specifically, the introduction of information meetings for workers and an increase in the amount of training and professional development for workers — which might be expected to impact upon the role of workers in the division. However, information about the extent and frequency of worker involvement in these activities, as well as information provided by an analysis of the associated qualitative data, suggested that the division's commitment to these activities, at least as initiatives intended to promote a more active and participative role for workers, was not strong. For example, information meetings were reportedly held only infrequently, attendance at these meetings was reportedly mandatory (i.e., it did not reflect worker self-motivation and interest), and the introduction of the meetings was seen largely as an attempt by management to quash increasing rumours associated with the threatened closure of the division. Similarly, training initiatives were seen primarily in the context of broader industry reforms (in particular, the current move to multi-skill workers through the restructuring of the award); they were not seen as organisation-specific (division-specific) initiatives designed to enhance the motivation and job satisfaction of individual workers.

It can be seen, then, that the overall picture of the role of workers in the tooling division, at least as suggested by the above 'activity histories', was that it had remained essentially the same over a prolonged period of time (possibly spanning the entire history of the division). As such, it would not be unrealistic to anticipate at least some resistance, by the members of this division, to any change which required divisional workers to assume a role fundamentally different from that to which they had become accustomed over the past years of their membership with the division. It might also be argued that knowledge of this kind may be of value to change agents (managers and/or consultants) in their efforts to develop strategies for change that take account of the particular context into which change is being introduced. For example, in order for change to be successful, change agents may need to provide much more information justifying the change than might otherwise be thought necessary. It might also be worth investigating organisation members' views regarding aspects of the past that they most value and that might be able to be preserved, and even further promoted. This would provide some continuity and a less marked disruption in activities than might otherwise occur.

The findings for the production division suggested a somewhat different picture of the role of workers in this division. Specifically, there was evidence that, in the relatively short history of the division, divisional members had been exposed to more changes than their counterparts in the tooling division with respect to this particular domain of their experience. These changes were associated with initiatives such as the introduction of group problem-solving for workers (initially as part of the broader team concept initiative, and more recently taking the form of QA meetings), the introduction of regular information meetings for workers, and an increase in worker responsibility for recording work-related information. Given their level of exposure to change, one might predict that, as a group, the members of the production division would be more accepting of future change than their counterparts in the tooling division. Clearly, however, the qualitative dimension of a group's change experience must also be taken into account. Of relevance here is the finding for the production division that, for all members of the divisional hierarchy, the experience of group problem-solving appears to have been a predominantly negative one. One possible implication of this finding for divisional management is that, in the event that some future reintroduction of similar group problem-solving initiatives is attempted, strategies may need to be developed for dealing with the residual effects (including cynical attitudes and resistance to change) of members' negative past experiences in relation to these initiatives. Thus, it might be anticipated that more direct involvement of, or support by, senior management would be needed to convince divisional members that the change is sincerely meant. Similarly, there may need to be more mentoring and support when difficulties arise, and such mentoring and support might need to be continued for much longer than initially thought necessary in order to convince members that a permanent change is intended.

The point can also be made that, given the different histories of each division, the strategies likely to facilitate such change in the production division may well be quite different from the strategies likely to facilitate such change in the tooling division. For example, in the production division, it might be useful to involve divisional members (including workers, supervisors, and managers) in group discussions about the perceived advantages and disadvantages of approaches to group problem-solving in the past. This information could then be used as the basis from which collaborative decisions could be made regarding how to modify past approaches to ensure their future success. In contrast, in the tooling division, management might be advised, if time and circumstances permitted, to adopt a more gradual approach to the implementation of group problem-solving. This might involve trialling the initiative in one section of the division only. Ideally, this would be a section comprising workers and supervisors most likely to be responsive to the initiative (possibly because of some positive experience of informal group problem-solving in the past). Furthermore, to ensure the group's success, the initial focus should probably be on simple rather than complex problems. As with the production division, collaboration among all of the participating members would be important, as would the dissemination of information about the initiative to non-participating members. To the extent that the initiative was found to be successful in the trial section, it could then be introduced gradually into other sections of the division.

In the context of the present discussion, attention should also be drawn to the finding that, among production division respondents, there was a perception that the level of worker involvement in activities not associated with direct production (e.g., training and group problem-solving activities) was, at any given time, contingent upon the level of production in the division (with the demands of direct production activities usually taking priority over the demands of indirect production activities). It might be argued that this perception, to the extent that it continued to be reinforced by experience, could lead to the development, among divisional members, of increasingly cynical attitudes towards initiatives introduced with the espoused intention of supporting a more active role for divisional workers. Such attitudes might, in turn, be expected to impact negatively upon members' responsiveness to these initiatives.

5. An understanding of the historical context of organisation members' experiences can provide insights into the process by which culture change may occur. The results of an analysis of data pertaining to the past and present contexts provided some evidence to suggest that culture change may occur as a gradual process, characterised by a series of incremental and possibly indiscernible shifts, over time, in organisation members' perceptions and thinking about their experience of organisational life. In other words, except in cases of cultural revolution or extreme cultural crisis, culture change is unlikely to occur as a single event, resulting in the sudden and radical transformation of the way in which organisation members 'see their world'. Some tentative support for this conclusion was provided by the finding that production division respondents (who were shop floor workers) tended to make positive evaluations of the communication relationship that they had with their own supervisor(s), while at the same time holding fairly negative views about the communication climate that prevailed in their division as a whole. One explanation for this discrepancy in respondents' perceptions of the 'specific' and the 'general' was that despite the reported change, in recent years, towards more open worker-supervisor communication (possibly reflected in, and reinforced by, the specific experiences of individual respondents), respondents' perceptions of the general situation with respect to worker-supervisor communication were continuing to be influenced by the residual effects of past experience (whereby more distant relationships between workers and supervisors had reportedly prevailed).

If this explanation can be accepted, and if one assumes that the culture of a work group is manifested more strongly in member perceptions of the group as a whole, rather than in their perceptions of their own specific situation, then one can begin to speculate as to the possible conditions under which culture change might occur. With respect to the present example, in order for divisional members to change the way in which they perceive and think about the overall communication climate in their division, it may be necessary, not only for the positive experiences of individual members to be continually reinforced by events which occur over some critical period of time, but also for these individual members to become aware of each other's positive experiences. Of course, this may require the use of some formal mechanism of communication to counteract the effects of informally communicated rhetoric about the past which may be negative in tone and which may serve to delay the emergence of a new consensus based on the positive experiences of individual organisation members.

The arguments above should alert managers to the need for considerable persistence and patience in their efforts to bring about culture change. If the aim is a benevolent approach to culture change (as opposed to an approach which involves a substantial rationalisation of the workforce, along with significant changes in personnel) then managers should be aware that this is unlikely to be achievable in the short term. In order to overcome the residual effects of past experience and bring about fundamental changes in the thinking of organisation members, managers will need to persist in their efforts to ensure that the desired change is consistently reinforced in the individual experiences of organisation members over a sustained period of time. This will be required to bring about a conscious consensus amongst members about this aspect of the culture. An even longer period is likely to be needed for such a change in the culture to become 'taken-for-granted'.

An additional recommendation suggested by the results is that, where organisation members have developed alternative explanations for change, which are counter to those espoused by management and which may undermine the potentially positive effects of the change (one example would be the perception among production division respondents that training for divisional workers was provided only when production demands were low), managers should seek to ensure that the future experience of organisation members is such that it consistently and repeatedly invalidates these explanations. In fact, one interesting direction for future research in this area would be to carry out longitudinal studies of organisation members' attributions during, and for some time after, the implementation of an organisational change program. One measure of the success of the program may well be the demonstration that positive attributions about the change continue to be made well after the initial implementation phase of the program is over. Conversely, the finding that alternative explanations are beginning to emerge may serve as a warning that the change effort is not proceeding as desired.

6. Organisation members' attributions about changes that they have experienced over time may constitute a valuable source of cultural data and, in addition, may provide clues as to the success of an organisation's culture change efforts. While a comprehensive analysis of all of the attributions data generated by the present study is beyond the scope of what is being attempted here[10], a preliminary analysis of the attributions data associated with experienced, rather than anticipated, change[11], provided some evidence to support the conclusion that such data may provide an important source of cultural information. In particular, organisations (organisational subgroups) may, to a greater or lesser extent, develop their own distinctive style of attributing cause, which differentiates them from other organisations (organisational subgroups). In other words, attribution style may be organisationally-determined (i.e., culturally-determined) rather than individually-determined and, as such, it may evolve through the same process of group learning thought to generate other forms of cultural knowledge. In the context of these comments, it is interesting to compare the attributions made by respondents from the tooling division (regarding changes over time in worker activities) with those made by respondents from the production division.

When considered as a whole, the attributions made by tooling division respondents conveyed the strong impression that, in this division, change was seen largely as a response to events (either internal or external) over which divisional members perceived that they had little control. For example, there were references to reactive change in the division such as that indicated in the widespread perception that information meetings for workers had been introduced primarily to combat the negative effects of rumours about the closure of the division. There were also references to changes perceived to be largely externally imposed. For example, the change towards more open worker-supervisor communication was commonly attributed to changes in the broader social context (such as changes in the educational level of people entering the workforce), which in turn were perceived to have changed employee expectations about how they should be managed. The broader social context was also seen as one factor contributing to the depressed social climate in the division (with workers today being seen as more self-interested and less community-minded than their peers in the past).

Similarly, changes such as the current trend towards more training for divisional workers, and the attempt in recent years to increase employee awareness of workplace safety, were seen primarily as externally imposed changes. Specifically, training initiatives were seen in the context of current industry-wide reforms (in particular, the move to multi-skill workers through the restructuring of the award) and the increased attention to workplace safety was seen as a response to changes in government legislation. Interestingly,

---

[10]This analysis constituted the focus of a follow-up study that is reported in Chapter 14, the final chapter in this volume.

[11]The latter will be dealt with in Section 12.5 in which the findings of an analysis of data pertaining to the future context are reported.

of all of the causal attributions made by respondents from the tooling division, there were none which suggested the perception that any of the changes reported had been motivated by an explicit commitment, on the part of divisional management, to develop a different, possibly more active role, for divisional workers.

Compared with the tooling division, the attributions data for the production division could be less easily classified to reflect a distinctive attribution style. Certainly, there were some similarities between the two divisions in the types of attributions made by respondents. For example, respondents from the production division, like their counterparts from the tooling division, perceived that some of the changes which they had experienced were essentially reactive changes, attributed in this case to the impact of increasing production pressure in the division over recent years. These changes (which were more or less widely reported) included: the decline, over recent years, in the level of worker involvement in group problem-solving activities (specifically QA meetings), in social activities, and in safety activities; the change towards workers today being more self-interested and less helpful towards their co-workers than workers in the past; and the change towards a growing tension in the communication relationship between workers and their immediate supervisors.

Production division respondents, like their counterparts from the tooling division, also reported changes that they attributed, at least in part, to the impact of external circumstances. For example, as for the tooling division, award restructuring and changes in government legislation were cited as factors influencing, respectively, recent training initiatives and recent workplace safety initiatives in the production division. The latter were also seen by some respondents from the production division, to be a response to rising compensation costs.

Despite the above similarities in the kinds of attributions made by respondents from each division, one important difference between the divisions did emerge. Unlike their counterparts from the tooling division, respondents from the production division commonly attributed changes that had occurred to changes in management personnel, in particular, the arrival in the late 1980s of a new divisional manager. Of greater significance, however, was the finding that this attribution typically included the perception that the new divisional management was more participative in its approach than divisional management in the past, and more committed to the development of the division's human resources. This different style of management was cited as one factor influencing a number of recent changes in the division including: the change towards more involvement of divisional workers in information meetings; the emergence of a more positive industrial relations climate in the division (whereby there was less industrial unrest today than in the past); the increase in the level of worker involvement in training; the development of closer communication between workers and their supervisors; and the introduction of an annual divisional barbeque which was seen as a somewhat unique event because of management's role in preparing the food, and serving it to workers. This finding provides some support for the view that leaders (managers) have an important role in shaping the culture of an organisation and that central to this role is the use of symbolic activity as a vehicle whereby leaders' values and beliefs are communicated to followers (Pfeffer, 1981; Schein, 1985, 1992, 2004, 2010).

It can be seen, then, that in the production division there was a perception that certain changes in the division had, to a greater or lesser extent, been driven by a commitment on the part of divisional management to develop a more active role for workers in the division and to effect some general improvements in divisional workers' experience of working life. One might anticipate that the existence of such attributions could have positive implications for the success of the particular change(s) with which these attributions are associated. In other words, if organisation members perceive that change is planned and positively motivated, as opposed to being reactive or driven entirely by circumstances over which the organisation has no control, then they may be more likely to be accepting of that change and, consequently, more likely to engage in behaviours which are conducive to positive change outcomes being realised. It might also be argued, however, that in order for any given change to be successful, such positive attributions about the change would need to be shown to have some stability over time. This is because events can occur which may change the way in which organisation members perceive, and attribute cause to, their experience of organisational life. In the present study, for example, there was evidence to suggest that the success of changes which were perceived to have been positively motivated (e.g., training initiatives, information meetings for workers, *etc.*) could well be undermined by the experience that, at times of high production pressure, the division's commitment to these changes was often not sustained.

It might also be predicted that, to the extent that the changes reported were seen to be due to the actions (behaviour, attitudes, personality, *etc.*) of a single individual (in this case, it was the management style of the current head of the division), an event such as the departure of this individual from the organisation could have the effect of making divisional members uncertain (perhaps even somewhat cynical) about the likelihood of these changes being maintained. This suggests that one important criterion for the long term success of any organisational (cultural) change may be the perception among organisation members that the change has survived, despite changes in the key personnel seen to have been the original architects of the change.

12.4.4 *An historical overview of the role of workers in each division*

It is worth noting that, to a large extent (though not entirely), the summary points above reflected insights that were obtained from an analysis of the prompt data rather than from an analysis of the open question data. This was because, in neither division, did an analysis of the data generated by the initial open-ended questions provide a particularly coherent picture of changes that had occurred, over time, in what the workers in each division did. The reader will recall that, while a majority of the respondents from each division

(67% from the tooling division and 89% from the production division) reported (in response to the open-ended questions) that there had been some changes, from the past to the present, in what the workers in their respective divisions did, in neither division was there much agreement among respondents about the nature of these changes. For example, in the tooling division, the most widely reported changes — described by the three activity categories, Primary Task, Specialisation, and Social — were referred to by only three respondents each. Similarly, for the production division, the most widely reported changes — described by the activity categories Technology and Group Problem-Solving — were referred to by only six respondents each. There was, however, some evidence from the open question data to suggest that the experience of change had been somewhat broader for members of the production division than for members of the tooling division. As indicated, the changes reported by the former in response to the initial open-ended questions could be described by 17 activity categories, whereas those reported by the latter could be described by only eight activity categories.

In the paragraphs that follow, an attempt has been made to describe, for each division, a profile of worker activities that is historically based, in the sense that it takes account of changes that have occurred, over time, in the activities in which workers have been engaged. In developing these divisional profiles, no distinction has been made between the findings suggested by the open question data and those suggested by the prompt data. Rather, these two sources of information about what workers do (and changes in what workers do) have been combined. The main purpose of this exercise has been to attempt to define the parameters of each division's experience with respect to the role of workers and, by so doing, provide a context within which to interpret and perhaps better understand respondents' subsequent accounts of both the anticipated future, and the ideal, role of divisional workers. A profile of worker activities is described, first for the tooling division and second for the production division.

Tooling division. As indicated, at the time of conducting this study, the primary job of the workers in the tooling division was reportedly to build the tools (including large dies and smaller assembly fixtures) which were used by the company's fabrication and assembly operations. There was little evidence to suggest that this job had changed much over time, except perhaps that, in the past, there had been more task specialisation than there was at the present time. In addition to this main job, the workers in the tooling division were reportedly currently engaged in a number of other activities. As indicated, the history of worker involvement in these other activities had been more or less stable over time. For example:

(1) The workers in the tooling division were currently all required to attend *information meetings*. These meetings were held infrequently (once or twice per year) and had been introduced only recently (approximately five years prior to the commencement of the present study), reportedly in an attempt by management to deal with increasing rumours about the closure of the division. In the years prior to the introduction of these

meetings, there appears to have been no formal mechanism by which work-related information was disseminated to workers.

(2) At the present time, there was some involvement of the workers in the tooling division in *training* activities. These activities typically took the form of off-the-job training courses, which provided training in specialised skills, such as welding, hydraulics, and pneumatics, and which were offered either in-house or externally through one of the local colleges of further education. Much of this training appears to have been made available in the context of the recent industry-wide reform to multi-skill workers through award restructuring. Prior to this time, the tooling division appears to have had a long history of little or no worker involvement in formal training, other than that which was provided to incoming apprentices. There was evidence to suggest that whether or not workers made use of the training opportunities that were currently available depended, to a large extent, upon the individual worker's motivation and initiative. Workers did not appear to be actively encouraged, by their supervisors or managers, to attend training and neither was there any sense of a commitment, on the part of divisional management, to the use of training as a tool to enhance workers' motivation and feelings of self-worth.

In addition to the above, there was evidence of some resistance, among members at all levels of the divisional hierarchy, to the current emphasis on multi-skilling. For example, the relevance and value of much of the training provided as part of this initiative was questioned on the grounds that the skills learned in training were subsequently often not applied on the job. There was also a perception that the training provided was of relevance to shorter serving (i.e., younger) employees only who, compared with their longer-serving counterparts, had a more certain future with the company. And finally, there was a perception that the multi-skilling initiative, which linked rewards such as pay and promotion to the number of skills acquired, discriminated unfairly against longer-serving employees who, it was argued, would be less likely than shorter-serving (younger) employees to cope with the 'academic' demands of the formal off-the-job training courses that were being offered.

(3) At the present time, there were a number of factors that constrained the extent to which the workers in the tooling division were able to *help one another* on the job if and when they needed help. For example, many jobs were designed to be performed by a single worker only, rather than by a team of workers. It was also the case that the boundaries that defined specific work areas/sections were typically fairly rigid, so that it was not practical (nor indeed was it approved of) for a worker from one section to go to a worker from another section for help. Associated with these structural constraints was an attitude (which was shared by supervisory/management staff and employees alike) that it was inappropriate for workers to seek help (particularly in relation to technical problems) from one another; rather, according to established authority relations in the division, they should seek help, first from a leading hand, and then from their immediate supervisor. Finally, some individual workers (tradesmen)

were more intent than others on 'protecting their turf' or, alternatively, more concerned than others with projecting an image of complete competence. These individual worker characteristics served to further limit the helpfulness of the workers in this division towards one another. There was little evidence to suggest that the role of the workers in the tooling division with respect to this activity category (i.e., providing one another with help on the job) had changed much over time.

(4) There was evidence to suggest that, at the present time, a majority of the workers in the tooling division engaged in some form of *communication with their supervisor(s)* on a daily basis. There were, however, a number of contingencies that influenced both the nature and the extent of the communication between workers and supervisors in this division. These included: the type of work being performed (it was argued that some jobs were more complex than others and, therefore, required closer monitoring and control by supervision); the communication style of individual supervisors (some supervisors reportedly favoured a larger 'power distance' between themselves and their subordinates than others); and the nature of individual workers (some workers were reportedly less responsive than others to the efforts of their supervisors to communicate with them). There was no evidence to suggest a division-wide pattern with respect to who was primarily responsible, whether workers or supervisors, for initiating worker-supervisor communication. The communication interactions that were initiated by supervisors were primarily concerned with giving workers information and discussing work-related problems with them. Few of these interactions were socially motivated, and fewer still were concerned with giving workers praise. There was little evidence to suggest that the nature of the communication between workers and their supervisors had changed much over the history of this division, although due to changes in the broader social context (such as, improved education for people entering the workforce, equal opportunity legislation, *etc.*), supervisors today may have been somewhat more open (i.e., more relaxed and less dictatorial) in their style of communication than their predecessors. Finally, there was good evidence to suggest that communication via a strict chain of command was still very much a communication norm in the tooling division.

(5) While the level of worker involvement in *industrial activity* (i.e., strike action) seemed to have fluctuated somewhat over the history of the division, there was evidence to suggest that, since the early 1970s (which marked the onset of a long period of considerable uncertainty about the future of the division), there had been sustained periods of reasonably high levels of worker involvement in such activity (with reports of between one stop work meeting every month to one stop work meeting every six months).

(6) All of the workers in the tooling division were currently involved in activities designed to promote awareness of *workplace safety*. These activities, which were reportedly held every one to two months, typically took the form of either safety talks by the section supervisor or safety handouts that were distributed to workers for them to read.

Every one to three months, there were also company-wide meetings of safety representatives (elected from among shop floor workers) and these were attended by two to three workers from each division. A strong shared history with respect to worker involvement in these activities did not emerge in the data for this division. However, there was some evidence to suggest that, around the mid-1980s, changes in government legislation regarding occupational health and safety may have effected an increase in the amount of attention given to workplace safety in this division. More recently (from the late 1980s onwards), however, the overall decline of the division was perceived to have contributed to the current climate of more lax attitudes towards workplace safety.

(7) The workers in the tooling division were currently involved, to a greater or lesser extent, in a range of *social activities*, the most commonly cited of which were film evenings, retirement functions, and the annual company picnic. There was good evidence, however, to suggest a marked contrast between the social climate (involving positive feelings about social activities) that prevailed in the division at the present time and the social climate that prevailed in the division in the past. The tooling division appears to have supported a long and very positive past history of social activity for divisional workers. The change towards the current less positive social climate in the division was commonly attributed to the general decline of the division. Reports of when this change had first become apparent ranged from 1972 to 1987.

(8) Finally, there was good evidence to suggest that the workers in the tooling division had never been involved, to any significant extent, in *planning activities*, *group problem-solving activities*, or the *recording of work-related information*. These activities were largely seen to be the domain of divisional personnel in more senior positions (i.e., supervisory and technical staff, and management).

Production division. At the time of conducting this study, the primary job of the workers in the production division was reportedly to manufacture production components for motor vehicles. This involved direct production activities, such as, the moulding, assembly, and painting of parts, as well as indirect production activities, such as, materials handling and quality control activities. As above for the tooling division, there was little evidence to suggest that the primary job of the workers in the production division had changed much over time except perhaps that, in the past, manufacturing techniques and processes were technologically less sophisticated than they were at the present time. Apart from their primary job, the workers in the production division were currently engaged in a number of other activities which, as indicated below, had varying histories with respect to the role of workers in this division. For example:

(1) The workers in the production division were currently all required to attend *information meetings*. While these meetings were reportedly held fairly often (every one to

three months), the frequency of their occurrence appeared to be contingent, at least to some extent, upon the demands of production in the division at any given time (such that, at times of high production pressure, the meetings were either not held or not attended by certain key workers or groups of workers). The meetings were reportedly a fairly recent initiative in the division (having been introduced approximately three years prior to the commencement of the present study) and their introduction was typically associated with the arrival, in the late 1980s, of the current divisional manager who was perceived to support a more participative approach to management than his predecessors.

(2)   The workers in the production division were currently involved, to a greater or lesser extent (depending upon the section in which they worked and also, to some extent, upon the stage of production of the current model) in the recording of *work-related information*. For most of these workers, record-keeping activities appeared to constitute an integral part of their job function and one that had been increasingly emphasised in recent years (from the late 1980s onwards) in an attempt, by divisional management, to increase the efficiency and effectiveness of production operations in the division. There was good evidence (from the attributions data, as well as from data pertaining to what kind of information was recorded and how this information was subsequently managed and used) to suggest that record-keeping served primarily a production control function and that its potential value as a motivational tool was currently not being realised.

(3)   At the present time, the extent to which workers and their immediate supervisors *communicated with one another* appeared to depend upon a number of factors, including the type of work being performed, the communication style of individual supervisors, and the personality and attitudes of individual workers. The communication interactions between workers and their supervisors were neither predominantly initiated by supervisors nor predominantly initiated by workers. When supervisors communicated with workers it was usually for the purpose of discussing work-related problems with them or providing them with work-related information. It was less often the case that these interactions were concerned with personal/social issues and it was on the rare occasion only that they were initiated for the purpose of giving a worker praise for her/his achievements. Despite their perception of a negative overall communication climate in their division, there was some evidence to suggest that the specific experience of individual workers (with respect to worker-supervisor communication) may have been quite positive.

Finally, there was evidence to suggest that the predominant style of communication in the division may have fluctuated somewhat over the history of the division. In the early years of divisional operations, it appears that a more closed autocratic approach to communication was supported. More recently, due to changes in management and supervisory staff, as well as to changes in the training available to personnel at these levels, this approach to communication appears to have been replaced by a more open democratic approach. And more recently still, due to an increase in production pressure in the division, there appears to have been a growing tension in the communication relationship between workers and their supervisors.

(4)   At the present time, all of the workers in the production division had some involvement (albeit of a fairly passive nature) in activities designed to promote *workplace safety*. These activities typically took the form of safety talks, which were presented by section supervisors and which all workers were required to attend, and safety handouts, which were distributed to workers for them to read and sign. On average, workers were involved in one or other of these activities every one to three months. In addition, there were several workers in the division who had been elected as safety representatives and these workers attended company-wide meetings of safety representatives, held every one to three months. There was some evidence to suggest that towards the end of the 1980s there had been an increased emphasis on the involvement of divisional workers in safety activities. This change was associated with legislative changes in occupational health and safety regulations, as well as the rising cost, in recent years, of compensation for work-related injuries.

(5)   At the present time, the workers in the production division *provided one another with help* if and when they needed it. However, the extent to which they did this appeared to depend upon a number of factors including: the section in which they worked, with the design of jobs in some sections (e.g., the moulding section) being such that the workers in these sections were not easily able to interact with one another; the nature of the relationship between workers (e.g., if the worker needing help was disliked or perceived by co-workers to be a 'bludger'[12], then she/he would be less likely to receive help); and the attitude, of some workers, that since they were not paid to be helpful towards one another, they were not obliged to engage in such behaviour. There was some evidence that from the late 1980s onwards the workers in this division had become less helpful towards one another than they had been in the past. This change was attributed to an increase in the production pressure in the division, as well as to a change in the nature of workers, such that workers today were perceived to be more self-interested than workers in the past.

(6)   At the present time, the workers in the production division had little involvement in *group problem-solving activities*. Where such activities were set up, these typically involved a total of no more than 3% to 5% of divisional workers at any given time. Furthermore, estimates of how often workers engaged in such activities varied considerably, ranging from once every six weeks to once in the last eight years. In the past, however, the workers in this division had had considerably more involvement in group problem-solving activities. In the early years of the division's operations, this took the form of participation in team meetings associated with the team concept and more recently, it took the form of participation in QA meetings. The former initiative,

---

[12]Australian vernacular to describe a person who is lazy and lives off the efforts of others.

which involved a radical change to the way in which work was done in the division — with self-managed work teams replacing the traditional supervisory control — was abandoned some three to six years after its implementation, reportedly because the objectives it sought to achieve were not being realised. This was attributed by respondents in the study to a number of factors, including the perception that the workers involved lacked the necessary attitudes, skills, and experience required for effective teamwork. The more recent QA meetings, in which a small group of divisional personnel (including workers, supervisors, and technical staff) would attempt to solve a specific work-related problem (that was usually assigned to the group by management), were reportedly phased out just prior to the commencement of the present study. This change was most commonly attributed to the increased production pressure in the division in recent years, associated with the introduction of a new model vehicle. There was good evidence to suggest that, for members at all levels of the divisional hierarchy, the experience of both of these initiatives (which suffered from some of the same problems, such as, lack of team/group leadership, negative worker attitudes, *etc.*), had been predominantly negative.

(7) Workers in the production division were currently involved, to a greater or lesser extent, in a range of *social activities*, the most commonly cited of which were company-sponsored film evenings, the company's Christmas party (a family event attended primarily by employees with young children), and the annual barbecue (which had special significance for employees because, on this occasion, management gave up their traditional role and became the "servants" of the workers, cooking the food and serving it to them). In this division, the history of worker involvement in social activities was not well defined. There were reports of no change from the past to the present with respect to this activity category, reports of a change towards more social activity at the present time than in the past, and reports of a change towards less social activity at the present time. Furthermore, where changes were reported, there was little consensus about the reasons for these changes.

(8) At the present time, there was some involvement of the workers in the production division in *training activities*. The training provided was either on-the-job (whereby new employees were assigned to work with experienced operators) or off-the-job (typically involving training in specialised skills, such as, die-setting). There was good evidence to suggest that training constituted a peripheral, rather than a central, activity with respect to the role of the workers in this division. In particular, the level of worker involvement in training at any given time appeared to be largely contingent upon production demands in the division (so that, at times of high production, training commitments were often forgone). It was also the case that respondents in the study variously expressed their concern about: (i) the quality of some of the training that was provided (in particular, on-the-job training); (ii) whether or not some of the training provided constituted 'real' training (or whether it was simply labelled as such, to enable the division/company to meet the requirements of the recently

introduced government Training Levy[13]); (iii) the current approach to the selection of workers for participation in training programs (whereby 'getting on well' with one's supervisor constituted a pre-condition for selection); and (iv) the attitude of some workers that they were not obliged to attend training, and neither did they have any interest in doing so, unless it was provided in company-time (i.e., unless they were paid to attend). While the history of worker involvement in training in this division was by no means clear, there was some evidence to suggest that from the late 1980s onwards the level of worker involvement in training may have increased somewhat. This change was associated with the industry-wide move to multi-skill workers through award restructuring. There was also a perception that current divisional management were more committed than their predecessors to the development of the division's human resources.

(9)   In the production division, the current level of worker involvement in *industrial activity* (in the form of stop work meetings) appeared to be relatively low. Reports indicated that between one and two stop work meetings were held per year. There was some evidence (although not strong) to suggest that, during the initial start-up years of the division, the level of industrial unrest may have been somewhat higher than it was at the present time.

(10) There was no evidence to suggest that, at any time during the history of the production division, had divisional workers been involved to any significant extent in *planning activities* (whether the decision-making involved was of a strategic nature and concerned with the future direction of the division, or of a more operational nature and concerned with such things as forthcoming work schedules).

12.5 The Future Context

The format of questioning adopted in relation to the future context was the same as that adopted previously in relation to the past context. Respondents were initially presented with two open-ended questions, which asked about anticipated changes (from the present) in the main duties and other activities of divisional workers[14]. To assist respondents in answering these questions, the interviewer provided a brief summary of the respondent's earlier comments regarding what divisional workers did (in terms of these main duties and other activities) at the present time. Following the presentation of the initial open-ended questions, respondents were then presented with the same prompt questions as previously.

---

[13]This legislation, which is now no longer operational, was in effect during the early 1990s.

[14]As indicated previously, the distinction intended by these two separate questions did not emerge consistently in the data, with the main duties described by some respondents being the other activities described by other respondents, and *vice versa*. For the purpose of reporting results, it was therefore decided to aggregate the data from these two questions (in cases where they had been asked separately). Furthermore, towards the latter stages of the interview administration (from questions about the future context and onwards), it was often the case that the two questions were combined and presented as a single question.

Again, each prompt question was typically preceded by a brief summary, by the interviewer, of what the respondent had said when asked that same question in relation to the present context. For example: "You have said that, at the present time, there is no involvement of the workers in your division in safety meetings, apart from the occasional safety talk given by the section supervisor. Do you think that this will change in the future?" Finally, in relation to each anticipated future change that was mentioned, the respondent was asked to indicate:

(1) When she/he thought that the change would occur (five *a priori* response categories were provided — *within the next six months*; *within the next year*; *within the next 2 years; within the next 5 years*; *more than 5 years away*); and
(2) Why she/he thought the change would occur.

The following discussion of the findings for the future context is presented in five main parts. First, we report the results of the analysis of the open question data. Second, we comment briefly on the discrepancy between respondents' spontaneous and prompted responses to questions about the future context. Third, we provide an overview of the main similarities and differences between the divisions that are represented by the future context prompt data shown in Tables 12.3 and 12.4. Fourth, drawing on both the open question and prompt data, we provide a summary of the key findings of the analysis of future context data, in particular, in terms of the additional insights of value that these data provided. Fifth, and finally, we discuss a number of important methodological issues that were highlighted by results of the analysis of the future context data.

12.5.1 *Findings for the open questions*

Tables 12.3 and 12.4 show that, for each division, there was a minority of respondents only (3/12 or 25% of tooling division respondents and 3/19 or 16% of production division respondents) who, in response to the initial open-ended question, gave either a "don't know" or a "no change" response. In other words, a majority of the respondents from both divisions indicated that they expected there to be some change, in the future, in the role of workers in their division.

Tooling division. Of the nine respondents from the tooling division (75%) who anticipated some future change(s), there was one who indicated that he was uncertain about the specific nature of this change. The remaining eight respondents made reference to changes that could subsequently be classified into eight activity categories. As indicated in Table 12.3, the best represented of these activity categories was Specialisation vs Multi-skilling, with five respondents (42%), including four wages employees and one senior supervisor, making reference to a change, in the future, away from task specialisation and towards multi-skilling. This change was clearly regarded as imminent, with some respondents suggesting that the trend towards multi-skilling was already being experienced and others estimating that the change would be likely to occur within the next two years. The decreasing size of the division over recent years was cited as the main factor precipitating the need for a multi-skilled workforce.

The next best-represented activity category was Technology. Four respondents (33%), including two wages employees and two first-line supervisors, made reference to the ongoing impact of new technologies on how work was done in the division. Technological change, to the extent that it was currently being experienced and was anticipated to continue into the future, was seen primarily as an attempt to keep abreast of trends overseas, thereby helping to ensure the international competitiveness of the company's tooling operations.

The only other activity category worth mentioning here is Responsibility/Accountability. Three respondents (25%) (two wages employees and one first-line supervisor) anticipated that, in the future, the level of responsibility and accountability of the individual worker would change. Two of these respondents believed that, in the future, divisional workers would have more responsibility and accountability than they did at the present time. This change was reportedly already beginning to be experienced and was attributed, in one case, to the decreasing size of the division (for the division to survive with a smaller workforce, individual workers would be expected to assume more responsibility/accountability) and, in the other, to changes in the broader social context (e.g., increased education of workers), whereby workers increasingly expected to have a more active and involved role (and by implication to have more responsibility/accountability) in organisational life. One respondent anticipated that, in the future (time not specified), workers would have less responsibility and accountability than they did at the present time. According to this respondent, the reduced size of the division would result in workers being seen even more as a "servant to production" (presumably suggesting a very passive role) than they were at the present time.

Production division. For the production division, there were 16 respondents (84%) who spontaneously (i.e., in response to the open-ended questions) made reference to some future change(s) with respect to what the workers in their division did. As indicated in Table 12.4, while the responses of these 16 respondents could be classified into 11 activity categories, there was only one category, namely Technology, which could be regarded as being well represented. Ten respondents (53%), including seven wages employees, two senior supervisors, and one first-line supervisor, made reference to the likelihood of ongoing technological change that would influence the way in which work in the division was done. This change was variously attributed to the need for the division to survive and remain competitive, and the need for the division to increase its productivity and reduce its operating costs.

As indicated in Table 12.4, the next best-represented activity category for the production division was Primary Task. Three respondents (16%), all wages employees, made reference to some change in the future that would impact on the primary task of the workers in this division. Two respondents argued that manufacturing in the car industry in Australia, at least in its present form, would effectively cease to exist in the future (time unspecified). It was predicted that all manufacturing would move offshore, leaving Australian automotive workers with assembly operations only. The third respondent predicted that the production operator's job was likely to become more difficult (again, time unspecified) because of the need to satisfy the increasing expectations of consumers regarding product quality.

Comparing the two divisions. It is interesting to note that, while almost half of the respondents from the tooling division commented on the trend away from specialisation and towards multi-skilling, there was only one respondent from the production division who made this same observation. It is possible that this finding reflects a cultural difference between the two divisions. It can be argued that, for members of the tooling division, their status and role as qualified tradesmen were linked inextricably to their acquisition, over many years, of highly specialised skills and abilities. In this sense, the change towards multi-skilling (which was part of an industry-wide reform) no doubt represented a more significant threat to the members of the tooling division than to their counterparts in the production division. The latter were predominantly production operators whose work was specialised only in the sense that it traditionally comprised performance of a single, relatively routine, task (or small number of such tasks). Of course, it may also be the case that the production division was more advanced with respect to the consolidation of the multi-skilling reform. In other words, respondents from this division may have considered that this was a change that had already occurred.

Taken as a whole, the above findings concerning respondents' unprompted views about how the role of divisional workers might change in the future suggest that the two divisions are roughly equivalent. It was also the case that in neither division was there much agreement among respondents about the range of changes anticipated. A further similarity between the divisions was that, in both, there existed a perception that technological change would somehow influence what divisional workers would do in the future[15]. As indicated, one possible difference between the divisions (which it was suggested may have some cultural significance) was suggested by the finding that respondents from the tooling division were more likely to make reference to the current (industry-wide) trend towards multi-skilling for workers.

---

[15]Respondents typically did not elaborate on the exact nature of this influence and neither were they asked to do so. Had they been prompted for this information, they may have been able to comment without hesitation. On the other hand, however, they might also have responded with considerable uncertainty. The point is that, while respondents may be well aware that changes in technology are imminent, they may have very little notion of (indeed, they might have given little thought to) the specific implications of these changes for their own role (if a worker) and for the role of workers in the division generally. Indeed, it will be recalled from Section 12.4 that the introduction of information meetings (which constituted the primary formal means by which management could disseminate information about the future of the organisation to workers) was a relatively recent phenomenon in each division. In this sense, it might be argued that, in neither division, did shop floor workers have a significant shared history of being well-informed, by management, about likely future developments which might impact upon them as individuals, as well as upon the organisation as a whole.

Finally, it is interesting to note that the above analysis of open question data provided little evidence of a perception, among respondents from either division, that divisional workers in the future might assume what would constitute a more active role. If indeed respondents believed that this was likely to be the case then one might expect that, given their exposure to the prompt set up to this point in the interview administration (initially in relation to questions about the present context, and then again in relation to questions about the past context), respondents might have offered this information spontaneously (i.e., in response to the open-ended questions). The fact that they did not might have some significance from a cultural perspective. It may be that, for respondents in both divisions, their past and present experience has been such that it has either provided no indication at all of a change towards a more active role for workers, or that what evidence there has been has been insufficient to convince respondents of a definite trend in this direction. The findings presented in the previous section suggest that, at least for the production division, the latter explanation might apply.

12.5.2 *The difference between open questions and prompted responses*

As previously, for both the present and the past contextual domains, the addition of prompt questions, following on from the initial open-ended questions, provided a somewhat different picture of anticipated future changes in the role of workers in each division than that which was provided by the open question data alone. This is clearly illustrated by the data pertaining to the activity category Attend Training. Tables 12.3 and 12.4 show that in response to the initial open-ended questions, there was only one respondent from each division who indicated that the current involvement of divisional workers in training might change, in some way, in the future. However, when specifically prompted, an additional eight respondents from the tooling division, and an additional 11 respondents from the production division, made reference to an anticipated future change with respect to this activity category.

This difference between open-ended and prompt questions has been observed previously in relation to questioning about both the present and the past contexts and, as previously, it is interesting to give some brief consideration here as to what it might mean. Again, it might be argued that the use of specific prompts (closed questions) may have had the effect of putting words into people's mouths[16]. In other words, the effect of asking respondents *directly* about specific changes that might occur (as opposed to allowing them to express their views spontaneously) may have been to increase the likelihood of their admitting to the possibility of such changes, without having previously considered this possibility. If this were the case, however, one would expect to have observed a marked difference between prompted and unprompted responses across the *entire* range of activity categories listed. As indicated in Tables 12.3 and 12.4, this was not the case. Rather, for both divisions, marked differences were observed for specific activity categories only.

---

[16]An account of the research concerning this claim is provided in Chapter 11, Section 11.1.2.

It seems reasonable to suggest, therefore, that the responses to prompting shown in Tables 12.3 and 12.4 are considered responses, rather than ad hoc responses. In other words, they can be taken to represent respondents' evaluations of how the role of divisional workers, with respect to specific activity categories, is likely to change, given respondents' experience to date with respect to these activity categories. The finding that this information was revealed only through prompting and not spontaneously, in response to the initial open-ended questions, is consistent with the view expressed earlier that responses to open-ended questions are likely to be based, not on some detailed schema that respondents have of all of the various activities which might make up the role of workers, but rather on respondents' perceptions of the most salient aspects of the more general (overall) role of workers. As indicated, to the extent that respondents anticipated any change in this more general role, it was associated, in both divisions, with anticipated changes in technology and, in the tooling division, also with the trend towards multi-skilling. Interestingly, both of these spontaneously mentioned changes can be seen as constituting general, industry-wide changes, the impact of which is likely to have been experienced (if not directly, then indirectly through socialisation with one's co-workers or with friends from other organisations, through the media, *etc.*) for some time. Changes of this kind, it might be argued, are likely to be very salient in the minds of organisation members and, hence, are more likely to be mentioned spontaneously than changes of a more specific and focussed nature, such as those which are asked about in the prompt questions.

The possible influence of the media on these reported changes suggests the need for researchers to consider the role of the media as an influence on organisational climate and culture. Media reports, either positive or negative, about the company's present or likely future performance might be expected to have more effect on the present climate than on the present culture of the organisation, if the former is defined as how workers feel about the organisation and particular aspects of its culture. However, media reports of this kind might also influence perceptions of the organisation's likely future culture and they might change the way in which the past culture is perceived. If, for example, media reports continued to suggest a decline in car manufacturing, with only one or two manufacturers likely to survive, this might promote a view of the past culture as 'the good old days'.

Finally, it is perhaps also worth highlighting the possibility that, had the interviews about the future been conducted with the company's senior management group (as opposed to shop floor workers and their immediate supervision), the kinds of changes mentioned spontaneously may well have been changes for which there was, as yet, little evidence at the level of the shop floor. In other words, senior managers typically have access to insights and information, not available to members at lower levels in the hierarchy, which make it possible for them to think with foresight about the organisation and where it is headed. However, it is also possible that senior managers' views would be more likely to be influenced by social desirability, that is, a tendency to answer in a way that would be approved of by the organisation. As it was, the changes that were anticipated were changes for which there were already clearly established trends.

12.5.3 *Prompt questions: Some initial findings*

Table 12.5 presents the results of prompting in relation to the future context for *both* the tooling division and the production division (previously these data were presented separately as part of Table 12.3 and Table 12.4 respectively). The number, and percentage (in parentheses), of respondents from each division who anticipated some future change with respect to each activity category is shown. Also shown is the percentage difference between the divisions. In addition, for each division, there is a column for missing data that shows the number of respondents who were not prompted with respect to each of the given activity categories. Typically, the decision to omit certain specific questions was based on the interviewer's awareness that time was pressing and that, without such omissions, it would not be possible to cover subsequent key sections of the interview (e.g., concerning the other and the ideal contextual domains).

It can be seen from Table 12.5 that the problem of missing data was not insignificant and was somewhat more marked for the production division than for the tooling division. It was also the case that the results of additional questioning pertaining to when anticipated changes were considered likely to occur, and why, suffered from a similar degree of incompleteness. This highlights a problem with the interview design, namely, that in its current form, it attempted to cover too much ground in the time available. (It will be recalled that this part of the interview, concerned with what workers do, constituted one part of a two-part interview that was designed to be administered over a period of approximately two hours.)

A more general implication of the problem of missing data, however, is that with any integrated approach to data collection there is likely to be some trade-off between the

Table 12.5. Future context prompt data: Number and percentage of respondents from each division anticipating future change and percentage difference between the divisions.

Activity Category	Tooling Division $n = 12$ Number (%) of Respondents	Missing Data	Production Division $n = 19$ Number (%) of Respondents	Missing Data	% Difference
Planning meetings	4 (36%)	1	3 (17%)	1	19%
Information meetings	4 (36%)	1	4 (35%)	3	11%
Group problem-solving	5 (45%)	1	6 (35%)	2	10%
Safety meetings	7 (64%)	1	6 (43%)	5	21%
Union meetings	2 (20%)	2	3 (20%)	4	0%
Help other workers	3 (27%)	1	3 (19%)	3	8%
Record work-related info	2 (20%)	2	10 (53%)	0	−33%
Attend training	9 (90%)	2	12 (67%)	1	23%
Social activities	5 (45%)	1	9 (53%)	2	−8%
Wkr-sup communication	3 (38%)	4	5 (31%)		7%

amount of structure that can be imposed, on the one hand, and the degree of flexibility that can be accommodated, on the other. In other words, assuming a set period of time in which to conduct an interview, respondents cannot be given more freedom (e.g., to elaborate on their responses or to introduce new, but potentially relevant, information) without there being an associated effort, on the part of the interviewer, to rein in the scope of the interview (in terms of the number of specific issues it seeks to address and the number of specific questions included in the protocol). Even where there are no formally negotiated time limits, factors such as respondent fatigue and the need to maintain an amicable research relationship with respondents will mean that an approach which seeks to pursue potentially important qualitative information through allowing respondents to elaborate on their responses will be likely to produce more or less incomplete results. These issues with respect to interviewing have implications for the kind of training required by interviewers in studies of organisational culture.

The difference data reported in Table 12.5 show that, for the future context, there were only two prompted activity categories out of 10 (Record Work-Related Information and Social Activities) for which a greater proportion of respondents from the production division than the tooling division anticipated a change. In other words, with respect to most of the activity categories about which they were prompted, tooling division respondents were more inclined than their counterparts in the production division to anticipate some future change. Interestingly, the reverse was true for the past context. As shown in Table 12.6 below, there were six activity categories (Planning Meetings, Information Meetings, Group Problem-Solving, Help Other Workers, Record Work-Related Information, and Worker-Supervisor Communication) for which a greater proportion of respondents from the production division than the tooling division reported a change. In other words, in

Table 12.6. Past context prompt data: Number and percentage of respondents from each division reporting a change from the past to the present and percentage difference between the divisions.

Activity Category	Tooling Division $n = 12$ Number (%) of Respondents	Production Division $n = 19$ Number (%) of Respondents	% Difference
Planning meetings	2 (17%)	6 (32%)	−15%
Information meetings	8 (67%)	13 (68%)	−1%
Group problem-solving	0 (0%)	16 (84%)	−84%
Safety meetings	7 (58%)	6 (32%)	26%
Union meetings	4 (33%)	6 (32%)	1%
Help other workers	2 (17%)	8 (42%)	−25%
Record work-related info	2 (17%)	9 (47%)	−30%
Attend training	12 (100%)	8 (42%)	58%
Social activities	9 (75%)	11 (58%)	17%
Wkr-sup communication	4 (33%)	13 (68%)	−35%

response to prompting, production division respondents were more inclined than their counterparts in the tooling division to report changes from the past to the present.

This finding may be interpreted in a number of ways. First, the difference data for the future context may reflect the current climate in the tooling division, whereby divisional members were feeling considerable uncertainty about their own future and the future of the division. Alternatively, as suggested by the difference data for the past context, it may be that some of the changes anticipated by respondents from the tooling division are changes that have already been experienced by production division respondents. In other words, the tooling division may simply lag behind the production division in terms of changes in specific worker activities that may ultimately affect workers across all divisions in the organisation. Indeed, while there was no explicit company policy which advocated that changes of the kind referred to above (i.e., associated with worker involvement in planning meetings, group problem-solving, *etc.*) should be introduced into some divisions before others, there is nevertheless some evidence, from a personal communication with the manager of the production division, to suggest that such changes may have been given a lower priority in the tooling division than in the production division.

This manager pointed to the different business contexts in which the two divisions were operating at the time. On the one hand, the tooling division was undergoing a major restructuring and downsizing, which followed on from the company's decision to move many of its major tooling projects offshore. There was, therefore, a perception, at least among senior management in the company at the time that the tooling division was of declining importance with respect to its role in the company's overall operations. On the other hand, the company had made a firm decision to retain its production operations and to develop them to a point where a highly competitive in-house service for the provision of production components was available. Given this goal, there was reportedly considerable pressure on the management in the production division to constantly strive to do better and this resulted in, among other things, a more committed and concerted effort to develop the division's human resources. As the reader will recall, it was also the case that the production division had originally been set-up partly as a demonstration model for the implementation of more innovative management practices (specifically, in the form of the team concept). As such, from its inception and at different points throughout its life, this division can be seen to have had more exposure to 'non-traditional' management practices than the tooling division.

As above for the analysis of prompt data pertaining to the past context, the more detailed analysis of future context prompt data involved, first of all, grouping prompted activities into those for which similarities between the divisions (in terms of the number of respondents anticipating some future change with respect to the activity) were indicated, and those for which differences between the divisions were indicated. It can be seen from Table 12.5 that there were seven prompted activity categories, out of ten, for which the difference between the divisions (in terms of the percentage of respondents anticipating a change in the future) was less than 20% (the nominated criterion for the classification of 'similarities').

From most similar to least similar, these categories included: (i) Union Meetings (a difference score of 0%); (ii) Worker-Supervisor Communication (7% difference); (iii) Social Activities (–8% difference); (iv) Help other Workers (8% difference); (v) Group Problem-Solving (10% difference); (vi) Information Meetings (11% difference); and (vii) Planning Meetings (19% difference). The proportion of respondents anticipating a change for each of these activity categories ranged from 20% to 45% for the tooling division, and from 17% to 53% for the plastics division. The important point is that, for only one of these activity categories, and in one division only, did the proportion of respondents anticipating a change exceed 50% (this was Social Activities for the plastics division). Thus, the similarity between the divisions with respect to these activity categories lay in the finding that the changes anticipated were noted by a minority (fewer than half) of the respondents from each division, rather than a majority.

It can also be seen from Table 12.5 that there were three prompted activity categories, out of ten, for which the difference between the divisions (in terms of the percentage of respondents anticipating a change in the future) was more than 20% (the nominated criterion for the classification of differences). These categories, in order from most different to least different, were: (i) Record Work-Related Information (a difference score of –33%); (ii) Attend Training (23% difference); and (iii) Safety Meetings (21% difference).

12.5.4 *The future context: Summary of key findings*

The summary results which are presented in this section draw on the findings reported above, as well as on the findings of the analysis of future context prompt data, reported in Kummerow (2000). These results are as follows:

1. Spontaneous responses regarding anticipated future change. In response to the initial open-ended question, a majority of respondents from both divisions anticipated a change, in the future, with respect to some aspect of the role of the workers in their division. In neither division, however, was there much agreement among respondents about the specific nature of the anticipated change. Among tooling division respondents, the most commonly cited change (mentioned by 42% of respondents) was the move away from specialisation towards multi-skilling. In the production division, technological change (and its implications for the downsizing of the workforce, and how work would be done in the future) was the most commonly cited change (mentioned by 53% of respondents). For neither division did the open question change data contain much evidence (in the form of the types of changes anticipated) to suggest a perception among respondents that the role of divisional workers would become more active in the future. This was despite the exposure of respondents, up to this point in the interview, to prompt questions suggestive of a more active role for workers.

2. Prompted responses regarding anticipated change. For both divisions, the addition of specific prompting in relation to the future context resulted in more changes being mentioned than had been mentioned previously in response to the initial open-ended question. However, as above for the spontaneously mentioned changes, the degree of consensus about these prompted responses was, in general, only marginal. For the tooling division, there were only two activity categories out of 10 (Safety Meetings and Attend Training), for which more than half of the respondents from the available sample antici-pated a change in the future; for the production division, there were three activity catego-ries (Record Work-Related Information, Attend Training, and Social Activities) for which this was the case[17].

There was also evidence that, as a group, tooling division respondents were somewhat more inclined than their counterparts from the production division to anticipate changes in the future in response to prompting. Specifically, there were eight out of 10 prompted activity categories for which the proportion of respondents anticipating a change in the future was greater for the tooling division than for the production division. That the reverse of this was true for the past context suggested the possibility that some of the changes that were anticipated by respondents from the tooling division were changes that may already have been experienced by respondents from the production division. This conclusion is consistent with the researcher's general impression (formed over several years as a researcher participant in each division) of each division's history with respect to the exposure of divisional members to change.

3. Extent of future-orientation of each division's culture. Considered as a whole, the findings of the analysis of future context data (both open question and prompt data) provided little evidence of the existence, in either division, of a strongly future-oriented culture, at least with respect to beliefs and assumptions about the fundamental role of workers.

This conclusion is not inconsistent with what one might expect given the nature of the sample drawn from each division. As indicated, participants in the study were predomi-nantly shop floor workers (wages employees) and their immediate supervisors. Had the study been conducted with more senior company (or indeed divisional) personnel, whom one might expect would be better informed about likely future trends (related to this and other issues), the findings might have been quite different. Similarly, had the site of the study been the company's research and development division or, alternatively, a different type of organisation altogether (say an organisation involved in the development of computer software), there might have been more evidence of the existence of a strongly future-oriented culture. Thus, organisations might differ in the extent to which they are concerned with different contexts, whether the past, the future, the other, or the ideal. Different sections of an organisation might also differ in this way. It might even be possible for there to be differences within an organisation's culture, such that for different categories of the basic beliefs and assumptions in Schein's (2010) typology, one finds a differential

---

[17]These calculations take account of the impact of missing data, referred to in Section 12.5.3.

emphasis on particular dimensions of context. Thus, for example, an organisation might be found to be more future-oriented with respect to its basic beliefs and assumptions about its relationship to the external environment; it might be found to be more past-oriented with respect to its basic beliefs and assumptions about the nature of human nature.

It is interesting to note that the above conclusion about the absence, in both divisions, of a strong future-orientation is also supported by the finding, for both divisions, that respondents' accounts of their experiences at the present time contained very few spontaneous references to the future context. In contrast, for both divisions, these same accounts contained many more spontaneous references to the past.

4. Nature of the changes anticipated. For both divisions, the changes that were anticipated (in response to the initial open-ended question and in response to prompting) tended to be changes that were perceived to be either already underway (and which respondents, therefore, already had some experience of) or likely to occur in the very near future (at least within the next two years). For the tooling division, this was the case for 93% of the anticipated changes for which time-line data were available; for the production division, it was the case for 72% of these changes. In other words, there was little evidence in these data of an awareness of changes likely to occur in the more distant future. For both divisions, only 5% of the changes for which time-line data were available were changes that were estimated by respondents to be *more than five years away*. This finding provides further support for the conclusion in point 3 above that neither division (at least at the shop floor level) appeared to support a strongly future-oriented culture.

The difference between what seemed to be the near future in the data presented, as opposed to a more distant future, raises the question as to how useful it might be to analyse contextual data in terms like this. While information about the past and the future could include associated real time estimates, these might not be as meaningful as psychologically distinct time frames. These time frames might differ for different organisations, divisions within an organisation, or between organisation members with different demographic characteristics. This distinction between near and far might also be useful in considering other contexts such as the ideal, in which the 'near ideal' might be considered more immediately realisable than the 'far ideal'. Similarly, with respect to the 'other', there might be a useful distinction between the 'near other', such as information about similar organisations or government regulations directly impacting the organisation, and the 'far other', which might include information about business or government generally or more general legislation, such as that related to younger workers or women. The extent to which such distinctions could be useful in understanding an organisation's culture would be a matter for empirical investigation.

5. Evidence of attribution style. An analysis of the attributions data for change respondents provided some evidence to suggest that the divisions might differ in terms of attribution style. This difference might be conceptualised broadly in terms of a reactive versus a proactive orientation to change (in this case, anticipated change). Among tooling division respondents, there was a marked tendency to see change as reactive, that is, as a response to events, circumstances, *etc.* over which the division was perceived to have little control. Anticipated changes in this division were commonly attributed to factors such as: (i) the downsizing and restructuring of the division, and its relocation to the site of the company's main manufacturing and assembly operations; (ii) the introduction of award restructuring (with its implications for job redesign and employee training); and (iii) increasing pressure (on the division and the company in general) to survive and remain competitive.

This same reactive attribution style also emerged in the production division data, with references, for example, to change being a consequence of: (i) increasing competitive pressure; (ii) the introduction of award restructuring; (iii) technological change; and (iv) the forthcoming introduction of a new model vehicle. However, in addition to attributions of this kind, there was also evidence in these data of a perception among respondents that change was more proactive, in the sense of being initiated from within the division and motivated by an explicit commitment on the part of divisional management (and supervision) to improve divisional operations and to enhance the experience of work for divisional members. In this sense, there were references to anticipated changes being a consequence of: (i) a drive on the part of divisional management to increase the efficiency of divisional operations and improve quality; and (ii) a commitment on the part of divisional management to develop the division's human resources (e.g., through fostering a more open communication climate between workers and their supervisors, keeping workers well-informed, implementing job enrichment strategies for workers, and encouraging the development of a positive social climate in the division).

The above conclusions are supported by the results of a subsequent analysis (albeit a fairly rudimentary analysis) which involved, first of all, listing all of the attributions made by respondents from each division (in relation to anticipated changes that were mentioned spontaneously and in response to prompting) and, secondly, classifying these attributions according to whether they were indicative of a reactive or proactive orientation to change. For the tooling division, 83% of respondents' attributions could be classified as reactive and 10% could be classified as proactive. In contrast, for the production division, 53% of respondents' attributions could be classified as reactive and 38% as proactive. (For both divisions, there were a number of attributions that could not easily be classified as either reactive or proactive.) Of course, these results must be interpreted with a degree of caution since they are based on numbers of attributions, rather than numbers of respondents. In other words, no consideration was given in this analysis to the extent to which single respondents made the same attribution in relation to a number of the changes that they anticipated.

6. Demographic differences. An analysis of seniority differences between the 'change' and 'no change' respondents for each division provided some evidence to suggest that, in the production division, these two groups might differ in terms of this demographic. For example, in response to prompting about the likelihood of future change (with respect to each of the listed activity categories), the supervisors from this division were more inclined, as a group, to give change rather than no change responses. Specifically, there were nine activity categories out of 10 for which the number of supervisors indicating change exceeded the number of supervisors indicating no change. Moreover, for eight of these categories, there were no supervisors represented in the no change responses (i.e., for each of these eight categories, all of the supervisors who were presented with the associated prompt question gave a change response). In contrast, the wages employees from this division were more inclined, as a group, to give no change rather than change responses. In this case, there were nine activity categories for which the number of wages employees indicating no change exceeded the number of wages employee indicating change. However, for all but one of these categories, there was some representation of wages employees in the change responses.

In contrast to their counterparts from the production division, supervisory staff from the tooling division were, as a group, no more inclined to give either change or no change responses. Specifically, there were five out of 10 activity categories for which the number of supervisors indicating change exceeded the number of supervisors indicating no change. The reverse was true for four of the 10 activity categories and, for one category the number indicating change was equivalent to the number indicating no change. The picture for wages employees from the tooling division was similar to that for wages employees from the production division. That is, as a group, wages employees from the tooling division were more inclined to give no change rather than change responses. Specifically, there were seven out of 10 activity categories for which the number of wages employees indicating no change exceeded the number of wages employees indicating change; the reverse was true for the remaining three categories.

Given the problem of missing data referred to previously, as well as the different representation of supervisory staff and wages employees in the two samples (e.g., supervisors represented 50% of the tooling division sample, but only 26% of the production division sample), the above findings must be interpreted with some caution. However, to the extent that they may be indicative of a more general trend in each division, it is interesting to speculate briefly as to what they might mean. The finding that, for both divisions, the wages employees were, as a group, more inclined to anticipate no change rather than change is perhaps not surprising and is consistent with the status of this group as generally less well-informed than their superiors about changes which are likely to occur in the future. The finding that supervisory staff from the tooling division were less likely than their counterparts from the production division to anticipate change is more difficult to explain. It may, however, reflect the general context in which evaluations by respondents from the tooling division were being made. As indicated, the tooling division had been in a state of decline for a number of years. It currently supported a considerably diminished workforce and, at the time of the present study, the downsizing effort was not yet complete. Some of the respondents in the present study had opted to accept a retrenchment package;

some had opted to remain with the company; and others were, as yet, undecided. As such, it seems reasonable to suggest that the context for tooling division respondents was one in which there was considerable uncertainty about what the future might hold (and hence, more ambivalence about whether or not change would occur).

7. Potential cultural significance of attitudinal data. Finally, the analysis of future context data provided some evidence to suggest that evaluative data — in the form of respondents' attitudes, whether positive or negative, to changes that they anticipated — may constitute an important source of cultural information. In particular, these data may provide clues about the extent of the group's resistance to, or support for, particular changes that the organisation might wish to implement. For example, it was found that there was considerable ambivalence among respondents from the tooling division about the anticipated change towards more involvement of divisional workers in training in the future. As noted, one of the main reasons for this ambivalence lay in a concern about the relevance of training for the division's older employees. These employees, it was argued, would experience more difficulty in adjusting to the academic demands of a return to training than their younger counterparts. There was also some evidence in this division of strongly negative attitudes towards the anticipated increase in the involvement of divisional workers in group problem-solving. On the one hand, problem-solving was considered to be a supervisory, rather than a worker, responsibility; on the other, it was argued that the types of problems which were typically encountered in this division were too complex to be solved by teams whose members included shop floor workers. Clearly, if the changes anticipated by these respondents were to be successfully implemented in this division, attitudes such as these would need to be taken into account, and explicitly managed as potential impediments to the change process. The point might also be made that such attitudes, even if shared by a minority of organisation members only (this was the case for the above attitudes to worker involvement in group problem-solving), are still likely to have an impact on the change effort, particularly if they are held by more senior, and hence more powerful, members of the organisation. Another consideration in this regard that might be important concerns the specificity of the attitudes expressed by an organisation's members. Are these attitudes confined to members' current organisation, or are they of a more general nature? For example, is resistance to involvement in group problem-solving restricted to members' current employment or would it apply to their employment in any organisation?

Unfortunately, because respondents were not consistently presented with questions about the desirability/undesirability of the changes that they anticipated, there was insufficient evaluative data upon which to draw any firm conclusions about emergent trends in either division. In fact, evaluative questions and direct questions asking respondents how they feel about culture or climate issues are not typically included in either assessments of organisational culture or assessments of organisational climate. However, information of this kind would seem to be very important, even critical, for change agents.

In our discussion of organisational climate in Chapter 4 of Volume I, we have argued that climate should be defined in terms of how respondents feel about particular aspects of the organisation at the present time. But knowledge of how respondents felt about those same aspects of the organisation in the past might also be important. Such knowledge might provide insights into the past culture of the organisation and might also be important for understanding the organisation's current climate. Because the deeper-level beliefs and assumptions of an organisation's culture are assumed to be mostly unconscious and taken-for-granted, one would not expect culture at this level to have an explicit affective component — unless, as we have argued in our discussion of organisational climate in Chapter 4 of Volume I, those beliefs and assumptions were to be challenged in some way, whether by an actual, anticipated, or even hypothetical change or threat. It was hypothesised that a strong negative emotional reaction to such a change or threat might be indicative of some underlying cultural belief or assumption of which the respondents might not be fully aware.

12.5.5 *Methodological issues arising from the findings for the future context*

A number of methodological issues arose in the course of conducting the analysis of future context data. These issues are outlined below and, where relevant, their implications for understanding culture in work organisations are discussed. Where appropriate, suggestions are also made about how this section of the present interview might be modified for use in subsequent research.

1. The trade-off between breadth and depth. As indicated, the data set upon which the above findings were based was somewhat incomplete. This problem of missing data arose as a consequence of the design of the interview schedule. Given the time available (a total of two hours for a two-part interview) and the fact that respondents were free to elaborate on, and qualify, their responses (this was a critical feature of the interview design), it is clear now that the interview schedule was too ambitious with respect to the number of issues which it attempted to address. It might, therefore, have been more realistic to seek information about fewer prompts. In this way, all of the questions associated with a particular issue could have been covered, with time available for respondents to provide important qualifying and elaborative detail.

An important lesson for the design of integrated approaches (such as the present approach based on a semi-structured interview) is that one should attempt, from the outset, to determine what constitutes a reasonable, and manageable scope, for the interview. In making this decision, one should be mindful of the inevitable trade-off in such approaches between the amount of structure that can be imposed and the degree of flexibility that can be accommodated. This issue has already been mentioned in terms of its implications for interviewing skills. In particular, there is a need to manage the interview session so that rapport is maintained, allowing the respondent to feel that she/he can elaborate on responses, but with the interviewer moving the interview along so that there is time to ask all questions and have them adequately answered. A temptation here, in order to save time, might be for the interviewer to inadvertently create an interview climate in which the interviewee feels under pressure to give formulaic responses, and responses that she/he believes are consistent with what the interviewer is expecting to hear, and in which the interviewer seeks no feedback from the interviewee regarding the accuracy of her/his responses.

2. Interpretive inconsistency. As for the analyses of past and present context data, conducted previously, the analysis of future context data revealed a degree of interpretive inconsistency among respondents. For example, there was evidence to suggest that respondents from the production division differed in terms of the criteria they used to evaluate the likelihood of a change, in the future, in the involvement of divisional workers in group problem-solving. The evaluations of some respondents were based on a consideration of the likelihood of a reintroduction of the team concept; for others, they were based on a consideration of the likelihood of a change, in the future, in the involvement of divisional workers in QA meetings. Interestingly, there were no obvious differences between these two groups in terms of respondents' tenure (i.e., it was not the case that the former were all longer-serving employees with experience of the team concept, while the latter were shorter-serving employees with experience only of the more recent QA initiative).

Clearly, it is important to know about interpretive differences of this kind. Such knowledge may have implications for understanding the culture of the group — how widely shared it is (a lot of interpretive inconsistency would suggest a lack of sharedness) and whether or not there are any subcultures operating within the group (with inconsistencies such as the above possibly serving as markers for subcultural boundaries). Other possible sources of inconsistency could include personality differences or broad political differences in how individuals interpret certain issues. Of course, where a high level of interpretive inconsistency exists, there are implications for the extent to which data can be aggregated and meaningful conclusions drawn from the findings. In the context of the present study, it is difficult to know how to deal with this problem and perhaps all that one can do is to simply acknowledge that it exists. A longer term solution, however, may be to revise the current approach so that, instead of breaking up the data for each individual respondent and then aggregating and analysing responses to specific questions, one might classify individual respondents on the basis of their overall pattern of responding and then group them according to similarities which emerge. It is possible that an approach such as this, whereby individuals rather than responses are aggregated, might be culturally somewhat more sensitive than the current approach — in the sense of providing a clearer indication of both the degree of sharedness of the group's culture and the extent to which different subcultures are supported within the group.

3. Future orientation and responsiveness to change. As indicated, the above finding that respondents from both divisions anticipated relatively few changes in the future, with respect to the role of the workers in their division, and that there was often not a lot of consensus about the changes which were anticipated, was interpreted to mean that, in neither division, was the prevailing culture strongly future-oriented. Such an insight, which it can be argued would not have been obtained had information about the future context not been sought, may have important implications for understanding organisational responsiveness to change. For example, it may be that change is easier to bring about in organisations where the members can be shown to have developed a reasonably well-articulated view of a future that involves the kind of change being proposed (through thinking and talking about it a lot) than in organisations where members' thinking appears to be more focussed on, say, the past context of their experience. The organisational climate associated with such views (i.e., the feelings, whether positive, negative, or neutral) would also be an important determinant of the ease with which that change could be implemented.

An interesting possibility for future research would be to repeat the present study with a group of respondents likely to be more future-oriented in their outlook than respondents comprising the present sample. (These respondents might be drawn from a higher level in the current organisation or, alternatively, from a different organisation altogether.) The findings of such a study, when compared with the findings of the present study, would allow for some assessment of the extent to which differences in time-orientation actually do exist. Furthermore, on the basis of comparative research of this kind, one could begin to address the issue of whether or not a group's time-orientation (whether past, present, or future) influences not only the type of culture that exists but also its responsiveness to change.

4. Integrating contextual domains. While an attempt was made, in the above analysis, to offer an historical interpretation of the future context data (i.e., to interpret data pertaining to the anticipated future in the context of data pertaining to the past and the present), this was often very difficult to achieve. In other words, the links between the three contextual domains considered thus far (namely, the past, the present, and the anticipated future) were not always evident. This suggests that organisation members' perceptions about what the future is likely to hold with respect to any given issue, will be influenced by more than just organisation members' history with respect to that issue. In other words, the former is not determined solely by the latter. This is not to say, however, that historical data (including data pertaining to the present context of organisation members' experience) have *no* relevance for the interpretation of future context data. For example, the finding in the present study that all but one of the available respondents from the tooling division anticipated an increase, in the future, in the involvement of divisional workers in training has meaning only when one has some knowledge about the history of worker involvement in training in this division. At the very least, one needs to know about how much training the workers in this division are receiving at the present time, since without this knowledge, there is no yardstick against which to interpret respondents' prediction that there will be 'more' training for divisional workers in the future.

5. The importance of attributions data. The findings of the analysis of future context data provided further support for the argument (made previously in the context of the analysis of historical data) that attributions data may constitute a valuable source of cultural information. It is suggested, therefore, that those questions that ask respondents about why particular changes will occur or, alternatively, why they will not occur, should be regarded as high priority questions, and hence every effort should be made to ensure their inclusion in the administration of the interview. The point can also be made that, to the extent that particular types of attributions emerge consistently in response to questions about both experienced and anticipated changes, then claims about there being an attribution style that is unique to the group, and that differentiates the group from other groups, are further validated.

6. The importance of evaluation questions. The above argument with respect to attributions data also applies to evaluative data. That is, given the potential cultural significance of evaluative data (for highlighting sources of resistance to, or support for, change), questions about the desirability or undesirability of anticipated changes should be regarded as high priority questions and hence presented consistently in relation to each of the changes that a respondent anticipates. As argued previously, the finding that particular attitudes — either highly positive or highly negative — are held by a small minority of organisation members only should not be dismissed as being insignificant. Such attitudes, particularly if held by senior members of the organisation, or influential persons in subcultures, may prove to be critical in either enabling or constraining the changes with which they are associated, should these be introduced.

Finally, it is worth noting that, in the current interview schedule, the above questions about the desirability or undesirability of anticipated changes can be seen as foreshadowing subsequent questions concerning respondents' beliefs about the ideal. In this sense, an individual's responses to each of these questions should provide some measure of the individual's consistency with respect to her/his reported beliefs and attitudes. For example, if the individual indicates that she/he considers an anticipated change towards more involvement of divisional workers in group problem-solving to be highly undesirable, then one might expect that the individual would subsequently argue against such a change when asked to comment on her/his beliefs about the ideal role for workers with respect to this activity.

12.6 The Other Context

The purpose of questioning in this section of the interview was to gain some insight into the extent of respondents' awareness of the role played by workers in other organisations and whether or not, in their experience, this role differed substantially from the role played by workers in their current organisation. Of course, as the reader will recall, the broader rationale for this focus on respondents' experience with respect to the other context was the argument, by some culture researchers (e.g., Louis, 1983; Wilkins & Ouchi, 1983), that an important condition for the development of highly cohesive and highly localised cultures may be the extent of the group's social isolation from other groups. Specifically, it has been proposed that, where a group has little knowledge of alternatives to its current experience, the emergent culture is likely to take the form of what Wilkins and Ouchi (1983) have called a clan culture; conversely, where a group has had significant exposure to alternatives which contradict its current experience, the emergent culture is likely to be more socially fragmented.

As indicated, the format of questioning which was followed in this part of the interview differed from that followed in the other sections in that only the initial open-ended questions were presented. These questions were not followed, as they were in the other sections, by the presentation of the closed questions, or prompts. As already indicated in the method section for Study 3 in Chapter 10, Studies 1 and 2 suggested that respondents would not have a particularly extensive knowledge of work in other organisations, whether other similar organisations or other organisations more generally. Specifically then, respondents were first of all asked whether or not they were aware of what it was that the workers in other organisations did. Where some awareness was indicated, information was then sought about the source of the respondent's knowledge, whether direct experience — that is, experience of having worked elsewhere — or indirect experience — in the form, for example, of: (i) knowledge acquired through professional or other work-related contacts; (ii) knowledge acquired through socialisation with people from other organisations (including the respondent's spouse and/or friends and acquaintances); or (iii) knowledge acquired via the media. These preliminary questions were then followed, where appropriate, by the two standard open-ended questions which asked respondents about whether or not they perceived any differences between their current organisation and their other[18] organisation, first of all, with respect to the main duties of workers (in this case, how workers went about performing their work), and secondly, with respect to the other activities in which workers were engaged.

The discussion in this section is presented in three main parts. First, we report the results of the analysis of the other context data, with the findings for the tooling division presented first, followed by the findings for the production division. The reader is reminded that, as for the analyses conducted previously, no distinction was made in the present analysis between responses to the two open-ended questions concerning, respectively, the main duties and other activities of workers. Again, the decision to aggregate the responses to these questions was made on the basis of inconsistencies that emerged in respondents' definitions of what constituted a main duty and what constituted an other activity. Second, we provide a summary of these findings, in particular, in terms of the key similarities and differences between the divisions that they revealed. And third, and finally, we discuss the

---

[18]In the event that a respondent had experience of more than one other organisation, she/he was asked to talk only about that organisation with which she/he was most familiar.

methodological implications of the findings and how other context data might usefully inform an understanding of the culture of work organisations.

12.6.1 *Results of the analysis of other context data*

The results of the analysis of the other context data are reported first for the tooling division and then for the production division.

Tooling division. As indicated in Table 12.3, there were six respondents from the tooling division (50% of the sample for this division) who indicated that they had no knowledge of what it was that the workers in other organisations did. These respondents included four supervisors (one senior supervisor and three first-line supervisors) and two wages employees (both with leading hand status). When prompted, five of these respondents attributed their lack of knowledge to their having either no work experience or very little work experience (which dated back many years) outside of their current organisation. The sixth respondent was somewhat unique, first of all because he was a relative newcomer to the tooling division (with only six years service) and, secondly, because he had, for many years prior to commencing his current job, operated his own "one-man" panel-beating business. This respondent indicated that, apart from his early apprenticeship training, he had no other experience in "a really big company".

The remaining six respondents from this division (50%) indicated that they had some knowledge of what it was that the workers in other organisations did. These respondents included two supervisors (one senior supervisor and one first-line supervisor) and four wages employees (including two leading hands and one shop steward). Three of these respondents indicated that they had direct experience of working in another organisation. In all cases, this experience involved work of a similar nature to that which the respondent currently performed. The remaining three respondents had knowledge of other organisations that was acquired through indirect experience. Specifically, all of these respondents had learned about other organisations from outsiders with whom they had some professional or work-related contact. For example, one respondent indicated that, in his prominent role in the governance of the Pattern Makers Association, he regularly attended meetings of this association and participated in visits to pattern shops in other organisations.

There was no difference between respondents who indicated no knowledge and respondents who indicated some knowledge, in terms of their length of service with the company. For the former, the mean length of service with the company was 27 years and for the latter, it was 24 years. However, among respondents who reported some knowledge, those with direct experience of working in another organisation tended to be shorter-serving employees than those whose knowledge had been acquired through indirect experience. For the former, the mean length of service with the company was 16 years and for the latter it was 33 years.

As shown in Table 12.3, of the six respondents who reported some knowledge, there was one who indicated that, in his experience, there was no difference between what workers did in his current organisation and what they did in other organisations with which he was familiar. The remaining five respondents mentioned a total of 14 differences (four respondents mentioned three differences each, and one respondent mentioned two differences) and these were subsequently categorised into the 12 difference categories shown in Table 12.3. As indicated, there was little consensus among these respondents in the differences that they reported. Specifically, 10 of the 12 difference categories were represented by only one respondent each, with the remaining two (namely Social Activities and Worker-Supervisor Communication) being represented by two respondents each. This finding is quite consistent with what one might expect given that each of these respondents was reporting experience (whether direct or indirect) which was associated with a different other context.

It is perhaps of more interest to note that some of the differences mentioned by these respondents were differences that one might associate with more general, possibly more observable characteristics of an organisation. For example, there were references to differences with respect to technological sophistication, production efficiency, the flexibility of work schedules, and the organisational climate (specifically, how "happy" workers were). The point should be made that this focus on general differences, rather than on differences more directly related to the role of workers (i.e., what workers do), was not unique to the data pertaining to the other context. As noted previously, this was a pattern of responding that emerged in responses to the open-ended questions about experienced changes (the past context), anticipated changes (the future context), and desired changes (the ideal context). As suggested previously, it may be that where respondents had difficulty answering these open-ended questions (perhaps because of difficulties in conceptualising the notion of the role of workers), they resorted to commenting upon differences/changes associated with more general, and perhaps more salient, characteristics of their work environment.

Given the broad rationale for the inclusion, in the present method, of questions about the other context, perhaps the most significant feature of the difference data for the tooling division is that they contained little evidence to suggest that the respondents concerned had significant knowledge (whether acquired through direct or indirect experience) of a more active role for workers. Of the 14 differences that were mentioned, there were perhaps three (21%) which might be interpreted as, at best, only suggestive of the possibility that the workers in respondents' other organisations might have a more active role than the workers in their current organisation. These differences included: (i) a reference by one respondent to there being a flatter hierarchy of authority in the other organisation and, as a result, closer communication between workers and their supervisors; (ii) a reference by a second respondent to workers in the other organisation being more humanely treated and trusted more; and (iii) a reference by a third respondent to workers in the other organisation having to be more flexible and multi-skilled. It should be noted that the single references to the three difference categories — Responsibility/Accountability, Information Meetings, and Safety Meetings — all involved negative comparisons. In other words, the workers in other organisations were reported to have less involvement in activities associated with each of these categories than the workers in the respondent's current organisation.

One possibility for the analysis of other context data that was suggested by the findings reported above was to attempt some classification of all of the differences that were reported in terms of whether they indicated a positive or a negative comparison. It may be that differences between groups in this regard — that is, in the extent to which groups draw consistently favourable, or consistently unfavourable, comparisons between themselves and other groups — are culturally significant. Of the 14 differences mentioned by respondents from the tooling division, eight (57%) could be classified as indicative of a positive comparison (in the sense that the other organisation was seen in a more positive light) and five (36%) could be classified as being indicative of a negative comparison (with the other organisation being seen in a more negative light). It should be noted that, in order to make some of these classifications, it was necessary to know about the respondent's more general evaluation — whether positive or negative — of the other organisation in question. This was the case, for example, for the difference indicated in the reference, by one respondent, to the workers in the other organisation being more flexible and multi-skilled. There was one difference out of 14 — a reference to the use of different materials, different equipment, *etc.* in the other organisation — which could not easily be classified as indicative of either a positive or a negative comparison. It should be pointed out here that these positive and negative evaluations were implied from the comparisons made by respondents; they were not the result of direct questions about what respondents liked or disliked.

Finally, an analysis of the other context data for common thematic content provided evidence of a perception, among some respondents from the tooling division, that differences between their current and other contexts, where these emerged, could be explained by organisational size. Specifically, there were four respondents from this division who shared the view that smaller organisations, by virtue of their size, provided workers with a qualitatively different (more positive) experience of work than larger organisations. For example, smaller organisations were able to support more social activities for workers than larger organisations; in smaller organisations, it was possible for there to be closer communication between workers and their supervisors; and in smaller organisations, workers had no option but to become multi-skilled and learn to do "everything that was available". It is perhaps worth making the point that this attempt to explain differences between organisational contexts in terms of organisational size (a variable which can be seen to be largely outside of the control of, say, operational management within an organisation) is consistent with the overall attribution style (of change being controlled by external forces) which appeared to prevail in the tooling division. We turn now to a consideration of the findings for the production division.

Production division. As indicated in Table 12.4, there were three respondents from the production division (16% of the sample for this division) who indicated that they had no knowledge of what it was that the workers in other organisations did. These respondents were all wages employees and included one female and two males. Two respondents attributed their lack of knowledge to their long years of service (in each case, more than 15 years) with the present company. The third respondent, who had only three years' service with the present company indicated that, prior to joining this company, he had only ever worked in a voluntary capacity. The implication was that he had no relevant experience elsewhere on which to base a comparison with his current experience.

There were 16 respondents from the production division (84% of the sample) who reported having some knowledge of what it was that the workers in other organisations did. These respondents included five supervisors (two senior supervisors and three first-line supervisors) and 11 wages employees. All of the former were males, while the latter included four females and seven males. In terms of the nature of their experience of other organisations, there were nine respondents who reported direct experience of having worked elsewhere and eight respondents who indicated that their knowledge of other organisations had been acquired through indirect experience[19]. For the former, their experience of work in other contexts was quite diverse. Some of these respondents reported past work experience that, as for their current experience, was also in manufacturing (e.g., reference was made to employment in a clothing factory and a table-tennis factory). For others, however, their past experience had been in quite different fields (with reference, e.g., to work as a furniture removalist, as a bricklayer in the construction industry, in a service station, in a laundry, in a school canteen, and in the army). This finding can be contrasted with the associated finding for the tooling division (whereby respondents' past work experiences tended to involve work that was similar to, rather than different from, that which they currently performed). The difference between the two divisions in this regard can probably be accounted for by differences in the occupational status of employees from each. All of the respondents from the tooling division were qualified tradesmen, while the majority of respondents from the production division required no formal qualifications for the work that they performed.

The eight respondents from the production division who indicated that their knowledge of other organisations had been acquired through indirect experience included: (i) six respondents who had friends and/or a spouse who worked elsewhere; (ii) one respondent who had been exposed to information about other organisations (specifically, examples of "excellent" companies) in the context of management training that he had received in his current organisation; and (iii) one respondent who had been required to visit other organisations as part of his current work duties, and who had also learned about other organisations through reading about them.

As for the tooling division, the 'no knowledge' and 'some knowledge' respondents from the production division did not differ in terms of their length of service with the company.

---

[19]One respondent indicated that he had knowledge of other organisations acquired through both direct and indirect experience. Hence, the number of respondents in these two groups totalled 17 and not 16.

For the production division, the mean length of service with the company for respondents in both of these groups was 13 years. However, and again as for the tooling division, this demographic did discriminate among respondents from the production division who reported some knowledge of other organisations. Respondents from this group who had direct experience of other organisations were, on average, shorter-serving employees than respondents whose experience of other organisations had been acquired indirectly. For the former, the mean length of service with the company was nine years, and for the latter it was 16 years.

As indicated in Table 12.4, of the 16 respondents from the production division who reported some knowledge of other organisations, there were four who indicated that there was no difference between their current and their other organisation, in terms of what it was that workers did (i.e., the role of workers). It is interesting to consider briefly the various grounds upon which these respondents based their evaluations of sameness. One respondent judged his current and other organisation to be similar on the grounds that the workers in both were engaged in housekeeping and social activities. A second respondent based his evaluation on his view that "...all large organisations are the same [in that] people on the bottom rung just get so frustrated". The third and fourth respondents both made reference to the subordinate role played by workers in their current and other organisation. In their own words, and with reference specifically to their other organisation:

> ...you still had someone you had to answer to, and be responsible to, and so really, you know, business is business wherever you are. (wages employee)
>
> It was just the same. You never saw the bosses. There was a leading hand, and they told you what to do, and showed you what to do... You wasn't involved in nothing, only your job. (wages employee)

These responses are of interest primarily because of the insights that they offer into how respondents see their current organisation. What emerges quite clearly in all of the above responses is a perception that the role of the workers in the production division is passive rather than active.

At this point, it should be noted that, of the 12 respondents represented in the difference data reported in Table 12.4, there were two who also mentioned similarities between their current and their other organisation. Interestingly, the above theme concerning the subordinate role of workers was also evident in these data. In one case, the respondent judged his current and other organisation to be similar on the grounds that, at the social functions held by each, one could always observe a clear separation between management and workers, such that they sat in different places and interacted very little with one another. The other respondent (a senior supervisor) argued that it was a feature of the Australian work culture in general for workers to feel frustrated by managers who consistently failed to acknowledge their worth to the organisation. As this respondent saw it, a commonplace attitude of workers towards management was that "[Management] are a bunch of bloody arseholes. They don't listen to us, they don't talk to us". The respondent went on to advocate a general change in management style whereby managers should become "less confronting and more working with [workers] as a team".

As indicated, there were 12 respondents from the production division who mentioned one or more differences between their current and their other organisation. In all, these respondents mentioned a total of 34 differences. The majority mentioned between one and three differences each, with the maximum number of differences mentioned by a single respondent (in this case, a supervisor) being seven. These differences were subsequently categorised into the thirteen difference categories shown in Table 12.4[20]. As for the tooling division, there was not a lot of consensus among respondents from the production division about the differences that they mentioned. Eleven of the 13 difference categories were represented by no more than three respondents each. The remaining two categories — Individual-Skills/Attitudes/Behaviours and Social Activities — were represented by five and six respondents, respectively. Again, this finding is hardly surprising given that the comparison made by each of the respondents concerned was in relation to a different other context.

It was also the case, as for the tooling division, that some of the differences that were mentioned were differences of a more general nature, rather than differences one might expect would have a direct bearing on the role played by the workers in an organisation. For example, there were references to differences with respect to workload (specifically, the "pressure of production"), with respect to various conditions of work including safety, pay and other benefits, and with respect to organisational recruitment practices. The explanation offered previously in relation to this particular feature of the present data set obviously also applies here.

In terms of differences suggesting knowledge (whether acquired through direct or indirect experience) of a more active role for workers, the findings for the production division were, again, similar to those for the tooling division. Of the 34 differences that were mentioned by respondents from this division, there were perhaps seven (21%) that could be classified in this way. These included: (i) a reference by two respondents to the workers in their other organisation having more responsibility and autonomy in relation to the work which they performed; (ii) a reference by two respondents to there being more training for the workers in their other organisation; (iii) a reference by one respondent to there being more positive worker-supervisor communication in his other organisation, such that "if [workers] had an idea, it had to be listened to — you couldn't sweep it under the carpet"; (iv) a reference by one respondent to there being more teamwork in his other organisation such that "there was a lot more interaction [between workers] and there was a lot more helping each other and

---

[20]The numbers in each of the difference categories shown in Table 12.4 are numbers of respondents, rather than numbers of differences. Given that some respondents mentioned more than one difference in a given difference category, the total number of differences mentioned (i.e., 34) is more than the sum of the tabled differences (i.e., 31).

trying to solve problems quickly and easily..."; and (v) a reference by one respondent to workers in her other organisation attending more information meetings.

The same classification of differences, in terms of whether they indicated a positive or negative comparison, was attempted for the production division as for the tooling division. Of the 34 differences mentioned by respondents from the production division, 23 (68%) could be classified as indicative of a positive comparison (in the sense that the other organisation was seen in a more positive light than the current organisation) and nine (26%) could be classified as indicative of a negative comparison (with the other organisation being seen in a more negative light than the current organisation). The remaining two differences could not easily be classified as being indicative of either a positive or a negative comparison. On the basis of these findings, there does appear to be a tendency among respondents from the production division to see their own organisation in a less favourable light than other organisations with which they are familiar. Of course, the question arises as to what such a tendency might signify more generally about the nature of the group in which it emerges. Perhaps it is indicative of an overall low level of job satisfaction among the members of the group? Alternatively, perhaps it is simply a manifestation of the more general human tendency to believe that the 'grass is always greener on the other side'?

It is perhaps worth mentioning here that the above classification of responses (as opposed to respondents) may exaggerate the picture somewhat. This is because a given respondent may judge her/his other organisation to be very similar, overall, to her/his current organisation, but may then go on to mention several specific, but possibly quite incidental positive (or for that matter negative) characteristics of the other organisation. The point is that, if one were to simply classify each respondent as having made either a favourable, or an unfavourable, judgement about her/his current organisation in relation to some other organisation, then one might get a more accurate picture of the extent to which the group displays a tendency towards either positive or negative comparisons with other groups. In order to determine which of these approaches to the presentation of data of this kind is likely to produce the most accurate account of an organisation's culture, it would be necessary to conduct a number of studies similar to the present study, in a range of other types of organisations.

Finally, as for the tooling division, the other context data for the production division were analysed for common thematic content. Nothing of particular interest with respect to culture was revealed by this analysis.

12.6.2 *The other context: Summary of key findings in terms of key divisional differences*

The above analysis of other context data revealed a number of similarities and differences between the two divisions in terms of respondents' exposure to other organisational contexts and their experience of the role of workers in other organisations. A summary of these similarities and differences is provided below.

1. Extent of experience of other organisational contexts. There was evidence to suggest that, as a group, the respondents from the tooling division had more limited, and narrower, direct experience of other organisational contexts than their counterparts from the production division. A similar pattern emerged in the findings for respondents whose knowledge of other organisations was based on indirect, rather than direct, experience.

It was suggested that the difference between the two divisions, in terms of the variability of respondents' experience of other organisations (whether direct or indirect), was probably a reflection of differences in the occupational status of respondents from each division. Given that respondents from the tooling division were all qualified tradesmen, one might expect that any experience of other organisational contexts which they had acquired either in the course of, or on becoming qualified, would be in areas similar to that in which they currently worked. In the same way it might be argued that, given that the majority of respondents from the production division lacked any formal work qualifications, they would be more likely, as a group, to have more varied employment experience.

2. Influence of respondent demographics. Given the relatively small number of respondents in the sample for each division, it is difficult to say anything conclusive about the extent to which the above findings might reflect differences in respondent demographics. Nevertheless, it is perhaps still worth commenting on some trends which emerged in this regard. For example, with respect to seniority, it is worth noting that four of the six supervisors from the tooling division indicated that they had no knowledge of what it was that workers in other organisations did. In contrast, all of the supervisors from the production division reported some knowledge. The point can be made that, such a trend, if it were to emerge in a larger population (whose findings could be subjected to statistical analysis), could have important implications for understanding organisational (divisional) culture. Specifically, one might predict the development of a more bounded culture in an organisation in which the majority of supervisory staff (whom one can argue are typically in positions of some power and influence) claim no knowledge of what Wilkins and Ouchi (1983, p. 473) have referred to as "institutional alternatives", than in an organisation in which the majority of supervisory staff report some knowledge of such alternatives.

As noted, respondents' length of service with the company failed to discriminate between the no knowledge and some knowledge groups for each division. While most of the respondents in the no knowledge group were, as one might expect, longer serving employees, there was one respondent in each of these groups who was a shorter serving employee. Both of these respondents reported that, while they had had past experience of working elsewhere, this experience had been such that it could not meaningfully be compared with their current experience. Length of service with the company did, however, discriminate among the some knowledge groups for both divisions. Specifically, for both divisions, respondents whose knowledge of other organisations had been acquired through direct experience (i.e., through having worked elsewhere) had, on average, shorter service with the company than respondents whose knowledge of other organisations had been acquired through indirect experience (i.e., through various work-related contacts and professional affiliations, through socialisation with friends and/or a spouse working elsewhere, and via the media). This finding is hardly surprising given that, to the extent that one has worked elsewhere prior to joining one's current organisation, there is likely to be less time spent in one's current organisation.

Finally, for the production division (where the sample included male and female respondents), there was no indication of a trend suggesting that the above findings might, in some way, be related to gender differences.

3. Criteria for evaluating sameness. Among the some knowledge groups for both divisions, there was a minority of respondents only — one out of six from the tooling division (17%), and four out of 16 from the production division (25%) — who reported no difference between their current and their other organisation. For the production division, an analysis of the criteria upon which these respondents made their evaluations of sameness provided some interesting insights into respondents' perceptions of their current organisation. In particular, there was evidence of a perception that the role of workers in the production division was predominantly passive and that there existed, in the division, a clear subordinate-superior relationship between workers and their supervisors.

4. Content of difference data. For both divisions, there was a majority of respondents in the some knowledge group who made reference to one or more differences between their current and their other organisation. As indicated, in neither division was there much consensus among these respondents about the differences they mentioned. The point was made that this finding was consistent with what one might expect given that the other contexts to which respondents were referring were, in all cases, different (i.e., no two respondents reported having had experience in the same other organisation).

As indicated, for both divisions, the difference data included a number of references to differences of a more general nature, such as, differences with respect to technological sophistication, production efficiency, workload, and various conditions of work. That the focus in these data was not (as intended) solely upon differences likely to have a direct bearing on the role of divisional workers was perhaps indicative of some difficulty, among respondents from both divisions, in conceptualising the notion of the role of workers.

It was also the case that the difference data, for both divisions, contained few references to differences that might be indicative of a more active role for workers. In other words, there was little evidence to suggest that, through their experience of other organisations (whether acquired directly or indirectly), the respondents from either division had gained much knowledge about a more active role for workers. In this sense, it might be concluded that the other context data that were generated by this study would, if anything, serve to confirm rather than disconfirm, respondents' existing views about the role of workers in an organisation.

5. Difference data as reflective of a positive or negative comparison. For both divisions, the difference data were analysed further to determine whether or not there were any trends in how respondents regarded their other organisation — whether more favourably, or alternatively more unfavourably, than their current organisation. For both divisions, a majority of the differences mentioned could be classified as indicative of a positive rather than a negative comparison (in the sense that the other organisation appeared to be considered in a more positive light than the current organisation). Two possible explanations were offered for this finding. On the one hand, it was argued that consistently positive comparisons with other organisations could be indicative of low job satisfaction with one's current organisation. On the other hand, it was suggested that such a finding may simply be a manifestation of the more general human tendency to believe that the grass is always greener on the other side.

6. Thematic content of other context data. As indicated, for both divisions, the other context data were analysed for common thematic content. Apart from some evidence in the tooling division data of a perception that, where differences between one's current and other organisations emerged, these could be explained largely by differences in organisational size, this analysis revealed little of interest. Again, this finding is not surprising given that, in all cases, the other contexts to which respondents referred were different.

12.6.3 *The other context: Methodological issues*

Having summarised the key findings of the above analysis of other context data, we turn now to a consideration of some of the methodological issues that were raised by this analysis. Of particular interest here is the extent to which other context data can contribute to our understanding of culture in work organisations. There is also the question of the adequacy of the present method for providing insights into the nature and extent of respondents' awareness of institutional alternatives. Specifically, what aspects of the present method should be retained and what revisions should be made? In the summary points that follow, each of these issues receives some attention.

1. Isolation from other groups is important. The findings above provided some support for the argument, in the literature, that a group's social isolation from other groups may be an important condition for the development of highly cohesive and highly localised cultures. As indicated, there was evidence to suggest that, as a group, respondents from the tooling division had more limited, and narrower, experience of other organisational contexts than their counterparts from the production division. This finding is not inconsistent with the overall assessment of the tooling division as supporting a somewhat more homogeneous, and definable, culture than the production division (this assessment being made on the basis of evidence from the present study, as well as impressionistic data gathered by the first author over several years in her role as a 'researcher participant' in each division). It would appear, therefore, that there is some empirical support for the inclusion, in the present study, of a focus on the other context of respondents' experience.

Of course, in order to more convincingly demonstrate the value of other context data, one would require a more extreme comparison — in terms of the degree of exposure of group members to institutional alternatives (particularly those which contradict members' current social reality) — than that offered by the two divisions in the present study. The reader is reminded that, even though respondents from the tooling division appeared to have been somewhat more socially isolated than their counterparts from the production division, in neither division was there much evidence of exposure to significantly different cultural alternatives. In fact, the point was made that, if anything, respondents' experience of other organisational contexts would have served to confirm, rather than disconfirm, existing views (in this case, about the role of workers in an organisation).

2. Importance of occupational status. As indicated, the above analysis of other context data provided some evidence to suggest that the occupational status of group members (in this case, the distinction was between members with trade qualifications and those with no formal work qualifications) may influence the nature of their exposure to other organisational contexts. While this finding is hardly surprising (and one might be criticised for stating the obvious), it nevertheless has important implications for understanding the role of other context experience in shaping the group's culture. In particular, one should be alert to the possibility that group members' experience of other organisational contexts may be acting primarily to reinforce occupational subcultures currently represented in the group.

3. Nature of other organisations is important. A third point, which is related to the second point above, is that, where a respondent indicates some knowledge (whether acquired directly or indirectly) of other organisations, one should go on to ask about the specific nature of those other organisations — whether they are in the same business as the respondent's current organisation, or whether they are different types of organisations altogether. Information of this kind may give some insight into the relevance of a respondent's experience of other organisations to her/his attitudes to, and evaluation of, her/his current organisation. For example, in the context of the present study, experience of work in another car manufacturing company (and, in particular, contradictory experience) would no doubt constitute more significant other experience (in terms of its influence on the current culture) than experience of, say, work as a bricklayer or as a furniture removalist.

4. Sameness criteria. As indicated above, some interesting insights into respondents' perceptions of their current organisation were provided by the analysis of the criteria upon which respondents judged their current and their other organisation to be similar. The implication of this finding for the analysis of other context data, in general, is that one should focus not just on the differences which respondents mention, but also on the similarities. The point can be made here that similar experiences in other organisations might serve to limit a respondent's options if asked about an 'ideal' with respect to their present organisation. Such a respondent might be more inclined to indicate that nothing much can be done to change an organisation because all organisations tend to be the same (e.g., with respect to relations between management and workers).

5. Favourable versus unfavourable comparisons. The analysis of other context data might also usefully include some assessment of the extent to which respondents consistently make either favourable or unfavourable comparisons between their current organisation and other organisations about which they have some knowledge. The value of information of this kind is that it could highlight differences between groups in terms of the cultures they support. However, as suggested by the results reported above, there is also a possibility that such information may constitute evidence of more generally held stereotypic views (in this case, the view that the grass is always greener on the other side). Given this possibility, one must be cautious about making claims, on the basis of information of this kind, to have tapped a cultural phenomenon that is unique to the group being investigated. Some clarification of this issue might be obtained by asking for specific examples of differences and how these impacted on the organisation and its workforce. While in the present data, positive and negative comparisons were assumed from the ways in which respondents described these differences, it might be useful in further studies to ask respondents directly about their attitude to their other organisation and, in particular, how they feel about it. It might even be possible to gauge the nature of these comparisons — whether more or less positive or negative — with respect to specific aspects of the respondent's current and other organisation.

6. Respondents versus responses? Finally, the results of the above analysis of other context data raised the question again as to whether, in the present study, it would have been better to analyse respondents (in terms of each individual's overall pattern of responding), rather than responses (to specific interview questions). As indicated, the latter approach can lead to some distortion in the representation of respondents' experience that is offered. Of course, this problem will be quite serious where there are many responses that represent the views of a minority of respondents only. Fortunately, this was not the case for the other context data that were generated by the present study. As indicated above, for both divisions, most of the respondents who mentioned differences between their current and their other organisation, mentioned between one and three differences each. In other words, it was not the case that most of the differences that were mentioned were from one or two respondents only. However, an important methodological question here is how to collect and accurately present data from individuals who might differ in the number of responses (including none) given in answer to a question.

12.7 The Ideal Context

Questioning in this section of the interview was designed to provide some insight into respondents' views about the ideal role for workers, that is, what it is that workers in an organisation, such as the respondent's current organisation, ideally should do. As indicated in the introduction to this study, findings from Study 2, along with arguments in the litera-ture concerning the prescriptive function served by cultural beliefs and assumptions (Sackmann, 1991; Smircich, 1983), provided the rationale for the inclusion, in the present method, of questions about the ideal. The possibility was suggested that responses to these questions might be expected to be more culture bound in organisations that support deeply embedded cultures than in organisations whose cultures are less entrenched.

The specific format of questioning which was followed in relation to the ideal context was, as indicated previously, the same as that followed in relation to the first three contex-tual domains, namely, the present context, the past context, and the anticipated future context. Respondents were first of all presented with two open-ended questions that asked about whether or not, if the respondent were in charge of an organisation such as her/his current organisation, there would be anything that the respondent would change about either the main duties of workers (i.e., their primary task) or the other activities in which workers were engaged. Respondents were then presented with the same prompt questions as previously. Again, where necessary, and in order to facilitate responding to the questions in this section, respondents were reminded of what they had said in their responses to these same questions (both the open-ended and the prompt questions) asked previously in rela-tion to the present context. By way of illustration (in this case in relation to a prompt ques-tion), an example of the kind of assistance that was given in this regard was: "You have said that, at the present time, there is no involvement of the workers in your division in safety meetings, apart from the occasional safety talk given by the section supervisor. If you were in charge of this division, would you want to make any changes to that, or would you be happy with the way it is?"

With respect to the format for reporting results in this section, it will be seen that, as previously for the past and future context data, the results of the analysis of open question data pertaining to the ideal context are reported first. This is followed by a discussion of the discrepancy between the spontaneous and prompted responses, and the presentation of the initial findings from the analysis of the prompt data. A summary of the key findings for the ideal context is then provided. In this summary, particular attention is given to similarities and differences between the divisions and what these might mean in terms of understanding the culture of each division. Following this, consideration is given to the question of whether or not a focus on the ideal context can contribute anything of value to an understanding of organisational culture. The section concludes with a discussion of some of the main meth-odological issues which arose in the course of conducting the analysis of ideal context data and which have implications for how the present method might subsequently be revised.

12.7.1 *Findings for the open questions*

The results of the analysis of the ideal context data elicited in response to the initial open-ended questions are reported first for the tooling division and then for the production division.

Tooling division. As shown in Table 12.3, in response to the initial open-ended question(s)[21], there were four respondents from the tooling division (33% of the sample for this division) who indicated that, in their opinion, there should be no change in what it was that the workers in their division did (either with respect to their main duties, or with respect to any other activities in which they were engaged). These respondents included three first-line supervisors and one wages employee (with leading hand status). All four respondents were longer serving employees (whose length of service with the company ranged from 25 years to 33 years).

The remaining eight respondents from the tooling division (67% of the sample) each advocated some change with respect to what it was that the workers in their division did (in terms of their main duties and/or their other activities). These respondents included three supervisors (one first-line supervisor and two senior supervisors) and five wages employees (including three leading hands and one shop steward). Four of these respondents were longer-serving employees (with between 17 and 40 years' service with the company) and two were shorter-serving employees (each with six years' service with the company).

In all, the eight change respondents advocated 20 specific changes[22]. The maximum number of changes advocated by a single respondent was four, and the minimum number was one (mean = 2.5 changes per respondent; median = 2.5 changes). As shown in Table 12.3, these changes were represented by 11 activity categories. Table 12.3 also shows that there was little consensus among respondents about the changes they advocated. There were seven activity categories (out of eleven) for which changes were mentioned by a single respondent only. Moreover, the maximum number of respondents advocating change with respect to a given activity category was only three (25% of the sample for this division and 38% of change respondents). This was the case for Responsibility/ Accountability and Social Activities. With respect to the former, all three respondents advocated some form of increased responsibility for the workers in their division. Specifically, one respondent advocated more involvement of divisional workers in "running the shop" and also suggested that there were some workers who could be involved in costing jobs. A second respondent argued that workers should be encouraged to follow a job through "from the beginning right to the end" and, in the process, learn how to solve their own problems rather than "having to be told what to do". And a third respondent

---

[21] In some cases, respondents were presented with two open-ended questions, the first asking about desirable changes with respect to the main duties (i.e., the primary task) of divisional workers and the second asking about desirable changes with respect to the other activities in which workers were engaged. In other cases, these two questions were combined into one so that respondents were simply asked about desirable changes with respect to any aspect of what workers did (whether in relation to their main duties or their other activities).

[22] As previously, the numbers shown for each category represent numbers of respondents and not numbers of responses (i.e., changes). Since some respondents advocated more than one change within a given category, the total number of changes advocated (i.e., 20) is more than the sum of the tabled changes (i.e., 17).

argued that workers "should be involved in their own shop as if it was their own home". This included having the power to change things (presumably associated with methods of work) that the worker did not like, and which he considered could be made more "practical". All three of these respondents were wages employees (with one being a shop steward and two being leading hands).

The three respondents who advocated some change with respect to social activities all argued for more involvement of divisional workers in such activities. These respondents included one wages employee (a leading hand) and two supervisors (one first-line supervisor and one senior supervisor). Specifically, one respondent argued that the tooling division should follow the example of the organisation in which his son worked, whereby, at the end of each week, employees got together for "drinks and nibbles and [a] yarn". This practice, it was argued, would serve to "make people happy, make them feel as though they are wanted". In a similar vein, a second respondent argued that there should be more socialisation of divisional members with one another (through informal gatherings as well as through clubs, such as sporting clubs) and suggested further that such a change could help to avoid "this 'them and us' business" between workers and their supervisors. And a third respondent, a supervisor, argued for the introduction of what he called "beer and bickie sessions" to be held "at least once a month". However, as illustrated in the following excerpt from the interview, the underlying purpose of these sessions, as the respondent saw it, was for the supervisor to surreptitiously learn about what workers really thought — that is, to learn about the things of real importance to workers, which workers would be likely to talk about with one another, but which they typically would not discuss in the presence of their supervisors:

> ...and usually after a few beers, they tell you what they think. And [you should] listen to that. *Interviewer:* So this would not be just social, but it would be a sort of feedback session about work? *Respondent:* Well, that is for you and me to know, that it would be feedback. But as you probably know, you go to any of those gatherings, the first beer is 'Ha, Ha', the second beer is 'How are you going, mate?', and the third beer they start to talk about things that they would never dare to tell you. (first-line supervisor)

This excerpt is of some interest, and has therefore been given some attention, because it provides a nice illustration of the way in which a respondent's elaborations and qualifications — in this case, in relation to the argument that there should be more involvement of divisional workers in social activities — can provide deeper level insights into how the respondent views her/his world. We learn, in this case, that the respondent's view of workers is such that, in order to know what workers really think, one must create a situation in which workers can, in a sense, be 'tricked' into saying things that, normally, "they would never dare to tell you". No mention is made by this respondent of the value of developing a climate of trust in which workers feel quite at ease to express their real concerns.

Perhaps the most noteworthy finding associated with the present analysis is that, despite the fact that, at this point in the interview, respondents had considerable exposure to prompt questions (asked in relation to the present context, the past context, and the anticipated future context), which might be expected to cue them to possible other activities in which workers might engage, the number of changes which respondents advocated spontaneously, in response to the open-ended questions about the ideal context, was relatively few. As above, there were four respondents who advocated no changes, and eight respondents who advocated, on average, 2.5 changes each. Moreover, it is interesting to note that only four (out of ten) prompted activity categories were represented by these changes. In other words, while there was reasonable scope for respondents to describe an ideal role for workers that differed from their current role — and indeed, if social desirability effects had been operating, one might have predicted such an outcome — this did not occur. It would appear, therefore, that there is some support for the conclusion that, as a group, respondents from the tooling division had a relatively bounded view of what it is that the workers in their division ideally should do.

While there was little evidence of social desirability responding in the present data, this might be an issue for careful consideration when dealing with more senior organisation members who might feel obliged to describe an ideal that is consistent with prevailing organisational rhetoric. For example, managers who are concerned about their responses being reported to their superiors might be inclined to argue that the present situation is close to the ideal, if they believe that this is the opinion of those in senior management. In cases such as this, anonymity of responding for a sample of managers interviewed by an outside consultant might reveal an ideal that is significantly different from the present situation.

Finally, in analysing the present data set, consideration was given to the extent to which the changes that were advocated could be classified as indicative of a more active role for workers. Of the 20 changes that were spontaneously mentioned by respondents from the tooling division, there were 11 (55%) that could be classified in this way. These included:

(1) Six references (by three respondents) to the desirability of some form of increased responsibility for divisional workers (these changes have been described above);
(2) One reference to the need for improved divisional communications whereby there would be more opportunities (meetings) for workers to "air their views";
(3) One reference to the desirability of introducing a profit-sharing scheme for workers;
(4) One reference to the desirability of more involvement of workers in planning related to the design of their jobs;
(5) One reference to the desirability of involving workers in group problem-solving with other divisional personnel (such as planners); and
(6) One reference to the need for workers to keep records of problem-solving decisions.

These changes were mentioned by five respondents in all (42% of the sample for this division, and 63% of the change respondents from this division), including four wages employees (one who was a shop steward and two with leading hand status) and one supervisor. Two of the wages employees were shorter serving employees, each with only six years' service with the company.

It should be noted that the argument above, concerning the potentially valuable insights that can be gained from an analysis of respondents' elaborations on, and qualifications of their responses, also applies here. This can be illustrated with reference to the specific changes described in points (5) and (6) above which advocated, respectively, more involvement of divisional workers in group problem-solving and more involvement of divisional workers in record-keeping. Both of these changes were advocated by the same respondent, namely the supervisor referred to above (and incidentally, the same supervisor whose data have been quoted in some detail above). It was clear from an analysis of the elaborations and qualifications associated with this respondent's initial reference to each of these changes that there were two key purposes which the changes were intended to serve, namely, quality control and cost control. Nowhere in these data was there any reference to the potential motivational function that might be served by such changes.

Thus, even though the specific changes proposed by this respondent might be classified as indicative of a more active role for workers, there was no evidence to suggest that this was consistent with what McGregor (1960) has described as a Theory Y view of workers. In fact, if one considers this respondent's interview as a whole, the impression gained is of a supervisor who is strongly Theory X in his views about workers. For example, one finds evidence of a belief that workers are motivated primarily by money (indicated in the perception that workers would not attend meetings, training courses, *etc.* that were held after hours, unless paid to do so); there was evidence of support for a rigid hierarchy of authority whereby workers were expected to always seek help from their immediate superior (typically a leading hand) and not from a fellow worker; and there was evidence of a belief that problems associated with quality and efficiency were best solved through increased supervisory control. On the basis of data such as these, one can again ask the question of whether or not, in the present study, the unit of analysis should have been the respondent (and her/his entire profile of responding), rather than the response.

The findings for this respondent can be contrasted with those for the other four change respondents who could be classified as advocating a more active role for divisional workers (with respect to one, or more, of the activities in which workers engaged). All of these respondents conveyed the impression of having some sense of the human resources implications of the change they advocated. For example, reference was variously made to:

(1) The increased loyalty and sense of belonging that would result from giving workers more responsibility (e.g., by involving them in quoting on jobs);

(2) The value of consulting workers on the shop floor because of their proximity to, and by implication their superior knowledge of, the job (and problems associated with the job); and

(3) The desirability of a "people person" approach, one characteristic of which was to involve workers "in their own shop as if it was their own home".

One possible methodological implication of these contrasting findings is that, in any future administration of the present interview schedule, it may be useful to seek information about why respondents see the change(s) they advocate as desirable. We turn now to a consideration of the open question data pertaining to the ideal context for the production division.

Production division. As indicated in Table 12.4, there were three respondents from the production division (16% of the sample for this division) who spontaneously expressed the view that there should be no change in what it was that the workers in their division did (either with respect to their main duties, or with respect to other activities in which they were engaged). All of these respondents were wages employees, with varying tenure (five, eight, and 19 years of service with the company, respectively).

The remaining 16 respondents from this division (84% of the sample) each advocated some change in what it was that the workers in their division did. These respondents included the five supervisory staff from this sample and the remaining 11 wages employees. Length of service with the company, for this group, was highly variable and ranged from three years to 30 years. In all, 49 specific changes were advocated by these 16 respondents. Most of these respondents advocated between one and three changes each, with the maximum number of changes advocated by a single respondent being eight (mean = 3.1 changes per respondent; median = 3 changes). As indicated in Table 12.4, these changes were represented by 14 activity categories[23]. In general, and as for the tooling division, there was little agreement among respondents from the production division about the changes they advocated. There were 10 activity categories (out of 14) for which changes were mentioned by no more than four respondents (i.e., by no more than 21% of the entire sample for this division or 25% of the change respondents).

As shown in Table 12.4, however, there was one activity category that was relatively well represented (in terms of the number of respondents advocating change within that category). This was Planning Meetings, with nine respondents in all (47% of the entire sample for the division, and 56% of the change respondents) arguing for more involvement of the workers in their division in some form of planning. These respondents included the five supervisory staff in the sample and four wages employees. Specifically, seven respondents made reference to the desirability of workers having a role with respect to the planning

---

[23] As indicated in the previous footnote, the sum of the tabled changes (in this case 46) is less than the total number of changes mentioned (in this case 49) because some respondents mentioned more than one change within a given activity category.

(design) of their own job(s) and/or the general layout of work in the plant as a whole. The following excerpts are illustrative of the comments made by this group:

> I think [I would get workers involved] in the planning of areas... I think that the best people that know how to plan a job are the people on the job. They know the easiest way they can get that job done... well most of the smart ones [do] anyway. (wages employee)
>
> [Workers] should be involved in the process planning... See everything runs on a process, what they call a process planning sheet. The engineers say 'It's got to be done this way' but they haven't tried it... They say 'Oh, we've got to do it this way, this way, this step, this step'. When you come and build it, it won't go together because they haven't tried it on the shop floor. (wages employee)
>
> There's a real need for operators to get involved in the way they process their product. I mean, they know best how to produce it, and some of those guys out there have had a lot of experience doing the types of work they're doing, but we tend not to find the time to draw that out of them... the way that they actually get around to building the part, they're the people out there that should be [doing it]. (senior supervisor)
>
> I would say 'Right, [we're] going to have a new concept. This Saturday, I'm bringing you all in on overtime [and] what we're going to do is we're going to completely strip the area out. What I want you to do is... here's the job we've got to do, figure out the best way we can do it... We've got to run at 350 a day. Do you think that moving the truck in here, or doing this here, is going to be dangerous?' ... [the work layout] has to be user friendly. They're the users — it's got to be friendly to them. (first-line supervisor)

The reader will note that a theme which is articulated more or less explicitly in each of the above excerpts is that, because of their 'hands-on' knowledge and experience of production tasks, shop floor workers are thought to be in a better position than many other divisional personnel to advise on decisions about job design and plant layout.

In addition to the above, there was one respondent (a first-line supervisor) who argued that workers should have some input into planning decisions about where they would work. In this respondent's own words:

> I think I would like to find out from the people what areas they would really like to work in. I don't think that happens a lot at the moment. I feel we've got a lot of people here who work in areas that they're not really suited to, for whatever reason. That would be one thing that I'd try... [to] find out exactly what they would like to do. Obviously, we've still got to build motor vehicles where you can't just shift everybody around. That would be something I'd have in the back of my mind... to try and get people in areas where they are happy to work. (first-line supervisor)

And finally, there was one respondent (also a first-line supervisor) who argued in favour of shop floor workers becoming involved in planning of a more strategic nature. The respondent cited the example of SPC, an Australian fruit processing company that used a collaborative approach to decision-making to help it survive a major financial crisis that it faced in the early 1990s. One important outcome of this company's approach was that all company personnel agreed to a four-day working week, thereby significantly reducing the company's expenditure on wages and salaries. It is worth commenting briefly on the context in which this particular change was advocated. When the respondent was first asked about whether or not, if he was in charge, he would make any changes to the main duties of the workers in his division, he replied by saying that, by way of a short-term solution to what he saw as the division's lack of competitiveness, he would de-unionise the plant and then he would employ all ethnic labour. In his own words:

> I will be quite honest with you. If I was a manager on the short-term, looking at it ... I would get myself right out of the vehicle industry and the union situation as it is at the moment... because by tying them up to a vehicle award, I am not competing with other production industries... then I would employ the place — and I will be quite honest with you — with Chinese or Vietnamese, or something like that. (first-line supervisor)

The respondent then proceeded to elaborate on what he described as his "other option" for dealing with the division's lack of competitiveness, namely, the change described above whereby divisional workers would have a role in strategic planning.

The important point illustrated by the above data is that one's interpretation of any given response, when it is analysed in isolation from the context in which it was made, can be quite different from one's interpretation of that same response, when analysed within the context in which it was made. The question again arises as to whether or not, in the present study, it would have been better to have treated respondents, rather than responses, as the primary unit of analysis. Such an approach could potentially provide a more coherent picture of each individual respondent in terms of what it is that she/he values and considers important. Of course, should such an approach be adopted, it would still be the case, as with the current approach, that qualitative data (in the form of elaborations on, and qualifications of, responses) would be critical to one's evolving understanding of the individual. There is an assumption in this approach that individuals will be consistent in their views, but this might not always be the case. While it might be possible to resolve apparent inconsistencies within individuals by questioning their responses, asking for examples, and talking to them about the contrary opinions they have expressed, it is also possible that some individuals may simply not have a consistent position on the topics about which they are questioned.

As shown in Table 12.4, after planning meetings, the next best represented activity categories were Job Rotation, Information Meetings, and Attend Training. Each of these categories was represented by five respondents (26% of the entire sample for this division, or 31% of the change respondents for this division). With respect to job rotation, the five respondents concerned — all wages employees — shared the view that there should be more job rotation for divisional workers. In each case, there was some reference to the quality of work life implications of such a change. In particular, it was felt that job rotation would serve to alleviate employee boredom. It was also suggested that job rotation could make for more friendly relations between workers, since it would alleviate the frustration that workers currently experienced — and which they inevitably took out on one another — as a result of being "stuck on the same job". Reference was also made to the implications of job rotation for improved work quality (the argument being that the longer one spent on the same job, the more likely it was that mistakes would go unnoticed), as well as for improved safety (i.e., fewer accidents).

In the case of information meetings, there were four respondents — all wages employees — who shared the view that workers should be better informed than they currently were. Two of these respondents made reference to the need for workers to have more specific job-related information (pertaining, e.g., to problems with parts, job design specifications, and quality criteria). One respondent made a general reference to the desirability of having more regular state of the nation meetings, and one respondent emphasised the importance of information meetings for keeping rumours in check. The fifth respondent — a senior supervisor — had a somewhat different perspective, in that he was concerned with the flow of information upwards, rather than downwards. This respondent argued that management should seek more information from workers — "draw on [workers'] experience" — about problems which they had encountered in the course of working on the current model. In this way, these same problems could be prevented from occurring in subsequent models.

Finally, with respect to attend training, all five respondents argued that the workers in their division should be more involved in training than they were at the present time. These respondents included three wages employees, one first-line supervisor and one senior supervisor. There was considerable variability among these respondents in the particular form(s) of training they were advocating. In one case, it was suggested that the more experienced operators in the division should be given responsibility for showing the less experienced operators "the wrong and the right ways of doing the jobs". A second respondent (the senior supervisor) expressed the view that workers should always be adequately trained in "new processes" before having to execute these processes in the actual production setting. This same respondent also advocated a form of train-the-trainer course for skilled operators. In his own words:

> ...they need to be better able to train the guy they're working with, if they're a skilled operator... because we've got some very skilled operators that aren't good at passing on their skills. (senior supervisor)

A third respondent argued that there should be more "formal" training for workers (in the sense of training provided by experts), specifically in the area of spray painting. According to this respondent, the situation at the present time was such that:

> ...the spray painting we got here is, if your overalls fit, you are sort of a spray painter. They don't have any sort of formal training or anything like that... there's a few of us that got

trained properly, and the rest of them nowadays just get thrown in the booth and they say 'This is the gun, this is the part, paint it.' (wages employee)

And finally, a fourth and fifth respondent argued for more training for workers in relation to some specific aspect(s) of their job. In one case, the emphasis was on training in relation to quality requirements as well as in relation to changes in job processes; in the other, the emphasis was on training for workers in problem-solving skills. In the words of the latter respondent (the first-line supervisor):

I'd like to train people up to basically solve their own problems, give them [the] tools if you like, to attack some of the problems that frustrate them as individuals. (first-line supervisor)

As for the tooling division, there was little evidence of social desirability responding in the open question data for the production division. The reader will recall the argument made previously that a likely indicator of social desirability responding would be the finding that many of the prompted activity categories were well-represented (in terms of the number of respondents mentioning change with respect to these categories). The main rationale for this argument was that, up to this point in the interview, respondents had had considerable exposure to the prompt questions (asked in relation to the present context, the past context, and the anticipated future context) which were designed to cue them to possible other activities in which workers might engage. In the case of the tooling division, it will be recalled that there were four prompted activity categories (out of 10) that were represented by the open question data. The level of representation was very low for three of these categories (in each case, change was mentioned by one respondent only), while for the fourth category it was somewhat higher (with change being mentioned by three respondents, comprising 25% of the entire sample for this division, and 38% of all change respondents).

In the case of the production division, the pattern of responding was somewhat different, with the representation of prompted activity categories being variable, rather than poor. As shown in Table 12.4, there were six prompted activity categories (out of ten) that were represented by the open question data for this division. One of these categories was relatively well-represented (with nine respondents, comprising 47% of the entire sample and 56% of change respondents, mentioning change in this category); a further two categories were represented to a reasonable extent (in each case, change was mentioned by five respondents, comprising 26% of the entire sample and 31% of change respondents); and the remaining three categories were relatively poorly represented (with change being mentioned by four or less respondents, comprising 21% or less of the entire sample or 25% or less of change respondents). This variable representation of prompted activity categories can also be seen as inconsistent with what one would expect if there was a social desirability bias influencing responding. In fact, what it does suggest is that, in responding to the open-ended questions about the ideal, respondents from the production division were exercising some judgement and voicing their own opinions. They were not responding indiscriminately to these questions.

Finally, and also as for the tooling division, the open question data for the production division were analysed to determine how many of the changes that were mentioned could be classified as indicative of a more active role for workers. Of the 49 changes that were mentioned, there were 20 (41%) that could be classified in this way. A number of these changes have already been described. These include:

(1) All nine changes that were advocated in relation to worker involvement in planning activities;
(2) Two of the changes advocated in relation to worker involvement in training (specifically, the reference by one respondent to the need for workers to be trained in problem-solving skills, and the reference by another respondent to the need for train-the-trainer courses for workers); and
(3) One of the changes advocated in relation to information meetings (with the specific reference being to the desirability of more upward communication whereby managers and supervisors should seek information from workers about problems which they were experiencing with the current model).

In addition to these changes, there were a further eight changes that were classified as indicative of a more active role for workers. Four of these changes were represented by the activity category Responsibility/Accountability[24]. Specifically, there was one respondent (a wages employee) who argued that workers should be involved in, and have some responsibility for, work carried out in the pilot phase of manufacturing a new model vehicle. According to this respondent, the situation at the present time was such that:

> It's only the leading hands that are involved in [pilot parts] anyway. ...we won't get to know about them until we actually have to. To be involved in the beginning would be nice, but we're not involved in the beginning... When they're all ready for us to produce and assemble, then we'll get to know about them. (wages employee)

This respondent also advocated more overall responsibility for the workers in her division:

> I think responsibility is important in your job, and you need to sort of feel you can handle it... I don't think they've got enough responsibility. You seem to have, like, [a situation

---

[24]These four changes were mentioned by three of the four respondents who spontaneously mentioned a change (or changes) associated with this activity category. The fourth respondent advocated a non-active change, arguing that the responsibilities of wages employees with leading hand status should change to include more involvement in direct production.

where you are told] 'You just stand there and push the buttons and put them in there, and we'll worry about the rest of it'.

A second respondent (also a wages employee) argued that divisional workers should have more responsibility for activities associated with the "running of the plant", such as stock control and quoting/costing activities. And a third respondent (a first-line supervisor) argued that divisional workers should have more responsibility for "[solving] their own problems".

A further two active changes were represented by the activity category Group Problem-Solving. Specifically, one respondent (a wages employee) argued for the reintroduction of the team meetings that had been held in the past as part of the team concept initiative. In the respondents own words:

> I think myself, I would go back to having a team meeting... Perhaps only once a month, but I would go back to that. I think there's a lot of good can come out of those. Because, there's a lot of people... We've got two or three very clever people here that are really good on ideas. (wages employee)

A second respondent (a senior supervisor) argued that there should be more collaboration between shop floor workers and "trades and maintenance type people" for the purpose of testing out workers' ideas as well as solving problems which workers encountered on the job. In this respondent's own words:

> The problem we've got in the past is that a lot of people come up with a lot of good ideas, but we haven't got anyone to make it, we haven't got the bits, or we haven't got the tool-maker to spare, or we haven't got the fitter to spare... if the assembly area have got a problem, I'd give them a maintenance guy and a toolmaker to work with them full time. If paint's got a problem, I'd give them a maintenance guy and a toolmaker to work for them, and do their jobs, and have these guys actually working for the shop floor people. (senior supervisor)

The remaining two active changes that were advocated by respondents from the production division were represented by the activity categories HRM-Reward and Worker-Supervisor Communication, respectively. With respect to the former, and as illustrated in the following excerpt, the respondent concerned (a supervisor) argued that the division's operating reward system should be changed to promote what was essentially a more active role for workers:

> ...I would change the reward system. Because at the moment a lot of the ideas that are coming from people on the floor, I feel that there's not a lot of rewards given back to them. If we as a group — and possibly this may happen in the future — if we as a supervisory group could reward a person fairly for using his initiative, coming up with an idea that we

know is going to work, and reward him a lot more quickly than what is happening at the
moment with our suggestion scheme... I think that would result in a lot more ideas coming
from the people themselves. (first-line supervisor)

With respect to the latter, the respondent concerned (also a first-line supervisor) argued for
a change in the nature of the communication between workers and their supervisors.
Specifically, he suggested that supervisors should encourage workers more to come up
with ideas and, further, that they should then "be good to [their] word" and act upon these
ideas.

The 20 active changes described above were mentioned by 11 respondents in all (representing 58% of the entire sample for this division and 69% of the change respondents).
These respondents included all five supervisory staff and six wages employees. There was
no difference between the active change respondents and the non-active change respondents in terms of either their length of service with the company (for the former, mean =
14.18 years and for the latter, mean = 10.75 years) or their gender.

At this point, the question arises as to whether or not, in terms of their overall pattern
of responding to the open-ended questions, respondents from the production division differed significantly from their counterparts in the tooling division. A review of the findings
associated with the quantitative data suggests that the divisions were, in fact, very similar.
Specifically, 84% of respondents from the production division compared with 67% of
respondents from the tooling division advocated some change with respect to what it was
that the workers in their division did; on average, production division respondents mentioned 3.1 changes each compared with 2.5 changes each for tooling division respondents;
the total number of activity categories represented by these change data was 14 for the
production division and 11 for the tooling division; and the number of prompted activity
categories represented by these data was six for the production division and four for the
tooling division. With respect to the analysis of active versus non-active changes, 41% of
the changes advocated by production division respondents were classified as active, compared with 55% for the tooling division; these data represented the responses of 11
respondents from the production division (58% of the sample for this division) compared
with five respondents from the tooling division (42% of the sample for this division).

As indicated, the conclusion suggested by these findings is that, in terms of their overall
pattern of responding, respondents from the two divisions appeared to be very similar.
Having said this, however, it is worth noting that, for all but one of the specific findings
reported above, the production division was better represented than the tooling division. In
other words, respondents from the production division were somewhat more likely than
their counterparts from the tooling division to spontaneously advocate change; the average
number of changes mentioned per respondent was slightly higher for the production division than it was for the tooling division; the number of activity categories represented by
these changes (essentially, the number of different types of changes that were mentioned)
was somewhat greater for the production division than for the tooling division; and so on.

This trend is consistent with the researcher's impression (gained over several years as a researcher participant in each division) of the production division as being somewhat less culture bound (and hence, possibly somewhat more accommodating of change) than the tooling division.

This trend can also be interpreted in the light of findings from the present study. For example, the analysis of data pertaining to the past context provided evidence to suggest that the production division had had more exposure to change over time than the tooling division and, moreover, that it had been exposed to more different types of change (including changes likely to challenge existing ways of doing things, such as, the introduction of the team concept). There was also evidence from the qualitative data associated with the above changes (i.e., the changes advocated in relation to the ideal context) that there would be more support in the production division than in the tooling division for what has been described as an active role for workers. In particular, respondents from the production division seemed better able than their counterparts from the tooling division to articulate (describe in detail) the active changes they advocated concerning changes in worker involvement in planning activities. It was also the case that these data typically contained more references than the associated tooling division data to the human resources management implications (in particular, the motivational implications) of the changes advocated.

Finally, it is interesting to note that, whereas three of the four no change respondents from the tooling division were supervisory staff, there were no supervisory staff among the no change respondents from the production division. In other words, all five of the supervisory staff included in the production division sample advocated some change with respect to what it was that the workers in their division did. Furthermore, of the three supervisors from the tooling division who advocated some change, two mentioned changes which, if realised, would be unlikely to influence, to any significant degree, the role of workers in the division (in terms of, say, a shift towards a more active role for workers). In contrast, all five of the supervisory staff included in the production division sample mentioned at least one change that could be classified as supportive of a more active role for workers. These findings may be of some significance given the argument that the more senior one's position in an organisation, the more influential one can be in either resisting, or enabling, changes which are proposed.

12.7.2 *Differences between the open and prompt questions*

From Tables 12.3 and 12.4, it can be seen that, for both divisions, the presentation of the prompt questions in relation to the ideal context served to provide additional information (over and above that provided by the open-ended questions) regarding respondents' views about what the workers in their division ideally should do. As the reader will recall, this discrepancy between responses to the open-ended questions and responses to the closed questions (prompts) has been noted previously in relation to each of the other contextual domains for which the format of questioning included both open-ended and closed questions (specifically, the present context, the past context, and the anticipated future context). The point should also be made that, in the case of the ideal context, the discrepancy suggested by the tabled data for each division might have been even more marked, had the problem of missing data in relation to the prompt questions not been so pronounced[25]. Nevertheless, the discrepancy is still evident and is particularly clear in the case of Information Meetings for the tooling division and Safety Meetings for the production division. With respect to the former, it can be seen from Table 12.3 that there were no respondents from the tooling division who spontaneously (i.e., in response to the initial open-ended question(s)) advocated a change in the role of divisional workers with respect to information meetings. However, when subsequently prompted, seven respondents from this division (out of 10 who were presented with this prompt) argued in favour of some change with respect to this activity category. Similarly, and as shown in Table 12.4, there were no respondents from the production division who spontaneously advocated a change in the role of divisional workers with respect to safety meetings. However, when subsequently prompted, 13 respondents from this division (out of 16 who were presented with this prompt) argued in favour of some change with respect to this activity category.

The question again arises as to what this discrepancy between spontaneous and prompted responses might mean. As previously, the argument that prompting may have had the effect of putting words into people's mouths was not well-supported by the data. That is, it was not the case, as one would expect if this argument were valid, that prompting consistently (i.e., across the entire range of prompt questions) resulted in significantly more respondents from each division advocating change. Instead, the size of the discrepancy between spontaneous and prompted responses varied considerably from one activity category to another (with this effect being more pronounced for the production division than for the tooling division). While supervisors might be expected to be more likely to give socially desirable responses than workers, there was no evidence of this in the responses from either division. Of course, it remains an empirical question as to whether or not social desirability effects might be more evident in the responses of more senior organisation members, such as managers, who have a vested interest in promoting a positive image of the organisation. To the extent that this was the case, one might expect an increase in responses related to prompts across all contextual domains.

In the case of the present data set, there are several other more plausible explanations for the discrepancy between spontaneous and prompted responses, all of which have been referred to previously in the course of discussing other findings from this study. These are as follows.

First, it may be that the unprompted data (i.e., the responses to the initial open-ended questions) represent respondents' perceptions (beliefs *etc.*) about those issues that are particularly salient to them at a given point in time. The prompt data, on the other hand, may represent respondents' perceptions (beliefs *etc.*) about issues that are of lesser

---

[25]This problem is described in more detail in Section 12.7.3 (see Table 12.7 and the associated discussion).

significance to them. With respect to the present findings, it might be argued that the issue of, say, worker involvement in planning (in particular, in relation to job design) was of greater, and more immediate, concern to the respondents from the production division — in the sense, perhaps, of being seen as in need of more improvement — than the issue of worker involvement in safety meetings. This explanation is consistent with the finding that a significant proportion of the respondents from this division spontaneously advocated a change with respect to the former, whereas the changes advocated with respect to the latter were elicited only through subsequent prompting.

It is perhaps worth making the point here that, in this section of the interview, respondents were essentially being asked whether or not they thought that the role of the workers in their division could be improved upon in any way, and if so, how. The findings for both divisions suggested that respondents felt somehow better equipped to answer this question than the previous open-ended question(s) concerning anticipated changes in the role of divisional workers in the future. It will be recalled that, in response to the latter, the anticipated changes that were mentioned tended to be changes of a very general nature (e.g., various technological changes), rather than changes that one might readily associate with the more specific issue of the role of workers. In contrast, the types of changes mentioned in response to the open-ended question(s) about the ideal were changes that were more obviously, and more directly, related to the issue of the role of workers. For example, there were references to the desirability of introducing job rotation for workers and to the desirability of supporting more involvement of divisional workers in planning activities, in training, and in social activities. The point is that it seemed easier for respondents to comment on how they thought the role of divisional workers could be improved upon than for them to comment on how the role of divisional workers might change in the future. This finding suggests that the four contextual domains of interest in the present study may not be equally accessible, in terms of the ease with which respondents can answer questions about each. This might reflect the amount of time that respondents spend talking and thinking about things (issues, events, experience, *etc.*) from the perspective of a given contextual domain. Thus, they may spend more time thinking about what ought to be the case (i.e., the ideal) than about what is likely to happen in the future. However, it is also possible that the accessibility of a given contextual domain may vary depending on the specific issue that constitutes the focus of the interview. It may be, for example, that if the issue had been technology (and not, as in the present case, the role of workers), then respondents might have found it easier to answer questions about the future context with respect to this issue than questions about the ideal context.

Another possible explanation for the difference between spontaneous and prompted responses, observed for the ideal context, is that respondents may have had a relatively poorly articulated notion of what might constitute an ideal role for workers. This might reflect their lack of information about the other context, which could provide evidence of more desirable alternatives, and/or it might reflect a long history of the same way of doing things in the organisation. Hence, in the absence of any prompting about this issue (i.e., in response to the initial open-ended question(s)), one might expect that respondents' accounts of how the current role of workers could be improved upon would be somewhat limited. With the addition of specific prompting, however, a more comprehensive profile of the ideal role of workers might be expected to emerge.

And finally, there is the argument that the prompt questions serve to reveal respondent knowledge that is assumed or taken-for-granted. With reference to the present data set, a case in point may be the prompt data for Safety Meetings for the production division. As indicated in Table 12.4, there were 13 respondents from this division (68% of the sample) who, when prompted, argued in favour of some change in the role of divisional workers with respect to workplace safety. A closer analysis of these data revealed that all but one of these respondents had advocated an increase in the involvement of divisional workers in safety activities. It can also be seen from Table 12.4 that there were no respondents from this division who spontaneously advocated a change with respect to this activity category. It is possible that, for these respondents, attention to safety was an area of assumed importance. Hence, respondents did not think to mention it in response to the initial open-ended question(s), but rather they required specific prompting to bring this information to the surface.

Of course, it is not possible to say with any certainty whether or not any one of the above explanations has more validity (in the sense of being more strongly supported by the data) than the others. It may even be that each explanation is valid insofar as it serves to explain some aspect of the data set under analysis. One possible approach to answering this question might be to ask respondents why they did not mention it in response to the open question and why other respondents might have failed to mention it. Responses, such as, "Well, I didn't mention it because it's obviously important", rather than "I just forgot to mention it", might provide some evidence of the assumed nature of such opinions.

12.7.3 *The prompt questions: Some initial findings*

Table 12.7 presents the results of prompting in relation to the ideal context for *both* the tooling division and the production division (previously these data were presented separately as part of Table 12.3 and Table 12.4 respectively). Specifically, Table 12.7 shows the representation of prompted activity categories for each division in terms of the *total* number of respondents from each division (also expressed as a percentage of the total available sample for each division) who advocated change with respect to each activity category. The number of respondents shown includes not only those respondents who provided this information in response to prompting, but also those respondents who provided this information spontaneously, in response to the initial open-ended question(s) (with the latter represented by the numbers in square brackets). In addition, for each division, there is a column for missing data which shows the number of respondents who were either: (i) not presented with the prompt question due to lack of time; or (ii) presented

Table 12.7. Ideal context prompt data: Number and percentage of respondents from each division advocating change.

Activity Category	Tooling Division $n = 12$			Production Division $n = 19$		
	% (Number) of Respondents		Missing Data	% (Number) of Respondents		Missing Data
Planning meetings	6 (55%)	[1]	1	16 (89%)	[9]	1
Information meetings	7 (70%)		2	13 (81%)	[5]	3
Group problem-solving	5 (56%)	[1]	3	8 (53%)	[2]	4
Safety meetings	2 (29%)		5	13 (81%)		3
Union meetings	2 (33%)		6	5 (36%)		5
Help other workers	2 (33%)		6	5 (42%)		7
Record work-related info	5 (56%)	[1]	3	8 (53%)		4
Attend training	4 (44%)		3	16 (89%)	[5]	1
Social activities	7 (78%)	[3]	3	9 (56%)	[2]	3
Wkr-sup communication	5 (100%)		6	12 (75%)	[4]	3

Note: The numbers in square brackets show the number of respondents, of the total indicated, who advocated change spontaneously, that is, in response to the open-ended question.

with the prompt question, but who misunderstood what was required and gave a response which subsequently could not be coded. This latter group comprised a small minority only of the missing data respondents.

It can be seen that, with respect to the above data set, the problem of missing data was quite pronounced[26], particularly in the case of the tooling division. As indicated, for this division, data were missing for six respondents (50% of the sample) for each of the following three activity categories: (i) Union Meetings; (ii) Help Other Workers; and (iii) Worker-Supervisor Communication. In view of the magnitude of this problem, the decision was made not to analyse the entire data set (i.e., the data for all 10 activity categories), but rather to analyse only those data pertaining to activity categories that were relatively well represented.

The specific criterion that was applied was that activity categories for which there were missing data for more than 25% of respondents, from either division, would be excluded from the analysis. Using this criterion, four activity categories were excluded, namely: (i) Safety Meetings (with excessive missing data for the tooling division); (ii) Union Meetings (with excessive missing data for both the tooling division and the production division); (iii) Help Other Workers (also with excessive missing data for both divisions); and (iv) Worker-Supervisor Communication (with excessive missing data for the tooling

---

[26] An explanation for the problem of missing data has been offered previously in relation to the findings for the future context (see Section 12.5.3). This same explanation also applies here.

division). Apart from these four activity categories, the data pertaining to a fifth category, namely Social Activities, were also omitted from the analysis. This decision was essentially a practical one, the main aim of which was to make the task of analysing and writing-up the data for this section of the interview more manageable. The decision to exclude Social Activities, rather than any of the other five remaining activity categories, was made on the grounds that the specific activities subsumed under this category could be seen as being less directly related to the issue at hand, namely, the role of workers, than the specific activities subsumed under the other categories.

The outcome of these various omissions was that the final analysis was reduced to those data pertaining to only five out of the original 10 activity categories. These were: (i) Planning Meetings; (ii) Information Meetings; (iii) Group Problem-Solving; (iv) Record Work-Related Information; and (v) Attend Training. It can be seen from Table 12.7 that similarities (in terms of the number of respondents from each division advocating change) were indicated for three of these categories, and differences were indicated for two. The former included Group Problem-Solving (with a difference score of 3%), Record Work-Related Information (also with a difference score of 3%), and Information Meetings (with a difference score of –11%). The latter included Attend Training (with a difference score of –45%) and Planning Meetings (with a difference score of –34%). The results of the analysis of data pertaining to each of these activity categories are reported, in full, in Kummerow (2000). It is these results, along with findings reported in this chapter thus far, that inform the summary of main findings that is offered below.

12.7.4 *The ideal context: Summary of main findings*

The main findings of the analysis of ideal context data can be summarised as follows:

1. General nature of spontaneously advocated changes. In response to the initial open-ended question, in which respondents were asked: "If you were running an organisation like this one, would you make any changes to what workers do (i.e., to the role of workers)?", a majority of respondents from both divisions argued in favour of some change. Specifically, 67% of tooling division respondents advocated change, compared with 84% of production division respondents. The point should be made that all of the changes mentioned by these respondents could be regarded as realistic and sensible, given respondents' respective work environments. In other words, while questions about the ideal could potentially encourage respondents to give extreme responses — that is, responses reflective of some utopian ideal, rather than reality-based responses — in the present study, this did not occur. For example, respondents variously talked about the desirability of divisional workers having more responsibility than they did currently, the need for more socialisation among divisional members at all levels of the hierarchy, the potential value of introducing job rotation for workers, and the need for improved training and communications in the division.

2. Number and type of spontaneously advocated changes. For both divisions, the number of changes advocated spontaneously (i.e., in response to the initial open-ended question) by any given respondent was small. For the tooling division, each respondent advocated, on average, 2.5 changes; for the production division, 3.1 changes were advocated, on average, by each respondent[27]. It was also the case that, for both divisions, there was little consensus among respondents about the nature of the changes they advocated. For the tooling division, spontaneously advocated changes fell into 11 change categories, with the best represented of these (namely, Responsibility and Accountability, and Social Activities) being mentioned by only three respondents each. For the production division, spontaneously advocated changes were classified into 14 change categories. One of these (namely, Planning Meetings) was reasonably well-represented, with nine respondents mentioning changes in this category. However, as for the tooling division, the remaining change categories for this division were relatively poorly represented. Specifically, there were three change categories (namely, Job Rotation, Information Meetings, and Attend Training) with changes mentioned by five respondents each and there were 10 change categories with changes mentioned by four or less respondents.

3. Divisional differences in the number of spontaneously advocated changes. With respect to the findings summarised in point 2 above, it was suggested that, while the magnitude of the difference between the divisions suggested by these findings was small, the direction of the difference was not inconsistent with what one might have expected, given both impressionistic data and data pertaining to the other contextual domains of interest. In other words, the finding that respondents from the production division spontaneously advocated somewhat more changes, on average, than their counterparts from the tooling division, and that there was somewhat more variability in the types of changes which they mentioned (as indicated in the number of activity categories represented by these changes) was not inconsistent with evidence suggesting that the production division was less culture-bound than the tooling division.

4. Divisional differences in the nature of spontaneously advocated changes. The analysis of spontaneously advocated changes in terms of whether they reflected an active or a passive orientation indicated that the two divisions were roughly equivalent in this regard. For the tooling division, 45% of the changes advocated in response to the open-ended question could be classified as unambiguously reflecting an active orientation[28], compared with 41% of changes advocated by production division respondents. Differences were, however, indicated in the number and seniority of the respondents advocating these changes. In the tooling division, the changes classified as active were mentioned by

---

[27] As reported previously, there was no difference between these mean scores and their associated medians.

[28] It will be recalled that, on the basis of qualifying data, two of the 11 active changes for this division were subsequently reclassified as passive changes.

a minority of respondents (4/12 or 33% of the sample for this division), all of whom were wages employees; in the production division, the changes classified as active were mentioned by a majority of respondents (11/19 or 58% of the sample for this division), and these respondents included supervisory staff as well as wages employees. In addition, the active changes advocated spontaneously by production division respondents appeared to be somewhat better articulated (in the sense of being described in more detail) than the active changes advocated by respondents from the tooling division. The degree of articulation might be an important indicator of the extent to which the ideal represents a realistic alternative to the present situation, rather than just a general dissatisfaction with it.

The above differences between the divisions were not inconsistent with findings from the other contextual domains suggesting that the production division was somewhat more Theory Y in its orientation to the role of workers than the tooling division. The point should be made, however, that while the ideal context data for the production division (when considered alone) might lead to the conclusion (e.g., by change agents) that initiatives consistent with Theory Y assumptions would be readily accepted in this division, findings pertaining to respondents' past experience of such initiatives suggest that this might not be the case. As indicated, there was evidence to suggest that past initiatives associated with the team concept were experienced negatively by some divisional members and, in this sense, one might expect there to be a degree of wariness in response to any reintroduction of such initiatives.

5. Divisional differences in the demographic profile of respondents spontaneously advocating change/no change. The analysis of responses to the open-ended question in terms of respondent demographics revealed that all five of the supervisory staff from the production division sample advocated change spontaneously, compared with three of the six supervisory staff from the tooling division sample. It was also found that all of the no change respondents from the tooling division sample (including wages employees and supervisory staff) were longer-serving employees (whose length of service with the company ranged from 25 to 35 years). For the production division, both the change and no change groups included longer-serving and shorter-serving respondents.

6. Influence of social desirability effects on spontaneously advocated changes. In neither division did responding to the open-ended question about the ideal context appear to be influenced significantly by social desirability effects. Effects of this kind might have been expected, given respondents' previous exposure, on three separate occasions — in the context of questioning about the present, the past, and the anticipated future — to prompting about worker involvement in a range of activities identified *a priori* by the researcher. As indicated, prompted activity categories were represented poorly in the open question data for the tooling division. Specifically, of the 10 prompted activity categories, only four were represented in the open question data for this division. Of these, three included a change (or changes) mentioned by one respondent only, and one included a change (or changes) mentioned by three respondents. In the case of the production division, while six of the 10 prompted activity categories were represented in the open question data for this division, the number of respondents advocating change (or changes) within each of these six categories was variable and ranged from two to nine respondents. If responding had been significantly influenced by a social desirability bias, one might have expected that prompted activity categories would have been better, and more consistently, represented in these open question data than was in fact the case.

7. Nature of the changes advocated in response to prompting. As for the other contextual domains of interest, the addition of closed (i.e., prompt) questions following on from the initial open-ended question served to provide a more complete picture of respondents' views about, in this case, the ideal context than if respondents had been presented with the initial open-ended question only. As above, the argument that this finding might simply be a consequence of social desirability responding (whereby prompting served to put words into respondents' mouths) was ruled out on the grounds that, for both divisions, the effects of prompting (in terms of the number of respondents advocating change in response to any given prompt) varied from one prompted activity category to the next[29]. In this sense, then, responses to prompting could be interpreted largely at their face value such that, where changes were advocated, they could be seen as changes which were regarded by respondents as being genuinely desirable. It was also the case that, where prompting resulted in a significant proportion of respondents arguing in favour of a given change, one could often identify the links between the desired change and some aspect of respondents' current, past, or anticipated future experience. For example, the finding that, in response to prompting, more than half of the respondents from the production division argued that there should, ideally, be more involvement of divisional workers in training could fairly readily be interpreted in the context of the drive for improved quality (one aspect of which was an emphasis on the importance of the training function) which was currently underway in this division.

With respect to the direction of the changes that respondents advocated in response to prompting, all of these changes but one involved a shift towards increasing, or otherwise improving, the involvement of divisional workers in the activity about which respondents were prompted. The exception was a change that was advocated by one respondent from the production division who argued that there should be less involvement than there was currently of divisional workers in record-keeping activities.

8. Divisional differences revealed by qualitative data associated with prompted responses. As was the case for the other contextual domains of interest, the analysis of respondents' elaborations on and\or qualifications of their responses (associated with the

---

[29]This was the case even taking into account the problem of missing data associated with this contextual domain.

five prompted activity categories referred to above) provided some interesting additional insights into similarities and differences between the two divisions, that would not have been obtained had the analysis focussed only on those data that could be easily quantified. Briefly summarised, some of these additional insights were:

(1) The no change respondents from the tooling division differed from their counterparts from the production division in that they were more likely to express explicit opposition to change. Moreover, this opposition tended to be underpinned by an allegiance to traditional views (e.g., about the respective roles of supervisors and workers and about how work should be performed and jobs designed). In contrast, respondents from the production division were not only less likely to express explicit opposition to change, but in the notable instance in which they did — some production division respondents indicated that they were opposed to more worker involvement in group problem-solving activities — the opposition arose from respondents' negative past experience of a team initiative in the division. Indeed, among the respondents from this division, a no change response was more likely to be indicative, not of opposition to change, but rather of satisfaction with things, as they were at the present time.

(2) The analysis of qualitative data provided evidence to suggest that, as a group, production division respondents were somewhat more fluent about, or better able to articulate, some of the changes that they advocated than their counterparts from the tooling division. For example, they tended to elaborate more on their change responses (this was particularly evident in the data pertaining to group problem-solving and planning), often providing good reasons for why they considered a particular change to be desirable. It was also the case that, for some of the prompted activity categories (notably, Information Meetings and Record Work-Related Information), there was more consensus among respondents from the production division than there was among respondents from the tooling division about the specific nature of the changes being advocated. The point was made that these findings probably reflected the greater past or current exposure of production division respondents, either to the specific activities in question, or to related activities.

(3) An analysis of the thematic content of the qualitative data provided evidence that respondents — in one or both divisions — held a number of themes in common. For example, respondents from both divisions, when arguing in favour of more worker involvement in record-keeping, made reference to the important control function that was served by this activity. Among those respondents from the production division who advocated more worker involvement in training, there was a shared view that such a change was necessary if the quality of production in the division was to improve. Interestingly, there was little recognition among the respondents from either division of the potential motivational value of increasing the involvement of divisional workers in either of these activities. This analysis also provided evidence of a perception, among the change respondents from both divisions, that while increased worker

involvement in planning activities was considered to be desirable, this involvement should be restricted to operational planning activities, and should not extend to strategic planning activities.

9. Divisional differences in the demographic profile of respondents advocating change/no change in response to prompting. The trends in respondent demographics that emerged from the analysis of the open question data (see point 5 above) were also evident in the data pertaining specifically to the prompted activity categories[30]. As previously, there was no representation of supervisory staff from the production division in the no change responses. This was the case across all five of the prompted activity categories that were included in this analysis. For the tooling division, supervisory staff were marginally better represented than wages employees in the no change data, while wages employees were better represented in the change data. With respect to the former, for three of the five activity categories, the number of supervisory staff who gave no change responses exceeded the number of wages employees who gave no change responses. With respect to the latter, there were four activity categories out of five for which the number of wages employees giving change responses exceeded the number of supervisory staff giving change responses. It was also the case for the tooling division that the no change respondents were more likely to be longer-serving than shorter-serving employees. No such trend in respondents' tenure was observed for the production division. Whether or not this finding has any cultural significance is hard to say given that longer-serving employees made up the majority of the tooling division sample, while in the production division sample, longer-serving and shorter-serving employees were more equally represented.

10. Integrating contextual domains. The analysis of ideal context data (pertaining to each of the five prompted activity categories) in terms of the broader context of respondents' experience produced somewhat variable results. That is, there were some activity categories for which, for either or both divisions, the links between the ideal context data and data pertaining to the other contextual domains of interest were more evident than they were for others. For example, these links were particularly evident in the case of the production division data on group problem-solving. One could see how, for some of the respondents from this division, their negative past experience of a team initiative, had influenced the way in which they thought about this activity in the ideal context. These respondents tended to be opposed to the idea of a change towards a more active role for divisional workers with respect to this activity. In a similar vein, the finding that, among other respondents from this division, there existed support for such a change could also be explained fairly readily. As

---

[30]The reader is reminded that some respondents spontaneously made reference to changes associated with prompted activity categories. The analysis of data pertaining to the prompted activity categories, in terms of respondent demographics, did not distinguish between these spontaneous responses and responses to specific prompting.

indicated, this finding might have been predicted given the positive attitudes towards a more active role for workers with respect to group problem-solving that emerged in the future context data. This finding was also consistent with what one might have expected given the considerable exposure, over recent years, of the members of this division to a range of activities intended to foster a more active role for workers.

As suggested by findings reported in Kummerow (2000), the links between the ideal context data and data pertaining to the other contextual domains were not always as apparent as they were in the case of group problem-solving above. One general trend worth mentioning in this regard is that, for some of the activity categories, the percentage of respondents from the tooling division who advocated change in the ideal context was somewhat higher than might have been expected given the limited exposure — in the past, at the present time, and in the anticipated future — of the members of this division to worker involvement in the activities associated with these categories. For example, despite the fact that respondents from this division reported no exposure to worker involvement in planning activities in the past or at the present time, and that a small minority of respondents only anticipated that this would change in the future, more than half of the respondents from this division (55%) subsequently, in response to prompting, espoused the view that divisional workers ideally should be involved in such activities. In attempting to explain a finding such as this, one cannot entirely rule out the possibility of there being some social desirability bias in responding. The observation that some of the changes advocated by respondents from the tooling division were poorly articulated, and that there was often considerable variability among respondents in the specific types of changes (within a given activity category) which they advocated, may in fact lend some support to this explanation. On the other hand, however, there is the explanation (offered previously) that, where support for change in the ideal context was espoused, it could be interpreted as indicative of a genuine desire for change on the part of respondents. In order to answer this question, an additional question asking why the changes were mentioned, or why the respondent did not advocate any changes might be informative.

Finally, there are two possible, and not unrelated, implications of the finding that ideal context data could not always be understood in terms of data pertaining to the other contextual domains. The first is that the contextual analysis attempted in the present study is likely to be limited by the fact that it was issue-specific — it was concerned with understanding the broader context of respondents' experience with respect to a single issue (whether worker involvement in training, planning activities, *etc.*) only. It may be that, for any given issue, the explanation for data pertaining to the ideal context (or any other context for that matter) may become apparent only through knowledge about some other issue. A good example of this is provided by the tooling division ideal context data on information meetings. On the basis of data pertaining to the other contextual domains, one could not readily have predicted the strong support for a change towards more and improved information dissemination for divisional workers (70% of respondents advocated such a change) that was indicated in the ideal context data. However, given knowledge about the current decline of the division and the prevailing climate of anxiety and uncertainty, it was hardly surprising that respondents expressed their desire for what, in effect, was improved communications in the division.

The second implication of a failure to establish strong links between ideal context data and data pertaining to the other contextual domains is that information about the ideal context is valuable in its own right. That is, it provides insights that would not otherwise have been obtained. To the extent that this is the case, there is support for the approach in the present study of including questions specifically concerned with respondents' experience in the ideal context. This leads us onto the next section in which a more detailed examination of the value of seeking information about the ideal context is offered.

12.7.5 *Information about the ideal context: What does it add?*

The findings of the analysis of ideal context data suggest that there are several important ways in which an attempt to understand the culture of an organisation (group) can benefit from the inclusion of questions about the ideal context of respondents' experience. These are as follows:

1. Information about the culture's degree of boundedness. Data pertaining to the ideal context can provide some insight into the boundedness of an organisation's (group's) culture. This is because questions about the ideal can be seen as inviting respondents to think beyond the boundaries of their experience (in their current organisation) and to imagine some alternative, and from their perspective, preferred way of doing things. In this sense, evidence that one is dealing with a relatively bounded culture would be suggested by the finding that respondents' notions of the ideal remain anchored in, rather than deviate from, respondents' existing experience.

The results of the analysis of ideal context data suggest that there may be a number of different sources of data — which should be considered as a whole, rather than singly — that can inform our understanding of the boundedness of the organisation's (group's) culture. In particular, consideration should be given to:

(1) The percentage of respondents in the group who advocate change. The finding that a high percentage of respondents advocate change — in particular, in response to the open-ended question, rather than in response to prompting — may be indicative that the group in question is not strongly culture bound.
(2) The average number of changes that are advocated per respondent. This information will give some insight into the group's breadth of vision for change. As above, where the average number of changes advocated per respondent is high, this may signal that one is dealing with a culture that is not strongly bounded.
(3) The specific types of changes which respondents advocate and, in particular, the extent to which these changes represent a departure from the way things are done at the

present time. In the present study, the classification of changes into whether or not they were indicative of an active or a passive orientation towards the role of divisional workers was a useful means of obtaining this information.

(4) The extent to which respondents' views about the ideal contain references to the past, or to tradition. In the present study, this information was derived from an analysis of the no change data — in particular, respondents' attributions about why they considered change to be undesirable. It can be argued that the more strongly bounded the culture, the more likely it is that references to the past will emerge in data pertaining to the ideal context.

(5) The extent to which respondents are able to clearly articulate the changes they advocate. A high level of articulation suggests that respondents have acquired some knowledge about the changes which they are espousing — whether through thinking or talking about them, or through some form of experience in the organisation or from knowledge of, or about, other organisations (which may, e.g., have increased their awareness of the need for, or desirability of, change). There is some evidence from the present study that respondents who are able to clearly articulate the changes which they advocate may be less strongly culture bound in their thinking than respondents who are less fluent in talking about change.

2. Information about the group's responsiveness to change. A second important way in which ideal context data can be of value is that they can provide some insight into the extent of support for change within the group. The specific data likely to be of most relevance/interest in this regard include:

(1) Data pertaining to the percentage of respondents who advocate change. A high degree of support for change would be suggested by the finding that a high percentage of respondents advocated change. This would be the case particularly where the need for change was argued spontaneously, rather than in response to prompting.

(2) Demographic data pertaining to the seniority of the respondents who advocate change. As argued previously, while there may be good support for change among respondents lower in the organisational (divisional) hierarchy, change efforts may ultimately be stymied by resistance from more senior members of the group. While the latter may be fewer in number than the former, they are likely to be more influential — because of their seniority — in determining the outcome of organisational change efforts. It can be argued, therefore, that information of this kind is likely to have important practical implications for approaches to the implementation of change.

3. A source of confirmatory information. A third argument in support of the inclusion of questions about the ideal context is that ideal context data can serve to confirm insights obtained from an analysis of data pertaining to the other contextual domains of interest. For example, in the present study, ideal context data served to confirm insights about:

(1) The value of qualitative data for making sense of quantitative data. As with the other contextual domains, the analysis of respondents' elaborations on their responses to questions about the ideal context helped to clarify the meaning of these responses. For example, it provided information about the specific types of changes respondents considered to be desirable and the extent to which these changes represented a departure from current practices. It also provided information about the meaning of no change responses — whether they were indicative of actual opposition to change or whether they implied satisfaction with current practices.

(2) The relative importance of particular themes. The finding that a particular theme emerges in the data pertaining to, not one, but a number of contextual domains lends support to the conclusion that the theme has considerable salience for respondents. For example, in the present study, it was found that respondents from both divisions shared the view that record keeping served primarily a control function. This theme emerged in the data pertaining to four of the five contextual domains of interest (with the exception being the other context).

(3) The value of including prompt or closed questions in addition to the initial open-ended question(s). As with the other contextual domains for which prompt questions were included — that is, the past, the present, and the anticipated future — prompting about the ideal context served to provide a more comprehensive picture of respondents' views about how things should change than if questioning had included the initial open-ended question only.

(4) The value of attributions data for understanding the culture of the group. As for the other contextual domains, respondents' attributions — in this case, about why particular changes were considered to be desirable or undesirable — constituted a valuable source of cultural data. For example, the reader will recall that the attributions data associated with the no change responses of tooling division respondents contained evidence of a strong allegiance to tradition among the members of this group.

12.7.6 *Methodological issues arising from the findings for the ideal context*

The above analysis of ideal context data served to highlight a number of problems with the present method, some of which would appear to be more readily resolved than others. It also provided information about how the present method might be revised in order to more fully capitalise on some of its strengths. A brief summary of these various methodological issues is provided below:

1. The trade-off between breadth and depth. As indicated, in this section of the interview, there was a considerable problem with missing data, associated specifically with the prompt or closed questions. The reader is reminded that this problem was encountered previously — albeit to a somewhat lesser extent — in relation to questioning about the future context. Moreover, it was suggested previously that the problem of missing data in the present study could be attributed to an interview schedule which attempted to cover more questions than was realistic given the time available.

While it is clear that any revision of the present method should involve a reduction in the length of the interview schedule, the question remains as to how best to achieve this. The reader is reminded that the broad aim of the interview was to tap organisation members' beliefs and assumptions about the essential nature of workers, as reflected in members' thinking about the role of workers. Interview questions were developed around two main topics, each of which was addressed in a separate interview lasting about one hour. The first topic was concerned with what workers do (in terms of their main duties and other activities in which they are engaged) and the second topic was concerned with the characteristics of good workers (the results for this topic being omitted from this analysis). One obvious strategy for reducing the length of the interview schedule would to be focus on one of these topics only. In this way, one could reasonably expect to present all of the questions pertaining to that topic (including open-ended and prompt questions, "Why?" questions, *etc.*) in the time available.

A second strategy would be to reduce the number of prompt questions. The reader is reminded that, for the section of the interview concerned with what workers do, there were six prompt questions (the first comprising six parts), all of which were intended to be asked, not once, but on four separate occasions — in relation to the present context, the past context, the anticipated future context, and the ideal context. Clearly, if the number of these prompts were to be reduced, the result would be a significant overall reduction in the length of this section of the interview protocol.

There are, however, two main arguments against adopting this second strategy. The first relates to the rationale for the design of prompt questions and to the fact that the present study was essentially investigative (i.e., concerned with the development of a new method, rather than with the evaluation of an existing method). As indicated, one important aim of the prompt questions in the present study was that they should cue respondents to information which they might have provided — but which they did not provide — in response to the initial open-ended question(s). Furthermore, in designing the prompt questions, an attempt was made to ask about activities (behaviours *etc.*) that could be classified according to McGregor's (1960) Theory X — Theory Y dichotomy. Given these two aims, and taking into account the investigative nature of the study, it was necessary that the prompt set (associated with each of the topics being explored in the interview) be reasonably inclusive (in the sense of representing a range of worker activities, behaviours, *etc.*). This is not to say, however, that with more research into the value of particular prompt questions, one could not reduce the number of these questions to a critical few. This might be most effectively done through the use of a pilot study that would aim to identify these critical questions.

A second argument against reducing the number of prompt questions is that, because the prompts (within a given prompt set) asked about activities (behaviours *etc.*) that were broadly related, the findings associated with one prompt (or with a number of prompts) could help to explain the findings associated with another prompt. A good example of this can be found in the findings for planning meetings for the ideal context reported in Kummerow (2000). As indicated, a large majority (89%) of respondents from the production division argued — with reasonable fluency — that the workers in their division should ideally be more involved in planning activities than they were at the present time. This finding, at first, seemed somewhat surprising given reports indicating that the workers in this division had never had any involvement in planning activities (such activities being potentially indicative of a more active role for workers). However, when considered in the light of data pertaining to some of the other activity categories in this prompt set (notably Information Meetings, Group Problem-Solving, and Attend Training), this finding could more readily be understood. As indicated, these data provided good evidence that the workers in this division had considerable exposure over time to activities that could be regarded as similar to planning in the sense of potentially contributing to a more active role for workers.

2. The 'individual' versus the 'response' as the unit of analysis. The above analysis of ideal context data drew further attention to a limitation of the present method that has already been well documented. This limitation concerns the argument that the unit of analysis might more appropriately have been the individual (and her/his overall pattern of responding), rather than the individual's response (to specific questions). One manifestation of this limitation in the ideal context was that, while a respondent could present as a strong advocate for a particular change (that might, e.g., imply support for a more active role for workers), knowledge of that respondent's overall pattern of responding may provide contradictory information about the respondent's likely 'in practice' support for such a change. In other words, inconsistencies between a respondent's espoused values and her/his likely values in practice are more easily overlooked when the individual's response is considered in isolation from the individual's overall pattern of responding.

3. General versus specific accounts of the ideal. A third limitation of the present method which was highlighted by the analysis of ideal context data concerned a tendency among some respondents to talk about the ideal in general, rather than specific, terms. This created a problem for the subsequent broader contextual analysis of data pertaining to the ideal context. For example, while a majority of the respondents from the tooling division (70%) advocated a change with respect to the activity category Information Meetings, the emphasis in these change data tended to be on the need for improvements in divisional communications, in general, rather than on the need for improvements specifically associated with the involvement of divisional workers in information meetings. In the subsequent contextual analysis of these data, one was therefore confronted with the problem of trying to interpret general information in the context of more specific information (which had been provided in response to questions about the past, present, and anticipated future).

4. The value of asking "Why?" With respect to 'what worked' in the present method, the analysis of ideal context data provided further evidence of the value of "Why?" questions for surfacing information of potential significance for understanding the culture of the group. Moreover, from this analysis, it can be concluded that attributions data associated with no change responses (in other words, explanations for why a particular change was seen as undesirable) proved to be as valuable in this regard as attributions data associated with change responses (i.e., explanations for why a particular change was seen as desirable). It is, therefore, recommended that, in any subsequent revision of the present method, it should be a requirement that respondents are asked "Why?" in relation to all of their change and all of their no change responses.

12.8 Conclusions

In this chapter, we have considered those results of Study 3 that were concerned with the operationalisation, in our proposed method, of the context of organisational culture in terms of five dimensions: the past, the present, the future, the other, and the ideal. As for the results reported in the previous chapter, and pertaining to the present context only, the combined use of open-ended and closed questions proved to be a valuable feature of the method in relation to other contextual domains. That is, these questions when used to elicit information about the role of workers in the past, the future, and the ideal, together provided a more comprehensive understanding of the respondent's views in this regard than would have been obtained had only one, or the other, of these types of questions (i.e., the open-ended questions only or the closed questions only) been asked. While the results reported in this chapter suggested that there was relatively little social desirability responding — of the kind that might be expected, particularly in response to questions about the ideal (how things could or should be) — they also drew attention to the importance of interviewing skills for maximising the quality and accuracy of the data obtained. In particular, interviewers involved in the kind of research reported here need to be skilled in establishing and maintaining rapport, and in striking a balance between encouraging respondents to qualify and elaborate on their responses and ensuring that sufficient time is available for key questions to be adequately addressed.

The results of the separate analyses of data pertaining to the past, future, other, and ideal contexts were found to provide meaningful additional insights over and above those provided by the previously reported results of the analysis of the present context data. In particular, information about these other contexts — in the form of quantitative data (e.g., the number of respondents reporting a change, or no change, from the past to the present), qualitative data (i.e., respondents' qualifications of, and elaborations on, their responses), and attributions (e.g., regarding the reason(s) for an anticipated future change) — provided a more in-depth understanding of the meaning of respondents' present experience in relation to the role of workers in their division. This information also drew attention to important differences between the divisions in this regard that would not otherwise have been revealed. Finally, given our conceptualisation of the context of organisational culture as multi-dimensional (with each dimension potentially influenced by, and influencing, every other dimension), the results reported in this chapter pertaining to the links between contexts enabled us to draw some tentative conclusions about possible differences in the contextual-orientation, and degree of boundedness, of the cultures of different organisations.

We turn now to Part Six of this volume, comprising the final two chapters of the book. The first of these chapters, Chapter 13, provides a comprehensive evaluation of the method developed for use, and trialled, in Study 3. The method is evaluated first in terms of each of its key features, and then more generally in terms of how it compares to other methods for assessing organisational culture. In Chapter 13, we also consider the possibilities for future research that are suggested by the combined results of the three studies that comprised the research reported in Parts Four and Five of this volume. Finally, in Chapter 14, we report the results of a follow-up study that we have conducted involving the more systematic and detailed analysis of the attributions data from Study 3. The aim of this follow-up study was to investigate more fully the possibility suggested by the results of Studies 1, 2, and 3, that questions about attributions might provide an important means of revealing deeper levels of an organisation's culture. It is our view that this study stands as just one example of the kind of future research into methodological issues in understanding organisational culture that might usefully be undertaken, and that we have advocated in Chapter 13.

PART SIX

EVALUATION AND FURTHER RESEARCH

Chapter 13

A Contextual Analysis of Organisational Culture: Evaluation and Recommendations for Future Research

The overall aim of Study 3 (reported in Chapters 10 through 12) was to develop a method for understanding organisational culture which would be more resource efficient than traditional ethnographic approaches, while at the same time offering insights into deeper-level culture that could not be obtained through the use of quantitative methods. The development of this method drew on insights from the two studies leading up to Study 3, as well as on the first author's understanding of the cultures of the two participating divisions of the research organisation (this understanding having evolved over a prolonged period of time spent in each division). Central also to the development of the method was a concern to bridge the gap (or at least go some way towards doing so) between the operationalisation of organisational culture and its conceptual treatment. A well-recognised problem in this area of research (e.g., Rousseau, 1990; Schein, 1985, 1992, 2004, 2010) is that, while conceptual treatments of organisational culture adequately convey its complexity (with references, e.g., to the taken-for-granted nature of cultural beliefs and assumptions and the grounding of these beliefs and assumptions in the organisation's history), operationalisations of culture often oversimplify the concept and fail to capture its true 'essence'. In attempting to address this problem, as well as to capitalise on insights gained from the first two studies, the method which was developed for use in Study 3 combined the following key features:

(1) It took the form of an 'issue-focussed' interview;
(2) The interview was semi-structured — it combined open-ended with closed questions and was sufficiently flexible to allow respondents to elaborate on, and qualify, their responses;
(3) The interview sought to operationalise key contextual variables thought to be important for an understanding of organisational culture; and
(4) The interview provided for the assessment of organisational attributions as a possible source of data from which inferences about culture could be made.

In the present chapter, an attempt is made to draw together the main findings of Study 3 (and the insights obtained from these findings) in order to provide some evaluation of the extent to which the aims of this study were met. The discussion in this chapter is divided into three sections. The first section provides an evaluation of each of the key features of the method in terms of its specific contribution to an understanding of organisational culture. The second section offers a more general evaluation of the method. Particular attention is drawn to the strengths and weaknesses of the method relative to other methods for understanding culture. And the third section considers some of the possible directions for future research which are suggested by the findings of Study 3. As indicated in the introduction to Study 3 (see Chapter 10), examples given to illustrate the use of the proposed method were drawn primarily from the main data set (concerned with the role of workers); however, as appropriate, examples were also drawn from the two associated data sets (concerned with the role of supervisors and the characteristics of good workers).

13.1 Evaluation of the Method: Key Features

As indicated, in this section we evaluate each of the key features of the method developed for use in Study 3. Consistent with our approach to this research throughout, the primary focus of the evaluation offered here is on methodological issues. Based on the findings of Study 3, what have we learned about each of method's key features? Is it useful insofar as providing information that, whether considered separately or in combination with other information, can help to reveal aspects of an organisation's deeper-level culture? Should the feature be retained as part of the method, or not?

13.1.1 *Issue-focussed interview*

The interview developed for use in Study 3 was designed to uncover cultural beliefs about the essential nature of workers. In terms of the typology that Schein originally proposed (Schein, 1985), beliefs in this area can be regarded as constituting a subset of the beliefs represented by his third category, The Nature of Human Nature[1]. Moreover, as Schein himself has acknowledged, there is a direct link between beliefs in this area and the beliefs with which McGregor (1960) was concerned in his Theory X — Theory Y classification of managerial assumptions. The specific focus of interviewing in Study 3 was on respondents' perceptions of the role of workers, elicited through questions about what workers did, in terms of both their primary or core activities and other activities in which they were engaged.

13.1.1.1 *Arguments in favour of an issue-focussed interview*

As indicated in the introduction to Study 3 (see Chapter 10) the exploratory nature of this work and the associated need to be able to evaluate the method's capacity for tapping

---

[1]As we have indicated previously, Schein later revised this typology (Schein, 1992, 2004, 2010), such that in its current form, beliefs about The Nature of Human Nature constitute a subset of a broader category that also includes beliefs about The Nature of Human Activity and beliefs about The Nature of Human Relationships.

cultural phenomena, was an important argument in support of the use of issue-focussed interviewing. In terms of an overall evaluation of this feature of the method, there are a number of additional, and to some extent more general, arguments which can be made in its defence. These are outlined below.

An issue-focussed interview has the advantage of allowing comparisons to be made across individuals and research settings (Sackmann, 1991). This was particularly important in Study 3 for two reasons. First, a key element of the validation of the method used in this study was the extent to which it could reveal differences between the participating divisions which the researcher[2] had become aware of through her involvement in each (on a relatively continuous basis over a period of approximately three years). Second, a hoped-for outcome of this research was that it would offer a practical means whereby aspects of an organisation's deeper-level culture could be systematically assessed. This would enable one to evaluate changes in culture over time, make comparisons between the cultures of different work organisations, and examine the relationship between organisational culture and change.

Another argument in favour of the use of issue-focussed interviewing — and one which has implications for the assessment of organisational culture more generally — concerns the pervasive nature of culture. This is the idea that "culture is not only deep, but also broad" (Pettigrew, 1990, p. 268) and that expressions or manifestations of it are likely to be found in all facets of organisation life. This characteristic of culture makes it naïve to think that one could arrive at an understanding of an organisation's (group's culture), in its entirety, in a single even though lengthy interview. At the same time, it can be argued that, given a culture's pervasiveness, the adoption of a focus for interviewing, *however narrow*, is still likely to provide insights into some aspect of the culture of the organisation (group) being studied. Indeed, it might even be argued that methods for understanding culture which are issue-specific enable a more in-depth analysis of culture than methods which are more broadly focussed. In this sense, the former might be better suited to revealing 'deep' culture, even though with respect to a single issue only, whereas the latter might be expected to provide more general, but also more superficial, insights into culture.

These speculations would need to be tested in empirical studies, the results of which might have implications for the choice of a method, based on the research question (whether it is broadly focussed and seeking surface-level insights only, or more narrowly focussed and seeking more in-depth insights). For example, an assessment of organisational attitudes to change, at a more surface-level, might be combined with a more in-depth assessment of the specific issue which is the subject of a change program. This would make apparent any discrepancy that existed between a surface-level willingness to change and deeper-level assumptions and beliefs about the issue that might be more resistant to

---

[2]As indicated previously, the first author undertook the data collection for the empirical studies that are reported in Volume II of this book. As such, any reference to 'the researcher' throughout this chapter is a reference to the first author.

change. For example, a surface-level willingness to participate in decision-making (reflected in comments along the lines of "Workers should be given a say") might be contradicted by an underlying belief, with respect to the issue in question, that it is the role of management to make decisions about this issue (and the role of workers to complain about these decisions). Studies of this kind might also provide information relevant to the development of more valid questionnaire measures of the surface elements of organisational culture. Specifically, insights into deep culture (even though they may be relatively narrowly focussed) may facilitate the construction of questionnaires in which the wording of items and/or their associated rating scales is more culturally grounded, and hence less prone to misinterpretation.

Finally, in the event that an organisation needs to conduct a cultural audit for practical purposes, issue-focussed interviewing, which can provide insights into highly specific aspects of the organisation's culture, is likely to be of more value than completely unstructured interviewing. For example, if the aim of the audit is to assess the organisation's 'readiness' for a particular change, it would be useful for change agents to know about those specific aspects of the culture, including contextual aspects, that are likely to have the most significant implications for the success of the change effort. Such knowledge could help to reveal sources of organisational resistance to change and may also provide insights into how to manage change more effectively. To take an example from the literature, knowledge that an organisation has traditionally supported values of innovation will help change agents to understand the resistance to change that is likely to be encountered if the organisation — perhaps for reasons of survival — decides to adopt an imitative strategy (Gagliardi, 1986). In the context of our Study 3, it can be argued that cultural beliefs about the role of workers are likely to have significant implications for the success of any organisational change effort which requires for its success a redefinition of the traditional role of workers. More will be said about this later in the discussion. It is of course possible that, in each of the examples above, there may be other aspects of the organisation's culture in addition to those cited (i.e., values of innovation, and beliefs about the role of workers, respectively), that could be relevant to an understanding of the issue in question. However, these aspects of the culture might be expected to emerge as part of the proposed assessment procedure. They might, for example, emerge in responses to questions about context and/ or they might find expression in organisation members' attributions concerning changes from one context to another (e.g., from the past to the present).

It should be noted that the above issue-focussed approach has been adopted in part by Schein (2010), in his role as a consultant to organisations (see Chapter 6 of Volume I for a description and discussion of Schein's 'clinical' approach to accessing, and using knowledge about, an organisation's culture to assist in dealing with practical issues in the organisation). Briefly, Schein provides what he claims to be a relatively quick clinical method — results can supposedly be obtained "in as little as half a day" (p. 326) — for accessing aspects of an organisation's deeper-level culture relevant to a specific organisational issue. The method involves the use of group discussions with insiders about the organisation's artefacts and values. Insiders are encouraged to explore any discrepancies that emerge between these artefacts and values, in order to identify the organisation's underlying cultural assumptions. Importantly, Schein's method does not use a standardised set of questions and this would seem to imply that it cannot be used to provide *direct* comparisons either of the cultures of different organisations or of the culture of the same organisation over time. Schein himself notes that a limitation of his method, at least when viewed from the perspective of the researcher, is that while the results of the assessment of organisational culture that it provides "may be completely clear to the insiders", these results may "still [be] puzzling to the outsider" (p. 325). From a practical perspective, Schein does not consider this feature of his method to be problematic. He argues that, if the goal of the assessment is "to help the organisation", then it is not necessary for the outsider to "fully understand the culture" (p. 325). However, if the aim is to provide the researcher with "enough clarity to be able to represent the culture to others" — and presumably this would entail having the capacity to compare the cultures of different organisations or to compare changes in one organisation's culture over time — then, as Schein suggests, "additional observational data and group meetings are likely to be necessary" (p. 325).

Schein does not elaborate on how specifically these additional data might be obtained or how long this process might take, but he does warn that ".... academic research or theory building ... requires real entry and involvement with the organisation beyond what questionnaires, surveys, or even individual interviews can provide" (p. 192). He also comments that: "... even if we have an intuitive understanding of an organisation's culture, we may find it extraordinarily difficult to write down that understanding in such a way that the essence of the culture can be communicated to someone else. We have so few examples in our literature that it is hard even to point to models of how it should be done" (p. 193). These comments suggest that Schein, like others who have taken a qualitative approach to culture, would be sceptical about the extent to which the method we are proposing could be successful in understanding and describing even relatively limited aspects of an organisation's deeper-level culture. However, those who have tried to assess the deeper levels of organisational culture might also be sceptical about Schein's claim that he can obtain such information within approximately a day, though they might readily accept that it is possible, and even likely, that the consultant or facilitator would not fully understand this information. The further claim that such information — gathered in so short a period of time, and not fully understood by the consultant or facilitator — can be useful in dealing with organisational issues, might also receive a sceptical response. What is needed here are studies that can determine whether or not Schein's clinical method is more valuable, insofar as providing culture-related insights into how to deal with organisational issues, than a method involving a discussion among insiders about their results on an existing (off-the-shelf) questionnaire measure of organisational norms or organisational values. As indicated in our discussion of Schein's method in Chapter 6 of Volume I, there is also a need to assess the extent to which this method produces accurate information about an organisation's culture, as would be evidenced, for example, by confirmatory data obtained from more in-depth follow-up investigations. And then there is the question of whether the value of Schein's method for facilitating organisational change derives from the actual data (i.e., the culture-related insights) that it generates, or whether the method gives rise to a kind of Hawthorne effect in which paying attention to cultural aspects of the organisation is, in and of itself, motivational for employees and secures their commitment to dealing with the particular problem or issue of concern. It is perhaps telling in this regard that Schein stresses the need to consider positive aspects of the culture in order to avoid unhelpful resistance or denial concerning negative aspects of the culture that might be revealed.

While we acknowledge the difficulties raised by Schein with respect to understanding and describing an organisation's deeper-level culture, we nevertheless maintain the view that a critical feature of any method for assessing deep culture is the adoption of a specific focus for interviewing. It might even be argued that investigations of organisational culture, more generally, could benefit from such an approach. The question remains, however, as to whether or not the issue of choice in Study 3 (namely, the role of workers) was relevant and appropriate given the aims of the study. Further to this, there needs to be some evaluation of the specific questions which were asked in order to elicit information about this issue. Were these questions the 'best' questions or can alternative, more useful, questions be suggested?

13.1.1.2 *The 'role of workers': An evaluation of the issue chosen*

With respect, first of all, to the relevance of the issue, the point can be made that this was largely established prior to Study 3 being carried out. As indicated in the introduction to Study 2, the choice of a focal point for interviewing was not made arbitrarily. On the contrary, there was good evidence — both from the previous empirical work in the participating divisions, as well as from the researcher's more general experience within the divisions — to suggest that the issue was one of considerable salience to participants in the research. Thus, one important confirmation of the relevance of the issue was its emergence in the data. Of course, one should be mindful here of the influence of the researcher's level of access to the organisation. The point has been made previously that the nature of the emergent issues in any data set is likely to be influenced significantly by the particular organisational level at which the research is being carried out. This, of course, has important implications for the *a priori* identification of a suitable issue. More will be said about this in a later section.

Apart from the emergence of the issue in the data, the fact that there existed, in the literature, a useful typology — namely that developed by Schein (1985, 1992, 2004, 2010) — for the classification of beliefs associated with this, and other issues, provided further confirmation of the issue's relevance. A third, and more general argument which validates the issue of choice for Study 3 is that, during the 1990s when this study was conducted, there was an emerging interest in the organisational change literature in the effectiveness, or otherwise, of organisational change efforts which required for their success a fundamental shift in organisation members' thinking about the respective roles of workers and supervisors (Clark, 1993; Dawson, 1994). For example, Total Quality Management (TQM) programs, with their emphasis on employee empowerment, the redesign of work around semi-autonomous and fully autonomous teams, and more open and participative styles of management, constituted a major focus of this literature (e.g., Dawson & Palmer, 1995; Kerfoot & Knights, 1995; Wilkinson, Marchington, Goodman, & Ackers, 1992).

The important point — at least in the context of the present discussion — is that much of this research (which often involved case study investigations of single research settings) documented the limited success of these change efforts and the equivocal results which they produced (e.g., Dawson, 1996; Guest, Peccei, & Fulcher, 1993; Meyer & Stott, 1985; Wells, 1982, cited in Blunt, 1986). Moreover, attempts to explain such findings often drew attention to the role of the organisation's culture in impeding the change effort. For example, in their case study account of a TQM program which was introduced into British Rail in the early 1990s, Guest *et al.* (1993) provide a nice illustration of the durability of organisational culture and its ability to slow the change process. They show how, despite extensive training of senior and middle management in the principles and practices of TQM, the behaviour of personnel at this level continued to reflect the beliefs and values of the organisation's traditional bureaucratic culture. While the TQM program had resulted in some excellent ideas for quality improvements being generated by junior members of the organisation, these ideas were typically not approved for implementation. Rather, the most successful ideas, in terms of implementation, were those which had been devised by senior managers. Thus, while there was support in principle for employee empowerment, in practice, the effects of a strongly bureaucratic culture were still very much in evidence.

The study by Meyer and Stott (1985) also provides a good illustration of how organisational culture can act to impede organisational change. These researchers were interested in why Quality Circles (QCs), which were a Japanese management innovation, were experiencing so little success in America. Their research took the form of a case study investigation of two companies which had introduced QCs. Of particular interest, in the context of our research, is the account provided by the authors of some of the main problems which the companies in their study had experienced in the running of team ('circle') meetings. Some of these problems quite clearly had their origins in the traditional (cultural) role expectations of participants in the meetings. For example, there were reports of supervisors dominating the discussion in meetings and attempting to impose their ideas on the group. There were complaints that, while supervisors were "open" (p. 38) in team meetings, they reverted to more traditional supervisory behaviour on the shop floor, rarely asking subordinates for their ideas, and ignoring subordinates' suggestions for change. And finally, some subordinates reported that, as a consequence of their supervisor's behaviour in team meetings, they had lost respect for their supervisor's abilities. The point can be made that, if there had been some assessment of the culture of these two organisations (with respect specifically to prevailing beliefs about the respective roles of workers and supervisors) prior to the introduction of QCs, it may have been possible to have anticipated, and devised strategies for dealing with, problems such as these.

On the basis of the arguments presented above, it can be concluded that the issue of choice for Study 3, namely the role of workers, constituted an appropriate and relevant focal point for interviewing. There remains, however, some uncertainty about the suitability of the specific questions that were asked in order to elicit information about this issue. The reasons for this uncertainty are elaborated upon below.

13.1.1.3 *The 'role of workers': An evaluation of the questions asked*

While the questions in Part A of the Study 3 interview (see Chapter 10, Section 10.3.1) were effective insofar as they generated 'rich' information about workers' activities (as perceived by respondents in relation to a number of different contextual domains), there was a sense in which they may have been too 'academic'. In other words, the questions that were asked — namely "What are the main duties of workers?" and "What else do workers do?" (modified, as necessary, and repeated for the past context, the future context, the 'other' context, and the ideal context) — may not be the kinds of questions that organisation members typically give much thought to. Another criticism of these questions is that they ask about an issue (i.e., workers' activities) which, to use Sackmann's (1991) terminology, could be seen to be more open to 'factual' definitions, rather than 'customary' (i.e., cultural) definitions. In other words, these questions may not have been as "sensitive to culturally specific interpretations" (Sackmann, 1991, p. 182) as was desirable, given the aims of the study.

The above argument that questions about workers' activities may not have been the most effective for eliciting information about the role of workers has important methodological implications. It suggests that, when designing questions for use in the assessment of organisational culture, one should not attempt to directly convert existing dimensions or categories of culture (of which many have been proposed in the literature) into questions. In Study 3, the question "What do workers do?" can perhaps be seen as too direct an attempt to elicit information about the role of workers. In this sense, the best questions may be those which are only indirectly related to the issue or dimension of interest, but which will nevertheless generate information from which inferences about the issue, or dimension, can be made. Attempts by psychologists to measure individual personality provide a useful analogy in this respect. Personality measures do not ask respondents directly whether they regard themselves as being, say, introverted or extroverted. Rather, respondents are presented with a number of more general questions (e.g., about activities in which they may like to engage) and, from their responses to these questions, inferences are made about their degree of introversion or extroversion.

13.1.2 *Semi-structured interview*

The choice of a semi-structured interview for use in Study 3 was based on the argument that such an approach could draw on the complementary strengths of qualitative and quantitative methods. On the one hand, it offered a means whereby rich data (of the kind usually associated with purely qualitative methods) could be generated and, on the other, it allowed for the systematic analysis and comparison of data (a particular strength of quantitative methods).

As indicated, the interview schedule included both open-ended and closed questions. The former permitted respondents to respond in their own terms and to voice their own thoughts and insights, while the latter required respondents to give a simple "Yes" or "No" answer or, alternatively, to choose their response from a number of predetermined response possibilities. A second important feature of the interview was that it was designed to be sufficiently flexible to allow respondents to elaborate on and/or qualify their responses (perhaps through the use of examples). And finally, while the aim was to maintain a relatively standardised format for questioning[3] — whereby all respondents would be presented with the same basic set of questions in roughly the same order — respondents were given some latitude to explore areas of interest not directly addressed by the interview questions, if they chose to do so.

The following discussion provides an evaluation of the use of a semi-structured format for interviewing in Study 3, with consideration given to the issues raised by each of the specific components making up this feature of the method's design.

13.1.2.1 *Open-ended and closed questions: Benefits of their combined use*

The main focus of the evaluation in this section is on that aspect of the method whereby respondents were presented with an initial open-ended question which was followed immediately afterwards by the presentation of a series of closed questions or prompts. As indicated, the former asked about what it was that workers did, in terms of both their primary task ('main' job) and other activities in which they were engaged. The latter asked about worker involvement in a number of pre-specified activities, identified by the researcher as possible activities in which workers might engage and chosen to represent McGregor's (1960) Theory X — Theory Y dichotomy. This particular combination of open-ended and closed questions was asked, first, in relation to the respondent's present experience and subsequently (and with appropriate modifications to tense *etc.*) in relation to the respondent's past, anticipated future, and ideal for the organisation.

---

[3]Clearly this was necessary if more systematic and comparative analyses of the data were to be carried out. There was also a concern to minimise the effects of researcher bias (e.g., the tendency of a researcher to explore some issues and ideas in more depth than others, based on her/his own interests and values), which has been recognised as a particular problem for interviews that adopt a more 'informal conversational' style (Patton, 1990).

Of course, there were other open-ended and closed questions, apart from these, with which respondents were presented. For example, there were questions which were designed to elicit information about the extent and frequency of worker involvement in particular activities, there were questions seeking information about the time frame of particular changes that respondents had experienced, or were anticipating, and there were "Why?" questions aimed at revealing respondents' causal beliefs or attributions. While the discussion in this section will consider the value of some of these questions, for others, their evaluation is more appropriately reported elsewhere (e.g., "Why?" questions are reviewed in Section 13.1.4 on 'Attributions').

An important finding of Study 3 was that the combination of the initial open-ended questions followed by prompt questions, which sought information about the *same* issue, consistently (i.e., for all four contextual domains) provided more information than would have been obtained had respondents been presented with the open-ended questions only or, alternatively, with the prompt questions only. Stated another way, while there was a degree of overlap between worker activities mentioned spontaneously and worker activities identified in response to prompting, the discrepancy between spontaneous and prompted responses was, for all four contextual domains, considerable. One conclusion suggested by this finding is that activities elicited only in response to prompting may be less salient to respondents — in terms of their definitions of what workers do — than activities elicited spontaneously. Indeed, the findings of Study 3 provided reasonable support for this conclusion. The reader is reminded briefly of the production division data on training. While there were no respondents from this division who spontaneously mentioned that divisional workers were involved in training, in response to prompting, almost two-thirds of respondents reported some worker involvement in this activity. However, a strong theme which emerged in the qualitative data associated with these responses was that workers' access to training was entirely contingent on production demands in the division, so that at times of high production, training activities tended to be suspended. It was argued, therefore, that training was likely to constitute a peripheral, rather than a central, activity in respondents' definitions of what workers do.

A similar, but somewhat more general conclusion which is suggested by the finding that there was a marked discrepancy between respondents' spontaneous and prompted responses is that the respondents and the researcher differed, at least to some extent, in the way in which they thought about the role of workers[4]. More specifically, activities which the researcher considered could be reasonably included in one's definition of the role of workers (i.e., 'what workers do') were different from many of the activities which emerged as being most salient in respondents' definitions. Of course, while this can be regarded as

---

[4]The reader is reminded that, in the Study 3 interview, the prompt questions related to the second open question only. That is, they asked about activities in which workers might engage *in addition to* their 'main' job. In this sense, the prompts were not intended to cover the range of activities that might be included in a comprehensive definition of the role of workers.

a useful insight in itself, it does raise the question of what specifically is to be gained from the addition of the prompt questions. There are perhaps four arguments of relevance here, each of which is outlined below.

(1) **Prompt questions provide additional information.** Study 3 clearly demonstrated that prompt questions offer a useful means for getting more information. Indeed, the point can be made, that with one exception[5], all of the prompt questions — whether they were asked in relation to the present, the past, the anticipated future, or the ideal — always generated some positive responses (i.e., "Yes" responses in the case of the present context, and 'change' responses in the case of the past, anticipated future, and ideal contexts). Moreover, for both divisions, prompting often generated a positive response from a *majority* of respondents in the sample. While it might be argued that the extra information provided by the prompts may lack salience for respondents, in terms of their definitions of the role of workers, when combined with the information generated spontaneously, it nevertheless gives one a more complete understanding of the issue (in this case 'what workers do') than one would otherwise have.

(2) **Prompt questions may elicit information which signals a culture in transition.** Another argument in favour of the presentation of prompt questions, in addition to the initial open-ended questions, is that prompting may elicit information about changes — in this case, in workers' activities — which could have implications for a future redefinition of the role of workers. In other words, while activities elicited in response to prompting may lack salience in respondents' *current* thinking about what workers do, such activities may, over time, become more central to prevailing definitions of the role of workers. Indeed, based on evidence from Study 3, such an outcome might reasonably be predicted for the production division. A number of respondents from this division shared the view that, over recent years, divisional management had become increasingly committed to the development of a more 'active' role for workers. Of course the success of management's efforts in this regard might have been evaluated with a readministration, several years later, of the Study 3 interview. If, on this second occasion, respondents' spontaneous accounts of what workers did were found to contain more references to activities indicative of a more active role (activities such as planning, group problem-solving, training, *etc.*), then one might reasonably conclude that management had succeeded in establishing a more active role for workers.

(3) **Prompt questions can be a stimulus for the emergence of themes and attributions.** The addition of prompt questions can increase the likelihood that particular themes and types of attributions which are associated with the issue being investigated will emerge. This is because the prompts provide respondents with additional focal points for their thinking about the issue (in this case, they ask about other activities in which

---

[5]For the tooling division, there were no respondents who reported a change from the past to the present in the involvement of divisional workers in group problem-solving.

workers might engage), thereby encouraging them to explore the issue in more depth than they might do if presented only with the initial open-ended question. This is important since, as will be argued subsequently, thematic and attributions data can offer critical insights into how respondents think about, and interpret, the issue.

(4) **Prompt questions can reveal assumed knowledge.** A fourth, and final, argument in support of the inclusion of prompt questions — and one which challenges the notion that information elicited in response to prompting will always have less salience for respondents than information elicited in response to the open-ended questions — is that prompting can potentially reveal assumed knowledge. This is the idea that there may, for example, be particular activities which are so central to respondents' definitions of the role of workers that they have come to be taken-for-granted and will require some form of prompting to bring them to the surface. The evidence in support of this argument came from the analysis of data pertaining to the qualities/characteristics of 'good' workers. Specifically, despite evidence suggesting that, in the tooling division, quality had always been very much on the agenda[6], a minority of respondents only made spontaneous reference to the importance of producing quality work, when asked about what one had to do to be thought of, by one's supervisor, as a good worker. However, when respondents were subsequently asked to rate the importance of this worker characteristic in determining one's status as a good worker, all respondents rated it as either *very important* or *moderately important*. A possible explanation for this finding is that, in this division, 'producing quality work' had come to be regarded as such a basic (taken-for-granted) requirement of one's role and status as a tradesman, that most respondents did not think to mention it in response to the initial open-ended question, but rather they required prompting in order to explicitly acknowledge its importance.

13.1.2.2 *Open-ended and closed questions: Do prompts introduce a social desirability bias?*

Of course, where there is a marked discrepancy between respondents' spontaneous and prompted responses, one also needs to consider the possibility that prompting is having the effect of 'putting words into people's mouths'. There was, however, little evidence in Study 3 of significant social desirability effects. First, the number of 'positive' responses to prompt questions — whether they were asked in relation to the present context, the past

---

[6]Historical data from the Study 3 interview provided evidence to suggest that the members of this division had a significant shared history (in most cases, spanning more than twenty years) in which there had been an emphasis on producing quality work. Study 1 also provided insights into the importance of quality in this division. There was evidence, for example, that notions of quality were central to the tradesman's sense of pride and self-worth and also helped to explain the position of considerable status which he occupied in the industry.

context, the anticipated future context, or the ideal context — was variable. That is, in some cases, a majority of respondents in the sample gave positive responses to prompt questions, whilst in others, positive responses were recorded for a minority of respondents only. If social desirability effects had been marked, one might have expected greater consistency in this regard than was observed. Second, social desirability responding would predict that, after initial exposure of respondents to the prompt questions (in relation to the present context), prompted activities would begin to be increasingly well-represented in respondents' answers to the subsequent open-ended questions. Thus, by the time one came to the open-ended question about the ideal role for workers, one would expect respondents to be well-primed to provide socially desirable responses to this question. In fact, what was found was that, for the tooling division, prompted activities were very poorly represented in open question data for the ideal context, and for the production division, the representation of these activities was highly variable. This finding not only constituted evidence of the relative absence of social desirability effects but it also provided some unexpected validation of these open question data (i.e., the data could be taken at their 'face value' as indicative of a genuine desire, on the part of respondents, for change).

It is interesting to speculate briefly as to the possible reasons for the relative absence of social desirability effects in Study 3. Four such explanations come to mind and these are outlined below.

(1) One explanation is suggested by the types of questions that were being asked. Questions which seek information about what workers do at the present time, or about what they did in the past (whether in the respondent's current, or other organisation), are essentially 'knowledge questions' (Patton, 1990). They are asking for factual information and, in this sense, may be less susceptible to social desirability effects than questions which ask about respondents' opinions, values, and feelings. However, these latter types of questions were also included in the interview (obvious examples being "Why?" questions and questions about the anticipated future and ideal contexts).

(2) It is possible that the in-depth nature of the inquiry, along with the intensive questioning of respondents about the issue (respondents were asked about their experience of the issue in relation to five contextual domains and, where relevant, were also asked for examples), had the effect of counteracting any tendency in respondents to provide quick responses that would satisfy some social desirability criterion. This kind of responding might be expected to be more prevalent in, say, questionnaire measures which require respondents to distinguish between their 'actual' and 'ideal' on a number of different dimensions — one example being Harrison's (1975) questionnaire for diagnosing organisation ideology, and its later revised edition Diagnosing Organizational Culture by Harrison and Stokes (1992). The method that we are proposing would help to overcome this possibility both by the in-depth nature of the questioning and by the fact that other contexts are also assessed to provide comparison data that can help to explain the relationship between the actual and the ideal.

(3) A third explanation lies in the fact that the respondents in Study 3 were all drawn from the lower levels of their divisional hierarchy (i.e., the sample comprised predominantly shop floor workers and their immediate supervisors). It may be that personnel at these lower levels are simply less well-informed about, and less aware of, what constitutes a socially desirable orientation towards any given issue, than say more senior divisional personnel (e.g., management personnel). The latter might be expected to have had more exposure, through their participation in training and development programs, to various ideas and concepts currently in vogue in academic thinking about the experience of work. They may also be more inclined to provide opinions that are in line with what would be acceptable to higher levels of management.

(4) A fourth factor influencing the absence of social desirability effects in Study 3 may have been the interviewing skills and experience of the researcher, which enabled her to establish a close and positive relationship with all participants in the study. This explanation has important practical implications for the use of our proposed method, a discussion of which will be provided in a subsequent section.

13.1.2.3 *Open-ended and closed questions: Additional issues related to the use of prompts*

On the basis of the discussion above, there would seem to be good support for the present approach of combining open-ended questions with prompt questions. This particular feature of the method did offer a means by which to obtain comprehensive information in a relatively economical way, while at the same time being faithful to the perspectives of respondents. Having said this, one revision to the method which has been suggested is a reduction in the number of prompt questions. The presentation of six prompts (the first comprising six parts) on four separate occasions (in relation to the present, past, anticipated future, and ideal contexts) did extend the interview time perhaps more than was desirable. This resulted in a problem with missing data in the last section of the interview which asked respondents about their views or aspirations with respect to the ideal context. While it has been argued that a reasonably inclusive prompt set was necessary given the exploratory nature of this research, a possible goal for future research in this area would be to reduce the number of prompt questions to a 'critical' few.

Another problem with the prompt questions — apart from there being too many of them — was that the attempt to identify, *a priori*, activities representative of McGregor's (1960) Theory X — Theory Y dichotomy met with limited success only. With the benefit of hindsight, this outcome might have been predicted. Whether or not a particular activity could be regarded as more or less indicative of a Theory X or a Theory Y orientation was dependent upon the meanings which respondents attached to the activity. For example, while the involvement of workers in record-keeping activities could reasonably be seen as indicative of an active (Theory Y), rather than a passive (Theory X) role for workers, there was little evidence from the Study 3 results to suggest that this was the case. On the contrary, a theme which emerged strongly in the qualitative data associated with this activity category (in particular, for the production division) was that record-keeping served primarily a quality control function. There was little recognition of the motivational value of involving workers in record-keeping — the idea being that workers' jobs will be enriched if they have some means of obtaining information about the effectiveness of their performance (Hackman & Oldham, 1976). These findings have important implications for the interpretation of the results of quantitative measures of organisational culture. The use of these measures is predicated on the assumption that the questions they ask, along with the ratings that respondents subsequently assign in responding to them, will be interpreted similarly by all respondents and, moreover, that these interpretations will be consistent with the meanings intended by those who constructed the measure.

While much of the above discussion has been concerned with the finding, in Study 3, that there was a marked discrepancy between respondents' spontaneous and prompted responses, the point should be made that, in some other research setting or with research participants drawn from a different level of the organisational hierarchy (e.g., senior management), one could conceivably get more overlap between these two sets of responses. Such a finding would suggest that the categories used by the research participants to describe their experience (in relation to the issue being investigated) were very similar to the categories which the researcher had identified (perhaps on the basis of her/his review of the literature) as being potentially relevant. In this sense, the open question data (respondents' spontaneous responses) could be seen as providing some validation of the categories represented by the prompt questions. Of course, one would also have to consider the possibility of there being a social desirability bias in respondents' spontaneous responses, particularly where respondents had been drawn from the more senior levels of the organisation's hierarchy. This is because, as suggested above, personnel at these levels are likely to be more aware of, and better informed about, what constitutes socially desirable thinking, than personnel at lower levels of the hierarchy.

13.1.2.4 *Open-ended and closed questions: The use of additional follow-up questions*

As indicated above, the interview developed for use in Study 3 included a number of other open-ended and closed questions, in addition to those already discussed. At this point it is appropriate to comment briefly on the value of some of these additional questions, in particular, the probe questions which were designed to provide more specific information about the activities in which workers reportedly engaged. It will be recalled that, for each of the worker activities which a respondent identified (not including the worker's main job or primary task), the respondent was asked to estimate the extent of worker involvement in the activity (e.g., "How many workers attend information meetings?") and the frequency of worker involvement in the activity (e.g., "How often do workers attend information meetings?").

The results of Study 3 suggested that one advantage of questions such as these is that they provide good information about the degree of consistency, or inconsistency, which exists in respondents' perceptions of the particular aspect(s) of organisational life about which they are being asked. Such information may be of value to management, particularly where it contradicts management's perceptions. For example, management may believe that there is widespread awareness in the organisation of its commitment to increasing the level of training for employees. Questions such as the above, however, may reveal that organisation members perceive the level of employee involvement in training to be very low. Alternatively, they may reveal that organisation members have highly variable perceptions of the level of employee involvement in training. Either way, information of this kind is likely to be useful to management. It may, for example, alert management to the need to more actively communicate the organisation's training efforts to all employees.

The results of Study 3 also provided evidence to suggest that the use of probe questions, of the kind described above, can provide more reliable information than questions which require respondents simply to provide a rating of the particular aspect(s) of their experience about which they are being asked. In other words, it is preferable to ask respondents direct questions, for example, about how many workers attend training, and how often, rather than ask them to indicate the level of worker involvement in training on a scale from, say, *a very high level* to *a very low level*. This is because respondents can differ markedly in their interpretations of the various response categories which are included in a rating scale. The same objective level of training can be interpreted by one respondent as *a very high level* and, by another, as *a very low level*. Moreover, there was evidence from Study 3 to suggest that interpretive differences of this kind may reflect differences in the historical context of respondents' experience (e.g., respondents who have had a long history in which the level of training activity has been very low are likely to judge any current increases in training as being more significant than would respondents who had considerably more exposure to training over time). This criticism of rating scales — namely, that there can be considerable variability in respondents' interpretations of the various response categories which they include — is not new, and has been addressed more directly, and in much more detail, by other researchers (e.g., Budescu & Wallsten, 1985; Clarke, Ruffin, Hill, & Beaman, 1992). These findings suggest that if rating scales are to be used in measures of organisational culture (and, indeed, also in measures of organisational climate), then they should be accompanied by descriptors to assist respondents in understanding the meaning associated with each rating.

13.1.2.5 *Elaborations and qualifications: Maximising the success of qualitative interviewing*

As indicated, an important feature of the method used in Study 3 was that the interview was designed to be sufficiently flexible to allow respondents to elaborate on and/or qualify their responses. This is not to say that respondents were free to 'ramble' unconstrainedly. On the contrary, the interviewer (in this case, the researcher) had a relatively active role in guiding respondents' elaborations and qualifications. Specifically, if respondents provided information that was quite clearly relevant to the issue about which they were being asked, then they were allowed to continue uninterrupted. If respondents offered no elaborative or qualifying information, and if time permitted, then the interviewer intervened with a prompt question, such as, "Can you tell me more about that?" or "Can you give an example?". And if respondents provided information which clearly lacked relevance to the issue about which they were being asked (this was typically not immediately apparent), then the interviewer attempted to redirect the focus of the interview with a comment such as "What you are saying is very interesting, and we might come back to it later. However, for now, I wonder if we can talk about…".

There are a number of factors likely to influence the success of the above approach to interviewing. First, while the approach is relatively straightforward in the sense that it requires no highly specialised skills for its use, it would nevertheless be desirable that the interviewer has received some basic training in interviewing skills[7]. These skills are needed to ensure that rapport is appropriately established and maintained, that accurate information is obtained in an effective and efficient way, and to minimise social desirability responding. A second, possibly more important prerequisite, and one which has been acknowledged in the literature on qualitative interviewing (Buchanan, Boddy, & McCalman, 1988; Patton, 1990), is that the interviewer should be the kind of person who is genuinely interested in the lives and experiences of others. Essentially, this is the argument that: "If what people have to say about their world is generally boring to you, then you will never be a great interviewer" (Patton, 1990, p. 279). Information of this kind might be available from an assessment of the performance of potential research interviewers in an interviewing training program. And third, consideration should also be given to the possibility that, in Study 3, the attempt to get good qualitative data was made easier by the researcher's relatively long association with the research organisation and the participants in the research. Of course, the question remains as to just how critical such an association might be. Is it the case, for example, that there is some minimum period of time which one would need to spend in the research setting, or that there are certain types of experiences which one would need to have, in order to maximise the usefulness of our proposed approach to interviewing? For example, would the experience of conducting pilot study interviews with a range of employees provide the researcher with sufficient information to gain an understanding of issues relevant to the assessment of the deeper levels of the organisation's culture?

13.1.2.6 *Elaborations and qualifications: Key benefits*

In terms of an overall assessment of this feature of the method, the results of Study 3 provided strong support for an approach in which respondents are given some latitude to

---

[7]The researcher's previous training as a psychologist was advantageous in this regard.

elaborate on and/or qualify their responses. Such an approach offers a number of important advantages, each of which is discussed below.

(1) **Qualitative data can provide insights into meaning.** Qualitative data (in the form of respondents' elaborations on, and qualifications of, their responses) can provide important insights into the meaning which respondents attach to those aspects of their experience about which they are being asked. More specifically, these data would seem to be critical for the interpretation of information provided in response to the standardised interview questions. For example, while the latter may reveal a perception among organisation members that the organisation supports a certain level of training activity, this information, by itself, tells us little about how organisation members think and feel about training, and what training actually means to them. Knowledge of this kind, which is highly context-specific, is unlikely to be revealed unless one has access to the kind of rich data that are generated when respondents elaborate on, and qualify, their responses.

To continue with the example above, a thematic content analysis of the elaborative and qualifying data on training provided evidence of a number of important themes in respondents' thinking about the involvement of divisional workers in training. Some of these themes were common to both divisions, whilst others emerged in the data for one division only. For example, respondents from both divisions shared the view that training was provided primarily in response to the organisation's needs, with little consideration given to the individual's needs and little recognition of the potential motivational value of involving workers in training. There was also a perception among respondents from both divisions that workers were reluctant to attend training if this required an investment of their own time for which they were not financially compensated. Differences between the divisions also emerged. For example, while there was evidence, in both divisions, of negative attitudes to training, these attitudes arose out of different concerns. In the tooling division, respondents were concerned about the lack of 'task' relevance of the training which was currently provided. They also expressed concern about the relevance of training for older workers and they questioned the fairness of the current expectation that older workers (along with their younger peers) should retrain for the purpose of becoming multi-skilled. In contrast, in the production division, respondents' negative attitudes to training were underpinned by their cynicism about the division's current efforts to satisfy government legislation (regarding an organisation's minimum acceptable commitment to training) by classifying, as 'training', almost any activity which did not involve direct production. The important point has been made previously that it is hard to imagine how insights such as these, which are highly context-specific, could have been obtained if a more structured quantitative approach to data collection had been used. It simply would not have been possible to have identified, *a priori*, the range of questions that one would need to ask in order to obtain this information. One possible way in which this assumption might be tested would be to compare the results of an analysis of data collected using an organisational culture questionnaire, with the results of an analysis of data, pertaining to the same issues, but collected using the method that we are advocating.

Given the widely accepted conceptualisation of organisational culture as comprising an organisation's system of shared meanings (Louis, 1983; Schein, 1985), it might be argued that the *sine qua non* of any method which seeks to understand organisational culture is that it should have the capacity to reveal meaning. As illustrated above, Study 3 provided good evidence to suggest that the qualitative data generated constituted an important source of information about meaning. There was also evidence from this study to suggest that the value of such information, apart from its general cultural significance, is that it can highlight similarities and differences within and between groups that might not otherwise be revealed.

More specifically, qualitative data of the kind referred to above can reveal inconsistencies — both between respondents and between respondents and the researcher — in the meanings which they attribute to the language and terms used in the interview questions. For example, in Study 3, it was found that respondents from the production division differed in their definition of the term 'training'. For some respondents, training was defined as encompassing both informal on-the-job training and formal off-the-job training whereas, for others, the term was interpreted to mean formal off-the-job training only. Of course, these different definitions influenced whether or not respondents gave a "Yes" or a "No" response in answer to the closed question: "Are the workers in your division involved in any training or professional development activities?" The apparent inconsistency which was suggested by the initial finding that some respondents reported that divisional workers were involved in training, whilst others reported that they were not, could be resolved by an analysis of the qualitative data which, in this case, suggested that a "Yes" and a "No" response could mean essentially the same thing (namely, that the training provided in this division was predominantly on-the-job training, rather than more formalised off-the-job training). One important methodological implication of a finding such as this is that one cannot assume that respondents who give a "Yes" response constitute a qualitatively different group from respondents who give a "No" response. More generally, the existence of any interpretive inconsistency raises questions about the extent to which data from one group (in this case, the reference is to data generated by the standardised interview questions) can be aggregated reliably and compared with data from another group. It also raises questions about the extent to which any apparent inconsistencies should be accepted as indicating a culture of disunity or ambiguity without further in-depth questioning. Of course, the resolution of such inconsistencies, as either genuine or due to different interpretations of questions, or different uses of rating categories based on different experiences, would depend on the skill of the interviewer to ask questions in such a way (e.g., with sufficient sensitivity) as to enable the issue to be resolved. Without such skills, the interviewer/researcher could interpret apparent differences as indicative of a culture of disunity or ambiguity, particularly if for practical or theoretical reasons, this is what she/he is expecting to find.

(2) **Qualitative data can reveal differences between groups.** A second advantage of qualitative data which was suggested by the findings of Study 3 is that they can reveal differences between groups (divisions) that may not be apparent in information provided in response to the standardised questions. For example, on the basis of such information, the tooling division and the production division appeared to be very similar in terms of respondents' current experience of the involvement of divisional workers in training. Specifically, all of the respondents from the tooling division and two-thirds of the respondents from the production division reported that the workers in their respective divisions attended training; in all cases, this information was provided in response to prompting, rather than in response to the open-ended question; and in both divisions, there was considerable variability in respondents' estimates of the extent and frequency of worker involvement in training. On the basis of this information, then, it was difficult to distinguish between the divisions. However, a subsequent analysis of the qualitative data associated with these responses provided evidence of some important thematic differences between the divisions. As indicated above, a theme which was unique to the production division concerned the perception that training was provided only when production demands were low. A theme which was unique to the tooling division concerned the perception that training was more appropriate for younger workers than older workers, and that it was unfair to expect older workers to retrain in order to become multi-skilled. The point can be made that differences of this kind, which are unlikely to be revealed using more highly structured quantitative approaches, may have critical implications for how managers and change agents should go about introducing and managing change (in this case, in relation to worker involvement in training) in each of these groups.

(3) **Qualitative data can expose superficial differences.** In contrast to the above, a third advantage of qualitative data is that they can show where differences, between individuals or groups, which are suggested by information provided in response to the standardised interview questions may be more apparent than real. Evidence for this might be indicated in the finding that the thematic content of respondents' elaborations and qualifications was the same, despite differences in their responses to the standardised questions. An example from Study 3 is that, in the production division, the qualitative data on training and information meetings, for both "Yes" respondents and "No" respondents (i.e., respondents reporting that workers were involved in these activities as well as respondents reporting that workers were not involved in these activities), contained evidence of the theme that worker involvement in non-production activities was contingent on production demands. One important implication of this finding is that, as above, it cannot be assumed that respondents who give a "Yes" response necessarily constitute a qualitatively different group from respondents who give a "No"

response. It has already been indicated above that the resolution of apparent differences and indeed, apparent similarities, within and between groups would require a certain amount of interviewing skill. The capacity of the method to reliably resolve such issues could be assessed partly by having different interviewers assess a different set of individuals from the same and/or different groups. It has been an assumption in qualitative research that the findings of research conducted by individual investigators who spend a considerable time in organisations are reliable as well as valid. But, as has been mentioned in previous chapters, the case of Margaret Mead's anthropological work and its questioning by Derek Freeman suggests that this assumption may be unwarranted and that such findings should be subject to reliability checks of the kind proposed.

13.1.2.7 *Elaborations and qualifications: The importance of a systematic approach to qualitative data analysis*

The discussion in the preceding sections has presented some of the main arguments in favour of an interview design which is sufficiently flexible to allow respondents to elaborate on, and qualify, their responses. Broadly speaking, this feature of the method allows for the generation of rich qualitative data, without which one's understanding of data generated in response to the standardised questions is likely to remain at a relatively superficial level. The point should be made, however, that in order to maximise the usefulness of this feature of the method, one's approach to the analysis of the qualitative data that are generated should be as systematic as possible. There are two main reasons for this.

(1) First, a systematic analysis of the qualitative data can provide one with relatively reliable information about the prevalence of (i.e., degree of consensus about) particular themes. This is important given the conceptualisation of organisational culture as an organisation's system of *shared* meanings (Louis, 1983; Schein, 1985), and also given the criticism that descriptive studies of culture often fail to demonstrate how much consensus actually exists (Rousseau, 1990). There are a number of sources of information which will be of value in determining a theme's prevalence. The most obvious is the number of respondents in the group who give responses which contain evidence of the theme. It is useful to know, for example, that a particular theme emerges in the responses of 80% of respondents, as opposed to, say, 10% of respondents. Of course, access to this information assumes that one's sample is sufficiently large for the theme, if it is present, to emerge. The point can be made that, if Study 3 had involved, say, two or three participants only from each division (instead, as was the case, 12 participants from the tooling division and 19 from the production division), then it is questionable whether some of the themes which emerged as being important, would have been identified at all. There is also an argument that, if one was seeking a comprehensive understanding of organisation-wide attitudes and opinions in relation to

some issue, then one may need to sample from different levels of the organisational hierarchy. This is because a theme which emerges in the data from respondents at one level of the hierarchy may not emerge in the data from respondents at another level.

The strength of a particular theme will also be indicated in the presence, or absence, of disconfirming evidence. For example, in Study 3, a small number of respondents from each division commented on the essentially passive role which workers played in information meetings. As they saw it, workers were either not asked to contribute in these meetings or, if they were, they were typically reluctant to participate. The point was made that, while this theme was not strongly supported by the data (in terms of the numbers of respondents who made comments reflecting the theme), the absence of any views to contradict it suggested that it might, in fact, be more central to an under-standing of the issue being investigated (in this case, the nature of workers' involve-ment in information meetings) than it had, at first, appeared to be.

A third source of information about the strength of a particular theme is the emer-gence of the theme in respondents' comments about a number of different issues. In Study 3, the production division theme that workers' involvement in non-production activities was contingent upon production demands emerged in the qualitative data associated with respondents' accounts of worker involvement in a number of different activities (including information meetings, training, and group problem-solving). As argued above, one advantage of the inclusion of prompt questions in addition to the open-ended questions was that it provided more opportunities for particular themes and types of attributions, if they were present, to find expression.

(2) Apart from the argument that a systematic approach to the analysis of qualitative data is necessary in order to demonstrate the degree of consensus that exists in relation to emergent themes, such an approach can also be advocated on the grounds that it allows the researcher to keep a check on her/his own biases. Given the widely accepted view that any research inquiry (regardless of the philosophical paradigm which informs the research design) is likely to be influenced, at least to some extent, by the researcher (Bryman, 1988; Easterby-Smith, Thorpe, & Lowe, 1991), it is not difficult to imagine how, in the present context, a researcher might be inclined to selectively report (even though unconsciously) those issues and themes that align most closely with her/his particular world view (personal predispositions, values, *etc.*). In this sense, a system-atic analysis of the data (which involves, e.g., providing quantitative evidence of the strength of particular themes) will go some way, at least, towards correcting this ten-dency. The validity of the method in this respect could be assessed, in part, by asking independent evaluators to draw conclusions about an organisation's culture from dif-ferent types and amounts of data, pertaining to a given issue, that are generated by the method. It would be expected that as more information is added, initial possibly diver-gent views would tend to converge on an increasingly consistent assessment of the organisation's culture.

13.1.3 *The operationalisation of context*

As has been argued previously, while conceptual treatments of organisational culture generally acknowledge the highly context-specific nature of cultural beliefs and assumptions, operationalisations of culture — both quantitative and qualitative — often fall far short of demonstrating a genuine commitment to context. With respect to this shortcoming, the method that we are proposing attempts to provide a systematic means of evaluating contextual aspects of culture. In this section, this feature of the method is discussed. Specifically, consideration is given to the relative merit of assessing each of the contextual domains of interest (in terms of what the information obtained contributes to an understanding of the culture), as well as to the value of integrating contextual information.

An appropriate starting point for this evaluation concerns the question of whether or not it is necessary to ask specific questions about context in order to obtain a context-specific understanding of respondents' experience. In Study 3 it was found that, to some extent at least, respondents did spontaneously refer to contextual domains other than the present context when commenting on their experience in relation to the present context. Moreover, an analysis of these spontaneous references to context provided some interesting, and potentially culturally significant, information. For example, in both divisions, there were more spontaneous references to the past context than to any other contextual domain (whether the anticipated future context, the other context, or the ideal context). It was also found that respondents from the production division tended to make more spontaneous references to the anticipated future and ideal contexts than did their counterparts from the tooling division. And, in neither division, did respondents' accounts of their present experience contain any significant spontaneous reference to the other context. The point can be made that these findings were not inconsistent with what one might have expected, given each division's particular circumstances. Of course, in other organisational cultures, the representation (spontaneously) of contextual domains other than the present context in data pertaining to the present context, may well differ.

The above results suggest that one can obtain some reasonably interesting contextual information without asking specific questions about context. The problem remains, however, that the amount of contextual information which is generated spontaneously is likely to be very limited. As reported previously, in Study 3, the number of spontaneous references by a single respondent to any given contextual domain, other than the present context, was typically very small. Moreover, there was considerable variability in the content areas represented by these spontaneous references. It can be argued, therefore, that if one's aim is to obtain comprehensive and systematic information about respondents' experience in relation to a number of different contextual domains, then one should ask specific questions about context, rather than rely on information on contextual data that are generated spontaneously. The results of Study 3 provided strong support for this argument insofar as the information generated by specific questions about context was indeed more systematic (in the sense that it provided a basis for comparative analyses) and more comprehensive than the information which respondents provided spontaneously in their accounts of their experience at the present time.

Of course, it is possible that there might be individual and group differences in the relative amounts of information about different contexts that emerge in respondents' spontaneous accounts of their present experience. For example, those from top management might be expected to refer disproportionately more to the future (because of their involvement in organisational planning); employees with professional affiliations, such as accountants, might be expected to refer more to the other (because of their knowledge of the experience of their professional colleagues in other organisations); union members might be expected to refer more to the ideal (because of their greater concern with improving conditions for workers); and older workers might be expected to refer more to the past (because of their more extensive experience of the organisation over time). It would be interesting in future research to compare such groups in terms of their non-prompted references to different contexts.

We turn now to a consideration of issues pertaining to the operationalisation of each of the contextual domains of interest, and the relative merits of their use, as suggested by the findings of Study 3.

13.1.3.1 *The past context: Advantages*

The contextual domain which emerged as being perhaps the most valuable in Study 3 — in terms of the quantity and quality of data generated by questions asking about respondents' experience in relation to this domain — was the historical context. In general, respondents (from both divisions) were able to talk with ease about how their past experience differed from, or was similar to, their present experience in terms of the various issues about which they were asked. The point has been made previously that, because the past constitutes an already experienced phenomenon (as opposed to something which one might expect to experience, or which one would like to experience), respondents may be better able to access and articulate information pertaining to their past experience than, say, information pertaining to their anticipated future, or ideal, experience. It may also be that, where the past context emerges as having particular significance, the culture of the group(s) being investigated may be more strongly rooted in the past than in any other contextual domain.

The findings of Study 3 provided evidence for a number of specific advantages associated with seeking information about respondents' experience in relation to the past context. Since these have been discussed in detail elsewhere, it is sufficient in this chapter to offer a brief summary only of the main advantages. These are as follows:

(1) **Knowledge of the past context of respondents' experience can facilitate the more accurate interpretation of data pertaining to respondents' experience in the present context.** This is the idea that past experience offers a kind of 'yardstick' against which respondents evaluate their present experience. Because this yardstick is likely

to differ for different individuals (groups), an understanding of it is essential if one is to make sense of present-time data. A nice illustration of this was provided by the tooling division data on training. There was evidence that the respondents from this division, because of their long history of little or no worker involvement in training, were more sensitive than were their counterparts from the production division (for whom a less well-defined training history emerged) to current shifts in the emphasis on this worker activity and, hence, more likely to interpret such shifts as instances of specific and significant change. It is worth making the point here that, in question-naire measures of culture, the historical context is likely to similarly influence respondents' interpretations of the various response categories contained within a given rating scale. To extrapolate from the above example, respondents may be asked to rate how often workers are involved in training — whether *frequently, occasion-ally,* or *rarely.* Evidence from Study 3 suggests that respondents (either within or between groups) may vary considerably in their interpretations of these response categories, depending on the nature of their past experience in relation to this worker activity. This is a problem that questionnaire measures of organisational culture fail to address.

(2) **Knowledge of the past context of respondents' experience can help to explain apparent inconsistencies and contradictions in data pertaining to the present context.** A good example of this was provided by the production division data on worker–supervisor communication. As indicated, respondents from this division (who were themselves shop floor workers) tended to hold negative views about the overall quality of worker–supervisor communication in the division at the present time, while at the same time making reference to the positive communication relation-ship which they, as individuals, had with their own supervisor(s). One explanation for this apparent inconsistency was that respondents' past experience in this regard (in the past, worker–supervisor communication had reportedly been very distant) was con-tinuing to influence their general, or overall, evaluation of their present experience, despite the existence of evidence, at an individual level, to negate it. The suggestion was made that, in culture change, there may well be a 'lag' between the occurrence, or experience, of any given change and the registration of that change in the 'world view' of organisation members. In other words, the residual effects of past experience may continue to influence organisation members' thinking about their present experi-ence for some time after the change has occurred. This may have important implica-tions for the evaluation of change programs in terms of how they affect the organisation's culture. While a more surface-level evaluation (e.g., using a norm indicator) might provide evidence of positive change, an evaluation that pushes to the deeper level of basic beliefs and assumptions might indicate that little has changed. This may reflect a view from those involved that, while the immediate effects of the change program appear to be positive, there is scepticism about whether these effects will last.

(3) **Knowledge of the past context of respondents' experience can highlight differences between groups that may not be revealed in data pertaining to the present context of respondents' experience.** For example, while the tooling division and the production division were found to be roughly equivalent in terms of the level of worker involvement in group problem-solving which they currently supported (for both divisions, this was reportedly very low), an analysis of the historical data associated with this activity category showed that the divisions had markedly different histories in this regard. Specifically, the tooling division had a long and stable history of little or no worker involvement in group problem-solving (i.e., the status of this worker activity was the same at present as it had been in the past). In contrast, there were two periods in the history of the production division in which divisional workers had considerably more involvement in group problem-solving than they had at the present time. The first was during the early years of the division's start-up when, as part of the Team Concept initiative, work was organised around semi-autonomous teams, and the second was associated with a more recent quality assurance initiative. Neither of these initiatives appears to have been particularly successful and organisation members' experience of both seems to have been predominantly negative. The point was made that information of this kind, which would not have been obtained had one's method of data collection focussed on the present context of respondents' experience only, is likely to have important practical implications for the implementation (in either division) of any future change in relation to this worker activity. For example, when embarking on a future change of this kind, it might be necessary to openly talk about organisation members' previous experiences and to explain to them how the present change effort differs from, and/or has learnt from, this past experience.

(4) **Knowledge of the past context of respondents' experience can provide important insights into the nature and extent of the individual's (and the group's) exposure to change.** There was good evidence from Study 3 to suggest that the two divisions differed markedly in this regard. While the details of this difference have been elaborated upon previously (in Chapter 12), the overall conclusion that was reached was that the tooling division had a long and relatively stable history (spaning some 20 years at least) during which the role of workers (as suggested by worker involvement in various activities) appears to have changed very little. In contrast, in the production division, there was evidence that divisional members had more exposure, during the ten years or so of this division's history, to changes of the kind likely to impact upon the role of workers. As suggested, an important practical implication of this finding is that the degree of a group's past exposure to change might be expected to influence the group's responsiveness to future change — with groups only minimally exposed to change likely to be more resistant to future change than groups in which the experience of change is more common. Of course, in the case of the latter, consideration should be given, not only to the quantitative dimension of the change experience, but also to the qualitative dimension. If the experience of a past change has been predominantly

negative (as in the group problem-solving example above), then one might expect to encounter resistance to, rather than acceptance of, a related change in the future.

13.1.3.2 *The past context: Specific versus general information about the past*

It is appropriate at this point to remind the reader that an important feature of the method used in Study 3, which distinguishes it from more unstructured qualitative approaches, was that it sought specific, rather than general, information about context. Thus, with respect to the past context, an attempt was made to establish detailed 'event histories' for individual respondents. In other words, for every change that a respondent mentioned (either in response to the open-ended questions or in response to a specific prompt question), she/he was asked to indicate: (i) when the change had occurred (approximate year); (ii) for how long before the change (i.e., for how many years) things had been the same; and (iii) why the change had occurred. If the respondent indicated that there had been no change from the past to the present, then she/he was asked to indicated for how long things had been the same (i.e., for how many years). The highly specific contextual information which was generated by these questions proved to be valuable for a number of reasons. First, it enabled a more thorough and more accurate assessment of sharedness to be made. Not only was it possible to establish the extent to which respondents agreed that a particular change had occurred, but it was also possible to demonstrate the extent of their agreement about when, and why, the change had occurred. Information of this kind can be used to further substantiate one's claims about the strength, or alternatively the weakness, of the group's culture. Moreover, as will be argued in a subsequent section (see Section 13.1.4), information about respondents' causal attributions may have important implications for one's approach to the implementation and management of change within the group. Of course, it is a matter for further research into our proposed method to determine how best to get this kind of information. What are the specific questions that might be asked to provide the most accurate information in a timely and efficient manner?

A second advantage of the information that was generated by the above questions was that it enabled some assessment to be made of the relative time span of respondents' experience. Thus, rather than being restricted to talking about a respondent's past in very general terms, it was possible to establish, for each event or change that was mentioned, just how far back the respondent's past actually extended. In other words, one could obtain highly specific information about the yardstick against which a respondent was evaluating her/his present experience.

The important point to make in the context of the present discussion is that, contrary to what one might have expected, this yardstick did not always bear a direct relationship with the respondent's seniority or, more particularly, length of service with the organisation (and/or division). In other words, what constituted a respondent's *psychologically salient* past often differed from what constituted her/his *chronological* past. A good example of this apparent inconsistency or ambiguity was provided by the production division data on worker–supervisor communication. Among the respondents from this division, there were some who reported that, in the past, worker–supervisor communication had been more open than it was at the present time, whilst there were others who argued that it had been more distant. An analysis of the time line data associated with these perceived changes showed that, in the case of the former, the reference or yardstick was the very recent past, while in the case of the latter it was the distant past. Moreover, these contrasting perceptions of change could not be explained in terms of respondents' length of tenure with the organisation (and/or division). Notably, those for whom the yardstick was the very recent past included both shorter serving and longer-serving employees. By way of a further illustration of this phenomenon, the reader is reminded that it was not uncommon for respondents from the tooling division to make reference to a past which extended beyond their date of commencement with the organisation. In other words, for these respondents, their reference or yardstick was past knowledge which they had acquired, not directly, but through socialisation with their co-workers.

The notion that a respondent's psychologically salient past may differ from her/his chronological past (as reflected in length of service with the organisation/division) has important implications for the delineation of groups for organisational culture research. It suggests that, contrary to the traditional delineation of groups in terms of boundaries suggested by respondents' demographics (e.g., age, tenure, seniority, functional unit, *etc.*), one might identify cultural groupings based on observed similarities in the *subjective* histories of respondents. To this end, it is clearly important that one's method is able to provide some fairly specific information about the nature and time frame of the events/changes which have made up each respondent's past experience.

The point should be made that this concern with how one should go about delineating groups for organisational culture research is not new. For example, Hofstede, Neuijen, Ohayv, and Sanders (1990) have argued that: "Determining what units are sufficiently homogeneous to be used for comparing cultures is both a theoretical and an empirical problem" (p. 289). In their major study of the cultures of twenty organisational units, Hofstede *et al.* dealt with this problem by seeking management's advice as to which particular units in their organisation were the most culturally homogenous and, hence, the most suitable for inclusion in the study. It was found that, while the results of the research failed to confirm management's judgement "in a few cases" (p. 289), the approach was nevertheless quite satisfactory. In an attempt to address this problem more directly, Rentsch (1990) conducted a study in which she examined the relationship between social interaction and organisational meanings[8]. Central to this research was the idea that, given the importance of social interaction in the development of shared meanings, one should be able to identify cultural groupings (groups of individuals who interpret events similarly) by focussing on individuals who interact with one another. While the findings of the

---

[8]A detailed account and critique of this study is provided in Chapter 6 of Volume I.

research were largely supportive of this idea, Rentsch herself posed the question as to what other variables, apart from interaction, might predict similar event interpretation.

It is clear that further research is needed in order to achieve some resolution of the different approaches to delineating groups for organisational culture research that have been proposed. This work will have important implications for establishing the validity of any claim that the similarities and differences between an organisation's members (suggested by the results of an assessment of the organisation's culture) are *cultural*, and that they confirm the existence of, and define the boundaries between, different subcultures.

13.1.3.3 *The future context: Advantages*

While respondents in Study 3 were able to talk with relative ease about their past experience with respect to the role of workers, and how it differed from their experience at the present time, they appeared to have some difficulty envisaging how the role of workers might change in the future. There was little evidence, in either division, of any significant orientation towards the future. In response to the open-ended question(s), very few changes per respondent were anticipated and there was little agreement among respondents about the nature of these changes. This picture did not change markedly with the addition of prompt questions in the sense that, for most of the prompted activity categories, a minority of respondents only from each division anticipated some change. It was also the case that anticipated changes (whether mentioned spontaneously or in response to prompting) tended to be changes that were either already underway or considered likely to occur in the very near future. And finally, the point can be made that, in response to the initial open-ended question(s), the changes that were mentioned tended to be changes of a very general nature (notably, an anticipated move away from specialisation towards multi-skilling in the tooling division, and general technological changes in the production division). While these changes would clearly have implications for the future role of workers, respondents typically did not elaborate (in their spontaneous responses) on what these might be.

While the above findings might lead one to conclude that, at least in our Study 3, future context data proved to be less valuable than data pertaining to the past context, such a conclusion denies the potential significance of what was found. In other words, the finding that a particular group is not strongly future-oriented and that its members have some difficulty envisaging what organisational life (or some aspect of it) might be like in the future, can be (indeed, should be) regarded as being of equal significance, from a cultural perspective, to the finding that a group is strongly future-oriented and that group members have a more clearly articulated view of what their future will be like. For example, with respect to change programs, the former workers might require a more detailed explanation than the latter of why proposed changes are necessary and what the advantages of those changes will be in the future. With this in mind, we turn to a consideration of some of the main advantages of including a focus on the future context, as suggested by the results of Study 3. These are as follows:

(1) **Data about the future context of respondents' experience can provide insights into the extent of a group's orientation toward the future.** The results of Study 3 provided some useful insights into the possible sources of this information. These include:

    i)   the number of respondents in the group who anticipate change;
    ii) the average number of changes anticipated per respondent;
    iii) the degree of consensus among respondents about the types of changes which they anticipate;
    iv) the time frame of the changes that are anticipated (e.g., whether already underway, likely to occur in the near future, or likely to occur in the distant future); and
    v) the level of articulation indicated in respondents' descriptions of the changes which they anticipate.

The point should be made that information pertaining to these various sources is probably best considered as a whole. In other words, the more pieces of evidence that one has which are suggestive of a strong, or alternatively, a weak, future orientation in the group, the more reliable one's judgement in this regard is likely to be. Further research with the method might, however, indicate that some of these measures may be more effective and/or efficient in obtaining the required information.

A possible practical implication of a group's future orientation is that it may influence a group's responsiveness to change. Is it the case, as one might predict, that change will be easier to bring about in a strongly future-oriented group in which group members have a well-articulated and positive view of their future, which is consistent with the change, than in a group in which there is a weak future orientation and in which members have a poorly articulated view of their future? Clearly, this is a question that has important implications for the implementation of change programs, and that might therefore usefully be explored through further research in this area.

(2) **Data about the future context of respondents' experience can provide insights into respondents' attitudes to, and attributions about, future change.** A second argument in favour of the inclusion of a focus on the future context is that, in Study 3, useful information was obtained about both respondents' attitudes to anticipated future change and their attributions about why change was considered likely to occur. As above, information of this kind is also likely to have implications for the group's responsiveness to change. For example, in the tooling division, there was evidence that some respondents were strongly ambivalent in their attitudes to an anticipated increase in the involvement of divisional workers in training. One of the main reasons for this ambivalence lay in a concern about the relevance of training for the division's older employees. There was also some evidence in this division of strongly negative attitudes to an anticipated increase in the involvement of divisional workers in group

problem-solving. Such a change was seen, by some, as a threat to the traditional authority and responsibility of the supervisor. Attitudes such as this, particularly if they are held by more senior organisation members (who are likely to have more responsibility for the change process and more power to influence it), could act to significantly impede change. In order for change to be successful, it would be important, therefore, for such attitudes to be both understood and carefully managed.

Attributions data were also interesting in this regard. There was some evidence that the two divisions differed with respect to respondents' attributions about why future change would occur. As a group, respondents from the tooling division were somewhat more inclined than their counterparts from the production division to see change (in this case, anticipated change) as 'reactive', that is, as a response to events, circumstances, *etc.* over which the division was perceived to have little control. Thus, the respondents from this division commonly attributed change to factors such as: (i) the downsizing and restructuring of the division, and its relocation to the site of the company's main manufacturing and assembly operations; (ii) the industry-wide initiative to multi-skill workers; and (iii) increasing pressure (on the division and the company in general) to survive and remain competitive. While similar kinds of attributions appeared in the corresponding production division data, these data also contained explanations for change which were indicative of a more 'proactive' orientation. For example, there were references by some respondents to a commitment, on the part of divisional management, to develop the division's human resources (by fostering a more open communication climate between workers and their supervisors, by improving information to workers, *etc.*), and there were references to a drive by divisional management to increase the efficiency and quality of production operations in the division. The question arises as to whether or not these different attribution styles might influence each group's responsiveness to change. In other words, is change more likely to be accepted if it is seen as proactive, rather than reactive? Again, this is an interesting question for further research with important implications for the successful implementation of change programs.

Of course, the attributions that organisation members make about the future changes that they anticipate are themselves likely to be influenced by the experience that organisation members have had of change in the past. To the extent that this experience was negative — perceptions of a past change program may have been that it was introduced only to obtain more productivity from workers, without any benefits in terms of increased pay, better conditions, or job satisfaction — then it might lead to negative attributions about a proposed new change program, which is seen as being introduced for the same purpose. This could have important implications for the process whereby it is proposed the new change will be implemented. Awareness of organisation members' negative attributions about the new change, and how these attributions were influenced by past experience, could lead change agents to devote considerably more time than they might otherwise have done, to explaining the reasons for the change and its benefits to both the company and the workers. Thus, seeking information about organisation members' attributions with respect to the future, and checking on the source of those attributions, might enable change agents to be better equipped to approach change in a way that will minimise resistance to it.

As for the past context, the findings and insights generated by the future context data could not have been obtained had respondents not been asked some very specific questions about their anticipated future experience. The reader is reminded that, for each of the changes which a respondent mentioned, she/he was asked to indicate when (i.e., in how many years' time) she/he thought the change was likely to occur, and why. While respondents were not asked specifically for their opinion as to the desirability (or undesirability) of the changes which they anticipated — this information tended to emerge in the elaborative and qualifying data — the potential importance of attitudinal data for understanding change suggests that a standardised question seeking this information could usefully be included in any revision of our proposed method.

(3) **Data about the future context of respondents' experience can serve to confirm, and indeed strengthen, findings associated with other contextual domains.** In Study 3, this insight derived mainly from the results of the thematic content analysis and the analysis of attributions data. With respect to the former, there were a number of themes which emerged in the future context data which had been encountered previously (i.e., in data pertaining to the present and past contexts). Examples include the shared perception among tooling division respondents that training was not relevant for older workers, and the shared perception among production division respondents that record-keeping served primarily a production control function. With respect to the latter, the tendency for respondents from the tooling division to attribute anticipated future changes to events perceived to be largely outside of their control (and their division's control) had been encountered previously in relation to changes that this group had already experienced. There was also some evidence from Study 3 to suggest that future context data — specifically, data pertaining to respondents' attitudes about the desirability/undesirability of anticipated future changes — may foreshadow respondents' views about the ideal context and, in this sense, provide some measure of the internal consistency of respondents with respect to their reported attitudes and beliefs.

(4) **Data about the future context of respondents' experience can provide additional support for one's methodological approach.** A fourth advantage, which is of interest from a methodological, rather than a practical, point of view is that, in Study 3, future context data served to further confirm the value of particular features of the method used. For example, these data provided further evidence of the value of qualitative data (in this case, providing insights into how respondents talked about anticipated future changes, and what their attitudes to these changes were) for giving meaning to responses to standardised questions (in this case, providing information about the content and time frame of anticipated future changes). Future context data also

provided further confirmation of the value of including specific prompt questions in addition to the open-ended questions. While a majority of the prompted activity categories were represented by a minority of respondents only from each division, it was still the case that there were some categories for which a majority of respondents in each division anticipated some future change (notably Safety Meetings and Attend Training for the tooling division, and Record Work-Related Information and Attend Training for the production division). The point can be made that this information would not have been obtained had respondents been presented only with the open-ended question(s) about the future context.

13.1.3.4 *The future context: Organisational culture as an influence on, and influenced by, future expectations*

A final issue which needs to be addressed in relation to this contextual domain concerns the extent to which the rationale for including a focus on the future context in our proposed method — namely, that a group's culture will influence, and be influenced by, the future expectations of group members — was supported empirically. Certainly, there was some evidence to suggest that respondents' experience in the past and present contexts might influence both their expectations about the likelihood of future change and their attitudes to that change. For example, the finding that, for both divisions, a minority of respondents only anticipated a future change in the involvement of divisional workers in planning activities was quite consistent with each division's history in this regard. As reported previously, in neither division had there ever been much involvement of divisional workers in such activities. An example of the influence of past experience on attitudes to anticipated future change was provided by the tooling division data on anticipated changes in the involvement of divisional workers in training. While a majority of respondents from this division anticipated an increase in the involvement of divisional workers in training in the future (a result largely of the current industry-wide initiative to multi-skill workers), the existence of strongly ambivalent attitudes to this change was not surprising given an historical context in which workers' (typically qualified tradesmen) technical skills were largely taken-for-granted, and in which any training beyond the training of new apprentices would probably have been regarded as superfluous. The point should be made that links, such as the above, between data pertaining to the historical context and data pertaining to the future context were more readily established for some worker activities than for others, suggesting that respondents' future expectations will be influenced by more than just the historical context of their experience.

With respect to the argument that a group's culture may be influenced by, rather than influence, the future expectations of group members, the results of Study 3 provided suggestive evidence only in this regard. In the tooling division, it was noted that respondents spoke about the future in terms of a continuing decline in the role of their division in the organisation as a whole. Respondents' expectations in this regard may have contributed to their less positive attitudes to additional training, particularly for older workers who, because of their limited remaining tenure with the organisation, would be less likely than their younger counterparts to reap the future benefits of any further investment in training.

The influence of future expectations on present culture might also be observed in situations where the group anticipates a change that is likely to challenge the group's established cultural beliefs. For example, a group's established cultural beliefs about the role of workers might be challenged by group members' knowledge that another firm, which is soon to take over their firm, supports a more Theory X, or alternatively a more Theory Y, approach to the management of workers. A more Theory X approach might be foreshadowed as involving a more regimented approach to work, with less involvement of workers in decision-making, and closer supervision and more overt performance-based evaluations of workers. A more Theory Y approach might be expected to involve more emphasis on outcomes, with more involvement of workers in decision-making, and more flexibility in the way they work. The anticipated change is likely to positively, or negatively, affect the group's current climate (in terms of how group members feel about the future) and this might mark the beginnings of a counterculture, depending on the way in which the group's established beliefs about the role of workers are challenged by the change in management style that is anticipated.

The higher education sector might constitute a relevant setting in which to more closely investigate the influence of a group's future expectations on its current culture. Over the last 30 years there have been a number of major changes in this sector, some of which have had important implications for the role of academic staff. Academics (in certain discipline areas at least) are now required to teach much larger classes than they were in the past, they have less decision-making authority than in the past (due to the appointment of 'professional' managers and the implementation of formal managerial controls), and the notion of 'academic freedom' has gradually been eroded by the implementation of formal systems of performance measurement designed to increase accountability in all areas of academic activity including teaching, research, and administration. For a detailed treatment of these, and other, changes in the higher education sector, see Parker, Guthrie, and Gray (1999). Given these changes it would be interesting to conduct a contextual analysis of the organisational culture within universities, comparing academics' beliefs about their roles as educators and researchers with respect to the past, the present, the anticipated future, and the ideal.

It also seems likely that the expectations that an organisation's members have about the future of the organisation might not only affect the present climate and culture of the organisation, but they might also affect members' views about the organisation's past. For example, in the above case, it might be predicted that older academics would provide increasingly positive accounts of their life in the university in the past, before the anticipated changes occurred.

13.1.3.5 *The other context: Advantages*

In Study 3, the analysis of other context data provided some evidence that, as a group, respondents from the tooling division had less experience of other organisational contexts than their counterparts from the production division and, moreover, that this experience had been less variable in terms of the types of work and organisations represented. This finding was not inconsistent with the overall assessment of the tooling division (based on evidence from Study 3 and also impressionistic data) as supporting a more homogeneous, and definable, culture than the production division. Study 3 therefore offered some empirical support for the argument in the literature (Louis, 1983; Wilkins & Ouchi, 1983) that information about a group's social isolation from other groups (i.e., other context data) can help to explain the strength or boundedness of the group's culture. At the same time, however, there was little evidence from Study 3 to suggest that either division was *strongly* other-oriented. Although respondents from the production division appeared to have been somewhat less socially isolated than their counterparts from the tooling division, the nature of their experience of other organisations had been such that (as for the tooling division) it would probably have confirmed, rather than disconfirmed, their prevailing beliefs and values (in this case about the role of workers). Of course, this finding is not to deny the value of seeking information about the other context. On the contrary, and as argued above in relation to the future context, the finding that a group is not strongly other-oriented is potentially as significant, from a cultural perspective, as the finding that a group has had considerable experience of other organisations which have offered exposure to culturally different ways of thinking.

The importance of the 'other' in the formation and maintenance of an organisation's culture might be particularly evident in certain professional subcultures, such as those represented by managers, accountants, and IT professionals in commercial organisations, teachers in educational institutions, and doctors and nurses in hospitals. In these cases, the basic assumptions that professionals acquire through their association with their professional training organisations, which might include universities, colleges, or institutes, might be expected to influence the nature and extent of the contribution of these groups, and the subcultures of which they are a part, to the overall culture of the organisation. Moreover, to the extent that there is relatively high turnover among the members of these professional subcultures, the influence of the other on the organisation's overall culture — the influence of employees' knowledge of 'how things are done' in other similar organisations — might be expected to be greater.

Overall, then, there would appear to be reasonable support for the inclusion, in our proposed method, of a focus on the other context of respondents' experience. However, as argued above (in relation to the past and future contexts), information about respondents' experience of other organisations is likely to be most valuable when it is specific, rather than general. The advantage of specific information is that it provides one with a clearer understanding of just what the relevance of the group's other experience might be, in terms of the potential influence of that experience on the group's culture. The findings of Study 3 suggest that there are a number of different pieces of information that might usefully be gathered in this regard. For example:

(1) Information should be sought about the number of respondents in the group who have some knowledge of other organisations (with respect to the issue about which they are being asked). Associated with this, one might also ascertain how respondents acquired this knowledge, whether directly (i.e., through working elsewhere) or indirectly (e.g., through some kind of professional or work-related association with other organisations, through interaction with friends or family members who work elsewhere, or through hearing about other organisations in the media). The distinction between knowledge acquired directly and knowledge acquired indirectly rests on the assumption that the former is likely to be more relevant (in terms of its potential influence on respondents' current thinking) than the latter. At the same time, however, the potential significance of the latter should not be ignored.

(2) Where direct experience is indicated, information might be sought about: (i) the type(s) of organisation(s) in which the respondent has worked previously (e.g., industry sector and type of industry); and (ii) the respondent's occupational status in her/his other organisation(s). With respect to the former, the greater the similarity between the respondent's current and other organisation(s), the more relevant is the comparison between the two likely to be. In Study 3, there was considerable variability among respondents from the production division in the types of organisations which were represented in their other context data. Some of these organisations were similar to the respondent's current organisation in that they were in the same industry sector (e.g., a clothing factory, a table-tennis factory), whilst others were very different (e.g., a petrol station, a school canteen). It might reasonably be argued that, in the case of the former, the respondent's current and other experience could more meaningfully be compared than in the case of the latter. It is perhaps also worth making the point here that there was one respondent from the production division whose current and other organisations were so dissimilar as to make it difficult for him to offer any comparison of his experience of each.

In Study 3, occupational status emerged as a second demographic variable of potential significance for understanding the relevance of respondents' other experience. The other context data for the tooling division were most revealing in this regard. Where direct experience of having worked elsewhere was reported, this involved, in all cases, work as a qualified tradesman (whether as a toolmaker, pattern maker, draftsman, *etc.*). For respondents in this division, occupational status also clearly influenced the nature of their indirect experience of other organisations (e.g., one respondent indicated that his knowledge of other organisations was based primarily on what he had learned as a result of work done in his prominent role in the governance of the Pattern Makers Association). These findings suggest that one advantage of seeking information about the respondent's occupational or professional status in her/his other organisation is that such information might alert one to the possible influence of occupational or professional subculture, as opposed to organisational culture (or subculture). As has been argued elsewhere (see Chapter 3 of Volume I), occupational or professional grouping constitutes an important source of subcultural development or emergence in work organisations, and one which, at least in the early decades of organisational culture research, was largely overlooked by scholars attempting to understand organisational cultures (Trice, 1993). Whether or not our proposed method should be revised to include a separate focus on 'occupational' context, in addition to the current focus on the 'other' context, is a question which remains to be answered.

(3) Finally, one should also seek to establish the extent to which respondents' other experience (in relation to the issue being investigated) is similar to, or different from, their current experience. It can be argued that similar experience in other contexts is likely to confirm or reinforce respondents' thinking about their current experience, whereas different, and in particular contradictory, experience in other contexts may lead to a questioning of current experience.

Study 3 provided some evidence to suggest that, where similarities are indicated, one might usefully examine the criteria upon which respondents' evaluations of 'sameness' have been made. This information can provide interesting insights into the respondent's perceptions of organisational life in the current context (in this case, in relation to the role of workers). For example, in the production division, evaluations of sameness tended to be made on the basis of observations that, in the respondent's other organisation (as in her/his current organisation), workers had little autonomy and were always answerable to the person above them, workers "never saw the bosses", and workers had little involvement in anything except their immediate job. As argued previously, these data suggested an underlying perception, among the respondents concerned, that the role of workers in the production division at the present time was essentially passive.

Where differences between respondents' current and other organisation(s) are indicated, consideration might be given to the number of differences mentioned per respondent (as a potential indicator of the significance of the group's other experience), as well as to the content of the differences mentioned. In Study 3, respondents from both divisions mentioned, on average, very few differences each (between two and three) and there was little consensus among respondents concerning the kinds of differences they mentioned. With respect to this latter finding, the important point has been made that, despite the diversity in the types of differences mentioned (this was hardly surprising given that no two respondents had experience of the same other organisation), the nature of these differences was such that they would have been unlikely to have seriously challenged respondents' thinking about the role of workers in their current organisation. It would appear, therefore, that in addition to examining the content of differences between respondents' current and other organisation(s), consideration should also be given to the values implicit in these differences.

Of course, the impact of a perceived difference between an individual's current and other organisation, in relation to any given issue (in this case, the issue was the role of workers), might depend upon the extent of the perceived similarities or differences in relation to other issues. For example, if a respondent perceives that her/his current and other organisations differ in relation to a single issue only — let's say that the other organisation is seen as more positive with respect to a particular aspect of its culture — then this difference might disproportionately influence the respondent's thinking about her/his current organisation. The respondent's attitude might be that, if everything else is so similar, why shouldn't my current organisation also be similar in terms of supporting the same positive cultural characteristic that is supported by the other organisation? If, on the other hand, the respondent perceives that her/his current and other organisations differ with respect to multiple issues, then the influence of the difference in relation to any single issue (in the example given, a difference pertaining to an aspect of the organisation's culture), might be expected to be considerably less. In this event, the respondent might reasonably conclude that there would be little chance of her/his current organisation being able to adopt an approach that would bring it into closer alignment with the other organisation, in relation to this particular issue. It is clear that further research is needed to determine the range of factors that might determine the relative influence of respondents' experience of other organisations on their thinking about their current organisation.

In Study 3, the analysis of elaborative and qualifying data associated with responses to questions about the other context was not particularly revealing. That is, there was no evidence of any significant common thematic content in these data. The point has been made previously that this finding was hardly surprising given that, in all cases, the other contexts to which respondents referred were different. It was also the case that the analysis of other context data in terms of respondents' demographics revealed little of interest. There was, however, some evidence that supervisory staff in the tooling division sample had less experience of other organisations than supervisory staff in the production division sample. The point was made that, if this finding was to be replicated in a larger sample (and its statistical significance established), it could have important implications for understanding the cultures of the groups in question. Specifically, one might predict a more bounded culture in the former than in the latter. In other words, the relative experience and/or knowledge that organisation members have of other organisations might provide a measure of relative boundedness of the organisation's culture or its subcultures.

It was also the case that the results of Study 3 provided some evidence to suggest that one might usefully examine the nature of the comparisons (whether favourable or unfavourable) which respondents make between their current and other organisation(s). The emergence of particular trends in this regard (i.e., consistently favourable or consistently unfavourable comparisons) may constitute evidence of respondents' satisfaction with their current organisation. That is, low satisfaction would be indicated in consistently positive references to other organisations, whereas high satisfaction would be indicated in consistently negative references. An alternative, and no less plausible, explanation for the emergence of such trends would, however, be that they are indicative of more general psychological tendencies (e.g., the tendency for people to believe that the 'grass is always greener on the other side'). Support for such an explanation would, of course, raise questions about the value of other context data for explaining the boundedness (or diffuseness) of the group's culture. One should, therefore, be alert to the possibility that the findings of an analysis of other context data may be confounded by the influence of psychological tendencies which may be widely distributed in the general population. A possible method for determining the extent of this confounding influence would be to ask respondents to identify the specific ways in which their current and other organisations differ, and to comment on how their current organisation would be improved by being more like their other organisation. It might be expected that the less specific and the more general a respondent's evaluative comments in this regard, the more likely that a 'grass is greener' response is being given.

A final consideration concerning the other context is the extent to which the concept of the other should be broadened beyond knowledge of, and/or experience in, other organisations. Essentially, this contextual domain, in it broadest conceptualisation, is concerned with possible influences, on a organisation's climate and culture, from outside of the organisation. In this sense, might it not also be reasonable to include in the other, knowledge that derives from external sources such as the media? While most organisations are unlikely to feature in the media, large organisations or government departments might be the subject of media reports concerning their relative success or failure, or concerning anticipated future trends, such as moving manufacturing in a particular industry (e.g., the car industry) overseas, or outsourcing or privatising certain government utilities or functions. To the extent that these reports come to the attention of employees, whether via the print media or television, and become the subject of discussion among employees, they might be expected to influence the current climate of the organisation as well as employees' expectations of likely future changes. The results of Study 3 provided evidence that the workers and supervisors in the tooling division anticipated that their division would decrease in size and importance in the future. While it was reasonable to conclude that such opinions were formed on the basis of organisational information, whether formal bulletins or the 'grapevine', it is also possible they were at least partly informed by media reports about the future of the car industry in Australia.

13.1.3.6 *The ideal context: Advantages*

In Study 3, the rationale for including a focus on the ideal context of respondents' experience was that data pertaining to this contextual domain could provide further insights into the boundedness of a group's culture (over and above those suggested by data pertaining to the other contextual domains). This view is consistent with conceptual treatments of organisational culture which emphasise the prescriptive function of cultural beliefs and assumptions (e.g., Sackmann, 1991; Smircich, 1983). If culture sets the boundaries for how organisation members *should* think about, and behave in response to, their experience of organisational life, then one would expect that, in strongly bounded cultures, members' responses to questions about the ideal (how they think things ought to be) would be likely to be more culturally constrained than they would be in less bounded cultures.

The results of Study 3 provided some support for this argument. That is, as one might have predicted, the tooling division emerged as being somewhat more culture bound than the production division in terms of respondents' views about the ideal (in this case, about how the role of divisional workers ideally should change). The open question data were particularly revealing in this regard. At this point in the interview, respondents had had considerable exposure (through presentation of the prompt questions) to a range of possible other activities (including activities suggestive of an alternative, more active, orientation to the role of workers) in which workers might become involved. Interestingly, the tooling division open question data contained no significant reference to any of these activities. These data also revealed that, as a group, respondents from the tooling division were somewhat less inclined than their counterparts from the production division to spontaneously advocate change (supervisors, in particular, argued for no change) and that, on average, respondents mentioned fewer changes each. It was also the case that respondents from the tooling division were often not as articulate as respondents from the production division about the changes which they mentioned (e.g., they elaborated less on these changes) and they were somewhat less inclined to advocate changes that were indicative of an active (as opposed to a passive) orientation to the role of workers. Where such changes were advocated, they were in all cases mentioned by 'wages' employees and not supervisory staff. Finally, there was more evidence in this group of explicit opposition to change which, in this case, was rooted in an allegiance to traditional views and practices (concerning the respective roles of workers and their supervisors)[9].

While it might be argued that, in Study 3, inferences about the boundedness of the cultures of the two divisions could have been made on the basis of historical data alone (e.g., there was good evidence that, in the tooling division, the role of workers had remained relatively unchanged for a long period of time), this is not to deny the important confirmatory value of data pertaining to the ideal context. There is also the argument that, where one is dealing with a culture which is undergoing change (the tooling division can be seen as an example of such a culture), it would be wrong to make predictions about cultural boundedness solely on the basis of historical data. In this case, the kind of evidence that

---

[9]The point has been made in the previous chapter (see Section 12.7.4) that, while the magnitude of the difference between the two divisions suggested by the above findings was quite small, the trends which emerged were in all cases in the expected direction.

would more convincingly demonstrate boundedness would be the finding that, despite the changes which organisation (group) members were currently experiencing, the influence of their past experience could nevertheless still be seen in their accounts of the ideal. Apart from these more general arguments in favour of a focus on the ideal context, the results of Study 3 served to highlight a number of specific advantages of seeking information about the ideal context of respondents' experience. These are described briefly below:

(1) **Data pertaining to the ideal context data can provide insights into the degree of support for, or resistance to, change which exists in the group.** The results from Study 3 provided evidence to suggest that potentially important indicators in this regard include the number of respondents in the group who advocate change, along with the number of changes advocated per respondent (the latter providing an index of the group's breadth of vision for change). Consideration might also be given to the level of articulation indicated in respondents' descriptions of the changes which they advocate. It may be that respondents who can talk quite fluently about particular changes (perhaps elaborating on why change is desirable) will be more accepting of these, and related, changes (should they be implemented) than respondents whose comments suggest that they have given little thought to the changes which they advocate.

(2) **On the basis of data pertaining to the ideal context, it may be possible to identify those group members most likely to support change and those most likely to resist it.** In Study 3, there was some evidence to suggest that, in the tooling division, supervisory staff may be less supportive of change (in relation to the role of workers) than wages employees, and longer serving employees may be less supportive of change than shorter serving employees. These findings are consistent with research reported in the literature (Poblador, 1990) suggesting that age and seniority are inversely related to adaptability to change. Interestingly, similar trends were not observed in the production division data. As reported previously, there was no representation of supervisory staff in the 'no change' responses (both spontaneous and prompted) for this division, and there was no evidence that length of service influenced a respondent's support, or lack of support, for change. Of course, findings such as these may have important practical implications for the selection of personnel for participation in, and possibly even the leadership of, organisational (group) change efforts.

(3) **Data pertaining to the ideal context can provide information about why there is resistance to change.** Study 3 provided evidence of an interesting difference between the two divisions in this regard. In the tooling division, resistance to change tended to be underpinned by an allegiance to traditional views (in this case, about the respective roles of workers and their supervisors), whereas in the production division, the opposition to change that was expressed (it will be recalled that there was less evidence of explicit opposition to change in the production division than in the tooling division) had its roots in respondents' negative past experience of a previous change initiative,

namely, the Team Concept. Again, information of this kind is likely to have important practical implications for how change agents might go about implementing and managing change within each division. The point should be made that the above insights emerged from an analysis of respondents' spontaneous elaborations on their 'no change' responses. Given the obvious value of such insights, it seems reasonable to argue that, in any subsequent revision of our proposed method, information should systematically be sought regarding respondents' perceptions about why particular changes are seen as desirable or, alternatively, as undesirable.

(4) **Ideal context data can provide information about the specific kinds of changes that are likely to be supported or resisted.** As suggested by the results of Study 3, this information may not always be evident from an analysis of data pertaining to the past context. For example, in their responses to questions about the ideal context, respondents from the tooling division espoused more support for an increase in the involvement of divisional workers in planning and group problem-solving activities than might have been predicted given their relatively long history of little or no worker involvement in these activities. The point can be made that these espoused changes might more readily be interpreted in the context of the division's current circumstances (e.g., a major downsizing effort was underway in the division and the division was being relocated to the main plant, which was perceived to support less traditional management practices) than in the context of past experience. In a similar vein, the support in this division for a change towards more, and improved, communication between workers and their supervisors is perhaps best understood as a response to the considerable uncertainty and anxiety which respondents currently felt in the face of their own, and the division's, changing circumstances. Given the view of organisational culture as dynamic, rather than static, a focus on the ideal context may therefore serve to highlight support for change which may be a product of a culture in transition.

Apart from information about the content of the changes which are advocated, consideration should also be given to the values implicit in these changes. The aim here is to establish the extent to which the changes advocated represent a departure from current thinking and practice. In Study 3, it was interesting that, while there was support in both divisions for an increase in the involvement of divisional workers in planning activities, the consensus was that workers should be involved in operational planning only and that it was inappropriate for them to be involved in planning of a more strategic nature. Another, perhaps more graphic, illustration of the importance of understanding the values implicit in the changes which respondents advocated was provided by one respondent from the tooling division (a first-line supervisor) who advocated an increase in the involvement of divisional workers in record-keeping activities. It was clear from this respondent's elaborations on his 'change' response that the main purpose of this change, as he saw it, was to provide supervisors with the means by which they could more effectively monitor their subordinates' performance.

(5) **Ideal context data can provide confirmation of findings associated with the other contextual domains.** In Study 3, the ideal context data that were generated provided additional evidence for the existence of particular themes that had emerged in respondents' accounts of their experience in relation to other contextual domains. These data also served to further confirm the value of particular aspects of the method (such as, the inclusion of prompt questions in addition to open-ended questions, the emphasis on allowing respondents to elaborate on, and qualify, their responses, and the inclusion of "Why?" questions).

On the basis of the discussion above, there would appear to be good support for the inclusion, in the proposed method, of a focus on the ideal context of respondents' experience. Not only can ideal context data provide general information about the boundedness of the group's culture, but they can provide additional highly specific information about the group's likely responsiveness, or resistance, to change (in terms of "How much?", "Who?", "What?", and "Why?"). Information such as this will clearly be of considerable value to personnel who are responsible for the implementation and management of organisational (group) change. In terms of our efforts towards the development of a method for assessing organisational culture, ideal context data are also of value insofar as they help to validate key findings and key aspects of the method.

In studies of organisational culture, the ideal is usually taken to involve a change or changes that could be carried out in the very near future, and within the existing resources of the organisation. However, it is possible to consider other forms of the ideal. For example, a distinction could be made between the above notion of the ideal in terms of what should be happening in the organisation but isn't (this might be an existing ideal of performance that is not currently being met), and one which envisages change that would lead to something new (and presumably better) for the organisation within a relatively short time frame. The ideal could also be seen in terms of a more fundamental change that would still be within the current resources of the organisation, but that might take more time to implement. Finally, in more strategic planning terms, the ideal could be depicted in terms of major changes to the organisation that would be beyond the current resources of the organisation and/or might depend on anticipated changes in technology, foreign markets, the nature and extent of the competition, or government legislation. For the respondents in Study 3, the notion of the ideal was most easily comprehended in terms of changes that could be made in the immediate future and within the current resources of the organisation. Such changes might include, for example, more consultation about work tasks. However, for higher levels of management, it might be necessary to specify the kind of ideal that is to be considered, since organisation members at this level might be more likely to think in terms of major changes, of a strategic nature, that involve longer timelines and considerable resources for implementation. Senior managers might also want to talk about a staged implementation for the ideal, such that the ideal is something towards which an organisation works in a series of discrete positive steps, or stages, that are implemented over a number of years.

13.1.3.7 *Integrating cultural contexts*

As indicated, a distinguishing feature of our proposed method is that it focuses on respondents' experience in relation to five contextual domains (i.e., the present, the past, the future, the other, and the ideal). In this sense, the method can be contrasted with established approaches to the assessment of organisational culture (whether quantitative or qualitative) that typically focus on respondents' experience in relation to a single contextual domain (i.e., the present) or at most two contextual domains (i.e., the present and the past, or alternatively, the present and the ideal). In the discussion above, we have considered the value, for understanding an organisation's (group's) culture, of seeking information not just about the present context of respondents' experience, but also about their experience in relation to the past context, the anticipated future context, the other context, and the ideal context. We have offered specific, and separate, evaluations of the additional insights that can be provided by asking respondents about their experience in relation to these other contextual domains. The question now arises as to what might be gained from integrating, or considering as a whole, the data across contextual domains. What, if anything, does the profile of organisation (group) members' experience, which is suggested by the combined findings for each domain, tell us about the organisation's (group's culture)? There would appear to be two main arguments in favour of integrating contextual information:

(1) **Integrating contextual information can enable one to build a more convincing case for the strength (or boundedness) of an organisation's culture than would be possible given access to information pertaining to one (or perhaps two) contextual domains.** In other words, to the extent that there are demonstrable links between the group's experience in relation to a number of different contextual domains — for example, if it can be shown that the group's past experience is consistent with members' future expectations or their attitudes to the future, and if members' accounts of the ideal can be shown to be, in some way, constrained by their past experience — then it can reasonably be argued that one is dealing with a culture that is strongly (rather than weakly) bounded. Moreover, to the extent that there is consistency in how members talk about, and explain, their experience in relation to these different contexts (indicated, e.g., in the emergence of common themes and attributions), then one has further support for a claim of cultural boundedness.

The results of Study 3 provided reasonable support for this argument. The profile of respondents' experience (suggested by the combined findings for each contextual domain) which emerged for the tooling division was more coherent than it was for the production division, suggesting a more bounded culture in the former than in the latter. As indicated, the tooling division had a longer and more stable past than the production division and it appeared to be somewhat more socially isolated (in terms of respondents' experience of 'institutional alternatives'); the division was not strongly future-oriented and there was evidence of opposition to anticipated future change which had its roots in an allegiance to traditional views and practices; and respondents from the tooling division were somewhat less likely than their counterparts from the production division to perceive a need for change in the ideal, and more likely to express opposition to such change. This distinction between the two divisions, in terms of the boundedness of their cultures, was consistent with impressionistic data (gathered over a prolonged period of time spent in each division), as well as with the findings of previous studies conducted as part of this research. The point can be made that, had the method used in Study 3 sought information about the present context of respondents' experience only, this difference between the divisions would not have emerged. While data pertaining to two contextual domains (say, e.g., the present and past contexts) would undoubtedly have been more revealing in this regard, a much more convincing case for any claim about boundedness can be made when one is able to draw on information pertaining to all five contextual domains.

(2) **Contextual information can provide insights into the relative impact of different contextual domains on the current thinking of organisation (group) members.** In other words, it can highlight the extent to which organisation members' thinking may be dominated by a particular contextual domain (whether the past context, the anticipated future context, the other context, or the ideal context). In Study 3, there was evidence to suggest that, for both divisions (but, in particular, for the tooling division), the contextual domain which was dominant (in terms of its influence on the current thinking of divisional members) was the past context. For example, for both divisions, respondents' accounts of their present experience contained more spontaneous references to the past context than to any other contextual domain; in neither division was there evidence of significant exposure of divisional members to institutional alternatives (the other context); in neither division was there evidence of a strong future orientation; and, for both divisions, the influence of past experience could be seen in members' expectations about, and attitudes to, the future, as well as in their accounts of the ideal.

Given the context in which Study 3 was carried out (i.e., the automotive industry, a company with a long history, and two divisions in which longer-serving employees were well represented, at least at supervisory and management levels), the finding above that the cultures of the two divisions appeared to be more strongly past-oriented (than, say, future-, other-, or ideal-, oriented) was perhaps not surprising. It is quite conceivable, however, that in different industry sectors, and in different types of organisations, the relative impact of these different contextual domains might be quite different. For example, one might expect that in high technology companies, where survival depends very much upon keeping abreast of rapid change, organisation members' thinking would be more strongly dominated by the future context (i.e., by members' expectations about the future) than by the past context. Employees from these companies might be expected to have a more articulate and longer-term vision of their future than respondents in our Study 3, as well as be more accepting of future change.

In management consulting firms, organisation members' thinking might be expected to be more strongly oriented toward the other context than the past context. Not only do these firms typically employ people from a number of different occupational groupings, but they also place a high value on individual flexibility and the recruitment of people with a proven 'track record' in other organisations. And in a government department concerned with policy development in, say, the area of workplace reform (e.g., with respect to discrimination on the basis of gender, age, ethnicity, *etc.*), one might expect that the ideal context would emerge as a dominant contextual domain. Clearly, one interesting possibility for future research would be to use our proposed method to verify predictions such as these.

There is also the argument that, given contemporary changes in the world of work — whereby new entrants to the workforce are likely to be highly mobile, in terms of both job and career changes (Naisbitt & Aburdene, 1990), whereby organisations are increasingly contracting out all but their most essential services, in addition to increasing their casual and part-time labour force (Handy, 1990), and whereby organisations are no longer 'stockpiling' people and notions of a 'job-for-life' have become a thing of the past (Handy, 1996) — the importance of the past context (for explaining organisation members' current thinking) is likely to decrease, relative to other contextual domains, simply because organisation members lack a significant shared history (in their current organisation). This possibility raises questions about the value of the organisational culture concept in the longer term. If organisational culture is dependent, for its evolution, on the passage of a considerable period of time — the 'coral reef' notion of culture (Kantrow, 1984) — then is it the case that organisations of the future will be increasingly unlikely to develop strong cultures because their membership lacks a significant shared history? Of course, it may not be shared time so much as shared significant history that is important in developing culture, particularly given the view that cultural beliefs form as a result of the organisation dealing successfully with its problems of internal integration and external adaptation (Schein, 1985, 1992, 2004, 2010). In this sense, it is possible that a younger organisation that has encountered, and successfully dealt with, a large number of significant challenges in a relatively short period of time, could have a more established culture than an older organisation that has encountered, and successfully dealt with, fewer challenges over a relatively long period of time.

Another possible external influence on the more rapid development of an organisational culture is common professional training. While this might be considered in terms of the past context, in this case the past constitutes the shared experience of trainee professionals, acquired outside of their current organisation (and often prior to entering their current organisation), as they complete their training towards their vocation or profession. This shared experience might affect an organisation's overall culture. For example, it might influence the culture of a new accountancy firm, or it might influence the development of an organisational subculture if, for example, as part of an expansion strategy, the organisation was to hire a number of accountants or IT specialists. In both cases, it might be expected that the similar training of professionals will lead them to adopt a consistent approach to dealing with the challenges that are faced by their organisation. This is not to say that all organisations that employ members of the same profession (all accountancy firms for example) will develop identical or even similar organisational cultures. This is because the initial contribution of the same professional training to the culture of a given organisation will be shaped by the relative success or failure of that organisation in coping with the unique challenges that it encounters. In terms of external influences, an organisation's culture might also be shaped by the union membership of employees, which in turn will lead to unions having more or less influence on an organisation's evolving culture. The growing, or alternatively declining, role of unions in an organisation might be expected to influence the organisation's culture via its influence on how members think about the role of unions in the past, at the present time, in the anticipated future, and ideally.

We made the point previously that, given the changed environment in which contemporary organisations operate, there is a possibility that the concept of organisational culture — if represented primarily as a phenomenon that evolves slowly over a long period of time — will become increasingly irrelevant to modern organisations. In view of this, we would argue that what is needed is a reconceptualisation of organisational culture that takes account of the possibility that culture is influenced, not just by present circumstances and past events, but by other domains of context that have been largely ignored in established treatments of organisational culture. If such a reconceptualisation were to occur, one may be able to demonstrate the existence of 'strong' cultures in organisations (groups) which lack a significant history in time, but in which members nevertheless share a common, and strongly held, view of their world which derives from the influence of some other contextual domain (e.g., the anticipated future, the other, or the ideal).

13.1.4 *Respondents' attributions and organisational (group) culture*

A final feature of our proposed method is its focus on respondents' causal attributions. It will be recalled that, for every change that a respondent mentioned (whether an already experienced change or an anticipated change), information was sought about why the respondent thought that the change had occurred, or would occur. In Study 3, the analysis of these attributions data provided evidence of an interesting difference between the two divisions. Among respondents from the tooling division there was a strong tendency to attribute change to circumstances perceived to be beyond the control of divisional members (including divisional management). Change was seen as primarily reactive — a response to pressure from the unions, compliance with government legislation, compliance with changes in company strategy, *etc*. In contrast, in the production division there was evidence of a perception (though not as widely shared) that change was the result of considered and planned action on the part of the division's new management, who were generally regarded as being more strongly committed than their predecessors to the development of the division's human resources. This difference between the divisions served to highlight the potential value of attributions data. In particular, it suggested that organisations (groups) may develop their own unique styles of attributing cause and that these styles may be culturally determined.

The analysis of attributions data from Study 3 also suggested the interesting possibility that causal attributions may provide clues as to the success, or otherwise, of planned change within an organisation. For example, if organisation members are consistently positive in their attributions about why change has been implemented, and if these positive attributions continue to be made even in the face of changing circumstances (say, e.g., the departure of a particularly charismatic manager who was the original architect of the change), then the change might be judged to have been successful.

The above hypotheses or hunches suggest that the study of attributions may constitute a very fruitful area for organisational culture research in the future. This theme is explored in more detail later in this chapter (see Section 13.3.1). Then, in the next and final chapter of this volume, we report the results of a follow-up study which uses the data from Study 3 to provide an example of how attributions might be more systematically investigated to inform an understanding of an organisation's (group's) culture.

13.2 Evaluation of the Method: Comparison with Extant Approaches and Practical Considerations

The aim of the first substantive section of this chapter was to offer some evaluation of each of the key features of our proposed method, namely, the use of an interview which was: (i) issue-focussed; (ii) semi-structured; (iii) designed to provide information about respondents' experience in relation to a number of different contextual domains; and (iv) designed to provide information about respondents' perceptions of the causes of experienced, as well as anticipated, events (i.e., attributions data). In the next substantive section, a more general evaluation of the method is offered in terms of how the method compares with existing approaches, both quantitative and qualitative, to understanding (assessing) organisational culture. In this context, consideration is also given to the potential value of the method as a tool for use in culture change. We then explore a number of practical issues regarding the use of the method that were raised by the findings of Study 3. For example, is there an optimal sample size beyond which the use of the method is likely to become unwieldy? How important is time spent in the research setting to the quality of the data gathered? What researcher skills are required? *etc.*

13.2.1 *Comparison with extant approaches*

Consideration is given, first of all, to the value of the method relative to existing quantitative approaches and, secondly, to the value of the method relative to existing qualitative approaches.

13.2.1.1 *Advantages when compared with quantitative methods*

One important limitation of questionnaire measures of organisational culture, as suggested by the results of Study 3, is that they typically focus on the present context of respondents' experience only, and pay no attention to any other contextual domain. Evidence from Study 3 suggests that, in the absence of information about the past context, for example, one's ability to accurately interpret and make sense of present time data is likely to be seriously limited. Perhaps more importantly, however, a broader contextualist approach, of the kind that we are proposing, can provide insights into the extent to which organisation (group) members are committed to particular ways of thinking and behaving. This is essentially the notion of boundedness, one indicator of which will be the extent to which members' beliefs about the ideal can be shown to be constrained by long-established ways of thinking and behaving. The problem with questionnaire measures of culture is that they provide no insight into the group's commitment to the culture as perceived at the present time. For example, norm indicators, such as the Norms Diagnostic Index (Allen & Dyer, 1980) and the Organizational Culture Inventory (Cooke & Lafferty, 1986), provide a measure of respondents' perceptions of the normative behaviours which prevail in the organisation at the present time. The issue of whether or not respondents are committed to these norms — in the sense that, at some basic level, they believe in their inherent worth — is simply not addressed. Sathe (1985) makes the important point that people can comply with behavioural norms without being committed to them, offering external justifications for their behaviour, such as, "We are doing this because it is required of us" (p. 246).

In this sense, questionnaire measures can be regarded as being of limited value only when compared with the method that we are proposing, in terms of their capacity to provide critical information about the organisation's (group's) likely responsiveness to change. The point is that one cannot assume that there will be resistance to change simply on the basis of the finding that particular behavioural norms are perceived to prevail which are inconsistent with (and perhaps even contradict) the norms required for successful change. This is not to say that quantitative measures do not have a place in assessing the prevailing norms and values of an organisation, but rather that the data generated by these measures need to be supplemented by a deeper level of analysis, such as that which we are proposing, if they are to be interpreted accurately from a cultural perspective. In fact, existing quantitative measures of organisational culture might benefit from a more contextualist approach. For example, consideration might be given to further supplementing these measures with assessments of norms, values, and/or artefacts in relation to other contexts. Thus, a measure such as the Kilmann–Saxton Culture Gap Survey (Kilmann & Saxton, 1983), which compares present and ideal norms of behaviour, could be expanded to ask about past norms, anticipated future norms, and norms in other organisations in which the respondent has worked, or which she/he knows about. In this way, quantitative measures could be made more flexible so that, for example: one could compare present and past norms or values in order to assess the results of a change program; or one could compare present and anticipated future norms in order to ascertain the extent to which changes are anticipated; or one could compare present norms with the norms of other comparable organisations as part of an evaluation of the organisation's standing with respect to its competitors. This contextual analysis might also be extended to organisational artefacts, such as uniforms and the layout of the organisation. As already indicated, however, in order to understand the cultural significance of the data generated (including, in particular, data pertaining to differences between contexts), a further and more in-depth analysis would be required.

A second limitation of questionnaire measures of organisational culture, which has been recognised in the literature (e.g., Rentsch, 1990), and which is confirmed by the results of Study 3, is that they provide no insight into the meaning, or interpretive framework which informs the individual's response to questionnaire items. The results of Study 3 provided evidence that differences in meaning could occur at a number of different levels. First, individuals (or groups) could differ in the meanings which they attached to, in this case, the various worker activities about which they were asked. There was some variability, for example, in respondents' definitions of activities such as 'training' and 'helping other workers'. For example, training was loosely defined by some respondents as incorporating both informal on-the-job and formal off-the-job training activities, whereas for other respondents, their definition was more narrow and included formal off-the-job training only. Similarly, helping other workers was defined by some respondents as simply "lending a hand", whereas for others it involved the formal provision, by experienced operators, of guidance and assistance to newcomers. While inconsistencies of this kind might be expected to be encountered in respondents' interpretations of the behaviours about which they are asked in norm indicators — behaviours such as training, feedback, cooperation, commitment, responsibility, opposition, *etc.* — these indicators provide no means by which such inconsistencies might be revealed. A clear advantage of our proposed method in this regard is that respondents are given the opportunity to elaborate on, and qualify, their responses. Indeed, it might even be argued that the use of various prompts (including "Why?" questions) encourages respondents to provide this information. An additional advantage of the more in-depth approach that we are advocating is that it could help to refine the questions that are used in quantitative measures. Thus, as suggested by the example above, a question about training may benefit from being more specific by differentiating between formal and informal training. However, even with such refinements, there may be other possible interpretations of the questions asked in quantitative measures, which will only be able to be revealed through a more in-depth inquiry.

Apart from inconsistencies in respondents' interpretations of the particular activities/behaviours about which they are asked, differences may also be encountered in the meanings which respondents attribute to the descriptive terms associated with these activities/behaviours. Thus, descriptors such as 'fair' (as in 'fair practices'), 'challenging' (as in 'challenging tasks'), 'effective' (as in 'effective communication'), which are frequently used in questionnaire measures of organisational culture, might be expected to mean different things to different people. The same argument applies to descriptive terms which have a quantitative dimension in the sense that they represent expressions of amount, degree, probability, *etc.* In Study 3, there was some evidence to suggest that respondents from the tooling division, because of their long history of no worker involvement in training, may have been more sensitive than their counterparts in the production division to changes in the involvement of workers in training, and hence also more likely to 'overestimate' the objective amount of training currently provided. The important implication is that, depending upon the yardstick which they use to evaluate their present experience, individuals (and groups) might be expected to differ in their interpretations of what constitutes, for example, *a lot* or *a high level* of worker involvement in any given activity. In the same way, respondents' interpretations of descriptors such as *regularly* (as in 'regularly plan', 'regularly review', or 'regularly meet'), *some* (as in 'some input'), and *moderately difficult* (as in 'moderately difficult goals'), which appear in questionnaire measures of organisational culture, are likely to be subject to differences in interpretation. Moreover, this problem is also likely to arise in relation to the response options from which respondents are expected to choose when completing questionnaire measures of organisational culture. For example, the Organizational Culture Inventory (Cooke & Lafferty, 1986) asks respondents to indicate, on a five-point scale, the extent to which organisation members are expected to engage in particular behaviours. The specific response categories include: 1–*Not at all*; 2–*To a slight extent*; 3–*To a moderate extent*; 4–*To a great extent*; and 5–*To a very great extent*. Evidence from Study 3 suggests that respondents' interpretations of these various response options may well differ depending upon the yardstick (or interpretive framework) which informs their evaluations of the behaviours in question. In the same way that a more in-depth approach might inform the refinement of questions in quantitative measures, it might also assist in refining the use of rating scales, in particular through the formulation of clear definitions of each rating along with examples to illustrate.

Finally, Study 3 provided evidence that emergent themes may constitute a third level at which differences in meaning could be encountered. This is the idea that the way in which people talk about the activities (or behaviours) about which they are asked can provide important insights into the unique meanings attributed to these activities (or behaviours). A nice illustration of this is provided by data collected as part of Study 3 which pertained to the activity category labelled Help Other Workers. While the two divisions were similar in that a majority of respondents from each reported that, at the present time, the workers in their division provided help to other workers, if and when they needed it, an analysis of the thematic content of the elaborative and qualifying data associated with these responses provided evidence of an interesting difference between the two divisions. Among tooling division respondents there was a shared view that 'giving help' was legitimate only in the context of the superior–subordinate relationships defined by the chain of command. Thus, while a qualified tradesman could legitimately give help to an apprentice, if he himself needed help, he should seek this help, not from a fellow tradesman (though this did happen in practice), but rather from his leading hand or immediate supervisor. In contrast, respondents from the production division emphasised the importance of interpersonal relationships in determining the helpfulness of the workers in this division towards one another. Specifically, if a worker was perceived to be a 'bludger'[10], then she/he was unlikely to receive help from a co-worker.

Data from Study 3 which were concerned with the characteristics of good workers provide a further illustration of how the thematic content of respondents' elaborations and qualifications can highlight differences in meaning (both within and between groups). While a majority of respondents from the tooling division indicated that, in order to be thought of as a good worker, it was either *very important* or *moderately important* for workers "to come up with ideas for how to improve things", an important contingency which applied to this behaviour was that it was valued only if the ideas were judged by those in authority (e.g., supervisors) to be 'good' ideas. Interestingly, there was no evidence that this same contingency applied to innovative behaviour in the production division.

The two examples above have been included because they have a direct bearing on questionnaire measures of organisational culture which ask about norms of support, on the one hand, and norms of task innovation, on the other. For example, in the Norms Diagnostic Index (Allen & Dyer, 1980), respondents are asked to indicate the extent of their agreement or disagreement with the statement that: "It's a norm around here for people to help each other with on-the-job and personal problems". In the Kilmann–Saxton Culture-Gap Survey (Kilmann & Saxton, 1983), respondents are asked to indicate which of the two norms, "Encourage new ideas" and "Discourage new ideas", best describes the actual norm operating in their group. In contrast to our proposed method, which offers a means whereby important contingencies (attitudes, qualifying comments, *etc.*) that might be associated with these behaviours can be revealed, questionnaire measures offer no means for generating understandings of this kind. As already indicated, it might be possible to refine the questions in measures such as these so as to make them less susceptible to interpretive variability among respondents. However, we would argue that even with the most carefully worded questions, it may be possible for respondents to impose their own meaning on them, particularly if certain words in those questions elicit strong emotional responses with respect to the present climate, or if they challenge underlying cultural beliefs. Answers may be provided in terms of what is of importance to the respondent rather than what is actually asked for in the question.

The failure of questionnaire measures of organisational culture to address this problem of differences in meaning — which, as shown above, can exist at a number of different levels — has two important implications. The first is that the aggregation of like responses to questionnaire items assumes a reasonable degree of interpretive consistency and, as evidence from Study 3 suggested, such an assumption would appear to be unfounded. The second is that questionnaire measures, by ignoring the meaning dimension of the data

---

[10]Australian vernacular referring to a person who is lazy, who seeks to avoid work, and who lives off the efforts of others.

which they generate, disregard what is potentially critical cultural information. In other words, differences in meaning (within or between groups) may be culturally determined and, as such, the analysis of meaning offers a potentially valuable source of cultural data. To draw on one of the examples above, what is important from a cultural perspective is not the extent to which organisation members share a perception that, say, selection and promotion practices in the organisation are 'fair', but rather it is organisation members' *beliefs about what constitutes 'fair practice'* with respect to selection and promotion. Notions of 'fairness' may be culturally determined and, as such, they may provide a basis for differentiating one group from another.

On the basis of the above arguments — and evidence attesting to the importance of both context and meaning as 'carriers' of cultural information — it would seem reasonable to conclude that questionnaire measures of organisational culture offer, at best, a superficial understanding of the concept only. Moreover, while it is true that advocates of the use of such measures admit that they are unsuitable for tapping culture at its deepest level (i.e., at the level of basic beliefs and assumptions) (Rousseau, 1990), the question remains as to just how different many of these measures are from measures of the earlier concept of organisational climate, which were developed in the late 1960s and early 1970s (e.g., Litwin & Stringer, 1968; Stern, 1970). As indicated in Chapter 4 of Volume I, a simple review of some of the items which appear in questionnaire measures of organisational culture and organisational climate (see Table 4.1) serves to illustrate just how similar quantitative approaches to the operationalisation of these two concepts are.

It will be recalled that, in Chapter 4 of Volume I, we compared and contrasted the concepts of organisational climate and organisational culture, in terms of their key similarities and differences. We argued that organisational climate might best be used to refer to organisation members' collective feelings about the surface elements of organisational culture (residing at Levels 1 and 2 in Schein's framework). At the same time, however, we suggested that these feelings might be precipitated by, or reflect, a conflict between the surface-elements of the organisation's culture — whether artefacts, norms, and values — and its deeper-level beliefs and assumptions (residing at Level 3 in Schein's framework). Moreover, while organisation members will be conscious of having negative feelings directed towards some aspect of the culture of which they are aware (i.e., its surface elements), they will not necessarily be able to articulate why they feel as they do. This is because the source of their discomfort lies in a conflict between the culture's surface elements and its deeper-level beliefs and assumptions which, for the most part, are taken-for-granted and unconsciously held. For example, a negative climate about imposed norms with respect to decision-making may be accompanied by the explanation that "It's just not right", without workers being able to clearly articulate what exactly it is that is not right. The use of the method that we are proposing — essentially, an issue-focussed semi-structured interview that asks about experience in relation to different contextual domains — might be valuable in helping, not only the interviewer, but also the interviewee, to understand and articulate the source of the problem (i.e., what exactly it is that is wrong). Specifically, this may become evident in the interviewee's responses to questions about differences between her/his experience of, in this case, decision-making in the organisation at the present time, and in relation to different contextual domains, and the reasons for these differences.

In addition to the above arguments in support of our proposed method, there are two further advantages which the method offers when compared with questionnaire measures of organisational culture. First, the use of open-ended questions facilitates the emergence of dimensions (in this case, activity categories) which are salient to respondents. A common criticism of quantitative approaches is that they are typically developed around researcher-derived categories, which may lack relevance in the particular context in which the research is being carried out (Jones, 1988; Ott, 1989). Second, compared with questionnaire measures of organisational culture, in which the focus is very much on generalities (i.e., norms, values, *etc.* which capture something about the group as a whole), the method that we are proposing can provide insights into the extent to which the individual's personal experience may be discrepant from her/his perception of the situation in general. The example has been given of how, in Study 3, respondents from the production division tended to make positive evaluations of the communication relationship that they had with their own supervisor(s), while at the same time holding fairly negative views about the communication climate that prevailed in their division as a whole. Moreover, the argument has been made that discrepancies of this kind (in respondents' perceptions of the 'specific' versus the 'general') may be an indication of culture change in progress, whereby the residual effects of past experience may continue, for some time, to influence organisation members' perceptions of the general, despite experience, at an individual level, which signals the onset of change.

13.2.1.2 *Advantages when compared with qualitative methods*

When compared with existing qualitative approaches to the study of organisational culture, the main advantage of our proposed method is that it is much more systematic and potentially time efficient in its approach to culture analysis. As such, inferences about cultural beliefs and assumptions which are suggested by the results are arguably more reliable, since they are made on the basis of data which are systematically collected and analysed. Moreover, this information can be obtained in much less time than would be required for a genuine ethnographic study of an organisation's culture (that is likely to involve in-depth interviewing, observation over an extended period of time, and/or detailed documentary analysis). The point can be made that, while qualitative accounts of culture often make for interesting and entertaining reading — they are typically highly descriptive and have some of the same qualities as a 'good story' — for this same reason, they can leave one feeling frustrated and seeking answers to questions about the research method (e.g., Just how much time did the researcher spend in the research setting? Just how many interviews were conducted and with whom, and what questions were asked?), the approach to data analysis (e.g., How did the researcher manage the data from 'multiple' interviews? Were conversational data treated differently from formal interview data?), and the reliability of the evidence presented (e.g., Just how widely shared is a view which is represented by the comments of one or two respondents and would another independent researcher using the same approach have come to the same conclusions?). The latter issue of reliability would seem to be of particular concern when conclusions in such studies support the theoretical views of the researcher.

The above concerns about qualitative (or ethnographic) accounts of organisational culture echo some of the more formal criticisms which have been made of ethnographic fieldwork in general. For example, Emerson (1987, cited in Bryman, 1991, p. 210) argues that much modern ethnography fails to adequately specify the "interactional practices" (essentially 'the method') and the "textual practices" (essentially, the approach to data analysis) which produce the ethnographic account. Emerson is also critical of the tendency for many fieldwork projects to be of very short duration and for participation in the research setting to be intermittent. With respect to this last point, and as noted previously, one ethnographic study which has been proposed as a model for how research into organisational culture should be conducted, namely Whyte's (1943) seminal study of Street Corner Society (Bryman, 1991), involved three years of continuous fieldwork. In qualitative studies of organisational culture, the time spent in the field is typically much less than this. Where the period of fieldwork is specified (and often it is not), it rarely exceeds one year (see, e.g., studies included in Jones, Moore, & Snyder, 1988). Moreover, it is not uncommon in qualitative accounts of culture to find references to the research having been conducted 'part-time', or 'over a period of [x] months', leaving open the question of just how much contact the researcher actually had with the research setting and the participants in the research.

The advantage of our approach, compared with extant qualitative approaches, is not only that it is more systematic in terms of its method and approach to data analysis (i.e., it offers a specific set of questions and a means for comparing data within and between groups), but it is also more systematic in terms of its attention to questions of sharedness and questions concerning the role of context in shaping culture. With respect to the former, and as suggested above, a source of frustration in reading qualitative accounts of organisational culture is that claims about commonality or sharedness (e.g., in relation to group members' interpretations, attitudes, perceptions, practices, *etc.*) are often made with very little supporting evidence. It is not uncommon to find such claims illustrated with the comments of one, or perhaps two, research respondents only, with no indication given of just how representative the views (attitudes *etc.*) of these individuals are. This can be the case even when the research has reportedly involved many hours of in-depth individual interviews with significant numbers of organisational personnel. A good example is provided by Bate's (1984) study of cultural impediments to change and problem resolution in three large manufacturing companies in the United Kingdom. Bate reports that the research in two of these companies[11] involved more than one hundred interviews (in all), generating 400 hours of audiotape. In addition, the data set for these two companies included 200 hours of recorded company meetings. On the basis of "repeated readings" (p. 49) of the transcripts of these interviews and meetings, Bate identified six dimensions of organisational culture which he argued would impact negatively on organisational problem-solving. What is noteworthy in the context of the present discussion is that the evidence documented in support of these dimensions takes the form of a series of individual quotes — between one and three — illustrating the various different aspects of each dimension. The respondents whose comments are quoted are not differentiated in terms of the organisation to which they belong, and no indication is given of how strongly their views are supported by other participating members of their organisation. For other similar examples, see Snyder's (1988) account of a culture change effort in an aircraft factory, Meyerson's (1991) study of ambiguity and the occupational culture of hospital social work, and Martin's (1992) multi-perspective study of the culture of a large Fortune 500 company. While studies such as these — which provide no empirical evidence of shared-ness despite clearly 'having the numbers' to do so — are commonplace, some exceptions do exist. For example, in their study of the role of the founder in the culture creation process, Martin, Sitkin, and Boehm (1985) not only address the issue of sharedness conceptually, but they also provide empirical evidence of the extent to which it is demonstrated in their data.

Of course, there are some qualitative accounts of organisational culture which provide very scant information about the research method, and in which there are no details whatsoever about the size or demographic characteristics of the sample (e.g., Bartunek & Moch, 1991; Fine, 1988; Young, 1991). Studies such as these are possibly open to even stronger criticism with respect to the cultural interpretations that they offer.

It can be concluded, therefore, that qualitative approaches, at least in practice, generally fail to offer convincing empirical evidence that particular views (attitudes, beliefs, *etc.*) are shared and can, in this sense, be regarded as cultural. Our proposed method offers a number of clear advantages in this regard. First, the use of standardised questions (asked about a specific issue) makes it relatively easy to assess the degree of unanimity, or diversity, of opinion which exists in the group. Second, the qualitative aspect of the method offers a means whereby group members are able to clarify their responses and this, in turn, facilitates the more accurate assessment of sharedness. Third, there is an emphasis on the systematic analysis of data (including qualitative data and data generated in response to the standardised questions) which, while it might be espoused in qualitative accounts of culture, is not always apparent from the way in which these accounts are constructed. And fourth, the method offers the possibility of sampling, not widely, but sufficiently well to provide insights into sharedness if it exists.

---

[11]The extent of the data collection effort in the third company is not specified.

In addition to being more systematic with respect to its treatment of sharedness, the method that we are proposing is also more systematic in terms of the attention it gives to context. The interview focuses on a single issue (in this case, the role of workers) and asks about respondents' experience of this issue in relation not only to the present context, but also in relation to the past context, the anticipated future context, the other context, and the ideal context. An examination of the links between respondents' experience in relation to these different aspects, or domains, of context can provide insights into the way in which respondents' thinking about the issue at the present time may have been shaped, and how it may be continuing to evolve. One important advantage of the method, in this sense, is that it provides a direct and systematic means of assessing, for example, the impact of respondents' past experience (whether in their current organisation or in some other organisational context) on their perceptions of, and thinking about, their current experience, their anticipated future experience, and their ideal experience.

This attempt in our method to operationalise specific dimensions, or domains, of context, and to make inferences about culture based on the linkages between them, contrasts markedly with the treatment of context which one finds in purely qualitative studies of organisational culture. While advocates of a qualitative approach espouse a commitment to context — and certainly the methods which they use, when compared with quantitative methods, are more likely to generate data which are relevant to the specific social milieu in which the research is carried out — the question remains as to how truly contextualist many qualitative studies of culture actually are. If one defines 'contextualism' as a commitment to understanding events, actions, *etc.* "in [their] wider social and historical context" (Bryman, 1988, p. 65), then can a qualitative study which is ahistorical and which reports only on respondents' perceptions, attitudes, *etc.* at the present time (the study by Bate, 1984, described above is one such example, and there are many others) be regarded as being genuinely contextualist in its approach?

Even though there are a number of qualitative studies in which the importance of the historical context is explicitly acknowledged, it is not always made clear how past events, and the meanings attributed to these events by organisation members, have influenced organisation members' thinking at the present time. For example, in his study of culture change in a British boarding school, Pettigrew (1979) espouses the value of a longitudinal approach for such a study on the grounds that, among other things, it allows one to examine "the impact of one drama [critical event] on successive and even consequent dramas" (p. 571). However, the empirical evidence which is subsequently offered in support of this argument is scant to say the least. There is a single paragraph only in which the author makes reference to certain myths which he argues were important in generating and sustaining organisation members' commitment to change. No data are presented which provide a convincing demonstration of how members' experience of past events, and their interpretations of these events, have influenced their thinking about subsequent events.

It is also the case that in studies of this kind, the link between the past and the present often seems to be more of an assumed link than a link which has been established through

independent and empirically derived evidence. For example, in Snyder's (1988) study c
culture change in the assembly plant of a large aircraft manufacturing company in th
United States, a link is made (it is not clear by whom — whether the researcher, or th
manager responsible for the change effort) between employees' current attitudes, behav
iours, *etc.* (e.g., low morale, fear of telling the truth, *etc.*) and their exposure, over time, t
autocratic and demeaning styles of management, as well as their history of "having bee
viewed as losers by other organizations within the company" (p. 198). While this lin
makes good sense intuitively, no data are presented which illustrate its veracity from th
perspective of the employees concerned. Our proposed method is able to avoid this criti
cism since it requires all respondents in the sample to be presented with the same basic se
of questions. Moreover, these questions seek highly specific information about the nature
timing, and perceived reasons for, changes which respondents have experienced (in thi
case, in the role of workers) from the past to the present. Another observation about the
Snyder study which is worth making is that, while it includes an account of two crises i
the history of the research organisation, nothing is said about the nature of the link betwee
these events and the subsequent experience of culture change in the particular division o.
the organisation (i.e., the assembly plant) which is the central focus of the research. I
other words, the primary purpose of the account would appear to be simply to 'set the
scene' in much the same way as a summary of respondents' demographics in a study such
as our Study 3 does. While this is entirely reasonable, it does alert one to the possibility
that qualitative accounts of organisational culture may include historical data without necessarily being truly contextualist in their approach.

With respect to their treatment of context, it is also the case that qualitative studies of
organisational culture, apart from their focus on the present context and sometimes also
the past context, typically pay no attention to other aspects of context which have appeared
in conceptual treatments of organisational culture (namely, the anticipated future, the
other, and the ideal). In contrast, our method offers a means whereby respondents' experience in relation to the range of different aspect of context which have emerged as being
conceptually important can be examined systematically.

Finally, the point can be made that, while advocates of qualitative approaches are
likely to object to the use of standardised questions in our method on the grounds that
they bias the research towards issues of interest to the researcher, and constrain the emergence of issues of interest to (and salience for) the respondents in the research, such
approaches are themselves not immune to the effects of this kind of researcher bias. A
classic illustration of this, to which we have made reference in a number of chapters of
this book, is Freeman's (1983) refutation of Mead's (1928) ethnographic account of the
experience of adolescence in Samoa. Freeman argues that Mead's depiction of Samoan
adolescence as a relatively idyllic period, devoid of the considerable emotional stress and
conflict associated with adolescence in America and elsewhere (a view which Freeman's
own research, and the work of others, subsequently challenged), was underpinned by her
strong commitment (and that of her supervisor and mentor) to the ideology of cultural

determinism — the notion that human behaviour is determined by cultural, rather than biological, influences. The argument can be made, therefore, that while a supposed advantage of unstructured qualitative approaches is that they are more faithful to the perspectives of the participants in the research, in practice, they may be equally susceptible to bias resulting from the researcher's particular interests and predispositions as are more structured approaches.

For the reader interested in gaining at least an introductory understanding of the Freeman–Mead debate, a useful resource is a YouTube video in six parts entitled *Margaret Mead and Samoa (1988)* that shows Freeman present at a later interview with one of the individuals that had previously been interviewed by Mead. This individual revealed that she and her female friends had more or less told Mead what they thought she wanted to hear in order to please her. Freeman's work created an ongoing controversy concerning the relative merits of both Mead and Freeman himself as anthropologists, but it is not the intention here to comment on the various arguments associated with this controversy. The important implication of Freeman's work for the study of organisational culture is that it suggests that a useful endeavour would be to undertake similar follow-up studies in organisational settings. The study of change programs in organisations would constitute a particularly interesting focus for a follow-up of this kind. This could involve reinterviewing CEOs, managers, supervisors, and workers quoted in earlier studies and/or interviewed in video clips for management training courses, to ascertain whether their opinions were still the same or whether they had changed over the intervening years. That such opinions may change over time is suggested by media interviews with retired politicians who indicate that they had reservations about certain decisions in which they were involved during their careers, but which were not apparent in the comments that they made, or failed to make, at the time.

13.2.2 *The proposed method: A tool for use in culture change?*

In the discussion above, consideration has been given to some of the main strengths of our proposed method when compared with existing quantitative and qualitative approaches to the study of organisational culture. While the method offers some clear advantages over these approaches — it is more focussed and systematic in its treatment of context, it draws attention to the importance of the meaning dimension, it deals with the issue of sharedness more convincingly, *etc.* — one important limitation of the method, it might be argued, is its very narrow focus on a single category of cultural beliefs only (in this case, beliefs about the role of workers). This characteristic of the method means that it is unable to deliver the kind of rich and comprehensive account of culture (with its multiple manifestations) that an intensive ethnographic study (such as that carried out by Whyte, 1943) is likely to produce. The point can also be made that, given that the method was designed to tap beliefs pertaining to just one of the broad categories in Schein's (1985, 1992, 2004, 2010) typology (specifically, beliefs about the nature of human nature), it would be unrealistic, within a single study, to try to use the method to generate a profile of an organi-sation's (group's) culture in which all of the categories included in Schein's typology were represented. Such a task would simply be unmanageable given the detailed and highly specific information which the method is designed to generate in relation to a single cat-egory of beliefs.

Notwithstanding the fact that our method might be criticised for being too narrowly focussed, there are two important points that we believe can be made in the method's defence in this regard. The first concerns the exploratory nature of the research that we have undertaken. As indicated previously, the aim of this research was not to produce a comprehensive description of the cultures of the two participating divisions, but rather it was to develop a method for understanding deeper-level culture which would have some predictive value, and which could be used to make systematic comparisons of culture (across research settings, over time, *etc.*). The choice of an issue-focussed interview for Study 3 was therefore very important from a methodological point of view.

The second point is that an issue-focussed approach is limited only if the aim of the research is to arrive at an understanding of an organisation's (group's) culture in its entirety (and it is questionable whether indeed that is possible). If, however, the aim is to under-stand some specific aspect of the culture — and this might be entirely appropriate in the context of, say, a specific organisational change effort — then a method such as our pro-posed method is likely to be of considerable practical value. The idea here is that, for any given (relatively focussed) change which an organisation might wish to implement, there are likely to be specific beliefs and assumptions, the presence or absence of which will have implications for the success of the change. Thus, an important question which change agents might ask is: "What beliefs and assumptions are necessary for the success of this change and are these beliefs and assumptions consistent with, or antagonistic to, those supported by the organisation's current culture?" Of course, this is a question that is not easily answered. A particular problem in this regard is that, while change agents might ask organisation members whether they support certain beliefs and assumptions which they regard as necessary for the success of a proposed change, a response in the affirmative cannot necessarily be taken at 'face value'. To repeat an example that we have used previ-ously, change agents might correctly assume that a change which has implications for a greater role for workers in decision-making will depend for its success on organisation members (at all levels) holding the belief that workers should be consulted in decision-making. However, while workers might agree in principle with this proposition, the reality, and their subsequent response to the change, might be very different if their basic beliefs are that it is the job of management to make decisions and the job of workers to accept those decisions, and also to complain about them. Similarly, asking managers whether they believe in management practices that constitute a Theory X or Theory Y approach may elicit social desirability responding that does not match their actual underlying beliefs and assumptions.

An important advantage of our proposed method is that it can readily be adapted to evaluate beliefs and assumptions which are specific to (in the sense of having implications for the success of) the particular change which an organisation might wish to implement. The point might also be made that, given the nature of basic beliefs and assumptions, it is unlikely that the influence of any particular set of beliefs and assumptions will be confined to a single domain of organisation members' experience only. Thus, even though our method deals with just one aspect of an organisation's (group's) culture, it is likely that the insights which it generates will have implications for a broader understanding of the organisation's (group's) culture as a whole. Of course, this does raise the question of the relative independence of the beliefs and assumptions in the various categories that make up Schein's typology. For example, using the in-depth method that we are advocating, how might the beliefs and assumptions in a given category — in this case, the nature of human nature and pertaining specifically to the role of workers — relate to the beliefs and assumptions in other categories? In using our method to assess a particular issue which is the subject of a change program, one would also need to be sensitive to possible subcultures — in particular, those formed around the less obvious groupings of age, gender, family status, and professional qualifications, rather than those formed around more obvious departmental or divisional boundaries — and the differences between them.

Given the above arguments, what is perhaps most distinctive about the method that we are proposing, when compared with existing approaches for assessing organisational culture, is its ability to inform one's understanding of, and approach to, organisational change. In particular, the method can provide insights into: (i) the likely resistance to a given change; (ii) where resistance to (and also support for) the change is located (e.g., in particular subcultures); (iii) the reasons for resistance to the change; and (iv) how well the change effort is progressing. A brief summary of some of the specific sources of data which are likely to generate these different insights is provided below.

(1) **Likely resistance to change.** Relevant data sources include:
   a. Historical data showing the extent of the group's exposure to change over time in relation to the issue of interest;
   b. Attitudinal data, including attitudes to anticipated future, and ideal, changes in relation to the issue;
   c. Data highlighting the extent of the group's future orientation in relation to the issue; and
   d. Other context data providing insights into the extent of the group's exposure to alternative ways of thinking about, and behaving in response to, the issue (i.e., 'cultural alternatives').

(2) **Where resistance to (and support for) change is located.** Time line data (pertaining to when particular changes in relation to the issue are perceived to have occurred, and how far back periods of 'no change' have extended) can be used to identify

organisation members who share similar histories. Groupings of this kind may, in turn, facilitate the identification of resistors to, and supporters of, change.

(3) **Reasons for resistance to change.** Relevant data sources include:

    a.   Historical data pertaining to the nature of the group's past experience with respect to the issue of interest (e.g., whether positive or negative);

    b.   Common themes which emerge in how organisation members talk about the issue;

    c.   Attributions data highlighting organisation members' perceptions about the reasons for experienced, or anticipated, changes in relation to the issue; and

    d.   Ideal context data highlighting reasons for a lack of support for change in relation to the issue (i.e., why organisation members see change as undesirable).

(4) **Progress with the change effort.** There are a number of possible indicators of the success of the change effort including:

    a.   Attributions data indicating the extent to which the change is seen as proactive, as opposed to reactive;

    b.   The prevalence of positive, as opposed to negative, attitudes in how organisation members talk about the change;

    c.   An emerging discrepancy between members' perceptions of the organisation as a whole (which may continue to be anchored in the past) and members' perceptions of their own individual experience (which may reflect the impact of the change); and

    d.   Changes over time in the pattern of responding to open-ended and closed questions.

In arguing that our method offers a potentially valuable tool for use in organisational culture change, consideration also needs to be given to the time that it would take to obtain information about organisation members' beliefs that might be used to facilitate a change program. While less time would be required to use an existing questionnaire measure of organisational culture, such a measure would not necessarily provide information directly relevant to the change program's central issue, and it would not provide the required in-depth information about organisation members' beliefs related to that issue. Given the design of our method, and the systematic approach it adopts, it would certainly take longer to administer than a questionnaire. However, it would be considerably more efficient in this regard than the kind of protracted qualitative inquiry that is entailed in ethnographic studies of organisational culture. Based on the results of Study 3, we would suggest that an allocated period of around two weeks full-time would be sufficient to administer our interview to around 20 individuals, with the numbers depending on the levels of the organisation to be represented, the departments to be represented, and whether or not there is an intention to examine suggested subcultural differences. A pilot study could be used to determine the best wording of the critical questions that constitute our proposed method, and to establish definitions for any ratings or estimates that might be used in the interviews.

It might be argued that, if the aim was to obtain an overall assessment of an organisation's culture prior to the implementation of a change program, our method would take too long to administer, since this would require an assessment of basic beliefs in each of the broad categories that make up Schein's typology. Moreover, if each respondent was to be interviewed about an issue related to only one of Schein's categories, then such an assessment would multiply the time and number of interviewees required, proportionally. It might be possible, however, to conduct this kind of assessment in a relatively short period of time if more than one interviewer were used, and if respondents could be interviewed in parallel. If respondents were prepared to be interviewed about more than one issue, then it might mean even less interview time on subsequent occasions, due to familiarity with the interview protocol. Again, a pilot study would be needed to determine the most appropriate questions to be used with respect to each belief domain. Of course, the organisation would need to be prepared to release the number of staff required, over the period of time required for the interviews. In terms of the number of staff required, it might be that initially a certain minimum number should be specified depending, as above, on the levels of the organisation, departments, and/or subcultures to be assessed, and that this number should be increased only if the results are inconsistent between respondents. Clearly, it would be a matter of accumulating experience in undertaking research of this kind, in order to determine the minimum time and minimum number of research participants required to provide a reliable account of beliefs and assumptions that are representative of the organisation's overall culture, across the range of categories of beliefs and assumptions that make up Schein's typology. While such a project would be major in scope, and might be expected to extend over several months, it might be considered worthwhile if research was to find that the information generated in this way contributed to much more successful outcomes for important change programs.

13.2.3 *Practical considerations in using the proposed method*

It has been argued above that our proposed method offers some important advantages over existing qualitative and quantitative approaches. It has also been suggested that the method might be most valuably used as a tool for understanding organisational change and, in particular, for providing insights into a group's likely cultural responsiveness to change. In this section, some tentative guidelines are offered regarding practical issues associated with the use of the method. Consideration is given to three key issues: (i) sampling and sample size; (ii) the need for, and optimal duration of, researcher involvement in the research setting; and (iii) the personality and skill requirements of the researcher.

13.2.3.1 *Sampling and sample size*

Given the relatively detailed and in-depth information which our proposed method is designed to generate, it would be unrealistic to attempt to use the method with very large samples, such as those which can be accommodated in studies using purely quantitative methods. Interviewing in our method (whether focussed on the current issue of the role of workers or on some other issue) is likely to take up to one and a half hours per respondent. Added to this is the time required for transcribing the interviews (this is recommended given the amount of qualitative data with which one will have to deal) and then analysing the data. While the data collection and analysis requirements of the method necessarily constrain the size of the sample that can be accommodated, the specific numbers of participants that might be included in any given study will clearly depend upon the resources available. Relevant considerations in this regard will include whether or not the research is being carried out by a single investigator or a research team (whose members could administer interviews in parallel), the time scale of the project (this may be set by the participating organisation and may, or may not, be able to be negotiated), and the availability of funds for administrative assistance (in particular, for interview transcription). The sample size is also likely to be influenced by the time commitments of individual participants in the research. More senior members of the organisation may be less accessible in this regard than members at lower levels of the organisational hierarchy.

On the basis of experience in the use of the method, it is our opinion that a sample size of around twenty participants could be managed by a single investigator, assuming reasonable participant availability, some administrative assistance, and working within a total time frame of around two months. This time frame might be substantially shortened by the use of a small team of researchers who could interview different respondents, or even small groups of respondents, simultaneously. As indicated in Chapter 6 of Volume I, while Schein is a strong advocate of the use of small group, rather than individual, interviews for assessing organisational culture, there is a need for further research to determine the relative merits, in terms of reliability and validity, of interviewing individually or in small groups.

A sample of about 10 to 20 would appear to be reasonable not only from a practical point of view but also from a methodological point of view. With a sample of this size (whether it constitutes a single group for study, or perhaps two subgroups), one can be reasonably sure of picking up on commonalities in the views, attitudes, *etc.* of group (subgroup) members, to the extent that these exist. A sample of this size is also sufficiently large to alert one to the possible existence of subgroup differences (which may be investigated through subsequent research involving wider sampling of the subgroup membership). Of course, preliminary pilot studies could be used to ask directly about the existence of any such subgroups or subcultures, as well as to ascertain whether the questions to be asked of members of these subgroups need to be customised in any way (e.g., in terms of the specific terminology to be used).

As with sample size, there are no hard and fast rules to guide decisions about the composition of the sample. The choice of participants for the research will depend upon a number of factors, not the least of which will be the purpose for which the research is being carried out. For example, if the aim of the research is to investigate possible subcultures that are defined by the formal structure of the organisation, as in the research presented in this book, then participants might be selected from different departments, divisions, or other formal groups in the organisation. If the aim is to investigate possible informal subcultures within a department or organisation, then a small number of pilot interviews might help to guide the selection of participants. By way of further illustration, if the aim of the research is to provide information about a group's likely cultural responsiveness to change, then one might be advised to sample from among those group members likely to be most affected by, and/or most influential in determining the success of, the change. Pilot interviews might again be required to determine just which organisation (group) members are likely to be important in any change program. For example, if the change involves the introduction of a work-family policy, then it would be necessary to assess those likely to be directly affected by the policy, such as workers who have children (and possibly also those planning to have children), particularly if they are considered to be valuable employees that the organisation wants to retain, either full-time or part-time, during the years in which they are having their children. It might also be essential to interview a sample of the managers and supervisors who will be involved in administering the policy, since the attitudes of these individuals to workers using the policy might be critical in its successful implementation. To the extent that managers or supervisors share deeply held beliefs that are consistent with a traditional and highly circumscribed role for workers — such that workers should not take time off other than for extreme circumstances (such as a death in the family), or that women with young children should not work — then this might result in workers being reluctant to use many of the work-family options that the policy makes available. Finally, it might be necessary to sample from other workers, not directly affected by the policy, to ensure that they understand and accept the implications of the policy for them in terms of, for example, the likely reallocation of work and/or the temporary replacement of the person who will be on leave.

Of course, given the well-documented influence of organisational gatekeepers on the process of carrying out research in organisations (e.g., Easterby-Smith *et al.*, 1991), the researcher may have little discretion in decisions about who should participate in the research and may be granted access to a narrow band of the organisation's membership only. Apart from these considerations, there are a number of other factors which may guide the selection of participants for research using the method that we are proposing. These are briefly as follows:

(1) To the extent that one is dealing with a relatively homogeneous group, in which members differ with respect to a range of demographic characteristics (such as age, gender, length of service with the organisation, *etc.*), sampling may be guided by an attempt to represent those demographics for which the most marked differences exist. If, for example, both longer-serving and shorter-serving employees are well-represented in the group as a whole, then one might select a sample in which this difference is reflected. If, on the other hand, shorter-serving employees are very poorly represented in the group as a whole, then one might sample from among the longer-serving

employees only. In the absence of any other information, representative sampling of this kind is probably advisable.

(2) Sample selection may be guided by existing theory or research which highlights the potential, or actual, importance of various personal (demographic) characteristics for understanding the issue being investigated. For example, if the aim of the research is to assess a group's likely cultural responsiveness to change, then, given research suggesting a positive relationship between age and resistance to change (e.g., Poblador, 1990), one might select a sample which includes both older and younger employees.

(3) Sample selection may be guided by information that becomes available only as the research unfolds. For example, data from a pilot study or from initial interviews may alert one to the potential importance of some personal (demographic) characteristic not previously considered. Subsequent sampling might then be guided by this information. Patton (1990) has suggested that this kind of flexible and emergent approach to sampling is entirely appropriate for qualitative research designs.

(4) Research participants might be selected on the basis of information provided by key informants. It will be recalled that, in his study of the cultures of twenty organisational units (from ten different organisations), Hofstede *et al.* (1990) relied on management's judgement as to whether or not a unit was culturally homogeneous and, therefore, suitable for inclusion in the study.

While it might be desirable to select a highly diverse sample in which participants' variability with respect to a range of personal (demographic) attributes is represented, the point should be made that there will necessarily be a trade-off between the number of subgroups that can be included in the sample, and the size of each subgroup. An obvious caveat in this regard is that the number of participants in each subgroup should be sufficiently large to enable subgroup differences, if these exist, to be detected, as well as to provide information about common themes *etc.* which cut across the subgroups. This might involve an initial small number in each subgroup which could be increased until any differences between subgroups become well-established.

One final point that can be made in relation to the issue of sampling and sample size concerns the possible use of quantitative methods. In terms of our own work, it can be argued that while research using our proposed method is unlikely to involve very large samples, this research could reasonably act as a precursor to research using more structured quantitative approaches involving much larger samples. For example, the former might provide insights into dimensions or aspects of respondents' experience which are of particular relevance, and these might constitute the focus of subsequent research using quantitative methods which are selected to focus on those dimensions[12]. The advantage of

---

[12]For a detailed discussion of the various ways in which qualitative research (in the context of this discussion, our proposed method is perhaps more appropriately classified as qualitative than quantitative) may facilitate quantitative research, the reader is referred to Bryman (1988, Chapter 6).

the latter is, of course, that they enable one to sample more widely, thereby allowing differences between groups to be tested using inferential statistics. Alternatively, this combination of methods might be used in reverse order. Thus, for example, large-scale sampling using quantitative methods to assess organisational norms and values might be followed by more in-depth interviewing, using our proposed method, in order to uncover deeper-level beliefs and assumptions that might underlie norms and values of particular interest. More specifically, a preliminary quantitative questionnaire might be used to assess norms and values assumed to be relevant to a change program and these norms and values could then be assessed at a deeper level using a much smaller sample of respondents.

13.2.3.2 *Researcher involvement in the research setting*

Experience with the use of our proposed method in Study 3 suggests that some involvement of the researcher in the research setting, prior to as well as during data collection, is highly desirable. The value of this can be argued on a number of grounds, including:

(1) To the extent that the researcher is able to spend some time participating in the research setting and building a relationship with the people who may subsequently be included in the study, the more reliable the information generated by the research is likely to be. Of course, this argument is particularly applicable where one is seeking information of a personal and/or potentially sensitive nature. It was the researcher's impression that, in Study 3, the relative absence of social desirability responding was due in part to the close and trusting relationship which had been established between the researcher and the research respondents (and which had developed over the course of conducting the research that led up to Study 3). It is worth cautioning, however, that the advantages of such a relationship might easily be compromised if the relationship is not handled professionally. For example, there might be requests, whether direct or implied, not to ask about or probe for information pertaining to certain, possibly sensitive, issues (e.g., respondents may be reluctant to talk about leadership), or to find and report results that are acceptable to the organisation or its management.

(2) Involvement of the researcher in the research setting can provide valuable information about how the method might be adapted to make it more relevant to the particular context in which the research is to be carried out. The type of adaptation required might be quite simple and may involve little more than changing some of the language (terms) used in interview questions. Alternatively, if the aim of the research is to provide information that will facilitate the implementation and management of a particular change, then a more substantial adaptation involving, for example, a shift in the central focus of interviewing, may be required.

(3) Knowledge of the research setting helps to ensure the selection of a suitable sample for study. The more time that the researcher is able to spend in the research setting, the better her/his knowledge of the setting is likely to be. In this sense, a flexible approach to sampling, whereby the identification of participants is gradual and depends on

insights gained over time, and as the research unfolds, will enable one to gain maximum advantage from the time spent in the research setting.

(4) Knowledge of the setting being studied facilitates the more accurate interpretation of the data that are gathered. It can also provide insights into the extent to which trends which emerge in the data may reflect more general characteristics of the group as a whole.

Clearly, there will be a number of practical considerations which will influence how much time the researcher is able to spend becoming familiar with the research setting. For example: (i) time constraints may be imposed by the participating organisation; (ii) if the research is being carried out in conjunction with a change effort, the time scale for the change may set the limits; and (iii) the researcher is likely to have other commitments which will influence how much time she/he can devote to the research. These considerations aside, given that research using the proposed method is concerned with understanding aspects of an organisation's (group's) deeper-level culture, it would be desirable for researchers using the method to try to negotiate a period of involvement in the research setting of around two to three months. Moreover, this involvement should, ideally, be continuous (say, two to three days per week) rather than intermittent. In the event that this ideal is unable to be realised, one's attitude should be that a period of say two weeks' continuous involvement of the researcher in the research setting is still preferable to no involvement whatsoever. More time- and resource-efficient methods for becoming familiar with the research setting might consist of a combination of relevant questionnaires on norms and/or values, followed by pilot interviews with a few key personnel, either individually or in a small group. These methods would need to be researched in order to determine their strengths and limitations as a means whereby to obtain relevant cultural information about the research setting.

13.2.3.3 *Personality and skill requirements of the researcher*

The point has been made previously that a researcher using our proposed method should ideally have some basic interviewing skills, as well as be the kind of person who has a genuine curiosity about, and interest in, the lives and experiences of others. Given the semi-structured nature of interviewing in our method and the requirement that each respondent be asked the same basic set of questions (presented in approximately the same sequence), it is not necessary for the researcher to have the kind of sophisticated interviewing skills (developed through long experience) required for entirely open-ended and unstructured interviewing. At the same time, however, the simple mechanical presentation of interview questions is unlikely to contribute to the development of a climate for interviewing in which respondents will willingly elaborate on, and qualify, their responses. In this sense, the researcher might be expected to possess at least some of the skills required for good qualitative interviewing, in particular, the ability to establish rapport, effective two-way communication skills and, associated with this, knowing when to probe for more information (whether for the purpose of clarification, elaboration, *etc.*) while at the same time being able to keep the interview focussed on the topic. Some indication of the skills required might become apparent from inconsistencies within and between respondents in their responses to initial interviewing that are shown, through subsequent checking, to be due to misunderstandings that might have been avoided had the interviewer been more skilled. It is also likely that repeated interviewing of this kind will lead to some refinement of the interviewer's skills, and the lessons learned in this regard could valuably be included in research reports.

While the success of our proposed method does not require the researcher to be highly experienced and skilled in the art of clinical interviewing, it is important that, over a period of some time spent in the research organisation, the researcher is able to establish and maintain a positive relationship with the people (including organisational gatekeepers, participants in the research, *etc.*) with whom she/he will be associated during the course of carrying out the research. As suggested above, this is because, among other things, the aim of the research is to understand deeper-level and potentially sensitive aspects of organisation members' experience. It is beyond the scope of the present discussion to provide a detailed account of the various practical issues involved in building and maintaining a positive research relationship in the context of research carried out in organisations. This is a subject which has received considerable attention in the literature on management and organisational research and it is appropriate, therefore, to refer the reader to sources such as Bryman (1988) and Easterby-Smith *et al.* (1991). Suffice to say that some of the skill and personality characteristics which will help to ensure the researcher's success in this regard will be:

(1) As above, an interest in, and curiosity about, the lives and experiences of others;
(2) Considerable interpersonal sensitivity;
(3) Good communication skills and an ability to respond empathically;
(4) An awareness of ethical issues and a commitment to protecting the interests of participants in the research;
(5) An ability to maintain a stance of impartiality and neutrality (i.e., a commitment to ensuring that one's own biases and prejudices do not unduly influence the research process); and
(6) An ability to work professionally within any negotiated constraints in terms of asking particular questions (e.g., with respect to leadership) and/or the reporting of sensitive information based on consultation with management and/or the governing board of an organisation.

While professional training in interviewing would not be essential for the method proposed, it would nevertheless be advantageous in ensuring that interviewing is carried out in a skilled and professionally appropriate way.

13.3 Suggestions for Future Research

The results of Study 3 (along with insights obtained from the other studies conducted as part of this research) suggest a number of interesting possibilities for future research. Each of these is described below and, as will be seen, each is concerned with providing information which will, in some way, contribute to our understanding of how best to go about measuring, or surfacing, culture in organisations. In other words, the main focus of these various research 'ideas' is on methodological issues. Three different types of studies are suggested, namely: (i) those which might be conducted using the existing data set (i.e., the Study 3 data set); (ii) those which involve collecting additional data using our proposed method (i.e., the method developed for use in Study 3); and (iii) those in which data collection involves the use of some of the other available measure(s) of organisational culture/climate, either alone or in combination with our proposed method.

13.3.1 *Research using the existing data set*

Insights from the Study 3 results suggest a number of interesting possibilities for future research that might serve to further advance our understanding of how best to decipher organisational culture. These are as follows:

(1) **The individual, rather than the response, as the unit of analysis.** In Study 3, the approach to data analysis was to aggregate individual responses to specific questions and then to look for any commonalities which emerge in these responses. One of the main problems with this approach, as suggested by the results of the study, is that it is not sensitive to intra-individual inconsistency. In other words, it does not pick up on inconsistencies between an individual's responses to specific questions and the overall pattern of responding for that individual. Such an approach is also somewhat limited when it comes to dealing with inter-individual differences, such as, differences between respondents in their interpretations of specific questions, and differences with respect to the amount of information that respondents provide (e.g., some respondents might mention many differences between, say, their current and their other organisation, whilst other respondents might mention only a few). The point has been made previously that a possible alternative approach to data analysis, which may help to overcome some of these problems, would be to adopt as the unit of analysis the individual, rather than the response. This would involve analysing the overall pattern of responding for each respondent, and then grouping respondents based upon the similarities which emerge (a kind of qualitative equivalent of a cluster analysis in quantitative research). Such an approach may be culturally more sensitive than the present approach in the sense of providing a clearer indication of both the degree of sharedness of the group's culture and the extent to which different subcultures are supported within the group. The value of such an approach could be explored empirically by conducting a reanalysis of the existing Study 3 data set.

(2) **Systematic analysis of time line data to differentiate subjective from chronological histories.** Study 3 provided some evidence that groups for organisational culture research might usefully be delineated in terms of similarities which emerge in respondents' subjective (as opposed to chronological) histories. An interesting study for future research would, therefore, be to conduct a more systematic analysis of the existing time line data (i.e., the data pertaining to respondents' perceptions of changes which have occurred from the past to the present, the timing of these changes, and the duration of the 'no change' periods prior to the onset of change). The aim would be to group those individuals who shared similar 'time line' data (with respect to the same changes of course) and then to examine the extent to which the resultant groupings were meaningful in other respects (e.g., homogeneous in terms of group members' attitudes, their way of talking about particular issues, their notions of the ideal, *etc.*). An alternative to this approach would, of course, be to use our proposed method solely for the purpose of delineating the groups for study. Having done this, one could then use a more superficial, and hence practical (with respect to data collection and analysis) measure of organisational culture (say, a norm indicator), to examine whether or not there were significant cultural differences between these groups.

(3) **Attributions as a 'window' into organisational culture.** As suggested previously in this chapter, the study of attributions may constitute a very fruitful area for organisational culture research in the future. Attributions may provide clues as to the strength of an organisation's culture (a high degree of sharedness in members' causal attributions may be indicative of a strong culture) and also to the content of the culture (i.e., the particular beliefs and assumptions which it supports). With respect to the latter, it can be argued that organisation members' attributions may be culturally determined such that certain kinds of cultures may give rise to particular attributions or attributional styles. This argument closely parallels Moscovici's (1984) argument in the social representations literature that representations (i.e., shared ways of knowing) determine the nature of the attributions that people make. If attributional style is culturally determined, then one might expect that attributions data would constitute a valuable source of information from which inferences about an organisation's underlying culture might be made.

While the study of attributions has traditionally been concerned with individual perceptions of causality (Greenberg & Baron, 1995), there is now a sizeable body of research in which the focus is on organisational (i.e., collectively realised) attributions (e.g., Bettman & Weitz, 1983; Martinko, 1995; Martinko, Harvey, & Dasborough, 2011; Salancik & Meindl, 1984; Smircich & Stubbart, 1985). However, as far as the present authors are aware, there is only one published account of research that has endeavoured to understand organisational culture through the analysis of shared attributions. This is a study by Silvester, Anderson, and Patterson (1999) in which attributions analysis is used to identify differences between key stakeholder groups involved in a culture change program, in terms of members' collective beliefs about the causes of the success (or alternatively, the failure) of the program. There is therefore considerable scope for further research in this regard. Drawing on our own research, a potentially fruitful avenue for inquiry would be to conduct a more sophisticated analysis of the attributions data contained within the Study 3 data set. The reader is reminded that the analysis of these data that was conducted for Study 3 was fairly rudimentary. The focus was on one set of attributions only, namely, those associated with changes (whether experienced or anticipated) that respondents reported, and these attributions were analysed in terms of a single dimensions only (i.e., a Proactive versus Reactive dimension). Future research might, therefore, explore the possibility of reanalysing these attributions using a more sophisticated coding system.

In Chapter 14 (the next and final chapter of this volume, and the final chapter of this book), we report the results of our own endeavour to conduct the kind of research envisaged here. Specifically, and as a follow-up to Study 3, the above attributions data — importantly these data included only attributions made in response to *direct* questioning regarding experienced and anticipated changes (or an absence of such changes) in the role of workers — were extracted from the Study 3 data set and subjected to a more systematic analysis. For the purpose of this analysis, we further developed and applied the coding system that was used by Silvester *et al.* (1999) — itself a version of the Leeds Attributional Coding System (LACS), developed by Stratton, Munton, Hanks, Heard, and Davidson (1988), for use primarily in family therapy contexts, and adapted in Silvester *et al.*'s study for use in organisational contexts. The LACS provides for the classification of attributions in terms of five bipolar dimensions: (i) Stable versus Unstable; (ii) Global versus Specific; (iii) Internal versus External; (iv) Personal versus Universal; and (v) Controllable versus Uncontrollable. As will be seen in Chapter 14, the advantage of this more systematic and more comprehensive analysis of the Study 3 attributions data is that it enabled a richer and more detailed comparison of respondents' attributions (both within and between divisions) to be made. It also provided for a more rigorous testing of the hypothesis that each of the participating divisions in our research supported its own unique style of attributing cause.

Finally, and again using the Study 3 data set, one might extend the attributions analysis (conducted for Study 3 and in the subsequent follow-up study reported in Chapter 14) to look at *all* of the attributions data contained within the Study 3 data set. In other words, rather than just focus on attributions associated with specific changes (these were made in response to the standardised and direct "Why?" questions), one could also look at *spontaneously generated attributions data*. It might be interesting, for example, to conduct a more systematic analysis of respondents' explanations for why the workers in their division did, or did not, participate in particular activities (such as training, information meetings, safety meetings, *etc.*). One might expect that the number and content of the spontaneous attributions that are made in this regard will be influenced by a number of factors including, for example, the seniority of respondents (whether managers or workers) and the stability of the issue about which respondents are asked (whether changing or about to change, or stable). The data for both divisions contained explanations for participation in particular activities, such as, "It's compulsory to attend", and "They go in order to avoid work", and explanations for non-participation, such as, "They have to do it in their own time" and "They don't get paid to attend". To the extent that attributions of this kind can be shown to be widely shared among the members of a group, one might reasonably infer that the culture of the group supports predominantly Theory X (as opposed to Theory Y) beliefs about the nature of workers.

13.3.2 *Research involving additional data collection with our proposed method*

Given the exploratory nature of the research that we have conducted using our proposed method, there is a need for additional research to more firmly establish the value of the method as a measure for deep culture. Some suggested possibilities in this regard include:

(1) **Differential involvement of the researcher in the research setting.** While it has been argued previously that researchers using our proposed method should ideally spend some time becoming familiar with the setting and subjects of their research, the question remains as to just how critical this might be to the effective use of the method. It would be interesting, therefore, to conduct a study comparing insights generated by the method when used with, and without, a period of researcher involvement in the research setting. Is it the case that the former are markedly more reliable and more in-depth than the latter? Of course, in conducting such a study, it would be important to control for interviewer skill, since a more skilled interviewer who has spent less time in the organisation may obtain more accurate data than a less skilled interviewer who has had a more protracted period of engagement with the organisation. A possible outcome, and advantage, of greater researcher involvement in the research setting, apart from improved rapport with participants in the research, is that certain revisions may be made to questions in the interview protocol. Of course, this would need to be taken into account when comparing the results for the "no involvement" group with those for the "some involvement" group. Continued research may reveal a set of critical questions that are more likely to access deeper aspects of organisational culture with respect to particular issues. It would also be interesting to compare the relative importance of researcher involvement in the organisation using the proposed method with the relative importance of researcher involvement using standard (i.e., off-the-shelf) organisational culture and organisational climate questionnaires.

(2) **Testing for researcher bias.** Given the possibility that researcher bias may influence the results of interviewing using our proposed method, a useful study for future research would be to compare the results of interviewing using a number of different interviewers. The participants for such a study would need to be selected from a culturally homogeneous group and then allocated randomly for interviewing by different

interviewers. One would also need to ensure that interviewers selected for inclusion in the study were similar with respect to the basic skill (formal training) and personality requirements for carrying out research using the proposed method. To the extent that interviewing using different interviewers produced discrepant results, one might then go on to look more closely at what the possible sources of bias may have been. We are unaware of any checks on this kind of reliability which have been carried out in relation to qualitative studies of organisational culture. Common biases in interviewing, such as those documented in relation to personnel selection interviews (e.g., Dessler, Griffiths, & Lloyd-Walker, 2007), could be assessed. For example, one might seek to ascertain whether the findings for different interviewers, to the extent that they are consistently different across a number of interviews, reflect differences between interviewers in their interviewing expertise and/or theoretical perspectives.

(3) **Contextual orientation as a defining characteristic of organisational culture.** The question of whether or not organisational cultures might be differentiated on the basis of contextual orientation (i.e., whether they are more past-oriented, future-oriented, *etc.*) is one that might readily be addressed through further research using our proposed method. As suggested previously in this chapter, the method could be used to test predictions about the likely dominant contextual orientation in a number of different kinds of organisations. Such a study might include: (i) a long-established, family-owned company with a stable workforce and operating in a relatively stable market (assuming such companies still exist) as an example of a company likely to have a strong past orientation; (ii) a high technology company as an example of a company likely to have a strong future orientation; (iii) a management consulting firm as an example of an other-oriented organisation; and (iv) a government department concerned with policy development in some area of, say, social or workplace reform as an example of an ideal-oriented organisation. The finding that different kinds of organisations did in fact support different contextual orientations would not only serve to validate the inclusion, in the proposed method, of a focus on these different aspects of context, but it would also raise important questions about the traditional conceptualisation of organisational culture as being determined largely by an organisation's past. Of course, one might also find that, within a given organisation, there may be different contextual orientations in relation to different issues. For example, an organisation may be future-oriented in its thinking about technology, but past-oriented in its thinking about, say, the role of workers. As a consequence, new technology, which could be used to enrich the role of workers, might be used in such a way as to reduce workers' autonomy further[13].

---

[13]The reader is referred to Zuboff's (1988) argument that many computer and information technologies can be used either to 'automate' or 'informate' aspects of work operations. The former involves replacing human skills, whereas the latter requires the development of new skills and competencies.

(4) **A closer investigation of organisational subcultures.** Our proposed method might be used to more closely investigate the nature of subcultures, their differences, and how they develop, are maintained, or change over time. For example, subcultures might be found to differ in their contextual orientation, and this might partly account for differences between them in the attitudes and behavioural responses to organisational change that are held by their members. This kind of research might show how and why different kinds of subcultures, such as enhancing, orthogonal, and counter-cultures, develop. For example, part of the reason that certain subcultures are found to oppose each other may be due to their different contextual orientations — with one subculture trying to preserve the past, and the other concerned with change for the future. A subcultural analysis of this kind could help to explain the existence of power and politics within an organisation, with different subcultures using power and politics to promote the interests that are associated with their dominant contextual orientation. One might also investigate the concept of overlapping subcultures and their influence on the exercise of power and politics. For example, can an overlapping social subculture which is predominantly focussed on the present context act to reduce the influence of the power and politics that might otherwise operate between more formal subcultures that have different contextual orientations?

(5) **A closer investigation of occupational and professional subcultures.** The proposed method might also be used to look more closely at the influence of occupational or professional subcultures. A possible implication of contemporary changes in the world of work, such as, the increasing mobility of the workforce (Naisbitt & Aburdene, 1990), is that the conditions required for organisation members to develop a significant shared history may be increasingly unlikely to exist. As such, organisational cultures may become increasingly diffuse and, in some organisations, the influence of occupational, or professional, subcultures may come to dominate. One might even predict a kind of 'shifting' culture in organisations in which the representation of different occupational, or professional, subcultural groupings is subject to change.

A possible study for future research in this area would be to use our proposed method to investigate the relative influence of organisational culture as opposed to occupational, or professional, subculture. One might do this by selecting two organisations (ideally, with different organisational cultures) each of which had a similar occupational or professional group, say, computer technicians. The study would involve the analysis and comparison of the cultures of four groups: two groups of computer technicians (one from each organisation) and two groups drawn from the general membership of each organisation. Ideally, individuals selected for participation in the study should be similar with respect to tenure. If it was found that the two computing subcultures had more in common with each other than either did with its respective 'organisational' culture, then one might conclude that, in this case, the influence of professional subculture was stronger than the influence of organisational culture. An obvious practical implication of such a finding would be the importance for managers to develop a good understanding of the professional cultures of the various occupational or professional groups which are represented in their organisation. For each of the above organisations, it would of course be important to determine the age of the particular professional subculture of interest (i.e., in terms of when it first became established in the organisation). The factor of time itself would be interesting to study with respect to the introduction of a professional subculture. Determining how and why it took on, or alternatively resisted, aspects of the host culture, or sought to isolate or defend itself (e.g., through the exaggerated use of professional jargon), could provide valuable information about factors affecting the development of different kinds of subcultures (e.g., whether enhancing, orthogonal, or countercultures), with important implications for the management of professional subcultures.

(6) **Seniority as a determinant of how cultural issues are perceived.** Another interesting study for future research would be to use our proposed method to explore the degree of insight which the members at one level of an organisation's hierarchy (say, managers) have into the experience (or culture) of members at another level of the organisation's hierarchy (say, workers). It will be remembered that the focus of interviewing in Study 3 was on the role of workers, that is, what workers do. As an extension to this study, it might be interesting to compare workers' perceptions of their own role with managers' perceptions of the role of workers and also with managers' expectations about how workers would be likely to see their own role. Alternatively, one could compare managers' perceptions of their own role with workers' perceptions of the role of managers and also with workers' expectations about how managers would be likely to see their own role. The finding that there were marked discrepancies between these different sets of perceptions and expectations may have important cultural implications. For example, if it was found that managers had very little insight into how workers perceived their own role or, alternatively, that workers had very little insight into how managers perceived their own role, then one might expect that a change effort which required for its success a change in the role of either workers or managers would be likely to encounter some problems. An important initial step in implementing such a change by management and/or consultants may be to identify, and seek to correct, misperceptions of this kind. Such misperceptions might account partly for the failure of some change programs, or for the fact that a program has not worked as well as expected. They might also account for the relative surprise among the members of certain subcultures (e.g., a management subculture) that the change program did not work as well as they expected it would.

(7) **The method as a tool for use in organisational change.** It has been suggested above that our proposed method might be most valuably used as a tool for understanding organisational change. A possible study which might go some way towards validating this claim would be to investigate the sensitivity of the method to changes in organisation members' experience (perceptions, attitudes, *etc.*) which might occur over time as a result of the implementation of a particular organisational change. In such a study, interviewing might be conducted before, during, and after the implementation of the change.

13.3.3 *Research involving data collection with other measures, alone or in combination with our proposed method*

Finally, there are a number of possibilities for future research that involve the collection of data using other methods, whether alone or in some combination with our proposed method. These are as follows:

(1) **Evaluation of different organisational culture measures in terms of their capacity to inform an understanding of organisational change.** Another study with essentially the same objective as the study proposed in point (7) above (namely, to validate the use of the method as a tool for understanding organisational change), would be to investigate the relative strengths of a number of different methods for assessing organisational culture (including our proposed method) in terms of their ability to provide information likely to be of value for understanding organisational change. The methods selected for review might include: (i) unstructured interviewing; (ii) interviewing using our proposed method; and (iii) a questionnaire measure such as the Organizational Culture Inventory (OCI) (Cooke & Lafferty, 1986). A possible approach would be to collect data, using each of these methods, just prior to the implementation of some change. Then, on the basis of the results obtained, one might try to predict how the change will proceed — its likely outcome (whether successful or unsuccessful), the kinds of resistance likely to be encountered, *etc.* These predictions could then be compared with the actual experience and outcome of the change. Given that the results of research using each of the different methods could not be made available to the participating organisation prior to the implementation of change, one might anticipate some difficulty in getting access to an organisation for the purpose of conducting a study such as this. While access is unlikely to be granted in the context of a major organisational change effort, it may however be able to be negotiated if the change in question is a relatively minor change.

(2) **Use of the proposed method in combination with an established, more structured, quantitative method.** It is possible that our proposed method might valuably be used in combination with an existing, more structured, measure for organisational culture (such as the OCI). Two alternative approaches can be suggested here. First, one might use our method to identify aspects of an organisation's culture that appear to be most relevant to the success of a change program. A more structured quantitative approach using questionnaires could then be employed to investigate those aspects of the culture with a more representative sample of the organisation's membership. Second, one might use the more structured approach for the initial identification of key dimensions, after which our proposed method could be used to explore these dimensions in-depth, as well as to clarify any inconsistencies in the data generated by the former.

(3) **Use of questions from the proposed method to refine established questionnaire measures of organisational culture.** The results of Study 3 provided some interesting insights into the kinds of questions that might be asked in order to obtain a

deeper-level (as opposed to more superficial) understanding of organisation members' experience. For example, questions seeking clarification of the meaning of responses, questions asking respondents to elaborate on their responses, and questions asking respondents to comment on their attitudes to particular events (changes *etc.*) emerged as being important in this regard. A useful study for future research would be to look at the extent to which existing quantitative measures of organisational culture (which can be criticised on the grounds that they offer only superficial insights into culture) might benefit from the addition of questions such as these. A possible approach would be to compare the quality of the information generated by a measure such as the OCI, administered in its current form and administered with revisions (i.e., with the addition of questions of the kind suggested above). For one group, the revisions could be presented in the context of a face-to-face interview, conducted after respondents had completed the questionnaire, and for another group, they could simply be written into the existing questionnaire format. While one might predict that the OCI (or other questionnaire measure) followed by interviewing would produce the best results, it may be that a simple written adaptation of the measure could also result in markedly better (i.e., richer, more in-depth) information being generated than that provided by the measure in its current form.

(4) **Towards the more explicit assessment of meaning.** Another potentially useful area for future research, as suggested by insights obtained from Study 3, would be to look more closely at the importance of understanding meaning in the analysis of organisational culture. One study that might be conducted in this regard would be to select items from an existing questionnaire measure, such as the OCI, and to ask members at different levels of an organisation (e.g., managers, supervisors, and workers) to describe how they interpret these items. The finding that there were marked differences in the interpretations of members at these different levels may have important cultural implications which one might subsequently investigate more closely. Of course, to the extent that marked interpretive differences did emerge (whether between or within the membership at these different levels), one would also have to address the methodological implications of such a finding. This is because an important assumption underlying the use of measures such as the OCI is that respondents' interpretations of the items in these measures will be the same and, moreover, that they will be consistent with the interpretations intended by the researcher. Such a finding would also have implications for the development and refinement of questionnaire measures of organisational culture and organisational climate.

(5) **A closer investigation of the cultural implications of differences between specific and general experience.** One final possibility for future research, as suggested by insights obtained from Study 3, would be to look more closely at the extent to which organisation members' individual experience with respect to any given issue, is consistent with their evaluation of (and attitude to) that issue at a more general, organisational level. An important finding of Study 3 was that respondents could hold negative

attitudes to some aspect of organisational life in general (e.g., the communication climate which prevailed in their division as a whole), whilst at the same time describe their individual experience in relation to that aspect of organisation life (e.g., the communication relationship which they had with their own supervisor) in very positive terms. As suggested, a possible cultural explanation for this incongruity may be that organisation members' perceptions of the 'general' may continue to be influenced by the residual effects of past experience, even after the implementation of certain changes (the initial impact of which may be registered at an individual or 'specific' level only) which may challenge those perceptions.

Given that questionnaire measures of organisational culture typically ask about the 'general', rather than the 'specific' — for example, in the Norms Diagnostic Index (Allen & Dyer, 1980) each item begins with "It is a norm around here …" — it would be interesting to conduct a study in which, following the administration of a culture questionnaire, respondents were asked to comment on their individual experience with respect to each of the core dimensions being tapped by the questionnaire. If the study was conducted in the context of a recently introduced change, one might anticipate that the experience of change may be reflected in the finding that, on a number of dimensions and for a significant number of respondents, there were discrepancies between these two sets of data. It is also possible that discrepancies of this kind might alert one to the existence of subcultural differences which would be unlikely to be detected using measures in which the unit of analysis is the organisation as a whole.

13.4 Conclusions

In conclusion, the research that we have reported in Chapters 8 through 12, and which involved a 'building block' design incorporating three sequential studies, was undertaken to provide some first steps towards the development of a method for investigating organisational culture which, on the one hand, is capable of accessing deeper-level cultural beliefs and assumptions and, on the other, is more practically useful than traditional ethnographic approaches. While the method proposed clearly requires further development in order to achieve the aims envisaged for it, the authors believe that efforts towards this further development — of the kind suggested by some of the above proposals for future research — would constitute a worthwhile endeavour. At the present time, our capacity to understand organisational culture is limited by the constraints of the methods available. On the one hand, there are quantitative measures which can provide insights into the surface elements of culture only and which are, therefore, of questionable value for informing our understanding of important organisational issues, such as organisational change. On the other hand, there are qualitative measures which can provide rich descriptions of organisational culture, but which are time consuming to use and which provide no means whereby systematic comparisons (e.g., of the cultures of different organisations or of culture in the same organisation over time) can be made. The hope is that the further development of methods such as that proposed will lead to a useful alternative to existing approaches, and will serve as the kind of methodological advance that scholars, such as, Ott (1989) and Reichers and Schneider (1990) have argued is needed in order for the organisational culture perspective to achieve maturity.

We turn now to the final chapter of this volume and of this book, in which we report the results of a follow-up study that we have conducted (involving the more systematic analysis of attributions data from Study 3), as just one example of the kind of future research that we have suggested, in the present chapter, might usefully be undertaken as part of a broad agenda for methodological advancement in the study of organisational culture.

Chapter 14

Developing Attributions Analysis for Assessing Organisational Culture

This chapter provides a more detailed investigation of the attributions data obtained in Study 3 (and reported in Chapters 10 through 12), in terms of the capacity of these data to reveal the deeper levels of organisational culture as described by Schein (1985, 1992, 2004, 2010). The research reported in this chapter follows on from one of the recommendations for future research made in the previous chapter, namely, the recommendation concerning the potential value of extending the analysis of the attributions data generated by the Study 3 interviews.

As described in the preceding chapters, the attributions data were obtained from workers and supervisors in two divisions of a large car company, who participated in an interview concerning the role of workers. Participants were asked about whether or not, in their experience, the role of workers had changed from the past to the present, and whether or not they anticipated it would change in the future. The explanations that they offered for the responses given — whether indicating a "change" or "no change" — constituted the attributions data that were subject to the more detailed analysis that is reported in this chapter. There was some evidence from a preliminary analysis of these data (reported in Chapters 11 and 12) that the particular line of questioning adopted — whereby explanations were sought for why things had changed or stayed the same, and for why things would change or stay the same — may provide a valuable means of accessing underlying beliefs and assumptions about an organisation's culture. The more sophisticated analysis of the attributions data that is reported in the present chapter puts this possibility to the test.

We begin this chapter by providing a brief introduction to the scope and limits of existing methods for assessing organisational culture. This is offered principally for the benefit of those readers who may choose to read this chapter as a 'stand-alone' chapter, and who will therefore not be familiar with the content of previous chapters of this book (in particular, Chapter 6 of Volume I) dealing with the assessment of organisational culture. We turn then to a consideration of the arguments in favour of using attributions analysis as a means whereby to decipher an organisation's culture and, in particular, those aspects of the culture that exist at a deeper, possibly unconscious level. Following this, the substantive content of the chapter is concerned with a discussion of the approach to, and results of, the more detailed analysis of the attributions data generated by the Study 3 interviews. Based on the findings of this more detailed analysis, an overall evaluation of the approach adopted is offered, along with a discussion of the content and implications for future research of a number of important methodological issues to which the approach gave rise. The chapter concludes with a statement of our wish that the methods proposed in this book will stimulate further research by others, so that the potential of our work to advance the study of how best to measure an organisation's (or group's) culture can be more fully realised.

14.1 Overview of Approaches to the Assessment of Organisational Culture

While the study of organisational culture has a history spanning more than 30 years, there is, as yet, no systematic and practically useful means whereby an organisation's deeper-level culture can be deciphered. Organisational culture scholars generally advocate the use of qualitative, rather than quantitative, methods for tapping culture at this level. The argument is that qualitative methods, including unstructured or semi-structured interviewing, participant observation, and documentary analysis (often used in combination) offer the kind of in-depth analysis needed to 'bring to the surface' the basic beliefs and assumptions thought to make up an organisation's 'deep' culture. Quantitative methods, on the other hand, are seen as more appropriate for the study of 'surface' culture. Such methods typically take the form of structured questionnaires that seek information about the more explicit and observable manifestations of an organisation's culture, such as, perceived organisational norms and values. While it seems reasonable to assume some kind of link between surface and deep culture, the exact nature of this link remains unclear and this has led some scholars (e.g., Ott, 1989, and Schein, 1985, 1992, 2004, 2010) to caution strongly against the use of surface or proxy indicators of organisational culture as a basis for making inferences about core cultural assumptions.

The use of qualitative methods for deciphering an organisation's deeper-level culture is, however, not without its problems. A major drawback of such methods is that, because of their generally unstructured nature, they provide no means whereby the data available can be systematically compared. As a result, there are many centrally important theoretical questions — concerning, for example, the pervasiveness or sharedness of an organisation's culture, the nature of cultural differences within, and between, organisations, the nature of culture change over time, and the influence of organisational culture on organisational performance and adaptability to change — which remain unanswered (Siehl & Martin, 1988). It is also the case that qualitative methods are limited with respect to their practical usefulness. In particular, it is not always possible for researchers to have the kind of prolonged and sustained involvement in the research setting that is required of 'good ethnography' (Emerson, 1987, cited in Bryman, 1991). Organisational gatekeepers may be unwilling, or unable, to grant extended periods of access to researchers, and there may be time constraints on the research itself. A related consideration, which reflects the growing instability of organisational environments, is that, during the course of a protracted investigation into an organisation's culture, the culture itself may change. In this sense, culture studies may increasingly need to be conducted within shorter, rather than longer, time frames.

14.2 The Case for an Attributions Analysis Approach

It can be seen from the above that there are both theoretical and practical arguments for the development of a method that allows for the more systematic and efficient assessment of an organisation's deeper-level culture. One potentially promising, yet relatively unexplored, avenue of inquiry in this regard is suggested by Silvester, Anderson, and Patterson's (1999) work on the use of attributions analysis as a means whereby insights into culture at this level might be obtained. Silvester *et al.* propose a 'socio-cognitive' model of organisational culture in which organisation members' shared attributions — collective explanations for work-related events — are regarded as the cognitive 'building blocks', or basic units, of organisational culture. Within this framework, attributions analysis is used to identify differences between key stakeholder groups involved in a culture change program, in terms of members' collective beliefs about the causes of the success (or alternatively, the failure) of the program. In articulating their model of organisational culture, Silvester *et al.* build an argument for why shared attributions can be conceptualised as constituting the basic (i.e., fundamental) units of an organisation's culture. Shared attributions, it is argued, have an important role in helping organisation members to 'make sense of' their experience of organisational life and render their environment more controllable; shared attributions evolve over time and can ultimately come to be stored in long-term memory (in the form of group-level causal schema), from where they are accessed through automatic, rather than conscious, processes; and shared attributions can be thought of as being socially generated and transmitted, through the everyday communication and interaction that occurs among organisation members.

While it might be argued that Silvester *et al.* claim too much for shared attributions — it remains open to question whether or not shared attributions are the 'basic units' of organisational culture or simply one of a number of manifestations of culture — the arguments they present nevertheless firmly establish a link between shared attributions and an organisation's deeper-level culture. The authors themselves acknowledge that there are "obvious similarities" (p. 3) between their treatment of shared attributions and Schein's (1985, 1992, 2004, 2010) definition of the shared basic assumptions and beliefs that, for him, constitute the 'essence' of organisational culture. This conceptual location of shared attributions at the level of deep, rather than surface, culture is important from a methodological point of view since it draws attention to the possibility that shared attributions may constitute a more valid indicator of organisational culture than other commonly assessed indicators, such as organisational norms and espoused organisational values (e.g., Cooke & Lafferty, 1986; O'Reilly, Chatman, & Caldwell, 1991).

A review of the organisational literature suggests that Silvester *et al.*'s (1999) socio-cognitive model of organisational culture offers the most explicit and comprehensive articulation, to date, of a conceptual link between organisational culture and group-level attributions. There appear to have been very few other contributions in this regard and those that do exist typically do not go beyond implying, or speculating about, the existence of a relationship between the two constructs. For example, in their work on the measurement and organisational behaviour correlates of occupational attribution style, Furnham, Sadka, and Brewin (1992) suggest the possibility that organisations might develop their own "corporate attribution styles" (p. 37) and that these styles are likely to be manifested in the organisation's climate and culture. There is, however, no development of this idea, which is simply offered as a speculative concluding comment. Similarly, in their case study analysis of the influence of top managers' causal attributions on their strategic response to organisational decline, Mueller, McKinley, Mone, and Barker III (2001) imply a link between shared attributions and organisational culture, but provide no conceptual development of this link. It is argued, simply, that organisational culture is the vehicle through which to develop the kind of attribution orientation that is likely to result in the organisation choosing innovation as a response to organisational decline.

One example of a study that does endeavour to more directly link organisational culture and attributions is Saxena and Shah's (2008) study of the relationship between different dimensions of organisational culture and the learned helplessness attributions of research and development professionals in the Indian pharmaceutical industry. A key finding of the study was that the eight cultural dimensions measured — represented by the organisational values of openness, confrontation, trust, authenticity, pro-action, autonomy, collaboration, and experimentation — were all negatively related to respondents' learned helplessness attributions. Without elaborating further on the details of this study, its main limitation from our point of view is its conceptualisation of organisational culture and attributions as separate constructs. In the study, organisational culture constitutes the main independent variable of interest, and respondents' learned helplessness attributions, the outcome or dependent variable. The possibility that the variables studied — perceived organisational values and attributions, in this case reflecting negative ways of thinking — may be manifestations of different levels of the same construct, namely organisational/group culture, is nowhere considered.

In building an argument about the link between organisational culture and shared attributions, it is useful to go beyond the organisational literature to a consideration of developments in social psychology which have drawn attention to a link between culture at a more general, societal level, and collective (causal) attributions. Of particular relevance in this regard is Moscovici's work on the concept, and theory, of social representations (e.g., Moscovici, 1984). As we have argued in Chapter 5 of Volume I — in which we offer a detailed comparison of the concepts of social representations and organisational culture — social representations can be thought of as the societal equivalent of the beliefs and basic assumptions that, for Schein (1985, 1992, 2004, 2010), constitute the essence, or core, of an organisation's culture. Stated another way, social representations and organisational culture can be thought of as being conceptually very similar, though concerned with a different unit of analysis. Whereas organisational culture researchers are concerned with culture (shared beliefs and basic assumptions) at the level of the organisation or organisational subgroup, social representations researchers are generally concerned with culture (shared representations, or ways of thinking) at the level of the wider society. The various arguments in favour of this view have been explicated in Chapter 5 of Volume I which discusses the possible integration of research in these two substantive, and previously unconnected, areas of inquiry on the grounds of similarities between social representations and organisational culture in their respective origins, conceptualisation, and dominant (preferred) methodology.

For Moscovici (1984), as for Silvester and her colleagues (1999), attributions and culture (in this case, social representations) are conceived of as being inextricably linked. As Moscovici (1984) notes, "...for those concerned with social representations" — the term 'social representations' is used here in its broadest sense to signify 'societal' — "the problem of causality has always been crucial" (p. 44). In a similar vein, Jaspars and Hewstone (1990) draw attention to the "essentially explanatory nature" of social representations (p. 131). This is a property of the phenomenon that they suggest is implicit in Moscovici's conceptualisation of social representations as 'common sense' knowledge, comprising "...a set of concepts, statements and explanations originating in daily life" (Moscovici, 1984, cited in Jaspars and Hewstone, 1990, p. 131). Importantly, however, and in contrast with Silvester *et al.*'s (1999) view, Moscovici (1984) sees attributions as being determined by, or arising from, social representations, rather than constituting, or being the 'cognitive building blocks' of, social representations. In other words, for Moscovici, social representations are more basic, in the sense of being more elemental or more foundational, than attributions. As common sense 'theories', or socially constructed patterns of meaning, social representations influence what we, as observers, take into account and the causes that we select in attempting to explain our experiences. Moscovici illustrates this view by arguing that our tendency to attribute a person's unemployment to dispositional factors (e.g., the person is lazy or, alternatively, too choosy), as opposed to situational factors (e.g., the person is the victim of an economic recession) is, at a very basic level, determined by our social representations. In the former case, the attribution can be seen to stem from a representation that emphasises individual responsibility, that is, that gives primacy to the role of the individual in solving individual and social problems; in the latter case, the attribution stems from a representation that emphasises societal responsibility, that is, that gives primacy to the role of society in helping to alleviate individual and social problems. This idea that our attributions are determined by our social representations lies at the heart of Moscovici's criticism of attribution theory which, he argues, continues to depict people as making judgements about causality — whether attributing effects to dispositional or situational causes — in a socially (or culturally) neutral context.

While Moscovici's conceptualisation of the relationship between social representations and attributions has considerable intuitive appeal, it presents a rather static view of social representations and fails to address the question of how such representations might themselves come to change. One possibility in this regard is that, to the extent that a particular explanation (attribution) suggested by a social representation ceases to be of value (in the sense that it no longer convincingly accounts for why an event has occurred), an alternative, more feasible explanation might arise which challenges the representation and which may ultimately change it. In this sense, it is not inconceivable that there exists a reciprocal, rather than a unidirectional, relationship between social representations and attributions. The more important point here is that, regardless of how one views the relationship between social representations or, in this case, organisational culture, and attributions — whether attributions are seen as constituting an organisation's culture, aris-ing from it, or existing in some kind of reciprocal relationship with it — there appears to be little doubt about the closeness of the link between the two constructs. This draws atten-tion again to the argument that attributions, and specifically group-level attributions, may be a more valid (in the sense of conceptually more accurate) indicator of an organisation's deep culture than either organisational norms or espoused organisational values.

Finally, in building the case for a close conceptual link between organisational culture and shared attributions, it is worth noting that, in social psychology, individual attribution style — the approach to attributing cause which an individual *habitually* adopts — is con-ceived of as a personality trait (Abrahamson, Seligman, & Teasdale, 1978). In other words, it is regarded as a characteristic of the individual which is relatively stable over time and across different situations, and which captures something unique about the individual and differentiates her/him from other individuals (Vecchio, Hearn, & Southey, 1992). In the same way, it might be argued that, to the extent that organisation members come to share a particular way of attributing cause, there could develop an organisational attribution style which might be seen as capturing something of the 'personality' of the organisation. And, with respect to this latter point, the interesting observation can be made that, in the organi-sational culture literature, the term 'organisational personality' as a synonym for 'organi-sational culture' dates back to the early work of Jacques (1951).

Apart from the above arguments, which have sought to establish the conceptual legiti-macy of using attributions analysis as a means whereby to gain insights into an organisa-tion's deeper-level culture, attributions analysis can also be advocated on the grounds of its practical utility. As indicated in Silvester *et al.* (1999), a number of researchers — the work of Antaki (1994), Moscovici (1984), Silvester (1997), and Weiner (1985), among others, is cited — have drawn attention to the accessibility of "spoken attributions" which, it is argued "can be isolated from discourse material and subjected to qualitative and quan-titative analysis" (p. 3). It might also be argued that spoken attributions, whether generated in the course of everyday conversation or in response to unstructured or semi-structured interviewing, are more likely to provide context specific understandings than attributions data generated in response to 'off-the-shelf' questionnaire measures of attribution patterns or attribution style. Of course, this is a particularly important consideration in organisa-tional culture studies, given the conceptualisation of organisational culture (and subcul-ture) as a unique and highly context specific phenomenon (Jones, 1988; Ott, 1989).

Despite the various conceptual and practical arguments in favour of an attributions analysis approach to understanding organisational culture, very little research has been undertaken to date to investigate the empirical validity of this approach. In fact, the only published account of research of this kind, of which we are aware, is Silvester *et al.*'s (1999) study. Of course, this is not to say that attribution theory has not been applied to the analysis of behaviour in organisational settings. On the contrary, there is now a considerable body of research in this area, the importance of which is attested to by Martinko's (1995) edited volume *Attribution theory: An organizational perspective*. As Martinko observes, however, the major focus of this work has been on *individual* attribution processes (how individuals attribute cause for their own, and others', outcomes) and the organisational behaviour correlates of these processes (in terms of, e.g., employee motivation, performance and job satisfaction, supervisory style, and decision-making behaviour). Thus far, very little attention has been given to the study of attribution processes in *group* and interactive contexts. Moreover, what work has been done has been concerned primarily with the impact of characteristics of the group on individual members' attributions for group performance. For example, in his study of cooperation failure in cross-functional teams, McDonald (1995) examines the impact of 'in-group' versus 'out-group' status differentials, operating within the team, on team members' attributions for the team's performance. In a similar vein, Ferrier, Smith, Rediker, and Mitchell (1995) consider the impact of different characteristics of the group — whether the group is high or low performing, the power of the group's leadership, and changes in the leader's power over time — on group members' attributions for the group's performance. The important point is that, in this research, attributions are of interest principally as outcome variables, operating at the level of the individual; no consideration is given to the notion of attributions as a collective phenomenon, the analysis of which might reveal something about the group. It is perhaps also worth noting that neither of the studies above were conducted in actual work organisations. McDonald's (1995) study was a laboratory study using undergraduate university students; Ferrier *et al.*'s (1995) study was an organisational simulation, also using undergraduate university students.

Interestingly, in a recent 'Incubator' article, Martinko, Harvey, and Dasborough (2011) argue that the application of attribution theory in the organisational sciences has yet to realise its potential. While the study of attributions and attribution style is well established in social psychology, the capacity of these constructs to inform answers to organisational research questions has not yet been fully explored. Martinko and his colleagues draw attention to what they see as two key areas for growth in this regard. The first concerns the possibilities for extending the application of attribution theory to the study of leadership, with particular emphasis given to the potential value of research into how a leader's attribution style might influence the way in which she/he seeks to develop the performance of subordinates. The second suggested area for growth involves the study of attributions and attribution style — constructs that, as Martinko *et al.* note, have traditionally been treated as individual-level constructs — at the *group*, or *collective*, level. More specifically, it is suggested that research into group-level attribution styles might provide valuable insights into group processes, such as risky-shift and groupthink. It is also suggested that group-level attributions and attribution styles may constitute important explanatory factors in understanding the extent to which the members of a group identify with, and feel a part of, the group. This call by Martinko *et al.* for attributions and attribution style to be conceptualised, and operationalised, as a group rather than an individual phenomenon, perhaps goes some way towards explaining the very limited use, to date, of attributions analysis as a means whereby to explore the collective phenomenon of organisational culture.

It is worth noting that, while empirical research into the link between organisational culture and attributions is still in its infancy, analogous work in social representations dates back to the early 1980s. As with the organisational studies cited above, however, this research is of limited relevance to the present analysis. In particular, the aim of the research — notable examples of which include a study by Hewstone, Jaspars, and Lalljee (1982) and a study by Augoustinos (1989) — is to show how social representations (associated with one's own, and others', social group membership) mediate and influence the kinds of attributions that people make (for their own and others' outcomes); in contrast with the approach taken in the present analysis, the research does not use attributions as a basis for inferences about the social representations (i.e., the culture) of the group. It is also the case that, whereas the present analysis uses naturalistic data, the studies by Hewstone *et al.* and Augoustinos are experimental studies, in which participants are required to make attributions for hypothetical outcomes, and in which causes are defined *a priori*. Finally, there is no social representations research of which we are aware that investigates the link between social representations and attributions at the more localised level of the work organisation, or work group.

14.3 Introduction to the Present Analysis[1]

In view of the above observations, there is a clear imperative for more empirical research into the link between organisational culture and attributions. The aim of the present analysis is, therefore, to add to the pioneering work in this area carried out by Silvester *et al.* (1999). As reported in Chapter 12, the preliminary analysis of the attributions data generated by the Study 3 interviews, provided evidence to suggest that organisational subgroups might develop their own unique style of attributing cause, and that this style might be culturally determined in the sense of being influenced by, or being a manifestation of, the group's culture. In particular, there was evidence to suggest that the two groups that were studied as part of this research (see below) differed with respect to members' collective perceptions about the extent to which they were able to control what happened to the group. Specifically, in one group, there seemed to be a predisposition towards attributing events and outcomes to external factors that were largely outside of the control of the group (e.g., changes in government legislation or the impact of overseas competition); in

---

[1]Throughout this chapter, we refer to the research undertaken as an 'analysis' rather than a 'study'. This is because the research is essentially a follow-up on Study 3, involving a more sophisticated analysis of data generated in Study 3.

contrast, in the other group, members seemed more inclined to attribute events and outcomes to internal factors that lay more within the group's control (e.g., employee attitudes and behaviours or group management initiatives for change). These findings drew attention to the possibility that a more in-depth and more systematic analysis of the attributions data from Study 3 might usefully be undertaken. To this end, the present analysis seeks to advance the initial progress made towards establishing a role for attributions in the elucidation and differentiation of, in this case, the cultures of two divisions of a large automotive company.

14.3.1 *Research participants*

As indicated in the introduction to this chapter, the attributions data for the present analysis were drawn from interviews conducted in Study 3. For those readers who may not have read the previous descriptions of the research organisation and participants (see Chapters 8 and 10 respectively), the following brief summary is provided.

The data were drawn from interviews conducted with employees from two divisions of the South Australian based manufacturing and assembly operations of a large automotive company. These interviews (conducted as part of Study 3) were designed to provide insights into respondents' beliefs about the fundamental role of the workers in their division (specifically, whether workers were believed to play a predominantly 'passive', or a predominantly 'active' role). A semi-structured interview format was used and respondents were interviewed individually for about one hour each. As above, the interview data of relevance to the present analysis were the attributions that respondents made when asked to explain their perception of the role of workers over time — specifically, whether it had changed from the past (in both their current organisation and any other organisation in which they had worked) to the present, or whether it had stayed the same, and whether they anticipated that it would change, or stay the same, in the future.

It should be noted that, for the purpose of the present analysis, the 'other' context — which constituted the focus of a dedicated subset of questions in the Study 3 interviews — was considered together with the past context. In Study 3, respondents reported changes from the past to the present in their experience of the role of workers. Some of these changes reflected a difference between respondents' *past experience in their current organisation* and their present experience in their current organisation, whereas other changes reflected a difference between respondents' *past experience in an 'other' organisation* in which they had worked, and their present experience in their current organisation. For the purpose of the present analysis, no distinction was drawn between the attributions that respondents offered as explanations for these various changes. The point should also be made that the ideal context — also the subject of a dedicated subset of questions in the Study 3 interviews — has no relevance in the context of the present analysis. This is because respondents in Study 3 were not asked to comment on why their particular depiction of the ideal was different from, or the same as, what they had already experienced. It was reasoned that a "Why?" question, asked in relation to the ideal context, had less obvious meaning than the same question asked in relation to the other contexts of interest, and would therefore be more difficult for respondents to answer. It was also reasoned that the inclusion of such a question would unnecessarily extend an already lengthy interview.

For the purpose of the present analysis, attributions data of this kind were extracted from 26 interviews: 12 with employees from the company's long established tooling division (this division had been in existence since the company's inception in the early 1930s), and 14 with employees from a more recently established production division (which commenced operations in the early 1980s)[2]. The main function of the tooling division was to provide an 'in-house' tooling service to the company's fabrication and assembly operations (this involved, among other things, the building and maintenance of press dies, assembly fixtures, and special purpose tools). The production division specialised in injection moulding, and the painting and assembly of plastic components, such as bumper bars, consoles, and facia plates for brake lights. At the time of conducting the interviews, the workforce of the tooling division numbered approximately 80 members, whereas that of the production division numbered approximately 320 members.

In terms of respondents' demographics, the sample for the tooling division comprised all males and included six hourly paid ('wages') employees and six supervisory staff. Respondents from this division had a mean age of 49 years (sd = 7.6 years) and a mean length of service with the division of 23 years (sd = 10.7 years). All of the respondents from this division were trade qualified. The production division sample included ten hourly paid employees and four supervisory staff. All of the supervisory staff were males, whereas four of the hourly paid employees were females and six were males. Respondents from the production division had a mean age of 41 years (sd = 8.7 years) and a mean length of service with the division of 8 years (sd = 1.8 years). The supervisory staff included in the sample for this division were all trade qualified, whereas the hourly paid employees were all assembly and production workers with no formal qualifications.

14.3.2 *Data for the analysis*

In the present analysis, the conceptualisation of an attribution which guided data extraction corresponded most closely to that recommended for use by Stratton, Munton, Hanks, Heard, and Davidson (1988). These authors, while drawing attention to the continuing debate surrounding the question of what attributions actually are, opt for what they consider to be the "most straightforward definition of an attribution to date" (p. 23), namely,

---

[2] While this component of the larger study involved interviews with 31 employees (12 from the tooling division and 19 from the production division), for the purposes of the present analysis, it was decided to use the data for 26 of these employees only (12 from the tooling division and 14 from the production division). This was essentially a practical decision, taken because of the exploratory nature of the present analysis, and also because of the magnitude of the attributions analysis exercise that was being undertaken.

that provided by Kidd and Amabile (1981). The latter, drawing on the work of the English philosopher Braithwaite, suggest that "an explanation [attribution] is any answer to the question 'why?'" (p. 310). While this definition accounts for both spontaneous attributions and attributions made in response to a *direct* "Why?" question, the important point should be made that, in the present analysis, only attributions of the latter kind were used. In other words, the data set included only those attributions made in response to *direct* questioning (of the respondent) regarding the respondent's perception of why the role of workers had, or had not, changed from the past to the present, and why it would, or would not, change in the anticipated future. This decision to exclude spontaneous attributions from the analysis, and focus only on prompted attributions, seemed appropriate given the exploratory nature of the analysis and the possibility that there might exist some kind of systematic difference between these two types of attributions. While spontaneous attributions might be more revealing and might offer more genuinely context-specific information, insofar as they might be less subject to social desirability biases, they might also be less well considered than attributions made in response to direction questioning. It was also reasoned that this approach would enable the two divisions to be more directly compared since, for each division, the assessment of attribution orientation would be based on responses to essentially the same set of questions.

A total of 553 attributions were extracted for analysis: 247 from interviews with tooling division respondents and 306 from interviews with production division respondents. While the divisions were similar with respect to the *average* number of attributions per respondent — on average, tooling division respondents produced 20.58 attributions each, compared with 21.86 attributions for production division respondents — tooling division respondents were somewhat less variable as a group (sd = 6.95) than their counterparts in production (sd = 10.41) in terms of the *actual* number of attributions per respondent. For the tooling division, the range from the minimum to the maximum number of attributions per respondent was 11 to 34, whereas for the production division, it was 9 to 44.

14.4 The Coding Framework

In the present analysis, as in the Silvester *et al.* (1999) analysis, attributions were coded using a modified version of the Leeds Attributional Coding System (LACS) (Stratton *et al.*, 1988). This system was developed for use in a family therapy context, for the purpose of coding causal beliefs arising during clients' natural discourse. In adapting this system for use in organisational settings, the present analysis has expanded on Silvester *et al.*'s (1999) important groundwork in this regard. The revised framework, while similar in some respects to that developed by Silvester *et al.*, differs in other respects; moreover, it is potentially more comprehensive in that it comprises more coding dimensions.

Before describing each of the coding dimensions making up this revised framework, the important point should be made that, given the nature of the data that were extracted for the present analysis, the decision was taken, in this case, not to apply the LACS distinction between 'speaker' (i.e., the person making the attribution) and 'target' (i.e., the person to whom the outcome, which is the subject of the attribution[3], happened). Of course, as indicated in the LACS, this distinction is necessary only for those attributions in which the speaker and the target are different people (i.e., when the speaker is someone other than the person who is affected by the outcome)[4]. In the present analysis, attributions by a supervisor (i.e., the speaker) — in this case, regarding his beliefs about why a particular change in the role of workers (i.e., the target) had occurred, or would occur — would qualify for such a distinction and such attributions might, therefore, have been coded separately for speaker and target. The main reason for not doing so was that the focus of the analysis was such as to limit the usefulness of this distinction. An example will help to illustrate. When coding the controllability of causes — the Controllable/Uncontrollable dimension is one of the LACS dimensions for which separate speaker and target codes are likely to have particular relevance — the aim, in the present analysis, was to ascertain the extent to which respondents from each division regarded the causes of, in this case, changes in the role of workers in the division, to be within, as opposed to outside of, *divisional control*. The question of whether or not supervisors regarded causes as more or less within their own, or the workers' control — a question to which the LACS speaker/target distinction might usefully be applied — was of considerably less interest.

The coding framework developed for use in the present analysis comprised ten coding dimensions in all. It included: seven dimensions for coding causes (one drawn directly from the LACS, three modified LACS dimensions, and three new dimensions); two dimensions for coding outcomes (both modified LACS dimensions); and one dimension for coding the causal statement as a whole (a modified LACS dimension). The coding categories for each of these dimensions included a *cannot code* category that was assigned a value of [8] and designated for use in instances where the attribution was judged to contain insufficient information to be coded according to that dimension. Each of the dimensions in the proposed framework is now described in some detail. Reference is made, as appropriate, to the various modifications to the LACS dimensions that were made and attention is also drawn to similarities and/or differences between the relevant dimensions and their corresponding dimensions in the Silvester *et al.* (1999) framework. The contents of this discussion are presented in summary form in Table 14.1.

Dimension 1: Stability of the Cause (modified LACS). This dimension is concerned with respondents' perceptions regarding how stable, or long-lasting, the cause is likely to be. In the LACS, causes can be classified as either *stable* (where they are perceived to have a high probability of influencing future outcomes) or *unstable* (where they are perceived to have a lower probability of influencing future outcomes) (Stratton *et al.*, 1988, p. 29).

---

[3] As indicated by Stratton *et al.* (1988), an attribution statement is essentially a causal sequence, comprising three parts: a cause, a link, and an outcome.

[4] By way of illustration, Stratton *et al.* (1988) give the example of a mother reporting that her son failed the exam because he is lazy.

Table 14.1. Summary description of coding dimensions, their organisational implications, and their congruence with the LACS (1988) and Silvester *et al.* (1999) frameworks.

Dimensions for Coding Causes: Description and Coding Categories	Organisational Implications	Congruence with the LACS	Silvester *et al.* (1999) Framework
1. Stability: Concerns the respondent's perception of how stable or long-lasting the cause is likely to be. [1] *Permanent*: Cause is unchanging, permanent in its effect(s), associated with tradition e.g., "In the future, workers will not be involved in meetings because it is not [the company's] 'way of doing things'". [2] *Semi-permanent*: Cause is likely to influence outcomes in the medium term (i.e., for at least the next 5 years) e.g., "…a lot more people will be involved in training with award restructuring". [3] *Temporary*: Cause is likely to influence outcomes in the short term (i.e., for several months only) e.g., "…we're in a slight change at the moment [with fewer information meetings for workers] because [current supervisor] drops out in a couple of weeks, and [new supervisor] takes over."	Scores on this dimension may provide insights into the group's exposure to change e.g., a preponderance of permanent causes may indicate little experience of change whereas a preponderance of temporary causes may indicate exposure to ongoing rapid change. Moreover, cultural change may be more difficult to achieve in groups with a bias towards permanent causes than in groups with a bias towards either temporary or semi-permanent causes.	The LACS includes two coding categories: *Stable* and *Unstable*. The current framework retains the essential meaning of this dimension, but has relabelled the coding categories (and included one additional category) to increase their relevance in an organisational, as opposed to clinical, setting.	Reportedly adopted directly from the LACS, but the interpretation of coding categories is not entirely consistent with that intended by the LACS.

(*Continued*)

Table 14.1. *(Continued)*

Dimensions for Coding Causes: Description and Coding Categories	Organisational Implications	Congruence with the LACS	Silvester *et al.* (1999) Framework
2. Globality: Concerns the respondent's perception of how pervasive the influence of the cause is likely to be. [1] *Global*: Cause is likely to have far-reaching effects; it will have many additional outcomes beyond the outcome specified in the attribution e.g., "Today, there is less involvement of workers in industrial activity because the pressure associated with the initial start up of the division has subsided". [2] *Specific*: Cause is likely to be very localised in its effects; it will have few additional outcomes beyond the outcome specified in the attribution e.g., "Today, workers have more information meetings [than they did in the past] because they put pressure on the management to have more of these meetings".	Scores on this dimension may provide insights into: • the group's cultural orientation towards 'optimism' (a style in which a few global causes account for multiple positive outcomes) or 'pessimism' (a style in which a few global causes account for multiple negative outcomes); • the required breadth of focus of a change effort (narrowly focussed for groups with a bias towards attributing outcomes to a limited number of global causes, and broader in scope for groups with a bias towards attributing outcomes to many specific causes); • the group's likely resistance to change (with change more difficult to effect in groups that support either overly optimistic, or overly pessimistic, cultures).	Adopted directly from the LACS.	Modified LACS, with *Global* used to denote causes that have outcomes that occur at a company level, and *Specific* used to denote causes with outcomes that occur at the level of a sub-section of the company (i.e., a division or specific group).

(Continued)

Table 14.1. (*Continued*)

Dimensions for Coding Causes: Description and Coding Categories	Organisational Implications	Congruence with the LACS	Silvester *et al.* (1999) Framework
3. Internality: Concerns the respondent's perception of the origin of the cause in relation to workers. [1] *Internal:* Cause originates in workers (their characteristics, behaviours, attitudes, etc.) e.g., "Workers had more social involvement in the past because there were more younger workers around, more families". [2] *External:* Cause originates outside workers (i.e., cause is situational or originates in the characteristics, behaviours, attitudes, etc. of other individuals or groups) e.g., "There is more involvement of workers in training today because of government legislation".	Scores on this dimension may provide insights into the group's ownership of the outcomes (both positive and negative) it experiences. Groups that support 'low ownership' cultures (i.e., cultures in which there is a bias towards attributing outcomes to causes external to workers) may be more resistant to change than groups that support 'high ownership' cultures. A realistic or 'healthy' orientation with respect to this dimension is likely to be one in which there is a good 'fit' between the group's perceived locus of causality and environmental contingencies.	The LACS evaluates locus of causality (whether 'internal' or 'external') in relation to the person being coded (not in relation to workers, as in the present framework); also, where appropriate, the LACS applies separate 'speaker' and 'target' codings for this dimension.	Adopted almost directly from the LACS, with the only difference being a simple expansion of the subject domain to include 'the person, *group or entity*,' being coded.

(*Continued*)

Table 14.1. (*Continued*)

Dimensions for Coding Causes: Description and Coding Categories	Organisational Implications	Congruence with the LACS	Silvester et al. (1999) Framework
4. Controllability: Concerns the respondent's perception of the controllability of the causal factor, whether: [1] *In the control of workers* e.g., "Group meetings were a waste of time because people [workers] weren't turning up and weren't being a participant of the group"; [2] *In the control of a sub-section of the division* e.g., "After I [section supervisor] introduced that [quality control] system, I never got a part back"; [3] *In the control of the division* e.g., "Information meetings were introduced [by divisional management] to make workers more aware of the problems that management have"; [4] *In the control of the company* e.g., "Workers [in the tooling division] don't know what they are doing because the company, in the early stages, employed people with a low level of expertise to make tools";	Scores on this dimension may provide insights into: • the group's likely responsiveness to change, such that groups with an internal locus of control (represented by a preponderance of causes that are scored 1, 2, or 3) may be more responsive to change than groups with an external locus of control (represented by a preponderance of causes that are scored 4, 5, or 6); • group members' motivation, with motivation likely to be higher in groups with an internal locus of control than in groups with an external locus of control.	The LACS includes two coding categories only — *Controllable* and *Uncontrollable* — compared with six in the current framework. In the LACS, evaluations of controllability are not restricted to an examination of the cause; controllability may be indicated in the causal sequence as a whole or in any of its component parts (whether the cause, the link, or the outcome). Where appropriate, the LACS codes separately for 'speaker' and 'target'; in the current framework, no such distinction is made.	Adopted almost directly from the LACS. Modifications include: • the expansion of the subject domain to include 'the person, *group or entity* being coded' (as above for Internality); • the classification of the dimension as a dimension for coding causes (a somewhat confusing treatment since, in this framework, evaluations of controllability are made in relation to the outcome, and not in relation to the cause).

(*Continued*)

Table 14.1.   (*Continued*)

Dimensions for Coding Causes: Description and Coding Categories	Organisational Implications	Congruence with the LACS	Silvester *et al.* (1999) Framework
[5] *Outside of the control of the company* e.g., "I think that [the current emphasis on multi-skilling] was a government directed change"; or [6] *Uncontrollable* e.g., "Workers today don't work as hard as they did in the past because they've got attitude problems...they just come to work to get paid and they don't want to do anything for the money".			
5. Content: Concerned with the content of the causal factor, whether: [1] *Human* e.g., "The team concept was a failure because none of us [workers and supervisors] had a real understanding of what a team concept means"; or [2] *Non-human* e.g., "In the future, union involvement could change with the introduction of award restructuring". [In addition to classifying each causal factor — as *human* or *non-human* — the actual factor (or some appropriate labelling of it) was also recorded on the attribution coding sheet.]	Following on from Bate (1984), scores on this dimension may provide insights into the group's ability to diagnose and deal effectively with its problems. Specifically, problem solving may be less effective, and change more difficult to bring about, in groups in which there is a preponderance of causes that are non-human along with a tendency to 'depersonalise' any human causes. [The analysis of the actual content of causes may provide insights into differences, within and between groups, in members' perceptions of the relative influence of particular causal factors.]	The LACS contains no dimension for coding the content of the causal factor.	The 'agent' (essentially the causal factor) and the 'target' (what, or who, it is that is acted upon by the agent) are classified according to a number of *a priori* content categories (e.g., 'the company', 'the program', 'senior management' and 'employees'). In this framework, there is no coding of the content of the causal factor in terms of whether it is 'human' or 'non-human'.

(*Continued*)

Table 14.1. (*Continued*)

Dimensions for Coding Causes: Description and Coding Categories	Organisational Implications	Congruence with the LACS	Silvester *et al.* (1999) Framework
6. Context: Concerned with the particular 'domain' of context within which the cause is located, whether:	Scores on this dimension may provide insights into:	The LACS contains no dimension for coding the context of the causal factor.	The Silvester *et al.* framework contains no dimension for coding the context of the causal factor.
[1] *In the past and no longer active* e.g., "Workers don't know what they are doing because...the company in the early stages employed people with an extremely low level of expertise";	• the group's cultural orientation with respect to different domains of context, i.e., whether the culture is more strongly rooted in the past, the present, the future, or the ideal (the latter being reflected in a pre-occupation with what is desirable and how things ideally should be);		
[2] *In the present* e.g., "Group meetings for workers have been introduced because we've got so many problems...that can be sorted out by group discussions";	• group members' perceptions of their experience in relation to different contextual domains (i.e., whether members hold a more or less positive or negative view of the past, the present, and the future).		
[3] *In the future* e.g., "There will be more involvement of workers in training in the future, with the new model coming in";	The contextual orientation of a group's culture may have implications for efforts to bring about change in the group. For example, past-oriented cultures may be more resistant to change than future-oriented cultures; and, in terms of a more fine-grained distinction, cultures with a bias towards attributing negative outcomes to past causes that are *still active* may be more difficult to change than cultures with a bias towards attributing outcomes to past causes that are *no longer active.*		
[4] *In the ideal* e.g., "Communication between workers and supervisors will improve because this is necessary for management to get the best from their workers";			
[5] *In the past and still active* e.g., "Workers don't trust management because we [management] haven't shown ourselves to be trustworthy in the past...we as a management team need to turn around and communicate a lot better than we have in the past";			

(*Continued*)

Table 14.1.   (*Continued*)

Dimensions for Coding Causes: Description and Coding Categories	Organisational Implications	Congruence with the LACS	Silvester *et al.* (1999) Framework
[6] *In the present and likely to be ongoing* e.g., "In the future, [workers] are going to have to do everything from start to finish instead of becoming specialists in a particular facet of their trade… because you've got a smaller group you have to do that; you have to have a versatile group"; or [7] *Timeless or perpetual* e.g., "Workers are sceptical about information meetings because, you know, these sorts of programs start and stop, start and stop".			
7. Desirability: Concerns the respondent's perception of the desirability of the cause, whether: [1] *Desirable or positive* e.g., "At present, workers seem to be a lot happier because of a change in management…I give [the new manager] a lot of praise because he has really got the place to get up and move, and not only work-wise…he's the sort of bloke that will turn a blind eye if you do have a bit of fun…as long as your work has been done and it's done correctly, he's not going to come down on you like a ton of bricks".	The organisational implications of respondents' scores on this dimension are highly speculative since the value of the dimension (as a useful, separate dimension) remains to be empirically established. Group biases, and inter-group differences may emerge, for example, in relation to: • the relative proportion of positive, negative, equivocal, and neutral causes; • the association between the desirability of a cause and the desirability of the outcome to which it gives rise;	The LACS contains no dimension for coding the desirability of the cause.	The Silvester *et al.* framework contains no dimension for coding the desirability of the cause.

(*Continued*)

Table 14.1.   *(Continued)*

Dimensions for Coding Causes: Description and Coding Categories	Organisational Implications	Congruence with the LACS	Silvester *et al.* (1999) Framework
[2] *Undesirable or negative* e.g., "I think the problem [of poor worker-supervisor communication] is that a lot of supervisors see themselves as little gods…it's the mentality of the person and unfortunately a lot of our supervisors…their egos get the better of them".	• the association between the desirability of a cause and the contextual domain in which the cause originates; • the association between a cause's perceived desirability and its perceived controllability.		
[3] *Equivocal* e.g., "Today, there is more consultation of workers because…a lot of the rules started to go, whereas wearing a brown uniform meant nothing. Something happened in the workforce where staff were no longer respected… You couldn't turn around and bully anybody because the people above staff didn't back them…and so the [division] started to relax and since then people started to get together better than what we had. [The reduced power/status of supervisors] is good… up to a point".	These biases and differences may be relevant in terms of understanding, and possibly changing, the group's culture.		
[4] *Neutral* e.g., "In the future, there will be [more involvement of workers in training] with the new model coming in".			

(Continued)

Table 14.1. *(Continued)*

Dimensions for Coding Outcomes: Description and Coding Categories	Organisational Implications	Congruence with the LACS	Silvester *et al.* (1999) Framework
8. Actuality: This dimension is used to differentiate outcomes that have occurred, or are occurring, from those that are seen as likely to occur in the future.	Scores on this dimension combined with scores on the Desirability of the Outcome dimension may provide insights into group members' optimism or pessimism regarding their actual versus anticipated future experience. For example, in a group with a bias towards optimism about the future (specifically, a group in which members believe that things will get better in the future), one might expect that the proportion of positive-anticipated outcomes will be high relative to the proportions of positive-actual, negative-anticipated, and negative-actual outcomes.	In the LACS, outcomes are classified according to whether they are 'actual' or 'hypothetical'. In the present framework, the focus on 'anticipated', as opposed to 'hypothetical' outcomes, reflects the view that outcomes perceived as likely to eventuate in the future will be more informative, in terms of understanding the group's culture, than outcomes perceived to be hypothetical possibilities only.	Appears to have been adopted directly from the LACS. However, in their framework, Silvester *et al.* treat 'hypothetical' outcomes — inappropriately it could be argued — as synonymous with 'future' outcomes.
[1] *Actual* e.g., "At present, workers are not consulted because…what management is afraid of is that for every one question you get asked that's got some validity, they'll get nine questions that are a bit stupid…But this is one thing I do agree with, with the Japanese. They never knock anything back". OR "Today, there are more information meetings for workers than in the past…We didn't used to get any at all to begin with, so it's since [the current manager] has taken over, he has sort of brought this in. It's been better with him".	Change may be more difficult to effect in groups with a pessimistic orientation towards the future (in which members believe that things will get worse in the future) than in groups with an optimistic orientation towards the future.		
[2] *Anticipated* e.g., "In the future, there will be more involvement of workers in training…because the company is trying to get the worker to feel as though he is responsible for what he's doing…I think any change in the area of people management is definitely very desirable". OR "In the future [worker-supervisor communication will remain poor] because the workers think the foremen are dickheads and the foremen think the workers are dickheads".			

(Continued)

Table 14.1. (*Continued*)

Dimensions for Coding Outcomes: Description and Coding Categories	Organisational Implications	Congruence with the LACS	Silvester et al. (1999) Framework
9. Desirability: Concerns the respondent's perception of the desirability of the outcome, whether: [1] *Desirable or positive* e.g., "In the future, there will be more involvement of workers in training because I think restructuring is going to make people go and do it…I think we're never too old to learn". [2] *Undesirable or negative* e.g., "At present, you wouldn't find many supervisors [who] talk to too many on the floor…they're far too busy in their own little worlds to be bothering about what's going on, on the floor. I don't think they spend enough time looking into the problems that the workers have". [3] *Equivocal* e.g., "Today we [i.e., supervisors] expect a person to be more flexible, to be able to do more than what he used to do. [This is because of] the downturn in the mid 1970s [and the consequent loss of workers]. It's good for them [workers], but bad for me". [4] *Neutral* e.g., "In the future, the involvement of workers in record-keeping will not change because there's not usually a lot that needs to be recorded in [the respondent's section]".	Scores on this dimension, considered separately from scores on other dimensions, may provide a simple measure of the degree of optimism versus pessimism in the group. For deeper-level practical insights, it might be more instructive to examine the pattern of responding that emerges in scores on this dimension combined with scores on other dimensions. As indicated, scores on this dimension might be linked in practically meaningful ways with scores on: Globality and Internality (the so-called 'optimistic' and 'pessimistic' attributional styles); Context; Actuality; and Desirability of the Cause.	The LACS includes three key coding categories: 'desirable or positive', 'undesirable or negative' and 'neutral'. It also includes a 'cannot code' category: 'undecidable but not neutral'. Data for the present study (specifically, attributions in which the respondent expressed ambivalence about the outcome) suggested the need to include the 'equivocal' coding category in the present framework.	Adopted almost directly from the LACS, with the only modification being that, in this framework, the dimension comprises two coding categories only: 'negative' and 'positive/neutral'.

(*Continued*)

Table 14.1. *(Continued)*

Dimensions for Coding the Attribution as a Whole: Description and Coding Categories	Organisational Implications	Congruence with the LACS	Silvester *et al.* (1999) Framework
10. Universality: Concerns the respondent's perception of the extent to which the causal statement applies at a very general, as opposed to more specific and localised, level. [1] *Unique to the division* e.g., "In the past, worker involvement in group meetings was a waste of time because of group members' attitudes...people weren't turning up, weren't being a participant of the group". [2] *Unique to the organisation* e.g., "In the future, workers will have to carry out more and more technical type jobs...where people control processes and the processes are carried out by equipment. It's seen by the organisation, I believe, as being more cost effective". [3] *General - applies to organisations in the same industry* e.g., "At present, workers have more involvement in training than they did in the past because of restructuring, you know, the government's restructuring program, retraining and so forth". [4] *General – applies to any organisation* e.g., "At present, there is more involvement of workers in safety because of the introduction of health and safety legislation". OR "In recent years, we've put more hours into [training for workers]...[This is because] companies now have to spend a percentage of their salaries on training".	Scores on this dimension may provide insights into the group's responsiveness to change. Groups with a bias towards 'general' attributions (whether coding category [3] or [4]) may be more resistance to change than groups with a bias towards 'unique' attributions (whether coding category [1] or [2]). In such groups, the tendency of members to believe that the problems they face are typical of organisations generally is likely to present a significant challenge for change.	The LACS includes two coding categories: 'personal' (for attributions that signify something unique about the individual being coded) and 'universal' (for attributions that could apply to any normal member of the appropriate reference group (e.g., men, women, children, etc.). In the LACS, universality is defined from the perspective of the individual, whereas in the current framework, universality is defined from the perspective of the group.	The Silvester *et al.* framework contains no dimension for coding the universality of the causal statement. The authors argue that the LACS Personal-Universal dimension is too clinically oriented to be of much value in their study (of attributions in an organisational context). There is, however, a parallel between this dimension (in the current framework and in the LACS) and the Silvester *et al.* Global-Specific dimension. Both dimensions seek some kind of differentiation of the general from the specific, or local.

In adapting this dimension for use in the present analysis, the existing coding categories were renamed — the terms *stable* and *unstable* carried clinical connotations that, it was felt, limited their usefulness in an organisational context — and a third coding category was introduced. Specifically, the three coding categories were: *permanent* (similar to the LACS coding category *stable*, and used to denote causes perceived to be unchanging, whether in the sense of their inevitability and the permanence of their effects, or their association with tradition and 'the way things have always been done'); *semi-permanent* (for causes perceived to have a likely medium term influence, i.e., an influence that extends for at least the next few years); and *temporary* (for causes perceived to have a likely short-term influence, i.e., an influence that extends for a period of several months only). These coding categories were scored [1], [2], and [3] respectively.

The practical significance of this dimension in the present context is that an observed bias in the group (whether towards a preponderance of permanent, semi-permanent, or temporary causes) may be indicative of the group's exposure to change. One might expect, for example, that in groups exposed to ongoing rapid change, there would be a preponderance of temporary causes; however, in groups that have experienced little change over time, and in which well-established traditions continue to influence behaviour, one might expect a preponderance of permanent causes. It might also be argued, from a cultural perspective, that culture change may generally be more difficult to achieve in groups with a bias towards permanent causes than in groups with a bias towards either temporary or semi-permanent causes.

Interestingly, while Silvester *et al.* (1999) claim to have adopted this dimension directly from the LACS (i.e., without modification), their interpretation of the LACS coding categories appears to be somewhat inconsistent with the interpretation intended by Stratton *et al.* (1988). Specifically, this inconsistency arises in the authors' example of an *unstable* cause, illustrated in the attribution statement: "Fortunately attitudes are changing, the old style of management may soon be a thing of the past" (Silvester *et al.*, 1999, Table 1, p. 7). The classification by Silvester *et al.* of 'changing attitudes' as an unstable cause would seem to be problematic. This is because there is an implied permanence, or stability, about the causal factor; changing (or changed) attitudes about what constitutes the appropriate style of management are likely to have relatively permanent or long-lasting consequences for managerial style in the organisation. In this example, then, the causal factor might more appropriately have been classified as stable.

Dimension 2: Globality of the Cause (same as LACS). This dimension was adopted directly from the LACS. It is concerned with respondents' perceptions regarding how pervasive the influence of the cause is likely to be. In the present system, as in the LACS, causes are classified as *global* if they are perceived to have far-reaching effects, that is, if they are perceived as likely to have many additional consequences (or outcomes) beyond the consequence (or outcome) specified in the attribution; causes are classified as *specific* if their effects are seen as more localised, that is, if they are perceived as likely to have few additional consequences beyond that specified in the attribution. A possible example of a global cause in an organisational setting would be a significant event such as a major technological change; a possible example of a specific cause would be a more localised event, such as a minor equipment maintenance problem. In the present analysis, global causes were assigned a score of [1] and specific causes a score of [2].

In terms of its organisational relevance, this dimension has been associated with the contrasting explanatory styles of 'optimism' and 'pessimism' (Seligman & Schulman, 1986), the former being an individual's predisposition to attribute *positive* events to causes which are stable, internal, and global, and the latter being an individual's predisposition to attribute *negative* events to causes which are stable, internal, and global. There is some evidence to suggest that, in occupational settings these styles may differentially influence individual work outcomes, such as, job success, job satisfaction, motivation, and performance. The general finding of research that has been undertaken in this regard — see, for example, Seligman and Schulman (1986) and Furnham *et al.* (1992) — is that the pessimistic style impacts negatively on such outcomes, whereas the optimistic style is associated with more positive effects.

The above findings suggest the possibility that, in the context of the present analysis, respondents' scores on this dimension may provide insights into the group's cultural orientation towards optimism or pessimism. One might expect, for example, that in a pessimistic culture, members' attributions would contain more negative than positive outcomes, and there would be a bias towards attributing the negative outcomes to global causes (i.e., causes likely to lead to many additional negative outcomes) and the positive outcomes to specific causes (i.e., causes unlikely to lead to many additional positive outcomes). By way of illustration, such a culture might be characterised by a shared belief, among organisation (group) members, that widespread problems in the organisation (group) are, for the most part, the fault of, for example, 'poor management'. Positive events, to the extent that they are experienced at all, are likely to be seen as the result of specific causes — for example, a single 'good manager' — with little influence beyond a highly localised domain. In the case of an optimistic culture, one might expect the opposite of this scenario to apply.

A group's orientation with respect to the Globality dimension[5] might also have implications for change efforts within the group. In particular, it might provide insights into the scope, or breadth, of any change effort required. A very focussed program may be required to bring about change in groups in which there is a bias towards attributing outcomes (whether positive or negative) to a limited number of global causes. Conversely, a program that is broader in scope may be needed to bring about change in groups with a bias towards attributing outcomes to many specific causes. A further implication for change is that there may be an association

---

[5]Throughout this chapter, capitals are used consistently for the labelling of all of the dimensions in the coding framework that we have developed. While this is contrary to the style protocol used in other chapters of this book, we have adopted this approach in the present chapter to facilitate the identification of these dimensions.

between a group's orientation with respect to this dimension and its likely resistance to change. Drawing on the above depiction of pessimistic and optimistic cultures, one might expect that, in groups that support overly pessimistic or even overly optimistic cultures, resistance to change may be a problem. With respect to the latter, such groups are likely to display a kind of unrealistic optimism, which may obfuscate members' perceptions of the need for change. A good example of this can be found in Halberstam's (1986) account of how, because of their long experience of success in the marketplace — experience which reinforced an overly-optimistic, even arrogant, belief in the likelihood of ongoing future success — the American automotive companies failed to take seriously the threat of the 1973 oil crisis, and its implications for their continued manufacture of fuel-inefficient vehicles.

With respect to the framework proposed by Silvester *et al.* (1999), this framework also includes the Globality dimension, but in a somewhat modified form. In this framework, *global* is used to denote causes that are perceived to have outcomes that occur at a company level, whereas *specific* is used to denote causes perceived to have outcomes occurring at the more localised level of a subsection of the company (e.g., at a divisional, or group, level). While this adaptation retains the essential meaning of this dimension (i.e., the meaning as originally intended in the LACS), it was not considered suitable for use in the present analysis because of the latter's focus on attributions (and their cultural significance) at a divisional, rather than a company, level. Thus, in the present analysis, causes that are perceived as having widespread effects on the division and its membership are classified as global causes (as indeed are causes which have company-wide outcomes), and not as specific causes, as would be the case if the Silvester *et al.* framework were to be applied. From a practical perspective, the present approach might arguably have greater utility than that proposed by Silvester *et al.*, since, in many instances, consultants and change agents direct their efforts towards unit-level, rather than organisation-wide, interventions.

Interestingly, in their adaptation of this dimension, Silvester *et al.* make the assumption that organisation members will assign a higher degree of importance to global causes (as defined in their framework) than to specific causes. In reality, however, the opposite may be true. That is, specific causes may be assigned more importance than global causes since, being more localised in their effects, these effects are likely to be more immediately, and more keenly, felt by organisation members.

Dimension 3: Internality of the Cause (modified LACS). This dimension is concerned with the perceived origin of the causal factor. In the LACS, causes that are perceived to originate in the person being coded are classified as *internal*; causes that are perceived to originate outside the person being coded — such causes may be "a characteristic or behaviour of another person, or a circumstance" (Stratton *et al.*, 1988, p. 75) — are classified as *external*. This dimension of the LACS is one for which separate speaker and target codings are applied, where relevant (see above).

For the purpose of the present analysis, this dimension was modified slightly to take account of the kind of attributions data being analysed (namely, attributions pertaining to the role of workers and changes in that role). In its revised form, the dimension is con-cerned with the perceived origin of the cause *in relation to workers*. Thus, causes perceived to originate in workers (their characteristics, behaviours, attitudes, *etc.*) are classified as *internal* and assigned a score of [1]; causes perceived to originate outside workers (i.e., situational causes or the characteristics, behaviours, attitudes, *etc.* of other individuals or groups) are classified as *external* and assigned a score of [2]. This modification rendered the LACS speaker/target distinction irrelevant.

In an organisational setting, a group's orientation with respect to this dimension may provide insights into the group's 'ownership' of the outcomes it experiences (whether posi-tive events, such as successes, or negative events, such as failures). Thus, in the present analysis, a preponderance of causes that are internal to workers may be indicative of a culture in which members display a high ownership of outcomes. Conversely, a preponder-ance of causes that are external to workers may be indicative of a culture in which owner-ship of outcomes is low. It is also possible that 'low ownership' cultures may be more resistant to change than 'high ownership' cultures. This is the idea that, if group members regard the outcomes they experience (in particular, their problems) as being caused by factors external to themselves, rather than by factors internal to themselves, then it may be more difficult to enlist their support for change.

In view of the above, it is interesting to consider the association of this dimension with the optimistic and pessimistic explanatory styles, previously discussed. According to Seligman and Schulman (1986), in the optimistic style, the individual is predisposed towards attributing positive outcomes (e.g., successes) to internal factors and negative outcomes (e.g., failures) to external factors (this is the so-called self-serving bias); in the pessimistic style, the individual is predisposed towards attributing negative outcomes to internal factors and positive outcomes to external factors. As indicated, in occupational settings, these styles have been associated with good and poor performance outcomes respectively and, accordingly, the optimistic style has been represented as 'healthy', and the pessimistic style as 'unhealthy' (see Furnham *et al.*, 1992). The question arises, how-ever, as to whether or not this same interpretation can be applied to group-level predisposi-tions. It might be the case, for example, that groups with a collective bias towards optimism are *unrealistic* in their perceptions of the locus of causality. In reality, environmental contingencies may be such that group successes do not *predominantly* originate in the group, and group failures do not *predominantly* originate outside of the group. Indeed, as suggested above, a bias towards optimism may be unhealthy for the group, since it may inappropriately deflect ownership of group problems (and possibly also responsibility for the resolution of group problems) away from the group. In this sense, what constitutes a healthy attribution style might more appropriately be evaluated in terms of the degree of 'fit' that exists between the group's perceived locus of causality and the contingencies that define the particular environment in which the group operates.

Whereas the present analysis adopted a somewhat modified version of the LACS Internal/External dimension, Silvester *et al.* (1999) apply this dimension essentially without change. Their only modification is to broaden the exclusively individual focus of the LACS — a product of this framework's development for use in clinical settings — to accommodate attributions in which the focus is on a group, or some other entity. Thus, in the Silvester *et al.* framework, a cause is coded as either internal or external depending upon whether or not it is perceived to originate with, or outside of, "the person, *group or entity*"[6] being coded (Silvester *et al.*, 1999, p. 7). In the Silvester *et al.* framework, as in the LACS, locus of causality is coded separately for the speaker and the target, where appropriate.

Dimension 4: Controllability of the Cause (modified LACS). In the present analysis, this dimension is concerned with respondents' perceptions regarding the controllability of the causal factor. The dimension has been adapted from the original LACS dimension and differs from it in a number of ways. First, in its current (i.e., adapted) form, the dimension focuses predominantly on the controllability of the *cause*. In contrast, the treatment of controllability in the LACS is broader, such that evaluations of controllability — in terms of a simple *controllable* versus *uncontrollable* dichotomy — can draw on evidence from a number of sources, including the causal sequence as a whole, or any of the component parts of the causal sequence (i.e., the cause, the link, or the outcome)[7]. Thus, in the LACS, the general rule is to code *controllable* in cases where "the speaker believes that the person being coded could normally manage to significantly influence the outcome in the absence of exceptional effort or circumstance"; in cases where the speaker believes that "the causal sequence is …inexorable or the outcome inevitable in normal circumstances", the rule is to code *uncontrollable* (Stratton *et al.*, 1988, p. 78). In developing the present framework, the decision to adopt a more bounded treatment of controllability was essentially a pragmatic one. Given the number of coding categories specified for this dimension (see below), the view was that it would be more practical (in the sense of more efficient) if the rater were to consider only the controllability of the cause (rather than base her/his evaluations of controllability on multiple sources of evidence). It was also felt that this strategy might give rise to more consistent judgements of controllability between raters.

A second important difference between the current (i.e., adapted) Controllability dimension and the original LACS dimension is that the former comprises six coding categories, compared with only two for the latter. This difference reflects the fact that, in the present framework, the dimension is designed to provide insights into respondents' perceptions of controllability in relation to *a number of different domains*. Thus, causes are classified (and assigned a corresponding score) according to whether the respondent believes them to be: *in the control of workers* [1]; *in the control of a sub-section of the division* [2]; *in the control of the division* [3]; *in the control of the company* [4]; *outside of the control of the*

---

[6] Emphasis added by the present authors.

[7] For an explanation of the rationale for this particular treatment of controllability, the reader is referred to pages 33–34 of the *LACS Manual* (Stratton *et al.*, 1988).

company [5]; or *uncontrollable* in the sense of being inevitable and unable to be influenced by any person, group, or entity [6]. Given the focus in the present analysis on attribution style at a group, rather than individual level — the group, in this case, being an organisational division — the first three of these coding categories can be seen to correspond broadly to the *controllability* category in the LACS, whereas the last three can be seen to correspond broadly to the *uncontrollable* category in the LACS.

A third, and final, difference between this dimension and the Controllability dimension in the LACS is that it does not require separate speaker and target codings. As for the Internality dimension, revisions made to the LACS coding categories for this dimension, rendered this distinction irrelevant.

In terms of its organisational relevance, a group's orientation with respect to this dimension may provide insights into the group's likely responsiveness to change. Specifically, change might be easier to bring about in a group in which controllability is perceived to lie largely within the boundaries of the group (in this case, whether at a divisional, sectional, or worker level) than in a group in which controllability is perceived to lie outside the boundaries of the group, or in which there are perceptions of uncontrollability. In order for a group of the latter kind to become more responsive to change, it may be necessary to enhance members' sense of control (i.e., to empower members). The organisational relevance of this dimension might also be argued on the grounds of the now well-established link between control and motivation (Hackman & Oldham, 1976). It may be, for example, that members' motivation will be higher in groups where control is located internally than in groups where control is located externally.

In the Silvester *et al.* (1999) framework, the Controllability dimension is conceptualised in much the same way as it is in the LACS. It comprises the same two coding categories, namely *controllable* and *uncontrollable*, and separate speaker and target codings are similarly applied. The definitions of the coding categories are also very similar, though, as above for the Internality dimension, the focus is no longer just on the 'person being coded' but on the 'person, group or entity' being coded. Unlike the Controllability dimension in the LACS, however, the Controllability dimension in the Silvester *et al.* framework is classified as a dimension for coding *causes*. That is, in the coding instructions, the rater is directed explicitly to *code the cause* — as *controllable*, in the event that "the speaker believes that the person, group, or entity being coded was able to exert substantial influence over whether or not the outcome occurred", and as *uncontrollable*, in the event that "the speaker believes that the outcome was inevitable and not under the influence of the person, group or entity being coded" (Silvester *et al.*, 1999, Table 1, p. 7). This treatment of the Controllability dimension is somewhat confusing because, as indicated in the above instructions, the *actual* evaluation of controllability is in relation to the outcome, but the code is applied to the cause. Unfortunately, Silvester *et al.* offer no explanation for this apparent incongruity.

Dimension 5: Content of the Cause (new dimension). This is a newly developed dimension that has no parallel in the LACS. It is concerned with the content of the causal factor, specifically, whether the causal factor is *human* or *non-human*. In the case of the former, a score of [1] is assigned; in the case of the latter, a score of [2] is assigned.

The significance of this dimension in the present context was suggested by Bate's (1984) research demonstrating that there are certain cultural orientations, or cultural traits, that can act to impede effective problem-solving and change in the organisations, or groups, in which they are present. One of these orientations — which Bate labelled 'depersonalisation' — is manifested in a reluctance on the part of organisation members to ascribe responsibility for their problems to specific (i.e., *named*) individuals or groups of individuals. To the extent that the human element contributing to the organisation's problems is recognised at all, members 'depersonalise' it with references to generic influences such as "management", "Head Office", "the unions", or some other group (p. 53). For the most part, however, members attribute their difficulties to non-human factors (such as, outdated machinery, production pressures, the economy, *etc.*). Bate conceptualises depersonalisation as a kind of avoidance behaviour and argues that, to the extent that such behaviour is widely practised and accepted in an organisation, the organisation will fail to diagnose and deal effectively with its problems.

Whereas Bate draws a clear distinction between human influences that are specific (i.e., named) and those that are generic, the application of the Content dimension in the present framework requires no such distinction to be made. As indicated, in this framework, the content of a cause is simply coded according to whether it is *human* or *non-human*. The point should be made, however, that as a more or less informal supplement to this information, the present authors have also made a note (on the attribution coding sheet) of the exact nature of the causal factor (e.g., whether 'the economy', 'divisional policy', 'worker attitudes', 'company culture', *etc.*). It was felt that these additional, more specific, data might subsequently prove useful insofar as they could inform an investigation of differences, both within and between the divisions, in members' perceptions of the relative influence of particular causal factors (as indicated by the frequency with which they were mentioned).

While the Content dimension has no parallel in the LACS, an analogy can be drawn between this dimension and the classification, in the Silvester *et al.* (1999) framework, of the content of both the 'agent' (essentially the causal factor) and the target (essentially, what or who it is that the causal factor acts upon, or influences). More specifically, in the Silvester *et al.* framework, agents and targets are coded in terms of a number of *a priori* content categories (examples of which include 'the company', 'the program'[8], 'senior management', and 'employees'). Beyond the requirement to classify content, however, there are few similarities between the present framework (in relation specifically to the content dimension) and that proposed by Silvester *et al.* Certainly, there is no requirement in the latter to code the content of causes in terms of the broad human versus non-human distinction that is central to the former.

---

[8] It will be recalled that Silvester *et al.*'s (1999) study was concerned with the causal beliefs of key stakeholder groups involved in a culture change program.

Dimension 6: Context of the Cause (new dimension). This dimension is concerned with the context, or frame of reference, of the causal factor. It is a new dimension, with no parallel either in the LACS or in the Silvester *et al.* (1999) framework. The decision to include a measure of context in the present framework was made on the basis of the findings of Study 3 (see, in particular, Chapter 12). These findings supported an approach to understanding organisational (group) culture in which particular aspects, or domains, of context — to which emphasis is variously given in conceptual treatments of culture — are operationalised. More specifically, the findings demonstrated that an understanding of organisational culture can usefully be informed by seeking information, not just about the present context of organisation members' experience, but about their experience in relation to the past, the anticipated future, other organisations, and the ideal (concerning members' views about how things ideally should be). In seeking to apply a contextual analysis to the attributions data being considered here, seven coding categories — each specifying a possible contextual domain in which the causal factor might have its origins — were identified. Accordingly, in the present framework, a cause is classified (and assigned a corresponding score) in terms of whether, from the respondent's perspective, it: *originates in the past and is no longer active* [1]; *originates in the present* [2]; *originates in the future* [3]; *originates in the ideal* [4]; *originates in the past and is still active* [5]; *originates in the present and is likely to be ongoing* [6]; or *is timeless or perpetual* [7]. The decision not to include a code for causes that originate in the 'other' context was made primarily on the basis that the coding framework already included two dimensions concerned with the perceived locus of control of the causal factor, namely, the Internality and Controllability dimensions. It was also reasoned that the inclusion of such a code in this dimension would have given rise to a degree of coding confusion, since causes that originated in an 'other' context may also be labelled as 'past' causes, or 'present' causes.

Respondents' scores on this dimension can be expected to provide some measure of the group's cultural orientation in relation to these different contextual domains, with some domains being more dominant (in the sense that the group's culture is more strongly embedded in these domains) than others. Thus, for example, a bias in the group towards attributing outcomes to causes which originate in the past (whether these causes are still active or no longer active), would be indicative of an historically-based culture, that is, a culture in which past experience and tradition continue to be major influences on current thinking and behaviour. Similarly, a bias in the group towards attributing outcomes to causes that originate in the present or anticipated future would be indicative of a more future-oriented culture, in which current thinking and behaviour are subject to more dynamic influences. From a practical point of view, these different contextual orientations are likely to have implications for the responsiveness of the group to change. It might be expected, for example, that change will be more difficult to bring about in groups that support historically-based cultures than in groups that support more future-oriented cultures.

In terms of the more fine-grained analysis that can be achieved with the coding categories for this dimension, there may be sound practical reasons for drawing a distinction, for example, between attributions in which the causal factor originates in the past *and is no longer active* and attributions in which the causal factor originates in the past *and is still active*. This distinction (as with the broader distinction above) may have important implications for change. For example, change may be more difficult to bring about in groups in which negative outcomes give rise to attributions of the latter kind — in these groups, problems are seen to be the result of causes which are still operational — than in groups in which negative outcomes give rise to attributions of the former kind — in these groups, problems are seen to be the result of causes which are no longer operational. A second practical implication of this distinction is that it may provide insights into how group members perceive, or think about, their experience in relation to different contextual domains. For example, a bias among group members towards attributing negative outcomes (i.e., problems encountered by the group) to present causes and positive outcomes (i.e., group successes) to past causes may be indicative of a culture in which members hold a very 'rosy' view of the past.

Dimension 7: Desirability of the Cause (new dimension). This is the last dimension in the present framework for coding causes. It is a new dimension and, as with Dimension 6 above, it has no parallel either in the LACS or in the Silvester *et al.* (1999) framework. The dimension is concerned with the respondent's perception of the desirability of the causal factor. There are four coding categories, such that causes are classified, and assigned a corresponding score, according to whether the respondent believes them to be: *desirable or positive* [1]; *undesirable or negative* [2]; *equivocal* (i.e., positive on the one hand, and negative on the other) [3]; or *neutral* (i.e., neither positive nor negative) [4].

In developing the present framework, consideration was given to the possibility that this dimension might prove redundant, given the inclusion of a related dimension for coding the desirability of the outcome (see below). The argument here is that the perceived desirability of any given cause may be determined, for the most part at least, by the perceived desirability of the outcome with which it is associated. Thus, negative outcomes will be perceived to be the result of negative causes, positive outcomes the result of positive causes, and so on. Another possibility, however, is that the scores on these two dimensions may be correlated only moderately, rather than strongly. Thus, for example, negative outcomes, instead of always being seen to be the result of negative causes, may sometimes be seen to be the result of, say, neutral, or even positive causes. If this were the case, then the current dimension (for coding the desirability of the cause) could be seen to be adding significant additional information. It was for this reason, and also to ensure the completeness of the coding system, that the current dimension was included.

Given that the value of this dimension (as a useful, separate dimension) is yet to be empirically established, it is difficult to offer any but the most speculative of comments about the potential practical significance of respondents' scores on the dimension. In terms of the possibilities in this regard, it is conceivable that particular patterns may emerge — whether in the scores for this dimension alone or in the association between these scores and the scores for other dimensions — that may have implications for under-standing, and possibly changing the culture of the group, and that may serve to differenti-ate one group from another. It is possible, for example, that group biases might emerge in relation to: (i) the relative proportion of positive, negative, equivocal, and neutral causes; (ii) the association between the desirability of a cause and the desirability of the outcome to which it gives rise (see above); (iii) the association between the desirability of a cause and the contextual domain in which the cause originates (e.g., past causes may be per-ceived to be predominantly positive, while present causes may be perceived to be pre-dominantly negative); and (iv) the association between the desirability of a cause and the perceived controllability of the cause (e.g., positive causes may be perceived to be more, or less, controllable than negative causes). As indicated, to the extent that particular biases do emerge, these may have implications for efforts to bring about change in the group. Thus, for example, a group in which negative outcomes are predominantly attributed to negative causes (e.g., the 'arrogant' attitudes of management or the 'laziness' of workers) may present different challenges for change than a group in which negative outcomes are predominantly attributed to more neutral causes (e.g., inevitable increases in competition or fundamental characteristics, or requirements, of the job).

Dimension 8: Actuality of the Outcome (modified LACS). This dimension is used to classify outcomes according to whether they are *actual*, in the sense of occurring in the pre-sent or experienced in the past, or *anticipated*, in the sense of being seen by the respondent to be likely to occur in the future. In the present analysis, actual outcomes were assigned a score of [1], and anticipated outcomes were assigned a score of [2]. This dimension is very similar to the associated LACS dimension, except that in the LACS, outcomes are classified as either *actual* or *hypothetical*. For the purpose of the present analysis, it was considered important to draw a distinction between hypothetical and anticipated outcomes. While both types of outcomes can be seen to be similar in that they are outcomes that have not actually occurred, hypothetical outcomes are likely to be much more speculative than anticipated outcomes, which are likely to be more firmly grounded in, and more directly shaped by, the respondent's actual experience to date. In this sense, it can be argued that data pertaining to anticipated outcomes are likely to be more relevant insofar as informing an understand-ing of the culture of a group (organisation) than data pertaining to hypothetical outcomes.

In the present analysis, the coding of attributions on this dimension was very straight-forward since, as indicated, the data for the analysis were drawn from interviews in which, among other things, respondents were asked specifically about anticipated future out-comes (whether an anticipated change of some kind in the role of workers, or the expected ongoing maintenance of the status quo). It is perhaps also worth mentioning that, consist-ent with the aforementioned commitment to a contextual understanding of organisational (group) culture, the interview as a whole sought information about the respondent's experi-ence in relation to a number of different domains of context: the present, the past, the anticipated future, other organisations, and the ideal.

With respect to the organisational relevance of this dimension, it may be particularly instructive to examine the association between respondents' scores on this dimension and their scores on the dimension for classifying the desirability of the outcome (see below). This could provide insights into the degree of optimism, or pessimism, among respondents regarding their actual versus their anticipated future experience. Specifically, by examining the relative proportions of positive (desirable) to negative (undesirable) actual and antici-pated outcomes, one may be able to answer questions such as: Is the group more or less optimistic, or pessimistic, about its experience to date? How optimistic, or pessimistic, are group members about their future? How does the group's view of the future compare with its view of what has already occurred (or is currently occurring) in the group? With respect to this last question, and by way of illustration, the finding that the proportion of positive-anticipated outcomes significantly exceeded the proportion of positive-actual, negative-anticipated, and negative-actual outcomes would be suggestive of a group in which members were more optimistic about their future than about events and outcomes they had already experienced (or were currently experiencing). Moreover, such a group might be expected to be more responsive to change than a group in which the prevailing view was that things would get worse, rather than better, in the future. In the case of the latter, to the extent that the group's pessimism about the future had become part of a deeply embedded group mentality, or mindset, this would be likely to constitute a significant impediment to change — a factor instrumental in preventing the group from moving forward.

With respect to the framework proposed by Silvester *et al.* (1999), this framework clas-sifies the actuality of outcomes according to the same *actual* versus *hypothetical* dichot-omy that is used in the LACS. Interestingly, however, Silvester *et al.* treat hypothetical outcomes as synonymous with future outcomes; they have not considered it necessary, as we do, to draw a distinction between these two types of outcomes. This difference aside, in the Silvester *et al.* study, the practical significance of the dimension is argued in much the same way as it is in the present analysis. Specifically, Silvester *et al.* suggest that the relative proportions of positive to negative actual and hypothetical ('future') outcomes will provide a measure of respondents' optimism or pessimism, in this case regarding the cur-rent, and likely future, effectiveness of the culture change program in which they are dif-ferentially involved as key stakeholders.

Dimension 9: Desirability of the Outcome (modified LACS). This dimension is con-cerned with respondents' perceptions regarding the desirability of the outcome. Coding on this dimension uses the same four coding categories that are used to classify the desirabil-ity of the cause. That is, outcomes are classified, and assigned a corresponding score, according to whether they are perceived, by the respondent, to be: *desirable or positive* [1]; *undesirable or negative* [2]; *equivocal* (i.e., positive on the one hand, and negative on the other) [3]; or *neutral* (i.e., neither positive nor negative) [4]. The dimension has been adopted from the LACS with minor modification only. In the LACS, the corresponding dimension contains three *key* coding categories, namely, *desirable or positive*, *undesirable or negative*, and *neutral*, along with what is essentially a 'cannot code' category, namely, *undecidable but not neutral*. In adapting this dimension for use in the present analysis, a fourth coding category was added, namely, *equivocal*. The rationale for this change was that the database for the present analysis contained a number of attributions in which the respondent was clearly ambivalent about the outcome, arguing that it was desirable, on the one hand, and undesirable on the other.

From a practical perspective, the scores on this dimension might usefully be analysed both individually and in association with the scores on other dimensions. With respect to the former, an analysis of the proportion of positive to negative outcomes might be expected to provide at least a rudimentary sense of the degree of optimism or pessimism in the group. With respect to the latter, attention has already been drawn (in the discussion above) to the potential practical value of examining the relationship between respondents' scores on this dimension and their scores on other dimensions in the present framework. Reference has been made, for example, to the practical implications of the so-called 'optimistic' and 'pessimistic' attribution styles that, according to attribution theory, will be revealed in the pattern of responding across three dimensions — the present dimension (for evaluating outcomes) and the Globality and Internality dimensions (for evaluating causes). Reference has also been made to the kinds of practically meaningful linkages that might be observed between: (i) scores on this dimension and scores on the Context dimension (for evaluating causes); (ii) scores on this dimension and scores on the Actuality dimension (for evaluating outcomes); and (iii) scores on this dimension and scores on the Desirability of the Cause dimension.

The Silvester *et al.* (1999) framework, like the present framework and the LACS, also includes a dimension for evaluating the desirability of the outcome. In this framework, however, this dimension comprises two coding categories only, with events or outcomes being classified as either *negative* or *positive/neutral*.

Dimension 10: Universality of the Attribution (modified LACS). This is the last dimension in the present framework. Unlike the other nine dimensions, for which coding is in relation to the cause specifically, or the outcome specifically, coding for this dimension is in relation to the attribution (i.e., the causal statement) as a whole. The dimension is concerned with respondents' perceptions of the universality of the causal statement — essentially whether the causal statement is believed to signify something that is of very general, as opposed to more localised, relevance. The dimension comprises two main coding categories — *unique* versus *general* — each of which consists of two subcategories. Specifically, for the unique category, causal statements are classified, and assigned a corresponding score, according to whether the respondent believes them to be *unique to the division* [1], or *unique to the organisation* [2]. For the general category, causal statements are classified, and assigned a corresponding score, according to whether the respondent believes them to be *general, in the sense of applicable to organisations in the same industry as the current organisation* [3], or *general, in the sense of applicable to any organisation* [4].

The dimension is an adaptation of the Personal-Universal dimension in the LACS. While the two dimensions are similar in that, in neither, is coding restricted specifically to the cause, or to the outcome — in the LACS dimension, coding can apply to the entire attribution or to any part of it, whether the cause, the link, or the outcome — they differ in that, in the LACS dimension, the main point of reference is the individual, whereas in the current dimension, it is the group. Thus, in the LACS, a causal statement is classified as *personal* if it is believed by the speaker to indicate something unique or idiosyncratic about the individual being coded. It is classified as *universal* if the speaker believes that it could apply to "any normal member of the appropriate reference group" ('appropriate' in this case being judged from the perspective of the speaker) (Stratton *et al.*, 1988, p. 77). By way of illustration, and drawing on an example from the LACS, the causal statement "She dropped it because she is a child" indicates a universal attribution, whereas the causal statement "She dropped it because she is clumsy" indicates a personal attribution. This difference between the current Unique-General dimension and the LACS Personal-Universal dimension is, of course, reflective of the different purposes for which these two frameworks were developed — the present framework, for the study of groups (specifically, group culture) in organisational settings and the LACS, for the study of individuals in clinical settings.

From a practical perspective, respondents' scores on this dimension may provide insights into the group's likely responsiveness to change. It might be expected, for example, that change will be more difficult to bring about in groups with a bias towards making general causal statements (i.e., statements that are applicable outside of the boundaries of the group's division or organisation) than in groups with a bias towards making unique causal statements (i.e., statements that draw attention to something that is particular to, or unique about, the group's division or organisation). In such groups, the development of a mindset whereby members believe that "It's not just our workplace that's like this, it's all organisations!" is likely to present a significant challenge for change.

With respect to the Silvester *et al.* (1999) framework, the authors are explicit about their decision not to include the LACS Personal-Universal dimension (or any modification of it) in their framework on the grounds that, since the dimension was "originally designed for use in clinical contexts", it was "not considered appropriate for this study" (p. 6). This argument aside, however, there is an interesting parallel that can be drawn between the LACS Personal-Universal dimension (both in its original form and as it has been adapted for use in the present analysis) and Silvester *et al.*'s modification of the LACS Global-Specific dimension. It will be recalled that, in the latter, causes are classified as global if they have outcomes that occur at a company level, and specific if they have outcomes that occur at a divisional level. The point is that, in terms of their basic intent, or essential meaning, both of these dimensions — the LACS Personal-Universal dimension (and its current modification) and the Silvester *et al.* Global-Specific dimension — are concerned with the broad distinction that can be made between attributions (or parts thereof) that signify something of very local relevance and those that signify something of more general relevance.

14.5 Results

We turn now to a consideration of the main findings of this study. By way of an introduction to these findings, we comment first on the extent to which the data could readily, and reliably, be coded using our proposed ten-dimension framework. Following this, we report the results of an analysis of differences between the divisions in their attribution tendencies with respect to each of the coding dimensions separately. Consideration is then given to similarities and differences between the divisions in the content of respondents' attributions — that is, the specific causes that they mention. And finally, we report the results of a multivariate analysis that sought to ascertain whether or not the divisions differed in terms of a more general attribution style, as reflected in the pattern of inter-relations among the coding dimensions in each division.

14.5.1 *Codability of the data*

Importantly, the data for the present analysis were not generated as part of a stand-alone study. As indicated previously, they were drawn from interviews conducted as part of Study 3, a larger and more broadly focussed study of organisational culture that is reported in Chapters 10, 11, and 12 of this volume. In view of this, an important initial consideration concerned the extent to which these data could readily be coded using the ten-dimension coding framework described above. Table 14.2 provides a summary of the codability of the data, separately for the tooling division and the production division. As indicated, for five of the ten coding dimensions — Globality, Internality, Content, Actuality, and Universality — the number of uncodable attributions (i.e., attributions classified as *cannot code* on the dimension in question) for each division was less than 5%. In other words,

Table 14.2. Percentage of attributions from each division that could not be coded on each dimension in the coding framework.

Dimension	Tooling Division (% of 247 Attributions)	Production Division (% of 306 Attributions)
1. Stability	4.5	23.9
2. Globality	0	0.3
3. Internality	0.4	1
4. Controllability	2	10.5
5. Content	0	0
6. Context	6.9	10.1
7. Desirability (Cause)	41.3	25.5
8. Actuality	0	0
9. Desirability (Outcome)	44.5	31.7
10. Universality	0	0.3

most of the attributions for each division contained sufficient information to be able to be readily coded on each of these five dimensions. Attributions were also fairly readily coded on the Controllability and Context dimensions; as indicated in Table 14.2, the highest percentage of uncodable data for these dimensions was 10.5% (for production division attributions on the Controllability dimension).

In contrast, there were three dimensions — Stability, Desirability of the Cause, and Desirability of the Outcome — for which the percentage of uncodable data was sufficiently high to be of concern. The latter two dimensions were particularly problematic in this regard, with a high percentage of attributions from both divisions unable to be coded on these dimensions. As can be seen from Table 14.2, 41.3% of tooling division attributions and 25.5% of production division attributions could not be coded on the Desirability of the Cause dimension; the corresponding figures for the Desirability of the Outcome dimension were 44.5% of tooling division attributions and 31.7% of production division attributions. Coding on both of these dimensions proved difficult because there was insufficient information — whether in the attribution statement itself or in the surrounding contextual data — upon which to base a judgement about the respondent's belief regarding the desirability, or alternatively, undesirability, of the outcome or the cause.

For dimensions such as these, where the level of uncodable data is high, questions arise as to the extent to which any meaningful conclusions can be drawn from the analysis of the codable data. In particular, there is a question about how confident one can be about the results of this analysis — whether a suggested difference between the divisions (say, with respect to the tendency of respondents to focus on undesirable as opposed to desirable outcomes) can be seen as indicative of an actual difference between the divisions. The problem of uncodable data also has important methodological implications. Specifically, if attributions analysis is to provide a valuable means whereby to obtain insights into an organisation's (group's) culture, then it might be necessary to seek a more comprehensive understanding of the contents of respondents' attributions. This would involve asking respondents specific questions (e.g., about the perceived desirability or undesirability of a given outcome, from the respondent's perspective) in order to fill information 'gaps' in these attributions. Further consideration will be given to this issue in Section 14.6 of this chapter.

14.5.2 *Coding reliability*

While the first author was responsible for independently coding all of the attributions in the data set, in order to establish coding reliability, the codes for 46 of these attributions, randomly selected from the attribution coding sheets[9], were compared with the codes subsequently assigned independently by the second author. While both coders were familiar

---

[9]These coding sheets contained each of the attribution statements (written across the page) that had been extracted for analysis, along with a series of ten columns (immediately below each statement), one for each of the coding dimensions in the coding framework.

Table 14.3. Coding reliability for each dimension, as calculated using Cohen's Kappa.

Dimension	Kappa	Significance
1. Stability	.313	.002
2. Globality	.618	.000
3. Internality	.734	.000
4. Controllability	.701	.000
5. Content	.822	.000
6. Context	.435	.000
7. Desirability (Cause)	.235	.007
8. Actuality	.948	.000
9. Desirability (Outcome)	.411	.000
10. Universality	.686	.000

with the findings of Study 3, pertaining to respondents' experience of the role of workers in relation to different domains of context, neither had previously considered the attributions data in the very detailed way required by the present analysis. The question as to whether or not some degree of contextual knowledge (even if this were limited to familiarity with the complete interview transcripts), and/or some experience in the use of the coding method, may be desirable insofar as enhancing coding reliability is an issue to which further consideration is given in the final section of this chapter.

For the present purposes, the coding reliability for each of the ten dimensions in the coding framework was assessed using Cohen's Kappa. Table 14.3 shows the value of Kappa for each dimension, along with its associated significance level. Using the interpretation of Kappa size proposed by Fleiss (1981, p. 218), and referring to the values in Table 14.3, it can be concluded that, for eight of the ten dimensions, coding reliability was acceptable. Specifically, there were two dimensions — Content and Actuality — for which 'excellent agreement beyond chance' (i.e., $K > 0.75$) was indicated and there were six dimensions — Globality, Internality, Controllability, Context, Desirability (Outcome), and Universality — for which 'fair to good agreement beyond chance' (i.e., $K = 0.40$ to 0.75) was indicated. For the remaining two dimensions — Stability and Desirability (Cause) — coding reliability was problematic. As indicated in Table 14.3, the K coefficients for these dimensions were less than 0.40, such values being indicative of 'poor agreement beyond chance'.

14.5.3 *Findings for individual dimensions*

A preliminary analysis of the data was carried out to ascertain whether or not there were any divisional differences in the attribution tendencies of respondents in relation to each individual coding dimension. The approach to this analysis involved, first of all, calculating the relative proportion of each respondent's attributions (expressed as a percentage of the total number of attributions made by that respondent) that fell into each of the coding categories for a given dimension. Drawing on the Content dimension to illustrate, for each respondent, the number of attributions in which the cause was classified as 'human', 'non-human', and 'cannot code', respectively, was calculated and expressed as a percentage of the total number of attributions made by that respondent (with the sum of these individual percentages being 100%). Following this, for each dimension, and for the two divisions separately, respondents' percentages for each coding category were summed and a divisional mean calculated for that coding category. Thus, in the case of the Content dimension, three mean scores for each division were calculated — a mean % *human*, a mean % *non-human*, and a mean % *cannot code* (with the sum of these mean percentages also being 100%). Independent samples *t*-tests were then used to ascertain whether or not the divisions differed significantly in terms of these mean scores. This exercise was repeated for each of the dimensions in the coding framework.

It should be noted that the present approach to analysing group (in this case, divisional) differences in attribution tendencies, for each separate dimension, contrasts with the approach adopted by both Silvester *et al.* (1999) and Stratton *et al.* (1988). The latter researchers rely on simple frequency counts of the data for *each group as a whole*, with no consideration given to within-group variability in the numbers of attributions made by individual respondents. Thus, for each group — with 'groups' in the Silvester *et al.* (1999) study being different stakeholders in a change program and, in the LACS research (Stratton *et al.*, 1988), being single families or groups of families, undergoing therapy — the researchers calculate the *total* number of attributions made by the group that fall within each of the coding categories for a given dimension. Again, using the Content dimension from the present analysis to illustrate, this is the equivalent of calculating, for each group, the total number of attributions in which the cause is classified as *human*, *non-human*, and *cannot code* respectively (with the sum of these 'category totals' being equal to the total number of attributions made by the group). Chi-square analysis can then be used to examine group differences in the observed frequencies[10].

As suggested, a limitation of this approach is that it ignores within-group differences in the numbers of attributions made by individual respondents. If, for example, most of the attributions that make up the data set for a given group are contributed by a small number of group members only, then the attribution tendency of the group with respect to any given dimension (as calculated using this approach) will be disproportionately influenced by the responses of these individuals. Moreover, this effect will be exacerbated if these individuals are also 'extreme scorers', that is, if they are strongly predisposed to attributing

---

[10] It is interesting to note that, while Silvester *et al.* (1999) report inter-group differences in attribution tendencies in relation to single dimensions (e.g., in relation to the desirability of outcomes, whether positive or negative), they provide no indication of the statistical significance of these differences. In contrast, Stratton *et al.* (1988) specifically advocate the use of chi-square analysis for the interpretation of such data.

Table 14.4. Differences between the Tooling Division (TD) and the Production Division (PD) in the mean proportions (%) of attributions for each category of each coding dimension.

Dimension	Category	TD mean %	PD mean %	TD sd %	PD sd %	t value	df	sig (2-tailed)
1. Stability	Permanent	43.84	18.58	16.57	12.32	4.45	24	.000***
	Semi-permanent	48.84	50.66	15.59	19.62	−0.26	24	.799
	Temporary	3.57	4.83	5.24	5.95	−0.57	24	.575
2. Globality	Global	85.88	72.22	11.68	19.17	2.15	24	.042*
	Specific	14.12	27.30	11.68	19.29	−2.06	24	.050
3. Internality	Internal	12.19	20.36	9.09	12.81	−1.85	24	.077
	External	87.38	78.92	9.67	12.95	1.86	24	.075
4. Controllability	Within division	31.80	49.26	15.66	14.53	−2.95	24	.007**
	Outside of division	63.43	30.07	14.90	8.53	7.14	24	.000***
5. Content	Human	38.96	55.32	18.12	10.58	−2.75	17.13	.014*
	Non-human	61.04	44.69	18.12	10.58	2.75	17.13	.014*
6. Context	Past, no longer active	4.36	9.26	5.74	11.09	−1.44	20.07	.181
	Present	23.33	9.50	21.67	6.93	2.12	12.93	.054
	Future	2.16	5.9	3.56	7.30	−1.62	24	.119
	Ideal	.00	.48	.00	1.78	−0.92	24	.365
	Past, still active	17.10	4.27	10.55	4.88	3.87	14.98	.002**
	Present, ongoing	33.00	45.86	22.78	19.08	−1.57	24	.130
	Timeless/Perpetual	12.08	12.77	12.43	6.67	−0.17	16.27	.866
7. Desirability (Cause)	Positive	20.55	29.42	15.51	21.25	−1.20	24	.243
	Negative	22.17	23.45	13.11	10.23	−0.28	24	.782
8. Actuality	Actual	67.78	66.12	14.53	18.61	0.25	24	.803
	Hypothetical	33.22	33.89	14.53	18.61	−0.25	24	.803
9. Desirability (Outcome)	Positive	26.73	35.89	16.59	22.68	−1.16	24	.258
	Negative	20.70	23.81	14.10	12.52	−.60	24	.557
10. Universality	Unique	70.03	82.34	9.81	11.05	−2.99	24	.006**
	General	26.18	12.03	9.58	11.95	3.29	24	.003**

$* p < .05$; $** p < .01$; $*** p < .001$.

Note: Where Levine's test for equality of variances was significant, the more conservative estimate of significance was used.

outcomes to, say, human as opposed to non-human causes. The present approach, whereby the tendencies of individual group members are averaged across the group, seeks to counteract this effect and provide a more accurate representation of the views of the group's membership as a whole.

The results of the analysis described above are reported in Table 14.4. It can be seen that, for each division and for each dimension separately, the mean percentage of

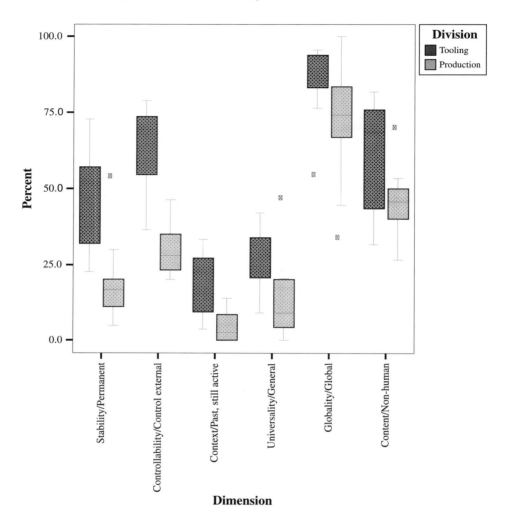

Figure 14.1.   Box plots showing dimensions (and their associated coding categories) for which significant differences between the Tooling Division and the Production Division were reported (see Table 14.4).

attributions falling within each of the coding categories for the dimension (with the exception of the cannot code category) is shown, along with the associated standard deviation. Also shown is the t value and, where relevant, its associated level of significance. In addition to the results reported in Table 14.4, the box plots shown in Figure 14.1 provide an alternative, and perhaps visually more informative, way of representing divisional differences in attribution tendencies in relation to each separate dimension. As indicated in Chambers, Cleveland, Kleiner, and Tukey (1983), box plots identify: the middle 50%, or 'body', of the data (represented by the shaded box); the median (represented by the horizontal line inside the box); and the extreme points (i.e., the minimum and maximum values of the data, represented by the small bar at the upper and lower boundary of each plot). It can be seen from Figure 14.1 that the box plots displayed pertain only to those dimensions and associated coding categories for which significant divisional differences were reported in Table 14.4 and for which the difference reported represented the *orientation of tooling division respondents*. Thus, for the Controllability dimension, since tooling division respondents were more inclined than their counterparts from production to attribute outcomes to causes that lay outside of the control of the division, the results for *control outside* were selected for inclusion in Figure 14.1, rather than those for *control inside*. In a similar vein, since tooling division respondents were more inclined than their counterparts from production to attribute outcomes to *non-human* causes — the Content dimension — it is the results for this coding category that are reported in Figure 14.1, rather than the results for the coding category *human*.

It can also be seen from Figure 14.1 that the box plots displayed are presented in order from the dimension and associated coding category for which there was the most significant divisional difference (as reported in Table 14.4) to the dimension and associated coding category for which there was the least significant divisional difference. The rationale for these choices about the content and format of Figure 14.1 was that, presented in this way, key findings would be more 'readable' and their interpretation and discussion could be more easily juxtaposed with the interpretation and discussion of the findings reported in Table 14.4. We turn now to a consideration of the main findings of the above analysis of divisional differences in attribution tendencies in relation to each separate dimension.

With respect, first of all, to the most marked differences between the divisions, it can be seen from Table 14.4 that there were two dimensions — Stability and Controllability — for which the difference between the divisions was significant at the level of $p < .001$. Specifically, respondents from the tooling division were significantly more likely than their counterparts from production to attribute outcomes to causes that were permanent or unchanging, as opposed to either semi-permanent or temporary (the Stability dimension) and to causes that lay outside of, rather than within, the control of the division (the Controllability dimension). The first two box plots in Figure 14.1 provide a visual representation of these findings. While it appears from these box plots that, for both dimensions (and the coding categories specified), respondents from the tooling division constituted a less homogeneous group than their counterparts from production, Levine's test for equality of variances indicated that, on neither dimension, was the difference in variability between the divisions significant.

With respect to the next most marked differences between the divisions, it can be seen from Table 14.4 that differences which were significant at the level of $p < .01$ emerged for the two dimensions Context and Universality[11]. Specifically, respondents from the tooling

---

[11] No reference is made here to the significant finding *(p < .01)* for the *within division* category of the Controllability dimension. This is because this finding is essentially the reverse of the finding, reported above, for the *outside of division* category of this dimension *(p < .001)*. That the *t* values associated with these findings, along with their corresponding levels of significance are not equivalent simply reflects the fact that there were a number of attributions that could not be coded on this dimension.

division were significantly more likely than their counterparts from production to attribute outcomes to causes that, while currently still active, had their origins in the past (the Context dimension). They were also more likely to make attributions that were general (in the sense of being applicable to any organisation, whether within or outside of the industry), as opposed to unique (in the sense of being specific to the respondent's division or organisation) (the Universality dimension). Again, Figure 14.1 provides a visual representation of these differences between the divisions. The difference in variability between the two divisions suggested by the box plots for the Context dimension was significant. Specifically, Levine's test for equality of variances indicated that, in terms of their tendency to attribute outcomes to past causes that were still active, tooling division respondents were significantly more variable, as a group, than their counterparts from production ($F = 13.72$, $p < .01$).

Finally, there were two dimensions, namely, Globality and Content, for which divisional differences which were significant at the level of $p < .05$ only emerged. As indicated in Table 14.4, tooling division respondents were significantly more likely than their counterparts from production to attribute outcomes to causes that were global rather than specific (the Globality dimension) and to causes that were non-human rather than human (the Content dimension). The last two box plots in Figure 14.1 provide a visual representation of these findings. Again, the difference in variability between the two divisions suggested by the box plots for the Content dimension was significant. Specifically, Levine's test for equality of variances indicated that, in terms of their tendency to attribute outcomes to non-human causes, tooling division respondents were significantly more variable, as a group, than their counterparts from production ($F = 6.60$, $p < .05$).

Considered as a whole, the above findings were consistent with expectations. As indicated previously, the tooling division was an older and more established division than the production division. At the time at which the data informing the present analysis were collected, it had been in operation for more than 60 years, whereas the production division had been in operation for some ten years only. The first author's experience, as the researcher in both of the divisions investigated in the three studies reported in this volume, spanned a period of some three years, during which time a consistently high-level of involvement with the research setting was maintained. Based on this experience and data (both qualitative and quantitative) collected as part of the research being undertaken, there was good evidence to indicate that the tooling division had a much more stable history than its younger counterpart (in the sense of having experience less change and fewer different types of change over time) and that its culture was more definable (i.e., more immediately identifiable) and more deeply embedded than the culture of the production division. As indicated above, there was also evidence to suggest that, in terms of members' collective perceptions of control, the tooling division supported a predominantly external orientation whereas the production division appeared to be more internally oriented.

This profile of general differences between the divisions corresponds closely with the contrasting attribution tendencies of tooling division and production division respondents, as reported in the present analysis. Specifically, the marked predisposition of tooling division respondents, compared with their counterparts from production, to attribute outcomes to permanent (rather than semi-permanent or temporary) causes (the Stability dimension) and to causes which had their origins in the past and which continued to influence outcomes in the present (the Context dimension), is consistent with what one would expect of a group with a relatively long and stable history. The findings of the attributions analysis were also consistent with the depiction of the tooling division as supporting a more definable and deeply embedded culture — such a culture is likely to pose problems for change in the group — than the production division. In addition to the findings above for the Stability and Context dimensions, the findings for the Controllability, Content, and Universality dimensions were also relevant in this regard. Specifically, tooling division respondents were more inclined than their counterparts from production to attribute outcomes to causes that lay outside of, rather than within, the control of the division (the Controllability dimension) and to causes that were non-human rather than human (the Content dimension). As discussed previously, both of these tendencies are likely to be associated with a higher level of resistance to change among group members. In a similar vein, the bias in the tooling division towards making general, as opposed to unique, attributions (the Universality dimension) is consistent with what one would expect of a group with a more embedded, and in this sense potentially more resilient, culture.

Unfortunately, it is difficult to say much about the practical implications of the finding for the Globality dimension. As indicated in the discussion of this dimension, the information that it provides is most useful when combined with information pertaining to the Desirability (Outcome) dimension. Specifically, scores on these two dimensions, considered together, can provide insights into a group's orientation towards optimism (a style in which a few global causes are seen as accounting for multiple positive outcomes), or alternatively, pessimism (a style in which a few global causes are seen as accounting for multiple negative outcomes). In the present analysis, however, the problem of uncodable data for the Desirability (Outcome) dimension — as indicated above, for both divisions, the proportion of attributions in which the desirability of the outcome could not be coded was high — meant that it was difficult to draw any meaningful conclusions about the extent to which the divisions differed in the degree of optimism, or pessimism, which they supported.

For the same reason, there were a number of other relationships of this kind that could not meaningfully be investigated. For example, it was not possible to establish, with any confidence, whether the divisions differed with respect to the relationship that existed between the Context and Desirability (Outcome) dimensions. Of particular interest in this regard was the question of whether or not the context of the causes of positive outcomes was different from the context of the causes of negative outcomes (it may be, e.g., that the former tends to be the past, whereas the latter tends to be the present). Further, do the divisions differ, if at all, in this regard? In a similar vein, the relationships between the Actuality and the Desirability (Outcome) dimensions and between the Universality and the Desirability (Outcome) dimensions could not be meaningfully analysed. With respect to the former, it would have been interesting to know whether or not actual versus antici-pated outcomes (the Actuality dimension) differed in terms of their desirability (whether positive or negative), and whether or not one division's profile of responding in this regard was different from that of the other division. As indicated in the discussion of the Actuality dimension, the relative proportions of positive-anticipated, positive-actual, negative-anticipated and negative-actual outcomes may provide insights into a group's level of optimism versus pessimism regarding actual and anticipated events and outcomes. With respect to the latter, there is the question of whether attributions for negative, as opposed to positive, outcomes are predominantly general (i.e., applicable to any organisation or, at least, to organisations in the same industry), as opposed to predominantly unique (i.e., applicable to the current organisation or division) (the Universality dimension). In other words, is there a perception among group members that the negative outcomes they expe-rience are typical of all organisations, rather than unique to their own organisation? Again, what differences, if any, are there between the divisions in this regard?

14.5.4 *The content, and commonality, of specific causal factors*

In addition to the above broad classification of the content of causes — as being either human or non-human — a more fine-grained analysis of the *specific* causal factors identi-fied by respondents was undertaken. The purpose of this analysis was to ascertain whether or not there were certain specific causes which had particular salience for respondents (in the sense of being mentioned more often than other causes, and by more respondents) and, if so, whether or not there were any divisional differences in this regard. The results of this analysis are shown in Table 14.5. In developing this table, it was decided that, for each division, only those causes mentioned by at least 25% of respondents would be reported. The decision was also taken to further classify the remaining causes into three specific levels of 'sharedness': (i) causes mentioned by 75% to 100% of respondents; (ii) causes mentioned by 50% to 74% of respondents; and (iii) causes mentioned by 25% to 49% of respondents. These criteria for the reporting and classification of the content data, while somewhat arbitrarily chosen, did take into account the small sample size for each divi-sion — this made it difficult to say anything meaningful about causes that were mentioned by fewer than 25% of respondents — and the potential interpretive value of designating causes as widely, moderately, or only somewhat, shared.

It can be seen from Table 14.5 that, for each of the causes reported, the *actual shared-ness* of the cause is indicated, along with the *average frequency* with which that cause was mentioned by each respondent. The former is simply the number (also represented as a percentage) of respondents from each division for whom the cause appeared in at least one of the attributions that they made. The latter is the proportion (percentage) of each

Table 14.5. Sharedness (number of respondents) and mean frequency per respondent of specific causal factors mentioned by respondents from each division.

Tooling Division (n = 12)

	Causal Factor	Number (and %) of Respondents	Frequency (%) Per Respondent: Mean (sd)
Causes mentioned by 75% to 100% of respondents	Award restructuring	12 (100%)	11.0 (7.1)
	Diminishing size of workforce/Decline of division	9 (75%)	14.6 (11.6)
	Expectations about the role of workers and/or supervisors	9 (75%)	13.2 (11.4)
	Divisional supervisor attitudes/behaviours/style	9 (75%)	12.5 (8.7)
Causes mentioned by 50% to 74% of respondents	Divisional worker attitudes/skills/behaviours/personality	8 (66.7%)	16.2 (6.5)
	Survival and competition imperative	7 (58.3%)	7.1 (2.5)
	Divisional management attitudes/behaviours/style	7 (58.3%)	6.4 (2.2)
	Company management attitudes/behaviours/style	7 (58.3%)	5.8 (4.1)

Production Division (n = 14)

	Causal Factor	Number (and %) of Respondents	Frequency (%) Per Respondent: Mean (sd)
Causes mentioned by 75% to 100% of respondents	Divisional worker attitudes/skills/behaviours/personality	14 (100%)	20.0 (10.7)
	Divisional management attitudes/behaviours/style	11 (78.6%)	16.8 (6.2)
Causes mentioned by 50% to 74% of respondents	Production demands	10 (71.4%)	6.3 (3.0)
	Expectations about the role of workers and/or supervisors	9 (64.3%)	8.4 (4.5)
	Divisional supervisor attitudes/behaviours/style	9 (64.3%)	13.2 (6.7)
	Award restructuring	9 (64.3%)	5.6 (2.2)
	Survival and competition imperative	7 (50%)	7.1 (2.7)

(Continued)

Table 14.5. (*Continued*)

Tooling Division (n = 12)			Production Division (n = 14)		
Causal Factor	Number (and %) of Respondents	Frequency (%) Per Respondent: Mean (sd)	Causal Factor	Number (and %) of Respondents	Frequency (%) Per Respondent: Mean (sd)
Job design/redesign	5 (41.7%)	7.3 (4.6)	Company management attitudes/ behaviours/style	4 (28.6%)	7.5 (4.1)
Divisional policy	5 (41.7%)	6.1 (2.2)	Job design/redesign	4 (28.6%)	6.5 (3.3)
Societal attitudes/behaviours	4 (33.3%)	9.4 (9.2)	The nature of the work (and changes in)	4 (28.6%)	4.6 (1.9)
The nature of the work (and changes in)	4 (33.3%)	5.4 (2.3)	Technological change	4 (28.6%)	6.5 (2.9)
Technological change	4 (33.3%)	6.0 (2.5)	Company culture	4 (28.6%)	6.4 (3.2)
Uncertainty (rumour) control measure	4 (33.3%)	8.3 (5.2)			
Union attitudes/behaviours	4 (33.3%)	4.5 (0.7)			
Organisation design/structure	3 (25%)	7.1 (3.8)			
Industrial relations policy/change	3 (25%)	8.1 (2.5)			
Company culture	3 (25%)	6.5 (3.6)			

Causes mentioned by 25% to 49% of respondents

respondent's attributions, on average, which contained the cause[12]. As indicated, for each cause, the average frequency along with its associated standard deviation is reported. The decision to exclude from Table 14.5 causes for which the level of sharedness was very low, or non-existent (i.e., causes that were mentioned by fewer than 25% of respondents) was based on the fact that these additional data would involve a substantial increase in the size of the table, while being of minimal empirical value only (at least insofar as providing insights into divisional differences in the types of attributions that had most salience for divisional members). The point should be made, however, that for both divisions, the proportion of attributions for which there was less than 25% agreement about the cause, was quite high. Specifically, this was the case for 38% of tooling division attributions and for 34% of production division attributions. This finding, together with the results reported in Table 14.5, draws attention to the overall diversity that existed in the specific causes identified by respondents from both divisions. The fact that so many different causes were mentioned suggests the important conclusion that the explanations that respondents offered for the outcomes they had experienced were considered responses, rather than superficial (i.e., 'off the top of the head') responses, that were more rhetoric than reality. Indeed, this may be one of the advantages of using an attributions analysis approach with naturalistic data (i.e., data drawn from the field, as in the present analysis) rather than with data derived from experimental studies.

An important initial observation that can be made about the findings reported in Table 14.5 is that there was considerable overlap in the specific causes that respondents from each division mentioned. While the number of causes mentioned by at least 25% of respondents was greater for the tooling division than for the production division (18 compared with 12), all but one of the 12 causes listed for the production division are also listed for the tooling division. The similarity between the divisions in this regard is not surprising. In addition to the divisions being part of the same organisation, it may well be that there are certain generic causes which are common across, if not all organisations, then the organisations within a given industry. For organisations within the manufacturing industry (the industry sector in which the current research was undertaken), one might reasonably expect that the kinds of causes likely to have this generic status (and upon which organisation members will, therefore, commonly draw in seeking to explain the outcomes that they experience) will include influences such as government legislation, management-labour relations, and overseas competition.

Importantly, however, in the context of the present analysis, it is not so much the commonality of the causes that are mentioned that is of interest, but rather the *salience* of these causes. Specifically, and as indicated above, the focus is on how widely shared each cause is within a division (i.e., whether it appears in the attributions of many, or just a few,

---

[12] Given that respondents varied with respect to the number of attributions that they made, this measure of frequency (based on proportions) was deemed more appropriate than simply calculating the average number of attributions, per respondent, in which the cause appeared.

divisional respondents), and on the frequency with which it is mentioned, on average, by each respondent (i.e., whether it appears in a number, or just one, of the respondent's attributions). When the divisions are compared according to the salience of the causes that are mentioned, a number of differences between the divisions emerge, along with a number of similarities. In the discussion that follows, the differences are considered first, followed by the similarities[13]. In discussing the differences, reference is first of all made to those causes which were either unique to the tooling division or which had more salience for respondents in this division than for respondents in production. Following this, reference is made to those causes which were either unique to the production division or which had more salience for respondents in this division than for respondents in tooling.

14.5.4.1 *Differences in causes between the divisions*

For the tooling division, there were five causes that were either unique to the division or that were more salient for respondents from this division than for their counterparts from production. The most salient of these causes was "award restructuring"[14], followed by "diminishing size of workforce/decline of division". With respect to the former, it can be seen from Table 14.5 that award restructuring was mentioned by all respondents from the tooling division, compared with just under two thirds (64.3%) of the respondents from the production division. This difference between the divisions in the sharedness of the cause was statistically significant (chi-square $= 5.31$, $p < .05$). It can also be seen that, for the tooling division, award restructuring was the cause in, on average, 11% of each respondent's attributions whereas, for the production division, it was the cause in, on average, only 5.6% of each respondent's attributions. This difference between the divisions in the frequency of the cause was also statistically significant ($t = 2.47$, $p < .05$). With respect to the latter, this cause was unique to the tooling division; that is, there was no mention of "diminishing size of workforce/decline of division" in any of the attributions made by production division respondents. It can be seen from Table 14.5 that this cause was mentioned by three quarters of the respondents from the tooling division; moreover, it constituted the cause in, on average, 14.6% of the attributions made by each of these respondents.

Of the five 'differentiating' causes for the tooling division, the next most salient was "company management attitudes/behaviours". As indicated in Table 14.5, this cause was mentioned by just over one half (58.3%) of the respondents from the tooling division,

---

[13] For the purpose of this analysis, a difference between the divisions of 20% or more in the level of sharedness of a causal factor was arbitrarily chosen as the criterion for the classification of 'differences'. A difference of less than 20% was the criterion for classifying 'similarities'.

[14] 'Award restructuring' was the name given to the major restructure of the vehicle industry award that was undertaken in the late 1980s. It was a tripartite initiative (involving the government, the unions, and local automotive manufacturers), which had as its main objectives the simplification of existing award classifications and the introduction of industry-wide procedures for increasing employees' skills and knowledge.

compared with just over one quarter (28.6%) of the respondents from the production division. In terms of frequency, it constituted the cause in, on average, 5.8% of the attributions made by the tooling division respondents, compared with 7.5% of the attributions made by the production division respondents. Neither the sharedness nor the frequency difference between the divisions was statistically significant. Finally, there were two additional causes that, while not particularly salient to respondents from the tooling division, were nevertheless unique to this division. These were "societal attitudes/behaviours", mentioned by one third of the respondents from the tooling division in an average of 9.4% of the attributions made by each of these respondents, and "uncertainty/rumour control measure", also mentioned by one third of the respondents from this division, in an average of 8.3% of the attributions made by each of these respondents.

For the production division, there were three 'differentiating' causes, one that was unique to the division and two which were more salient for respondents from this division than for respondents from the tooling division. The most salient of these causes was "divisional worker attitudes/skills/behaviours/personality". As indicated in Table 14.5, this cause was mentioned by every respondent from the production division compared with two-thirds of the respondents from the tooling division. This difference between the divisions in the sharedness of the cause was statistically significant (chi-square = 5.52, $p < .05$). For both divisions, the frequency with which individual respondents mentioned this cause was similarly high. As indicated, it constituted the cause in, on average, 20% and 16.2% of the attributions made by each of the production division and tooling division respondents respectively. The next most salient cause for the production division was "divisional management attitudes/behaviours/style". Table 14.5 shows that this cause was mentioned by just over three quarters (78.6%) of the respondents from the production division in, on average, 16.8% of the attributions made by each of these respondents. In contrast, it was mentioned by less than two-thirds (58.3%) of the respondents from the tooling division in, on average, 6.4% of the attributions made by each of these respondents. While the difference between the divisions in the sharedness of the cause was not statistically significant, the difference in the frequency with which each respondent, on average, mentioned the cause was significant ($t = -5.10$, $p < .001$). The final 'differentiating' cause for this division was "production demands". This cause was unique to the division. It was mentioned by just under three-quarters (71.4%) of the respondents from this division in, on average, 6.3% of the attributions made by each of these respondents.

14.5.4.2 *Similarities in causes between the divisions*

Turning now to a consideration of the similarities between the divisions, there were a number of similarities for causes that had a moderate to high-level of sharedness (i.e., 50% or higher) among respondents within both divisions, and a number of similarities for causes that were less widely shared (i.e., with a level of sharedness within a division of 25%–49%). With respect to the former, there were three causes in this group: "expectations about the role of workers/supervisors"; "divisional supervisor attitudes/behaviours/style"; and "survival and competition imperative". Specifically, and as can be seen from Table 14.5, the first two of these causes were each mentioned by three-quarters of the respondents from the tooling division and just under two-thirds (64.3%) of the respondents from the production division. In terms of frequency, the proportion of attributions per respondent in which "expectations about the role of workers/supervisors" was the cause was 13.2% for tooling division respondents and 8.4% for production division respondents. For "divisional supervisor attitudes/behaviours/style", these proportions were 12.5% and 13.2% for tooling and production division respondents respectively. Finally, "survival and competition imperative" was mentioned by just over one half (58.3%) of the respondents from the tooling division and by exactly one half of the respondents from production. For both divisions, it constituted the cause in 7.1% of the attributions made by each of these respondents.

With respect to causes that were less widely shared among divisional respondents, there were four for which similarities between the divisions emerged. These were: "job design/redesign"; "the nature of the work (and changes in)"; "technological change"; and "company culture". With respect to the first of these causes, it can be seen from Table 14.5 that just over one-third (41.7%) of tooling division respondents and just under one-third (28.6%) of production division respondents made reference to "job design/redesign". It can also be seen that this constituted the cause in, on average, 7.3% of the attributions made by the tooling division respondents and 6.5% of the attributions made by the production division respondents. For both "the nature of the work (and changes in)" and "technological change", the sharedness for the tooling division was the same, as was the sharedness for the production division. Specifically, and as indicated in Table 14.5, each of these causes was mentioned by one-third of the respondents from the tooling division and by just under one-third (28.6%) of the respondents from production. In terms of frequency, "the nature of the work (and changes in)" constituted the cause in 5.4% of the attributions made by the tooling division respondents and in 4.6% of the attributions made by respondents from production. The corresponding frequencies for "technological change" were 6% and 6.5% for the tooling and production divisions respectively. Finally, "company culture" was mentioned by one quarter of the respondents from the tooling division in, on average, 6.5% of the attributions made by each of these respondents. Similarly, this cause was mentioned by just over one quarter (28.6%) of the respondents from the production division in, on average, 6.4% of the attributions made by each of these respondents.

14.5.4.3 *Summary of findings concerning the content of causal factors*

By way of summary, the above findings illustrate that, in terms of the specific content of the causes that respondents mentioned, there were a number of similarities between the divisions as well as a number of differences. In terms of the similarities, there were, as indicated, three causes that had a relatively high level of salience for respondents from both divisions. These included: divisional members' expectations about the respective roles of workers and supervisors; the behaviours, attitudes, and/or 'style' of divisional supervisors; and the demands created by the increased pressure to compete and survive. Commonalities of this kind may well reflect an aspect of organisational, as opposed to divisional, culture (e.g., role expectations and supervisory behaviour/attitudes/style might be organisation-specific rather than division-specific). Alternatively, they may even be indicative of an industry-wide culture (this might arguably be the case for a cause such as increased competition and survival pressure).

In terms of the differences, the two most salient causes that were mentioned by respondents from the tooling division, and which differentiated these respondents from their counterparts in production, were represented by references to the restructuring of the award and to the decline of this division and its diminishing workforce. In contrast, the corresponding causes for respondents from the production division were represented by references to the particular characteristics (whether behaviours, attitudes, skills, *etc.*) of divisional workers, on the one hand, and divisional management, on the other. Of course, the dimensionality of these differences has been commented on previously. Specifically, reference has been made to the non-human versus human distinction between the divisions, with respondents from the tooling division more inclined to attribute outcomes to non-human causes, and respondents from production more inclined to attribute outcomes to human causes. Reference has also been made to the greater sense of ownership of outcomes displayed by respondents from the production division when compared with their counterparts from tooling. This is reflected in the above specific causes whereby, for production division respondents, it is the divisional members themselves (notably divisional workers and divisional management) who are perceived to be the dominant cause of the things that happen in the division. In contrast, for tooling division respondents, causes such as award restructuring and the decline of the division, which are more external and more outside of the control of the division, are seen as particularly influential.

It should be noted that in the above analysis of the specific content of causes, the divisions were differentiated on the basis of both *common* causes (which were more or less salient for respondents from one division than another) and *unique* causes. While differences with respect to both types of causes may be equally important insofar as understanding differences between the divisions in their respective cultures, it is possible that unique causes (in particular, those with a relatively high level of salience for divisional members) may represent a more defining characteristic of the division in which they arise than common causes. It was certainly the case in the present analysis that the unique causes that were most salient, namely, "diminishing size of workforce/decline of division" for the tooling division and "production demands" for the production division, each captured a characteristic of its respective division that could be seen to be critical to an understanding of the 'way things were done' in the division. This suggests that highly salient unique causes might warrant particular consideration.

In terms of the practical value of the present approach, information about the specific content (as opposed to the dimensionality) of causes that have most salience for group members is likely to be useful insofar as informing an understanding of *what* might need to change in the group. It might be, for example, that there are particular causes (e.g., poor worker-supervisor relations) that are commonly perceived to be associated with negative outcomes for the group. In this event, a training program for group members could be developed, the aim of which would be to make such causes explicit and endeavour to manage them in such a way as to improve outcomes for the group. Alternatively, it may be that group members have collectively misjudged the cause (or causes) of a particular outcome. Again, training could be undertaken to correct such misperceptions. Following on from this, the training that has been provided could be evaluated by monitoring changes, over time, in the salience for group members of the causes that have been the subject of the training.

14.5.5 *Interrelations among dimensions*

The final analysis of the data that was undertaken involved examining whether or not the divisions could be differentiated based on the pattern of interrelations that existed among the dimensions in the coding framework. The question of interest here was whether or not each division supported its own unique style of attributing cause, this style being represented by a predisposition towards making particular 'types' of attributions (with 'type' in this case being a multidimensional, rather than a unidimensional, characteristic).

The statistical procedure that was used to carry out this analysis was Multiple Correspondence Analysis (MCA) (Benzecri, 1992; Hirschfeld, 1935), an exploratory technique for the analysis of multivariate categorical data[15]. As suggested by some scholars (e.g., Greenacre & Hastie, 1987), MCA can be regarded as a variant of principal components analysis adapted for use with categorical, as opposed to, continuous data. MCA is an extension of simple Correspondence Analysis; it is used with multi-way, rather than two-way, contingencies tables. The results of Correspondence Analysis are typically presented in the form of a graph, or map, which shows the categories of interest and how they are

---

[15] While the LACS researchers (Stratton *et al.*, 1988) recommend the use of log linear analysis (another multivariate technique) for examining the interrelations among dimensions, this technique could not be used in the present analysis because of limitations with the sample size. Specifically, there were too few attributions for each division, given the number of dimensions (and associated coding categories) in the coding framework. A problem with the use of MCA in the present analysis is that the assumption of independent observations (whereby each observation — in this case, each attribution — should be contributed by a different respondent) has been breached. Interestingly, while not acknowledged by the LACS researchers, this same problem arises with the use of log linear analysis for investigating relations among dimensions in the LACS data. An alternative to both MCA and log linear analysis, which can cope with multiple observations per respondent, is the Generalized Estimating Equation (Liang & Zeger, 1986). An attempt was made to use this technique in the present analysis, but again, this was unsuccessful due to the restricted sample size.

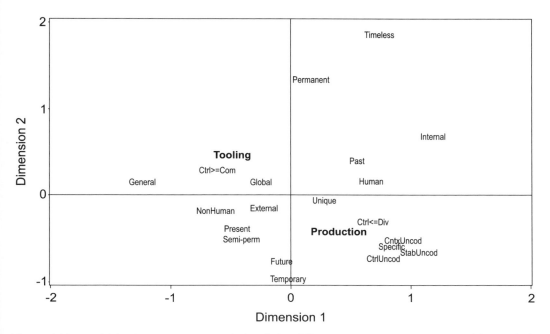

Figure 14.2. Multiple Correspondence Analysis of the difference between the Tooling Division and the Production Division in terms of the interrelations among the coding categories of the attribution coding dimensions.

associated in relation to the first two principal axes, or dimensions, found to underlie the data. In terms of interpretation, the categories (represented by points on the graph) considered to be most closely associated are those that are located in approximately the same region of space and in approximately the same direction from the origin (represented by the point at which the two principal axes intersect). While the distance between categories is sometimes also used as an indication of how closely categories are associated, it has been argued (Greenacre & Hastie, 1987) that the interpretation of this measure, particularly in MCA, is far from straightforward.

Figure 14.2 shows the results of the Multiple Correspondence Analysis of the present data set. The point should be made that, for the purpose of this analysis, it was decided to exclude the data pertaining to three of the dimensions of the coding framework. These dimensions were: Desirability (Cause); Actuality (Outcome); and Desirability (Outcome). With respect to the Desirability dimensions, it will be recalled that, for both divisions, the proportion of uncodable data for each of these dimensions was very high. In other words, the data available provided no clear picture of either individual, or group-level, predispositions regarding the perceived desirability (or otherwise) of causes or outcomes. In view of this, it was reasoned that, if these data were included in the present analysis, they might conceal or even distort the patterns of relations that might exist among those dimensions for which more complete information was available. With respect to the Actuality dimension, in the present analysis, the findings for this dimension were more a function of the design of the interview protocol than of any *natural* predisposition of group members towards mentioning actual outcomes as opposed to anticipated outcomes (or *vice versa*). It will be recalled from Chapter 10 (see Section 10.3 on Research Method) that respondents were specifically asked to comment on outcomes (in this case, changes in the role of workers) that they had experienced (actual outcomes) and that they anticipated experiencing in the future (anticipated outcomes). The information provided in this regard was therefore prompted, rather than spontaneously offered, as was the case for the other dimensions. This peculiarity of the Actuality dimension made it inappropriate, at least in the present analysis, to combine data pertaining to this dimension with data pertaining to the other dimensions.

In terms of the underlying dimensionality of the data pertaining to the seven coding dimensions with which the present analysis was concerned, it can be seen from Figure 14.2 that the second dimension is more readily interpretable than the first. Specifically, this dimension differentiates most clearly along the categories of Context (namely, Timeless, Past, Present, and Future) and Stability (namely, Permanent, Semipermanent, and Temporary). In essence, this would appear to be a dimension that is broadly concerned with *time* — whether the location of a cause in a particular context of time (the past, the present, *etc.*), or the perceived likely duration of a cause (whether long-lasting, or more temporary, in its influence on outcomes). Indeed, one would expect a reasonable degree of association between the scores on the Context and Stability dimensions. In particular, causes that are timeless (in the sense of 'cutting across' all time contexts) are also likely to be permanent rather than temporary (in the sense of continuing to influence outcomes over the longer term). In contrast, there is no such clear differentiation of categories for the first underlying dimension. While this dimension does appear to differentiate along the categories of Universality (namely, Unique and General), Internality (namely, Internal and External), and Content (namely, Human and Non-human), the degree of differentiation of these categories is by no means as strong as it is for the categories represented by the second dimension. Moreover, this combination of categories suggests no readily identifiable interpretation of the first dimension.

It can be seen from Figure 14.2 that neither of the underlying dimensions described above clearly differentiates the tooling division from the production division. Rather, the categories most closely associated with each division (i.e., the categories located in the same quadrant as the division) spread and contrast along the diagonal axis (specifically, the axis from top left to bottom right), rather than along either of the principal axes. A review of the content of these categories provides evidence to suggest that each division may, indeed, support its own unique (and multidimensional) style of attributing causality. It can be seen that, for the tooling division, this style is represented by a tendency towards making *General* attributions (i.e., attributions that apply to any organisation within, or even outside of, the industry), in which the cause is *Global* (i.e., far-reaching in its effects) as well as perceived by respondents to be largely outside of the control of the division (specifically, control is located at the level of the company or beyond, signified by

Ctrl>=Com). In contrast, the style for the production division is characterised by a tendency towards making *Unique* attributions (i.e., attributions that apply to the respondent's division or organisation), in which the cause is *Specific* (i.e., more localised in its effects) as well as perceived by respondents to be largely within the control of the division or divisional subsection (signified by *Ctrl<=Div*). As indicated in Figure 14.2, it is also the case that the production division style somehow incorporates causes that could not be coded in terms of their Context (*CntxUncod*), Stability (*StabUncod*), or Controllability (*CtrlUncod*). It is not entirely clear how this finding should be interpreted.

It should be noted that the divisional differences described above are entirely consistent with findings of the earlier research that prompted the present analysis. Specifically, and as indicated in the introduction, the results of Study 3 (in which attribution style was a comparatively minor focus) depicted the tooling division as more externally focussed than the production division, with members displaying less ownership of, and accountability for, the outcomes they experienced than their counterparts in production. The above results are also consistent with the divisional differences that emerged, in the present analysis, when the tendencies within each of the Universality, Globality, and Controllability dimensions were examined separately. Given these consistencies, it would seem reasonable to conclude that the above results provide at least preliminary evidence of a divisional difference in what might be referred to as 'attribution style'. The advantage of conducting a multivariate analysis of the kind described here is that it can reveal group differences in the pattern of relations among dimensions that may not be evident from, or may not be well-represented by, the differences suggested by an analysis of the tendencies within each separate dimension. Indeed, in the present analysis, whereby the results for each dimension were considered separately, there was evidence of divisional differences in relation to six of the ten dimensions of the coding framework. The results of the multivariate analysis, however, indicated that there were only three of these dimensions for which the tendencies observed occurred simultaneously (i.e., for which respondents' attributions were simultaneously more or less Universal, more or less Global, and more or less Controllable). Clearly, it is information of this latter kind that is most useful in terms of understanding differences between groups in attribution style.

14.6 Summary and Methodological Implications

As indicated in the introduction to this chapter, research into the use of attributions analysis as a tool for deciphering deeper-level organisational (or group) culture is currently still in its infancy. While a strong case can be made for a conceptual link between shared attributions and deeper-level culture — the relevant arguments in this regard have been elucidated in Section 14.2 — the empirical validity of this link is yet to be firmly established. Clearly, the work of Silvester *et al.* (1999) constitutes an important initial contribution in this regard. It would also seem reasonable to suggest that the findings of the present analysis are of sufficient interest to justify some commitment to ongoing research in this area.

As indicated, these findings provided evidence to suggest that groups — in this case, two divisions of the same organisation — can differ in terms of: (i) attribution tendencies in relation to single coding dimensions; (ii) the specific causal factors that have most salience for group members; and (iii) attribution style, as represented by the pattern of relations among coding dimensions. Importantly, the specific differences that emerged in the present analysis were consistent with differences suggested by the findings of Study 3, the more broadly focussed and more qualitative study from which the data for the present analysis were drawn. As indicated, the results of Study 3 provided preliminary evidence to suggest that there were differences, between the two divisions studied, in members' causal beliefs. Moreover, the impression was that these differences had a cultural basis. They appeared to operate at a collective, rather than an individual, level and there was a sense in which they had some history in time. In seeking to confirm the findings of the present research, and thereby go some way towards validating the method, attention can also be drawn to Silvester *et al.*'s finding that each of the groups in their study could be described in terms of a different 'cognitive map' (the latter being a visual representation of the nature of the group's collective causal beliefs). Clearly, this finding is broadly consistent with the finding from the present analysis that there were divisional differences in what might be described as group-level attribution style.

Based on the evidence available to date, one might feel at least cautiously optimistic about the possibilities for attributions analysis as a tool for deciphering organisational cultures and subcultures. The technique, first developed by Silvester *et al.* and subjected to considerable refinement in the present analysis, offers a number of advantages over the measurement tools (whether quantitative or qualitative) that have traditionally been used in organisational culture research. For example, compared with existing quantitative measures for which the content (including questionnaire items, response categories, and the core dimensions being investigated) is typically formulated in advance, the technique being proposed here makes use of naturalistic data, that is, data drawn from the actual field. Specifically, the data take the form of causal attributions that are made, not about hypothetical outcomes and events, but rather about outcomes and events that respondents have actually experienced. In this sense, the data being used are more directly grounded in the reality of respondents, and more specific to the context in which the investigation is being carried out, than the data generated by traditional quantitative techniques. It is also the case, as already argued, that the proposed technique has the potential to provide insights into an organisation's deeper-level culture. In contrast, existing quantitative techniques are usually regarded as suitable for accessing surface-level culture only.

When compared with existing qualitative techniques, the proposed technique offers a number of additional advantages. These derive principally from the potential of the technique to overcome some of the major limitations of qualitative techniques, to which reference has been made previously. In particular, the proposed technique offers a more systematic means whereby to investigate the sharedness of the content of an organisation's culture (in this case, to investigate the extent to which particular attribution orientations, and indeed particular attributions, are shared among organisation members); it offers a more systematic means whereby organisational cultures and subcultures can be compared and whereby changes in culture over time can be evaluated; and it is a technique that is potentially more practical insofar as requiring less researcher time in the field than existing qualitative techniques.

Despite the suggested benefits of the proposed technique, the findings of the present analysis make it clear that there are a number of important methodological issues that have yet to be resolved if the technique is to gain acceptance as a theoretically valid and practically useful technique for the assessment of an organisation's (or group's) deeper-level culture. The remainder of this discussion is devoted to a consideration of these methodological issues and their implications for the kinds of research studies that might usefully be undertaken in this area in the future.

The first issue concerns the value of the coding framework developed for use in the present analysis. As indicated, this framework, like that developed by Silvester *et al.*, was essentially an adaptation — for use in organisational as opposed to clinical settings — of the framework developed by the LACS researchers (Stratton *et al.*, 1988). Seven of the ten dimensions in the present framework were either modified LACS dimensions or dimensions taken directly from the LACS framework. The remaining three dimensions (all dimensions for coding causes) were new dimensions, not included in either the LACS or the Silvester *et al.* (1999) frameworks. There was evidence from the present analysis to suggest that these ten dimensions may differ in terms of their centrality to an understanding of collective, or cultural, attribution orientations and styles. Of the ten dimensions there were six — five for coding causes (Stability, Globality, Controllability, Content, and Context) and one for coding the attribution as a whole (Universality) — for which differences between the divisions in their orientation with respect to each separate dimension were indicated. Importantly, these six dimensions included two (Content and Context) that were unique to the present framework. It was also the case that, of these six dimensions, there were three — two for coding causes (Globality and Controllability) and one for coding the attribution as a whole (Universality) — that, in combination, underpinned the difference between the divisions in attribution style. The fact that the direction of these various differences between the divisions was consistent with expectations (formed on the basis of the first author's protracted involvement with the organisation while undertaking Studies 1, 2, and 3) suggests that the six dimensions concerned have at least some validity with respect to the assessment of organisational and group-level attributions.

In the case of the remaining four dimensions — these included two dimensions for coding causes (Internality and Desirability (Cause)) and two dimensions for coding outcomes (Actuality and Desirability (Outcome)) — there was no evidence, either from the single- or multiple-dimension analyses, of any divisional differences associated with these dimensions. While this finding might be able to be taken at face value — the divisions really did not differ with respect to these dimensions — an alternative conclusion is that some further development of these dimensions, as least as they were used in the present analysis, might be required. As already indicated, due to a problem with uncodable data, it was difficult to interpret the findings for either the Desirablity (Cause) dimension (a new dimension) or the Desirability (Outcome) dimension. While the value of the Desirability (Outcome) dimension has been well established in previous attributions research — for example, this dimension has been shown to be central to the assessment of the so-called optimistic and pessimistic explanatory styles (Seligman & Schulman, 1986) — the paucity of data pertaining to this dimension and the Desirability (Cause) dimension in the present analysis makes it difficult to comment on the comparative value of these two dimensions. The question remains, therefore, as to whether the new Desirability (Cause) dimension provides additional useful information (over and above that provided by the Desirability (Outcome) dimension) or whether it is a redundant dimension.

Attention has also been drawn to a problem with the use of the Actuality dimension in the present analysis. As indicated, a characteristic of the design of the interview protocol meant that the findings for this dimension did not, as they ideally should, provide insights into whether or not respondents from either division were *naturally* more inclined to mention actual (i.e., experienced) outcomes as opposed to anticipated outcomes (or *vice versa*). Clearly, for this dimension to be of value, the method of data collection must be sufficiently unstructured to allow respondents to *spontaneously* refer to outcomes which they expect to experience in the future, as well as to outcomes which they have already experienced or are currently experiencing.

Finally, based on the results of the present analysis, there is a question about the value of the Internality dimension for use in organisational settings. While this dimension is clearly important in clinical contexts — for example, the knowledge that an individual is predisposed towards attributing negative outcomes to causes that are internal (i.e., inherent in the individual herself/himself) rather than external, is likely to have important implications for therapy — it is not clear what the unit of analysis should be when adapting this dimension for use in organisational contexts. In the present analysis, causes were coded as being either *internal to workers* or *external to workers*. It is possible, however, that a more appropriate unit of analysis — one possibly more sensitive to group differences — might have been 'the division', making the coding categories *internal to the division* and *external to the division*.

The above comments, considered as a whole, draw attention to the clear research imperative that exists to more convincingly establish the validity of each of the coding dimensions included in the proposed coding framework. Up to this point, questions regarding which dimensions to retain, which to change, and which to exclude, remain only partially answered. From a practical perspective, there are of course good arguments for working towards a more parsimonious model. Clearly, the more coding dimensions (and associated coding categories) that are included in the framework, the more onerous the task of coding the data becomes, and the more data are required in order that meaningful analyses can be carried out.

A second methodological issue to which the findings of the present analysis draw attention concerns the 'completeness' of the information that is contained within an attribution.

This is directly reflected in the level of uncodable data for each of the dimensions in the coding framework. Essentially, the more 'complete' the attributions information, the more dimensions for which the level of uncodable data is very low. It will be recalled that the attributions data that were extracted for the present analysis could be more easily coded on some dimensions than on others. For example, all of the attributions for both divisions could be coded according to whether the cause was a human or non-human factor. In other words, for neither division, were there any uncodable data for the Content dimension. In contrast, for both divisions, there was a high level of uncodable data for the Desirability (Cause) and Desirability (Outcome) dimensions. At least one quarter of the attributions for both divisions (and up to almost one half for Desirability (Outcome) for the tooling division) could not be coded according to these dimensions.

An important methodological implication of this variability in the codability of data according to different dimensions is that, in order to obtain more complete attributions information (and thereby enhance the value of the technique), there will be instances where it will be necessary to question respondents further regarding gaps in the attributions information they have provided. Drawing on the present findings to illustrate, where a respondent's views about the desirability of a particular cause, or a particular outcome, cannot be ascertained, either from the information contained within the attribution or from the surrounding contextual data, additional specific questions will need to be asked to determine what these views actually are.

Of course, it is easy for researchers to make assumptions, whether consciously or unconsciously, about the meaning that participants in their research attribute to the data that they provide. It is important, however, that researchers — in particular, those working in the area of organisational culture, which regards the 'insider's perspective' as critical — are mindful of this tendency and actively seek to avoid it. In the present analysis, for example, it might easily have been assumed, in the absence of qualifying information to the contrary, that any anticipated increase in the involvement of workers in training in the future would be regarded by respondents as a desirable, rather than an undesirable, outcome. Indeed, such an assumption would be consistent with the tenets of good management practice. Interestingly, however, there was evidence (mostly from the original, larger study from which the attributions data for the present analysis were drawn) to suggest that respondents from the tooling division, and in particular the older respondents from this division, were at best ambivalent about this outcome, and at worst, actively opposed to it. These respondents indicated that they regarded training as more appropriate for younger workers and argued (possibly in an attempt to disguise certain anxieties about having to "go back to school") that they were "too old to learn new tricks". It can be seen, then, that what might be regarded as a desirable outcome from the researcher's perspective can be regarded very differently from the perspective of participants in the research.

This tendency for researchers to impose their own systems of meaning on the interpretation of their data, rather than to 'see the world' from the perspective of those whom they are studying (Blumer, 1969, cited in Bryman, 1988), should not be underestimated, and neither should its effects be seen as inconsequential. Mention has been made a number of times, in various chapters of both volumes of this book, of a classic illustration of researcher bias (or at least claimed researcher bias) in anthropology. The reference here is, of course, to Freeman's (1983) refutation of Mead's (1928) ethnographic account of the experience of adolescence in Samoa. Based on the findings of his own study of Samoan culture (conducted some 20 years after Mead's original work), and the findings of research conducted by a number of his contemporaries, Freeman argued that the experience of adolescence in Samoa was far less idyllic than Mead had portrayed it to be. In fact, this later research provided good evidence to suggest that there was a universality about the experience of adolescence, such that Samoan youth suffered many of the same emotional stressors and conflicts as their counterparts in the United States and elsewhere. In challenging Mead's research, Freeman argued that her findings appear to be largely an artefact of her particular theoretical bias — in this case, a commitment to the ideology of cultural determinism, that is, to the notion that human behaviour is determined by cultural, rather than biological, influences. While the interpretation of the relative value of the research undertaken by Mead and Freeman has remained controversial, the issue of potential researcher bias should be of continuing concern in the fields of both organisational and anthropological research.

It is interesting to note that, in the attributions analysis research conducted by Silvester *et al.* (1999), there is no reference at all to the issue of gaps in attributions information. While the coding framework developed by the authors includes an *uncertain* category (for attributions which were ambiguous with respect to a particular coding dimension, or which contained insufficient information to be coded according to that dimension), the authors provide no information about the relative proportions of attributions that could not be coded according to each of the six dimensions in their framework. It appears, however, that in the case of their dimension for coding the desirability of the outcome, there were no uncodable data. In the authors' own words: "Of the 1230 attributions extracted from the transcripts, 617 (50.16%) described positive or neutral events and 613 (49.84%) described negative events" (p. 9). This finding is surprising particularly when one considers that, for the corresponding dimension in the framework developed for use in the present analysis, the proportion of uncodable data for both the tooling and production divisions was so high. Moreover, contrary to what this finding might suggest, the interview protocol that Silvester *et al.* used to generate their attributions data was even more unstructured than that used in the present analysis. There is also no indication by the authors that they specifically requested any additional qualifying information from their respondents. Given these observations, it is difficult to imagine how the reported complete codability of *all* attributions, in terms of the desirability, *from the perspective of respondents*, of the outcomes (events) to which these attributions referred, could have been achieved.

A final point to make regarding this second methodological issue concerns the question of how to obtain the additional qualifying information that might be required to better understand the meaning, from the respondent's perspective, of any given attribution. The answer to this question would appear to depend upon whether the method of data collection used to generate attributions is very unstructured, or alternatively very structured. If attributions are drawn from very unstructured interviews, comprising mostly open-ended questions, then it is unlikely that the researcher could obtain the additional information required in the course of conducting the actual interview. This is because, in natural conversation of the kind that unstructured interviewing seeks to encourage, it is not always obvious (except in cases where the question "Why?" is specifically asked) when an attribution is being made; it is even less clear when there is certain attributions information that is lacking (e.g., information pertaining to the desirability of the outcome which is the subject of the attribution). Thus, with this method of data collection, it may well be necessary to conduct a second interview in which the respondent is prompted about the meaning of specific aspects of the attributions that she/he has made. If, on the other hand, a more structured method of data collection is used — this might take the form of some kind of issue-focussed interview that explicitly seeks information about the causal beliefs of respondents — then it might be possible to incorporate into the actual method specific questions that could be asked, immediately an attribution has been made, to obtain any qualifying information that might be required about that attribution. Of course, the question of whether attributions data are best drawn from structured or unstructured interviews is itself an important one. It is considered in some detail later in the discussion, as a fourth methodological issue raised by the findings of the present analysis.

Apart from the above finding that there were cross-dimensional differences in the codability of the data, coding reliability across dimensions was also found to differ. In other words, the attributions extracted for analysis could be coded more reliably on some dimensions than on others. Thus, for the Content and Actuality dimensions, there was very good agreement among raters about the coding of the data on these dimension, whereas for the Stability and Desirability (Cause) dimensions, inter-rater agreement was problematic. This finding draws attention to a third important methodological issue, namely, the question of how to improve coding reliability. Clearly, for the proposed method to be of value, the data must be able to be coded reliably on all dimensions established as valid for inclusion in the coding framework.

As suggested previously, coding reliability is likely to be influenced by, among other factors, the extent to which coders are similar with respect to both their training and/or experience in the use of the method and their knowledge of the context in which the attributions data were generated. With respect to the latter, contextual knowledge might simply take the form of coder familiarity with the complete interview transcripts. Such knowledge, whilst requiring some time and effort to acquire, is likely to be of value insofar as the meaning of an attribution may lie, not in the attribution statement itself, but rather in the data which immediately surround it. Of course, contextual knowledge is usually thought of as knowledge acquired through actual exposure to the setting and subjects of the research. Knowledge of this kind might be expected to be particularly influential in determining a coder's interpretation of the data being analysed. A good example from the present analysis involves the coding, according to the Context dimension, of the following attribution by a respondent from the tooling division:

> Workers [in this division] have no say in planning decisions because all those decisions are taken at a supervisory level, or even above a supervisory level, and then passed on down to the shop floor.

It will be recalled that the Context dimension is a dimension for evaluating the context of the cause (whether the past, present, future, *etc.*). In the absence of any qualifying information, a naïve coder might be expected to rate the cause in this attribution — essentially, the division's approach to decision-making — as being located in the present. In the same situation, a more conscientious coder, perhaps with training in the use of the method, may decide that the attribution contains insufficient information for a judgement to be made. However, a coder with good contextual knowledge might be more likely to recognise that there is a cultural basis to the cause in this attribution. Essentially, the culture of the tooling division was such that the traditional, and still legitimate, role of supervisors in the division was to make decisions and the traditional, and still legitimate, role of workers was to abide by those decisions. Given this information, the cause in this attribution might therefore be coded more appropriately as 'timeless or perpetual'.

The above example is not intended to imply that all coders should necessarily have extensive knowledge of the context in which the data being analysed were collected. While this would arguably ensure more accurate understandings of the meaning of the data, such a requirement is clearly unrealistic in terms of the practical utility of the method. The critical point is, simply, that similarities and differences among coders, with respect to their contextual knowledge — and indeed with respect to each of the other factors to which attention has been drawn — are likely to influence coding reliability. The question remains, however, as to the actual extent of this influence. Is coding reliability improved markedly, or only marginally, when coders are similar, rather than different, with respect to characteristics of the kind mentioned? This is an empirical question that is, unfortunately, not able to be answered by the findings of the present analysis. Interestingly, while Silvester *et al.* (1999) might have offered some useful insights in this regard, they make no reference in their paper to the requirements for achieving good coding reliability. In their study, coding reliability was established using three independent coders, each with varying experience (from none to considerable) in the use of the method, and varying knowledge (from none to extensive) of the research site and subjects. These parameters suggest that, in this study, it ought to have been possible to compare the inter-rater agreement of those coders that were most similar with respect to the specified characteristics with the inter-rater agreement of those coders that were most different with respect to these characteristics. Clearly, the issue of coding reliability is one to which future research might usefully be directed.

As indicated, a fourth methodological issue that was raised by the findings of the present analysis concerns the source of the data for analysis — whether these data should be drawn from highly unstructured, or highly structured, interviews. While it has been suggested that each type of data is likely to require a different approach for dealing with gaps in attributions information, there are really no theoretical, or technical, reasons for why the proposed method should be restricted for use with one kind of data or the other. Ultimately, the decision about which type of data to use is a practical decision that should be guided by a consideration of what it is that one hopes to achieve with the research. If the overall aim of the research is to gain a general understanding of the culture of the group — in this case, in terms of the group's characteristic style of attributing cause — then it would seem reasonable to use a relatively unstructured method to generate the data required. On the other hand, if the research is designed to provide more specific information about the group's culture — for example, the aim might be to ascertain group members' beliefs about the role of management with respect to a particular change initiative — then the data required could only be generated using a more structured technique involving some kind of issue-focussed interview.

A possible limitation of the former approach is that, in a highly unstructured interview, very little attributions data may be generated. Rather than being a limitation, however, such an outcome might prove to have some empirical significance. Specifically, the finding that group members produce very few attributions in the course of what is essentially an informal conversation, may constitute evidence of a relatively stable and embedded group culture — one in which members' collective understandings about 'the way things are' are largely taken-for-granted and unspoken. Conversely, the finding that many attributions are generated might be indicative of a culture in transition — one in which the experience of uncertainty has created an imperative for members to actively seek to explain 'the way things are'. Clearly, further research is needed to determine whether or not 'attribution density' (arguably an appropriate term for the phenomenon described here) *actually* has the empirical significance that is suggested. With respect to the latter approach, consideration should be given to the possibility that, in a highly structured interview, there may be a greater tendency towards social desirability responding than is the case in a more unstructured interview. Managers, in particular, might be expected to give answers to "Why?" questions — for example, questions about why particular changes have been made — that are based more on rhetoric than reality. In a structured interview, therefore, it would be important to word questions in such a way as to minimise the likelihood of their presupposing the answer or 'putting words into the interviewee's mouth'. Again, further research is needed to determine whether there is empirical support for the suggested differential influence of rhetoric, both on the attributions made by the members of different groups (say, e.g., managers and workers) and on the attributions produced in the context of structured, as opposed to unstructured, interviews. With respect to the latter, a useful starting point would be to compare the attributions data drawn from the everyday conversations of a sample of group members with the attributions data drawn from structured interviews with these same group members.

A fifth methodological issue — the last to be considered here — that was raised by the findings of the present analysis, concerns the size of the data set available for analysis. It will be recalled that, in the present analysis, some 550 attribution statements (approximately 250 from interviews with tooling division respondents and approximately 300 from interviews with production division respondents) were analysed. It will also be recalled that, while the size of this data set was entirely adequate for examining divisional differences in attribution tendencies in relation to single dimensions, it posed considerable problems for the analysis of divisional differences in the pattern of relations among dimensions. Importantly, it is this latter analysis — which provides insights into group differences in attribution style — which is of most interest from an organisational culture perspective. As indicated, in the present analysis, there were simply too few attributions from each division for this analysis to be carried out using the statistical procedure judged to be most appropriate to the task. The procedure that was ultimately successfully applied was at least partially compromised in its use because, in this instance, this involved a breach of one of the procedure's methodological assumptions.

Unfortunately, the issue of the size of the data set is not one that Silvester *et al.* (1999) address in their research. Their data set was certainly larger than that available for use in the present analysis; it comprised some 1200 attributions drawn from interviews with respondents from three different groups. No assessment is made, however, of the adequacy of this number of attributions in relation to the kinds of statistical procedures that the authors deemed appropriate to apply to the analysis of their data. The authors do acknowledge that their attempts to apply log linear analysis were unsuccessful, but in their explanation of this outcome, no reference is made to the size of their data set.

The conclusion suggested by the above observations is that, in order to more firmly establish the validity of attributions analysis as a tool for deciphering organisational (and group) culture, there is a need for future research involving the use of the proposed method with data sets that are larger than that used in the present analysis and possibly also larger than that used in the Silvester *et al.* study. Interestingly, the LACS researchers draw a similar conclusion in their summary of the status of attributions research in clinical settings. They argue that, for research in this area to advance, it will be necessary to have access to "more substantial bodies of data than have been available until now". Only then will it be possible to "be able to fully investigate issues such as the existence of attribution styles, and the prevalence of specific patterns in different populations" (Stratton *et al.*, 1988, p. 109).

14.7 Conclusions

In this chapter — the final chapter of this volume and of the book — we have explored the use of attributions analysis as a means by which to more effectively and efficiently uncover an organisation's (or a group's) deeper-level culture. Importantly, the attributions data that informed the analysis reported in this chapter were drawn from a larger study that itself was an exploration of a proposed new method for deciphering deep culture. As indicated, this new method involves the use of open questions and prompts to ask respondents about their experience of a given issue (in this case, the role of workers) in relation to a number of contextual domains, including: the past, the present, other organisations, the future, and the ideal. Questions are also asked about respondents' perceptions of the causes of changes (whether experienced or anticipated) across these different domains of context, and if no changes (whether experienced or anticipated) are reported, respondents are asked about why things have stayed, or would stay, the same. Importantly, while we started out primarily with a contextual approach, the work done in this regard provided evidence that the analysis of attributions — and, in particular, attributions generated through specific questioning about context — may offer further insights into an organisation's (or a group's) deeper-level culture. The subsequent more sophisticated attributions analysis that is reported in this chapter has gone some way towards confirming that possibility.

Our hope for this book is that it will stimulate renewed debate about the inevitable methodological challenges that are faced with any attempt to push beyond the surface manifestations of an organisation's (or a group's) culture to an understanding of the deeper-level beliefs and assumptions that make up the essence of that culture. We hope also that this book will encourage others to undertake research towards the further development and refinement of the methods that we have proposed and, at least partly, put to the test. We are optimistic that continued work involving a contextual analysis of organisational culture will be of value in helping to meet the long-recognised need for methodological advancement in this area. Such work may, we believe, be the key that enables organisational culture to achieve its early promise as a construct that, meaningfully operationalised, can provide unique and practically important insights into how organisations develop, operate, and change, and how they can most effectively realise their task- and person-related goals.

References — Volume II

Abramson, L., Seligman, M., & Teasdale, J. (1978). Learned helplessness in humans: Critique and reformulation. *Journal of Abnormal Psychology*, 87, 32–48.

Alderfer, C.P. (1972). *Existence, relatedness, and growth: Human needs in organizational settings*. New York: Free Press.

Allen, R.F. & Dyer, F.J. (1980). A tool for tapping the organizational unconscious. *Personnel Journal, March*, 192–198.

Augoustinos, M. (1989). Social representations and causal attributions. In J.P. Forgas & J.M. Innes (eds.), *Recent advances in social psychology: An international perspective* (pp. 95–106). North Holland: Elsevier Science Publishers.

Barley, S.R. (1983). Semiotics and the study of occupational and organizational cultures. *Administrative Science Quarterly*, 28, 393–413.

Bartunek, J.M. & Moch, M.K. (1991). Multiple constituencies and the quality of working life: Intervention at FoodCom. In P.J. Frost, L.F. Moore, M.R. Louis, C.C. Lundberg, & J. Martin (eds.), *Reframing organizational culture* (pp. 104–114). Newbury Park, CA: Sage Publications.

Bate, P. (1984). The impact of organizational culture on approaches to organizational problem-solving. *Organization Studies*, 5/1, 43–66.

Benzecri, J.P. (1992). *Correspondence analysis handbook*. New York: Marcel Dekker.

Bettman, J. & Weitz, B. (1983). Attributions in the board room: Causal reasoning in corporate annual reports. *Administrative Science Quarterly*, 28/2, 165–183.

Blunt, P. (1986). *Human resource management*. Melbourne, Aust.: Longman Cheshire.

Bryman, A. (1988). *Quantity and quality in social research*. London: Unwin Hyman.

Bryman, A. (1991). *Street Corner Society* as a model for research into organizational culture. In P.J. Frost, L.F. Moore, M.R. Louis, C.C. Lundberg, & J. Martin (eds.), *Reframing organizational culture* (pp. 205–214). Newbury Park, CA: Sage Publications.

Buchanan, D.A., Boddy, D., & McCalman, J. (1988). Getting in, getting on, getting out, and getting back. In A. Bryman (ed.), *Doing research in organizations* (pp. 53–67). London: Routledge.

Budescu, D.V. & Wallsten, T.S. (1985). Consistency in interpretation of probabilistic phrases. *Organizational Behavior and Human Decision Processes, 36/3,* 391–405.

Chambers, J.M., Cleveland, W.S., Kleiner, B., & Tukey, P.A. (1983). *Graphical methods for data analysis*. Belmont, CA: Wadsworth International Group.

Clark, J. (1993). Full flexibility and self-supervision in an automated factory. In J. Clark (ed.), *Human resource management and technical change* (pp. 116–136). London: Sage Publications.

Clarke, V.A., Ruffin, C.L., Hill, D.J., & Beaman, A.L. (1992). Ratings of orally presented verbal expressions of probability by a heterogeneous sample. *Journal of Applied Social Psychology, 22/8*, 638–656.

Cooke, R.A. & Lafferty, J.C. (1986). *Organizational Culture Inventory*. Plymouth, MI: Human Synergistics Inc.

Dawson, P. (1994). *Organizational change: A processual approach*. London: Paul Chapman Publishing Ltd.

Dawson, P. (1996). *Technology and quality: Change in the workplace*. London: International Thomson Business Press.

Dawson, P. & Palmer, G. (1995). *Quality management: The theory and practice of implementing change*. Melbourne, Aust.: Longman Cheshire.

Dessler, G., Griffiths, J., & Lloyd-Walker, B. (2007). *Human resource management: Theory, skills, application* (3rd ed.). Australia: Pearson.

Dick, B. & Dalmau, T. (1988). *To tame a unicorn: Recipes for cultural intervention*. Queensland, Aust.: Interchange.

Donaldson, G. & Lorsch, J.W. (1983). *Decision making at the top: The shaping of strategic direction*. New York: Basic Books.

Easterby-Smith, M., Thorpe, R., & Lowe, A. (1991). *Management research: An introduction*. London: Sage Publications.

Ferrier, W.J., Smith, K.G., Rediker, K.J., & Mitchell, T.R. (1995). Distributive justice norms and attributions for performance outcomes as a function of power. In M.J. Martinko (ed.), *Attribution theory: An organizational perspective* (pp. 315–330). Delray Beach, FL: St. Lucie Press.

Fiedler, F.E. (1967). *A theory of leadership effectiveness*. New York: McGraw-Hill.

Fine, G.A. (1988). Letting off steam? Redefining a restaurant's work environment. In M.O. Jones, M.D. Moore, & R.C. Snyder (eds.), *Inside organizations: Understanding the human dimension* (pp. 119–127). Newbury Park, CA: Sage Publications.

Fleiss, J.L. (1981). *Statistical methods for rates and proportions* (2nd ed.). New York: John Wiley.

Freeman, D. (1983). *Margaret Mead and Samoa: The making and unmaking of an anthropological myth*. Cambridge, MA: Harvard University Press.

Furnham, A., Sadka, V., & Brewin, C.R. (1992). The development of an occupational attributional style questionnaire. *Journal of Organizational Behavior, 13*, 27–39.

Gagliardi, P. (1986). The creation and change of organizational cultures: A conceptual framework. *Organization Studies, 7/2*, 117–134.

Gibson, J.L., Ivancevich, J.M., & Donnelly, J.H. (2000). *Organizations: Behavior, structure, processes* (10th ed.). Boston, MA: Irwin/McGraw-Hill.

Greenacre, M. & Hastie, T. (1987). The geometric interpretation of Correspondence Analysis. *Journal of the American Statistical Association, 82/398*, 437–447.

Greenberg, J. & Baron, R.A. (1995). *Behavior in organizations: Understanding and managing the human side of work* (5th ed.). Englewood Cliffs, NJ: Prentice Hall.

Guest, D.E., Peccei, R., & Fulcher, A. (1993). Culture change and quality improvement in British Rail. In D. Gowler, K. Legge, & C. Clegg (eds.), *Case studies in organizational behaviour and human resource management* (pp. 126–133). London: Paul Chapman Publishing Ltd.

Hackman, J.R. & Oldham, G.R. (1976). Motivation through the design of work: Test of a theory. *Organizational Behavior and Human Performance, 16/2,* 250–279.

Halberstam, D. (1986). *The reckoning.* London: Bloomsbury.

Handy, C.B. (1990). *The age of unreason.* London: Arrow Books Ltd.

Handy, C.B. (1996). *Beyond certainty: The changing world of organizations.* Boston: Harvard Business School Press.

Harrison, R. (1975). Diagnosing organisation ideology. In J.E. Jones & J.W. Pfeiffer (eds.), *The 1975 annual handbook for group facilitators* (pp. 101–107). La Jolla, CA: University Associates Publishers, Inc.

Harrison, R. & Stokes, H. (1992). *Diagnosing organizational culture.* San Diego, CA: Pfeiffer & Company.

Herzberg, F., Mausner, B., & Snyderman, B. (1959). *The motivation to work* (2nd ed.). New York: John Wiley & Sons.

Hewstone, M., Jaspars, J., & Lalljee, M. (1982). Social representations, social attribution and social identity: The intergroup images of 'public' and 'comprehensive' schoolboys. *European Journal of Social Psychology, 12/3,* 241–269.

Hirschfeld, H.O. (1935). A connection between correspondence and contingency. *Proceedings of the Cambridge Philosophical Society (Mathematical Proceedings), 31,* 520–524.

Hofstede, G. (1980). *Culture's consequences: International differences in work-related values.* Beverly Hills, CA: Sage Publications.

Hofstede, G., Neuijen, B., Ohayv, D.D., & Sanders, G. (1990). Measuring organizational cultures: A qualitative and quantitative study across twenty cases. *Administrative Science Quarterly, 35,* 286–316.

Jacques, E. (1951). *The changing culture of a factory: A study of authority and participation in an industrial setting.* London: Tavistock Publications Ltd.

Jaspars, J. & Hewstone, M. (1990). Social categorization, collective beliefs, and causal attribution. In C. Frost & G. Gaskell (eds.), *The social psychological study of widespread beliefs* (pp. 121–141). New York: Oxford University Press.

Jones, M.O. (1988). In search of meaning: Using qualitative methods in research and application. In M.O. Jones, M.D. Moore, & R.C. Snyder (eds.), *Inside organizations: Understanding the human dimension* (pp. 31–47). Newbury Park, CA: Sage Publications.

Jones, M.O., Moore, M.D., & Snyder, R.C. (eds.) (1988). *Inside organizations: Understanding the human dimension.* Newbury Park, CA: Sage Publications.

Kantrow, A.M. (1984). *The constraints of corporate tradition.* New York: Harper & Row.

Kerfoot, D. & Knights, D. (1995). Empowering the 'quality' worker? The seduction and contradiction of the total quality phenomenon. In A. Wilkinson & H. Willmott (eds.), *Making quality critical: New perspectives on organizational change* (pp. 219–239). London: Routledge.

Kidd, R.F. & Amabile, T.M. (1981). Causal explanations in social interaction: Some dialogues on dialogue. In J.H. Harvey, W. Ickes, & R.F. Kidd (eds.), *New directions in attribution research, Vol 3* (pp. 307–328). Hillsdale, NJ: Lawrence Erlbaum Associates.

Kilmann, R.H. (1984). *Beyond the quick fix: Managing five tracks to organizational success.* San Francisco, CA: Jossey-Bass.

Kilmann, R.H. & Saxton, M.J. (1983). *The Kilmann-Saxton Culture-Gap Survey.* Pittsburgh, PA: Organizational Design Consultants.

Kluckhohn, F. & Strodtbeck, F.L. (1961). *Variations in value orientations.* Evanston, IL: Row, Peterson, and Company.

Kummerow, E.H. (2000). *Towards the measurement of organisational culture.* PhD Thesis: The University of Adelaide, South Australia.

Lewis, A. (1990). Shared economic beliefs. In C. Fraser & G. Gaskell (eds.), *The social psychological study of widespread beliefs* (pp. 192–209). New York: Clarendon Press.

Liang, K.Y. & Zeger, S.L. (1986). Longitudinal analysis using generalized linear models. *Biometrika, 73/1,* 13–22.

Litwin, G.H. & Stringer, R.A. (1968). *Motivation and organizational climate.* Boston: Harvard University.

Louis, M.R. (1980). Surprise and sense making: What newcomers experience in entering unfamiliar organizational settings. *Administrative Science Quarterly, 25,* 226–251.

Louis, M.R. (1983). Organizations as culture bearing milieux. In L.R. Pondy, P.J. Frost, G. Morgan, & T.C. Dandridge (eds.), *Organizational symbolism* (pp. 39–54). Greenwich, CT: JAI Press.

Martin, J. (1992). *Cultures in organizations: Three perspectives.* New York: Oxford University Press.

Martin, J., Sitkin, S.B., & Boehm, M. (1985). Founders and the elusiveness of a cultural legacy. In P.J. Frost, L.F. Moore, M.R. Louis, C.C. Lundberg, & J. Martin (eds.), *Organizational culture* (pp. 99–124). Newbury Park, CA: Sage Publications.

Martinko, M.J. (1995). *Attribution theory: An organizational perspective.* Delray Beach, FL: St. Lucie Press.

Martinko, M.J., Harvey, P., & Dasborough, M.T. (2011). Attribution theory in the organizational sciences: A case of unrealised potential. *Journal of Organizational Behavior, 32/1,* 144–149.

Maslow, A.H. (1954). *Motivation and personality.* New York: Harper.

McDonald, D.M. (1995). Fixing blame in *n*-person attributions: A social identity model for attributional processes in newly formed cross-functional groups. In M.J. Martinko (ed.), *Attribution theory: An organizational perspective* (pp. 273–288). Delray Beach, FL: St. Lucie Press.

McGregor, D.M. (1960). *The human side of enterprise.* New York: McGraw-Hill.

Mead, M. (1928). *Coming of age in Samoa: A psychological study of primitive youth for western civilization.* New York: William Morrow.

Meyer, G.W. & Stott, R.G. (1985). Quality circles: Panacea or Pandora's box. *Organizational Dynamics, 13/4,* 34–50.

Meyerson, D.E. (1991). Acknowledging and uncovering ambiguities in cultures. In P.J. Frost, L.F. Moore, M.R. Louis, C.C. Lundberg, & J. Martin (eds.), *Reframing organizational culture* (pp. 254–270). Newbury Park, CA: Sage Publications.

Moscovici, S. (1984). The phenomenon of social representations. In R.M. Farr and S. Moscovici (eds.), *Social representations* (pp. 3–69). Cambridge: Cambridge University Press.

Mueller, G.C., McKinley, W., Mone, M.A., & Barker III, V.L. (2001). Organizational decline: A stimulus for innovation? *Business Horizons, 44/6*, 25–34.

Naisbitt, J. & Aburdene, P. (1990). *Megatrends 2000*. London: Pan Books Ltd.

O'Reilly, C., Chatman, J., & Caldwell, D. (1991). People and organizational culture: A profile comparison approach to assessing person-environment fit. *Academy of Management Journal, 34/3*, 487–516.

Ott, J.S. (1989). *The organizational culture perspective*. Pacific Grove, CA: Brooks/Cole Publishing Company.

Parker, L., Guthrie, J., & Gray, R. (1999). *Exploring social construction and commodification in accounting and management research*. Working paper, Graduate School of Management, Macquarie University, Sydney.

Patton, M.Q. (1990). *Qualitative evaluation and research methods* (2nd ed.). London: Sage Publications.

Pettigrew, A.M. (1979). On studying organizational cultures. *Administrative Science Quarterly, 24*, 570–581.

Pettigrew, A.M. (1990). Is corporate culture manageable? In D.C. Wilson & R.H. Rosenfeld (eds.), *Managing organizations: Text, readings and cases* (pp. 266–272). London: McGraw-Hill.

Pfeffer, J. (1981). Management as symbolic action: The creation and maintenance of organizational paradigms. In L.L. Cummings & B.M. Staw (eds.), *Research in organizational behavior, Vol. 3* (pp. 1–52). Greenwich, CT: JAI Press.

Poblador, N. (1990). Change and adaptation. In R.I. Westwood (ed.), *Organisational behaviour: Southeast Asian perspectives* (pp. 387–404). Hong Kong: Longman Group.

Reichers, A.E. & Schneider, B. (1990). Climate and culture: An evolution of constructs. In B. Schneider (ed.), *Organizational climate and culture* (pp. 5–39). San Francisco, CA: Jossey-Bass.

Rentsch, J.R. (1990). Climate and culture: Interaction and qualitative differences in organizational meanings. *Journal of Applied Psychology, 75/6*, 668–681.

Rotter, J.B. (1966). Generalized expectancies for internal versus external control of reinforcement. *Psychological Monographs, 80/1*, 1–28.

Rousseau, D.M. (1989). Psychological and implied contracts in organizations. *Employee Responsibilities and Rights Journal, 2/2*, 121–139.

Rousseau, D.M. (1990). Assessing organizational culture: The case for multiple methods. In B. Schneider (ed.), *Organizational climate and culture* (pp. 153–192). San Francisco, CA: Jossey-Bass.

Sackmann, S.A. (1991). *Cultural knowledge in organizations: Exploring the collective mind*. Newbury Park, CA: Sage Publications.

Salancik, G.R. & Meindl, J.R. (1984). Corporate attributions as strategic illusions of management control. *Administrative Science Quarterly*, *29/2*, 238–254.

Sathe, V (1985). How to decipher and change corporate culture. In R.H. Kilmann, M.J. Saxton, & R. Serpa (eds.), *Gaining control of the corporate culture* (pp. 230–261). San Francisco, CA: Jossey-Bass.

Saxena, S. & Shah, H. (2008). Effect of organizational culture on creating learned helplessness attributions in R&D professionals: A canonical analysis. *The Journal for Decision Makers*, *33/2*, 25–45.

Schein, E.H. (1985). *Organizational culture and leadership*: San Francisco, CA: Jossey-Bass.

Schein, E.H. (1992). *Organizational culture and leadership* (2nd ed.). San Francisco, CA: Jossey-Bass.

Schein, E.H. (2004). *Organizational culture and leadership* (3rd ed.). San Francisco, CA: Jossey-Bass.

Schein, E.H. (2010). *Organizational culture and leadership* (4th ed.). San Francisco, CA: Jossey-Bass.

Seidel, J., Kjolseth, R., & Seymour, E. (1988). *The Ethnograph, V3.0: A programme for the analysis of text based data*. Amherst, Mass: Qualis Research Associates.

Seligman, M.E. & Schulman, P. (1986). Explanatory style as a predictor of productivity and quitting among life insurance sales agents. *Journal of Personality and Social Psychology*, *50/4*, 832–830.

Siehl, C. & Martin, J. (1988). Measuring organizational culture: Mixing qualitative and quantitative methods. In M.O. Jones, M.D. Moore, & R.C. Snyder (eds.), *Inside organizations: Understanding the human dimension* (pp. 79–103). Newbury Park, CA: Sage Publications.

Siehl, C. & Martin, J. (1990). Organizational culture: A key to financial performance. In B. Schneider (ed.), *Organizational climate and culture* (pp. 241–281). San Francisco, CA: Jossey-Bass.

Silvester, J., Anderson, N.R., & Patterson, F. (1999). Organizational culture change: An inter-group attributional analysis. *Journal of Occupational and Organizational Psychology*, *72/1*, 1–23.

Smircich, L. (1983). Concepts of culture and organizational analysis. *Administrative Science Quarterly*, *28/3*, 339–358.

Smircich, L. & Stubbart, C. (1985). Strategic management in an enacted world. *Academy of Management Review*, *10/4*, 724–736.

Snyder, R.C. (1988). New frames for old: Changing the managerial culture of an aircraft factory. In M.O. Jones, M.D. Moore, & R.C. Snyder (eds.), *Inside organizations: Understanding the human dimension* (pp. 191–208). Newbury Park, CA: Sage Publications.

Stern, G. (1970). *People in context: Measuring person-environment congruence in education and industry*. New York: Wiley.

Stratton, P., Munton, T., Hanks, H., Heard, D., & Davidson, C. (1988). *Leeds attributional coding system manual*. Leeds, UK: Leeds Family Therapy & Research Centre, University of Leeds.

Taylor, F. (1911). *The principles of scientific management*. New York: W.W. Norton & Co., Inc.

Trice, H.M. (1993). *Occupational subcultures in the workplace*. Ithaca, NY: ILR Press.

Trice, H.M. & Beyer, J.M. (1993). *The cultures of work organizations*. Englewood Cliffs, NJ: Prentice Hall.

UnusedName1. (2012). Margaret Mead and Samoa [Video file]. Retrieved from http://www.youtube.com/watch?v=lyOD-qNaiL0 (Accessed 8 April 2013).

Vecchio, R.P., Hearn, G., & Southey, G. (1992). *Organisational behaviour: Life at work in Australia*. Sydney, Aust.: Harcourt Brace Jovanovich.

Whyte, W.F. (1943). *Street corner society*. Chicago, IL: University of Chicago Press.

Wilkins, A.L. & Ouchi, W.G. (1983). Efficient cultures: Exploring the relationship between culture and organizational performance. *Administrative Science Quarterly, 28/3*, 468–481.

Wilkinson, A., Marchington, M., Goodman, J., & Ackers, P. (1992). Total quality management and employee involvement. *Human Resource Management Journal, 2/4*, 1–20.

Woodward, J. (1965). *Industrial organization: Theory and practice*. London: Oxford University Press.

Young, E. (1991). On the naming of the rose: Interests and multiple meanings as elements of organizational culture. In P.J. Frost, L.F. Moore, M.R. Louis, C.C. Lundberg, & J. Martin (eds.), *Reframing organizational culture* (pp. 90–103). Newbury Park, CA: Sage Publications.

Zuboff, S. (1988). *In the age of the smart machine: The future of work and power*. Oxford: Heinemann Professional Publishing.

Author Index — Volume II

Subject Index — Volume II